Praise for *My Thoughts Be Bloody*

"This is narrative history at its most engaging and edifying: the forgotten story of a sibling rivalry, shot through with Shakespearean overtones, that played itself out tragically on the national stage. With the authority of a historian and the dramatic talents of a novelist, Nora Titone has written a book full of surprises that will fundamentally change the way Americans think about John Wilkes Booth

Part of the World

"Nora Titone's energetic   story must add
to its indictment of Boot   *Henry and Clara*

"Premonition looms in every chapter, even in each epigraph, as the course of the war turns in favor of the North and the mind of John Wilkes Booth grows more warped. The narrative *races* ahead to the fraternal clash because Ms. Titone's control is wire-tight; and the end, which we know anyway, is crushing."   —James Cornelius, Curator of the Lincoln Papers at the
Abraham Lincoln Presidential Library

"The Booth family, like most involved with creative endeavors, produced brilliant eccentrics. What began as sibling rivalry transformed into something darker and deadly as national divisions became mirrored in family squabbles. How ironic that the greatest family of the American theater produced the assassin of the greatest President who supported American theater. For anyone wanting to know how this could happen, *My Thoughts Be Bloody* is the book to read."   —Thomas F. Schwartz, Director of Research,
the Abraham Lincoln Presidential Library and Museum

"Why did John Wilkes Booth do it? In *My Thoughts Be Bloody* young historian Nora Titone is one of the few to have genuinely explored this question. In doing so, she has crafted a fascinating psychological drama about one of the central events of the Civil War: the assassination of Abraham Lincoln. This book promises to stimulate lively historical debate and will be a treat for every Civil War buff who always pondered that haunting question, 'what made him pull that trigger?' Bravo on a marvelous achievement."
—Jay Winik, author of *April 1865* and *The Great Upheaval*

"Titone uncovers a narrative as old as Cain and Abel. She also casts the nineteenth century's greatest True Crime story in a new light."
—*New England Quarterly Review*

"The new light [Titone] shines on the Booth family provides some compelling context for the Lincoln assassination." —*The Dallas Morning News*

"*My Thoughts Be Bloody* is an impressively researched and smoothly written narrative. . . . It will become essential reading on the Booth family and the Lincoln assassination." —*The Civil War Times*

"A panoramic tour of nineteenth-century America, from the streets of 1840s Baltimore to the gold fields of California, from the jungles of the Isthmus of Panama to the glittering mansions of Gilded Age New York." —*University of Iowa*

"A splendid narrative, by turns amusing, surprising, and suspenseful, which illuminates the theatrical world of the nineteenth century and provides the context for the most memorable murder in American history." —*Tulsa World*

"An astonishing, tangled family saga." —*American History*

"Finding a patch of nineteenth-century American history that hasn't already been well traveled is rare. Like any good storyteller, Titone spins this yarn in a riveting, theatrical style that is both fun to read and informative." —*Chicago Sun-Times*

"Well-researched and smartly written . . . [an] engrossing tale." —*San Jose Mercury News*

"A very well done examination of the trials and tribulations of a remarkable family." —*Booklist*

"The author does a remarkably thorough job of illuminating the lives of [John Wilkes Booth's] parents and siblings . . . the multiple portraits display hidden facets of all the Booths." —*Kirkus Reviews*

"Provocative and revealing, Titone's first book provides another dimension to an iconic national calamity by alleging that John Wilkes Booth assassinated Abraham Lincoln in part to establish his own importance within a family of theatrical rivals. . . . Titone's theory adds to the narrative without dismissing the political and cultural reasons for Wilkes Booth's plot—his Confederate and proslavery sympathies have often been noted. She is most impressive in her use of primary sources and in her literary style." —*Library Journal* *f*P

THE BITTER RIVALRY

THAT LED TO THE ASSASSINATION

OF ABRAHAM LINCOLN

MY
THOUGHTS
BE BLOODY

NORA TITONE

FOREWORD BY DORIS KEARNS GOODWIN

Free Press
New York   London   Toronto   Sydney

Free Press
A Division of Simon & Schuster, Inc.
1230 Avenue of the Americas
New York, NY 10020

Copyright © 2010 by Nora Titone

All rights reserved, including the right to reproduce this book or portions thereof in any form whatsoever. For information address Free Press Subsidiary Rights Department, 1230 Avenue of the Americas, New York, NY 10020.

First Free Press trade paperback edition May 2011

FREE PRESS and colophon are trademarks of Simon & Schuster, Inc.

For information about special discounts for bulk purchases, please contact Simon & Schuster Special Sales at 1-866-506-1949 or business@simonandschuster.com.

The Simon & Schuster Speakers Bureau can bring authors to your live event. For more information or to book an event contact the Simon & Schuster Speakers Bureau at 1-866-248-3049 or visit our website at www.simonspeakers.com.

Designed by Akasha Archer

Manufactured in the United States of America

10 9 8 7 6 5 4 3 2 1

Library of Congress has cataloged the hardcover edition as follows:

Titone, Nora.
    My thoughts be bloody : the bitter rivalry between Edwin and John Wilkes Booth that led to an American tragedy / by Nora Titone ; foreword by Doris Kearns Goodwin. — 1st Free Press hardcover ed.
        p.   cm.
    Includes bibliographical references and index.
1. Booth, John Wilkes, 1838–1865.   2. Booth, John Wilkes, 1838–1865—Family.   3. Booth, Edwin, 1833–1893.   4. Assassins—United States—Biography.   5. Actors—United States—Biography.   6. Brothers—United States—Biography.   7. Lincoln, Abraham, 1809–1865—Assassination.   8. Sibling rivalry—United States—Case studies.   I. Title.
    E457.5.T57   2010
    973.7092—dc22
    [B]
    2010034297

ISBN 978-1-4165-8605-0
ISBN 978-1-4165-8606-7 (pbk)
ISBN 978-1-4165-8616-6 (ebook)

For Jason and Nick

Let me lament,
With tears as sovereign as the blood of hearts,
That thou, my brother, my competitor
In top of all design, my mate in empire,
Friend and companion in the front of war,
The arm of mine own body, and the heart
Where mine his thoughts did kindle,—that our stars,
Unreconcilable, should divide
Our equalness to this.
                    —*Antony and Cleopatra*, 5.1

How all occasions do inform against me
And spur my dull revenge!
. . . O, from this time forth,
My thoughts be bloody, or be nothing worth!
                    —*Hamlet*, 4.4

CONTENTS

PART ONE

1821–1852

PART TWO

1853–1860

CONTENTS

PART THREE
1861–1865

FOREWORD

Filled with ambition, rivalry, betrayal, and tragedy, this story of the celebrated Shakespearean actor Junius Brutus Booth and the two sons, Edwin and John Wilkes, who competed to wear his crown, is as gripping as a fine work of fiction. Yet, given the role that the younger son played in murdering President Abraham Lincoln, *My Thoughts Be Bloody* is simultaneously an important work of history—the best account I have ever read of the complex forces that led John Wilkes Booth to carry a gun into Ford's Theatre on April 14, 1865.

Spanning nearly three-quarters of a century, the book carries us back to early nineteenth-century London, where Junius Booth, handsome, tormented, and brilliant, is the toast of the town. Married with a small child, he falls in love with nineteen-year-old Mary Ann Holmes. Abandoning his family, he flees with his mistress to America, where he begins a new family and becomes a towering star, traveling from one city to the next, delivering passionate performances of Richard III, Hamlet, and King Lear.

Early on, Nora Titone convincingly argues, two of Junius's four surviving sons give promise of following in their father's footsteps. But which of the two would succeed—the more intelligent, sensitive Edwin or the handsomer, more aggressive John Wilkes—is unclear. When Junius chooses the older son, Edwin, to accompany him on the road, a fierce jealousy begins to fester in John Wilkes. Though Edwin finds traveling with his hard-drinking father difficult, he begins to experience the magic of the theater. On his own, he memorizes long passages from Shakespeare; he absorbs his father's gestures, accents, and facial expressions. He hungers for the fame his father has achieved.

Edwin's chance comes when Junius suddenly dies. As throngs of mourners gather for the funeral procession, the nineteen-year-old Edwin assumes his father's mantle and soon becomes a greater star than Junius ever was. In contrast to his father's bombastic style, he mesmerizes audiences with the naturalness of his performances and his conversational tone. Critics rate his first performance as Richard III "a blaze of genius." Moving from one triumph to another, he becomes a wealthy man when still in his early twenties.

When John Wilkes comes of age, he too becomes an actor. His handsome features and well-proportioned body hold promise, but he possesses neither the talent nor the discipline to become a star. Edwin fears that his brother will dilute the family name and that two Booths on the same circuit will cut into his profits, even though he is, by far, the better known. He has power to wield, however, so he divides the United States into two regions. Each brother would perform in his own region, never crossing into the other's territory. Edwin takes the populous North, including New York City, Boston, and Philadelphia, while John Wilkes is relegated to the less populous South, where audiences and profits are much smaller. John Wilkes begins his first Southern tour in 1860, as the country itself is dividing along the same lines as his brother's map.

Toiling in the South, John Wilkes begins to sympathize with the Confederate cause, increasing tensions with his Union-loving family. After performing in New Orleans, where he meets up with members of the Confederate Secret Service, John Wilkes finally finds his chance for stardom by joining the conspiracy to kidnap President Lincoln. His decision, Titone persuasively argues, is forged as much by his failed career, his squandered earnings, and his jealousy of his brother's success, as by his politics or his hatred for Lincoln.

In short, this book forces us to look at the familiar story of Lincoln's assassin in a new way—through the lens of his tangled family history. Moreover, by placing Edwin Booth at center stage, it brings back to vivid life a fascinating figure whose achievements have been obscured by his brother's murderous deed. We see Edwin performing before President Lincoln, dining with Secretary of State William Seward, befriending Julia Ward Howe and Adam Badeau, General Grant's aide-de-camp. We learn that no other actor in the golden age of nineteenth-century theater was ever held in higher esteem. Still, as Titone appreciates, through a final desperate performance, John Wilkes Booth accomplished by death what he had never been able to achieve in life—he finally upstaged his brother.

—Doris Kearns Goodwin
    April 29, 2010
    Concord, Massachusetts

PROLOGUE

THE PLAYERS

All the world's a stage,
And all the men and women merely players;
They have their exits and their entrances,
And one man in his time plays many parts . . .
—*As You Like It*, 2.7

ON THE LAST DAY OF 1892, A TEMPEST HIT MANHATTAN. A HEAVY, day-long downpour filled the avenues of the city with ankle-deep water. Fifty-mile-an-hour winds tore umbrellas inside out, chased pedestrians off the streets, and hurled gusts of rain against roof and window. This weather kept most people home for New Year's Eve, but three hours before midnight a coach carrying the president-elect of the United States started southward, directly into the path of the storm. It was not an easy journey. For forty-five blocks the driver had to urge his balking horses to bring the president to his destination. Only a serious commitment would call a person out in a gale like this one, particularly Grover Cleveland, a good-natured but torpid man who generally avoided physical exertion. Yet tonight he dressed in a white tie and black evening coat, left the comfort of his mansion on East Sixty-eighth Street, and set forth on the wet and blustery drive without complaint. He was going to a party to give a speech in honor of the actor Edwin Booth.

Paying tribute to an actor would be a delicate mission for any president at the close of the nineteenth century. Most stage stars, no matter how popular, were social outcasts. As a guardian of New York's high society once explained, acting, like other forms of moneymaking artistic work, was scorned by the nineteenth-century ruling classes "as something between a black art and a form of manual labor." Adding to the difficulty of Cleveland's task was that, over the past half century, perhaps no name had been at once more beloved and more reviled by the American people than that of Booth. On an earlier occasion, John Hay, who had lived and worked with Abraham Lincoln in the White House and was like a son to the martyred president, chose to send his speech honoring Edwin Booth by mail. General William T. Sherman, hero of the Grand Army of the Republic and an enthusiastic admirer of Edwin Booth, would be present at tonight's party but would not address the crowd.

Cleveland agreed to deliver the night's keynote, encouraged perhaps by the official limbo he found himself in this season. By a strange twist of timing, Cleveland was president tonight, and yet he was not. The only chief executive to win the White House, lose it, and win it back again four years later, this New Year's Eve Cleveland was at once an ex-president and the president-elect. Benjamin Harrison would hold the real title to the highest office in the land until March 3, 1893, when Cleveland would be inaugurated for the second time.

Booth had made a special request that Cleveland speak for him tonight. Having a president, even one of indeterminate status, make a personal address meant everything to the actor. On this New Year's Eve, out of friendship and love for Edwin Booth, Cleveland was happy to play a president's part. After four years of exile from the White House, Cleveland wanted to wear the mantle of the office again. "What shall be done with our ex-presidents?" he had demanded before his reelection, impatient with the routines of civilian life. "Take them out and shoot them?"

Wind shook Cleveland's coach as it moved downtown, heading for Gramercy Park. This private square, planted with elms and willows, ornately fenced, and surrounded by some of the finest mansions in the city, was a world unto itself. A proud list of pedigreed American families made their homes in the quiet enclave three blocks from Fifth Avenue—Joneses, Coopers, Ruggleses, and Van Rensselaers all had lived here. Former president Chester A. Arthur kept an address on Gramercy Park, as had, from time to time, such celebrated names as Herman Melville and Edith Wharton. In 1888 Edwin Booth had staked out a permanent place for himself in this patrician nook when he bought the Greek Revival residence at No. 16. His exceptional talents, his status as a nationally recognized "genius," his immense wealth, and his international fame guaranteed the star a respectful welcome, even here.

Yet from behind window curtains of taffeta and embroidered velvet, the park's blue-blood residents watched in consternation as construction work began at No. 16 after Booth's purchase. The actor moved his personal possessions only into the third floor of the mansion. His plans for the rest of the space came as a surprise to all. Over a lunch at Delmonico's early in 1888, Booth and a handful of his well-known friends—Mark Twain and General William T. Sherman among them—signed articles of incorporation to establish a private club, called The Players, within the walls of No. 16. It was said that the best men in New York, perhaps in the entire nation, would be invited to fill the ranks of this secretive new society. But, it was understood, Edwin Booth would reign supreme over the elite company as the club's founder and lifetime president.

Gramercy Park's denizens watched as metalworkers soldered a massive gold-toned plaque into place above No. 16's doorway. A sunburst of bronze rays surrounded two masks, the emblems of Comedy and Tragedy, one frozen in a rictus of laughter, the other set in a grimace of despair. Quoting Shakespeare, Edwin explained his choice for his new club's insignia: "all the world's a stage, and all the men and women merely players." The laughing and crying masks were eerie reminders of the actor's peculiar personal history and probably unsettled his neighbors. When carpenters hung two iron lanterns crowned with foot-long spikes on either side of those masks, some muttered about the garish addition to the neighborhood's refined architecture. Every evening the gas-fed light from these lamps suffused the park with a green brilliance, marking the path to Booth's door.

Even in the thick of the New Year's gale, The Players' beacons did their work. Cleveland would have seen his destination well enough as the carriage entered Gramercy Park, where the wind whipped the leafless elm trees. December 31, 1892, was the fifth anniversary of The Players' existence. Edwin Booth's club had grown in that time to almost eight hundred members, and brought unaccustomed traffic to the pavements of Gramercy Park. President Cleveland himself had been a Player in good standing since 1889; his carriage stopping before the clubhouse was by now a familiar sight to park dwellers. Tonight, bundled in a greatcoat, Cleveland struggled to the ground and made his way to the shelter of the porch. Dozens of storm-rattled coaches pulled into line behind Cleveland's, delivering a procession of figures in high hats and long-tailed coats to the same entrance. The club's illustrious membership was arriving. They have been described as "the foremost men in every walk of life." Every New Year's Eve, on the anniversary of their club's creation, The Players gathered to pay tribute to their founder, Edwin Booth. This year, Grover Cleveland would lead the assembled greats in a ritual honoring the white-haired actor.

A waiter divested Cleveland of his enormous coat in the club's white marble entry hall. When political opponents dubbed Cleveland "the Beast of Buffalo," they were not only referring to the former mayor's rumored penchant for seducing shop girls in that city. Weighing in at three hundred pounds, with his thick neck and massive jowls, Cleveland was practically bison-sized. As he climbed the curving mahogany steps to reach the club's main hall, his tread made the boards creak. The room at the top of the stairs was dazzling to the eye, but Cleveland had become inured to its splendors. When Booth chose No. 16 as the home for his private society, the thirty-five-year-old architect Stanford White, Booth's friend and a founding club member, labored long over The Players' interior design. Every detail of the rooms and all the furnishings were chosen to gratify the tastes of the eminent men Booth hoped to entice into joining. *Century Magazine*, a leading periodical of the day, published an illustrated account of White's designs when the club first opened its doors. Readers across America learned that the club's millionaire members were donating portions of their art collections to The Players, turning the building into a miniature museum, a treasure house of antiques, rare books and manuscripts, paintings, and curios. A number of fireproof steel bank safes bolted into the walls held the more precious items, including Second, Third, and Fourth Folio editions of Shakespeare, but the rest of the club's riches were displayed for members to use and enjoy.

Yellow and gold wallpaper lined the reception hall. Blue frescoes covered the ceiling. A fireplace built from slabs of African marble dominated the west end of the room. Zebra and tiger skin rugs covered the glossy oak floors. In the light of crystal chandeliers and lamps selected by Louis Comfort Tiffany, the club's mahogany furniture glowed. Paintings by Velázquez, Sir Joshua Reynolds, and Childe Hassam sat in gilded frames. For Founder's Night, every room, corridor, and even the balustrade of the grand staircase descending from the second-floor library to the main hall was decked with pine boughs and flowers. Blooms and greenery adorned a life-size portrait of Edwin Booth near the main fireplace, like offerings at a saint's altar.

Pressing his way through the crowd of guests, Cleveland would have smelled the club's rich atmosphere of cut flowers and cigar smoke. Smoking was habitual at The Players, tobacco the recognized currency of fellowship. Cuspidors abounded.

A knot of men standing before the central fireplace caught sight of Cleveland and hailed their master of ceremonies with welcoming shouts, ushering him through a pair of sixteen-foot-high sliding doors into the Grill Room, where dinner awaited. Visitors lucky enough to have a meal here found the space magnificent. Branches of stag's antlers had been transformed into candelabra and affixed to the room's mahogany-paneled walls. Oak beams criss-crossed the ceiling, evoking the inner hold of a ship. The head of a ten-point buck, shot by a club member, jutted over a fireplace at one end of the room. A portrait of Edwin Booth's father, the great actor Junius Brutus Booth, hung opposite. Long tables covered in white damask and set with fine old pewter plates and silver goblets awaited President Cleveland, Edwin Booth, and dozens of other distinguished guests.

The Players was an unusual society. Nothing like it existed anywhere else in the country. Too ill and infirm to act onstage any longer, the sixty-year-old Booth had devoted his remaining energies to creating a club where the brightest minds and biggest talents in America could meet and mingle. Membership in this society was limited, by Booth's own decree, to a small number of actors and a lengthy list of men who had proved themselves giants or geniuses in their chosen fields of endeavor. When the actor had approached leading figures in the arts, finance, law, publishing, politics, and science, all submitted their names for membership. Not only William T. Sherman and Grover Cleveland answered the call, but J. Pierpont Morgan, Cornelius Vanderbilt II, and assorted scions of the Astor and Carnegie families. Inventors Nikola Tesla and Peter Cooper Hewitt, author Samuel L. Clemens (always known as Mark at The Players), architect Stanford White, painter John Singer Sargent, designer Louis Comfort Tiffany, and sculptors Frederic Remington and Augustus Saint-Gaudens all sought admission along with poets, judges, book publishers, magazine editors, diplomats, and art patrons.

The Players comprised a field of accomplishment so varied that Booth's bookkeeper was led to devise odd abbreviations to keep track of its members' multifarious occupations. In the official club records, the terms Bish, Bnkr, CP, Expl, Lyr, Mag, Mer, Min, Orn, RE, and RR denote Players who identified their professions, respectively, as Bishop, Banker, College President, Explorer, Lyricist, Magician, Merchant, Mining executive, Ornithologist, Real Estate magnate, and Railroad baron.

Women were barred from the club's door. On one day each year, Shake-speare's birthday, April 23, the wives and daughters of members were permitted to cross the threshold, and then only between the hours of two and four, to drink tea. Club rules also forbade gambling and card playing. Plentiful food and drink, a well-stocked library, camaraderie, and conversation were the only diversions on offer.

Booth considered The Players his lasting gift to America. He hoped the society's members, through continual association, would find new ways to invigorate the nation's cultural, intellectual, and economic life for generations to come. In private, the actor confessed to another goal in mind. He had been born to a family of stage performers, and learned from childhood that Americans viewed actors as second-class citizens; they were hardscrabble illusionists, hucksters who mimed and dissembled before crowds for money. Refined people disapproved of theaters and looked down on anyone who made a living inside them. Even while clamoring for tickets, respectable folk recoiled from social intimacy with the traveling Bohemians they applauded, fearing a taint of immorality. So actors lived apart, in a closed and clannish subculture of their own.

Edwin Booth knew better than most that an actor's isolation from the mainstream could have disastrous consequences. He wanted The Players to bridge the gap between the real world and the realm of the stage, with himself as chief ambassador. "We actors do not mingle enough with minds that influence the world," the Founder explained. "We should measure ourselves through personal contact with outsiders." A club composed only of theater people, Booth said, "would be a gathering place of freaks who come to look upon another sort of freak. I want real men there." Of the 750 men who belonged to the club in 1892, 150 were actors. The rest were "real men."

Edith Wharton, chronicler of the American upper class in the waning years of the nineteenth century, once observed that "the attempts of vulgar persons to buy their way into the circle of the elect" rarely succeeded. Perhaps only a man of Edwin Booth's caliber could have accomplished it. Toward the end of his life, newspapers called Booth "the Actor King." In the last decades of an almost fifty-year career, the millionaire star traveled from city to city by private railroad car, performing Shakespeare for audiences paying up to a hundred dollars per ticket. Booth could earn fifty thousand dollars in four weeks on the road—roughly the equivalent of $2 million in modern currency. When the train towing his car approached a station, bands of musicians gathered by the tracks, alongside parades of citizens and delegations of local officials, to salute him. Edwin Booth, opined one newspaper, "is the foremost actor of a nation of sixty millions, an honor to his time and to his country. No other actor of any age has ever been held in higher esteem." The head of one of Manhattan's ruling families put it another way. "Edwin Booth is a man of genius," he said simply, "and a most charming person to meet—which is not always the case with men of genius, you know."

Hundreds of Players were making the trip through the New Year's storm for the midnight ritual honoring the actor, but a small circle of club members arrived early to share a formal dinner with Booth and President-elect

Cleveland. Immense fortunes had been made in the quarter century since the end of the Civil War, years some historians have referred to as "the most shameful period ever seen in American life." It was a time of collusion between government and private business over land rights, coal and mineral deposits, supply contracts, and tax exemptions. This period witnessed the rise of mammoth trusts and corporations, many of which owed their existence to the rulings of federal courts, Congress, and a White House that saw "the acquisition of wealth as the single worthy aim." Contemporaries called it "the Great Barbecue"; a small number of individuals had the choicest cuts of meat while the mass of Americans, it was said, made do "with the giblets." Many of the men seated in rows along the tables in the Grill Room for Booth's private banquet tonight had seized some of the biggest portions.

One guest, the Player calling himself Mark Twain, had written a novel whose title gave these years their enduring name, "the Gilded Age." Twain lampooned the spectacle of new American wealth by revealing the mendacity and fraud that had accompanied it. The age was gilded, not gold, Twain argued, because one scratch of this gleaming façade revealed the layer of dross underneath.

The same might be said of Booth's palace on Gramercy Park, and not because its owner, decades earlier, led a vagabond's existence, stealing chickens when hungry and sleeping off his hangovers in the gutter. Every man at the table tonight knew who Edwin Booth's younger brother was, though it was forbidden to speak the dead youth's name within the club's walls. Outside The Players, the same newspapers and magazines hailing Edwin Booth as a national treasure observed a similar ban. Everyone knew of the actor's refusal to discuss his brother or his brother's crime. Close friends always took care to warn visitors to The Players that the Founder "had no brother by the name of John Wilkes Booth."

In the twenty-seven years since Abraham Lincoln's death in 1865, the actor refused to set foot in the nation's capital, declining a personal invitation from President Chester A. Arthur to perform there in 1885. Even when a host of United States senators, Supreme Court justices, and cabinet members joined the call for Booth's appearance, the star remained unmoved. He would perform in Baltimore, but no closer. When Booth refused to act in Washington, the capital made a pilgrimage to Booth. A line of first-class railroad cars shuttled President Arthur and his administration to and from Baltimore for a full week. "Night after night," Booth's manager recalled, "the Great World came to him." "Official, Diplomatic, Social Washington," he said, occupied front-row seats in an auditorium forty miles away from Ford's

Theatre, honoring Booth with tearful ovations. Such demonstrations left the actor unmoved.

Once, during a social evening over brandy and tobacco, a young player eager to curry favor with the Founder forgot this taboo, and asked,

"How many brothers and sisters did you have, Mr. Booth?"

A hush fell over the company as the actor replied, slowly, between puffs on a pipe, "I forget the lot of us. I'll name them. You count them for me! Junius Brutus—after my father, of course—Rosalie, Henry, Mary, Frederick, Elizabeth—I come in here—Asia, Joe—how many is that?"

"Nine, Mr. Booth," answered his questioner, mortified at committing such a gaffe. "What big families they used to raise!" the Founder marveled, continuing to smoke, and the topic of conversation was changed. Everyone listening that night knew there was a tenth Booth sibling, but during the Founder's lifetime he was omitted from the count.

When John Wilkes Booth shot Lincoln, a Maryland resident remembered, "extreme prejudice and wild excitement ruled the hour, and was intensified, for the time, in hearing the sound of the name of 'Booth.'" Lynching parties were formed by grieving citizens, and many actors, regardless of their connection to the assassin, went in fear for their safety. Nearly three decades later, such excitement had long been extinguished. "The innocent no longer suffer for the guilty," rejoiced one of Edwin's admirers. "Time sets all things even." A president was present at The Players tonight to garnish the Booth name with laurels, to give a hero's salute to the reputation of an artist who felt tainted by the events of April 14, 1865. The actor had created a living monument to the Booth name and his own celebrity when he founded The Players, but he planned tonight's banquet and special ceremony in order to set things further even. These honorary gestures, one contemporary perceived, established the fact that Edwin Booth was "loved, honored and respected for his transcendent talents and law-abiding citizenship, fully as much as it would be possible to accord him had his reckless brother never committed the insane act."

For most of the guests this Founder's Night, memories of the Civil War were distant. Edith Wharton herself recalled the year 1892 as "the dark time of our national indifference." "The war seemed much less a part of us," she wrote, feeling as if her country had "buried the whole business out of sight, out of hearing." Nobody talked about it anymore, certainly not the men assembled that night to honor Edwin Booth. They, like the rest of the country, accepted the prevailing explanation for what happened in Ford's Theatre. Booth's brother was "no hired assassin," one theatrical old-timer explained. "The spirit of exaltation that made him exclaim as he leaped upon the stage after the fatal shot: 'Sic Semper Tyranis' was but the natural outcome of the distemper that lay in the blood and ill-regulated mind of the father which skipped the other children and lodged in the superficial brain of the mad Wilkes." "The fiend in human shape who committed a deed which has no parallel in atrocity in the world" had been insane. The unsuccessful actor, it was said, inherited the Booth taint of madness, but missed the spark of genius his father and his older brother Edwin possessed. A demented enthusiasm for the South's lost cause and an obsessive hatred for Abraham Lincoln, it was assumed, drove the Founder's brother to his desperate act.

The Founder's Night feast, like the surroundings, was magnificent. An hour before midnight, after the plates were cleared away, the small company rose and passed into the main hall to greet the mass of other Players now arriving. Men in evening dress crammed every room, spilling into the hallways, even occupying steps of the staircase. Younger, more nimble members of the club perched on the banister for a better view of the spot before the central fireplace where the night's ritual would take place. A rain-soaked reporter from the *New York Times* had managed to make his way past the door. When the club's grandfather clock struck midnight and Grover Cleveland claimed the floor to speak, the reporter's pen would be ready.

Grover Cleveland was the first Democratic candidate to capture the White House since the South seceded from the Union. He composed his speech honoring Edwin Booth tonight with care. Not an eloquent man but a single-minded one, Cleveland was known for his defense of millionaires' interests and for his veto of a bill awarding pensions to Civil War veterans. Allergic to art and a stranger to reading material other than the Bible, Cleveland held literature and high culture in low esteem.

Some people who knew Cleveland intimately marveled at how this corpulent nonreader could brave the intellectual atmosphere of The Players. There, the gathering of artists, innovators, and thinkers would make any ordinary man feel like a voyager to a foreign land. Cleveland, perhaps with a sense of his own limitations, referred to Booth, Twain, and other exceptional members of the club as "the bright lights." Stories were told of the president being seized with paralyzing shyness when hobnobbing with Players "to whom he attributed superior learning or cultivation." But these attacks were momentary. Cleveland was no stranger to drink, and after a few glasses, the president lost his reticence and became "one of the raciest talkers and raconteurs" in the city.

When drinking and trading stories in the club's Grill Room, Cleveland could feel at home, but his strongest connection to this congregation of "bright lights" was the Founder himself. Edwin Booth and Grover Cleveland first met while summering on nearby Connecticut estates during Cleveland's first term. The actor and the president discovered an immediate rapport. In hot July weather, wearing broad-brimmed straw hats and linen trousers, the two trooped off with fishing lines and tackle. The president considered Booth an excellent sport, and easily set aside the crime the actor's brother had committed so many years ago. Cleveland's voting public could find nothing unseemly in this friendship. Almost three decades had gone by since the tragedy. For an equal period, the highest echelons of society had embraced Edwin Booth. In fact, it was widely known that the idea for creating The Players had first come to Booth while he was taking a pleasure trip on a steam yacht belonging to the financier Elias C. Benedict, President Cleveland's closest, most trusted friend.

Spending warm-weather holidays on the New England coast was a long-standing habit in the Booth family. Edwin and two of his brothers, in a rare period of peace among them, vacationed on Long Island Sound during the last summer of the Civil War. One of them kept a diary for July 1864, noting the brothers spent quiet days together "sunning and rowing . . . loafing, reading and smoking." If, when walking the same beaches with Grover Cleveland decades later, Edwin's memory ever turned to that faraway time, it is unlikely he ever mentioned it to the president.

After dinner, President Cleveland made his way through the throng in the main hall to reach the central fireplace. The club's maître d'hôtel, dressed in severe black, directed him to stand before the hearth in preparation for the ceremony. The backdrop for Cleveland's midnight speech could not have been grander. The marble mantel, heavily carved, was over a foot thick. A large medallion stamped with The Players' masks of tragedy and comedy loomed over the flames. Bronze candelabra, weighing hundreds of pounds, supported blazing candles on either side of the fireplace. John Singer Sargent's life-size portrait of Edwin Booth filled the wall. Reaching nearly to the ceiling, the picture showed the star at middle age. Booth seemed to be striding out of the gold frame, on the verge of speaking. Sargent was no flatterer. Before posing for the penetrating, all-seeing portraitist, Edwin Booth was advised by fellow club members to "lock yourself in a dark room and sandpaper your soul." Sargent certainly painted the actor as he saw him: an egotist and a depressive, an artist at once compassionate, ruthless, morbidly sensitive, and filled with tension and grief. The Players loved this honest image of their Founder, and complimented club member Sargent on his triumph.

Cleveland needed only to look at the difference between this portrait and its white-haired, hollow-cheeked original to understand why his presence as speaker tonight had been requested so urgently. The living Edwin Booth had taken his place at Cleveland's side in an armchair before the fireplace. He looked a decade older than his fifty-nine years. Rheumatism, a stroke, and an assassination attempt by a Lincoln-loving audience member while Booth was performing in Chicago in 1879 had all taken their toll. Rumors that Booth's health was failing, that perhaps he was not long for this world, seemed to be accurate.

Cleveland grasped Edwin's hand to wish him Happy New Year then stepped aside to make room for other well-wishers. The actor was heard to say in a low voice, "You drink tonight to my health. A year from tonight you will drink to my memory." Friends reproved Booth for the gloomy prediction, but he only smiled and shook his head. Walter Oettel, the headwaiter, placed a small table next to Cleveland and poured a bottle of champagne into the three-handled silver cup the president would use when toasting Booth at midnight. The Players drank from this ceremonial vessel every year during the ritual pledge of fidelity to the Founder.

When the Players' clock indicated five minutes to midnight, the noise in the hall subsided and all guests turned to where President Cleveland stood beside the Founder. The waiter held the three-handled cup ready as Cleveland smiled at his audience. He was here tonight, before prominent witnesses, to honor a man who had been waiting nearly thirty years for such a gesture. The *Times* reporter stood in the crowd, noting Cleveland's words and demeanor. A transcript of the speech appeared in the papers the next day. Perhaps it was the exalted company, or perhaps it was the weightiness of the task before him, but Cleveland's hearers were surprised at the man's unaccustomed eloquence.

"Gentlemen," he began, "this is one of the occasions which remind me that the best things in life are not found in struggle or turmoil, nor in the sad pursuit of a favorite phantom. There is something within our reach more valuable, more satisfying, more ennobling, than all that wealth, or social distinction, or even professional success can give us. I speak," he said, "of friendship." A storm of applause interrupted here, and for a few moments Cleveland was unable to proceed. When the clapping subsided, the president faced Edwin Booth again and resumed. "We rejoice that the opportunity is here and now afforded us to express our love and admiration for our Founder, whose name is a sacred word within these walls, and of whose fame, we, as his brothers, are doubly proud. You honor us all, Mr. Booth, and you know how affectionately and heartily we wish you a 'Happy New Year.'" The *Times* reported that the Players burst into "a fervent chorus of acclaim" while the actor rose slowly from his chair to bow to the room.

Men standing close to him noticed Booth was crying. The clock was striking twelve as the Founder, with hands that trembled, accepted the massive silver cup of champagne from the president. When he raised it to his lips to drink, the Players cheered again. Cleveland took the cup back from Edwin, sipped, and handed it into the audience. Every club member would drink from it in turn. Silence settled over the company. One man standing in the crowd that night remembered shivering at the sight of Booth and Cleveland, and feeling "the chill at the heart" that comes from experiencing an unforgettable moment in history. This is a president of the United States, people were thinking, and this is the brother of the man who shot Lincoln. The midnight ritual complete, the frail actor stepped into an elevator and ascended to his private apartment on the mansion's third floor. Less than a year later, Edwin Booth would be dead.

The actor made his exit from his last Founder's Night ceremony almost dropping with exhaustion, but despite the late hour he could not close his eyes. The yellow-canopied four-poster in Booth's bedroom had a wishful motto painted over it, "Now blessings light on him that first invented sleep." Every night in his luxurious sanctum at The Players, the insomniac star stayed fitfully awake, smoking a pipe in silence, waiting often until the hour of dawn for rest to claim him. Edwin called this sleepless stretch between midnight and morning "my vulture hours," telling friends that crowding memories kept him awake through the night, preying on him like scavenging birds.

Booth wrestled with his thoughts alone, he said, "in the aching gloom of my little red room." He never talked about what troubled him, or invited a friend to share his all-night vigils. Edwin Booth served out a sentence imposed by his tireless memory inside the walls of The Players, spending five years in this bedroom where sleep was a stranger. "Nothing of fame or fortune can compensate for spiritual suffering," Edwin wrote to his daughter on the twenty-fifth anniversary of Abraham Lincoln's murder. "I'd sooner be an obscure farmer, or a cabinetmaker as my father advised," the actor stated, than endure "the penalty of greatness. But Nature cast me for the part she found me best fitted for, and I have to play it, and must play it, till the curtain falls." On June 7, 1893, at one o'clock in the morning, in that bedroom, the end came. He was sixty.

Booth's room remains unchanged and undisturbed still, over a century after his death. Visitors are rare. A framed chalk rubbing over his writing desk, taken from the inscription on Shakespeare's tomb at Stratford-upon-Avon, reads like a warning: "Good friend, for Jesus' sake forbear to dig the dust enclosed here. Blessed be the man that spares these stones, and curst be he that moves my bones." It would be a fitting epitaph for Edwin Booth. To enter his chamber now is to confront a puzzle. The place is a jumble of images and artifacts testifying to a darker drama beneath the surface of this actor's long and extraordinary career.

To the left of Edwin's bed, placed so as to be at eye level with the actor as he reclined against the pillows, is a photograph of his brother John Wilkes in street clothes, dating from the Civil War. The handsome face of their father, Junius Brutus Booth, flushed with the boundless energy of a nineteen-year-old, shines from a gilt frame over the doorway. This portrait could be of any young British gentleman: his hair is combed to perfection and his cravat is crisply tied over a high collar. A photograph of the same man, taken decades later in America, provides a startling contrast: this Junius Brutus Booth wears mismatched garments, his features are roughened by drink and exposure to the sun, and a fanatic gleam lurks in his eyes. A cameo of the Booth boys' London-born mother, Mary Ann Holmes, rests on a dresser near the bed, and on the far wall is a picture of the young actress Edwin married on the eve of the Civil War. The day of their wedding, John Wilkes was the only member of the Booth family who agreed to be a witness.

Below this picture, a dagger dangles in a scabbard. Edwin and his brothers were skilled fencers and fighters, able to enact the gymnastic swordplay of *Macbeth, Romeo and Juliet, Richard III, Hamlet,* and *Julius Caesar.* Stagecraft was in Edwin Booth's bones. From his famous father, the star had learned how to set a scene and dominate it. John Wilkes Booth had not been apprenticed to his father, but the training he acquired on his own was on full display the night of April 14, 1865, when the twenty-six-year-old made his show-stopping entrance in the third act of *Our American Cousin.* John choreographed his surprise performance at Ford's Theatre in part to secure himself a permanent place in national memory and knock his celebrated older brother off his pedestal forever. Every aspect of the brief, violent scene was carefully planned by a narcissistic player who cast his victim in a minor role, a bleeding stage prop. The firing of Booth's pistol was not a signal to bring down the curtain, but the attention-grabbing announcement of his own grand entrance. After shooting Lincoln, the killer planted himself at center stage, stalking across the boards in a slow, menacing crouch. He slashed a dagger before the footlights, shouting scripted words of defiance. This was a star's turn, and many in the theater that night perceived the assassin was acting.

Even the shooter's wild leap from the balcony of Lincoln's box was contrived, not improvised. Dizzying fifteen-foot jumps were among Booth's signature tricks. Theater owner John T. Ford had seen John Wilkes make the same jump three years earlier: while playing *Macbeth* in Baltimore, Ford stated in his court testimony, Wilkes made his entrance by plummeting to the stage from a precipice, startling Shakespeare's witches as they toiled over the cauldron. Edwin Booth's closest friend, Adam Badeau, a theater critic and Union Army officer, was in the field as an aide-de-camp to General Ulysses S. Grant when Lincoln was killed. From his post in Virginia, Colonel Badeau, who knew John Wilkes well, immediately recognized the assassination as a performance. "It was exactly what a man brought up in a theater might have been expected to conceive," Badeau wrote. "A man, too, of his peculiar family, the son of Junius Brutus Booth, used all his life to acting tragedies."

When Junius Brutus Booth died before his time—stricken with dysentery in 1852 aboard a Mississippi River steamboat—he bequeathed a contest to his two favorite sons. At the first news of the actor's demise, theater people could predict the nature of this competition. This towering star, beloved by audiences from New York to New Orleans, left "a kingless kingdom" behind him. The elder Booth's "vacant throne and unworn crown were waiting," a family friend explained, for one of his sons, Edwin or John Wilkes, to seize. While yet in their teens, the two brothers dedicated themselves to a fight for their father's legacy. Not only fame was at stake between the two siblings, but also money. On the crowded boards of the nineteenth-century American theater business, there was room for only one Booth.

Four years older and ruthlessly competitive, Edwin Booth used every advantage he had to lock his younger brother out of a stage career, denying John Wilkes the mentoring and professional help he might otherwise have provided. The younger brother was forced to make his bid for stardom largely alone, encouraged only by his mother, Mary Ann, and his sister Asia. As the race progressed, it became clear only one of the brothers had inherited their father's genius. John Wilkes lacked the qualities that made his brother a star. Time and again in the course of his brief life, the younger Booth stood by as Edwin scored victory after victory, amassing large profits and raising the bar of achievement higher. Edwin had been furious when he heard of his brother's crime. He interpreted Lincoln's murder as a direct attack on the celebrity he worked so hard to win. "Oh where has my glory gone?" Edwin once lamented. "John's madness," he later wrote, appeared "to set the seal on my destiny."

The race between the brothers Booth did not end with the president's death, or when the assassin was killed on the run. Edwin pressed on with greater intensity than before, striving to outpace the notoriety his brother achieved and to restore honor to the Booth name. Theater audiences fueled the now one-sided contest. As a New York theatrical agent of the Civil War period explained, "Edwin Booth was devoured with a thirst for fame—a very wise ambition, for fame brings money—and he drew the largest profits after his brother's assassination of Lincoln." Only six months after the president's body was laid in the ground at Springfield, Illinois, the brother of Lincoln's killer gave notice that he would walk the stage once more, pulling off one of the most audacious comebacks in American history.

THE ACTOR'S NOW FRAYING BEDROOM ON THE THIRD FLOOR OF THE PLAYERS is the domain of one whose outsize talents were instrumental in changing the course of history. It is the place where a tormented man privately weighed the meaning of his success and measured his share of responsibility for a brother's epic crime. Edwin's dramatic gifts, his accomplishments, the magnitude of his victory over his sibling, had played a part in costing Abraham Lincoln his life. These thoughts, pawed over in silence night after night, year after year, brought Edwin Booth's "vulture hours" down upon him. Even when a president of the United States led a room of eminent Americans in praise of the Booth name, the knowledge remained. As much as Lincoln's murder was the result of the war between the North and South, it also was the climax of a dark struggle between two brothers who never wore the uniform of soldiers, except onstage. Until his dying day, Edwin Booth lived with the fact that he himself loomed as large as President Lincoln in what a family friend called "the vortex of hell-born dreams" driving John Wilkes to pull the trigger. A confession of sorts burst from Edwin at the end of his life. "I am glad I have not sons," he said. "When a name becomes important it had better die with the one who made it distinguished."

After Mark Twain, one historian has observed, Edwin Booth was one of the most recognizable American artists of the late nineteenth century. His features were familiar to millions; quite a feat in a day before motion pictures. When Booth walked abroad in cities, strangers recognized him. Thus did many Chicagoans observe the star making a pilgrimage one Sunday morning to the statue of the slain president that stands in a park on the shores of Lake Michigan. Thinking he was unseen, Booth removed his hat and stood for some minutes contemplating the statue's face. A witness to the scene said the actor then "took a flower from his button hole and placed it at the martyred President's feet. When he reached his carriage he turned and made a gesture which said everything that was in his heart. He drove away."

The visitor to Edwin Booth's room today will see the glass cabinet with mirrored shelves that holds the paraphernalia of a dedicated smoker. Here the actor kept his collection of pipes, some carved from bone or molded from clay, some slender and long-stemmed, others short, rounded, and fat. When the "vulture hours" of memory plagued him, he filled and lit one of these, and sat contemplating a line from *Don Quixote* he had painted in green and gold lettering over his fireplace: *"And when the smoke ascends on high, then thou beholds the vanity of worldly stuff, gone with a puff. Thus think, and smoke tobacco."*

Together, Edwin and John Wilkes Booth enacted one of the strangest stories in American history, one with twists and turnings as improbable as any saga from Shakespeare. To trace the plot of their intertwined lives and to understand its violent climax, we must follow this tale of two brothers back to the beginning, to the moment the Booth family first arrived on these shores. The parents of Edwin and John Wilkes Booth came here from London in the infant years of the Republic. Forging a life in a new land changed the couple, altering them in ways that would have a profound effect on their children.

Their father, Junius Brutus Booth, was an extraordinary figure. His genius onstage won him the admiration and regard of several United States presidents—including John Quincy Adams, Andrew Jackson, and Martin Van Buren. But Booth's membership in the theatrical profession, his taste for alcohol and violence, his heretical religious beliefs, and his recurring attempts at suicide consigned him to the company of misfits and outlaws. The boys received another unhappy legacy from their parents. Junius Brutus Booth and Mary Ann Holmes lived together for thirty years, unmarried. All of their ten children were illegitimate, a Baltimore lawyer proved, the "fruits" of "adulterous" intercourse. Born into these circumstances, it is no surprise that the brothers Booth conceived a lifelong hunger for social and professional prestige. Even before their ill-fated race for fame began, the boys played their parts in a painful family drama filled with episodes of humiliation and betrayal so extreme, only a playwright, it might seem, could have imagined them.

PART ONE

———◆———

1821–1852

ONE

A FAMOUS REBEL

Both young and old rebel,
And all goes worse than I have power to tell.
—*Richard II*, 3.2

ON JUNE 30, 1821, A SCHOONER—THE *TWO BROTHERS*—SAILED INTO PORT at Norfolk, Virginia. Bound from Madeira with a cargo of wine, the vessel made its way through a forest of tall ships in the harbor. *Two Brothers* belonged to the smallest class of freighters on the high seas, and was not fit to carry passengers. The only private space on board belonged to the captain. Yet for this trip, he had cut a deal with a man and a young woman who said they were anxious to reach America. An appeal to chivalry—the woman was pregnant—may have persuaded the captain to give up his cabin, but more likely it was her partner's offer to pay for their passage in gold. Money changed hands, and the captain duly listed his two passengers, "Junius Brutus Booth and lady," as "Actors" in his manifest. Only in hindsight does the name of the ship assume an aura of destiny.

They claimed to be husband and wife. This was a lie, one they planned to pass off as truth in the strange land coming into view over the prow. In reality, they were runaways. Booth was running from his wife and his three-year-old son in London. Nineteen-year-old Mary Ann Holmes was on the run from her parents. She had slipped out of her bedroom in the dark of night, not bothering to tell mother or father of her plan to elope with a married man, and start a new life overseas. It had taken them forty-four days to reach Norfolk from Madeira. Before that, the two made their escape from London by riding a stagecoach out of the city in secret. Stopping at a smugglers' haven on the English Channel, they found a ship leaving for the island of Madeira and had started on the first leg of their long voyage west.

The pair now stood on deck surrounded by their worldly goods, a little mountain of trunks embossed in bold letters, J. B. BOOTH. One box contained Mary Ann's hastily packed books and clothing. The rest were crammed with the costly wardrobe of a Shakespearean actor: a crown and cloak of purple velvet for *Richard III;* a toga, Roman sword, and sandals for *Julius Caesar;* Hamlet's black doublet and hose; the turban, scimitar, and sash of *Othello;* Shylock's black hat and prayer shawl; the boots and tunic belonging to Macbeth. Packed between layers of costumes were pots of theatrical makeup, wigs, playbills and posters from old shows, a collection of fan mail, and some rave reviews clipped out of London newspapers.

The two wayfarers had turned their backs on what was then the largest city in the world. Over a million people teemed in London's streets, where palaces and cathedrals, libraries and museums stood monument to centuries of Western civilization. Norfolk, by contrast, was a blank on the map, a place seemingly without history. From the deck of the *Two Brothers,* Junius and Mary Ann would have seen a handful of wooden buildings and low warehouses huddled onshore. Like so many other American settlements, Norfolk looked rough and primitive, "like a child's toy," one English visitor sniffed.

The town clung to a patch of ground on the edge of the Great Dismal Swamp. Eight thousand people scratched out a living here, in the shadow of an immense, alien wilderness. This ancient forest was filled with trees half submerged in brackish liquid, their trunks and branches choked by vines and insectivorous plants. It stretched for eight hundred square miles, populated by reptiles, bears, wildcats, and a species of wild boar the local people called "tuskers."

Only the promise of treasure could have lured settlers to this inhospitable spot. In 1682, the British first braved the swamp's ground in order to harvest live oaks. The trees were hard to find and difficult to extract from boggy turf, but they were beloved by shipbuilders. Live oak timber was legendary for its resistance to water, showing unbeatable strength and longevity at sea. The Great Dismal Swamp's rich supply had kept loggers and carpenters busily at work in Norfolk for over a hundred years. In colonial times, her shipwrights made fast, durable crafts for the British navy. After the Revolution, the town built nearly a hundred ships a year for the United States merchant marine.

Immigrants were scarce here. Most new arrivals hoping to build a future in America put in at Baltimore, New York, or Philadelphia, populous places with plenty of opportunity for employment. Norfolk was a stopover for traders. Captains discharged cargoes of coffee, sugar, and molasses at the warehouses. Crews visited the few brothels and gambling dens onshore before loading up their ships with tobacco cultivated by Virginia's slaves. Occasionally, a luxury item, like an English harpsichord or a statue of Italian marble, arrived at Norfolk's docks, destined to grace the mansion of a wealthy planter owner living inland, up the James River.

A crowd met *Two Brothers* at the dock. Agents swarmed to register the cargo, stevedores hauled out the wine casks, and a pack of boys came to gawk. Junius Brutus Booth and Mary Ann Holmes would have been a notable sight anywhere, but here, in this rough way station on the edge of a swamp, the two were unforgettable. Eyewitnesses remembered the couple's arrival for years afterward, and histories of the port always record the incident. Booth was small, not above five and a half feet tall, but he made an outsize impression. People saw a "handsome youth with a look betraying no ordinary degree of intelligence" step off the ship. He had arresting features, blue eyes, and long dark hair. A pair of gold hoops dangled, pirate-like, from his ears. His pile of initialed luggage excited much interest, but his female companion was the most interesting object of all. One person described Mary Ann as "exceedingly beautiful, with rare personal attractions," while another flatly asserted she "was the handsomest woman I ever saw."

The residents of Norfolk were starved for amusement. Some regularly inhaled nitrous oxide, or laughing gas, to relieve their boredom. "Forty doses as usual will be prepared, and the first 30 who may leave their names at Mr. Hall's Bookstore shall have the gas administered to them," read a weekly notice in the *American Beacon*, the local paper. Beyond hard labor, heavy drinking, and church attendance, little existed to distract them from the vast wilderness that pressed at the margins of their town. In 1821, most of North America remained unexplored, unexploited, and undisturbed by Europeans. Only ten million people scattered mainly along the eastern seaboard.

In this lonely place, the coming of an entertainer was cause for celebration. Yet Junius Brutus Booth was not just any actor. He was a prodigy, a star, a man internationally renowned for his dramatic genius. He was a European import as rare and precious as the ivory-keyed harpsichords, intricate timepieces, or gold-rimmed telescopes unloaded at the docks for the delight of Virginia's plantation owners.

Booth had come into the world, as he himself was the first to aver, with "a wonder-working mind." He was born in 1796 to a highly educated clan of Jewish lawyers and silversmiths on his father's side, and to an Anglican family on his mother's, in the Bloomsbury section of London. While still a toddler, he showed a startling facility for language. His father instructed him in Latin, Greek, and Hebrew at an early age, and the ambitious child went on to study Arabic, Portuguese, Dutch, French, and Italian before reaching maturity. By his early teens, Booth was stringing verses together like a seasoned poet. He painted and sculpted with skill. Yet to his career-oriented family, the boy's polymath abilities presented a troublesome riddle. They apprenticed him first as a clerk in a law office, then signed him on as printer's devil, then he did a turn in an architecture firm. Junius failed at every post. Oppressed by the tedium of repetitive tasks, he wailed that these jobs were too small for his intelligence. His attention wandered and he shirked assignments. The family then enrolled him at an art academy, but cut off his tuition when a pregnant household servant took the teenager to court for child support.

In 1812 the sixteen-year-old Junius, restless and adventure-hungry, decided to enlist in the British navy. His trunks were packed and midshipman's uniform purchased when his father, Richard, abruptly canceled the arrangement. The United States and Great Britain were at war that year: the elderly attorney did not want his only son to fire cannon at American targets. Lawyer Booth idolized "any and all things appertaining to America," Junius later explained. His father even made an ironclad rule that all visitors to the Booth home bow before "the picture of General Washington that hung up in our parlor." Though such sentiments made Richard Booth extremely "unpopular" in their London neighborhood, Junius remembered, it was a point of family pride to "cherish" the vibrant new nation across the Atlantic where freedoms of religion and self-expression were guaranteed.

Filled with talents that could find no proper outlet, Junius burned with frustration. Finally, in 1813, as one Booth relative remembered, "genius pointed out the path." All London was wild that year for Edmund Kean, the undisputed king of the English stage and greatest actor of his generation. Critics could not find fault with him, worshipping his work in every part he chose to play. Samuel Taylor Coleridge said watching Kean act was "like reading Shakespeare by flashes of lightning." Lord Byron became so overwrought during a Kean performance, he fell into "a sort of convulsive fit" and had to be carried home from the theater, fainting, by friends. Aristocratic admirers showered the star with laurel crowns, flowers, and purses full of gold coins.

Acting, Junius informed his father, was the answer to his dilemma. Onstage, his multitude of talents would all be engaged. To act was to become sculpture animated, poetry brought to life. Not a single word of Shakespeare's works was lost to the boy's extraordinary memory. Junius had acquired fluency in seven languages with ease; learning scripts by heart was the work of a single reading. With Richard's consent, the seventeen-year-old joined a troupe of Shakespearean actors shipping out on a tour of European capitals.

Booth and his fellow players arrived in Brussels in August 1814 not long before the Battle of Waterloo. The Duke of Wellington's army—nearly seventy thousand strong—soon would encamp around the city. Napoleon's forces were gathering as well, preparing to meet for battle. In the coming months, the novice would find himself honing his stagecraft in front of an extraordinary audience. High-ranking British officers, the Duke of York, Prince William of Orange, and Wellington himself sought diversion at the Brussels theater from the mayhem of war. Young Booth was undaunted by the task of entertaining these larger-than-life military heroes. He felt no stage fright. Confidence in his own gifts made him calm, even careless, about the work. When the Prince of Orange made a special request for Junius to play *Macbeth*, the teenager showed up drunk and late for his command performance. Grinning at the prince, Booth explained his tardiness. He had been detained at a brothel by "two interesting mademoiselles," he said, who badly wanted to teach him Dutch. Fortunately for Booth, the prince only laughed at his insouciance and sat back to enjoy the play in good humor. When the actor returned home at last, he was a seasoned player, bold, arrogant, and ready to take London by storm.

In a twist of luck that now seems like a cliché from theatrical legend, Booth's chance at fame arrived in 1817. One night, Edmund Kean, reigning star of London's stage, failed to appear for a scheduled performance. A harried stage manager pushed twenty-year-old Booth on in Kean's place. The play was a melodrama popular then, though long forgotten now, *A New Way to Pay Old Debts*. If Kean produced flashes of lightning, the newcomer showered comets on the crowd. Booth gave the audience, he later boasted, "the god-damnedest" show they had ever seen. Waking up the next morning, he discovered he was a star.

Eager theatrical agents booked Booth at the Covent Garden theater. The announcement drew thousands of people to clamor outside the building, "hungering and thirsting," one critic reported, for the new favorite. Critics proclaimed the young man's gift for Shakespeare was unprecedented. Since Queen Elizabeth's time, they said, few actors had presented the Bard's characters with such wildness and originality.

Edmund Kean was furious to discover that in one night, a young upstart had toppled him from his throne. The jealous star lost no time trying to destroy his challenger. Kean sent men to disrupt Booth's performances at Covent Garden. Night after night, when Junius walked onstage, gangs of rowdies hired by Kean shouted, hissed, and waved insulting signs. The twenty-one-year-old bellowed out his lines, but he could not make himself heard over the confusion. Booth's legions of fans fought back. For over a month, riots erupted as "Boothites" and "Keanites" battled for supremacy in the theater while Junius tried to perform. The uproar at times forced him to run off the stage to escape the rotten vegetables thrown by Kean's supporters. Only a threat by the lord chamberlain to close all the theaters in London put a stop to the trouble. Kean's rabble-rousers were silenced. Junius was free, one of his admirers exulted, to use his talent to achieve "the highest pinnacle of fame."

Richard Booth could not have been happier. His son, far from being a delinquent, now earned a thousand pounds per year onstage, an income some lawyers and architects might envy. Junius had distinguished himself at last. A biography of the dramatic prodigy was rushed into print, telling the story of Booth's rise to stardom. The memoir contained "some passages of his life and a comic song written by Booth and accounted very witty by those who read it." The young actor had won himself a place in the circle of radical British artists calling themselves Romantics. These youthful visionaries wanted to do for painting, drama, and literature what Thomas Jefferson, Benjamin Franklin, and John Adams had done for political liberty. They saw themselves as rebels in art, creating works that celebrated the individual, worshipped the natural world, and expressed unrestrained human emotion.

Francisco Goya painted scenes of violence and suffering; J. M. W. Turner captured avalanches and hurricanes on canvas; Mary Wollstonecraft Shelley plumbed the depths of horror in her masterpiece, *Frankenstein;* the poems of Lord Byron and Percy Bysshe Shelley promoted the sublime experiences of sex, passion, and rebellion. Yet Booth, the actor, in a sense surpassed them all. His creations are lost to us now, but with his body and his voice alone, he channeled the murderer's fury, the avalanche's force, the weirdness of a human monster, and the soaring sensations of love. His art was alive, immediate, in the flesh—not trapped in the pages of a book or nailed to a museum wall—and he could be seen nightly, by anyone, for the price of a theater ticket.

Booth's showdown with Kean did more than demonstrate his acting mettle: it publicized the young star's talent overseas. British newspapers circulating in the United States carried news of the actors' contest. From Albany to New Orleans, from Washington, D.C., to Norfolk, many in the United States had heard the name Junius Brutus Booth.

Those who watched this meteoric talent arrive on American shores did so with intense curiosity. One mentioned how surprised he was to find the famous actor not pompous or puffed with self-regard, but boyish, friendly, and completely open in his manners. A citizen on Norfolk's docks that hot July day in 1821 caught a glimpse of the actor as he arrived, noting Booth "was nearly twenty-five, but looked seven years younger, wore an old straw hat and a linen roundabout; and, without the least shadow of pretension, he sauntered along, gazing at everything he saw."

Junius and Mary Ann followed dirt lanes from the harbor to Main Street, cutting through a slum of brothels and taverns to reach the center of town. No doubt it was on this walk that the couple saw American slaves for the first time. While both slaves and free blacks lived in Norfolk, the physical sufferings of enslaved people were impossible to miss. Many were hungry, poorly clothed, and showed signs of brandings, whippings, or other forms of abuse. In Virginia at the time, though the Booths did not know it yet, teaching a slave to read was a greater crime than killing one. Junius and Mary Ann may have paid a shilling to a female slave tending one of Norfolk's "tea wagons" near Market Square. Because potable water was hard to obtain, carts with barrels of tea brewed from well water could be found on most street corners.

Visitors to Norfolk complained that the smell of human waste, rising from ditches and puddles in the streets, overwhelmed the marshy town. Its cluster of makeshift wood houses appeared "slovenly" to visitors used to the orderly brick buildings of Boston, Philadelphia, and Washington, D.C. But after forty-four days at sea, Junius and Mary Ann surely found Norfolk's Main Street a cheerful sight. Here were carts and bright-painted carriages and a motley, busy pedestrian crowd. Scottish, French, Portuguese, and Spanish-speaking people called Norfolk home. Junius also tuned his ear to the tones and phrasings unique to the American South that were audible in Norfolk. Virginians, the language-loving actor noted in his travel diary that day, pronounced *cow* as "kyow" and offered to "tote them there things along" when they meant "carry."

The travelers craved fresh food and information. They hurried, therefore, to the Exchange Coffee House, the hub of Norfolk's activity. This institution was so important to town life that most business in Norfolk would have come to a halt without it. When President James Monroe visited the Great Dismal Swamp two years before, he and Secretary of State John C. Calhoun dined at the Exchange. The place was a restaurant, travel agency, newsstand, reading room, and informal town hall all in one. The Exchange kept schedules for all the steamboat lines, stagecoach routes, and packet ship systems in the region. Newspapers from the principal American cities, indexed by date, were held in a small library for the benefit of travelers and traders. Citizens could track the arrival and departure of ships, identify cargoes and passengers, ascertain the weather in different parts of the country, and keep up with national and international events. People also might discover where cholera or smallpox had broken out, vital information for anyone planning a journey.

For an actor needing to drum up some paid work, the Exchange was the place to start. "All the news, rumors true or false, scandal and title-tattle centered there," one old-timer remembered. "It was a useful place of resort where a-body could meet a-body." A body also might drink a mint julep, consume a beefsteak, or order a dandelion salad. Scanning local papers while eating their first good meal in weeks, the couple would have seen the Dismal Swamp Canal Company's advertisement for loggers. Men willing to risk life and limb cutting timber might earn fifteen dollars a month. Mary Ann and Junius must have laughed at their good fortune: once the actor found a theater, he could earn ten times the money in a single night.

People at the Exchange told the actor that a grand playhouse, the Marshall, had just been completed in Richmond. Theaters were scarce in Virginia. This new structure, sizable and well appointed, seemed heaven-sent for Booth's American debut. Junius learned that the steamboat *Powhatan* could carry him and Mary Ann up the James River to Virginia's capital for seven dollars apiece. His trunks of costumes went free of charge.

Chugging through a swamp by steamboat filled Junius with elation. He relished novelty and hard traveling. Touring Brussels and Antwerp in the wake of Napoleon's armies, the actor had recorded in a leather-bound diary scenes of what he called "the terrible effects of the late war." Booth had seen looters being beheaded by guillotines in Brussels, watched prostitutes and soldiers transacting their business "in the public streets at day," and walked past houses and churches "beaten almost to pieces" by cannon fire. Now he scribbled a new round of impressions in a black account book, describing the strange sensation of steam-powered travel.

His companion was not such an experienced traveler. Mary Ann Holmes, born and raised in London, probably never dreamed of leaving her home city or of leading a life different from that of her working-class parents, until she crossed paths with Junius Brutus Booth. Less than a year earlier, the young woman had bought a ticket to see Booth act. The experience changed her life, she later explained, and was the reason she followed the actor to this place where sixteen-foot-long alligators patrolled the riverbanks. It was the reason she agreed, unmarried and five months pregnant, to risk a ride toward an uncertain future aboard the *Two Brothers*, and now, the *Powhatan*. Mary Ann Holmes had been seduced by genius.

She was born in 1802 to an industrious, deeply pious Anglican couple in Marsh Gate, a poor area of London. Mary Ann, an only child, learned to read and write in a household where scripture was the only reading material allowed. Money was short, which may explain why the parents, who ran a plant nursery, decided to use Mary Ann's exceptional beauty to boost business. Mr. Holmes sent his daughter to the market at Covent Garden with trays of fresh flowers for sale. Here, in the crowded square before the city's leading theater, Mary Ann wandered among farm stalls, food venders, jugglers, and fortune tellers, selling bouquets to the audiences who packed the playhouse nightly.

In 1820, Junius Brutus Booth was starring in a hit production of *King Lear* at Covent Garden theater. His interpretation of the character was so sensational, London newspapers complained the actor was driving the city "Lear-mad." Day and night, Booth's admirers howled loudly through the streets, echoing the speeches of the demented king. When Mary Ann saw the play on October 9, she was starstruck. The girl's attitude toward Booth's talent, one of her family members said, was nothing less than "reverent." No record exists of how the flower girl managed to come face-to-face with the actor she idolized. She may have stopped Booth in the market square as he left the theater, or he may have noticed her on his own. However the encounter happened, the meeting left a deep impression on Junius. He placed a large "X" in his diary next to the date October 9, 1820. Years later, one of Mary Ann's children wrote the words "the night mother first saw my father" beside his inked mark.

Booth was infatuated with the beautiful stranger. He began composing feverish letters to her: in one, he addressed Mary Ann as "my own soul," and signed the page "your worshipper, Junius." The actor wrote nearly a hundred letters to the girl in the space of three months, scribbling his feelings onto paper backstage, in his dressing room, nightly from the date of their first meeting to the moment in January 1821 when she at last agreed to run away with him. Junius did not mail these declarations of love to the Holmes household. They were smuggled to Mary Ann in secret, probably pressed into her hand by a messenger as she sold her bouquets in Covent Garden.

The girl told no one about the actor's letters. Her Anglican parents, Mary Ann later confessed, were "very religious and severe." Mr. and Mrs. Holmes would have put a stop to the intrigue if they had discovered it. Letters of the kind Booth was writing to their daughter could have only one aim, and it was not honorable. The actor belonged to a higher social class than their own. He possessed a gentleman's classical education, a refined accent, and money. Whatever other promises he could offer Mary Ann—romance, adventure, material luxuries, entrée to a world beyond the working-class sphere of her birth—marriage was not among them. Junius Brutus Booth already had a wife.

Booth had met Adelaide Delannoy in Brussels in 1814. With the city's hotels crowded to capacity with officers, diplomats, and journalists, the players in Booth's troupe were billeted in a large house belonging to Adelaide's mother, described as "a gentlewoman of good birth and education, having three daughters." Adelaide was the liveliest of the Delannoy girls. She fell hard for the dashing young player, and when he returned to London, she followed him. French-speaking Adelaide was "not pretty," Booth's friends complained. She was also a Catholic, and almost ten years his senior. Yet the Belgian woman was impressively well educated. Junius had been captivated by her quick mind and head for business. The two exchanged vows before an Anglican minister in Bloomsbury. "I am married to Booth since the 8th of May," Adelaide boasted in an 1815 letter home to her mother. "I am the happiest of women." She proved a helpmeet to the actor as he soared to fame, advising the younger man on his dealings with fans, newspaper critics, and theater managers. They lived in Booth's childhood home with his elderly father, in the house where General Washington's portrait hung in a place of honor on the parlor wall. The couple's only son, Richard Junius Booth, was born in 1819. Yet the instant he met Mary Ann Holmes, Junius Brutus Booth seems to have made up his mind to leave Adelaide and their shared life completely behind.

If ever there was a moment for a married man to abandon his family on a whim, 1820 was the year to do it. By then, many of the leading artists and intellectuals of Booth's generation—poets Lord Byron and Percy Bysshe Shelley, pioneering feminist Mary Wollstonecraft, and philosopher William Godwin—had declared war on the institution of marriage. Byron's one-man campaign of free love created a public sensation. The aristocrat had affairs with hundreds of women—married and unmarried, blue-blooded and common, youthful and mature—and liked to celebrate his exploits in witty, wildly popular verses. One of his poems, "The Corsair," sold ten thousand copies in a day. London gossips whispered the insatiable Byron pursued young men as well, and even shared a sexual relationship with his half sister. Shelley was no less scandalous. This poet seduced Mary Wollstonecraft's sixteen-year-old daughter, Mary Godwin, deserting his own wife to take the girl to a love nest in Switzerland. Nine months later, the precocious teenager had given birth to Shelley's illegitimate child and composed literature's first work of science fiction, *Frankenstein*.

To these Romantics, marriage was a form of slavery. The lifelong legal bond was an impediment to freedom and self-expression, stifling the creative force of human passion. "In the cold, formal English world," one devotee of Shelley explained, "the yoke of marriage is an iron one that crushes those who have once thrown it over their necks." Booth agreed. The actor idolized Byron and Shelley, taking inspiration from their bold, rebellious philosophy. Junius told Mary Ann the men were always in his thoughts. "These are my companions," the actor declared, indicating the extensive collection of Byron's and Shelley's writings he owned and obsessively read. "With them, time never wearies, and the eloquent teachings that fall from their leaves are counselors and guides."

Booth's letters alone were not enough to part Mary Ann Holmes from her family. Adultery was a serious step for a young woman to contemplate, especially one raised in a pious household like the Holmeses'. If she cast her lot with Booth, Mary Ann risked life as an outcast. English society expelled Byron and Shelley for their sins. The two poets died in exile, yearning for home. Adulterers wore their brand for life, and their offspring suffered a hard fate. Any children she bore to Booth would have no lawful right to their father's surname and could not inherit his property. They would be persons in limbo, portionless and without a legal identity. The benefits of her future at this actor's side would have to outweigh the considerable costs.

Desperate to press his case, Junius presented the eighteen-year-old with a ten-volume edition of Byron's *Works* beautifully bound in leather. Cautiously hiding the expensive volumes in her bedroom, Mary Ann remembered, she would "get up at night and read these books at her window by moonlight," evading her mother's watchful eye. Most right-thinking parents banned Byron from the shelves of schoolroom and parlor, seeing his poetry as a danger to girlhood purity. The poet laughed at this prohibition. "There has been an eleventh commandment to women not to read [my work]," he crowed. "But that can be of little import to them, poor things—for the reading or non-reading of a book will never keep down a single petticoat." The author underestimated his own writing. Mary Ann later indicated to her children that it had been Byron's poetry that tipped the balance in her mind in favor of accepting Booth's proposal.

Most teenagers found Byron's catalog of sexual escapades fascinating, but the poems' real danger lay elsewhere. In everything he wrote, Byron taught his youthful readers one lesson: life held no greater reward than romantic passion. His verse, like a rhyming, titillating Declaration of Independence, urged young people to defy their parents and pursue true love, whatever the cost. Mary Ann was intoxicated by the message. Decades later, twelve-year-old John Wilkes Booth would recite Byron's poem "The Giaour" to his mother and father. The gesture was perhaps the child's way of celebrating the renegade beginnings of his parents' love affair.

Mary Ann was awed to discover that Junius and the author of these poems belonged to the same circle. Byron had sat on the board of directors of Drury Lane, the theater where Booth often performed. Byron prowled the greenroom for sexually available actresses, and picked drinking companions from the company of male stars. To show his admiration for Booth's genius onstage, the actor told Mary Ann, Lord Byron had sent Booth his portrait. This tiny watercolor was a treasure, a miniature of Byron's face painted in detail on an oval of ivory. Instead of a wedding ring, Booth gave the poet's picture to Mary Ann. Taking the ornament to a jeweler, he requested it be "backed in gold and set for a lady's brooch."

She finally eloped with Junius Brutus Booth on January 18, 1821. Packing for her escape, the flower girl tucked the ten-volume set of Byron's poems into her trunk, but she left the actor's letters behind. At the throat of her dress, she pinned Lord Byron's cameo. She wore it proudly, a badge of her newfound belief in free love. A distraught Mr. and Mrs. Holmes woke the next morning to find their daughter gone. They ransacked her room for clues to her whereabouts. To their horror they found "ninety-three letters from Booth and a dark lantern," the device that helped Mary Ann read secretly after lights out.

The runaways could not stay in London. Actors' reputations were fragile things, and audiences fickle. A charge of bigamy could put an end to Booth's stardom. Lord Byron owned vast estates in the north of England. Shelley was the pampered heir of a baronet. Their inherited fortunes freed them to defy social rules, but Junius Brutus Booth was no aristocrat. This middle-class son of a lawyer had a living to earn.

A solution came in the form of a letter from Romantic philosopher William Godwin. Godwin was infamous for his attacks on the institution of marriage. The lifelong bond, he wrote, was "the worst of all laws" and "the most odious of all monopolies." Marriage was "evil," Godwin declared, "a fraud," "an irretrievable mistake." It would be far better, he argued, for men and women to pursue "sensual intercourse" and "affairs" freely, according to "the unforced consent of either party." Like most London Romantics, Godwin was a great admirer of Booth's volcanic acting. His letter to the young star was filled with praise and encouragement. Reading it, Junius must have felt as if this man, whose daughter had had an affair with Shelley, was sanctioning his and Mary Ann's adulterous plans. Godwin knew what it was like to feel "the brutal outcry" of public disapproval, he said. The best way to avoid scandal, the philosopher told Booth, was to leave the country: "the whole British dominions [are] before you, which you may visit with undiminished fame."

Booth acted on Godwin's advice. He chose a destination for himself and Mary Ann that he hoped would ensure a happier ending to their story than Byron's or Shelley's. In America, the two young people could keep the truth about their illicit relationship hidden. They would make a fresh start overseas, in a place where any children they might have would never feel the shame of illegitimacy, a place where Mary Ann could not be labeled an adulteress. Of all nations on earth, America seemed made for them. In its short history, the Republic proved a happy resort for separatists, individualists, risk takers, and sectarians. The new country, they believed, nurtured every stripe of Protestant, as well as Catholics, Jews, Quakers, and Shakers. Surely it would welcome two secret devotees of free love? Booth knew that Lord Byron so admired the United States and what he imagined were its tolerant, freethinking ways, he declared he would "rather have a nod from an American than a snuff-box from an Emperor." History would prove him to be misguided on this point.

Adelaide Booth did not know her husband was abandoning her. She had no idea Mary Ann Holmes existed. Junius hid his intentions from the strong-minded Catholic woman. He spun her a story about British audiences tiring of his acting. A tour of United States, he declared, would rejuvenate his career and bring new wealth to the family accounts. "Never creature was more ardent for fame than I am for yours," Mrs. Booth replied, praying that "honor" would come to him in the country across the Atlantic "as fast as [his] impatient spirit could desire." She loyally offered to go with him, but Junius hastily objected. Their three-year-old son, he said, was "too young for the voyage." Booth warned his wife he might be gone for several years. He gave her money enough to live on for the next twelve months, promising to send "50 pounds a year" or more, as his future success in America allowed.

Only Junius's father knew the truth. After the actor and Mary Ann made their escape from London, Richard Booth paid a visit to Mary Ann's parents. In words that destroyed all hope, the lawyer explained to Mr. and

Mrs. Holmes that their daughter was on her way to America to "live with Booth." He assured them Junius would provide well for the girl, even though he could not marry her.

Mary Ann Holmes called herself Mrs. Booth now. In the summer of 1821, as the couple leaned on the rail of the *Powhatan* and watched the water of the James River flow past, they were hopeful and confident. Booth had the promise of an engagement in Richmond, Virginia. Mary Ann's pregnancy seemed to be progressing well. Booth had packed William Godwin's letter blessing their enterprise in his luggage. Mary Ann had Byron's portrait to wear. The letter and the oval brooch survived all the tumultuous decades of the couple's future life together. Long after their parents were dead, the children of Junius and Mary Ann would value these items among their family's most prized possessions, tangible proofs of the people and ideas responsible for launching the Booths' fortunes in America.

TWO

O BRAVE NEW WORLD

O, wonder!
How many goodly creatures are there here!
How beauteous mankind is! O brave new world,
That has such people in't!

—*Tempest*, 5.1

AFTER TWO DAYS LISTENING TO *POWHATAN*'S ENGINES CHURN, MARY ANN and Junius probably longed to see the city of Richmond appear around a bend in the James. Riverboat accommodations in 1821 were far from luxurious. Close to a hundred passengers crammed into a main cabin that was divided by a curtain into gentlemen's and ladies' salons. Twice a day, this barrier was pushed aside to allow a meal of corn bread, steaks, and hot coffee to be served on a makeshift table of long planks laid across the length of the room. Water for the passengers to drink was hoisted directly from the muddy river. Stewards always dipped their water buckets off the port side, while chamber pot refuse was tipped over the starboard rail.

Male passengers played cards and chewed tobacco to pass the time, females did "fancy work," and everyone "became more or less intimate," one river traveler remembered, as the steamer "puffed and paddled its way along." Mary Ann and Junius might have climbed to the boiler deck where "gaping armchairs" awaited those who wished to sit peacefully, smoke a pipe, and take in the view.

After a quick and intense courtship, this couple was learning to know one another better. Mary Ann would have noted Booth was almost hysterically sensitive to the physical suffering of animals. Any overworked horse or abused farm animal spotted along their journey could move Booth to melancholy tears. Even an insect in plight sent the actor springing to the rescue. Blind to social convention, he would plunge his hand into a dining partner's cup of milk or wine to save a fly from drowning.

Mary Ann discovered that Booth was obsessed with vegetarianism. Like Percy Shelley, Junius refused to eat fish or meat. "Man was not intended to make Earth a Slaughter-house of innocent animals," he told her earnestly, echoing the poet he idolized. Some Romantics demonstrated their love for Nature in this way, arguing humans had a sacred responsibility to protect all creatures. Pointing to the abundance of food freely available from plant sources—beans, peas, grains, fruits, vegetables—Booth concluded that "it is unnecessary for Man to eat Animal flesh." Such principles were more than a century ahead of social acceptance. Advocates of vegetarianism in the 1820s were widely considered freakish, even deranged. To Mary Ann's dismay, Booth did not keep his controversial views private. She might be mortified at any moment in a restaurant or tavern if Booth was in the mood to evangelize. Seeing someone eating so much as an oyster, the actor's brow would darken and he would whisper "Murderer! Murderer!" at the offending person in sepulchral tones.

Booth showed similar distress when he saw America's wilderness being destroyed at a breathtaking pace. Tourists on the James River at this time recalled that "the eye was pained" by the sight of primeval forests along the riverbanks being laid to ruin by fire and the axe. Novelist Charles Dickens, one of many to ride *Powhatan*'s route, wrote that "it was quite sad and oppressive to come upon great tracts where settlers had been burning down the trees, and where their wounded bodies lay about, like those of murdered creatures." In years to come, Junius Brutus Booth became notorious for his angry, futile protests against the hunting of native species and the cutting down of forests. "I wish to testify, in some public way," he would say with anguish, "against this wanton destruction of life."

Powhatan reached Richmond on July 3, 1821. The city's grand residences and buildings perched on a range of steep hills near the water. The biggest structures were the workshops where Virginia's tobacco crop was chopped, scented, and flavored for smoking and chewing. Knowing that General Washington, the man he had been taught to "revere and hallow" since childhood, once danced "minuets, reels and congos" at Galt's Tavern on Main Street filled Booth with amazement. Equally marvelous was the knowledge that the author of the Declaration of Independence lived and breathed nearby. Thomas Jefferson's great mansion, Monticello, was less than fifty miles away. Filled with patriotic enthusiasm, Booth wanted to make his debut the very next night. It had to be explained to the actor that July Fourth was a sacred and solemn occasion. Parades by local militia, ceremonial readings of the Declaration of Independence, and salutes to the heroes of 1776 would occupy Richmond's citizens.

Booth met with the manager of the Marshall Theatre, an impresario named Gilfert, the day he arrived. Anticipating huge profits, Gilfert signed the Covent Garden celebrity to a two-week contract, agreeing on July 6 for opening night. Booth did not like the man. "There is something in Gilfert which occasions an involuntary shudder," Booth wrote. The manager did have something to hide. There was a grisly backstory to the Marshall Theatre's existence, a tale that surely would have put Booth on the alert had he known it. In time, the Booth family's history would prove sadly intertwined with the Marshall. A decade later, a messenger would track Booth to the Marshall's stage with news that would change the actor's life forever. Two of his sons would perform at the Marshall as well, with ill-fated results. But for now, few people wanted to discuss why they needed to build a new theater in Richmond. In the words of one resident, the explanation was "too shocking to dwell upon."

Ten years before, a gem of a theater, the Old Academy, stood proudly at the center of Richmond. It had been the favorite resort of Virginia's plantation aristocrats, politicians, and social elites. On Christmas Eve 1811, six hundred people dressed in the height of fashion—including the governor of Virginia, his wife, and his daughter—packed the Academy's three-tiered auditorium to enjoy a musical performance. At half-past ten o'clock, a rain of fire fell from the Academy's ceiling onto the people below. As the clothes of actors and audience burst into flames, one witness remembered, the theater rang with "blood-chilling" screams and panicked shouts. Chaos erupted as audience members tried to shield "an affectionate wife, a tender child, an aged parent" from burning. The scene outside was no better. People tried to escape the fire by jumping out of the Academy's third-story windows. They died on hitting the frozen ground below, or were crushed by others jumping after. The governor managed to exit safely, but a crowd of onlookers saw him turn around and dash back into flames. His wife and daughter were trapped within; he died at their side.

The fire claimed nearly a hundred lives. Many victims hesitated to flee the burning theater because they believed a slave uprising in the streets outside was responsible for the fire. Only later was it learned that actors, not slaves, were to blame. It was the job of performers to guard the massive oil lamps that shed light on the stage. To be on "swabbing duty," as it was then called, meant standing near one of these lamps with a water-soaked mop, ready to extinguish escaping sparks. Distracted by the night's holiday music, one swab neglected his work. A stray flame flew up to the ceiling unseen, setting the rafters on fire.

Richmond's civic leaders banned all public entertainments as penance, they said, for "the most horrid disaster" ever to strike their city. After the bodies and charred wreckage had been cleared away, Robert Mills, architect of the Washington Monument, built a church on the site, consecrated to the memory of those who died in the theater disaster. Mills's Monumental Church stands there today.

By 1821, boredom had eaten away at the city's puritanical resolve. Sources of amusement were scarce. Books and paintings were hard to come by for most people, while objects like pianos, harps, and music boxes were rarer still. Richmond's citizens were hungry for entertainment. Ten years after the fire, they were willing to tempt fate inside a theater once more, lining up by the thousands to see Junius Brutus Booth in the gory spectacle of *Richard III*.

The actor chose to give the city Shakespeare's bloodcurdling tale of fratricide and conspiracy because this was the role that had lifted him out of obscurity in London and made him a star. British audiences loved to watch Richard kill everyone ahead of him in line to England's throne. His victims included women and small children as well as his own loving brother, John. Richard murders his rivals in inventive ways, poisoning, impaling, beheading, and even smothering them to death with pillows. Worst—or perhaps best—of all was the scene where the evil genius plans for his brother John to be shoved headfirst into a cask of malmsey until drowned.

Booth made his entrance in silence, sidling before the footlights in Richard's hitching, hunchbacked gait. Dangling a sword in front of him as he walked, he kicked moodily at the blade while an uncomfortable silence built in the theater. Booth mumbled the play's first line, "Now is the winter of our discontent," one witness remembered, like a "school-boy repeating a lesson." The Richmond crowd traded incredulous glances. Manager Gilfert had promised them the "best actor living." People started muttering that Booth was an imposter and that they had been duped. At this instant, Booth performed the frightening trick that never failed, the poet Walt Whitman would later testify, to make "a shudder [go] through every nervous system in the audience." He let the audience watch the spirit of Shakespeare's power-hungry monster slowly possess his body.

Booth, now fully in character, ordered a beheading, making a chopping motion with one hand. A sickening note crept into the actor's voice as he plotted the deaths of two little boys, nephews ahead of him in line to the throne. "Why, I can smile, and murder whiles I smile," he purred. Booth's supporting actors stopped in their tracks, dumbstruck by the change in him. Some forgot their lines, standing speechless until the star momentarily broke character, poked them in the ribs, and whispered "Go on, go on!"

In the climactic battle scene, newspapers reported next morning, the actor dashed to the edge of the stage "his face the ashy hue of death, his limbs trembling, his eyes rolling and gleaming with an unearthly glare, and his form convulsed with intense excitement." Sweat oozed grotesquely from his forehead, drenching his hair and pasting it to his cheeks. Richard's dying words—filled, critics said, with "despair, hate, and grief"—echoed from every corner of the Marshall. The *Richmond Enquirer* declared Booth's acting "the most striking we have ever beheld."

Letters from theater managers in New York, Philadelphia, Boston, New Orleans, and Baltimore poured into Richmond, offering Booth generous terms and expressing their "anxious desire to see him." The most important invitation came from Manhattan's Park Theatre. Eager to build on his Richmond success with an appearance in what was even then America's cultural capital, Junius and Mary Ann packed their trunks once more. They rode *Powhatan* back down the James River to Norfolk, where they could catch *Fidelity*, an oceangoing steamboat, to New York.

A week's journey up the desolate Atlantic coastline ended with *Fidelity* joining a parade of other steamboats, ships, and barges pressing across New York harbor, flags fluttering and smokestacks billowing white, to reach the wharves. The city of New York, according to residents in those days, was "an immense hive teeming with human bees." The most populous place in the country, it was twice the size of its nearest competitors, Philadelphia and Baltimore. In 1821, over 120,000 people swarmed the southern tip of Manhattan, intent on earning a living. Even then the natives boasted, "New York is a *fast* city. The very *fastest* in all creation. Its men are *fast*, its women are *fast*, and so are its horses. Everything goes with a rush."

THE CITY WOULD SEEM TINY NOW. THE METROPOLIS THEN COVERED ONLY a small quadrangle of land, bounded by rivers, between Tenth Street and the Battery. Above Tenth, all was vegetable gardens, cornfields or pasture, with here and there a country house. Gramercy Park, where Junius and Mary Ann's future son would stake his mansion and play host to a president, was then an empty lot overgrown with grass and gooseberry bushes. The tall buildings that would make Manhattan a maze of steep-sided canyons were a century away. For now, modest structures lined the avenues, built of brick or wood. But as one city dweller predicted at the time, "the mighty magician of Progress" was waving his wand over the place: "the march of New York is onward."

The Park Theatre stood at the edge of a public garden between Fulton and Chambers streets, steps from City Hall and bordered by the homes of Manhattan's merchant princes. Like the choice real estate around it, the Park was "stylish and select," charging steep admission to keep out undesirables.

Junius's old nemesis Edmund Kean haunted him even in New York. The London star had played the Park only months before, scoring, reviewers agreed, "a complete triumph" in the city. Booth found himself needing to surpass his older rival once again. Luckily for Junius, one resident of the city wrote at the time, "in New York the wheels of Fortune are always revolving—one man goes *up* today, and another goes *down* tomorrow."

Ever since Richmond, Mary Ann had had work to do. A skilled seamstress, she took charge of unpacking and repairing Booth's costumes. The costumes had lain too long in their steamer trunks. Musty velvets needed to be brushed and aired, the matted fur trim on robes and tunics repaired. She helped Booth sort through jewel-encrusted stage weapons, royal scepters, collars, and crowns, securing any glass gem, bead, or stone that had fallen loose. She learned to help him put on stage wigs, mustaches, and beards, and even mastered the trick of buckling Richard III's prosthetic hump over the actor's shoulders.

The hardest job behind the scenes, she soon learned, was keeping Booth cheerful. Adelaide Booth, in her role as wifely dramatic coach, often talked the star out of what she called his "vexations." As his fame increased, Junius developed a capricious, perfectionist temperament. Some nights, if he did not feel inspired to act, or if he believed the audience would misunderstand his work, he plunged into a black mood and refused to go onstage. Professing to "hate" acting, Booth would croak he never wanted to do it again. It then fell to Adelaide, and later to Mary Ann, to soothe his qualms and coax a performance out of him. Sometimes a glass of brandy helped the star recover his will to act. The night of October 6, 1821, Mary Ann probably did not have to worry. Winning New York's favor was crucial to Booth's plans. If the couple were to have a chance at a prosperous life together in the United States, the actor knew, he needed to make his appearance in this reigning city a hit.

Rainstorms soaked Manhattan that night, flooding streets and immobilizing the traffic on Broadway, but the *New York Evening Post* reported that a capacity crowd braved the elements to see Booth in action. After the curtain fell on *Richard III*, two thousand rain-drenched New Yorkers jumped to their feet, roaring, cheering, stomping feet, and clapping hands in an ovation that lasted for nearly ten minutes. Junius was so overcome he could not speak. Stepping before the worshipful crowd, newspapers reported, the actor bowed silent thanks, his entire body shaking with emotion. The verdict on Booth's genius was unanimous. "We cannot withhold from him our highest praise," announced the *Post;* "he made an extraordinary impression." Booth "broke through all rules and all traditions," another critic wrote, achieving something "beyond any of his kind on record."

During his first American season, Booth's profits from sold-out shows topped one hundred dollars per night. Performing for a week to ten days each in Richmond, New York, Baltimore, Charleston, Savannah, New Orleans, Boston, Providence, and Washington, D.C., he raked in thousands. Mary Ann kept pace with Booth's grueling tour schedule until her pregnancy became too advanced. In December 1821, while Junius traveled down the Mississippi River to dazzle audiences in New Orleans, Mary Ann gave birth alone in a boardinghouse in Charleston. She named her newborn Junius Brutus, Jr. When Booth rejoined her and the baby several months later, he was flush with new wealth and the news that he could afford to buy a comfortable estate for her and the "dear darling child."

The actor's eye had fallen on a piece of property in Harford County, Maryland. It would prove a fateful choice as things turned out, but the decision seemed practical to Junius at the time. "No city in the world has a more beautiful countryside around it than Baltimore," a tourist wrote in 1821. Harford County lay beyond the city limits, a sleepy place where fruit orchards and plots of rich farmland made little islands of human activity in what was otherwise a wilderness. Booth, lured by the promise of privacy, made a down payment on 150 acres of forest there in May 1822. "Tis a lovely spot," a visitor later said, but "remote and lonely."

Travelers had to follow twenty-five miles of rough country road northeast from Baltimore, then thread their way through a "thick growth of trees" to find the clearing where Booth's log cabin stood, plastered white, with bright red shutters. Massive beech trees, oaks, and walnuts cast the farmhouse in constant shadow. Because he was not an American citizen, the laws of Maryland barred Junius from owning land in the state. The English actor escaped the provision in the customary way, by paying Richard Hall, original owner of the cabin and its acreage, for a lease of one thousand years.

Mary Ann Holmes was not used to country quiet. The Londoner born and raised craved nothing more, she told Booth, than "the social world, and the amusements which present themselves, in so many shapes, in populous towns." Yet the cabin Junius chose for her was hemmed in by a forest so vast and thick, one visitor remembered, it was like an impenetrable green wall stretching "as far as the eye could reach." Such isolation was a hard prospect for a young woman who had been seduced away from city life by promises of romance and adventure.

The spotlight of celebrity shone more brightly on this couple in the United States than either of them had anticipated. After Booth's successes in Richmond and New York, newspapers started tracking the actor's movements and showed an interest in his beautiful traveling companion. Norfolk papers ran sightings of "Mr. Booth and Lady" when the pair disembarked from a steamboat or checked into a hotel, and other port cities were the same. So much ink was expended on the actor that one journal ran an editorial defending its Booth obsession: "Next to political and economical concerns, there is no more legitimate object of newspaper attention than the most respectable and classical of public spectacles, the Stage." Junius was alarmed by the press scrutiny, worrying the story he told of his and Mary Ann's legal union would eventually be exposed as fake. He also discovered that ships crossed between New York and London rather too frequently for his peace of mind. Many British actors visited Manhattan, and all of them knew Junius Brutus Booth. They might ask questions about the young woman and infant at his side, and perhaps carry stories back home to Adelaide Booth.

The only way to keep his mistress and her baby a secret was to hide them deep in the country. There they would be far from the notice of gossiping actors and scandal-minded journalists, and safely beyond the reach of his wife.

The few families with farms near Booth's new home guessed the actor was looking for a hiding place. Mrs. Elijah Rogers, Junius's neighbor for thirty years, later told an interviewer that the actor's "object in moving to our county was to seclude himself as far as possible from all acquaintances." Booth's children agreed, saying their father's "chief delight" in his property "was that it was so perfectly shut in, and away from the world." It must have been hard for Booth to imagine the past catching up with him and Mary Ann here. Once a week, a postman on horseback tossed a packet of mail over the fence surrounding what the actor liked to call his "Big Woods"; otherwise no one disturbed the sanctuary. There was a tiny village, Bel Air, three miles distant where a general store sold necessities like coffee, whiskey, candles, sugar, soap, and writing paper.

A glance at a map of the United States in 1821 reveals the other reason the actor chose Harford County for his home base. Booth needed money.

Supporting two households, Adelaide's and Mary Ann's, was going to be expensive. Audiences across the twenty-four states promised to reward the actor's talents generously, but to reach these paying crowds Booth had to travel thousands of miles. Throughout the fall, winter, and spring he would be gone, riding stagecoaches, riverboats, and ocean steamers to destinations along the demanding nine-month touring route typical of a traveling star. To turn an annual profit, Booth visited a dozen or so cities on a circuitous path from Albany and Boston in the North to Charleston and New Orleans in the South. The port of Baltimore, only a day's ride from Booth's cabin in the forest, was an ideal transportation hub.

Junius broke the news to Mary Ann that he could afford to spend only the three summer months with her on their new property. Faced with the reality of being stranded alone in the woods for most of each year, she was crushed. "What could he do else?" the actor wrote. "Was he not forced to make money?" For company, Junius bought the young woman three huge New-foundland dogs. It was a small gesture, but a significant one: Lord Byron himself was devoted to the breed. Byron had written a famous ode praising the animals' fidelity and capacity for friendship. He even declared he should be buried next to Boatswain, his beloved Newfoundland. Mary Ann gave the same name, Boatswain, to one of her new pets. She chained them close to the cabin during the daytime, but freed them to roam the acreage at night. The animals warned off anyone who bothered her. Years later, neighbors re-membered how "Mrs. Booth" had "three very large dogs as protectors" while the man they presumed to be her husband was away from home. Neighbors knew little else about how the British woman spent her days, remarking she "did not visit" anyone.

Junius asked his widowed father, sixty-three-year-old Richard Booth, to close his London law practice and join Mary Ann in the wilderness. The elder Booth agreed, landing in Baltimore in the fall of 1822, his trunks packed with books in Latin and Greek. He was a curious sight, this ama-teur classical scholar, with his long white hair, a hobbling walk, and eccentric eighteenth-century garments. As much as he loved his son, Richard Booth took no interest in farming. Complaining that the cabin in the forest felt as desolate as "Robinson Crusoe's Island," the elder Booth buried himself in the work of adapting Virgil's *Aeneid* into an English-language drama.

The actor had plans for his country property. Maryland's rich soil and temperate growing season produced crops in abundance. Local people cul-tivated tomatoes, sweet corn, okra, potatoes, rhubarb, grapes, peaches, pears, apricots, and apples in addition to wheat, barley, and other grains. If the work could be done to clear fields for planting and if orchards, vineyards, and gardens could be established, Booth's farm might in time come to supply all the family's needs. Junius hoped his father would take a break from his studies to help Mary Ann supervise the many construction projects and agricultural schemes he had in mind, but this was not to be. All too soon, Richard Booth embarked on a love affair with the locally distilled whiskey he could buy from the Bel Air General Store for nineteen cents a gallon. Booth was dismayed, but perhaps not surprised, at his father's weakness. "I have witnessed often with regret the terrible ravages [drinking] has made both on your mind and Body," he wrote to his father while on tour in 1822. "Refrain from that destructive and Sense-depriving custom of getting intoxicated. Madness will be the result if you persist." Junius wrote that Richard's drinking made it impossible to entrust him with the work of "overlook[ing] the Servants and Laborers, that I many not be cheated and robbed on every side."

Condemned to this strange, isolated existence with Booth's difficult parent, Mary Ann made the best of her situation. She took charge of carrying out the actor's instructions for improving the farm. Junius had leased a team of slaves from a neighboring farmer. A group of men and women were bound to the actor by labor contracts renewable each year. Joe Hall, a tall, soft-spoken man who traced his origins to the island of Madagascar, was hired by Booth to plow his fields, plant his gardens, and tend his livestock. In time, Hall was able to purchase the freedom of his wife, Ann, a slave from a nearby farm. Ann Hall then came to work in the Booth cabin, cooking, cleaning, and washing clothes. A group of carpenters from Baltimore built a barn, dairy, and stables near the cabin to shelter horses, oxen, cows, flocks of sheep, hogs, and chickens. A peach orchard was put in, and a large grove of apple trees. Bricklayers came to build an outdoor oven for bread baking, while carpenters made a cider press and constructed vats for winemaking.

Joe Hall was the leader of the workforce in Junius's absence, the person Mary Ann relied on to carry out the actor's commands. Booth's letters to his home overflowed with assignments: "Joe had best soon get up the potatoes & bring them carefully," read a typical note. "Joe must fit up the Garden Paling so as to prevent the fowls getting in, and it is time now to sow Radishes and Carrots. Beets and Parsnips will do the latter end of this month. Peas and cucumbers the beginning of next." Observing with approval that Joe was not "fond of using the infernal whip" when driving horses or oxen to plow, Booth charged this man, whom local people described as a "Madagascan Prince," with caring for the livestock. "Pray see all my quadrupeds be taken care of,"

Booth instructed him, "and not overworked as they are not too strong this Season of the Year." The vegetarian continued, "should the cows have calves, I don't wish them to be made meat for the Butcher as it is in direct opposition to my Religion."

Each summer, the actor took a break from touring and returned home, spending time with Mary Ann and pitching in to the work of the farm. "Soon after sunrise," a family member recalled, the travel-weary star would rush rejuvenated out of bed to "dig in his garden, whistling while he worked." Junius took the most happiness, however, one neighbor recalled, from the sight of his and Mary Ann's growing flock of children being cared for and fed.

"Nearly all the children were born in that house, log as it was," recalled one of Mary Ann's neighbors, marveling at the young woman's fortitude. There was a doctor in nearby Bel Air, but Mary Ann sent for him only in emergencies. She gave birth usually in late autumn or early winter when Junius was on the road, presumably laboring before a fireplace in one of the cabin's upstairs bedrooms. Enemas of salt and pig fat were popular treatments for the pain of childbirth. Mary Ann might also have gulped an opiate tea brewed from poppies, soaked her feet in hot water, or chewed pieces of ice to alleviate discomfort. A sheet knotted around the bedpost was to pull on when the birth pangs grew unbearable. At the crucial moment, a midwife inserted a hand "well greased with lard" into the birth canal to help the baby emerge safely.

Mary Ann's firstborn son, Junius Brutus Jr., was called "June," an echo of Byron's *Don Juan*. He was followed by a daughter, Rosalie, in 1823. In 1825, Mary Ann's second son, Henry Byron, named in honor of her favorite poet, arrived. Eighteen twenty-seven brought another daughter, Mary, and 1829 a third son, Frederick. A baby named Elizabeth was born in 1831. Away from these children for months at a time, Junius wrote letters home from wherever he happened to be—New York, New Orleans, Philadelphia—that overflowed with solicitude. "Let nothing be neglected to keep them in health," the anxious father instructed. "Particularly their feet should always be dry & good shoes provided for them." The toddlers especially "must not go out in the wet. Nothing is more dangerous."

Junius Brutus Booth rarely expressed fear for Mary Ann's health in these letters, though puerperal or "childbirth" fever—an infection spread to laboring women by a physician's unwashed hands—killed many women in the nineteenth century. Mary Ann avoided it because the women hired to work on the Booth property were excellent midwives. People from different parts of Africa or the Caribbean brought a wealth of skills and specialized knowledge to the places of their enslavement. Little is known about Ann Hall's origins, but with her help and that of other skilled women, the mother of the Maryland Booths never contracted childbirth fever. Even Joe Hall practiced a custom from his native place when Mary Ann gave birth. One Booth child remembered watching this man, who worked grueling hours in the fields by day, spending "long winter evenings" weaving straw of different colors into "cradle-baskets for the babies."

The first decade Mary Ann Holmes and Junius Brutus Booth spent in the United States was a prosperous one. All along Booth's tour route, ticket sales boomed. American theater managers in the 1820s considered him a "highly successful" draw and were eager to book the British star. "I have seen him act Richard many times as no other man could or can act it," one New Orleans theater proprietor remembered, "and have seen the whole house, pit, boxes and gallery, on their feet to do honor to Booth."

Junius was earning enough to keep his father, Mary Ann, and her children in comfort. He could even afford to splurge on some luxuries. One of his first major expenditures, unrelated to improvements on his farm, was commissioning a portrait of Mary Ann Holmes. He could not marry the mother of his growing flock of children, but he could show his devotion to her with costly gifts. In 1823 the actor learned Thomas Sully, the premier American portrait artist, was renting a studio in Baltimore. Sully was fresh from a long residence with Thomas Jefferson at Monticello, where he had been at work on his masterpiece, a full-length portrait of the ailing, eighty-year-old Founding Father. Sully was expensive to hire. The leading families of Boston, New York, and Philadelphia were his clients, as well as occupants of the White House from John Adams to Andrew Jackson. For Junius Brutus Booth to hire Jefferson's portraitist to paint his mistress's picture—even before he had accumulated enough money to make the final payment on his Maryland farm—was a grand gesture indeed.

Junius Brutus Booth tried to maintain a balance between his families on each side of the Atlantic. After Sully completed the portrait of Mary Ann, the actor hired a London society artist to paint Adelaide Booth and her seven-year-old son, Richard. The artist, a Mr. Williams, sent a flattering note to Junius along with the bill: "my greatest ambition would be to attempt your portrait in one of your favorite characters."

Junius continued to postpone the date of his London return, but Adelaide was unconcerned. Her husband's letters to her in this period, written three or four times a year, were long and affectionate, concealing the truth about the existence of his second family. He wrote openly to Adelaide about the ambition burning inside him, his love for his art, and his struggles with an emotional sensitivity that at times threatened to sour his relationship with the American public. She in turn wrote back encouraging words, urging Junius to treat audiences with respect so as to secure their loyalty for the next season, and their money. Curtain calls, she said, were crucial. "I can easily understand it would be preferable to drag our weary limbs and exhausted frame to our dressing room," she advised the actor, but the audience's desire to have "the pleasure of looking on you" after a show must be respected. Junius kept up an intimate correspondence with her, Adelaide marveled years afterward, "as though nothing had happened." Booth sent his wife a share of his stage profits along with each letter. For many years cash arrived from him, Adelaide testified later, "with promptitude, and often in excess of what was promised."

But Booth was haunted by fear of discovery. Isolation in the country kept Mary Ann away from the notice of American newspapers, but in 1825 an anonymous item ran in London's *Sunday Monitor* accusing Booth of "deserting his wife and child—stripping them of even common necessities—and seducing from the roof of a father an infatuated girl to follow a traitorous husband to another quarter of the world." The source of the story was not given—perhaps the angry parents of Mary Ann Holmes were striking a blow at the man who ruined their daughter. Fortunately for Junius, the report did not go far. Adelaide remained in the dark. She was visiting her mother in Brussels at the time the short article appeared.

In 1826 a souvenir-crazed theater fan broke into Richard Booth's luggage while the elderly man was staying at a Baltimore hotel. The thief stole some personal letters, craving samples of Junius's handwriting. The actor was terrified by this theft. The letters he wrote to his parent often listed the payments he made to Adelaide, and on occasion discussed arrangements for Mary Ann and her illegitimate children to inherit his property upon his death. "The prosperity of Bel Air of course I shall bequeath to Mary Ann, Junius, Rosalie and Henry Byron," the actor had written to his lawyer father, explaining that Adelaide and her son should be given the Booths' London-based assets. Anyone reading those words would hold the key to the family's reputation, to Mary Ann and her children's good name. Junius warned his father to be on guard in the future. "Lock well your trunk!" he cried. "Or if there be aught [in] my letters that should not be hawked about as 'Neighbor's News' always destroy it as soon as read."

The delicate equilibrium Booth established between his wife in London and the new family he had hidden away in the Maryland woods could not last. Welcoming his return to the farm each summer, Mary Ann gradually observed a change, a slow unraveling, in the man who had brought her there. The actor's annual treks to every corner of the United States were altering him in ways no one could have anticipated. The serious, ambitious actor whose foremost wish—after building a new life with the woman he loved—had been securing his fame as an artist, started to falter onstage. He became careless and erratic, and the family's prosperity suffered. The star's steady decline had consequences for Mary Ann and her children, especially Edwin and John Wilkes, two sons unlucky enough to arrive as their father accelerated toward disaster. Sol Smith, a theatrical manager who knew Junius well, explained what happened. Booth "was a truly great actor and continued to be so," Smith wrote, "until he fell into bad company in New Orleans, and took to hard drink." This dedicated artist who once viewed his father's drinking with dismay became a new, self-destructive man. Thereafter, Smith opined sadly, "Booth was nobody's enemy but his own."

THREE

THIS BE MADNESS

Though this be madness, yet there is a method in't.

—*Hamlet, 2.2*

In 1823, Booth was in Washington, D.C., at the height of his second national tour of the United States. At the Washington Theatre, Booth offered members of President James Monroe's administration a bill of Shakespeare for their evening entertainment, playing Richard III, King Lear, and Othello. After curtain, Junius Booth could be found at O'Neale's Tavern near Capitol Hill "industriously circulating the bottle," as one witness described his method, with a pair of American folk heroes, the great Daniel Webster and a new member of Congress from the backwoods of Tennessee, Sam Houston.

Houston had volunteered as a lieutenant under the command of General Andrew Jackson in the War of 1812, surviving an arrow shot to his leg and two rifle balls in his arm while battling British-backed Creek Indians for control of the Arkansas Territory. Elected to Congress in 1823, he would rise in little more than a decade to become governor of Tennessee, a major general in the United States Army, and the first president of the Republic of Texas. Houston's impassioned belief in America's westward expansion and his talent with a sword, one historian wrote, "altered the destiny of a continent." It was Sam Houston who would lead the U.S. Army to victory at the Battle of San Jacinto in 1836, vanquishing Mexican general Santa Anna and redrawing the map of America.

But in 1823, Houston's great deeds were yet to come. Instead, Webster, the elder statesman from Massachusetts, and Booth, the British actor, were teasing the young man about which type of oratory he would bring to the floor of Congress in his freshman efforts. Webster, one drinker remembered, "professed chagrin that the Tennessean should prefer the manner of Booth, while the tragedian affected disappointment because so promising a pupil had selected Webster for his model." An impromptu display of public speaking followed. In years to come, Booth and Houston would enact this scene together many times over in different saloons. Witnesses said the men always seemed as intoxicated by the words they recited as by the brandy they consumed.

"Now Booth, let's have a speech to liberty—one of those apostrophes to old Roman freedom," the inebriated Houston would cry. The actor always obliged, witnesses said, leaping to his feet to perform for his friend "those electric passages in defense of liberty with which the English drama abounds." Houston, whose "spirit seemed to take fire" at Booth's words, repeated every line Junius delivered, copying the actor's gestures and intonations exactly. Later, when the Tennessean delivered a stirring speech to the House of Representatives, Booth pushed his way through the admiring crowd to embrace him. "Houston," the actor reportedly said, "take my laurels."

A friendship was born in 1823 between Houston and Booth that would have important consequences for the actor's family. As their paths continued to cross in the ensuing years, the Tennessean's hard-drinking habits rubbed off on the actor. Sam Houston was chief among the "bad company" Sol Smith blamed for introducing Booth to liquor. The bond between these two "great cronies," as one newspaper described the pair, had another result as well. Decades later, after time and distance had dimmed the intensity of their relationship, Booth spent hours regaling his impressionable sons, Edwin and John Wilkes, with tales of the frontiersman's superhuman exploits. In 1888, a few years before he died, an ailing Edwin Booth traveled to San Antonio to seek out General Houston's daughter. His pilgrimage was "prompted," Edwin said, "by a desire to meet the daughter of the man who had been the hero of so many of his father's anecdotes." Admirers called Sam Houston a "magnificent barbarian." Junius Brutus Booth declared in his diary that his beloved friend was nothing less than a "singular genius." This American original would replace Booth's former idols, Lord Byron and Percy Shelley, and Booth's family would suffer the results.

In November 1827, Sam Houston received word in his rooms at the Nashville Inn that he had been elected governor of Tennessee. It was a week later, when Junius Brutus Booth arrived by steamboat to give a string of performances in Nashville's New Theatre, that the pair likely rekindled their association. Thereafter, whenever Booth met up with the governor on his regular dramatic tours between Cincinnati and New Orleans, Houston was the British man's personal guide to the colorful, dangerous world of the American frontier.

That year, the farthest reach of U.S. authority was a tiny garrison at Little Rock, in what is now Arkansas. Most of the land west of the Mississippi River was unincorporated territory, the property of Mexico, or Indian lands occupied by Shawnee, Choctaw, Osage, and Cherokee. In the late 1820s, pioneers traversed America's sparsely populated western holdings on three major rivers—the Cumberland, the Ohio, and the Mississippi. The watershed of these rivers created a slow-winding, two-thousand-mile path leading from Pennsylvania—with stops in Tennessee, Kentucky, Indiana, Illinois, Missouri, and Mississippi—all the way to Louisiana. In his history *Life on the Mississippi*, Mark Twain recalled, the waterways "were an awful solitude then."

In 1828, a nineteen-year-old Abraham Lincoln joined a crowd of Mississippi bargers and flatboatmen, river laborers who favored a uniform of flannel shirts, leather leggings, moccasins, and red sashes. He and another youth together guided a raft stacked with corn and barrels of salt pork from Little Pigeon Creek, Indiana, to New Orleans. The journey took the young men nearly two months, but Junius Brutus Booth and the governor of Tennessee were able to cover the same route by steamboat in less than three weeks. These "ungainly water buildings" had evolved since Junius and Mary Ann's 1821 ride on *Powhatan*. Now three stories high and fantastically adorned with carpets, cupolas, and filigreed railings, a single steamboat might convey thousands of cotton bales and hundreds of passengers with ease. By the 1840s they would dominate the shipping on the Mississippi.

With the Tennessean at his side, Junius immersed himself in the rough, thriving culture of river life. Houston and Booth on a drunken spree became a familiar sight along the Mississippi after 1827: on riverboats, in the taverns of Cincinnati and Nashville, and as Sol Smith has suggested, in New Orleans. They made an unforgettable, and unintentionally comic, impression on observers. Houston had a theatrical streak almost as wide as Booth's own. He would dress for these benders in full Cherokee ceremonial regalia, or wrap his tall form in a striped Indian blanket. Weaving drunkenly arm in arm down a street together, the six-foot-six adventurer would dwarf his pint-sized friend. Booth, dressed nattily in the British style, stumbled gamely at Houston's side, his hat knocked awry, his legs tangling in the skirts of his frock coat. "Thus they marched," one newspaper reported, "little Booth clinging to the arm and with difficulty keeping pace with the sturdy strides of the hero."

Strong drink was not hard to come by on the frontier. Addiction was a constant peril for westerners on and off the rivers, and it may be that even without Houston's lead, Booth would have succumbed to its lure. In the early days of his Springfield law career, Abraham Lincoln gave a speech on the problem of intemperance, as alcoholism then was termed. When he was growing up in southern Indiana, Lincoln remembered, "intoxicating liquor" was "recognized by everybody, used by everybody and repudiated by nobody." Whiskey distilled from native corn was the pioneers' drink of choice. "To have a rolling or a raising, a husking or a hoe-down anywhere without it," the young lawyer said, "was *positively insufferable*." Though he himself escaped temptation, this future president believed it was the sensitive and highly intelligent young men who were most likely to become, in his words, "habitual drunkards." "There seems ever to have been a proneness in the brilliant to fall into this vice," Lincoln observed. "The demon of intemperance ever seems to have delight in sucking the blood of genius."

The case of Sam Houston and Junius Brutus Booth certainly lends credence to Lincoln's hypothesis. The two men shared what Booth liked to call, simply and emphatically, with an expressive gesture to the forehead, "Mind." The actor and the Indian fighter believed they were rare beings, separated from the common walk of humanity by the possession of incredible talents. Where Booth learned nearly a dozen ancient and modern languages as a teenager, Sam Houston by the age of eighteen made a linguistic achievement staggering in its own right. Having spent three years living among the Cherokees as a youth, Houston managed, he boasted, to "thoroughly acquire the Cherokee language." The tribal tongue "is so difficult," Houston's biographer stated, "that it is said never to have been learned by an adult." Each young man had a driving need to achieve, and had fueled his fantasies of future glory with epic poetry. Where Junius thrilled to the daring exploits of Byron's Romantic heroes, young Sam made sure to bring a copy of Homer's *Iliad* with him into Cherokee country when he ran away from home. He read the account of "those gigantic heroes from the ruins of Greece and Rome" so many times, Houston told one interviewer, "he could repeat it almost entire from beginning to end."

Until the frontiersman won immortality at San Jacinto, he was often, like Booth, oppressed by feelings of failure. In his lowest moments, Houston said, he "was strongly tempted ... to end my worthless life." During one episode, Houston said his hand was stayed when an eagle plummeted from the sky and "swooped down near my head." The man raised by Cherokee shamans believed the creature was a messenger from the spirit world. His gloom lifted, and he took heart. "I knew then," he wrote, "that a great destiny awaited for me in the West."

Houston taught Booth how, in his words, to "bury sorrow in the flowing bowl." Friends recalled that whenever "a dark cloud" fell on the Tennessean, he "gave himself up to the fatal enchantress," alcohol. The actor learned quickly. By 1829, the pair had parted ways. Houston abdicated the governorship to return to his old life among the Cherokee in their lands west of the Tennessee River. His adopted relatives, seeing what Houston had become, changed his tribal name from "Col-lon-neh," the Raven, to "Oo-tse-tee Ar-dee-tah-skee," the Big Drunk.

Booth now drank with strangers. According to his onetime manager Noah Ludlow, whenever Junius played New Orleans, hordes of well-lubricated river men formed the mainstay of his audience and rallied to the actor's side wherever he went. If Booth and other actors proceeded to a bar after curtain, these boon companions appeared, eager to buy their favorite a drink. Holding glasses of brandy and roaring out the words to old river songs, their arms slung across each other's shoulders, they drank the night away. The actor's mental storehouse of poetry and Shakespeare placed him in high demand. The sound of ice clinking in silver cups, and the rich sheen of the mahogany bar in the saloon at New Orleans's St. Charles Hotel formed as much of a backdrop for the actor as the stage itself. Booth gave in to the brotherhood of these barrooms, rarely refusing patrons' alcohol-soaked calls for performances—Coleridge's "Rime of the Ancient Mariner" was a particular favorite. Booth was not unaware of the changes overtaking him. It was easy for an actor to fall victim, he wrote home to his father, to "boisterous circles of intoxicated fools."

A small retinue of Cherokee friends sometimes trailed Big Drunk when he went out at night, to keep the tall man from trouble. Booth was not so fortunate. Lurching on foot from tavern to hotel "whilst he was drunk," one witness stated, the star "barely escaped several times being run over by carriages." Other dangers waited. Once, in a fit of maudlin generosity, the actor signed over a thousand-dollar stock certificate to a stranger he met at a bar. "I must have been insane," Junius wrote to his bankers, seeking to cancel the transfer of money, but to no avail. More drains on his finances occurred when he missed performances. Either he was too drunk to stand and act, or, afflicted with hangover, he failed to wake up in time to catch the stagecoach or steamboat to his next destination. Theater managers who printed playbills advertising the star's appearance for a certain night would be left with stacks of worthless paper. "It is best in my humble opinion," Booth warned prospective employers, "not to announce until the Beast arrives." Mary Ann Holmes must have been worried. It was clear Junius's far-flung travels were taking a toll. His letters home at times contained no money.

Booth's mistress was not the only one to notice the change. Audiences took note as well. By 1829, stories of Booth's transformation began to surface in newspapers, inspiring such alarming headlines as "Lunacy of a Tragedian." Performing *Richard III* at New York's Bowery Theatre, the star refused to die in the last act as stipulated in the script. Instead he kept battling out his fight scene with such fury that he forced his bewildered opponent off the stage, up the aisle, and out the doors of the playhouse into the street. Witnesses recalled "the amazing spectacle of two armor-clad individuals, swords in hand, wigs and plumes a-stream, racing and clanking under the street-lamps." Playing Boston that winter, Junius burst into tears midscene. Turning to the audience he screamed, "take me to the Lunatic Hospital!" and ran sobbing toward the exit. The stage manager stepped forward to announce, "Ladies and gentlemen, Mr. Booth cannot appear this evening. His reason has left him." The curtain dropped, and the audience departed. Days later, the thirty-three-year-old actor was found sleeping in the woods outside the city, burrowed under a pile of leaves.

Fans puzzled over these fits. Was Booth, like Shakespeare's Hamlet, "putting an antic disposition on," or had he actually gone insane? Sol Smith, the New Orleans theater manager who blamed "bad company" for the actor's problems, disagreed with the insanity charge. "I never believed him to be a crazy man except when he was excited by liquor, and that was pretty often—nearly all the time in fact," Smith contended.

In February 1833 Booth was in Richmond, acting at the ill-starred Marshall Theatre. The play was *Hamlet*. Everything went well until the star walked onstage for the fifth act, in which the melancholy Prince pays a visit to the graveyard of Elsinore Castle. A fellow actor, engaged in shoveling up the bones of the court jester Yorick, tossed Booth a cranium out of the open grave, as called for in the stage directions. When Junius opened his lips to speak the line, "Whose was it?" he choked. Instead of the man's skull they had used in rehearsals, Booth found the bleached head of a small child in his hands. It was a nasty prank. Junius later recounted he felt an awful premonition in that moment, certain this was a portent of evil to come.

And so it was that later in the week Booth played *Richard III*. Before the curtain rose on the second act that night, a newspaper reported, "a messenger covered with dust rushed behind the stage," shouting Booth's name. The man was fresh from Baltimore with urgent news: cholera had found its way to the Booth farm. The disease was a fast-working killer, causing fevers and diarrhea so severe that some victims perished of dehydration within hours of showing symptoms. Junius's six-year-old daughter Mary was already dead; four-year-old Frederick and two-year-old Elizabeth were seriously ill. Twelve-year-old Junius, Jr., was sick, but Rosalie, ten, and Henry Byron, eight, thus far had escaped contamination. Booth's daughter died and was buried on February 4, but it had taken the courier several days to reach Richmond with this news. There was no telling what events had transpired since then.

Witnesses backstage at the Marshall said the actor grabbed his temples in agony when he heard the report, "as though trying," one remembered, "to clutch the brain beneath." He stormed his way out of the theater, still wearing the spangled dress of his character, and ran headlong to the steamboat landing on the James River. He made the journey home at record speed.

The scene at the small cabin under the trees was a desperate one. Mary Ann Holmes was so undone by grief, it was said, she was suicidal, but Junius's return did nothing to improve the situation. The dead child, local residents remembered, "had been buried a week or more" in the soil by the time its father arrived. Nevertheless, Booth ordered Joe Hall to open her grave. Mrs. Rogers, living on a nearby farm, remembered Junius commanded the man "to take the child up and bring it to the house so it would come to life again." A horrifying interlude followed, with Booth "gibbering in idiotic madness and caressing the corpse of his little one," according to one newspaper that got hold of the story. Neighbors, perhaps summoned by Joe Hall to help the Booths in their emergency, burst into the house, reclaimed the little girl's body, and forcibly confined the actor to a bedroom, where he raved until falling into a deep sleep. "When he woke," Mrs. Rogers recalled, "he was all right." His son Frederick and daughter Elizabeth died of cholera in the following weeks, but Booth's frenzy was spent. He did not disrupt their burials.

Ground was cleared for a family graveyard beneath a stand of willow trees on the farm, the perimeter edged with an ornamental fence. The three headstones raised there, inscribed with names, were the only proofs that Mary, Frederick, and Elizabeth had ever lived. Other than in the pages of the family Bible, the unmarried parents could make no legal record of these children's births. In spring, Mary Ann planted flowering althea bushes over the small graves.

Junius harbored odd notions as to why the epidemic had hit his farm, diminishing his family by half. In the end, he blamed himself. A lapse in his vegetarian principles, he believed, caused the children to die. "Every Death Its Own Avenger Breeds," the actor told his father a month after the calamity. "Partaking of dead flesh and letting the children do the same, after a considerable prohibition of it on my part, brought on our recent afflictions."

He may not have been far off the mark. We now know the cholera bacterium spreads through contaminated food and water. When trade vessels from London carried the disease to the port of Baltimore in 1832, it took root among the abundant goods and close-packed crowds of the city's famous market houses. Sixty thousand people bought their food there daily— fish and mollusks from the Chesapeake; vegetables, mutton, and beef from local farms; wild duck and pheasant, breads, coffee, sugar, and flour. It was a place where many hands turned over the produce, where fishermen and farmers carelessly packed their wares in unclean barrels. When the Booths ordered bushels of herring and oysters from this source, cholera most likely traveled with the delivery wagon to their remote farm.

Mary Ann could only watch in bewilderment, she later recalled, as Junius embarked on a punishing regimen of "penance" and "reparation" for the deaths of his three children. The actor "put hard peas in his shoes and walked all day about the house and land," she reported. "Another time," Mary Ann said, "he fitted heavy soles of lead to the inside of his shoes and walked from Baltimore to Washington."

Though unfit to travel or to act, Booth had no choice but to go back out on the road. His manager was irate at him for skipping out on his engagement and threatened to sue Booth for breach of contract. Junius could not risk going to court: the truth about his two families would be exposed in a trial. The death of a wife or a legitimate child might excuse a brief absence from the stage, but Mary Ann and her offspring were not Booth's legal family. No businessman standing to lose thousands of dollars in ticket sales would grant an actor freedom to console his mistress or mourn a brace of bastards. "I am in his power," Booth wrote. The manager "is at liberty to sue whenever it may suit his humor. As things are, I must proceed with the devilish Contract."

Returning to the stage now, a crushed Junius confessed to a friend, "was so hard." The work of acting felt like drudgery. Only alcohol gave him the strength to act with the kind of passion his audiences craved. "He could not perform as he would like," Mrs. Rogers, the actor's neighbor, recalled him saying to her, "till he would drink some wine, and then he would get crazy." This reliance on alcohol was making the actor's offstage demeanor alarming. When he played in Louisville, Kentucky, in January 1834, near the one-year anniversary of the death of his three children, locals recalled "his fellow-actors were afraid of him." Backstage, they said, Junius "looked terribly earnest" and "spoke to no one." He would sit immobile on a chair between scenes, "looking sternly at the ground."

Booth's unhappiness, which he nursed at night with bottles of brandy in his hotel room, burst forth in an act that not only landed him in jail, but confirmed his growing reputation as a madman. It would be the first and only time Booth used the methods of the theater not to entertain, but to make a public statement about his private beliefs.

There was an immense swath of beech trees along the stretch of the Ohio River where Louisville sat. In 1834 this forest was home, one resident naturalist estimated, to "more than twenty-two hundred millions" of *Columbia migratoria*, the American passenger pigeon. The mammoth flock did not last long: they were a cornucopia of food for hungry local people. Hunters attacked the creatures at night when they returned to their trees to roost. Gangs of torch-bearing men fired guns and swung clubs and poles at the bird-laden branches. A hundred thousand birds might be killed in a night. The next day, carcasses were sold in town by the wagonload.

This local practice appalled the actor, and he was not alone. After British naturalist John James Audubon witnessed a Louisville pigeon shoot, he said he would never forget the "terrifying" scene of "devastation." The noise of the dying birds was so deafening, Audubon testified, "even the reports of the guns were seldom heard, and I was made aware of the firing only by seeing the shooters reloading."

The vegetarian Booth, already hypersensitive to animal suffering, became fixated on these massacres during his visit to the town. Angry at the "brutal Americans," as he called the hunters, Booth was spurred into action. He summoned James Freeman Clarke, then minister at the Louisville Unitarian Church, to his hotel. Forty years later, Clarke recalled the interview with perfect clarity. Entering Booth's suite of rooms, an astonishing scene met the clergyman's eyes. The actor, sitting at a table with a Bible open before him and a bottle of wine by his side, was surrounded by bushels of dead birds. The feathered bodies were piled on floors and furniture, draped in white sheets. As Clarke watched, Junius pulled back the sheets and began weeping over the birds, stroking their blue wings and red tail plumes, gathering up the corpses, Clarke remembered, and "press[ing] them to his heart." Booth told the minister he was planning to stage a burial for the birds at the Louisville churchyard. Making a sweeping gesture at the corpses, Junius said, "You see these innocent victims of man's barbarity? I wish to testify, in some public way, against this wanton destruction of life. And I wish you to help me. Will you?" Clarke declined.

"I heard, in a day or two," the minister wrote in his memoirs, that Booth "had purchased a lot in the cemetery, had a coffin made, hired a horse and carriage, and had gone through all the solemnity of a regular funeral." Junius wrote a speech protesting the bird killings in his diary, which he no doubt shared with the crowd of locals who gathered to watch his bizarre proceedings at the graveyard. "What Rage, what Fury and Madness incite you to commit such Carnage?" the actor asked. "It is the innocent, the harmless, the gentle creatures you take and kill, although Nature seems to have created them only for Beauty and Delight." He praised the birds' "fair and beautiful color," their "sweet and tunable" voices, their "quickness and subtlety of spirit," and "neat & clean life." Booth begged the townspeople to stop the slaughter, and to show the passenger pigeon "mercy & forbearance."

At first the crowd may have taken Booth's words as a joke, but when the actor argued that Jesus Christ had been nailed to the cross not in penance for the sins of mankind, but for the crime of eating meat, things turned ugly. Being drunk and disorderly in antebellum Kentucky was not enough to land a man in jail, but informing the citizenry that "had there been no miracle of [the loaves and] fish there would have been no crucifixion" and shouting "the Hindoo religion is the only one I believe to be at all like the Truth" were acts guaranteed to bring the sheriff running. Authorities may have locked Booth in the jailhouse as much for his own protection as for causing a public disturbance. The actor wrote in a letter to a friend that he had been imprisoned for the "unprofitable" crime of "telling Truth to Scoundrels." After tensions in the town settled, Junius slunk onto a steamboat bound for Pittsburgh, the site of his next engagement.

"Ah Junius, Junius, will you never have done with these mad freaks?" Booth's father asked in despair. Without a chaperone, the actor's touring was a disaster. He required constant supervision to prevent him from engaging in more outrageous acts. June Booth, now twelve, accompanied his father on a few short trips, but the child failed to keep the parent steady. Booth's closest friend was a British actor and comedian named Thomas Flynn. He seems to have loyally stepped into the role of guardian. Mary Ann Holmes was the best guarantor of Booth's well-being, but her constant pregnancies made long journeys difficult. Less than a month after half of her children had died, the thirty-one-year-old found she was pregnant again. It would be for the seventh time.

When Mary Ann's labor pangs started November 13, 1833, the birth did not progress as expected. More concerned than usual after the bereavements of the past year, her midwives may have advised sending for a doctor. June, Mary Ann's oldest boy, was the chosen messenger. As he headed out on the back of a mule hours before daybreak with Joe Hall as his companion, June recalled that in the darkness above, thousands of meteors started raining downward. Baltimore's papers reported the next morning that many people believed the world was coming to an end. Others were certain the meteors "prognosticated some dreadful war." Only astronomers seemed unafraid, "viewing the phenomenon wonderful." The shower lasted for a full hour. One meteor exploded with a bang over northwest Baltimore, lighting the clouds like a sunrise and leaving a fiery, thirty-foot trail.

June Booth and Joe Hall fetched a doctor to Mary Ann's bedside. Her newborn emerged safely, but he had a transparent layer of skin swathed around his face, a rare phenomenon known as a caul. Since medieval times, folk wisdom held that any infant delivered thus was destined for greatness. Shakespeare called the mark "fortune's star." Mary Ann saved the bit of membrane carefully in a box. Years later, she would show it to her grandchildren as proof of this one baby's special fate. If the superstitious Booth family was going to rely on one son, out of all others, for salvation and support, how could it not be the one who arrived with cosmic fanfare and a caul? The mother named the unusually silent, alert child Edwin Thomas Booth.

It was in May 1836 that news of General Sam Houston's triumph at the Battle of San Jacinto reached Andrew Jackson in the White House. His old drinking partner had found his destiny at last, Booth marveled in his diary. The actor's own star still shone brightly despite his near-constant intoxication. Junius had been a perennial favorite with D.C. audiences since the Monroe administration, but he won particular acclaim during Andrew Jackson's two terms in office. Booth and General Jackson were friends, close enough that the actor fondly addressed the president in written communications as "you damned old scoundrel." He even visited with the chief executive at the Hermitage, Jackson's plantation outside of Nashville. The actor's impassioned portrayals of Iago and Othello, recalled a Washington resident of the 1830s, "were a delight to the refined scholar" but especially thrilling to "the uncultivated backwoodsman" then occupying the presidency.

The same year, a crushing blow fell on the actor when he least expected it. Hoping to clear the melancholy fog from his mind, Junius agreed to return once again to London's Drury Lane Theatre. In the autumn of 1836, the entire Booth family boarded an oceangoing steamer: Junius, Mary Ann, fifteen-year-old June, twelve-year-old Rosalie, ten-year-old Henry Byron, three-year-old Edwin, and Mary Ann's latest, a four-month-old named Asia. All received smallpox vaccinations before the voyage, but within a month of their arrival in England, Henry Byron fell sick. As if a swarm of bees had attacked him, thick clusters of red pustules appeared all over the child's skin, even covering his eyelids and the lining of his mouth. The ten-year-old died in agony, vomiting and writhing with fever. June and Rosalie escaped untouched; toddler Edwin and infant Asia experienced only a mild sickness.

Something snapped inside Junius when Henry Byron died. "So proud as I was of him, above all the others," the father wailed. The actor always had scanned his children for signs of greatness similar to his own. "Can [he] read?" Junius inquired impatiently of a four-year-old son. His first two children were unremarkable. Little June was a dogged student but showed no talent for books; he preferred physical sport. Rosalie, according to neighbors, was the spitting image of her father, "not pretty, but a noble girl," yet silent and withdrawn. Henry Byron, in contrast, was everything Junius could have hoped. The child had his mother's dark good looks as well as his father's mercurial wit, terrific head for languages, and dramatic spark. Henry Byron seems to have replicated the best in Booth. The actor could not bear to tell his father, Richard, waiting back in Maryland, that this prodigy was gone. Only when "time had somewhat softened the horror of the event," Junius said, was he able to write the words "our dear little Henry is dead." Henry Byron Booth was buried in a London cemetery beneath a headstone Junius himself designed for the child. It reads, "Oh, even in spite of death, yet still my choice; Oft with the inward, all-beholding eye, I think I see thee, and I hear thy voice."

The family would never be the same. Their ill-fated voyage, Junius wrote, "cost me the price of a Son's life." It also brought him into the orbit of his legal wife and child. Adelaide Delannoy Booth learned that her husband would be performing in London. From her mother's house in Brussels, she wrote begging for assistance with their eighteen-year-old son Richard's education. Absorbed in mourning for Henry Byron, Booth did everything he could to avoid a face-to-face meeting with Adelaide. If she remained in Europe, the actor pledged to send her more money than usual. He would make another visit to London in a few years' time, Booth assured his wife, to "look after" Richard's prospects.

This was an empty promise. The actor was desperate to slip off the constraints of this world. Despite Mary Ann becoming pregnant with yet another baby, her ninth, by the time the bereaved family had returned to their

Maryland farm, Booth could not shake the urge to die. On March 7, 1838, on his way from New York to an engagement in Charleston, South Carolina, Booth's traveling companion, Thomas Flynn, left him alone in the main cabin for a moment. The actor seized his chance at oblivion, rushing on deck and leaping over the railing into the open ocean. Though the steamer was far from shore and puffing south with great speed, the captain stopped the engines and sent out a rescue party. Booth's body was spotted in the water; sailors pulled him from the freezing Atlantic and restored him to consciousness.

When newspapers reported this escapade, Booth's fame only increased. Such manic displays, it was thought, were proof of the artist's sensitivity and genius. "We consider him not only as the ornament and glory, but the victim of his profession," stated a lead editorial in the *Charleston Mercury* after the star jumped overboard. "The public have forgiven in him eccentricities which would scarce have been tolerated in another." With no knowledge of his private life, no information about the deaths of his children, the editors could only conclude that Booth's unhappiness flowed from his dwelling too little in reality and too much in the imaginary world of Shakespeare. The actor had so deeply explored the madness of King Lear, the melancholy of Hamlet, and the passion of Othello, that now the "painted scenes turned to solid castles, frowning forests and bustling streets, and he himself stepped into the shadow of the poet's dreams, as no simulated hero."

Edwin Booth later claimed that his earliest memory dated from the first week of May 1838. It was his fourth year of life, two months after his father tried to drown himself, and only days before his brother John Wilkes would come into the world. The image fixed in the child's mind is the interior of a backstage dressing room at Baltimore's Holliday Street Theatre. His mother, Mary Ann, eight months pregnant, was with him. Together they sat listening to the distant sound of Junius Brutus Booth's voice from the stage, the little boy making use, he later said, of "the theatrical wigs and paint-pots for his toys." When he became tired, Edwin remembered, "he was put to bed in a chest of drawers that held his father's wardrobe."

He needed whatever rest he could get, for the minute Junius took his final bow and entered the dressing room to remove his costume, the boy would be awakened and dandled before his father to divert him from disappearing into a tavern for the rest of the night. If mother and son failed to sufficiently entertain him, Junius would be off to drink and the night's wages would be lost. The star had become so insatiable in his habits, his neighbor Mrs. Rogers remembered, that Mary Ann Holmes "had finally to go with him and take care of his money." Of all the children then on the Maryland farm, thoughtful, dark-haired little "Teddy," as Edwin was called, seemed to hold the most appeal for the troubled actor. "When his mother used to accompany his father to the playhouse," Edwin later said, he "was taken with them."

Mary Ann's ploy to distract Booth from drinking sometimes worked and sometimes did not, but she brought an urgency to the task that the perceptive four-year-old learned to emulate. For all his concern about protecting animals from suffering, Booth when drunk was physically abusive. A Philadelphia doctor who once treated Mary Ann Holmes's children blamed the actor, he said, for suffusing her life with "misery" and "fear." Disturbing proof of Junius's temper under the influence came on March 13, 1838, when the actor almost killed his best friend, Thomas Flynn. A dispute the two men were having over Mary Ann, then seven months pregnant, ended in violence. According to backstage gossip, Flynn was attacked because he tried to stop Booth from "having a fair shake at his wife." Whether Junius intended to beat Mary Ann or have intercourse with her is unclear: the old slang phrase had variable meanings. Newspapers reported the drunk, irate Booth seized an iron poker from a fireplace and struck Flynn across the face and head with it. Mary Ann's defender made a narrow escape.

John Wilkes Booth was born at the family farm in Harford County on May 10, 1838, in an interlude of comparative peace that followed the outrageous events of March. No stars fell from the sky that night, as they had at the hour of Edwin's birth, but the infant's father was electrified nonetheless. It was rare for Booth to be present when Mary Ann went into labor. Watching this baby come into the world seems to have left a deep impression on the forty-two-year-old actor, perhaps healing some of the pain he felt for his lost favorite, the son so much like himself, Henry Byron. After this strong, healthy baby arrived, Junius appears to have made no further attempts at suicide.

The baby's grandfather, Richard Booth, then in his seventy-fifth year, was given the honor of naming the child. He settled on John Wilkes, a striking choice, a hopeful choice, one filled with personal significance for Richard and no doubt pleasing to Junius as well. In retrospect, the name seems the elderly man's way of conferring his blessing on the Booth family's haphazard enterprise in the United States, which thus far had earned equal shares of glory and infamy.

The old lawyer plucked a famous figure from the Booth family tree to stand as namesake: Richard Booth's mother had claimed the politician John Wilkes as a relative. A member of the British Parliament from 1775 to

1790, Wilkes had been a strident defender of the rights of American colonists to rebel against the Crown and organize themselves into an independent nation. His views were all the more brave, one biographer notes, for being "flung in the teeth of power and popular feeling." In 1774, scant weeks after Boston's Sons of Liberty staged their Tea Party, John Wilkes rose in the House of Commons to make an inflammatory prediction: "the Americans will rise to independence, to power, to all the greatness of the most renowned States, for they build on the solid basis of general, public liberty." By his command, Wilkes's tombstone bore the epitaph "A Friend of Liberty."

The name of this prophetic Englishman seemed to fit the promising new baby, who, its family hoped, would enjoy a rich inheritance of American freedom and the spark of the Booth genius. The original John Wilkes was not born a gentleman, but instead had propelled himself from social obscurity to public distinction by his quick wit and charismatic manner. An illegitimate son of Junius Brutus Booth—a man whose fame and popularity were "as grand," one contemporary wrote, "as his private life was intemperate and eccentric"—easily could make the same journey.

In decades to come, other names would be given to this child. The baby's sister Asia would call him, years later, "Absalom," after the biblical King David's favorite son. In the Old Testament story, Absalom was a boy warrior who brought trouble upon his family and disaster to his father's kingdom when he conspired to destroy his older brother.

FOUR

A POPULOUS CITY

There's many a beast then, in a populous city, and many a civil monster.
—*Othello*, 4.1

THE LOG HOUSE IN THE WOODS WHERE EDWIN AND JOHN WILKES SPENT their earliest years of life was sturdy, but mean-looking. A Harford County farm family had built the cabin in the early 1800s as a temporary shelter. Before Junius Brutus Booth bought the structure in 1822, it had stood empty for years. Locals called the cabin "unattractive." The boy's sister Asia used a kinder word. Their birthplace was "humble," she said. In her memoirs, Asia describes a home of Quaker-like simplicity. The ground floor, a single low-ceilinged room, was furnished with a table, some "straight-backed, hard and uncomfortable" mahogany chairs, a mirror, a china cupboard, and a spinning wheel. On the east wall was a fireplace flanked by bookshelves. A desk crammed with the actor's journals and correspondence stood in a corner. This was not a place where the younger members of the household were welcome to play. Too much work happened in it: wool was spun for blankets and stockings, lengths of store-bought cloth were cut and sewed for Booth's costumes, account books were balanced, dough was kneaded for the day's bread. As long as the weather allowed, from early spring through the late autumn, Mary Ann Holmes's six surviving children spent their days outdoors.

A cherry tree growing on the lawn in front of the cabin partly made up for the limitations of this overcrowded dwelling. For much of the year, the tree was the favorite haunt of June, Rosalie, Edwin, Asia, John Wilkes, and Mary Ann's youngest, little Joseph Adrian. Long before they had been born, the cherry had been grafted so that five thick branches would radiate outward from the main trunk, at the perfect height to enable young climbers. By the time Edwin and John Wilkes were of an age to clamber up, the tree was a "grand" size, Asia remembered, "very tall and straight." The old cherry was strong enough, she wrote, to support the half-dozen Booth children who spent hours in its branches, talking, playing, "or doz[ing] away . . . a sultry afternoon."

This old tree was the first theater Edwin and John Wilkes ever knew. Decades after the Civil War, the brothers' childhood friends still told the story of "how, from the crotch of the tree, which separated like five great fingers from a hand, the Booth boys used to declaim passages from Shakespeare." Against the changing backdrop of flowers, fruit, and leaves, the children imitated their famous father in piping voices, parroting parts from Booth's repertoire while swinging on tree branches.

They could speak the lines before they knew how to read, for Edwin, John Wilkes, and their siblings grew up with the phrases of Shakespeare ringing in their ears. When their father came home to Harford County each summer after a long season of touring, he sang or spoke Shakespeare aloud all day long. His sons could not help but hear. Whether from irresistible compulsion, or whether this was a device he consciously employed to stay sober and keep darker thoughts at bay, the actor, when at home, was a fountain of language. Booth's vocal habit mystified the local people. One resident remembered: "my grandfather told me of the times [Booth] would ride his horse from his homestead to Bel Air, reciting Shakespeare, to the wonderment of the neighbors, adding to their thoughts he was 'peculiar.'"

When they reached adulthood, Asia and Edwin wrote about what it was like to spend a childhood with Junius Brutus Booth. Their memoirs are painful to read. As they try to paint a portrait of the father they knew, the emotions of awe, admiration, anger, resentment, and hurt mingle together. Asia recalled an evening when Booth gathered his offspring in a circle on the floor before his armchair so he could read aloud to them speeches from *Coriolanus* and *King John*. These tragedies were advanced fare for so young a crowd, the meat of the stories being the twisted passions of family conflict and dynastic struggles for power. As Booth read, he paused to instruct his small listeners on the fine points of diction and enunciation that separated educated British speech from the looser rhythms of American English. "He was particular that we should imitate him," Asia remembered. Her father especially warned the children not to drop the "the final 'g' of words," she said, as many Americans made a habit of doing.

One of the stranger contradictions Booth presented to his family was that even as he filled their imaginations with the plots and poetry of Shakespeare, even as he dazzled them with his dramatic ability and taught them rudiments of oratory, the actor drew a sharp, forbidding line between his children and life in the theater. They were not invited to watch him perform before an audience, they were not told anything about his work or artistic methods, and many of their clumsy efforts at playacting were, at times, brutally discouraged by him. "In the youth of his children," Edwin wrote, "everything connected with his profession was carefully avoided, as if he feared, by intercourse or allusion, to throw that glamour over its reality which might delude the senses and engender romantic desires for excitement." Booth had come to find the grueling life of a traveling star to be physically unbearable. At times, he said, going through the motions of a play was impossible for him without the stimulus of alcohol. Junius hoped his sons would pursue careers less damaging to body and mind. He also feared what would happen if one of his children harbored fantasies of stardom but lacked the dramatic genius to achieve it—a fear that would prove to be justified.

Booth's efforts to discourage his children's love of acting were wasted. The household he and Mary Ann had created was in effect a miniature theater. Even when Booth himself was far from home, his presence filled the place. Anyone entering the cabin could see it belonged to an actor's family and became enthralled by its aura of celebrity and theatrical "glamour." Costumes were everywhere, one of Edwin's friends recalled. An avalanche of old cloaks, armor, swords, velvet slippers, long-haired wigs, and assorted stage "toggery" spilled out of wardrobes and dresser drawers in the bedrooms upstairs. On the main floor, Mary Ann was constantly employed in repairing Booth's worn-out stage "dresses," as they were called, or devising new ones. Weeks after giving birth to her last child, Joseph, in 1840, the tireless seamstress completed an elaborate dress of wool gabardine for Booth to wear in *The Merchant of Venice*, as well as a classical Greek garment for his part in the ancient tragedy *Orestes*.

Piles of playbills were scattered about, a family friend remembered, some on shelves, some cluttering the closets and bureaus. Set in bold typeface to catch the eye of prospective ticket buyers, the posters fascinated visitors. Printed in cities across Europe and America and proclaiming in large, fat letters the name BOOTH, the copious bills offered a graphic guide to the actor's roving, rollicking career. There were leaflets from his 1815 tour of Brussels and Amsterdam, a trip made in the teeth of the Napoleonic wars. Enormous sheets, printed in London in 1817, trumpeted the boy prodigy's sensational showdown with the great Edmund Kean. Smaller broadsides proclaimed Booth's 1821 debut on American shores, and his subsequent triumphs across the country. Posters from the star's decades of appearances in Washington City were carefully preserved, forming a record of how Booth entertained a slew of U.S. presidents.

The shelves by the fireplace were stocked with plays "in every language," a guest on the farm reported. Between them, Junius and his father, Richard, had amassed an impressive library of scripts. Books in Latin and Greek, French, Spanish, Italian, Portuguese, and English, "all thumbed and marked," dominated the room, representing dramatic classics from every nation and era. "Terence and Lope de Vega, Shakespeare and Tait, Ben Jonson and Racine, lay side by side," recounted a friend, "some marked for the stage and full of directions; some with famous autographs on the fly-leaf." There were plentiful copies of a play Booth himself wrote and published in 1840. Always gifted in the poetic line, the actor had dreamed up a seamy blood-bath of seduction and murder set in seventeenth-century Venice. He titled it "Ugolino." No doubt on a special shelf, out of reach of young hands, were Booth's diaries of his travels, his secretive communications with his wife, Adelaide Delannoy Booth, and his priceless mementos of Lord Byron, Shelley, and other Romantic writers from the actor's London heyday.

The cabin in the forest was undeniably an actor's house, and it was filled with an actor's progeny. Language came easily to many of them. They showed a love for music and had other creative inclinations. Booth could not help passing on some of his own gifts to his children. His daughter Asia was dark-haired and beautiful like her mother, sharp-tongued—at times spiteful, with a forceful personality. Sharing her father's facility for language, Asia was afflicted like him with fits of moodiness and melancholy. She was a keen observer of the personalities around her and would become the chief chronicler of Booth family life. Asia once wrote that Mary Ann Holmes treated her sons with the same reverence she paid to Booth himself. There was an element of "eager worship" in Mary Ann's mothering, Asia said, an emotion she could only describe as a "mysterious . . . hungering Love."

The intensity of Mary Ann's maternal feelings may have been a legacy of watching four promising young children die. And Mary Ann's four surviving sons did not inherit equal shares of their father's talents. A childhood companion of June, Edwin, John Wilkes, and Joseph Adrian observed that the four boys "were as wide apart as points of the compass." "They all differed," he said.

June, the eldest, was a disappointment to his parents. The boy had been carefully trained by his grandfather Richard in the mysteries of Latin and Greek. A neighbor remembered June's father intended him "to be a lawyer or a doctor." But June was stagestruck, she said, and "did not wish anything but the theater." He made his debut in a supporting role in Philadelphia in 1839, aged eighteen. It was a poor decision. Though he had a leading man's good looks, his fellow actors spoke of June in damning phrases, noting he was "fairly good," "slow in speech," "great in nothing," and competent "to the limit of his ability." Privately, the youth's famous father suggested "June would make a better merchant than an actor."

In 1840, the youngest Booth child, Joseph Adrian, was a newborn, an unknown quantity. As years passed, however, he was so far from showing signs of his father's greatness, he did not even measure up to older brother June's mediocre mark. "Of dramatic fire Joe had not one spark," reported a family friend. He was unremarkable in all respects, a colorless, amiable person, having a talent only, his companions said, for "ease, comfort and good fellowship."

Edwin and John Wilkes were another story. As children, the pair excited interest in all who met them. "Nature seems to have favored Edwin and John with all the charms that go to make [an actor] perfect," a friend observed. "These two sons," he continued, were worthy of the "erratic genius" who fathered them. Booth himself acknowledged that Edwin and John Wilkes were promising in different ways, "but which one will excel," he muttered darkly in 1850, "remains to be seen."

The boys presented a stark contrast. John Wilkes's face was "perfect" in its handsomeness, friends said, uncannily like his father's. The child "was an exact counterpart," neighbors declared, "of the elder Booth." For this reason, and perhaps because he brought to mind the beloved Henry Byron, Edwin claimed that John Wilkes was "his mother's darling," favored by her above all her other children, Even as a toddler, this pint-sized version of Junius Brutus Booth was passionate, outgoing, noisy, and appealing. His hazel eyes were "piercing and most expressive," observers noted, with "long, up-curling lashes."

Edwin looked nothing like his famous parent. "I do not remember a father and son more unlike in figure," remarked one of Booth's contemporaries. Edwin was a "slender, sallow-faced little youngster," a family friend remembered, whose delicate features closely resembled his mother's. The child was painfully shy, with dark eyes that seemed too large for his face, and a sad expression. An actor meeting the silent ten-year-old for the first time commented that Edwin's sensitive, melancholy looks made "an immediate and powerful impression."

Being scanned for signs of their father's remarkable gifts was not unusual. This was, after all, the household of a man who spoke ten languages, composed poetry and plays, and had won international fame before he was twenty-five. The Booth cabin was a place where creativity, talent, and quick wit never failed to win praise. Literary, poetic, and artistic impulses were encouraged at all times: pen and paper were readily available, musical instruments were put in the hands of those who wanted them, books were never off-limits. Next to his livelier siblings Asia and John Wilkes, Edwin faded into the background. Describing the spirit of competition for the actor's attention when he was at home, Booth's "other children were more vivacious and amused him," Edwin remembered. "He almost ignored me."

Growing up as they did, with the tools of their father's profession and the tokens of his fame all around them, it is not surprising Booth's sons showed an interest in drama. Booth's theatrical paraphernalia was all the more alluring given the family's lonely situation in the Maryland woods. With few neighbors and no diversions besides one another's company, Edwin said, the Booth children experienced "a sense of estrangement" from the outside world. The feeling of apartness instilled by early years of isolation became such a habit with the family, Edwin said, it was "never eradicated," even after the clan took up residence in more populous places. And neither, no doubt, was the impression that an actor's life was a ticket to adventure.

To this family marooned on the farm their grandfather called "Robinson Crusoe's Island" for its suffocating remoteness, Junius's summer homecomings were like the arrival of an emissary from a faraway land, with tidings of a tumultuous nation beyond the forest. He may have remained silent about his acting work, but Booth thrilled his family with tales of the famous men and the wondrous cities encountered on his travels. When the actor was in the mood, he talked of friendships with General Sam Houston, Daniel Webster, and President Andrew Jackson. Booth the international star, try as he might to discourage his offspring from following in his footsteps, could not hide the truth about his own life story, which from the very start had been no mere tale, but an epic.

ONE COLD EVENING IN 1839 WHEN BOOTH HIMSELF WAS OFF ON TOUR, a chapter from the actor's past life came back to haunt his family. Mary Ann's Newfoundland dogs—descendants of the original trio Booth had bought her for company nearly twenty years before—began barking, breaking the farm's nighttime quiet. A band of strangers was coming up the winding, tree-lined dirt road toward the cabin. Visitors were a rare, almost unheard-of occurrence. These would prove a nightmare for the Booths. Mary Ann Holmes had never seen them before, and at first could only marvel, her daughter Asia recalled, at the group's "grotesque" appearance. Ten in all, they were filthy, travel-worn, and ill-dressed against the cold. Some were in rags; others were draped in oddments and bits of finery cadged from the costume stores of a Baltimore theater. At least one was barefoot.

Their leader was a malevolent, sneering man named James Mitchell, Asia wrote, garbed in a "long-tailed green velvet coat." He had once been a servant in the Booths' London house, a lowly "bootblack and knife-scourer," neighbors later said. Junius Brutus Booth's younger sister, Jane, despite her status as a "very beautiful" and "highly educated . . . gentleman's daughter," shocked everyone by falling under Mitchell's spell and eloping with him. In the ensuing family uproar, Richard Booth disowned his youngest child and refused to speak to her ever again. Soon thereafter, Junius and Richard had immigrated to America. Over the years, Jane Mitchell had not had an easy time. She bore eight children to Mitchell, who revealed himself to be indolent, physically abusive, and a heavy drinker. The family's life in London was one of desperate poverty.

The Mitchells boarded a ship for Baltimore. Had they not done so, Asia recalled, "they could have starved and filled the graves of paupers." Upon landing, this family, with no money or luggage, made their way to the nearest theater, begging actors and stage managers for food, clothing, and help on the strength of Booth's name. Dressed in cast-off costumes and equipped with directions to Bel Air, James and Jane Mitchell traced a path to the actor's isolated farm, where they made clear to a startled Mary Ann and an irate Richard Booth, they expected to be fed, housed, and supplied with money for the long term.

One historian has suggested that James Mitchell threatened Booth with blackmail, dangling the hint of exposing Junius and Mary Ann's adulterous relationship. Such a threat, however, may not have needed to be made outright. Mitchell was a drunkard. Junius could not have wanted this troublesome brother-in-law loose in Baltimore, carousing in taverns and spreading tales of the legal wife and legitimate son the great Booth kept in London, or of his elopement to America with a Covent Garden flower girl. The publication of this story would make bastards of Mary Ann Holmes's children, perhaps even lead to a scandal that would put an end to Booth's career. To stave off this fate, room was made for the newcomers. The Mitchells broke up the fragile contentment Mary Ann had established at her home. Mitchell's hold over Mary Ann and Junius brought the exposure they had always feared uncomfortably near. However high the price of harboring this difficult family, it was worth paying them off to prevent the unveiling of the secret.

The arrival of the Mitchells furnished spicy gossip for the Bel Air neighborhood. Much was made of poor "Mrs. Booth," whose tiny cabin now was wretchedly overcrowded, and who was being forced, it was said, "to assist and wait upon her sickly and delicate sister-in-law." Jane Mitchell, contemptuous of the woman her brother had run away with, took to her bed and treated Mary Ann Holmes like a servant. Her husband's behavior was even more mystifying to outsiders. It was widely known that Mitchell performed no work on the farm, spending his days in ill-tempered idleness. "Mr. Mitchell would not do anything," exclaimed Mrs. Rogers, the Booths' nearest neighbor, "not even cut the wood at the door," yet "Mr. & Mrs. Booth [continued on] supporting them all." To relieve the crowding in the cabin, Mrs. Rogers recalled, "Mr. Booth repaired the carriage house and Mr. Mitchell moved in there."

How the Booth children grappled with the invasion of their home is not clear. Asia's memoirs reek of resentment for the pack of interlopers who cut up her privacy and turned her mother into a drudge. There was no love lost between the two sets of cousins; jeers and taunts were traded freely. Edwin turned to studying music as a way of escape. In his sister's words, there was a "clever, self-taught negro musician" in the neighborhood, an expert guitar player and singer. This man, whose name is not mentioned in Booth family papers, taught seven-year-old Edwin to pluck intricate melodies on the five-stringed banjo, an instrument devised by slaves whose ancestors were among the lute-playing peoples of western Africa. Edwin learned the words to dance songs and work songs, and memorized the rhyming meditations on the perfidy of women and the persistence of bad luck that are now recognized as the basis of American blues. Asia and John Wilkes were less musically inclined, but the young Booths seem to have redoubled their enthusiasm for singing and acting as a way of shutting out the Mitchell cousins and demonstrating the talents they bore as the offspring of the famous Booth.

Imitating their father from the boughs of the old cherry tree had been a start, but Edwin, Asia, and John Wilkes progressed to demanding their mother pitch them a tent on the lawn to use as a theater. Harriet Kennett, the daughter of a leased slave named Hagar who worked on the Booth property, recalled how she used to "run over the farm together" with the young Booths at a time when putting on stage melodramas was a popular game with them. Kennett recounted to an interviewer, "sometimes they had a kind of show over there, thunder and lightning I called it. Many a day they put up a tent in the yard."

Just as the great tragedian excelled, so critics said, at "depicting the passions of hate, fear, terror, revenge, scorn, despair and the like," his children relished spectacles that were as bloodthirsty and action-packed as possible.

The play their father wrote, *Ugolino*, furnished an ideal plot. The star-crossed hero, driven mad by jealousy, kills his true love, Angelica, after he discovers and slays a rival for her affections. "Was it not well done?" Ugolino demands of the audience while clutching Angelica's bleeding corpse to his chest. "Look here! She loved me . . . and I—I killed her!" As the curtain falls on the final scene, Ugolino is supposed to commit suicide. "Come, my bride . . . to Hell's center! In my heart I plunge this reeking sword!" he shrieks. Acted out on the Booth lawn, with twigs for swords and filched scraps of cloth for costumes, *Ugolino* would have been "thunder and lightning" indeed.

Such scenes could draw a sizable audience, even in the woods. By the early 1840s, with the coming of the Mitchells, there were upwards of twenty people, black and white, free and slave, living on the Booth farm. A majority of this number were children: eight Mitchell cousins, five Booth offspring, and several belonging to Joe and Ann Hall. Harriet Kennett was interviewed when she was in her late seventies. She retained a memory of Mary Ann Holmes's impartiality toward the young people. "Mrs. Booth was a handsome woman," she said. "She didn't mind the colored children playing on the place at all. She used to give us food just the same as she did her own children."

As hard as it was for Mary Ann to bear the Mitchells, the situation was even worse for the Hall family. Junius Brutus Booth had leased Joe Hall, a slave, from a neighboring plantation in 1822. Local tradition holds that the actor immediately decided to buy Hall from his owner in order to set him free. The "peculiar" Mr. Booth, it was said, "surely could not have approved of slavery." Over several years, Joe Hall earned the five hundred dollars he needed to buy his wife's freedom. Ann Hall was owned by the nearby Rogers family. Once emancipated, she came to work on the Booth farm. "Her freedom did not bring her much happiness," Ann Hall later told an interviewer, because a number of her "little ones," she said, including an infant, remained in slavery on the Rogerses' plantation. Neighboring people remembered Ann as a "devoted mother." In addition to working grueling hours for the Booths, Ann said, she and Joe hired themselves out to others in the area for odd jobs "until they had a hundred and ten dollars with which they bought their baby" from the Rogers. The couple's next goal was to buy their own cabin and a piece of land where they could raise their free children, but the arrival of the Mitchells meant extra work and new worries for the Halls. The couple had less time to work for other families, meaning a longer deferment of their dream. Worse, Ann and Joe had concealed what money they had earned in the wall of the carriage house where the Mitchells now lived.

Richard Booth was so outraged by the presence of his disgraced daughter and obnoxious son-in-law, Mrs. Rogers reported, "I don't think he ever spoke to Mr. & Mrs. Mitchell." To have the man who had blacked the boots in his London household now lording it over him in America was too much for the old lawyer. He packed his trunks and left the farm for good, moving to a rented room in Baltimore. The seventy-six-year-old Englishman died not long after, "alone in the night, supposed to have been seized by a cramp in the stomach." An undertaker named Weaver, whose business was next door to Baltimore's Front Street Theatre, took charge of the corpse, knowing Junius would pay him for the service when he returned from tour. Richard Booth's body was buried in Baltimore Cemetery under a marble slab bearing lines of Hebrew poetry chosen by his son. "I take my departure from life as from an inn—hence, to the stars!" the stone proclaimed to those who could read the language.

Money had been tight for the Booths before the Mitchells came. Audiences showed up in droves wherever Junius was billed to perform, but the unreliable star did not always appear before curtain. Benjamin Perley Poore was a longtime fixture of society in Washington, D.C. Over the span of three decades, he watched Booth entertain U.S. presidents from John Quincy Adams to John Tyler. Noting it was common knowledge that Booth was "a slave to intoxicating drink," Poore marveled at how forgiving the actor's admirers were. Even though the star "often disappointed his audiences," Poore admitted "his popularity remained unabated." Booth's incessant struggles with alcohol meant the day-to-day fortunes of his children dangled from a thread; by 1840, the ten Mitchells had doubled the number of dependents the actor needed to support.

Pinched for cash, Mary Ann Holmes had no choice but to commandeer Booth's wages whenever she could. If he had an engagement in Baltimore, Mary Ann would make the twenty-five-mile trip into the city by stagecoach, a friend recalled, in order to "collect her husband's salary a few hours before it was due, else the family would see none of it." Sympathetic theater managers, well aware, as one put it, that "the family had a hard time owing to the father's habits," were more than happy to hand over the money to her. For extra income in summer and fall, Mary Ann fell back on the trade she practiced in her London days. With Joe Hall at her side, she took cartloads of apples, peaches, potatoes, and beets into Baltimore, hawking them to the crowds who thronged the city's Lexington Market.

Mary Ann Holmes spent nearly twenty years in the log cabin, but the coming of the Mitchells put an end to her year-round residence there. The

Booths still would summer on their farm, when waves of cholera and typhoid plagued Baltimore, but the rest of the year the family lived in the city. By the fall of 1840, Mary Ann, Rosalie, Edwin, Asia, John Wilkes, and baby Joseph occupied a rented house on Baltimore's North High Street. They had left behind "Robinson Crusoe's Island," as Richard Booth jokingly dubbed his son's secluded farm, and were now plunged into the tumult of an industrial city one hundred thousand people strong. For the next dozen years, the family made their home in the same modest neighborhood of brick row houses on the east side of Baltimore. Shopkeepers, butchers, and sea captains favored the place: the tree-lined streets were inexpensive but presentable, in easy walking distance to the city's theaters, markets, and wharves. On Sundays, Asia remembered, when the playhouses were closed, Junius Brutus Booth would shepherd his children on the six-block walk to the inner harbor, where "admiring the shipping" became a favorite family pastime. The family's Newfoundland dogs, Veto and Rolla, went along on these outings and proved helpful in preventing the younger Booths from toddling off the piers into the water.

In 1840, Baltimore was the third-largest city in the Union. Intent on outpacing higher-ranked Philadelphia and New York, her civic motto was "Death, or Go-Ahead." A group of forward-looking business leaders, alive to the potential of steam power, railroads, and telegraphy, were catapulting the city into the industrial future. Gone was the peaceful hamlet ringed with farms that charmed Junius and Mary Ann in 1821. Now the place was smoke-choked cacophony. A writer passing through the city said the transformations wrought by new technology were so "astounding and incredible," newcomers felt jolted to the core. One could only conclude, he wrote, that Baltimore "has studied ugliness, practiced it long and toilsomely, made a philosophy of ugliness and raised it to a fine art, so that in the end it has become a work of genius." The result, as elsewhere, was a rising tide of consumerist and middle-class living.

The years the Booths spent in Baltimore would prove a crucial period not only in that city's history, but in America as a whole. Families were leaving farms and making their way to urban centers, abandoning eighteenth-century ways of living and adapting themselves to the accelerated rhythms of nineteenth-century life. On walks across the city, the Booths were surrounded with the increasingly familiar hum of steam-powered machinery. Three blocks from the harbor, in the heart of downtown, the children could feel the thudding of the printing press in the basement of the *Baltimore Sun* building through the soles of their shoes. Thousands of people worked the steam-driven cotton mills on the east end of town, where a clatter rose from mechanized looms weaving sailcloth for clipper ships and calico for dresses. There were flour mills, sawmills, brickyards, manufacturers of bullets and chemicals, dye houses, carriage makers, furniture factories, oyster-packing warehouses, and a five-story piano factory. Everywhere, the air tasted of soot.

Degrees of wealth and poverty never before seen emerged in Baltimore in this decade. Marble-fronted mansions springing up off Monument Square and along pricey Lexington Street made earlier standards of opulence obsolete. These dwellings, some equivalent in cost to a new locomotive, possessed all the modern conveniences: wallpaper, gaslights, bathrooms, hot and cold running water, and central heat. Such luxuries were undreamed of by Baltimore's growing underclass of tenement dwellers, a population swollen each year as refugees from Ireland's potato famine and the struggling poor of England and Germany arrived on passenger ships, desperate for work. The poorest of these lived not in the slums but on the streets, barefoot, beset by illness and hunger.

Half the population fell somewhere between these two extremes. Baltimore's middle class was sizable, one that sparked a building boom of row houses to accommodate the many engineers, railroad clerks, haberdashers, machinists, glaziers, cabinetmakers, chemists, schoolteachers, piano tuners, booksellers, innkeepers, and physicians all earning good money. Where the Booths should fit into this kaleidoscopic array of middling classes and professions was a problem the family never solved during the dozen years they lived in the city.

What happened to the Booth family between 1840 and 1852 would leave Edwin and John Wilkes Booth with a corrosive, lifelong anxiety about their status in the world. Hurled from the sleepy solitude of their native Harford County forest into this complicated, fast-changing city, the family would be forced to find a place for itself under difficult circumstances. Before they left Baltimore in 1852, the Booths would be as famous as the families of the merchant princes occupying the palaces on Monument Square, but as despised as the "filthy vagabonds," in the mayor's words, who begged for coin at every steamboat landing and public market in the city.

By 1846, despite the actor's erratic earnings and the drain of supporting the Mitchell family in idleness on the Bel Air farm, Junius and Mary Ann were able to buy a two-story brick house on North Exeter Street. The Booths' new home boasted a basement, a separate dining room, a front parlor, an attic for storage, and a backyard with a wooden gazebo. No longer would the cooking be done over an open fireplace, as in the old cabin: this house had a sturdy Franklin stove. At the front entrance was a wide stone stoop, identical to those of the other houses along the block. The Booths advertised their pretensions to middle-class gentility by wallpapering the parlor in green and gold, and acquiring several pieces of what Asia called "lofty and important" factory-made furniture, including a highly polished sideboard that Mary Ann kept stocked with glassware, fresh flowers, and fruit.

This new residence certainly was a far cry from the Booth farm. The shriek of steam whistles from Baltimore's east-side mills might be heard morning and night. A few blocks away workers noisily were building the terminus of a railroad line. North Exeter was the kind of street where children played on the cobblestones past nightfall, where parents sat on front stoops in the cool of the evening and watched the girls dance ring-around-the-rosy, and where mothers and fathers soundly beat their male offspring for minor infractions. Slang and ungrammatical speech were not unknown here. The Booths, like several of their neighbors, could be seen at the public markets on Saturday nights, washing dirt from wagonloads of potatoes to sell in the hopes of clearing a few extra dollars.

To be a recognizable member of the middle class in 1840s America, one had to live in a decent house, speak beautifully, dress handsomely, be well versed in etiquette, and refrain from coarse language and rowdy behavior. Mary Ann Holmes had her eyes on this goal, knowing North Exeter Street was a better place to begin working toward it than in the Bel Air woods. Though Mary Ann's eldest, June, had wasted his Latin lessons and some early training in the law by running away to join a theater company, her younger boys would succeed in being raised to respectable professions, she trusted, where June had failed.

Determinedly, she set about putting a polish on the children. She enrolled Asia, Edwin, and John Wilkes in a Baltimore finishing school where they were instructed in the fine points of social deportment, and drilled in the paces of the waltz, the quadrille, and the mazurka by a French dancing master, J. R. Codet. She also found money to send all three children to a private academy run by a woman named Susan Hyde, where they might study elocution, spelling, arithmetic, and small lessons in history and literature. Mary Ann, Booth's wardrobe mistress, now labored over a new kind of costume: fashionable street clothing for her family. She sewed flounced dresses and pinafores for the girls, gray pantaloons, trim jackets, and gold-buttoned long coats for the boys and their father. She even bought a silver-topped cane and high black hat for Booth to wear on his Sunday walks by the harbor.

Mary Ann Holmes's hopes for establishing her children as secure members of the middle class may well have seemed justified at the time. Baltimore was a city where culture was valued by the citizens. Charles Dickens visited Barnum's Hotel on Monument Square in 1842, where he shared a drink with a struggling local author named Edgar Allan Poe, himself the son of itinerant American actors. Inspired by the great novelist, Poe wrote and published his masterpiece, "The Raven," in Baltimore that very year, to tremendous popular acclaim. Baltimore's workers spent their wages at the theater. The temples of entertainment where Booth performed were among the grandest structures in the city.

The house Booth purchased was a few blocks away from Baltimore's Front Street Theatre, a white stone building decorated with columns and a pediment in imitation of the Greek Parthenon. Booth easily packed this cavernous space, where three thousand seats ringed an arena large enough to hold equestrian shows and circus animals. Whenever their father played here, the building's giant façade trumpeted the words MR. BOOTH. The children were proud that their father's name was a byword for genius in Baltimore. At the same time, they knew his trade was low on the social scale, and that his mental aberrations and hard-drinking habits meant their own fortunes were never quite secure. Wherever they went with their father in Baltimore, Edwin and Asia recalled, people of all classes stared and pointed at the famous actor, but few ever addressed him. Tales of Booth's alcohol-fueled oddities were common coin in Baltimore, but his embrace of world religions was the real scandal. Junius's visits to a synagogue on High Street, where he discussed the Talmud with a Bavarian rabbi, were known. He freely quoted the Koran, fraternized on terms of equality with Arabic-speaking peoples, and had been heard to assert that Hinduism was a perfect system of belief. These heresies were more outrageous than reports of Booth's suicide attempts. As Edwin later would write in a memoir of his father's life, it was the necessary fate of Booth's family "to become isolated, and ill at ease in the presence of other than their own immediate relatives."

"Actors in those days," Asia Booth remembered, "knew themselves to be an exclusive, if not entirely excluded, class." Yet the goal of acceptance was important enough to Mary Ann that she marshaled Junius into carting the children to the West Side of the city for their weekly dose of dance lessons and etiquette training from Mr. Codet. The crosstown trip meant Edwin, Asia, and John Wilkes endured a bone-rattling ride over two miles of cobblestone streets to the corner of Hanover and Lombard, where their class convened in an assembly hall near the Baltimore & Ohio Railroad station. Edwin was a natural dancer. The slender youth was lithe and graceful, capable of showing, his sister wrote, "a princely . . . repose" in the ballroom. John Wilkes, who even as a little boy was broad in the shoulders, muscular, stiff-backed, and somewhat bowlegged, was out of place here. His physical abilities showed better in athletic feats, Asia wrote, than on the dance floor.

The children's dancing master accepted Booth's money, but he did not give these pupils a very warm welcome. Speaking to an interviewer years later, Codet acknowledged it would been more proper to have kept Edwin, Asia, and John Wilkes "set apart" from the other students, he said, "because their father was an actor." With a touch of contempt, Codet recalled that whenever Junius arrived at the school to pick up his children, he muddied the dressing room with his clumsy farmer's boots. He also struck an unfashionable note by wearing a "horrible, flat, hard, glazed cap on his head, like a Dutch baker." The actor, Codet sniffed, "resembled closely the ordinary hay-seed."

The little Booths received better treatment from Susan Hyde, the schoolteacher who valued Edwin highly for his "intuitive intelligence" and "quickly receptive mind." Learning came easily to this book-loving boy. He applied himself to it with the same focus and skill he had brought to learning the banjo and blues melodies on the Bel Air farm. Miss Hyde's pupil John Wilkes was another matter, showing none of his brother's mental speed.

Wilkes was a plodder. The younger boy "was not quick at acquiring knowledge," his sister later recalled; he had to "progress slowly step by step." Wilkes's typical pose in the schoolroom, apparently, was hunched over his desk, head gripped between two hands in frustrated determination. Spelling stumped him, and arithmetic, he confessed, "drives me mad." Wilkes explained the technique he developed for dealing with troublesome numbers and letters: imagining the figures as "so many foes in a line," he was able to "attack them with a vigor which he declared nothing else could inspire." Keenly aware that his nimble-witted older siblings had no difficulty with book learning, Wilkes early on took to calling himself a "dullard."

If Edwin, age twelve in 1846, felt most at home with the Third Reader and in the ballroom of Codet's dancing academy, eight-year-old John Wilkes found his own natural habitat on the streets of Baltimore. Many neighborhoods of the city in the 1840s were dominated by mobs of children—and not the hoop-skirt-wearing, chinchilla-muff-carrying variety to be found on what Asia Booth called the "respectable" streets. Rather, as Baltimore's mayors warned citizens time and again, these were a rowdy, raucous, uncontrollable class of urchins, "boys from ten to eighteen or nineteen years old" who assembled in the city's markets, on street corners, and near the engine houses of fire companies, bent on pranks and mayhem. North Exeter Street had its own squad of unruly boys. All the "fighters of our little neighborhood," Asia remembered, "enrolled themselves under a twelve-year-old leader and gloried in the title of 'Bully Boys of Baltimore."

Baltimore native George Stout grew up with Edwin and Wilkes in the area around North Exeter Street, and testified that the younger Booth brother was widely admired for his quick fists and scrappy disposition. "Wilkes Booth was always ready for a fight," Stout said. "He was a regular athlete and a good fighter." Edwin's perfections might shine in the schoolroom, but on the streets and in their own father's eyes, Wilkes was unquestionably the star. Like Henry Byron, the beloved, long-dead son, Wilkes was, in Booth's words, "the strongest child I ever saw." His face was the mirror image of his father's, and the actor doted upon the handsome, book-challenged child for his strength and bravura. Junius could find no fault with his eight-year-old "bully boy," who seemed likely to become an adventurer in the mold of Booth's old friend General Sam Houston, now a hero of the Mexican War. Wilkes came to pride himself on this pugnacity, a quality that set him apart from his older brother.

Edwin cut a hapless figure on Baltimore's streets. He wore his black, curling hair long, and often sported, it was said, "a short Italian cloak," like Shakespeare's Romeo. These girlish affectations did not endear Edwin to the local toughs. One of the brothers' childhood friends recalled the typical scene that unfolded when "a big boy of our neighborhood insulted Edwin by ridiculing his personal appearance." A one-sided battle followed, in which Edwin, cowering and covering his face with his hands, sustained all the damage.

Some fair-minded boys on North Exeter Street took it upon themselves to protect Wilkes's quailing, fragile older brother from regular beatings. George Stout was one of these guardians, explaining years later, "I did [Edwin's] fighting for him." Stout said his "worst" memory of street conflict happened when Edwin was walking home from the Baltimore Museum with a set of fencing foils for his father. The child was stopped by a local tough whom Stout described as "a terror." The assailant grabbed Booth's stage props, snapped them in two, and hurled them into the gutter. "Edwin began to cry," his friend remembered. "I sailed into the terror. The battle began on Holliday Street but was adjourned to a little alley running from Baltimore Street near Gay, and finally wound up on Calvert Street. It was a tough tussle, but at last I came out victorious and the boys rode me on their shoulders in triumph." Such conflicts were straightforward, settled simply by brute force. From 1847 onward, however, nothing about life on Baltimore's streets would be straightforward for either Edwin or John Wilkes again.

NOT LONG AFTER JAMES MITCHELL, HIS WIFE, JANE, AND THEIR EIGHT children imposed themselves on the Booth farm, Mary Ann Holmes had made up her mind to move her family to Baltimore. Throughout the subsequent years of their residence in the city, she and Junius provided the Mitchells with shelter and money, and they in turn kept their side of the implicit bargain: silence. No whisper of scandal emerged about Junius Brutus Booth having a wife and child in London. The fact that Mary Ann and her children June, Rosalie, Edwin, Asia, John Wilkes, and Joseph had no legal claim to the Booth name remained completely hidden. But in March 1847, the long-held secret burst into the open at last, in a way more humiliating than the family could have imagined.

Only indirectly were the Mitchells responsible. After they came to Harford County, the cost of keeping them was such that Junius could not afford to make his annual payments to Adelaide Delannoy Booth on schedule. The Brussels-born woman, who had enjoyed frequent and generous payments from her estranged husband for nearly twenty years, was thus put on the alert. Adelaide was intelligent and resourceful. She began subscribing to American newspapers, whereby she assured herself that "the great Booth" indeed was acting in various cities and continuing to earn well. In the fall of 1842, she dispatched her son, Richard Booth, now twenty-five years of age, to the United States to meet his father, to discover his reasons for failing to pay, and to reestablish the flow of money. Young Richard had been raised a devout Catholic. Unlike his father, he was tall, straitlaced, and obsessed with propriety; yet, like Junius, this son could speak and write Latin and Greek, French, Dutch, and English. In London, he had earned his living teaching languages.

Adelaide directed Richard to stick with his father, to travel with him and keep an eye on his money. For over three years, until 1846, this young man dutifully accompanied Junius Brutus Booth on his regular tours of American theaters. Booth told his estranged son nothing about his half sisters and brothers living in Baltimore. He told him nothing about Mary Ann Holmes. Instead, Junius pretended he had lived alone in America for two decades. How Booth succeeded in this deception for three years, during which time he made frequent solo visits to Baltimore to live with Mary Ann and the children, we cannot know. What we do know is how Richard Booth finally heard the truth about his father's double life.

Years later, Adelaide's son told his mother's story to a newspaper reporter, providing letters, court documents, and Adelaide's private papers as proof of the strange tale. "One night behind the scenes," she reported, "some person accused [Richard] of putting on airs, and called him the illegitimate son of the great actor, taunting him with the fact that his father had a large family living in Baltimore." The priggish Richard could not rest until he verified this story. Quitting his father in a fury, Richard wrote to his mother, summoning her to Baltimore "to establish his legitimacy." Money was at stake here as well as honor. Richard and Adelaide believed themselves legally entitled to Booth's entire fortune—whatever it might be—and wanted not a penny to be spent on the actor's unknown mistress and bastard children.

Adelaide Delannoy Booth would prove an implacable adversary. She instantly boarded a ship in London bound for the port of New York. Her vessel sank off the coast of Newfoundland during a storm, but Adelaide pressed on, transferring to a Canadian ship and reaching Baltimore in mid-December 1846. Together she and Richard set out to play a game of cat and mouse with the family on North Exeter Street. "Nobody here has any notion that I am the wife of the famous tragedian," Adelaide wrote. A lawyer she consulted secretly in the city assured the woman she could sue Booth for "5000 francs"—the combined value of the actor's Baltimore row house and Harford County farm—but Adelaide did not bring suit immediately. The winter theatrical season was in full swing, and Booth was gone from the city, touring. "I don't want to do anything to prevent him from making money," she wrote to her mother in Brussels, laying out a plan of attack. "So I shall wait until he comes to Baltimore, and as soon as he arrives my lawyer will fall on his back like a bomb." In the meantime, the mother and son amused themselves by hiring a carriage and riding up and down North Exeter Street to spy on Mary Ann Holmes. The drab look of the house somewhat surprised Adelaide. "The Holmes residence," she commented, "has not a very grand appearance."

Junius Brutus Booth returned in the first week of March 1847. Adelaide probably saw posters proclaiming the star's weeklong engagement at the Baltimore Museum, a huge theater fronting Baltimore Street, one of the city's main thoroughfares. The Museum was five stories high, occupied almost the entire square block, and had the words GALLERY OF FINE ARTS emblazoned in large white capitals over its arched entrance. Gas lanterns, two cupolas, and a massive American flag surmounted the roof. Adelaide had her choice of settings in which to confront Booth with her bomblike revelation. She did not summon him to her lawyer's office, nor did she pound the brass knocker on the door of their home. She had a scene to play. She would surprise the husband she had not seen in two decades on the stage of a theater, making her way there with her son during Booth's rehearsal time.

Before an audience of stagehands, actors, and the manager at the Baltimore Museum, Adelaide announced her identity to Booth. The stage manager discreetly ushered the stricken actor and his long-lost wife into the theater's business office and closed the door. It made no difference. The screaming argument that erupted between them was audible to all. Junius raged at Adelaide to go back to London. She refused, threatening to never leave Baltimore until it was proved in the courts of the state of Maryland that her son was the legitimate child of Junius Brutus Booth. The combatants reached no resolution. Junius stormed home to Mary Ann.

Adelaide wanted money. She offered to forestall a lawsuit in exchange for two thousand dollars from Booth—the equivalent of roughly eighty thousand dollars in modern currency—and the renewal of her annual stipend. Helpless, the actor agreed, though he knew full well that his finances could not support it. The alcoholic star had a difficult time holding on to cash. "To avoid drinking, I make every effort," Junius had written to Mary Ann in an 1846 letter, but when alone on tour and far from home, he squandered his income on drinking sprees, gave large sums to strangers in compulsive fits of generosity, and invested in ill-conceived business schemes. He also frequently surrendered to depression and refused to act, and was then required to compensate theater managers for lost business. The family could not begin to pay Adelaide Booth what she demanded unless the actor from that moment on had a constant guide, a watchdog and keeper capable of forcing the star not only to perform on schedule, but also to bank his earnings safely or send the money home.

Mary Ann Holmes once performed that duty, but she could do so no longer. The task of raising her remaining children—minding little Joseph, keeping Asia and the others in school—was too great. June Booth was now twenty-five years old, a player of bit parts in New York and Philadelphia theaters. He was married, and at times still sent money home to his mother, but June had found his own life. He would not work as his father's caretaker. This left either Edwin, age twelve, or Wilkes, age eight, for the job.

The choice of which brother to keep at home and which to send out on the road with the actor was perhaps a foregone conclusion: Edwin was four years older, after all. Mary Ann already may have taken the measure of Edwin's "reticent and singular, profound and sensitive" character, as the boy's friends later described him, and trusted the child's maturity, if not his physical strength, for the job. Mary Ann herself had traveled with Junius as companion and dresser; she knew the risks the twelve-year-old would have to face to get the money home. The actor could be physically abusive when drunk. Sober, he was often moody and foul-tempered, or stonily withdrawn. Traveling the two-thousand-mile theatrical circuit from Boston to New Orleans posed other hazards. Mishaps occurred on steamboats. Stagecoaches could be late or overturned, stranding passengers in inclement weather. Hotels were poorly heated, meals were catch-as-catch-can, and sleep was a rare and precious commodity. Exposure to diseases like whooping chough, typhoid, cholera, and influenza was a danger in every new city visited.

John Wilkes Booth, stronger and much healthier than frail Edwin, had legitimate qualifications for this kind of journey. He was his father's favorite. John had not witnessed, as four-year-old Edwin had done in 1838, the violence and destructive rage Junius was capable of in unstable moments. He had little fear of his parent. John's fighting bravura, appetite for adventure, and bold disposition never failed to delight the eccentric actor. But Mary Ann's own devouring affection for John was a powerful counterclaim. Her preference for him, above all her other children, was proverbial in the family. John Wilkes was "his mother's darling," Edwin later wrote. She wanted him with her in Baltimore.

It is one of the curious chances of history that the boys' parents made the choice they did. The brother who was so ill-suited to the work of the classroom was kept at his books, while the one seemingly least equipped to face the hardships of the road was sent away. The chosen one "was envied," Asia remembered, "because of these trips with his father." John, like the other Booth children, believed Edwin's assignment was "a golden holiday," and that he himself had been "ill-used" by being left behind. John Wilkes no doubt resented Edwin's escape from the torment of book learning. He also may have felt supplanted from what he believed was his rightful place at the side of an idolized father. Worst of all, staying behind in Baltimore meant that John was forced "to answer charges of bastardy," as his father put it, on the streets alone. The humiliating truth about Mary Ann Holmes was in the open now, exposing her children to jeers and slurs. Junius had paid Adelaide a large sum to keep the matter out of the courts, but rather than returning to London with the cash, Adelaide and Richard Booth remained in Baltimore. Mother and son took an apartment on the west side of the city, making no more efforts to conceal their identity as the famous actor's legitimate family. Adelaide seemed to enjoy causing Booth to worry what her next move would be.

Edwin, for his part, argued that his brother's jealousy could not have been more misplaced. It was "my punishment," Edwin said, to quit life at home and become his father's keeper. "My youth! ah, what a mockery," he exclaimed bitterly in 1863. "My sorrows began at so green an age," he said, "'twas old age for me." Keeping a twenty-four-hour watch on a hard-drinking, uncontrollable genius would have been difficult even for an adult.

Walking away from this appointed role was impossible. Without Edwin as the linchpin, the family finances would collapse. Mary Ann, Rosalie, Asia, John Wilkes, and Joseph would lose the house on North Exeter Street. There would be no money to pay the mortgage, and none to spend on tuition, music lessons, dance training, new clothing, and furniture. Not much would be left to distinguish the Booths from another drunkard's family, the Mitchells. A silver lining: once the secret of Booth's marriage to Adelaide was exposed, the actor's putative blackmailer had no further hold over his victim. He was forced off the Bel Air farm. Mitchell, his wife, and eight children disappeared into the squalid slums of Baltimore's Sixteenth Ward. By last report, Edwin and John Wilkes's cousins had been sent out to work in a factory.

So the twelve-year-old shouldered his burden, family friends lamented, "when he ought to have been sleeping all night and playing out of doors in the daytime," like his brothers and sisters. Edwin later wrote that 1847 marked the end of his childhood and began his introduction to a life so "grotesque," so filled with "hideousness," it would have been unimaginable to his more fortunate siblings.

FIVE

STAND UP FOR BASTARDS

Now, gods, stand up for bastards!

—*King Lear*, 1.2

Nᴇᴡ Yᴏʀᴋ ʜᴀᴅ ᴄʜᴀɴɢᴇᴅ ɪɴ ᴛʜᴇ ǫᴜᴀʀᴛᴇʀ ᴄᴇɴᴛᴜʀʏ sɪɴᴄᴇ ᴀᴜᴅɪᴇɴᴄᴇs ᴀᴛ the Park Theatre first hailed young Junius Brutus Booth as a star. When the actor and his teenage son visited Manhattan together in 1847, the city's population had tripled and the old Park Theatre had been eclipsed by other, grander halls. Amusements to suit every taste and income level now flourished in a new part of the city.

Anyone looking for a good time now went to the Bowery to find it. This legendary street on the Lower East Side, the favorite destination of Manhattan's entertainment-hungry masses before the Civil War, was known in its heyday as "the broadest and brightest in the city." All classes and kinds converged on the Bowery. For those without private carriages or the means to hire a cab, rail lines ran up and down the avenue for passenger cars to glide on, pulled by teams of horses. Day or night, visitors testified, there was "no end to the sights to be seen" on the gaslit route.

Denizens liked to boast that "every second door" on the street opened to a saloon. Liquor did flow freely here, even on Sundays, and prostitutes were easily found. Young men with money in their pockets, after downing a few rounds, might stop at bowling alleys, pistol galleries, dance halls, or boxing rings. At special establishments, male patrons were invited to sit in darkened rooms and watch "tableaux vivants." These were highbrow peep shows where women in transparent draperies stood on rotating platforms, striking poses inspired by ancient Greek statues while harp music played discreetly.

Edwin came to this part of Manhattan as many as eight times with his father between 1847 and 1852. Each trip proved lucrative for the hard-pressed actor. Of all the thrills and spectacles on that busy street, Junius Brutus Booth in a bill of Shakespeare was a favorite. Walt Whitman, then editor of the *Brooklyn Eagle*, was one of thousands who packed the Bowery Theatre to see Booth. Whitman later recalled Booth's "genius" at the Bowery as "one of the grandest revelations of my life, a lesson of artistic expression." Whenever the star was in town, Whitman said, the city's "leading authors, poets, editors"—including such giants as Washington Irving and James Fenimore Cooper—crowded the dress circle seats. Some nights, he noted, one of "the great national eminences, Presidents Adams, Jackson, Van Buren and Tyler," might be spotted as well, accompanied by their richly dressed wives.

Elites were not the mainstay of Booth's popularity in New York. The men whose money made the actor's time on the Bowery so profitable were the carpenters, machinists, typesetters, butchers, cart drivers, and mechanics glorying in the title "Bowery B'hoys." Their presence was unmistakable. Most sported the same uniform—a thick mustache, a "stovepipe" hat, red shirt, close-fitting black trousers, and high-heeled black boots. Such a rig was incomplete without a hulking physique to match. When Booth was at the Bowery Theatre, these B'hoys, many of them drunk, crowded the pit, one habitué reported, like "a horde of unchained demons." They came to cheer on their beloved star, Whitman remembered, with all the "electric force and muscle" that "2000 full-sinewed men" could muster.

The Bowery's velvet curtain parted exactly at seven-thirty. While waiting for the show to start, the "B'hoys" made forays to the concession stand at the back of the theater for slices of cherry pie, hot pigs' knuckles, pickles, and oranges. Nothing stronger than ginger beer and sarsaparilla was served at the counter, but the mood in the pit was as volatile as if it were a tavern. If the curtain did not go up on time, there were angry shouts of "H'ist dat rag!," rude noises, boot stomping, and outbursts of scuffling. The pit was the exclusive realm of the toughs; no refined person or out-of-towner dared enter it. Actors disappointed such bruising fans at their peril.

The workaday men and women of Manhattan's Lower East Side—for the wives, mothers, and sisters of Bowery Boys took their seats in the balcony, safely above the fray—passionately loved Shakespeare. They came to drink up the universal human themes—sibling rivalry, conflicts between parents and children, ambition, jealousy, hatred, and unconquerable passion.

No one conveyed trickery and wickedness more believably, more thrillingly, than Booth. Even in 1847, when the actor's once-handsome face was weather-worn and battered, his nose broken in some forgotten brawl, his addiction to alcohol sometimes bringing his performances to a halt, he could still hold an audience transfixed with "acting," as one witness said, "so intense and natural that the mimic scene seemed really to have happened."

The Bowery Boys also thrilled to the unpredictability of the genius whose drunken stage fighting often devolved into real battle. There were times when Booth's opponent, sober and terrified, struggled to save himself from being seized by the neck, choked, and thrown to the ground. At fifty-four years of age, one of his children recalled, Booth had a "powerful, thick-set" frame. He looked and moved like an aging pugilist.

At the Bowery, the swordplay had to be sensational. The men in the pit were connoisseurs of fisticuffs. In their own street conflicts, they used flagstones and brickbats for weapons, or carpenters' tools like mallets and files. They came to see Booth's fencing moves, to marvel at the footwork of this trained duelist, and to root for his villainous characters.

Edwin Booth was like an assistant at a prizefight. Violent stage battles exhausted Junius, and he often needed to run into the wings, where his son waited with a bottle of brandy for refreshment. The twelve-year-old would heave the contents of the bottle into his father's mouth. Booth would drink thirstily between panting gasps for air, then dash onstage again to resume pummeling his enemy. "[I] could not imagine how [my] father swallowed the draught and got back to his place in time," Edwin later confessed to a friend, "but he did, and the great scene went on." Junius dashed backstage for other forms of help from his son. Sometimes the boy had to pound his father's back to get him to cough up a pasted-on mustache swallowed in the thick of fighting, or to bind a sprained finger with tape and a stick so the star could continue his swordplay.

It was Edwin Booth's job to make sure his father's Bowery audiences got what they wanted. The success of these nights that Walt Whitman still remembered at fifty years' distance rested on the shoulders of the cringing child almost lost in the crush of call boys, sceneshifters, prompters, and supernumeraries that filled the wings backstage. It was Edwin who steered his father away from the alluring doorways of saloons, and who managed to keep liquor out of the actor's hands in the perilous hours of leisure before showtime. The boy learned to recognize the onset of his father's craving for drink. As Edwin later told one of his biographers, Junius would make "a peculiar gesture, sawing the air with his right hand beside his head, and when, as sometimes happened, [I] would try to separate him from his boon companions, Father would use that ominous gesture, saying 'Go away, young man, go away! By God, Sir, I'll put you aboard a man-o-war, sir!' "

It required all of Edwin's charm and ingenuity to turn Booth from his purpose. The boy told jokes, or he tried to engage the adult in an interesting conversation. When those failed, Edwin took out his banjo and played.

Susceptible to minstrel tunes with a lively beat, Booth would close his eyes and sway to the rhythm. If Edwin played well enough, he recalled, his father might jump to his feet to demonstrate the popular dance moves of those days, "jig, double shuffle, turn and twist, round and round the center . . . the fancy heel and toe touch," until he dropped in a chair, breathless with fatigue. "I could do more with him than anybody else at such times," Edwin later said.

Even when Edwin succeeded in keeping his father sober, Junius might refuse to act anyway. The star would declare he was not in the mood to perform, or claim a sudden illness. Then Edwin would have to start a litany of persuasive arguments, flattering his father on "how splendidly he had acquitted himself at rehearsal," or appealing to Booth's sense of obligation to the theater manager and supporting cast who would lose a night's income. "What will they do without you, Father?" the boy would implore. Edwin had a strong motivation for persuading Booth to work. If he failed to get his father onstage, there would be no money to send home to his mother and his siblings in Baltimore.

Her brother, Asia said, was "an excitable, nervously-organized youth." He had been, she believed, "particularly impressed by the great responsibility devolved upon him" by Mary Ann Holmes. Edwin believed the family's financial future depended on him alone. The child's "imaginative mind," Asia wrote, was "sensitively alive" to the consequences of failing, yet this was no job for a child. It was misery to dance attendance on a drunkard. Foul-tempered from headaches, sick to his stomach after drinking binges, Junius was prone to ugly moods. "Sleepless nights and lonely days are not the proper lot of boyhood," Asia mourned, but Edwin never relaxed his vigilance. He worked around the clock as his father's companion, guardian, and conscience. Theater people who encountered Booth and son traveling together in the late 1840s painted a sad picture of the situation. "The boy lived almost a servant's life," one testified. It was "a pathetic sight," another confessed, to see little Edwin trailing Junius with a worried, pleading look on his thin face.

Edwin's work did not end when the curtain rang down. Of course there were costumes to pack away, the makeup box to put in order, wigs to be brushed in preparation for the next performance. But a more grueling task waited when the two left the theater for the night. After a show, Junius was restless and excitable, game for any bizarre escapade. He might hop a steamboat to an unknown destination, or simply disappear into the woods. The child had to keep his father in constant view while the actor worked off the adrenaline of his performance. One night, Junius sprinted through the streets of Louisville for hours after a performance of *Richard III*, trying to shake his son's pursuit. Sobbing with exhaustion and fearful he would lose his parent in the darkness, Edwin chased Junius down alleys and through the stalls of an empty marketplace. While running, Edwin later recounted, he succumbed to bouts of hysterical laughter at the weirdness of the situation, but he did not stop his pursuit. At sunrise, unable to outrun his watchdog, Junius returned abruptly to their hotel.

Only once did Edwin try to stop his father from these all-night rambles, but Booth's reaction proved so frightening, the boy never attempted it again. They were staying at the Pemberton House in Boston, a respectable hotel, when Junius declared he wanted to go out. Unwilling to face another night of torture, Edwin summoned his courage and blocked the exit from their room. "You shall not!" he quavered. The child expected a beating for such insubordination, but something worse happened. Junius, stone-faced, barricaded himself in a closet and refused to emerge. As the minutes ticked by and no sound came from the actor, Edwin began to fear the worst. Knowing Junius had tried to commit suicide in the past, Edwin hammered on the closet and begged for a word of reassurance from his father, but there was no response. Just as he was ready to summon the hotel's staff to break down the door, Junius stepped out quietly, and ignoring Edwin completely, went to sleep on his bed as if nothing upsetting had taken place.

"It was an odd and dangerous way to bring up a boy," a family friend once said of the years Edwin spent with his father on the road, but it was, perhaps, the best way to bring up an actor. Despite the traumas and terrors of dealing with an unstable adult, Edwin found himself immersed in the glamorous realm Junius previously placed off-limits to his children. Edwin's ticket backstage as his father's companion was what made these trips seem like "a holiday" to the envious siblings left behind in Baltimore.

In barring Edwin, John Wilkes, and Joseph from aspiring to the stage, Junius was only trying to protect his remaining sons. The star blamed the work of acting, he said, for creating those "oddities" in his "nervous system" that "were a source of suffering to him." Lacking the modern concept of psychology, nineteenth-century people often used the phrase "nervous system" to talk about conditions of the mind. Junius hoped his boys "would engage in some more healthful work." The father said he wanted them to find professions rooted in "anything that was true, rather than that they should be of that unreal world where nothing is but what is not."

Even though Edwin's formal education was a sometime thing, he did discover how his father created kingdoms of illusion onstage: the magic generated in theaters nightly was a kind of reward. Any time Junius did not need Edwin's services, he ordered the boy to shut himself in a dressing room and study his schoolbooks. Edwin was quick to disobey. Throwing aside his lessons, he put his ear to the dressing room's keyhole and listened to the great voice booming from the stage. "By this means," Edwin later explained, "at an early age my memory became stored with the words of all the parts of every play in which my father performed." The child would creep to a safe vantage point behind the scenes where he could watch and memorize his father's gestures, expressions, and characteristic poses.

The temptation to spy was irresistible, for Edwin had assisted Junius in his preparations for the night's given role. The child had been trained to oversee the costumes, their cleaning and repair, and he was in charge of maintaining order in the dressing case where his father's stage makeup was stored. Most actors carried such a case, typically weighing from ten to fifteen pounds and containing a complete kit for self-transformation and disguise. There were paste-on mustaches and beards; a hare's foot for dusting cheeks with powder; waxy sticks of pigment in an array of flesh tones and shades of blue, orange, yellow, and gray used to add color and contour to the face. There were pots of oily carmine gloss for the lips, watercolor paint to darken the eyelashes, and even a set of scissors and curling tongs for barbering hair and producing ringlets. Most important were the tins of powder that, when mixed with cold cream, became the foundation layer that turned an actor's skin into colors the manufacturer variously labeled as "Juvenile Flesh," "Fresh Pink," "Sallow Old Age," "Sunburnt," "Dark Brunette," or "Indian."

Watching a new face emerge beneath the brushstrokes of his father's practiced hand fascinated Edwin, but even this interesting process had its dark side. Once Booth donned his makeup, he went into character and stayed that way until the show was over. As he put on his Richard III costume, Edwin later recalled, Junius "seemed to put the character on with it. From that moment he was Richard. He wished to be spoken to by nobody." If Edwin had the temerity to break his father's concentration by commenting on the size of the crowd in the auditorium, or remarking on the weather, his father, he remembered, "would glare at me like a fiend." Edwin learned to adapt to the actor's method of preparing for a role, sitting in silence as Junius spoke Hebrew all afternoon if Shylock was to be his evening's work. "If Othello was billed," the son recalled, "disregarding the fact that Shakespeare's Moor was a Christian, [my father] would wear a crescent pin on his breast that day and mumble maxims of the Koran."

It was Edwin who brought the genius Booth to audiences. Without the child's help, curtains would lift on an empty stage. He could be forgiven for feeling a sense of accomplishment. The timid, nervous boy began to see the result of his achievement, as, in theaters across the country—New York, New Orleans, Philadelphia, Albany, Boston, Louisville—night after night, audiences surged to their feet, roaring for Booth. Edwin would mouth Shakespeare's mighty couplets as Junius bellowed them onstage, finding some compensation for his work merely by basking, he confessed, "in the full sunlight of [my father's] genius."

LIFE IN BALTIMORE SHOULD HAVE BEEN PEACEFUL FOR MARY ANN Holmes after Booth and Edwin started touring together in 1847. She supervised the house on North Exeter Street, worked on designing new costumes for Booth, conducted her children to school, and sent them to their special classes in deportment and dancing. Mary Ann also took charge of making a profit from the produce of Booth's Harford County farm, now emptied of the troublesome Mitchells. Whatever Joe Hall harvested from the family's vegetable plots and fruit orchards, Mary Ann sold in the markets of Baltimore. One of Edwin's jobs before becoming his father's traveling companion had been to wash the dirt from cartloads of potatoes and other produce before it was offered for sale. For Baltimoreans, market vending was "a family affair. The husband, wife, son and daughter all . . . act as salespeople." John Wilkes, nine years old in 1847, probably started helping his mother with this work after Edwin left home.

The biggest market day was Saturday, and Lexington Market was the most crowded in the city. Thousands of shoppers descended on hundreds of small vendors whose carts and stalls choked the intersection of Lexington and Eutaw streets. Sellers touted their goods in singsong calls, using voices loud enough to carry over the milling crowds. Even in this open-air pandemonium, the Booths managed to stand out. Residents of the city in the late 1840s remembered how the long-suffering woman they called "Mrs. Booth" could be seen "presid[ing] over a market stall" during the actor's frequent absences from Baltimore. It was not Mary Ann Holme's still-vivid beauty that attracted so much attention. Rather, she became memorable for a series of painful and humiliating scenes that erupted in front of her produce stall whenever she arrived to do business.

Adelaide Booth, not content with the payment she extracted from her husband in April 1847, had her eyes on a bigger goal. She wanted to prove the legitimacy of her son Richard Booth. She wanted to establish as a matter of public record that Mary Ann Holmes was the actor's mistress and her children were illegitimate. The only way for Adelaide to do this was to sue Junius for divorce on the grounds of adultery. Baltimore attorneys had assured her she would win this case, and thereby be entitled to claim Booth's income and estate as her own property. She had a certificate of marriage to Junius, witnessed and signed in a London church. The only thing standing in Adelaide's way was time. As a foreigner, she needed to reside in Maryland for a period of three years before her petition would be admissible in a court of law.

Living with her son in a drafty, uncomfortable apartment on the east side of Baltimore, Booth's wife vented her frustrations in letters home to her family in Brussels. She complained of the inferiority of American food and of the excessive cold of the American climate. She was angry her son could not afford to hire a servant to cook for them and clean their small flat. She was impatient for more of Booth's money.

She became obsessed with her husband's second family. She had paid clandestine visits to the Booths' row house on North Exeter Street, trying to spy on them. Emboldened now by Junius's periodic absences from Baltimore, Adelaide found a more satisfying way of venting her anger. She made it her business to pursue Mary Ann Holmes in the city streets, surprising the unsuspecting mother, who often had a child or two at her side, with a burst of invective.

"It was a custom with [Adelaide] to haunt the Baltimore markets," reported the *Baltimore American*, "for a chance meeting with the woman who had usurped her place in the heart and home of her husband. These encounters were as much avoided by the one as sought for by the other." When she found Mary Ann's vegetable stand, Adelaide showed no mercy. The Belgian woman attacked her victim, a journalist wrote, "with violent, often coarse language and opprobrious epithets." It is not difficult to imagine what insults Adelaide screamed at her husband's mistress in front of the startled market day crowds. She no doubt decried Mary Ann Holmes as a harlot and called whatever child was with her a bastard. Mary Ann never acknowledged or responded to her husband's wife, witnesses said, but merely packed up her belongings in silence and put an end to the scene "by the speediest exit."

The Booths' market stall was portable. Mary Ann could shift her location from the high-traffic trade on Lexington Street to any of the other half-dozen farmers' markets in Baltimore. It then became a matter of luck for Adelaide to track her quarry down, and a matter of some suspense for Mary Ann to venture forth with a load of produce to sell. Yet the two women crossed paths often enough for Adelaide's tirades to become familiar to local people. Booth's wife had her wish. Long before 1850, the year her suit for divorce would be taken up by the Maryland courts, it was whispered widely through the city, the *Baltimore American* wrote, "that the children . . . Edwin, John Wilkes, Joseph and the sisters, are of illegitimate birth."

Junius Brutus Booth already exemplified the supposed degradation of the acting profession. Apostrophized in newspapers as "a frequent victim of the bottle," and as a godless nature worshipper, the star was exonerated for these eccentricities on the grounds of his genius. The sin of siring ten children out of wedlock was harder to overlook. As the *Baltimore American* phrased it, these ugly family dramas in the market square "unlocked the secrets of the [Booth] family charnel-house," shaming Mary Ann Holmes and stigmatizing her children.

With father and older brother away for months at a time during the 1847–48 theatrical season, John Wilkes faced this humiliation on his own. Adelaide Booth's harassment of Mary Ann—a pattern of pursuit and attack, the newspaper noted, that seemed to intensify in frequency when Booth was out of town—no doubt took a toll on the boy. Left behind in Baltimore with his mother, two sisters, and little brother Joseph, John Wilkes probably took upon himself the role of family protector. It amplified this child's already strong pugnacious streak to fight back against the taunts and ridicule that must have come from the other children on west Baltimore's streets. Classmates said "Jack" Booth, as they called John Wilkes, "was a bad boy." "Jack was a bully," one student remembered, who seemed to enjoy treating "the smaller boys cruelly." Asia took a more sympathetic view of her younger brother. She saw him as a hot-tempered son fiercely loyal to his mother; an intense, emotional child bristling with wounded pride.

Marooned on North Exeter Street in a household dominated by females, John Wilkes envied his older brother's travels with their father. Whatever work was involved in corralling the madman from theater to theater between Albany and New Orleans must have seemed a fair price to pay for a ticket out of Baltimore. His older brother "Ned," it appeared, had won an easy escape from the ugly scenes in the marketplace with Adelaide Delannoy Booth.

Craving the adventures he believed his brother was finding on the road, John Wilkes started his own career as a streetwise prankster and mischief maker. This was a part in which he excelled. Years after the world's first telegraphic message arrived at the Baltimore & Ohio Railroad depot in 1844, the event loomed large in the imagination of the city's youth. It became a common sight to see young people, armed with wire and firecrackers, trying to imitate the new invention. On North Exeter Street, where maple and mulberry trees lined the sidewalks, groups of children devised the perfect telegraph game to play at dusk. Stringing their wires across the road and tying the ends to tree branches opposite, boys and girls sent firecrackers whizzing along these pathways from one side of the street to the other. Such fast-flying "Morse code messages" lit up the twilight to the delight of all.

According to his sister Asia, John Wilkes gave this telegraph game a new twist. He looped his wire across the road at head level. When an unsuspecting adult came strolling by, the youth sent a firework across. One of these well-timed "transmissions" exploded near the head of a pedestrian, knocking off a man's hat. Asia, retelling the story decades later, downplayed this as a harmless trick, but the escapade seems to have been more serious than she admits. In chaotic 1840s Baltimore, only serious acts of juvenile delinquency could catch the attention of an overtaxed police force. Uproarious deeds committed by the gangs of children who spent their days on the streets was nothing new or surprising; newspapers of the time abound with complaints about children "frequently behaving in a manner that is extremely impolite." The fact that an officer appeared on the scene and arrested John Wilkes as the ringleader is a measure of how dangerous this joke seemed.

A policeman grabbed the boy's arm and prepared to haul him off to the Old Watch-House on North Street, a dank and squalid eighteenth-century jail only a few blocks away. The culprit quietly agreed to go, pausing only to disconnect his "telegraph" line. "Just let me coil up the wire, officer," John Wilkes said, "or we'll have a horse's head off—that'll be worse than a man's hat, won't it?" All the other children on the street had fled. To his sister Asia, who alone stayed by his side, the boy said reassuringly, "Don't frighten mother; I'll go all right."

At the Watch-House, John Wilkes found the victim of his prank angrily awaiting him. His case was tried by "a magistrate" and two other representatives of the law. In the end, the child was ordered to pay a fine. Because their father was gone from the city on tour, a friend of the Booth family paid the money to secure the boy's release.

Brushes with the law may have given John Wilkes Booth something to brag about to friends, but his juvenile pranks in Baltimore were no match for his older brother Edwin's steamboat odyssey in the winter of 1848. Junius and Edwin traveled down the Mississippi River to New Orleans, where the star was booked at the American Theatre for three weeks in January 1849.

"Of all the places in the world for the study of humanity in all its variety of light and shade, in all its grotesqueness, picturesqueness and kaleidoscope changes of character," wrote a passenger to New Orleans in the same decade, "give me the Mississippi steamboat." Crammed with scores of other travelers in the main cabin for weeks at a stretch, Junius and Edwin met people from all walks of life. The youth, who at times yearned desperately for the peace and quiet of his Baltimore schoolroom, came face to face on the riverboat with "a thousand chapters of human history," his fellow passengers providing him enough material "to fill a book of mental observation with curious and valuable notes."

Edwin was a born observer and a quick study. Just as he had picked up the songs and guitar skills of the black musician on his father's Harford County farm, the teenager proved a deft mimic of the strange accents and characters he encountered on board. He turned a ready ear to the talk of waiters, sailors, plantation owners, card sharks. He learned the different sounds of Southern speech, Kentucky-born or raised in Mississippi. He heard the lilting rhythms of Irish laborers, the accented English of German immigrants, and the round vowels of native speakers of Choctaw, Creek, and Osage languages. This was a kind of early training invaluable to the later actor, training that Edwin's younger brother John Wilkes, stuck at home in Baltimore, never received. And if the Mississippi riverboat ride was a crash course in human nature, the weeks Edwin spent with his father in New Orleans amounted to another order of schooling entirely.

By 1848, when the fourteen-year-old first set eyes on New Orleans, slaves on cotton plantations in South Carolina, Georgia, Alabama, and Mississippi harvested around 500 million pounds of cotton each year, nearly two-thirds of the world's annual supply. On steamboats, barges, and flatboats, the lion's share of this yield made its way to New Orleans, where the bales were loaded in thousand-ton ships for points around the globe. The trade in cotton and in sugar, another major crop, kept the port awash in cash. A river of money flowed through the city, waiting to be skimmed. Merchants, investors, traders, small businessmen, bankers, and lawyers arrived here from all over America and the western territories, looking to profit. Gamblers, pirates, and adventurers came too, angling for their own opportunities to strike it rich. Wherever money was being made, legitimately or illegitimately, a horde of actors was never far behind. Theater folk would not miss a chance to do what Shakespeare's Iago advised: "put money in thy purse."

The St. Charles Hotel was the first stop for every Yankee steamboat passenger who had enough money to pay for a good meal. Junius and Edwin would not have omitted a visit to its cavernous, pillared dining room where more than one hundred items appeared on the famous menu. Diners might begin with an appetizer of gumbo file, clam chowder, or mock turtle soup. Next they could sample pigeon compote, buffalo tongue, or wild turkey in oyster sauce. The main courses—there were thirty in all—included bear, venison, veal, and a choice of four species of duck (mallard, canvasback, black, or teal) prepared four different ways. When traveling with his vegetarian father, Edwin had to be content with eating only vegetables—but at the St. Charles, at least these would be simmered in cream, baked with cheese, or dressed in vinaigrette. As Junius drank iced ale or chilled punch blended with egg at the end of the meal, his teenage son must have gazed longingly at the desserts: pyramids of nougat, French gâteaux, quivering mounds of champagne jelly, and citrus-flavored soufflé.

New Orleans's pleasures came at a price. Many who flocked here annually never returned to their homes, but remained in the city permanently, residents of the graveyard. Summer epidemics of yellow fever struck down unseasoned newcomers by the score. The native population seemed largely immune to the sickness, but out-of-towners dropped like flies from "yellow jack," as it was called. A remedy for the deadly fever was unknown; some sufferers went so far as to ingest doses of mercury, believing that the salivation this poison induced would cure them.

The toll yellow fever wreaked on New Orleans tended to imbue the corridors and bedrooms of the city's hotels with an eerie quality. Imaginative new arrivals, like Edwin Booth, reported feeling haunted by the ghosts of unlucky travelers from years past. Waiting for sleep to come, wary visitors wondered how many previous guests had succumbed to yellow jack on the very same bed, men whose final hours of life had been made bitter by thoughts of home and family far away. To Edwin, who had lost three siblings to cholera and one to smallpox, the prospect must have been terrifying.

The boy had to work harder here, perhaps, than in other cities to keep his father on the straight and narrow path. New Orleans acted on Booth like a drug, bringing back memories of glory days with Sam Houston, when the American soldier first introduced the British actor to the delights of bad company and strong liquor. But after traveling with Junius for so many months, Edwin was becoming better at his job. Now Junius talked about his son being indispensable to him while he was working, and would even announce to booking agents—almost as a guarantee of sobriety and good behavior—in advance of coming to a theater, "my son is with me."

Before his death in 1893, Edwin Booth told a member of The Players how his time on the road with Junius forged his character. "Those long wanderings by night and day," he said, "and that close and intimate companionship with that strange, wild genius" marked his developing mind with "gloom and radiance" in equal measure. Exhausted from the work of guarding his father, drained of emotion by being kept in a constant state of anxiety and suspense, Edwin longed for the moments of homecoming, the returns, at intervals, to Baltimore when he would see his mother again and be allowed to attend school like his brother John Wilkes.

Father and son often arrived by stagecoach after a long journey, late at night, and Edwin always remembered the sensation of being hoisted half asleep out of the conveyance and helped to stand upright. "Your foot is on your native heath!" Junius would say.

Reunions with Mary Ann and the children on North Exeter Street were blissful for Edwin. Yet every time father and son returned home, it was obvious to all how many changes were coming over Edwin. As a family friend testified, it was clear the boy had been "rapidly learn[ing] things that can never be got by books." Before the year 1848 drew to a close, the fourteen-year-old had spent time with his intemperate parent in all the major cities of the country, enduring a painful crucible of experience. His exposure to the world behind the scenes of various theaters, his experience of human nature in all its perplexing variety, made him different from his peers. The youth's intellect, friends noted, "was better rounded [at fourteen] than most young men's at twenty-one." Edwin Booth had ceased to be the cringing whelp who relied on other boys to do his fighting for him.

He was no stronger physically than he had been before, and he had not grown into a scrapper like his brother John Wilkes, but Edwin was a leader now. He was bossy, single-minded, and filled with dreams of emulating his father onstage. Edwin took charge of John Wilkes and a small gang of boys handpicked from the brothers' neighborhood friends. He had a plan: to start a theatrical company. "Sometimes one boy will influence the taste of many others," observed Celia Logan years later. Logan, a Baltimore native, spent her girlhood playing with the young brothers. Edwin Booth's ambition to be an actor, she wrote, "fired the emulation and the soul of the other boys."

George Stout, one of the children drawn into the ragtag company, told an interviewer after the Civil War, "Oh, it seems very long ago, but I think we'll all remember it till we die." The experience changed all the boys: each one would grow up to work in the theater, though none of them achieved the fame and eminence that their young founder did.

Edwin called a "secret council," Stout remembered, and unveiled his plans to train a troupe of boy actors to perform a series of fantastic plays and to charge neighborhood children admission. All the boys were thrilled by the idea. "Our fire would not be quenched," Stout laughed. In addition to George Stout and ten-year-old John Wilkes Booth, Edwin involved three others. He included a typesetter's apprentice named Stuart Robson, a squeaky-voiced child who "made everyone laugh who saw him." John Wilkes's particular friend Theodore Hamilton also was invited, and so was twelve-year-old John Sleeper Clarke, known as "Sleepy" among the Exeter Street boys.

As childhood games went, Edwin's idea was inspired. Acting, seemingly, was the perfect answer to the Booth boys' troubles. Edwin could put to use everything he had observed on travels with his father. John Wilkes's after-school hours now would be filled with a happier purpose than defending his mother's honor. There was no better way of facing down the brewing scandal of their parents' illicit relationship—not to mention their own illegitimate status—than launching a bold scheme. The boys lacked a space to perform in, they had no scenery, no backdrops, no costumes, and, worst of all, no capital—but solving these problems proved a gleeful obsession for the children. The exploits of the "Tripple Alley" players, as the boy actors soon came to be known, absorbed the Booth brothers' attention, lifting their spirits and distracting them from the troubling persecution of their father's wife. As George Stout fondly remembered, their game felt special and exciting. It was a way "of distinguishing ourselves among our fellow boys," Stout said, and of earning a few dollars while they were at it.

Edwin had found a hotel at the center of the city, on Calvert Street, three blocks from the harbor, with a cellar that was commodious, empty, and entirely unused. A line of windows set high in the wall overlooked the Calvert Street sidewalk and let in natural light. A single entrance, off Tripple Alley, the lane behind the hotel, kept the space private. The janitor of the hotel agreed to let the boys turn the cellar into a theatrical "auditorium," Stout recalled, "and keep our doings from the people overhead, if we allowed him to be door-keeper and take half the proceeds." The deal was made, and the boys set to work. With scrap lumber, they built benches for the audience at one end of the room. "Boards were put up" at the other end, Stout said, "within which sufficient dirt was dumped to create a stage." Each child scrounged his family's attic for old quilts. These the boys stitched into a curtain that might be raised or lowered with the tug of a string. When Kilmiste Garden, a failing Baltimore playhouse, announced the sale of old set pieces and backdrops, Edwin was keen to get his hands on one—it would supply the finishing touch—but money was an object.

At this juncture, Stout recalled, "it was pointed out to Stuart Robson that an old iron stove belonging to his mother might conveniently be converted into cash." Poor Stuart balked at purloining his mother's property—"she did not spoil him by sparing the rod," he explained—but Edwin and the others urged him to the crime. The proceeds from the stolen stove—a dollar and five cents—were enough to buy a scenic flat with a painting of a house on it. The boys would use this in all their productions, no matter if the setting of the play was on the high seas, in a castle, or on a field of battle. "It was a plain little house set," Stout recalled, "but it was a real stage setting, real actors had played before it, and in our eyes it was a precious thing."

The first offering, penned by "Sleepy" Clarke himself, was a gory melodrama titled *Allessandro Massaroni, or The King of the Bloody Thieves*. Geared to the appetites of neighborhood boys and girls, and guaranteed, in Clarke's words, "to give a feller lots of fun," the play starred all the founding members of the company: Edwin, John Wilkes, Sleepy Clarke, George Stout, Stuart Robson, and Theodore Hamilton. Fifty children packed the cellar opening night, paying three cents each for bench seats. Standing room was a penny. An organ grinder had been paid to crank out music for the audience as the curtain rose. By the light of whale oil lamps, the assembly watched the villainous King, played by Edwin, commit atrocious robberies. Justice triumphed in the end: the final scene showed the bloody King tied to an executioner's block, while Stuart, axe in hand, stood nearby, ready to chop off his head.

The Tripple Alley players started a sensation among local children, who craved beheadings and bloody scenes. They eagerly scraped together coins for the shows, and the janitor was happy to continue taking in his dollar's profit each night. Despite the success of this game, harmony among the six players did not last long. As George Stout explained, "jealousy developed in the company." Stuart Robson was more frank, blaming Edwin's high-handed, commanding behavior as the cause of the discord. "Ned Booth was but two years senior of [some] of the other members," Robson said, "but he looked down on them all." The veteran of so many theatrical campaigns with his famous father, Edwin could not help but lord his expertise over the rest of the crew. He claimed the best roles for himself, ordered the younger boys into minor parts, and ruled the band with ruthless authority. John Wilkes chafed under his older brother's control, and perhaps disliked being upstaged. When trouble came on the company, taking Edwin by surprise, a disgruntled John Wilkes was the driving wedge.

Toiling under his father's thumb for so long had given Edwin a hunger to be a star in his own right. Stout remembers his friend showing a "predilection" for monopolizing leading roles. When Edwin suggested the Tripple Alley gang do a production of *Richard III*, there was no question in his mind who would play the hunchbacked villain. As one of the younger members, it seems, John Wilkes was not given a role in this particular production. Edwin, intent on his own ambition, pursued the scheme without giving any thought to his younger brother's hurt feelings or disaffection.

It was a habit with the boys, Stout said, "to hunt about and get anything big and gaudy for our costumes," but the part of Richard posed a dilemma, for the fighting usurper "naturally required armor." The temptation to take what he needed from his father's trunks in the attic on North Exeter Street proved irresistible. He crept to the attic and rooted through the collection of gabardines, silks, velvets, and furs to find an old Shylock robe with metallic spangles decorating its front. Once Edwin snipped these off and sewed them onto an oilcloth tunic, his costume armor was perfect.

Any apprentice who oversteps the boundaries of his training runs a risk. Unfortunately for Edwin, his thieving came to light at the worst moment. Before packed benches in the Tripple Alley cellar, the play was in full swing and Richard delivering the thrilling line, "A horse! A horse! My kingdom for a horse!" when the dreaded sound of the parental voice, booming with fury, was heard at the doorway. Junius Brutus Booth stormed into the dark basement and headed straight for Edwin, resplendent on the mounded-dirt stage in his stolen spangles. The boy jumped for the window to escape onto Calvert Street, but the father was too quick. He caught his son by the legs, and according to George Stout, who stood nearby, started beating the culprit "with a vigor that produced realistic shrieks from Richard."

A timely tip from John Wilkes, Stout later said, sent Junius "hastening to the cellar" off Tripple Alley with "his anger now at the boiling point." The actor happened to be looking over his wardrobe earlier in the evening and discovered scissors had been taken to his Shylock robe. John Wilkes, on hand at home because Edwin had not invited him to perform in the show, helpfully informed his father "that Edwin was responsible, and moreover that he was wearing the stolen ornaments." Stout never forgot the scene, describing the intensity of Booth's "towering passion" as he "belabored [Edwin] unmercifully." The shouting and crying was so loud, it attracted a policeman to the scene, who joined in the fray, believing a crime was taking place. The boys and girls in the cellar received more than their three cents' worth of entertainment that night, as the noisy and confusing spectacle unfolded.

At home, John Wilkes informed his hurt, humiliated brother that he had had no choice but to tell their father the truth about the stolen costume. John Wilkes said the actor had threatened him with a "thrashing" otherwise. This explanation does not seem to have mattered to Edwin. A chill settled over the relationship.

The bad feelings between the brothers intensified when John Wilkes devised a plot to sabotage the Tripple Alley players, bringing Edwin's fledgling theatrical venture crashing to the ground. According to Celia Logan, John Wilkes and his friend Theodore Hamilton "broke into" the basement auditorium to steal Edwin's most prized possession, the stage backdrop from the Kilmiste Garden. Logan claimed John Wilkes stole the set piece because he wanted "to start an opposition show" in another Baltimore basement— presumably, a show where the younger boy would have a chance to play a leading role. Angering bossy Edwin was, no doubt, a side benefit to John Wilkes's scheme. "When Edwin and the rest discovered the foul theft," Logan remembered, "there was mounting in hot haste!"

George Stout described a bitter feud springing up between Edwin and John Wilkes, each brother backed by a set of loyal friends. These rival gangs of boys battled for ownership of their prize. Edwin, Stout, and John Sleeper Clarke plotted together to retrieve the set piece from where John Wilkes had hidden it, and take revenge. "Of course we went after it, and after a fight, got it back," Stout remembered. "But we were fearful of losing it again, and many a night in Baltimore has that precious set been transported from one hiding place to another, with a devoted band of boys armed with clubs and sticks guarding the treasure."

Edwin and John's theatrical game devolved into street fighting. As the gangs' attacks against one another increased in fervor, the precious set piece ultimately "was torn to shreds," Logan wrote, along with any hope for reconciliation between the warring boys. Mary Ann Holmes reportedly exclaimed in despair over her two antagonistic sons, "A plague on both their houses!"

The parents of the two opponents were concerned enough about the rivalry to institute some changes in their family organization. Whether they felt Adelaide Booth's public attacks were having an effect on John, or whether they disliked what appeared to be his slide into hooliganism, Junius and Mary Ann decided it was time to take the boy off the streets. In 1849, at great expense, they enrolled John Wilkes in Milton Academy, a Quaker boarding school in Cockeysville, Maryland, which promised "to prepare youths for college, or for a professional or mercantile life." The place was presided over by a white-haired Friend named John Emerson Lamb, who had a reputation for being able to civilize and pacify the unruliest of delinquents. This minister's "gentleness" was so exemplary, Asia Booth wrote, he was thought to be able to tame "even the boys with lupine propensities who entered [his] home-like circle."

John Wilkes Booth certainly belonged in the "lupine" category. To hear his classmate James Shettel tell the story, more fighting went on at Lamb's academy during John's tenure than perhaps ever had been known before. "I attended that school . . . when Booth was there and slept next bed to him in the dormitory," Shettel wrote. "Jack . . . used to fag the smaller boys cruelly." None of his classmates liked John Booth, Shettel claimed. The children at the school were jubilant when a new student arrived and proved strong enough to "turn on Jack and thrash him terribly."

During John's vacations from Milton, Junius Brutus Booth took a hand in his son's education. Trying to direct the boy's ambitions away from acting, the father had a carpenter's shed erected in the backyard. This little "workshop," as Booth called it, was stocked with boards, nails, tools, and devices calculated to tempt the building and tinkering instincts of the boy. Asia believed her father was striving, as she put it, "to excite in [John Wilkes] a love of mechanical pursuits." The actor, apparently, after showing the new toy to his son, pedantically quoted the Latin motto of the Freemasons, "Laborare est orare," or, "To work is to pray." Such an adage may have won the antebellum equivalent of an eye-roll from the streetwise adolescent.

Junius did everything in his power to place John Wilkes well apart from the unhealthy lure of the theater, keeping his son three years at the Quaker school where, the father hoped, John Wilkes would be groomed for a future as a Maryland country squire. To cement these plans, Junius went so far as to put a down payment on a tract of farmland in Cockeysville, close to Milton Academy, "to provide," the father said, "a home and occupation" for John Wilkes "when [he] should have completed [his] school life."

THE ACTOR HAD A VERY DIFFERENT FUTURE IN MIND FOR EDWIN. DESPITE his outward fury at the boy's raiding his costume trunk, Junius privately was "elated" by his son's dramatic "undertakings," Asia claimed. It was clear to the star that his son Edwin had inherited his dramatic spark, maybe even his genius. As Edwin continued regular travels with Junius in 1849, he found himself being given more to do than wait in the dark backstage.

On September 10, 1849, father and son were in Boston; the play for the night was *Richard III*. Junius surprised Edwin before curtain time by ordering him to dress for a small part in the show, a messenger from the battlefield named Tressel, who gallops to King Richard's side with tidings of a defeat. Looking the boy's costume over with a narrow eye, Junius asked Edwin in a terse, impatient tone, "Who was Tressel?"

"A messenger from the field of Tewksbury," the boy answered nervously.

"What was his mission?"

"To bear the news of the defeat to the King's party."

"How did he make the journey?"

"On horseback."

"Where are the spurs?"

Edwin looked to his feet, clad only in soft leather shoes. With an air of import, Booth said to Edwin, "Take mine."

Edwin knelt down, unbuckled the metal spurs from his father's boots, and fixed them to his heels. On cue, he made his entrance and spoke his few lines.

After the show, the sixteen-year-old waited anxiously to hear his father's verdict. True to form, Booth said nothing, offering neither praise nor criticism. He only glared at Edwin as usual, and demanded "Give me my spurs."

No further discussion of the night's work passed between father and son, but Edwin was filled with new excitement. Wearing Junius's spurs in the part of Tressel was a milestone in Booth family tradition. Edwin's brother June, now twenty-eight and an actor in San Francisco, had made his stage debut as Tressel to their father's Richard a decade before. When Booth allowed a son to wear one of his precious costume pieces onstage, he was giving the youth his blessing, inviting him to try to become an actor.

For the next three years and more, as Junius and Edwin toured cities—Providence, Pittsburgh, Charleston, Philadelphia, New York, Washington, D.C., Richmond—the son now put on his own makeup and costume each night, in addition to assisting his father. He had the thrill of seeing his own name printed on playbills and posters everywhere they went, in smaller lettering beneath his father's. The boy played Laertes to Booth's Hamlet, Richmond to his Richard III, Gratiano to his Shylock, Macduff to his Macbeth.

Edwin had yearned to act ever since his travels with Junius began, but now that he achieved his dream, the hard work of keeping Booth out of saloons felt more excruciating than ever. He longed to be released from this responsibility. Compared to the strain and anxiety of being his father's keeper, Edwin wrote, even "the monotony of school life would have been preferable."

In 1850, Mary Ann Holmes agreed to give the exhausted sixteen-year-old a few weeks' vacation at home, sending Junius alone to an engagement at the

Marshall Theatre in Richmond, Virginia. Without Edwin at his side, the actor disappeared immediately. Notified of her husband's nonappearance by the irate manager of the Marshall, Mary Ann put Edwin on a train to Virginia to track down his father. The boy located Junius, drunk and deranged in the countryside, all his money gone. Father and son had to borrow fifty dollars from friends in Richmond in order to buy train tickets for the journey home. After this incident, there was no question of Edwin having another holiday from his caretaking duties.

John Wilkes's three years at Milton Academy cost the Booth family nearly $250 in tuition. They were able to pay this bill—as well as the cost of educating young Asia and little Joseph—largely because Edwin succeeded in keeping Junius on task and on time to his various engagements. As the family's expenses increased, Edwin's work as his father's shadow threatened to become a permanent position. Even when he begged to be released, hoping to take a six-dollar-week job as a bit player in Baltimore's Holliday Street Theatre, Mary Ann refused. Her son was more valuable to the family on the road, ensuring that the family wage earner, Junius Brutus Booth, continued to reach his destinations.

IN FEBRUARY 1851, THE RECKONING THAT JUNIUS AND MARY ANN HAD tried for three decades to escape came due at last. Adelaide Delannoy Booth had her revenge: on that day, she filed for a divorce before the judges of the Baltimore County Court. The news was a shock to Junius. When contacted by lawyers, the actor wrote that after his hefty cash payment to Adelaide in 1847 "I of course thought . . . all was well, and no further imposition by her would be attempted." Booth could not have been farther from the mark. The imposition, after her three years of residency had elapsed, was as severe as Adelaide could devise. Her petition became a permanent part of Maryland's public records. Adelaide claimed her motive for divorcing Booth was "the vindication of her own rights," not, she was careful to aver, "any desire to add infamy and disgrace" to the reputations of Junius Brutus Booth and Mary Ann Holmes.

"For more than twenty-nine years," her text began, Junius Brutus Booth and Mary Ann Holmes had lived together and been "in the constant habit of adulterous intercourse." Junius was guilty, she wrote, of abandoning her for another woman and committing the "grossly insulting" act of rearing "a large family of children [who were] the fruits of adulterous intercourse." The truth was out—not just as a shouted slander in the marketplace, but as a legal fact.

Junius and Mary Ann had no grounds for contesting Adelaide's accusations. Mrs. Booth showed the court her 1815 certificate of marriage to Junius. This small piece of paper, accepted in the docket, proved that all ten of Mary Ann's children—Junius Brutus, Jr., Rosalie, Edwin, Asia, John Wilkes, Joseph, and the long-dead Mary Ann, Henry Byron, Frederick, and Elizabeth—were illegitimate. Defeated at last, Booth admitted in a sworn affidavit that "the facts as stated" in Adelaide's bill were all "true." As one Baltimore newspaper noted, Edwin and John Wilkes had no right to the Booth estate; "the dissoluteness of the father and the shame of the mother" were now established.

Junius Brutus Booth had been deriding society's rules and living by his own code for most of his fifty-five years. This pioneering Romantic did not betray much concern about the scandal over his divorce. Only once, in New York, did he give a sign something was amiss. On April 5, 1851, less than an hour before the curtain was supposed to rise at Manhattan's National Theatre, Junius was struck by one of his extraordinary moods. "He announced that he was too ill to perform," Edwin recalled. "Nothing I could say seemed to move him in the least."

"If you are so anxious to have Richard acted, go and act it yourself," his father growled at him. Edwin, terrified, "hurried to the theater to announce to the manager that father refused to appear and had commanded that I should take his place."

"No matter," answered the imperturbable manager; "you can do it."

The seventeen-year-old struggled into his father's costume, "a long, belted, purple velvet shirt, ornamented with jewels, and an armhole cloak trimmed with fur." The audience was stunned when the youth walked out in his father's place, but they remained seated, and applauded Edwin's freshman effort after the curtain fell.

"When I returned to the hotel," Edwin remembered, "I found father in the same position as when I had left him. He questioned me briefly as to my reception and then dismissed the subject, but I have reason to believe that he witnessed the whole performance and had not been wholly dissatisfied with my humble but earnest endeavor to fill his place."

Soon after this episode, he and his father were visited by an old British actor who had known Booth for decades.

"Upon which of your sons do you intend to confer your mantle?" the gentleman asked curiously.

Edwin held his breath, eager to hear this answer. Junius did not speak, but instead, with grave and deliberate intent, lifted his hand and laid it upon Edwin's head. The moment filled Edwin with a wave of emotion. The boy "felt certain that his father meant all that the gesture implied," he told a member of The Players nearly half a century later. "My father had to reach up to put his hand on me," Edwin recalled. "I was taller than he." Booth's choice of a successor had been made.

PART TWO

1853–1860

SIX

IN THE DUST

Seek for thy noble Father in the dust.

—*Hamlet*, 1.2

On February 22, 1847, General Zachary Taylor fought a decisive battle in Mexico's Sierra Madre mountains. His five thousand inexperienced troops faced twenty thousand seasoned soldiers commanded by Mexico's Santa Anna. Over two days of fighting, at times through thunder and rain, "Old Rough and Ready," as General Taylor was known, guided the outmatched American forces to victory.

News of America's triumph at what became known as the Battle of Buena Vista broke on the home front with sensational force. Journalists compared Buena Vista to the Battle of Agincourt in 1415, when Henry V's small band of English heroes vanquished the armies of France. The Virginia-born, sixty-three-year-old Taylor was hailed as a military genius on par with Caesar, Hannibal, and Napoleon.

The national flag, carried by Taylor's men and by those of General Winfield Scott, continued to sweep across Mexico, waving victoriously at Vera Cruz, Cerro Gordo, and Mexico City. The Treaty of Guadalupe Hidalgo that ended the fighting in 1848 added an immense piece of territory to America's map: Texas was secured, as were thousands of square miles later to become California, Utah, and New Mexico. Hero worship surged for veterans of the Mexican conflict. In 1848, popular enthusiasm catapulted Zachary Taylor to the presidency.

In Baltimore, the Booth family felt connected to these great events. Junius Brutus Booth's friendship with Sam Houston was one of many ways the westward tide of American empire tugged at the family. Houston had beaten Santa Anna in 1836, in the first drive to annex Texas from Mexico. Once he was named president of the Lone Star Republic, Houston had pushed for full admission to the Union, aggravating the outbreak of war in 1846.

This frontier giant, Edwin Booth said, was "the hero of so many of [my] father's anecdotes." When telling Houston stories to his sons, Booth could show them the "genuine Indian dress"—complete with a chieftain's feathered headgear—that Houston gave the actor long ago on one of their Mississippi River adventures.

General Taylor's victories in Mexico became tangible for John Wilkes Booth soon after the fighting ended, when Junius brought home an unusual package for his sons. Slender, unwieldy, and eight feet long, it proved to be a lance captured from one of Santa Anna's cavalry officers at Buena Vista. This "relic of the Mexican war," Edwin later explained, was "given to father by some soldier who served under Taylor."

John Wilkes claimed the exotic weapon as his exclusive property and put it to use in solitary reenactments of battle. "While at the Farm in Maryland," Edwin later recalled, his brother "would charge on horseback through the woods, spouting heroic speeches with [this] lance in his hand." Whether John pretended to be in the thick of fighting in the Sierra Madre, or whether, shouting "Who thundering comes on blackest steed, with slackened bit and hoof of speed?" he dreamed he was a Byronic character riding into combat, cannot be known. Alone, armed with his lance and drunk on poetry, John threw himself into fantasized realms where valor held sway.

Edwin dismissed these juvenile flights of fancy as "rattle-pated" and "quixotic." The older brother, who left his childhood behind at age twelve when he was put to work for his father, might have been more understanding. After 1848, as one historian has written, "the country was filled with would-be great men whose every bosom beat high with aspirations." The recent victories in Mexico filled many American youths with a desire to win fame through military exploits. Young people were crazed for the novels of Sir Edward Bulwer-Lytton and the works of Byron because those authors excelled at evoking battlefield heroics and the manly virtues of gallantry, honor, and daring. The bookshelf in John's room was crammed with these works.

When his father was at home, John Wilkes imbibed the actor's every word about his meetings with real-life military heroes: not only Sam Houston, but General Andrew Jackson, the warrior-poet Lord Byron, and the legendary Duke of Wellington. John, like the other Booth children, heard the stories about Junius's trips down the wild Mississippi in the 1820s and his performances for officers of the British army in Paris and Brussels before the Battle of Waterloo. Raised on this diet of adventure narratives— some real, some fictional—it is no wonder that John, who never had traveled far beyond Baltimore in his fourteen years of life, should thirst for excitement.

ON JUNE 21, 1852, JUNIUS BRUTUS BOOTH AND TWO OF HIS SONS STOOD ON the deck of a side-wheeled Atlantic steamer puffing its way out of New York harbor. The vessel was en route to the Isthmus of Panama, with stops at the islands of Cuba and Jamaica on the way. Once ashore in South America, the Booths planned to cross the narrow land bridge separating the Atlantic and Pacific oceans, then proceed by another steamship up the coast of Mexico. They were bound for the fertile, temperate wilderness of California. This, the newest state in the Union, was America's last Eden, a place where the mountain ranges were blanketed in ancient forests, and where the riverbeds allegedly glinted with gold.

To visit the paradise won by General Taylor's victories in Mexico likely would have been a dream come true for the adventure-hungry John Wilkes. For the lance-wielding boy, the trip had the added attraction of being a high-stakes mission: once again, the fortunes of the Booth family needed rescuing, and in California lay their hope of recovery. But, in what may have been one of the greatest disappointments of his life, the fourteen-year-old was left behind, while his older brothers, Edwin and Junius, Jr., embarked as their father's chosen companions on this perilous journey.

Nuggets of gold, some as large as six ounces, first were spotted in April 1848 by a crew of laborers working along the American River near Sacramento. So much of the precious metal was visible at the water's edge, gleaming just beneath the surface of the sand, the men had no hope of concealing their discovery. News sped through settlements at San Francisco, Santa Cruz, and Monterey that, as one correspondent wrote, "the banks and bottoms" of California's northern rivers were "impregnated with gold." These towns, the first to be seized by what local people called "the gold or yellow fever," emptied overnight. Every able-bodied person made for Sacramento, one prospector later remembered, "each ravenous to be in at the rich harvest before the others." Farmers left their crops standing in the fields and crews deserted their ships, leaving vessels stranded in San Francisco Bay.

"People here are perfectly crazy," a resident exclaimed; "we can hear nothing but Gold Gold Gold." Extracting the treasure was a swift and simple process. A man working alone on a riverbank with a shovel and sieve might earn as much as a hundred dollars in a single hour. According to some reports, prospectors unhinged by greed stood waist-deep in cold river water for hours on end, frantically scooping and sifting "until they die[d]." Secretary of State James Buchanan received an estimate from one government correspondent that "over half a million [dollars]" might be "dug out" of California's soil every month—the equivalent of roughly $20 million in modern currency.

A young historian named Hubert Howe Bancroft shipped out for the gold fields from New York only three months before the Booth family did in 1852. When "the yellow fever" pandemic hit America's East Coast, Bancroft wrote, it sparked one of the greatest "uprising and exodus of the nations" the world had ever known. The discovery of gold was coincident with two other events: the annexation of California from Mexico by treaty of war, and the advent of a trans-Isthmian steamship network that cut the travel time between New York and San Francisco from four months to four weeks. By 1849, the promise of wealth drew a flood tide of dreamers and strivers from the eastern states to the wilderness in the West. America, always viewed as a land of opportunity, suddenly seemed to offer limitless possibilities for advancement.

John Wilkes Booth's feelings as he watched his father and brothers embark must have been powerful indeed. The California journey was dangerous. Afterward, Edwin Booth came to believe he survived it only because he brought with him his caul, the bit of membrane covering his face at birth that his superstitious mother had carefully saved.

Migrants taking the arduous overland route to California by covered wagon succumbed to sickness and hunger in Death Valley and in the Sierra Nevada mountains where the Donner Party met its fate in 1846. Ships sailing the four-month route to San Francisco around the tip of South America foundered in storms off Cape Horn. Steamship networks whisked emigrants to their destination via Panama in one-quarter the time of either a "prairie schooner" or a Baltimore clipper, but this speedy journey was no less hazardous. Robbers and bandits preyed on travelers once they left the safety of Atlantic steamships to straggle on pack mules over the rough terrain of the Isthmus. In the week required to complete the trek, Panama's fever-ridden jungles took a toll on the unseasoned and the weak.

In 1852, Lieutenant Ulysses S. Grant was thirty years old, an experienced campaigner after his tour of duty in the Mexican War. On July 5 of that year, two weeks after the Booths themselves sailed from New York for the Isthmus, Lieutenant Grant embarked by steamer on the same route with over six hundred U.S. soldiers. These men had been deployed to northern California because the federal government wanted the army firmly in place, their orders read, "to protect the growing settlements from the depredations of Indians."

More than one hundred people in Grant's party—soldiers, officers, and their wives and children—died of cholera during or immediately after the march across the Isthmus. Dozens were buried along the route through the tropical rain forest. Many others survived the march only to do die of cholera once the company reached Panama's harbor.

Grant's was not the first group of Isthmian travelers in the Gold Rush years to be struck by illness. Why would the Booths, who had suffered huge losses to cholera already, dare such a risk? As with so many other decisions this family made, they had a desperate need for money.

In the spring of 1852, Booth and Mary Ann's eldest son, Junius, Jr., nicknamed June, turned up on the doorstep of 62 North Exeter Street. He had not been home in a long time. Some years earlier, theater folks were fond of gossiping, youthful June "had been caught in the toils of matrimony" by an older actress, Clementina DeBar, who hoped to profit by her connection to the famous Booth name. When this marriage soured in 1849, June absconded for "the freer atmosphere" of the western wilderness. He sailed from New York in the very first wave of California gold seekers, bringing with him a beautiful young actress, Harriet Mace.

When June and Harriet arrived, San Francisco had fewer than two hundred buildings and no more than a thousand civilian residents, predominantly male. Women were so rare a sight in the muddy streets, an old-timer remembered, the arrival of one like Harriet was "an absolute and unmitigated wonder." She was as startling, it was said, "as an elephant or a giraffe would be now." The unmarried couple set up housekeeping in a clapboard shanty on Telegraph Hill.

June Booth was an affable and modest man, admired by peers for his calm temperament and kind, sympathetic character. Like his father, June was strikingly handsome, with classic Roman features and a noble profile, but he showed not a drop of the dramatic genius that characterized his parent. "The Booth Face," as the family called it, was June's only inheritance. Lacking his father's divine spark did not prevent the son from wanting to work in the theater. He had struggled for roles on the East Coast, but found his niche in San Francisco. There he helped mount the first dramatic productions ever to entertain the thrill-seeking "Forty-Niners." A terrific swordsman and a bruising boxer, June made his mark as an action man in fight sequences and as a reliable, workaday supporting actor. More importantly, behind the scenes of the earliest playhouses in San Francisco and Sacramento—some of them no more than mud-floored tents with canvas walls and log benches—June showed a rough-and-ready talent for directing and stage management.

It was in his capacity as a manager that June now made the perilous trip back to Baltimore. He had a business proposition to put before his parents. During June's three-year residence, San Francisco had blossomed from a pioneer outpost into a boomtown of fifty thousand people and growing. A new kind of American civilization was taking shape in the city and in nearby Sacramento, one where three institutions were essential to daily life: saloons, newspapers, and theaters. Californians were passionate about entertainment. It is a remarkable fact that playhouses were among the first public structures erected by the Forty-Niners, receiving more attention and investment than town halls, schools, courts of law, and churches.

"The craving for excitement," one old-timer explained, "had become second nature" to the legions of gold-seeking men. The adrenaline rush of hunting treasure by day gave the early waves of prospectors, and those who followed after, a taste for thrills. Drinking, gambling, and prostitution were diversions easy to come by in the frontier cities, but the experience of first-class acting, and the heart-racing storytelling found in the best plays, were valued even more highly for being so rare. The people of San Francisco and Sacramento, June informed his father, were desperate for dramatic amusement. To see a star like Junius Brutus Booth they would pay handsomely.

A huge theater, the Jenny Lind, seating capacity two thousand, stood in San Francisco's Portsmouth Square. June Booth was stage manager there. According to a family friend, June was bursting "with enthusiasm for the new El Dorado, [and] beseeched his father to try his fortunes there." He explained to both parents that for months past "he had been earnestly solicited by the Californians" to bring his legendary father on a visit to the Pacific coast. June assured Junius that the profits awaiting him there would fully compensate for the hardships of the journey. Western audiences had been known to hurl purses heavy with gold at the feet of performers who pleased them best.

The fifty-six-year-old star was harassed by money worries and eager for retirement; otherwise he might never have agreed to the proposal. A profitable California tour promised to bring riches enough to secure all his future plans. Junius and Mary Ann had started to build a house on their farm in Bel Air, a place where the couple looked forward to living out their life in privacy and quiet. After his divorce from Adelaide in 1851, Junius Brutus Booth at last was able to marry Mary Ann Holmes, making their thirty-year relationship legitimate. The couple chose May 10, their son John Wilkes's birthday, as their wedding day. Now they were planning to leave Baltimore permanently and take up residence in an elegant new home on their Bel Air farm.

This portrait of John Wilkes Booth was taken December 3, 1862, during what may have been the happiest period of his life. His domineering older brother Edwin spent much of 1862 in Europe. Edwin's absence freed John, for the first time, to perform wherever he wished on American stages.

Cartes-de-visite (Booth, John Wilkes), Harvard Theatre Collection, Houghton Library, Harvard University.

Junius Brutus Booth as he appeared in London in 1817, at the start of his acting career. The twenty-year-old dramatic prodigy soared to fame overnight, thrilling British audiences with his innovative portrayals of Shakespeare's villains. At right, Booth is dressed for Richard III, his greatest role.

Booth sat for this portrait (*above*) in Matthew Brady's New York studio circa 1850. Thirty years of life in America transformed the once disciplined star into a brawling, uncontrollable drunk. Booth's genius never left him, but under the influence of alcohol his artistry was erratic.

Clockwise, from top left: LP-1427T, Taper Collection, Abraham Lincoln Presidential Library & Museum; Courtesy of the Rare Book & Manuscript Library, University of Illinois at Urbana-Champaign; By permission of the Folger Shakespeare Library; Library of Congress, LC-USZC4-6711.

Mary Ann Holmes, Junius Brutus Booth's mistress and the mother of his ten illegitimate children—including Edwin and John Wilkes. Though he could not marry her, Booth paid artists to capture her beauty, including the famed Thomas Sully. In Sully's portrait (*at left*), Mary Ann wears no wedding ring and smiles as she displays a book, most likely a work by Lord Byron, the Romantic poet whose seductive odes to free love changed her life.

From top: Library of Congress, LC-USZ6-2065; Skinner, Inc., Boston and Marlborough, MA.

When the Booths moved to Baltimore in the 1840s, Mary Ann Holmes hoped to elevate her children's low social status by placing them in good schools. The family's Exeter Street town house and the Baltimore Museum of Fine Arts, where Junius Brutus Booth often starred, are shown.

In 1933, Joseph Edwin Hall stands beside the grave of his mother, Ann Hall, the freed slave who worked on the Booth family farm for decades and helped to raise Edwin and John Wilkes Booth.

From top: By permission of the Folger Shakespeare Library; University of Chicago Library; Stanley Kimmel Collection, Macdonald-Kelce Library, University of Tampa.

Edwin Booth was removed from school at an early age to be his father's valet. This is how the pair looked in 1852, before embarking from New York for the California gold country—a dangerous trip from which Junius Brutus Booth did not return alive. Below is the steamboat ticket from his final trip up the Mississippi River, preserved by his family.

CROSSING THE ISTHMUS TO CALIFORNIA, 1852.

Lieutenant Ulysses S. Grant and a regiment of U.S. infantry crossed the Isthmus to California two weeks after the Booths did in 1852. More than a hundred of Grant's soldiers died of cholera along the way, but Edwin and his father proved more fortunate.

Clockwise, from top left: By permission of the Folger Shakespeare Library; From the collection of Louise Taper; University of Chicago Library.

Tudor Hall, the house in Bel Air, Maryland, where John Wilkes, his mother, and his sisters went to live after the death of Junius Brutus Booth. Mary Ann tried to make the farm profitable, but to no avail. The volatile John, inflamed by the racial and ethnic tensions sweeping Maryland in the 1850s, started fights with farm laborers, both black and white.

Asia Booth, John Wilkes's older sister, was his closest companion at Tudor Hall, encouraging him in his dreams to become an actor. After John's death, Asia became the chief chronicler of Booth lore, publishing biographies of her father and her brother Edwin. Asia kept the memoir she wrote of John Wilkes Booth a profound secret from the rest of her family, suppressing its publication until long after Edwin had died.

From top: By permission of the Folger Shakespeare Library; Special Collections Research Center, University of Chicago Library.

Edwin Booth's romantic relationships with two different actresses sped his rise to stardom. Eighteen-year-old Mary Devlin (*top left*) gave up the stage to marry Edwin, manage his career, and help him conquer his alcoholism. Many years his senior and internationally renowned, Laura Keene chose Edwin to be her leading man. Their love affair ended in 1855; a decade later, Keene's fame turned to notoriety when Lincoln was shot during her performance of *Our American Cousin.*

Clockwise, from top left: By permission of the Folger Shakespeare Library; Library of Congress, LC-USZ62-55263; Cabinet photograph (Booth, Edwin), Harvard Theatre Collection, Houghton Library, Harvard University.

The Boston abolitionists Julia Ward Howe and Samuel Gridley Howe adopted two protégées in 1858: Edwin Booth and John Brown. While Julia introduced Edwin into high society and published poems about his acting talent in the *Atlantic Monthly,* her husband helped John Brown plan his attack on Harpers Ferry.

From top: Library of Congress, LC-USZ62-8221; Library of Congress, LC-USZ62-26637.

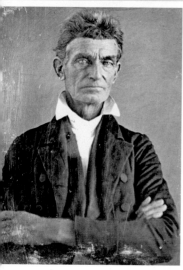

n Brown (*below, left*), abolitionist, photographed in 1856. At Brown's hanging 1859, pictured above, John Wilkes Booth stood near the scaffold, in the costume a Virginia militia group. Dissatisfied with his life as a lowly extra at Richmond's rshall Theatre, John Wilkes (*below, right*) talked his way onto the train carrying itiamen to Brown's execution.

wise, from top: Library of Congress, LC-USZ62-37868; Boston Athenæum; Cartes-de-visite (Booth, John es), Harvard Theatre Collection, Houghton Library, Harvard University.

The physical resemblance between John Wilkes Booth and his renowned father
clear in this portrait (*at left*) of Junius Brutus Booth by artist Robert Sully. Thou
he could not act, John Wilkes was the image of a younger Junius, inspiring nosta
in theatergoers. Fans flocked to see John despite his bad reviews.

From left: By permission of The Players; By permission of the Folger Shakespeare Library.

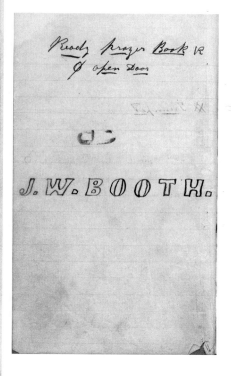

MRS. JNO. DREW'S
ARCH STREET THEATRE

Acting and Stage Manager,   -   MR. WM. S. FREDERICKS
Business Agent and Treasurer,   -   MR. JOS. D. MURPHY

JOHN WILKES BOOTH
In his Great Character of PESCARA.

This Evening, Thursday, March 5th, 1863
Will be presented, 1st time in 3 years, the

APOSTATE!

PESCARA, 1st time here,   JOHN WILKES BOOTH

Florinda,	Mrs John Drew
Hemeya,	Mr Barton Hill
Malec,	Mr Albaugh
Hamet,	Mr Little
Haley,	Mr Craig
Alvarez,	Mr Wallis
Gomez,	Mr Fisher
Ordi,	Mr Saphore
Officer,	Mr Rogers
1st Spaniard,	Mr Wilson
2d Spaniard,	Mr Worth
Moor,	Mr Jones

Moors, Spaniards, Guards, Monks, &c.

SCENE,   GRENADA

The Orchestra, led by Mr. CHARLES R. DODWORTH, will perform a Popular Overture, and other Musical Selections.

To conclude with the Musical Burlesque, entitled

Mazeppa, or the Untamed Rocking-Horse

POLES.

Olinska, Pearl of Poland,	Mrs Chas. Henri
Zamilla, her Tiring, not to say Fatiguing Maid,	Mrs Stoneall
The Castellan of Lairinski, a stern Parent, and a particular'y upright Pole,	Mr Wallis
Mazeppa, alias Cassimere, a Page of Mystery, an Ambitious, Towering, and A-spiring Boy, with a soul far above his buttons,	Mr Frank Drew
Count Premislaus, last of his Race, and Sole Prop of an Ancient Line,	Miss E. Price
Drolinsko,	Mr Ringgold
Rudesroff, a Major Domo,	Mr Fisher
Huski, Boskroff, Piffiki, small Poles, but by no means Sticks,	Charles, Clair & Hooper

TARTARS.

Abd-r Khan, King of Tartary, in very low water indeed,	Mr Craig
Thamer, a Rebellious Chief,	Mr Chas. Henri
Kosoar, a regular Tartar,	Mr Saphore
Kadac, "	Mr Wilson
Zemba, "	Mr Rogers
Kinto, "	Mr Little
Oneiza, the Maid with the Milking Pail,	Miss Adams

To-Morrow, Friday,

First Benefit of Mr. JOHN WILKES BOOTH!
When he will appear as "Shylock" and "Petruchio."

Doors open at 7 o'clock.   To commence at half-past 7.

U. S. Job Print, Ledger Buildings, Phila'a

Critics derided John's attempts to reprise his father's famous roles, like "The Apostate," which he performed for dissatisfied audiences at the Arch Street Theatre in Philadelphia in 1863. John never found the success he wanted, but he persisted in meditating on his future as a star, if the graffiti he scrawled in the margins of his play scripts is any indication.

Clockwise, from top: TS Promptbook Sh154.332, Harvard Theatre Collection, Houghton Library, Harvard University; TS Promptbook Sh154.332, Harvard Theatre Collection, Houghton Library, Harvard University; LP-1434T, Taper Collection, Abraham Lincoln Presidential Library & Museum.

The New York City Draft Riots in July 1863 were the closest Edwin and John Wilkes Booth came to combat during the Civil War. Union officer Adam Badeau was recuperating from a battlefield injury at Edwin's New York mansion when the riots broke out. John helped hide Badeau and an African-American medic from the lynch mobs, arsonists, and anti-Union gangs that filled the streets.

From top: Library of Congress, from LC, #B 812-9637; Library of Congress, LC-USZ62-47037.

When Edwin became manager, director, and star of Broadway's Winter Garden Theatre, he boasted his daughter Edwina would "be an heiress." Edwin's vast income, coupled with his refusal to make his brothers into business partners, strained the already tense relationships among the siblings. Below, the three Booths are dressed for a performance of *Julius Caesar:* John Wilkes is Mark Antony, Edwin is Brutus, and Junius Jr. is Cassius.

From top: Cabinet photograph (Booth, Edwin), Harvard Theatre Collection, Houghton Library, Harvard University; National Portrait Gallery, Smithsonian Institution.

In June 1864, John abandoned the stage to prospect for oil in western Pennsylvania, but his investments yielded nothing. The former actor papered the walls of his wooden shack in Venango County, like the one pictured below, with photographs of his famous family. Edwin, meanwhile, enjoyed the most successful year of his professional life, giving command performances for Abraham Lincoln in Washington, D.C., to celebrate the third anniversary of the president's inauguration.

Clockwise, from top left: By permission of the Folger Shakespeare Library; Cabinet photograph (Booth, Edwin), Harvard Theatre Collection, Houghton Library, Harvard University; Library of Congress, LC-USZ62-42794.

| ...ordung des Präsidenten Abraham Lincoln. | **Assassination of the president Abraham Lincoln.** | L'assassinat du président Abraham Lincoln. |

...m Badeau, Edwin's lifelong friend and the aide-de-camp to General U.S. ...nt, later wrote that John Wilkes Booth's assassination of Lincoln was "exactly ...t a man brought up in a theater might have been expected to conceive. A man, ...of his peculiar family, the son of Junius Brutus Booth, used all his life to acting ...edies."

...ry of Congress, Rare Books and Special Collections Division, Alfred Whital Stern Collection of Lincolniana.

After 1865, Edwin Booth's already booming stage career became unstopp[a]
Critics whispered this beloved celebrity only started to draw "the largest profit
ter his brother's assassination of Lincoln." After earning a fortune many times [o]
Edwin founded The Players, a private Manhattan club whose members incl[u]
some of the greatest figures of nineteenth-century America—Mark Twain, Ni[k]
Tesla, Grover Cleveland, William Tecumseh Sherman, and J. Pierpont Mor[r]
This portrait by John Singer Sargent shows Edwin Booth as he appeared in 1[
the year The Players began.

Private Collection, Courtesy Adelson Galleries, New York.

The old log cabin on the Booth farm, the shelter in which so many of Mary Ann's children had been born, was to be given to the former slaves Joe and Ann Hall. Booth now commissioned an architect, James Gifford, to build him a gentleman's country residence in "the Elizabethan style." It is worth noting that, a decade later, theater manager John T. Ford would hire the same man to design Ford's Theatre in Washington, D.C. Work on Booth's house started in 1851. "Tudor Hall," as the actor wished to name the place, promised to be a beautiful structure, two-storied, with decorative windows, a quaint gabled roof, and a solid foundation of quarried stone.

As always, money was a sticking point. The fine materials required by this project were costly, and skilled labor proved equally so. True to form, nature-loving Booth would not consent to a single tree being harmed during construction. Workers were forced to move slowly and carefully, sparing the grove of locust trees that surrounded the building site.

More pressure came from the court of Baltimore, which had ordered Booth to pay his ex-wife's legal fees and to provide her with a money settlement as a condition of the divorce. Another drain, perhaps the one of utmost importance to Mary Ann, was the cost of tuition for John Wilkes and his younger brother Joseph. She wished to send the boys to St. Timothy's Hall, a prestigious boarding academy in Catonsville, Maryland, serving the sons of prosperous Baltimore businessmen and Harford County landowners. All that remained of the actor's income after paying these expenses went into constructing Tudor Hall.

In need of cash, Junius Brutus Booth accepted his son's proposition to make a bid for the West. The elder actor's original plan was to travel to San Francisco with June as his only guide. The San Francisco stage manager knew every step of the Isthmian route and was awake to the many dangers posed by bandits. Taller and stronger than his short-statured father and brothers, June Booth had worked hard in gymnasiums to build his muscular physique, fencing and boxing "with skill and power," friends remembered. His sword arm and fists were reassuring assets: on this trip, June would be a reliable protector.

Edwin later wrote how relieved he felt that his father "left me at home, in compliance with my mother's wish." Mary Ann wanted Edwin to go to school once more. In six years of service to his father, the eighteen-year-old had missed the academic training his sister Asia and younger brothers received. Mary Ann may also have believed her son was due for a rest. June's appearance on the scene, ready to take on the jobs of managing the aging Booth and bringing new income to the family coffers, lifted a burden from

Edwin's shoulders. The exhausted young man might remain at home with his mother for a little while, away from the dominion of his maddening father.

June and Junius left for New York City, but within a day, before the pair could board their scheduled steamer for Panama, the fifty-six-year-old actor's courage failed him. Without his shadow Edwin at his side, Booth told a friend, "a sense of loneliness attacked him at once." Though he never showed his gratitude, Booth knew exactly how often his son had pulled him back from the brink of disaster. The actor sent a telegram to Exeter Street summoning the boy to New York in time to catch the next steamer, or else the trip to California would be canceled.

Reading the telegram undid Edwin's hopes of freedom. "While not [my father's] favorite," he later wrote, this summons was proof that "my presence [was] necessary to him." Mary Ann's emotions as she packed for Edwin's journey cannot be known. She scrambled to provide him with duplicates of her husband's traveling gear: two straw hats to protect from rain and sun, linen trousers for the tropical heat, sturdy shoes for the hike over the Isthmus. A few costumes, for Edwin's supporting parts in *Richard III, Brutus, or The Fall of Tarquin* and other plays, were included in the waterproof valise.

As for John Wilkes, everything known indicates that the latter half of 1852 was a difficult time for the fourteen-year-old. The boarding school where he had been placed, St. Timothy's Hall, was a "nursery of heroes," one of many military academies for boys that became popular with middle-class parents after the Mexican War. This expensive finishing school delivered the kind of education deemed useful to the next generation of American soldiers and officers. Like all the other students, John was required to wear a cadet's "steel-grey uniform" and to conduct himself with a soldier's discipline and obedience to authority.

Mary Ann Booth, who envisioned a gentleman's prosperous future for her favorite child, could not have been happier with his new school. The students lived and took their lessons at the main hall, a stately three-story brick edifice topped with a cupola and flags. Wide green lawns and playing fields surrounded the building, on which the cadets trained and marched in formation. A small, pretty chapel stood nearby, where the boys worshipped daily.

John Wilkes took an instant dislike to the place. "Something is rotten in the State of Denmark," he wrote home to his mother and sister. The Episcopalian minister Libertus Van Bokkelen, who presided over St. Timothy's, did not believe in coddling the young. He devised a harsh regimen of military drills and religious study to occupy his pupils' time. A clanging bell startled the two hundred students awake at five-thirty every morning of the week. They were expected to jump out of bed and proceed in an orderly line to the bathroom, where a communal trough filled with ice-cold water awaited them. After scrubbing their hands and faces, the boys marched to the school-room for a barrage of early-morning exercises in "penmanship and mental arithmetic." Only afterward were they permitted to sit down to breakfast in the dining hall.

John Wilkes fought against this jail-like environment. He seems to have fomented an uprising at St. Timothy's, leading a gang of his schoolfellows on a wild escapade in which they killed the chickens that furnished the dormitory kitchen with eggs, then ran away into the woods to revel in their vandalism. St. Timothy's headmaster immediately contacted the parents of the guilty parties, demanding that the fathers come directly to the school to discipline their unruly sons. When the summons came to North Exeter Street, John Wilkes's father was far beyond reach.

THE STEAMER SHUTTLING JUNIUS, JUNE, AND EDWIN ON THE FIRST LEG OF their California odyssey was a powerful machine. The 1,250-ton behemoth, belching soot, churning the ocean to froth with its paddle blades, plowed steadily southward. Proceeding at the steady speed of ten miles per hour day and night, she moved from the gray swells of New York harbor to the warm blue waters of the Florida Keys, where cream-colored shells of swimming nautilus were visible in the waves. She carried five hundred emigrants to the gold fields, along with their luggage and mining equipment—pickaxes, sieves, sluicing devices, water pumps. Most travelers were well armed, packing guns to protect against claim jumpers and thieves. Actors were an exception in this crowd, bringing with them trunks of stage costumes, their only tools for harvesting a share of California gold. Every theater had a table equipped with calibrated scales for weighing miners' dust by the ounce, in exchange for tickets.

The Booth men likely paid for three berths on the main deck of the steamship, taking their meals with the captain, officers, and other first-class and second-class passengers. The low-cost alternative was to bunk in the dark and evil-smelling compartment below the vessel's waterline, in steerage. There, travelers consumed the dregs of the meals brought to the first-class tables. Penned belowdecks for the duration of the seven-day ride, steerage passengers, one Isthmian voyager remembered, "were bedded like swine and fed like swine" in a cramped environment perfect for breeding sickness.

"Their sufferings," he recalled, "and whether they lived or died, were matters of their own."

The Booths were free to pace the steamer's open decks, sampling the changing atmosphere daily as they descended into the lower latitudes. Progress depended on the labor of the vessel's firemen, ceaselessly shoveling coal into the blazing furnace. When a fireman collapsed from exertion, he was dragged from the heat of the boiler room to the fresh air of the main deck and revived in a vat of ice. When the vessel put in at Cuba and Jamaica for more coal, first-class passengers marveled at the island women doing the refueling. Ranging in age from girlhood to grandmotherdom, these workers sweated their way up the gangplanks balancing sixty-pound bundles of coal on their heads, which they hoisted and tipped into the hold.

The Isthmus of Panama, a ribbon of land between the present-day nations of Costa Rica and Colombia, separates the Pacific Ocean from the Caribbean Sea. For many migrants in 1851, approaching the east coast of the Isthmus in a steam-powered mechanical monster was an eerie experience, akin to time travel. A castle dating from the days of the conquistadors stood on a cliff at the mouth of the Chagres River, their vessel's destination. The fortification's crenellated walls and high towers were overgrown with vegetation. Flocks of seagulls roosted in the partially collapsed structure, while fragments of old cannon lay crashed and rusting on the beach below. It was a scene straight from one of the historical novels that John Wilkes Booth so admired. These were the shores of what once had been called Darien by the old explorers, the place Sir Walter Raleigh spoke of when he advised ambitious Queen Elizabeth, "Seize the Isthmus of Darien, and you will wrest the keys of the world from Spain."

Dumped unceremoniously at the base of this ruin with their trunks and bags, the Booths saw little to reassure them. Several dozen rough shelters built of bamboo poles and palm fronds edged the shore. A crowd of returning California travelers waited there to board the steamer, anxious to make their way back to New York—some appeared diseased, all were burned by sun and weather, and many, their coats bulging with little bags of gold, stood together guardedly, "armed to the teeth," one traveler remembered, against brigands.

June negotiated seats for himself, Edwin, and Junius in a dugout canoe for the next stage of their journey, the ride up the Chagres River. Teams of local men, near naked in the heat, laboriously poled the Booths upriver for two days and nights. It was a ride out of a dream. The river wound through dense rain forest, a moist habitat where daylight hours were steaming hot and the nights were chilly and filled with rain. The Booths alternately sweltered and shivered, but under such conditions the jungle bloomed frenziedly with alien flowers—red, purple, yellow—and pendant fruits like avocado, banana, and mango. A profusion of birds and butterflies filled the forest's upper canopy, while the branches of trees overgrowing the river were alive with snakes and other creeping reptiles.

When the Booths reached Gorgona, the next stage of the Isthmian crossing, the landscape changed to rocky and mountainous. The men spent a night here, resting in hammocks, before taking their places on packmules bound for Panama City. All the Booths were nervous. Edwin later said he never closed his eyes, so terrified was he that the local men armed with machetes and paid to conduct them to the port of Panama City would rob and murder him if he slept. He could be excused for feeling this way; Gorgona was like a graveyard. So many travelers had died of fever here, or were killed for the gold they carried, that everywhere one looked, rough-hewn crosses marked impromptu burial sites. Lieutenant U. S. Grant, two weeks behind the Booths, would lay many of his men to rest in this place.

It was a relief to reach the comparative safety of Panama City. The sixteenth-century Spanish city was a haven of citrus groves, hundred-year-old adobe houses, monasteries, and an immense cathedral. The Booths holed up in a hotel for a week, shunning other travelers out of fear of catching cholera, often a risk in this city, while they waited for the Pacific Mail Steamship Company's vessel *California* to carry them north on the final phase of their thirty-seven-day journey.

After the terrors of the Isthmus crossing, the two-week ride up the coast of Mexico and California was an easy one. The Booths could lounge on deck, watching the sunset over the ocean or catching glimpses of dolphin schools and migrating pods of whales. They could nap, and leisurely contemplate the bill of fare posted each afternoon in the main saloon. A typical dinner included fresh salmon, lamb in caper sauce, lobsters, tapioca pudding, and fruit pies.

On July 28, 1852, Harriet Mace stood waiting at the wharf, craning for a sight of *California* as the ship entered San Francisco Bay. Steamers reached this remote place twice a month. Whenever a lookout on Telegraph Hill spotted a smudge of smoke on the horizon, he raised two black bars—like outspread arms—on a tall pole at the top of the hill. "Everyone knew this signal," a Forty-Niner remembered. Hordes of people rushed to the waterfront, eager to meet the vessel that was their only connection to the outside world. "One can hardly understand now, the excitement created by the signal for a side-wheel steamer."

The whole company of actors belonging to the Jenny Lind Theatre stood with Harriet to greet the legendary star. The delegation whooped and whistled, happily waving hats and handkerchiefs, when *California* chugged past Alcatraz Island and announced her arrival with a salvo of gunfire. "We all recognized the father from his pictures—the Booth family all resemble each other strongly," recalled J. J. McCloskey, an actor at the wharf that day. The Booths' trunks and sacks were lifted by willing hands and carried to their hotel.

The design of the Jenny Lind Theatre proved the truth of the claim that, as June had reported, entertainment was the cornerstone of San Francisco civilization: "No matter what happened, no matter how their fortunes climbed or sank, the Argonauts must have their newspapers, their saloons, and no less imperatively, their playhouses." In 1852, the structure was the biggest, costliest building in the five-year-old city.

Junius and Edwin Booth, arriving for rehearsal at the Jenny Lind's entrance on the eastern side of Portsmouth Square, were confronted with a gleaming monstrosity of pink stone, shipped over from Australia at great expense. A parade of voluptuous female statues lined the roof, catching the eye of all passersby; "whether muses, nymphs or angels, we never yet could learn," joked one resident. The Jenny Lind would not last long. San Francisco was in need of a city hall, and for size and centrality of location the theater could not be rivaled. Even as the Booths arrived for their two-week engagement, plans already had been made by the city's fathers to purchase this bordello-like confection for two hundred thousand dollars and convert it into a civic building. The father-and-son Shakespeare act would be the last major bill of the theater's existence.

Those present at the Jenny Lind on July 29, 1852, for Junius Brutus Booth's first rehearsal noticed conflict brewing between the great actor and his younger son. Junius was in one of his rare hardworking moods that day; Edwin, it appeared, was the one who had been drinking. In recent years, he had joined his father in partaking of adult vice. The eighteen-year-old was sullen, uncooperative, and slow to respond to his father's stage directions. "He didn't take anything seriously," J. J. McCloskey remembered of Edwin's first rehearsal in San Francisco; "he slurred his words." McCloskey never forgot the sight of Junius, "a leonine figure with the grand manner," scolding his recalcitrant son.

"That won't do! Come, come, come!" the father snapped, after the boy spoke his part badly.

Edwin muttered the lines again, refusing to gesticulate or to bring any expression to bear on his assigned words, "The weary sun has made a golden set."

"For God's sake!" interrupted Booth. "Where does the sun set? Well, show it then! Point to it! Nod your head! Do something!" Junius stalked forward in frustration and forced his son's arms and head through the proper motions. Infuriated, Edwin stormed out of the theater, saying to McCloskey, "Oh come on! Let's cut all this and go out and see the town!"

Despite Edwin's lack of cooperation, Junius Brutus Booth "performed nightly" in San Francisco, one critic remembered, for fourteen days. "The houses were immense," he recalled of the crowds who came to see the star. "The aging senior . . . was a splendid ruin, aged and crumbling, but majestic and magnificent even in decay." On his last night in the city, Booth played Iago to June's Othello and Edwin's Cassio. Whether admiring fans tossed purses filled with gold on the stage, records do not show.

On August 15, 1852, the three Booths left the Jenny Lind for Sacramento and points inland, closer to the gold fields. The companionship that had sustained these travelers across the Isthmus of Panama seems to have frayed. Something changed in Edwin Booth during his journey from Baltimore to San Francisco, something that turned this once reliable and responsible guardian into a resentful, rebellious eighteen-year-old. Years of being Junius's shadow had worn him down. Edwin, who had not wanted to go on this voyage, felt only frustration now toward a father whose "seeming indifference," he later wrote, "was painful [to me]." His older brother June, a veritable stranger to Edwin, may have been an inspiring figure. June had slipped the bonds of family responsibility early in life; getting to know this brother may have persuaded Edwin to believe that after six years of taking care of his father, he had done enough.

The actors' luck ran out in Sacramento when heavy rains brought all gold-mining activity to a standstill. The river flooded, filling the streets of the settlement with mud. Theaters closed, transportation was difficult, food supplies began to give out, and inflation spiraled. Junius Brutus Booth, impatient with the situation, declared he wanted to go home to Baltimore immediately. Though he had made no money in Sacramento, the star insisted on leaving California with the full sum his son had promised him when he first proposed the journey west. To hold thirty-year-old June Booth to a bargain like this in the middle of "hard times," Asia Booth later wrote, "seemed harsh" and "severe." Paying his father this money—$2,000, the rough equivalent of $80,000 in modern currency—left the stage manager bankrupt.

Edwin seized this moment of familial discord to make his bid for liberty.

Not yet nineteen, and equipped with little more than what his friends described as "a worn-out hat, short monkey-jacket and shoes that told of something like pedestrianism," Edwin announced to his father and brother that he did not want to go back to Baltimore. Instead he wished to join a group of itinerant actors on a tramp across the Sierras, aiming to entertain laborers in the mining camps of Grass Valley and Nevada City. After six years in the harness, Edwin was ready to abdicate responsibility for being his father's caretaker. Junius Brutus Booth would make the journey home across the Isthmus of Panama alone.

On October 1, 1852, Booth waited at the San Francisco steamboat docks to board the vessel that would carry him to Panama City. In his trunks, along with his costumes and a collection of seashells he gathered on the beach at Acapulco, was a sizable quantity of gold. The heavy bags of dust represented both his earnings from performances in San Francisco and the large sum he had demanded as payment from his son June.

Edwin never forgot the scene of his father's departure. The teenager watched in silence, he later remembered, as the gray-haired actor "anxiously superintended the transportation of his baggage to the boat." Because the sailor who took charge of loading Booth's trunks was careless and rude, the star spoke sharply to the man, demanding to know, "What are you employed for? Who are you?"

The seaman growled in answer, "I am a thief."

At this ruffian-like reply, Edwin remembered, his father burst out laughing, then mugged and leered, making to shake the sailor's hand.

"Give me your hand, comrade," Booth rasped theatrically, in the accent of a sea dog, "I am a pirate!" He followed the seaman companionably down into the hold.

As he waved good-bye to the steamship that would convey Junius on the week-long voyage south to Panama City, Edwin told himself his father looked "in excellent health." The actor's condition did not last long. At some point on the long journey, Junius ran into difficulty. He may have been unable to find a reliable guide to lead him safely through the mountain passes and thick jungles of the Isthmus. He may have started drinking, and relaxed his vigilant supervision over his precious trunks.

Before he reached the port of Chagres, on the Caribbean coast of the Isthmus, Junius Brutus Booth was robbed of his treasure. Every sack of gold dust was taken. Penniless and stranded, with no means to reach home, Booth received help from a rich Texan, a man named Reid, who later explained he had recognized the legendary actor and felt pity for his state of "distress."

Reid gave Booth enough money to book his steamboat passage from Chagres to New Orleans, where, from November 14 through 19, Booth performed at the St. Charles Theatre, earning a little over one thousand dollars for his work. He then boarded another steamboat, *J. S. Chenoweth*, which was headed up the Mississippi River to Cincinnati. From that point, Booth planned to ride the train home to Mary Ann in Baltimore.

On the first day out from New Orleans, James Simpson, another passenger on *Chenoweth*, saw Junius Brutus Booth "walking back and forth in the saloon, with his hands behind him, his head bowed in deep thought." The other passengers stared at the actor in awe, whispering to one another, "That is the tragedian Booth." The next day, Booth was nowhere to be seen. Simpson inquired after him, and was told by porters that the actor, feeling weak and feverish, had retired to his berth. There, drinking "freely of the Mississippi water, which greatly increased his disorder," he began to show symptoms of dysentery. Without anyone to take him off the ship for immediate medical attention, Booth quietly succumbed to the illness. Several days later, Simpson knocked on Booth's stateroom door to offer help. Finding the actor "neglected" and "very sick," Simpson testified that he "had the room cleaned out, clean linen put on him and on the bed; ordered some gruel made for him, as he was too weak for nourishment." Booth apparently tried to explain to this would-be rescuer the story "of his travels in California," Simpson recalled, "but I could understand nothing but that he had suffered a great deal and been exposed very much."

Hoping to contact a member of Booth's family, Simpson asked the actor if he had a wife.

The semidelirious Booth replied with great effort, "Certainly I have."

"I then asked if he had any message to send her, but I could not understand him," Simpson later told a newspaper reporter. "He seemed to say in his look and features, 'Oh that I could talk!' But, poor man, his power of utterance was so impaired that he could scarcely utter a word distinctly."

On November 30, 1852, Mrs. Mary Ann Booth received a telegram. It came from a stranger, the captain of the Mississippi riverboat *J. S. Chenoweth*, and was datelined Louisville, Kentucky. She was informed her husband was seriously ill, and was ordered to meet him at the boat's next destination, Cincinnati. Leaving daughters Asia and Rosalie behind, Mary Ann left immediately by train for Ohio. When she arrived, she found Booth's trunks strapped and stacked in the steamship office. A clerk conducted her to the vault of a Baptist church in the city where she saw an iron coffin, tightly sealed, with a thick window of glass set in its lid. Through this, the face of her husband—

so often red-eyed and glaring with drink, grief, or anger—could be seen, smiling faintly in repose. There was nothing to do but take the body back to Baltimore.

Mary Ann, her daughters, and her sons John Wilkes and Joseph—presumably summoned to make the thirteen-mile train ride from St. Timothy's in this emergency—kept vigil by Booth's remains for three days and nights in the green and gold parlor at 62 North Exeter Street. White sheets, a sign of mourning, had been hung on the walls. Mirrors and paintings likewise were swathed in cloth. A line of visitors streamed through the house to pay their respects to the deceased.

The family was paralyzed with shock. None of them could stop, Asia later wrote, "musing over the sudden loss." Mary Ann tried to piece together the circumstances of how her husband came to die on the voyage home, and what arrangement had been made among father and sons such that the actor had been allowed to travel by himself. As the story of Booth's last weeks of life became clear to her, it seemed to prove the common wisdom of many nineteenth-century American travelers that "once seized with sickness and without a faithful comrade, a man's chance for recovery was small, for . . . a pale, fever-stricken stranger was too often shunned like a leper."

Mary Ann and Asia experienced bitter emotions as they watched over the coffin in the parlor. The two repeatedly envisioned Booth's lonely last moments aboard *J. S. Chenoweth*. "Recounting the circumstances of his sad and neglected dying hours," Asia remembered, her mother said, " 'Yes, yes—that was just what he thought right to do; to endure patiently, to suffer without a complaint, and to trouble no one.' " Without someone there to keep disaster at bay, Mary Ann implied, Junius Brutus Booth would willingly allow death to overtake him.

Life was about to become much harder for Mary Ann Booth and her children in Baltimore. With the loss of the family's sole wage earner, their home, as Asia put it, was "broken up forever." She, her mother, John Wilkes, Rosalie, and Joseph had not been provided for: Booth left no will, and for a man who easily earned a thousand dollars in a week of work, he left behind a pitifully small amount of money. In his thirty-year career, the actor had been drained by his many dependents and by his own folly. All that was left of decades of profits was $4,729; this sum included the value of his house in Baltimore, the worth of Tudor Hall and his farmland in Bel Air, and the resale price of his furniture, books, and musical instruments. According to a family member, the cash holdings of the estate amounted to "a few hundreds."

Creditors swarmed on the family, as did Richard Booth and his mother, Adelaide. The pair sued Mary Ann for everything they could get and accused the actor's second wife of hiding secret reserves of cash. There was little to hide. As we have seen, the gold Junius earned in California had been stolen from him during the Isthmian crossing. Booth's profits from his last appearance in New Orleans were his widow's only defense against dire need. Mary Ann found nearly five hundred dollars in cash when she examined the contents of her husband's trunks. The metal box holding his corpse had been pried open by doctors before its trip to the cemetery. Only some seashells Booth gathered in Mexico and his steamboat ticket were found on his person. The actor's most prized possession—his collection of stage costumes— alone survived the trip from California intact.

Not even these personal effects escaped the grasp of Adelaide Booth. She and her son claimed the costumes—valuable creations in their own right—as their inheritance. Seamstress Mary Ann Booth struck back against such claims, arguing she had made these costumes "with her own hands." She won her case. The state of Maryland declared the beautiful stage garments were "personal apparel not to be accounted for in the estate of the deceased." Booth's widow would later present these costumes to her son John Wilkes as his special inheritance, writing the young man's initials in dark ink on the inner lapels and hems. One who saw the collection described a "black-beaded Hamlet hauberk," a "cut-leather jerkin with slashed green velvet sleeves," "a gorgeous robe for Othello made of East India shawls," and Junius's favorite, his costume for Richard III, "a long, belted, purple velvet shirt trimmed with jewels, and an armhole cloak trimmed with fur."

Junius Brutus Booth's status in life was measured by the crowds of mourners who assembled for his funeral procession. Though a crunching carpet of ice covered the streets of the city and a heavy snow was falling, more than a thousand citizens of Baltimore, white and black, actors and theatergoers, marched with John Wilkes, his mother, and his siblings behind the casket to the Baltimore Cemetery. Adelaide Booth and her son Richard, a city newspaper noted, were pointedly absent. In the freezing winter twilight, men went hatless and wore armbands of black ribbon as marks of their grief. As news of Booth's death traveled the telegraph wires, letters to his widow poured in from across the country. Poets composed odes to the "matchless Booth"; newspapers from New York to New Orleans printed solemn memorials to the "jewel of Booth's dramatic genius," now lost to American audiences forever.

• • •

WORD OF JUNIUS BRUTUS BOOTH'S DEATH REACHED SAN FRANCISCO before any letter of Mary Ann's. Sixty thousand pieces of mail, including newspapers from principal East Coast cities, were delivered each month to the United States post office on Portsmouth Square. A line of men formed outside this building as soon as the signal post on Telegraph Hill hoisted its black bars to tell of a mail steamer's approach. Twenty-four hours could pass before the busy postal employees—hired for their ability to read letters addressed in Chinese and Russian, French, Italian, and Spanish—sorted the mountains of correspondence prior to distribution. In that time, the columns of homesick men, hungry for news from "the States," stretched from Portsmouth Square all the way into the fields of chaparral ringing the town. They waited all night for the clerk's window to open, rolling dice, smoking, or snoozing in their bedrolls. Those impatient to pick up a special letter bribed their way with gold to the front of the line.

June Booth, presumably, was one of these men waiting in December 1852, desperate for a letter from his mother. The terse message he received from Baltimore has not survived—much of the family correspondence from the period after Booth's death was deliberately destroyed—but June described its contents to a friend. For her sons who failed to safeguard the family interests, Mary Ann had one command: "Do not come home." Her "wants," she said, "were not to be considered." June and Edwin "would do well to remain [in California]."

Unlike June Booth, Edwin remained unaware of his father's fate for a while longer. He had set forth happily in October 1852 with his newfound friends. Traveling "on horseback, on muleback and sometimes on footback," as one of Edwin's companions joked, the players wended their way through redwood forests, listening for the calls of unfamiliar birds—vultures, eagles, raptors of all kinds—and the noises of bobcats or bears.

His lack of warm clothing, the scarcity of food, and danger of losing the way did not trouble Edwin, who was elated at being free from his father. Excitement sustained him on the rough hike over the snowy Sierra Nevada. "He was jolly, full of mirth," one of his companions marveled. "He was never despondent and showed the spirit of a true Bohemian, ready to subsist on a crust." The boy started to show the spirit of a true actor as well. The stubborn sullenness that dampened his showing at the Jenny Lind Theatre was gone. The young man exerted himself to impress the Forty-Niners of California's remote mountain areas. Edwin played Iago so perfectly for a group of half-drunk Grass Valley gold diggers, a witness later wrote, "the audience, which had not seen a new play for years, was so much incensed at his apparent villainy that they pulled out their shooters in the middle of the third act, and began blazing away at the stage." Edwin dived to the floor, crawling to safety as the overstimulated audience cursed Iago for being an "infernal sneaking cuss."

In late December 1852, Edwin and his companions were stuck by heavy snowfall in one of these barely civilized mountain settlements, a desolate place called Red Dog, the actor later remembered, "where gold-diggers had undermined the houses and left deep and yawning gulches in the roads." The report of Junius Brutus Booth's death finally caught up with him here, when a mail carrier managed to struggle through the snowdrifts with a bundle of newspapers and letters.

"What news is there?" the youth cheerfully asked members of his troupe. When he heard the answer, friends testified, Edwin became "half-distracted." No one could comfort the young man. Edwin kept protesting that he could not "forgive himself" for "the desertion of his father," and "for having allowed [him] to undertake the homeward journey alone."

Edwin had no money. Regardless, the teenager left his friends the next morning and struggled fifty miles through deep snow to Marysville, a town with stagecoach connection to Sacramento. The physical pain of making this two-day hike without sufficient food or clothing did not begin to cauterize Edwin's grief. Sympathetic strangers in Marysville, shocked by his half-starved appearance, gave the son of the famous actor ten dollars to buy a seat on the coach. Others helped by feeding the distraught youth and helping him find conveyance from Sacramento to San Francisco.

At nineteen, Edwin Booth felt harrowed by life. His years on the road with Junius Brutus Booth had marked him with melancholy. "From my earliest childhood," he confessed to a friend, "I have felt a dark and heavy cloud hanging over me." Guilt for abandoning his parent made that "heavy cloud" more burdensome. As Edwin explained, "I feel the deadness of an outcast soul." In later years, he would be driven to consult mediums and psychics in an attempt to communicate with his father, trying to make amends.

Edwin appeared at his brother's cottage on Telegraph Hill in January 1853, looking, June Booth remembered, "considerably the worse for wear" after his empty-pocketed trek from Red Dog. By some accounts, Edwin was almost suicidal. Harriet Mace took charge of the situation, mothering the frantic and lost-looking youth, cooking for him and patching his clothes. She was not the only one to try to remedy Edwin's unhappiness. Many members of the city's tightly knit acting community now stepped forward, adopting the son of the great Booth as one of their own. One later explained to an interviewer how the bereaved Edwin possessed a mysterious "power to win love from other men."

"Yes, I use the word love advisedly, the actor clarified. "It was not mere good-fellowship or even affection, but there was something so strong and sweet in his nature, that it won the love of those who knew him."

June's cottage overlooked Portsmouth Square, the heart of California's pioneer culture. The Gold Rush had made San Francisco, for that brief moment, the most bustling crossroads in America. People from countless nations and ethnicities paraded the streets—there were Chinese, Australians, Englishmen, Europeans, Russians, Africans, Pacific Islanders, Mexicans, Malayans, Peruvians, Turks, native Californians, and Americans from every one of the Union's thirty-one states. There were no class divisions here, a Forty-Niner remembered. "Every man—ruffian, gambler, laborer, scholar— was on terms of equality. So small a matter of one being born a gentleman and another a common laborer was of here no account." Because a single turn of fortune's wheel in the mines or at the gambling table could transform a pauper into a man of means, or the other way around, the condition of one's birth—legitimate or illegitimate, rich or poor—had become irrelevant.

Yet this freewheeling frontier democracy was for whites only, a resident recalled. "The native Indian did not rank high enough in the scale of humanity to command the deliberations of any august popular meeting. If he dared strike a blow, whatever its object might be, even in defense of wife and children, an outcry was raised, and mounted men with rifles would ride to the rancheria and shoot down men, women and children promiscuously." One of the first acts of the new state's all-white legislature was to pass laws barring Chinese and Mexican people from mining gold for profit.

San Francisco's heterogeneous thousands congregated in Portsmouth Square night and day, drawn by its theaters, saloons, restaurants, hotels, and brothels. High-rolling card players, sporting brooches made of gigantic gold nuggets, were everywhere. They tucked squirrel tails in their hat brims, and carried little silver handbells with them into saloons, used to summon waiters with liquor and new decks of cards. Well-to-do San Francisco businessmen dressed in velvet cloaks, sombreros, and spurs. Miners favored red shirts and wool serapes. Most packed knives or pistols.

Plunging into this whirl lifted Edwin out of his dark mood. Now that the Jenny Lind Theatre was the seat of city government, June Booth had a job managing a new playhouse, called San Francisco Hall. He signed his younger brother on as a bit player in the company, paying only a pittance for salary. Edwin played every part handed him. He obediently donned blackface, thumped his banjo, sang minstrel tunes, and hoofed it in clogs. He acted comedies, melodramas, burlesques, variety shows, and farces. He took the minor parts, the roles old-timers called "the small business," and made something interesting of each one. He proved to be a dramatic chameleon, a hardworking, good-natured jack-of-all-trades. Audiences found him "lovable"; fellow actors called him "disciplined" and "courteous and considerate." "Ned" Booth was a general favorite.

David C. Anderson, a kindly character actor of Junius Brutus Booth's generation, now took Edwin under his wing. "Uncle Dave" did what he could to help the star's son deal with his lingering grief and guilt. The pair learned that a group of actors were camping out in a shantytown built on deserted government land east of the city. The settlement, located near present-day Third Street and the Mission Dolores, was dubbed "Pipesville." Edwin and "Uncle Dave" moved right in, hammering scrap lumber and old crates together into a rickety shack for themselves and a lean-to shelter for their Mexican ponies. They strung canvas hammocks from a nearby tree. When they weren't rehearsing or performing, these friends reveled in bachelor freedom, drinking by the fire all night, sleeping in the day, and subsisting on an unvaried diet of buckwheat pancakes and fried kidneys with onion. Sometimes, when memories of his father troubled Edwin, the two friends drunkenly warbled the refrain to a song about a dead actor: "He has sung his last song, he has played his last farce; His curtain's rung down—and cold is his arse."

JUNIUS BRUTUS BOOTH MAY HAVE TAKEN ALL HIS SON JUNE'S MONEY WITH him when he departed California, but he left something important behind— at least, something important within the private world of the Booth family. The aging actor handed his two sons his jeweled crown, the sacrosanct costume piece he wore to play Richard III. Perhaps it was Booth's way of passing the torch: a tacit admission by the star that he knew he might never reach home.

On April 21, 1853, less than six months after his father's coffin was buried in Baltimore, Edwin walked onstage at San Francisco Hall wearing his father's crown. June Booth, always angling after an opportunity to earn cash, energetically publicized the event. An immense audience assembled to watch the nineteen-year-old's entrance as Richard III. Ferdinand Ewer, a Harvard-educated drama critic for San Francisco's *Times and Transcript*, gaped at the teenager's stunt. "It was a tremendously bold thing to attempt," Ewer later scolded the actor, "when the real Richard III had just left California and the echoes of your father's voice were still sounding amid the scenery of the stage." Ewer feared that Edwin "couldn't do it."

Beneath his carefree, Bohemian surface, bit player Edwin Booth had been concealing a powerful ambition. His months of toiling as a humble utility player, cheerfully taking any role that came to him, now looked like a practical joke. Edwin Booth had only been biding his time; he knew what he was capable of achieving.

Ewer stumbled out of the theater that night in a daze, heading straight for his favorite bar. Each night for the following week, as Edwin took on, one after another, his father's great roles, Ewer could be seen at work in a saloon on the corner of Washington and Montgomery streets, scribbling long after midnight his dawning impressions of California's new star.

The first performance was a "blaze of genius," Ewer wrote. The nineteen-year-old actor could only be called "a Diamond." "There is an undeveloped genius now in San Francisco," Ewer announced, "whom they of London and New York know not of." On April 22, 1853, the critic became the first to predict that Edwin was the son "worthy to receive the mantle of the father, and sustain the reputation of that name, which has been carved so high upon the monument of histrionic fame."

SEVEN

BROTHER, YOU HAVE DONE ME WRONG

CASSIUS: Most noble brother, you have done me wrong.
BRUTUS: Judge me, you gods! Wrong I mine enemies?
And if not so, how should I wrong a brother?

—*Julius Caesar,* 4.2

"IT IS A DREADFUL MISCHANCE TO BE EARLY CAST UPON THE WORLD without a guide or a protector," a friend of the Booth family once observed. Without his father, John Wilkes Booth would come of age with no strong hand to corral him, no mentor to show him the way. The youth now was the sole defender of his mother and sisters, a job considerably complicated by his father's legacy of scandal. Difficult as life had been for John in the days when Adelaide Delannoy Booth shouted insults at his family in the Baltimore streets, it became worse in his new home, the Booth family farm in remote Harford County.

After the funeral, Booth's widow made the twenty-five-mile journey out of Baltimore by stagecoach to the farm at Bel Air. A drayman's cart, piled high with furnishings from their Exeter Street home, had gone ahead, conveying bed frames, bookcases, a dining table and heavy sideboard, mahogany chairs, glassware, china, quilts, lamps, paintings, mirrors, and a bust of Shakespeare. The post road they traveled was as lonely as it had been in 1822, the year Mary Ann Holmes first made the drive into Harford County. The only change to the landscape was a line of telegraph poles now planted in the tall grass by the roadside, their tar-coated cables swaying in the winter wind.

"Love is terrible," seventeen-year-old Asia wrote, observing her fifty-year-old mother's sufferings. "Love is the turning point in life, the one great cast for happiness or woe." The daughter knew Mary Ann's history, how the naïve Covent Garden flower girl, drunk on the poems of Byron, recklessly chased love, looking, she explained, for "some rock to break her heart upon." Asia understood the truth of this disappointing life story, remarking that "the failure of all your brighter dreams and hopes will embitter the heart and divest life of all romance and sentiment."

In Junius Brutus Booth, Mary Ann had found the rock to break her heart upon. Telling a friend what a "sudden . . . dreadful affliction" his loss had been to her, Mary Ann confessed, "I have been scarcely able to collect my thoughts." The work of sorting and organizing the actor's personal effects was too upsetting. All his belongings—diaries, correspondence, papers, costumes—she decided to leave behind, padlocked in trunks in the basement of the Exeter Street house. Booth's body remained behind as well, unburied. The airtight coffin she had met in Cincinnati only weeks before sat in a mausoleum, waiting for the warm weather of spring, when the frozen turf of the Baltimore Cemetery would thaw enough to permit the digging of a grave.

Asia wrote that after his death, it became clear to her that her father's "monetary affairs, as far as his children were concerned, were pitiable failures." She and her brothers, Asia stated, "were left unprovided for." Mary Ann agreed, admitting the job of supporting four children on her own was going to be "painful." After the courts settled the claims against Booth's estate, his widow discovered only "a few hundreds [of dollars were] left standing in her name." For decades, the actor had collected rental income from a Booth family property in London, but that reliable source now dried up. Mary Ann's children, proved to be illegitimate in the 1851 divorce, were not eligible to receive it. The income now transferred to Adelaide's son Richard, Junius's only legitimate child.

Mary Ann found tenants for the Exeter Street house who could pay thirty-five dollars per month in rent; but taxes, mortgage payments, and lawyer's fees ate much of this. Even after removing her youngest boys from their expensive military academy and relocating to Bel Air, the widow knew there would not be enough money to keep her family going. She had no prospect of making an income until fourteen-year-old John Wilkes and twelve-year-old Joseph Adrian grew old enough to help run the 150-acre farm.

IT WAS A STRANGE HOMECOMING, LEAVING BEHIND BALTIMORE, A METROPOLIS of 170,000 people. Now, the Booths were cutting through the dark woods of their family land in the depth of winter, following the zigzag path to the clearing where the old log cabin loomed, now occupied by longtime Booth family servants Joe and Ann Hall. Here, everything was quiet. Here, the same two families—the Rogerses and the Woolseys—had lived on acreages touching the Booth property for more than thirty years. It was a place where locals knew each other's business, and where most people—black and white, free and slave—were bound together in a thick web of legal ties and family associations.

Booth had spent the bulk of his earnings from the past few years on building the house that stood ready to receive his widow and children. Tudor Hall was so new, its oak floors gave off a pungent odor and its paint was fresh. A formal dining room graced the first floor. Diamond-shaped panes of glass glinted in the mullioned windows of the upper story. There was an ornate central chimney, a colonnaded porch, and a handsome pair of carved doors at the main entrance.

Tudor Hall was an elegant place, but there was nothing decorous or refined about the conflicts that raged inside it once the Booths arrived. The house the patriarch built was not the haven he hoped it would be for his family, but more like a hell. Over the next four years, dark moods predominated in this gabled manor under the locust trees, moods Mary Ann's children later would describe variously as "gloom," "mania," and "insanity." Family tensions roiled, and desperate feelings at times exploded into acts of violence.

The bedrooms on the second floor of the house contained too many miserable people in too close quarters. One of Asia's first acts upon moving in was to nail a picture of Job, the Old Testament character scourged by God with undeserved punishments, to her bedroom wall. At night, she confessed to a friend, "I lie abed praying for strength to imitate his patience." Besides a bitter and unhappy Mary Ann, there was her eldest daughter, twenty-nine-year-old Rosalie, an eccentric woman who rarely spoke, except in whispers; Asia, a seventeen-year-old beauty as brilliant as her father and as turbulently emotional; little Joseph Adrian, a timid twelve-year-old who suffered from what he called episodes of "melancholy"; and John Wilkes Booth.

John was the eye of this family storm. Restless and troublesome, the boy was filled with pent-up emotions that found release, Asia remembered, in intense displays of feeling. The youth would be moved almost to tears, she wrote, by the scent of the forests around their house in springtime. He would hurl himself onto the earth and inhale the woodsy smells. When a much-loved family pet bit John unexpectedly, he was inconsolable, taking the incident personally, saying he felt betrayed by the creature. In one of several accounts of the family she would write as an adult, Asia blamed her brother's reading of "unhealthy" adventure stories for "[feeding] to fever-heat" the volatile passions he displayed at Tudor Hall.

Reading fiction probably was less upsetting to John Wilkes than the real-life adventure narrative responsible for turning his world upside down. His father and brothers' trek across the Isthmus, their quest for California gold and its disastrous outcome, could have been plot points in a cliff-hanging tale from a penny press. To this Shakespearean family, however, the events may have seemed more like an echo of *King Lear*, with June and Edwin taking the parts of Goneril and Regan, the selfish, ungrateful daughters of the old king. In the play, the children's cold treatment of their father is "sharper than a serpent's tooth": they steal his crown and send him into the wilderness alone. In a letter she wrote soon after moving to Tudor Hall, Asia told a friend that the chain of events leading to her father's death had "broken up forever" her "bright happy home."

"When I was a little boy," Edwin Booth wrote with a touch of self-pity in 1872, "I had no opportunity to learn the different games and sports of childhood, for I was traveling [with my father] most of the time." Starting in January 1853, Asia, John, and Joe had a glut of playtime. Lack of money to pay for tutors meant that outdoor games and sports consumed the children's waking hours. Bundled in wool coats, they investigated the boundaries of their country home. Perhaps it was inevitable these young people would devote their time to acting out playful versions of their father's final, epic adventures. Asia wrote that she and her brothers made believe they were explorers crossing into strange lands. Armed with "long poles" they went "leaping from stone to stone" over streams and brooks, cheering as they took possession of virgin territory. Like Isthmian travelers, they constructed hammocks "out of guano bags and ropes" and pretended to sleep in the jungle. They even mimicked gold miners. Asia remembers taking up "the spade and pick" with John Wilkes and excavating a sizable "trench."

The first in a series of angry outbursts from John Wilkes put an end to the siblings' good relations. Spring arrived, and with it the necessity of preparing the ground for the cereal crops—acres of wheat, corn, and rye—that Joe Hall planted annually. Mary Ann encouraged young John Wilkes and Joseph Adrian to take a hand in the process, hoping they might learn something of farming. The boys decided to build a cabin near the largest field, a place to rest and refresh themselves during the anticipated labors of harvest time. With axes and tools in hand, they set out to clear a patch of woods and raise their shelter. Before long, two figures came stumbling up the grassy rise toward Tudor Hall, clothes filthy, bodies contorted in pain, features bloated and bruised. One of the workers on the farm headed for the creek, where she scooped up cool, sticky mud to make compresses for their hurts. While hovering females "daubed their faces" with this soothing remedy, John Wilkes told his mother that he and his brother Joseph had been attacked by a swarm of bees.

Something about his story did not ring true for Mary Ann. The nature of her sons' injuries, and perhaps their unequal distribution, suggested another explanation. One boy was wounded so severely the swelling around his eyes prevented him from seeing for a day. "Very soon afterwards," Asia reported, Joseph Booth "went to a boarding school at . . . Elkton."

Tuition was a luxury the cash-strapped Mary Ann could ill afford. Yet she would keep her youngest son at Elkton for the next four years. After Joseph departed, John Wilkes confessed what his mother suspected all along, that there had been no stinging hornets. As John told the story, he and his brother, disagreeing about the best way to build their hut, fought one other in frustration until they were black and blue.

At fifteen, John Wilkes Booth was a seasoned fighter. He had been the terror of Reverend Lamb's Quaker school, and the ringleader of the chicken-slaughtering cadets at St. Timothy's. Even Baltimore's "Bully Boys" praised him for his ready fists. Joseph, by contrast, was two years younger, spindly and slightly built. He was a nervous, dreamy, anxious child who once wistfully told his family he wished he had been born a "sea-gull" because "they are the happiest of God's creatures." A fight between these two very different boys would not have ended in a draw.

With Joseph exiled to boarding school, John became the only male in his mother's home, sole recipient of all female attentions. Rather than being punished for sowing trouble with his brother, he was rewarded. Mary Ann saw to it John was provided with a fast horse, a fine saddle, and cash to spend at the local tavern. His older sisters Asia and Rosalie tiptoed past his bedroom as if it were a shrine. John's room had uncarpeted floors, tall windows that let in the eastern light of morning, and was dominated by a set of antlers on the wall, from which dangled in scabbards and holsters a fearsome collection of weapons. A cupboard in the corner held copies of Byron, Bulwer-Lytton, Longfellow, Poe, and Shakespeare.

NONE OF THE BOOTHS COULD SHAKE AN INSULT THAT HAD COME TWO days after Junius's funeral. A knock came at the door of their Exeter Street house, and the Browns, elderly next-door neighbors, entered with pious faces. Mrs. Brown announced to Mary Ann that she and her husband intended to "engage in prayer for your conversion to Christianity, my dear." Booth's interest in Islam and Hinduism, his visits to Baltimore's synagogues, his adherence to the poet Shelley's godless, naturecentric philosophy, had tarred his family as heathens in the eyes of many. "Canting hypocrites!" Asia hissed after the departing Browns. "These egotistical little people teaching us our prayers," she fumed, were "trying to make us accept [Father's] death as a judgment for our wickedness." Little did the Browns know, Mary Ann was a devout Christian who had raised her sons and daughters in that faith. John Wilkes had been preparing for his confirmation at St. Timothy's when his father died. A large and respectful delegation of Baltimore's actors, arriving to pay somber tribute to the star's genius, took some of the sting out of the Browns' visit.

In Harford County, population twenty thousand, the Booths were open targets for neighbors' gossip. Many residents over the past three decades had witnessed firsthand some of Junius Brutus Booth's worst crises, especially his manic and suicidal episodes that followed the deaths of his children in 1833 from cholera. Each time calls for help emanated from the Booth farm in those years, neighbors came running to the rescue. Locals had admired Booth's evident genius and took a certain pride of ownership in their local celebrity. Yet his death, and the return of his widow to the area, revived many dark stories of the man known among them as an "oddity," one who "at times appeared to be insane."

Asia and John were forced to withstand neighborly retellings of tales about their father's freakish behavior. Folks paying calls on Mary Ann, eager to talk over old times, trotted out the familiar "funny anecdotes" that showed some mental infirmity of Booth's. Some of these tales were "horrible," Asia later wrote, while others were flat-out obscene, and most of the residents within a certain radius of Bel Air knew them by heart. A favorite was the grisly spectacle of the actor's grief in 1833, the year he and Mary Ann lost their three children. Booth had cut open his dead daughter Mary's veins, the story ran, and, vampire-like, sucked her blood in an attempt to restore circulation to her heart. The teller of this tale would not hesitate to describe the aftermath of the failed experiment: the deranged father dragging the girl's body through the woods at night, hiding it in different places, until Joe Hall, faithfully hunting "with dogs and lantern," found the corpse in "some thickly-planted bushes near the house" and laid it to rest in the graveyard.

John Wilkes hated to hear such talk. They "are only lies," he cried, "disgraceful falsehoods." As often as he could, the youth defied anyone who repeated them, stopping a storyteller in his tracks by declaring loudly "I cannot see why sensible people will trouble themselves to concoct ridiculous stories of their great actors." His angry, defensive reactions left neighbors feeling "snubbed," Asia remembered. While she too was mortified by the gossip, she kept her annoyance to herself, only confiding in letters to a friend in Baltimore how she "detested" the "prudish, cold-hearted, narrow, judging" Bel Air neighbors.

Even as Mary Ann and the children were troubled by the scandals Booth sowed in his lifetime, the family set out to follow the patriarch's rules, clinging to the actor's guiding principles at a time when they felt rudderless and abandoned. Keeping faith with Booth's views on vegetarianism, Mary Ann and Asia doggedly consumed "salad[s] of beets and potatoes," with mustard-vinegar dressing, lima bean succotash, and large droughts of buttermilk so sour, Asia complained, they "never [would] go down without drawing my face awry." Mary Ann continued to preach Booth's antislavery beliefs. "Pardon me," she would quietly interject when the topic was raised in social gatherings, "we have never owned a slave. We have not done so on principle—our people are hired or bound for a term." If someone objected that there was little difference between leasing a slave's labor and purchasing him or her outright, Mary Ann hastily contradicted them. "It is very very different," she asserted.

Junius Brutus Booth had believed that the "importance and dignity" of every person should be "respected," Asia reported. "He delighted to seek out the destitute and the unfortunate, and to aid them." She marveled that he "encouraged even the low and vile to approach him as friends." In the dead of winter, the actor might startle his family by inviting underdressed, often shoeless, Irish laborers off the streets into the warmth of the green-papered parlor of his Baltimore town house. He offered the freezing men glasses of Madeira wine from the sideboard as graciously, Asia exclaimed in horror, "as he would have done to Daniel Webster." "Here's to your perfect health, Mr. Booth, sir, here's to your eternal salvation," one man typically said, drinking through chattering teeth.

With such "little deeds of kindness," his daughter remembered, Booth "thus sought to impress upon the minds of his children the lessons of humanity to man." When it came to interactions with the family's hired workers, slave and free, Booth's lessons could not have been clearer on that point. The actor chastised Asia for being rude to an elderly black woman employed by the family. Only after the girl made a formal apology to the older woman, saying, "Please excuse me, Eliza, I did not mean to offend you," was her father satisfied. When a young slave named Amenda, the property of a Baltimore neighbor, was dying of typhoid, Junius insisted that his daughter visit the girl's sickroom to say good-bye, even though she went at the risk of catching the fatal fever. The actor officiated at the burials of many black residents of Bel Air, giving emotional performances of the Lord's Prayer at gravesides.

Unfortunately for the rest of the Booths, John Wilkes did not share his father's common touch; he was a stickler for hierarchy, eager to exact from his employees, both black and white, the full measure of a "Master's" due. In the fall of 1853, when Mary Ann gave her son the job of overseeing the work of Joe Hall and the field hands hired take in the harvest, disaster struck. Asia called this unhappy interlude, which resulted in a diminished harvest and much consternation among the women of the family, "the first evidence of an undemocratic feeling in Wilkes."

As one historian of this border state has explained, "there were two Marylands by 1850: one founded upon slavery, and the other upon free labor." The Booths had set their roots in the freer half of state, Baltimore's northwestern hinterland. The Census of 1850 recorded that only 5 percent of the people in northern Maryland were slaves, while greater numbers of free black people lived in that region than in any other part of the Union. Conditions supporting slavery in the upper half of the state had been in decline for decades, as tobacco farms steadily gave way to fields of wheat and corn. Cereal crops, unlike tobacco, did not demand hard labor all the year round. It was more profitable for farmers to sell off their human property and instead make short-term contracts with free workers during planting and harvest time. Conveniently, a new source of cheap white labor had begun to flood port cities like Baltimore. Between 1845 and 1854, nearly three million European immigrants arrived on American shores. More than half were refugees from famine-stricken Ireland, destitute, unskilled, desperate for work. On the Booth acreage in the fall of 1853, Irish immigrants, hired slaves, and free blacks scythed wheat together, side by side.

When white men worked the harvest, it was a local custom for them to leave their black coworkers in the fields at dinner and supper, and to join the landowner's family at the table in the main house. John Wilkes was uneasy with this arrangement. Her brother "loved equality," Asia contended, but felt strongly that any "white laborer" must be "kept . . . from free association with his employer or his superior." The youth instructed his mother and sisters to stay upstairs during these meals; he would eat with the Irishmen alone. Offense was swiftly taken at this break in custom. Several men wondered "If the ladies thought themselves too mighty good to eat with us 'hands'?"

A mutinous mood settled over the daily guests at Tudor Hall. They deliberately left large smears of jam on the tablecloth, their efforts in the field turned grudging, and jeering comments were made in Gaelic accents about the Booths having "dirty British blood." Showing their contempt for John Booth's hidebound class prejudice, the men spat that "being mixed up with Southern ideas" had made John Wilkes Booth even "dirtier." "We were not a popular family with our white laborers," Asia remembered.

John managed to antagonize the black laborers as well. Halloween night, falling at the end of harvest season, was traditionally the time when local people vented the tensions and grudges of past months by committing pranks on their neighbors. Under cover of darkness, vegetables might be uprooted from gardens, tools taken from sheds and scattered across lawns, livestock turned loose in the fields. John, ranging abroad that night on his own missions of mischief, was fired at in the darkness by a free black farmer named Stephen Hooper. The lead pellets flew over John's head: it was a warning shot, presumably intended to chase the boy away from Hooper's cabin. Some of Stephen Hooper's children had worked under John's supervision at the Booth farm that harvesttime, Asia wrote, and Hooper "nursed a smiling hatred" for John Wilkes, but she did not explain why. Harford County's unique situation, and the bloody consequences of the recently passed Fugitive Slave Law, may provide a clue to the hostility between them.

Tensions between whites and blacks ran high in Bel Air and neighboring villages in the 1850s. For those who were enslaved, freedom's boundary was tantalizingly close. The Pennsylvania state line lay less than twenty-five miles north of Bel Air. The Underground Railroad had been shuttling fugitives through this part of Maryland to abolitionist communities in Pennsylvania for years. Christiana, a predominantly black settlement in Lancaster County, Pennsylvania, was a common destination for escaped slaves.

On September 11, 1851, a group of abolitionists and Underground Railroad volunteers in Christiana killed Edmund Gorsuch, a Baltimore County slave owner whose wheat plantation was within a day's ride of Tudor Hall. John Wilkes Booth knew the dead man's son, Thomas, referring to him in later writings as "my bosom friend" and "my playmate." The boys had gone to school together at Milton Academy. The Gorsuch family entered Maryland's history books when a group of slaves from their plantation escaped to Pennsylvania. Empowered by the Fugitive Slave Law, Edmund Gorsuch gathered a party of gunmen, including some U.S. marshals, and boarded a train for Christiana. The law gave slave owners like Gorsuch the authority to cross into a free state, recapture runaways, and, with the help of federal marshals, return escaped slaves to bondage.

Gorsuch and his men approached the farmhouse where the fugitives were living. A shoot-out erupted between the quarry and the slave catchers that left no one hurt, but brought two dozen antislavery townspeople running to the scene with rifles, pitchforks, and shovels. A yelling match ensued, with Gorsuch quoting biblical passages in support of slavery, while the men inside the house loudly questioned the constitutionality of the Fugitive Slave Law. Seeing they were outnumbered, the federal marshals recommended leaving, but Gorsuch, gun drawn, would not back down. He remained outside the house, shouting for the return of what he called "my property," until the residents of Christiana killed him. No one would be convicted for his death: the Maryland runaways fled to Canada. When Stephen Hooper fired his gun at John Wilkes Booth, echoes of what came to be called the "Christiana Riot" were still ringing on both sides of the Maryland-Pennsylvania border.

At this time in northern Maryland, one historian has written, black people were suffering "the agony of slavery's slow death, but not the deliverance." So many free blacks living beside a smaller number of people in bondage produced wrenching and painful contrasts. It was common for families to include both slave and free members, a state of affairs that gave, one historian wrote, "an extra measure of bitterness" to the lives of loved ones trapped on opposite sides of this legal divide.

Joe and Ann Hall, for example, lived in constant anxiety. Though Joe had been able to buy his wife's freedom from the Rogers family decades earlier, many of their children remained slaves on that nearby farm. If the Rogerses had a bad harvest or needed extra money, one or more of the Hall youngsters might be sold downstate.

The Halls faced an impossible situation. Joe and Ann were trying to earn enough cash to buy back their children, while at the same time they had to make the calculation of whom to buy, and in what order. Two of the Hall children, unable to wait any longer, made a bid for freedom. One boy and one girl lit out from the Rogers farm, presumably aided by some money their parents had earned. According to a Hall descendant interviewed in 1935, both young people reached Harrisburg, Pennsylvania, safely, but at a cost. They would not see their mother and father again for over a decade, not until after the Civil War.

For all of Junius Brutus Booth's imperfections, when he had lived in Bel Air the actor had been able to pour oil on the troubled waters of that mixed community. John Wilkes seems to have done the opposite. When he superintended the labor of blacks and whites, he exacerbated conflicts and brought tensions to a boil. Mary Ann wisely decided to remove her son from a position of authority.

In the spring of 1854, she rented her fields to a white farmer, one who would take charge of sowing the crops, reaping them, and managing the laborers. Even then, John's temper and penchant for conflict plunged Mary Ann into distress, driving away the tenant and incurring legal trouble.

A confrontation started in late July, as the fields of wheat stood ripening in the heat of summer. Mary Ann had questioned the tenant's farming methods, worrying he was spending too much money on fertilizer and working the black field hands too hard. The man's response was "very insolent," Asia remembered. He called her mother "vile names," she said. When sixteen-year-old John heard about the words that had passed between the adults, he became enraged. Making a cudgel out of a stout piece of wood and marching to the tenant's cabin, he threatened to beat him unless he apologized instantly to the ladies of the house.

"First find your *ladies*," the farmer sneered. For John, no more provocation was needed. He swung his cudgel, striking the man about the head and upper body.

"I knocked him down, which made him bleed like a butcher," he boasted to a friend afterward. "In a couple of weeks I have to stand trial. For assault and battery as you call it."

John's description missed the part where the farmer, blood spurting from his nose, ran to the nearby Woolsey plantation, screaming "he was killed and murdered." Woolsey, no friend of the Booths, sent for a sheriff.

Asia describes the strange tableau that followed in the parlor of Tudor Hall. A magistrate of the court and a law clerk entered the house to find, she wrote, "my mother in her widow's weeds, my gentle invalid sister, Wilkes, very handsome, and I, very cross."

John was put on probation, according to Asia, "bound over to keep the peace."

Several small children who lived on the Booth farm, including Joe and Ann Hall's six-year-old daughter, Nancy, made a singsong rhyme about John's sentencing, which they often sang while playing on the lawn that summer.

> *We's bound over to keep the peace, to keep the peace, to keep the peace,*
> *We's all bound over to keep the peace,*
> *Glory Hallelujah!*

John Wilkes Booth now enjoyed a life of leisure at Tudor Hall. All he did, day in and day out, the youth said in a letter to one of his old Baltimore playmates, was "gun, ride, sleep and eat." By his own admission, he became "a very late riser." His main interest seems to have been "cutting a dash" with the several pretty girls who lived in the neighborhood. Mounted on Cola di Renzi, his all-black colt, John spent hours showing Asia how to ride her mare, Fanny, "with and without a saddle," she recalled. In the springtime, brother and sister would ride through the woods breathing in air that was "fragrant," Asia remembered, "with the fresh smell of early violets." Little by little, the siblings began to participate in the social life of Bel Air, attending "strawberry-eatings," fairs, and reenactments of medieval jousts at Deer Creek, a spectacular rock formation popular with picnicking locals. John discovered, too, the Travelers' Home, a tavern in a town next to Bel Air, where men gathered in the daytime to drink, play cards, and do business.

It was perhaps through regular visits to the Travelers' Home that John Wilkes found a fresh diversion: politics. The Order of the Star-Spangled Banner, otherwise known as the Know-Nothing Party, was sweeping northern Maryland and most of the free states in the fall of 1854. The freshman political organization was highly successful, winning the governorships of eight states and sending a hundred new representatives to Congress. The Know-Nothing creed embraced two principles: hostility to new immigrants— particularly Irish Catholic ones—and opposition to slavery's expansion into new territory.

John joined the Harford County chapter of this new party, the memory of insults hurled at him by Irish workers still fresh in mind. In the year 1854 alone, four hundred thousand émigrés landed in the American Northeast. Capping a decade of unprecedented immigration rates, this year was the high-tide mark. An 1854 editorial in the *New York Tribune* called the latest surge of newcomers "a social phenomenon with few, if any, parallels." Asia Booth's plainspoken bigotry reflected the nativist spirit of the times: she talked about Irish people as a "filth" that must be "washed . . . from our Country." Know-Nothing candidates pledged to push back against the Irish, protecting the rights of native-born citizens by keeping foreign voters away from the polls.

Know-Nothings also promised to stamp out sectional antagonism. Mary Ann and Asia were avid newspaper readers. John absorbed the talk of the older men congregating at the Travelers' Home. In 1854, widespread disgust over the Kansas-Nebraska Act dominated public discourse and was another reason for Know-Nothing success. A violent controversy broke that year when Stephen A. Douglas, a senator from Illinois, proposed that the territories of Kansas and Nebraska be opened to settlement by slave owners and free men alike. Douglas reasoned that people moving into the territory could be left to decide slavery's future among themselves, at the ballot box.

Historians have described the Kansas-Nebraska Act as "the most monstrous and fatal of all political errors," for it was an outright invitation to war—people settling Kansas in 1854 had a pioneer experience unlike any other. Anarchy ruled as pro- and antislavery neighbors shot one another, community leaders were scalped and beaten, and opponents burned each other's farms. Roving gangs of gunmen terrorized newcomers to the area, demanding to know which side they were on, that of slavery, or of freedom. If a person gave the wrong answer, one veteran of the conflict recalled, he "was marked for destruction." The barrel of a gun, not the ballot box, was the tool used to determine that territory's future.

Know-Nothing candidates argued that the two old parties, the Whigs and the Democrats, had unleashed this bloody furor. Voters hungry for a fresh solution flocked to the new party's banner. Being part of this fledgling political movement was a thrill for John Wilkes Booth, whose days of luxuriant idleness were paling into boredom. The proceedings of the new organization held a mysterious allure, for the Know-Nothings were a fraternal association as well as a political party, complete with clandestine passwords and private rituals. Members joined by invitation only, lodge meetings were held in hidden locations, and those pledged to the brotherhood swore a special oath of allegiance. It is likely John's pledge was similar to one sworn by a Know-Nothing initiate to a New York chapter that year, assuring fellow members of his "belief in the existence of a Supreme Being," avowing his status as "a native-born citizen, a Protestant," and asserting he was "not united in marriage with a Roman Catholic." John's illegitimacy and his father's adherence to aspects of Islam and Hinduism seemed not to have been barriers to membership.

When Henry Winter Davis, a Know-Nothing candidate for Congress, came to Bel Air for a rally in November 1854, the lodge tapped sixteen-year-old Booth to be a steward. John Wilkes would wear the party's badge and carry a banner at the event. Mary Ann spent money she did not have to dress her son exquisitely for his role. He sported a wine-red coat trimmed in velvet, gray trousers, and a fawn-colored vest. Mounted on his prancing horse, he was every inch the neighborhood heartthrob. John "looked remarkably handsome," Asia recalled.

Women attending the rally gasped in distress when John, cantering toward the speaker's platform with the party colors, suddenly plunged into a roadside ditch. His horse had tripped and stumbled to its knees, perhaps spooked by its rider's waving flag. Asia writes that her brother "leaped off, hoisted the colt, and by aid of the flagstaff, without touching the stirrup, sprang lightly into the saddle and dashed off again, only looking back at us with a reassuring smile." When Asia and her mother reached him, they found John surrounded by a crowd of women smoothing the dust from the shoulders of his new coat, praising him for his athletic prowess. Attention like this was balm to John's feelings. Plagued by neighbors' gossip, his own quick temper, and the status-bucking attitudes of country laborers, John preened himself on minor achievements like this one.

AROUND THIS TIME, AN UNNAMED VISITOR TO THE BOOTH FARM— someone Asia referred to only as "a man of letters"—gave John and his sister Asia a new purpose in life. The guest warned Booth's widow and children to busy themselves publishing an official memoir of the great actor. If they did not, unscrupulous journalists who sought to profit from the star's name would beat them to the task, writing an account of Booth's life as one long scandal.

John Wilkes and Asia embraced this project. Protecting the family name and the memory of their father's genius was a mission these siblings craved. Asia also may have hoped that the work would be a healthy pursuit for John Wilkes, filled as he was with so much purposeless energy. With their mother's consent, an expedition to Baltimore was launched to fetch their father's trunks from storage. Sitting in a farm wagon with the cargo, Asia remembered she and John felt "elated" on the bumpy homeward ride.

Pondering the best way to tell their father's story, the pair settled down to unpack and sort his treasures. "Truly we delved and worked like moles," Asia remembered. Countless old "letters and journals, as well as books, were open to scrutiny," testified a family friend who saw these riches spilled across the floor of Tudor Hall, including "engagements offered to Junius Brutus nearly half a century ago, and particulars of his quarrel with Kean." Here was the sum total of Booth's greatness, documented in sheaves of playbills and posters of every size and shape, dating from 1817 to 1852, telling of his debut in London and subsequent decades of American success.

Reading, touching, even smelling these old possessions brought Junius back to his children with new vividness. Asia and John pored over diaries and memoranda for clues to his character. His trespasses and betrayals forgotten, they lost themselves in admiration for their father's achievements.

John and Asia's excitement at becoming biographers, however, quickly turned to dismay. Their mother, usually a model of restrained temperament, broke at the sight her husband's things. Seized with a "morbid grief," Asia records, the widow burned Booth's archive. John and his sister clung to one another in disbelief as Mary Ann shredded, ripped, and set fire to thirty years' worth of letters. The actor had left his correspondence in beautiful order, the envelopes indexed, dated, and bundled with ribbon into appropriate categories. She tore these open, scanned their contents, and dropped them ruthlessly in the stove. As their father's life story went up in smoke, the children tried to stop her.

"Oh Mother, give us some autographs—some old letters—for remembrance!" cried Asia.

John accused his mother of succumbing to what he called "homicidal mania." "You are leaving nothing," he stormed at her, torn between anger and pleading. "Supposing someone should write father's life? Such a lot of false statements will be made. Give us the proofs, and everything that can be of service."

Mary Ann Booth refused to discuss the matter. Pressing on in silence, she did her best to erase large swaths of her husband's history.

Stymied, the young biographers worked furtively on the few papers that survived the wreckage. Mary Ann spared some relics from Booth's younger days in London, proofs of his association with great Romantic artists like Lord Byron. Their father had been obsessed with the poet's heroic mission to Greece, where Byron rushed to join the efforts of Greek freedom fighters who were trying to oust the occupying Turkish army.

Junius Brutus Booth, delighted with the poet's heroic mission, sent money to help his efforts. Part of the proceeds from the star's 1824 performances would be donated, his playbills promised, "for the benefit of the Fund in Aid of the Greeks."

Her brother "spent many hours . . . reading aloud from Byron's poems" during this period of his life, Asia later recalled. John learned, however, that before Byron could even strike a blow against the Turks, before he ever organized a raid, the poet died, his end hastened by inept doctors. After catching a fever on one of his daily rides along the beach, Byron was bled by local surgeons. Opening the poet's veins with lancets one night, they drained too many pints of blood. Weakened to the danger point, Byron lapsed into a coma and died on April 19, 1824. His death was mourned as an international event.

According to Mary Ann, when Junius heard the news of Byron's death, he was so crushed he wore black "crape [sic] on his arm thirty days for this poet." Newspapers in England and Greece memorialized Byron as a hero.

His scandals and sexual misadventures forgotten, statues were raised in his honor.

John Wilkes Booth, absorbing the lessons of his father's stardom and of Byron's bold achievement, began to build, Asia remembered, "fantastic temples of fame." He was obsessed with thoughts of his own potential. "For my brother," she remembered, "no visions or dreams were too extravagantly great." Junius Brutus Booth's writings encouraged such thinking. The actor's few surviving diaries, somehow held back from the flames, revealed to John Wilkes his father's private thoughts on celebrity and genius. Fame was a marvelous prize, the elder Booth suggested, open to anyone who had talent, no matter what their parentage. "Mind happily belongs to no age, clime, sex or condition," the actor had scrawled in a thick, decisive hand on the lined pages of a notebook. "Instances can be quoted when even from the most despised classes Genius has developed itself and towered above all the circle of the human race." Booth listed famous men of mixed heritage and undistinguished birth—Galileo, Napoleon Bonaparte, Hannibal of Carthage, Christopher Columbus, and himself—to prove his point.

How John Wilkes Booth would make his mark on the future was an open question as 1854 drew to a close. "Our childhood was waning fast," Asia mused that winter. John Wilkes, she wrote, "like the other [brothers], must go out and do his work in the world." The mess he had made of the plantings and harvests over the past two years proved he was not fit for farming. While Asia acknowledged that one of John's "dearest ambitions" was to be a soldier, the heaps of paraphernalia filling Tudor Hall pointed to a more immediate plan. They could not write a biography of their actor father, but Asia could try to help her younger brother become an actor himself. His good looks, his athleticism, and the strength of the family name encouraged them in this shared ambition. Asia states that their mother took no part in the venture. "Lost," Asia noted, in "obsessive grief," the widow left her son and daughter to their own devices.

Mary Ann Booth burned her husband's papers but she did not touch the star's vast collection of costumes. A fortune's worth of stage dresses lay about the second floor of the house. These "toggeries," as Booth once called them, were individual works of art, each lavishly trimmed with metalwork, brocade, ermine, or lace. His collection of stage jewelry was equally fine—earrings, bracelets, rings, medallions, scabbards, and shoe buckles, all studded with glass beads, or inlaid with semiprecious gems. Boxes held tall boots, Roman sandals with lacings, curly-toed slippers, and a plethora of hats. Last but not least was the makeup case, the contents jumbled just as Booth had left them after his last performance in New Orleans—hare's foot, blunted sticks of greasepaint, musty-smelling face powder, a smudged cotton apron worn while making up at the mirror.

They had the tools, but not the understanding. Neither Booth child had the faintest idea how to begin John Wilkes's course of theatrical training. Asia had a schoolgirl's familiarity with elocution, but no more. They had not been exposed to their father's work onstage more than a handful of times. The barricade Junius Brutus Booth built between his younger children and his public performances had been effective.

Asia and John's first impulse was to turn to the plays themselves. Pulling volumes of Shakespeare off the shelves, the pair set to work studying speeches. Asia called her brother "my slow student," describing his dogged "struggles with the ever-opened manuscript." John Wilkes examined an illustrated version of the classic plays, one that showed the main characters in various poses—martial, loverlike, kingly, sorrowing—then tried to mold his own body to match these images. A visitor to Tudor Hall years later who opened this book reported seeing the phrase "Form this picture" scrawled in a boyish hand beneath one of the illustrations.

Through his seven years of apprenticeship to Junius Brutus Booth, Edwin "imbibed" all the works of Shakespeare "by ear," learning by careful listening where to breathe in the long speeches, understanding how to pace his respiration, finding places where pauses would not break the flow of language. Only those raised in the theater from childhood received that kind of specific instruction. Edwin's knowledge of Shakespeare passed to him by oral tradition.

In the one recording of Edwin Booth's voice that survives today, made with a primitive wax cylinder device in 1890, Othello's speech to the Venetian senate rolls in natural, modulated, and melodious waves. His accent when speaking Shakespeare's lines is British, not American, partly indebted to the London theatrical tradition that produced his father. It is a riveting performance, one whose rhythms and soaring intonations exactly fit the meaning of the difficult passage. He displays the measured, subtle vocal inflections of a master at his craft. There are shifts in mood within couplets; touches of humor suggested by a lifting note here, a falling one there; precise, yet effortless-seeming, enunciation; layers of meaning conveyed through the smallest changes in tone.

Without an experienced teacher, John Wilkes had no hope of achieving this kind of mastery. He could only stumble, unguided and alone, through the complicated thicket of Shakespeare's words. Committing long passages to memory, he went outside and ranted them in the woods, shouting the words in a way that did not illuminate their true sense. These performances were bewildering to brother and sister both. "Whether wrong or right, by rule or emphasis, neither he nor I could tell," Asia recorded. John's sister saw and heard what his lack of training, coupled with vehement urgency, produced: it was "sound and fury, signifying nothing." A teacher—a "Master," Asia wrote—was needed "to prune, cultivate, subdue and encourage" her brother's efforts. In desperation, she scrounged a text on breathing, *Dr. Rush on the Voice*, but it had been written by a medical doctor, not an actor, and was of no use to them. Nothing their father left behind could help John solve the riddle, they realized, of "the inflection and guidance of the voice."

Lack of a mentor and teacher was a serious obstacle to John's dramatic ambitions. But as the winter of 1854 shaded into the spring of 1855, and their tussles with Shakespeare continued, Asia identified one final barrier to John's success. It was a realization the young woman probably kept to herself, only committing the observation to paper in a few leaves of private memories produced for her son, Wilfred Booth Clarke, in 1885. Becoming an actor was not simply a matter of training, Asia wrote, but of aptitude. John Wilkes did not have the gift his brother Edwin was born with. When her brother was still a small child, Asia stated, it had been obvious to their parents that the plays of Shakespeare "were intuitively made clear to Edwin's comprehension." At a young age, for example, the boy asked his father, "When Hamlet says, 'I am too much i' the sun,' does he mean a play upon words, is it a pun?"

"Who told you that?" Junius had demanded, startled.

"No one; I only thought it meant so when I heard you speak the line."

Even before he began traveling with and learning from their father, Asia recalled, the child Edwin found "lines of seeming ambiguity" in Shakespeare perfectly "intelligible and clear"—even such grammatical riddles as Hamlet's comment "Since no man knows aught of what he leaves what is't to leave betimes?"

John Wilkes could not have been more different. He did not have his brother's knack for words, and his lackluster performance in school was noted by his peers. Asia, after many months of helping John Wilkes learn to act, confessed that only Edwin seemed able intuitively to grasp and convey the full spectrum of Shakespeare's darker emotions. He alone could "dissociate," as she put it, "the grotesque from the pathetic and highly tragic, for too often one merges insensibly into the other."

John Wilkes seemed to realize the impossibility of becoming an actor without a teacher. His frustration burst forth, Asia remembered, in impatient, despairing exclamations at the dinner table at Tudor Hall. "How shall I ever have a chance on stage?" the youth moaned. "Buried here," he demanded, "what chance have I of ever studying elocution or declamation?"

In the spring of 1855, batches of letters arrived at Tudor Hall from the long-absent Edwin, containing photographs of himself and some surprising news. The family read with amazement a record of the young man's recent adventures. Since 1853, he had risen to become a "chief player" in San Francisco, costarring with internationally known actresses like Catherine Norton Sinclair and Jean Davenport. Sinclair and Davenport were mature stage professionals, older than Edwin, already well established. For forty-three nights straight in 1853—an unprecedented run in San Francisco for that time—Mrs. Sinclair and Edwin held audiences spellbound with a melodrama called *The Marble Heart*. The actress wore a $1,200 costume from Paris for the show, "at a time," one newspaper commented, "when $19 was thought ruinous for a leading lady's gown." Even so expensively attired, Mrs. Sinclair, critics said, was cast entirely in the shade by Edwin's talent.

Years later, Jean Davenport laughingly recalled the contrast between twenty-year-old Edwin's onstage poise and offstage immaturity. At nightly performances, she wrote, Edwin "played with the very soul of genius in him. Never had I seen grief so naturally portrayed. I was carried out of myself." Yet the next morning, he would arrive late to rehearsal carrying a dirty hat filled with seagull's eggs. "Oh Miss Davenport, see what I have brought you!" the young star enthused. "It's such fun to hunt nests on the Pacific Coast! I do wish, Miss Davenport, you could have been along!"

Most impressive of all to Edwin's family at Tudor Hall, however, was the news that the young man had launched an international tour with the famous British actress Laura Keene. Born Mary Frances Moss in 1826 to a working-class London family, this future star had been married young to a hard-drinking tavern keeper. When her intoxicated husband started abusing her, Mary traded the misery of life with an alcoholic for the freedom and opportunity of the stage. Calling herself Laura Keene, the intrepid girl won instant acclaim. Popular in London, twenty-five-year-old Keene then took New York by storm and never looked back. This self-made woman had big dreams: she wanted to own and manage her own theater in America. To raise the money, like so many other actors of her time, she had headed for California.

Keene was famous not only for her perfect portrayals of romantic and comic heroines, but also, one reviewer admitted, for her proven ability to captivate masculine audiences with her "tall graceful body" and "statuesque poses." In 1854, gold prospectors left their outposts by the thousands at the news that Laura had arrived in San Francisco. The miners came in from the wilderness in droves, hungry for what they called the "revivifying" sight of the voluptuous Miss Keene.

When Laura Keene first met Edwin Booth, Benjamin Baker, a San Francisco theatrical agent recalled, she had to get in line to start a romance with him. "Ned" was "one of the handsomest fellows in the world," Baker said. Another old-timer who knew Edwin in these years gave an interview to a magazine at the dawn of the motion picture era. "Talk about your matinee idols these days!" the octogenarian exclaimed. "Ed Booth would have lost them all!" Despite differences in age and experience, the pair fell in love. In the summer of 1854, Edwin, twenty, and Laura, twenty-eight, embarked for Australia, planning to make some money by bringing Shakespeare to the prosperous cities of Sydney and Melbourne.

The seventy-two-day voyage across the Pacific Ocean was an idyllic one. Laura loved her melancholy, intelligent co-star. "They were inseparable," recalled a friend, "as happy together as a pair of turtledoves." The two spent hours spinning grandiose schemes for a future of joint stardom. The thrill of their romance was heightened by the unexpected dangers of the journey. Pirates attacked their ship, the *Snow*, as it lay off the island of Samoa. A small team of men climbed aboard and tried to dash the vessel on a coral reef, Edwin later explained, in an effort to claim salvage rights. The quick-thinking captain managed to grab the wheel in time and steer to safety. As if that episode were not exciting enough, a mutiny of the crew followed. When the first mate rang the alarm, Edwin told his family, all passengers on board raced to "arm themselves with every available object." He and other actors dashed to their costume trunks, seizing rapiers and broadswords. These "stage properties," he boasted, "presented a formidable array as they were brandished to defend the Captain."

The mutiny quelled, Edwin and Laura returned to the work of rehearsing their scenes on deck, running through Portia and Shylock's parts in *The Merchant of Venice* as the *Snow* plowed through the Coral Sea toward Sydney. Strange birds cried overhead, and the rush of the waves at times drowned out their dialogue. White beaches and emerald jungles of "wonderful beauty," Edwin remembered, passed by on the horizon.

True love ended abruptly when the vessel docked in the British colony of Australia in October 1854. Sydney was an attractive place, with plenty of shops, churches, fine houses, and an extensive botanical garden. There were also saloons. Ever since his father's death, Edwin Booth was prone to alcoholism. Though his habit had been kept at bay by shipboard liquor rationing and Laura's attention, the instant Edwin set foot on land he disappeared into the harborside taverns for days, only to show up at Laura's hotel much later, a friend recalled, in a "lively and oblivious condition." An inebriated Edwin began to shout abuse at the British colonial government and clumsily tried to raise a United States flag on the lawn of the hotel. "Though very patriotic from an American stand-point," reported a witness, the actor's display "was decidedly unpleasant from an English point of view."

Public sentiment in Sydney turned against him, with audiences of loyal British subjects refusing to buy tickets to see Edwin perform. Laura Keene was furious. Her careful planning, the risky voyage, her hopes for a profitable run, all were ruined. Far worse was her lover's transformation into a copy of the hard-drinking husband she had left London to escape. Once the effects of his spree wore off, a repentant Edwin tried to apologize but Laura refused to listen. She broke with him completely. "There was no more turtle-doving between them," a journalist later acknowledged. "Edwin Booth and Laura Keene were never friends again." The young actor notoriously joked at the time that he felt Laura's rejection "Keenely."

READING HIS OLDER BROTHER'S EPISTOLARY ACCOUNTS OF ADVENTURE ON the high seas—undoubtedly condensed and expurgated for their mother's eyes—John Wilkes must have yearned to share them. Edwin's homeward journey had included stops in Samoa and Tahiti, as well as in the Sandwich Islands. On Oahu, Edwin spent eight weeks in the beautiful village, Honolulu, that lay in the shadow of an extinct volcano. He performed *Richard III* for King Kamehameha IV.

Americans were still reeling from Herman Melville's titillating accounts of his experiences in the islands of the Pacific, *Typee* and *Omoo*, published in the 1840s. Melville had evoked island women in minute detail, describing "their jet-black tresses streaming over their shoulders and half-enveloping their otherwise naked forms." These "savage" beauties, unfamiliar with clothing and untutored in the fine points of Christian morality, Melville informed his readers, would swim out to American vessels, carrying with them seashells filled with palm oil as they swam, and climbing aboard, proceed to engage crews in "the grossest licentiousness," permitting "every species of riot and debauchery." Compared to Edwin's exploits in the Pacific—with pirates and mutineers, with Laura Keene, and, presumably, with native females—

John Wilkes's flirtations with Harford County girls and his participation in a Know-Nothing rally probably seemed like small beer to both brothers.

Edwin's letters to their mother contained, Asia recalled, his "promises soon to be home." The California star had found a business manager to promote his career in the East, theatrical agent Benjamin Baker. Baker went on ahead, crossing the Isthmus in the summer of 1856 to negotiate advance contracts for Edwin to act up and down the Atlantic Coast. Baker promised bookers that Booth's son was a talent big enough "to fill the void left by his father's death." Edwin had started to worry that if he did not leave the West soon for the eastern United States, other actors, as he wrote, would "take the position that should be his." It was important for Edwin to stake his claim now, he believed, "while his father's memory was dear to the American heart."

Mary Ann Booth was holding out for Edwin's return as she would for a rescue. With no tenant farmer to put in crops that spring, she had not been able to raise enough to eat. Her small store of cash was gone. The widow and her children went hungry over the winter of 1855–56. "We came near to sickness through want of nourishing food," Asia remembered of that season. "Sheer necessity led us to set traps beyond our own precincts." Even poaching opossum and birds on their neighbors' property could not supply the family's wants. Mary Ann dispatched John on a money-raising errand: the youth drove the family's small herd of cattle to a livestock market, where he sold the animals for over sixty dollars in cash. Beyond these efforts, seventeen-year-old John Wilkes seems to have been unable to help his mother improve their situation.

Edwin Booth arrived by stagecoach at Tudor Hall in September 1856. Now twenty-two, he had been absent for more than four years. A crowd of "country lads," Asia remembered, rushed to meet the young actor as he stepped down from the coach. As the world traveler sauntered up the drive, the youths hoisted Edwin's heavy trunks on their shoulders, speculating out loud "at the weight of the supposed contents," imagining boulder-size lumps of California gold. "He's from the diggin's!" they exclaimed.

Edwin Booth certainly walked with the assurance of a rich man. All the family, including John Wilkes, were amazed at the sight of him. He had the same long, curling black hair and bright black eyes, but now, like a Portsmouth Square gambler who had hit a winning streak, Edwin wore a huge diamond pin in his cravat and a velvet cloak. The splendor of his California style took the lean and threadbare Booths aback. Edwin's cheerful mood and expensive jewelry posed a startling contrast to this family's recent miseries and the desperate state of their finances. Edwin's report of his easy homeward journey across the Isthmus of Panama only brought to mind the sufferings of their father, robbed of his gold during a solo crossing on foot. Now, travelers sped through the jungle in the pampered comfort of a railway car. The days of life-threatening slogs through the wilderness, at the mercy of bandits and malignant fevers, were over.

When Edwin walked through the door of his father's house, Asia and Mary Ann closely examined the stone pinned at his collar. The diamond was set in a large nugget of pure gold. This eye-catching ornament, the actor told his astonished mother and sister, had been a "farewell gift from the ladies of San Francisco." Edwin carried in his trunks other evidence of his artistic achievements: in addition to rave reviews from San Francisco papers, and playbills from Sydney, there was a copy of a resolution passed in his honor by the California state legislature. The text of this proclamation referred to Edwin Booth as a treasure, a gift of great value that the people of California were bestowing on the rest of the United States. The Booth talent, the resolution announced, was moving from "the Western portion of the Continent to the Eastern." The public testimonial was a "manifestation," the authors informed Edwin, "of the esteem in which you are held, not only as a talented and notable exponent of the Drama, but as a citizen of the State of California."

Best of all, on his belt, beneath the Spanish cloak, Edwin Booth carried a purse heavy with gold. Mary Ann Booth almost wept with relief. Her son's farewell performances in San Francisco had earned him the equivalent of twenty thousand dollars in modern currency. Decades after the Civil War, General William Tecumseh Sherman still retained the memory of young Booth's final California engagement. Sherman, then a lowly lieutenant who recently had resigned from the U.S. Army, sat night after night on the veranda of his hotel, listening to "the thunders of applause" rolling from the playhouse opposite, as the star took his last bows.

For John Wilkes Booth, the return of this talented older brother was a mixed blessing. Over the past four years, the Booth family's existence at Tudor Hall had become increasingly untenable. Neither John Wilkes nor his mother, Mary Ann, had been able to figure out how to make a living off the farmland. Now the Booth family had a new theatrical wage earner to depend on for their fortunes. Edwin seemed poised to take on his father's role.

It is clear that John Wilkes had hoped he would be filling that place. After a year of laboriously studying Shakespeare and practicing speeches in the woods, John Wilkes Booth stole away from Tudor Hall to make his own first stand on a stage. On August 14, 1855, he took a small part in a production of *Richard III* at Baltimore's Charles Street Theatre. This stage, "the least important," locals said, of the city's five playhouses, was a second-floor ballroom near the city docks. John Sleeper Clarke, one of the Booth brothers' old friends from Exeter Street, had invited John Wilkes to try his luck there. Clarke was a natural showman. Looking to draw attention to this unpopular stage, he hoped that adding the teenager's famous last name to the playbills would cause a sensation. Clarke was not wrong. A capacity crowd turned out to see if Booth's son was "worthy of wearing the mantle of his father."

Returning home the morning after the show, seventeen-year-old John announced to Mary Ann and Asia that he had made his debut. Mary Ann was furious. Their mother "thought it was premature," Asia remembered, telling John Wilkes he had been manipulated "by others who wished to gain notoriety and money by the use of his name." Her husband had made the name Booth a synonym for genius. Mary Ann did not wish a raw, untrained son to risk his father's legacy.

Anticipating her objection, John had not informed Mary Ann of his plans beforehand. This was typical for a youth who was "affectionate . . . toward his mother," friends said, "without being obedient." Nor did John tell her the full story of his first night onstage. The attempt had been a decided failure. As one local recalled, "before a crowded place, Booth played so badly he was hissed." Another two years would pass before John Wilkes Booth attempted to act in public again.

EIGHT

A DELICATE AND
TENDER PRINCE

. . . A delicate and tender prince,
Whose spirit, with divine ambition puff'd,
Makes mouths at the invisible event,
Exposing what is mortal and unsure
To all that fortune, death, and danger dare,
Even for an eggshell.

—*Hamlet*, 4.4

ALL THROUGH THE WINTER OF 1858, THE DOORS OF WILLIAM WHEATLEY'S Arch Street Theatre in Philadelphia opened at six-thirty every evening except Sunday. February 23 was a Tuesday. Playgoers who arrived early waited outside, stamping their feet and blowing on their fingers, impatient to enter the warmth of the auditorium. Their gloved hands pushed coins across a ticket counter to the box office treasurer. Fifteen cents admitted one to the balcony, fifty cents to a seat on the main floor. Black Philadelphians were welcome, too, though they paid double the amount whites did and sat in a separate "Gallery for Colored Persons."

For ticket seekers, the wait in the cold was an annoyance worth bearing. Tonight's performance was a historical tour de force, programs advertised, of "Beauty, Grandeur and Great Acting." Patrons looked forward to three hours of enchantment and escape: Manager Wheatley, by means of theatrical magic, promised to transport them through time and space to Renaissance Venice.

The strains of a sixteenth-century Italian song wafted from the orchestra. The house lights dimmed, and the curtain lifted to reveal the façade of a palace, its arched marble entrance and curved steps fronting a terrace dotted with statues. Beyond, the Grand Canal could be seen bathed in moonlight. The stage manager, Mr. Fredericks, cued the sound of rushing water and sent gondolas passing to and fro. It was Carnival night in Venice. Lords and ladies promenaded the stage in cloaks and painted masks. The leering mouths, beaked noses, and staring eyeholes evoked an ominous mood, for tonight's story was a tragedy.

Suddenly the music turned threatening. Six Italian cavaliers dashed on-stage to warn the audience of the story about to unfold.

One cried, "There never was a tale more full of horror! There never was a deed more black and damning!"

After a short pause, a second cavalier stepped forward. It was nineteen-year-old John Wilkes Booth, about to deliver the opening line of his first big speaking role since that humiliating night in Baltimore two years before, when his debut in a dockside theater earned hisses from a crowd.

"Aye, a dark and bloody deed," he said, "perpetrated by some malicious demon, who revels in blood and crime!"

The play was Victor Hugo's assassin melodrama, *Lucretia Borgia*, trans-lated from the French and adapted to American tastes, and it was a perfect opportunity for John Wilkes Booth to make a hit. He had made the transi-tion from Tudor Hall to Philadelphia in 1857 when William Wheatley hired him for work as a bit player.

The nineteen-year-old could thank John Sleeper Clarke, one of the origi-nal Tripple Alley players, for his new job. Ten years before, Clarke had been a member of that small band of Baltimore street urchins who joined Edwin and John Wilkes in starting a children's theater in a Baltimore basement. Even then, "Sleepy" Clarke had shown a gift for making people laugh. He was now a comedy star in Philadelphia, a friend of William Wheatley, and an investor in many of his productions.

Clarke helped John Wilkes find a job because it won him favor in the eyes of Asia Booth. Clarke's romance with John's older sister was progressing slowly, and he wanted to prove his devotion. As one Philadelphia actor re-membered, "Wilkes induced J. S. Clarke, who was then addressing his sister, to obtain him a position in the company of the Arch Street Theatre." It had not been difficult for Clarke to persuade Wheatley to hire a son of Junius Brutus Booth. Though he was untrained, John's resemblance to his parent was unmistakable: he had the dark hair, the high forehead, the clean-lined Roman profile. It was an enviable face, and the nineteen-year-old seemed to have something of the elder Booth's charisma and energy.

For months John Wilkes Booth had labored in Wheatley's large company as a lowly "supe," or supernumerary, the name given to extras in nineteenth-century stage productions. So far, John had appeared in 165 performances at the Arch Street Theatre, mostly playing background roles, the soldiers, servants, peasants, and noblemen with no lines to speak, but whose costumed figures helped set the scene. Tonight, John's fellow supes—the two dozen young men and women in Carnival regalia—envied the chance that was his.

Supernumeraries, as a rule, were a competitive bunch of beginners. The only way to rise from their place at the bottom of the actors' hierarchy was to land a credited role and make an impression with it. Hungry for advancement, supes showed energy. These minor players studied all the major parts, hoping a leading man or lady would fall sick and the stage manager would send them on instead. Such absences happened often enough, in those days, that young and talented underlings maintained a state of constant readiness, waiting for their chance to break out of the ranks of the unknown.

When John Wilkes walked into Wheatley's greenroom the second week of February 1858, he learned his chance had arrived. Prominent on a central wall was the call board, where rehearsal schedules and cast assignments appeared. John probably had been checking this board impatiently since he started at Wheatley's in August 1857, six months before. Now he saw his name announced for two good speaking parts in full-length plays: tonight he would play Ascanio Petrucca, a Venetian swordsman in *Lucretia Borgia*. Tomorrow he would appear as Dawson, a villain from London's criminal underworld, in an eighteenth-century British classic, *The Gamester*.

Both of these were midlevel parts, nothing a star would stoop to, yet they were good stepping-stones for a striver. A clever supe would find a way to make something out of even this small opportunity. He or she could try to steal a scene, to be original and different, to win a burst of applause or an appreciative shout from the audience—anything to be remembered. John had "studied faithfully," he later said, to perfect his twenty-odd lines. Experienced actors looking back on these maiden performances never forgot the agony of preparation that went into their small part. One supe recalled how she had practiced her one first line with a professional company over and over again, "putting the emphasis first on one word, and then on the other," for hours, in "dress rehearsals all by myself."

JOHN WILKES BOOTH COULD NOT HAVE ASKED FOR A BIGGER CROWD TO witness what was, in effect, his tryout. Theater managers in general considered *Lucretia Borgia* "a sure card," meaning it was the kind of spectacle, one newspaper explained, guaranteed to pack in audiences "as closely as herrings in a barrel." For Wheatley and his stage director, Mr. Fredericks, the stakes riding on tonight's show were high. They were pitted in battle with the rival Walnut Street Theatre. Founded in 1809 and renowned for introducing gas footlights to stage technology, the Walnut had a strong claim on the affections of the city (as it does to this day). In recent weeks, crowds of Philadelphians had flocked there to enjoy *White Lies*, a melodrama that nightly inspired no fewer than eight standing ovations. A shortage of ladies' handkerchiefs in local department stores was blamed on the tear-jerking effect of this show. Even "stout gentlemen," one correspondent reported, were observed "absolutely sobbing out loud" at the finale. Determined to recapture these crowds, Wheatley played his strongest hand: the grisly and thrilling *Lucretia Borgia*.

In the 1850s, a new kind of theater audience was coming into being, one with tastes different from the kind Junius Brutus Booth had catered to in 1840s with his trademark gladiatorial violence and displays of emotional mayhem. As the old prejudice against playhouses as dens of sin and moral degradation eroded, members of a newly prosperous American middle class—the wives and children of businessmen, skilled artisans, railroad officials, newspaper editors, lawyers, and doctors—were now entering theaters on Saturday afternoons to enjoy tasteful dramatizations of popular novels by Charles Dickens, Sir Walter Scott, and Alexandre Dumas, along with other family-friendly fare. Never one to miss a chance, Wheatley and other impresarios in the Northeast threw out lures to keep these worthy, well-paying customers coming back for more.

The Arch Street players mounted ninety-eight different plays in the thirty-six weeks of the 1857–58 season, a busy parade of new attractions that pushed Wheatley's company of actors at a furious pace. Wheatley offered an ever-changing mix of drawing-room comedies, tragedies, adventure stories, sentimental dramas, mysteries, romances, and mistaken-identity capers. He switched genres at will, gauging when the popular mood demanded a special-effects stunner like the lava-spitting volcano at the end of *The Last Days of Pompeii*, or a cautionary tale about the dangers of card playing and drinking, such as *The Gamester*. Wheatley drew the line at entertainments as vulgar as *Mazeppa*, the racy hit beloved by male patrons of New York's Bowery Theatre. The climax of this piece involved a half-naked actress, lashed with leather thongs to the back of a horse, galloping up and down the theater's aisles and finally onto the stage, where horse and rider reared and plunged until the curtain came crashing down.

To distance his productions as much as possible from the uncouth spectacles offered by rougher establishments, Wheatley renovated his theater annually, laying down new carpets and putting fresh wallpaper on the walls. Such improvements made clear that the Arch was no noisy, disorderly pit, but a wholesome theatrical venue.

Wheatley even managed to persuade a prominent New York divine, the Reverend Dr. Bellows, to express his approval of play going. "I cannot trust the man that never laughs, that has no apparent outlets for the natural springs of sportiveness and gaiety that are perennial in the human soul," Bellows intoned in the pages of *Wheatley's Gift*, a free magazine available at the box office. "It gives me a sincere moral gratification to see innocent pleasures and popular amusements resisting the religious bigotry that frowns so unwisely upon them." Indeed, according to this Christian minister, evil consequences awaited anyone who, out of misguided piety, denied himself the pleasure of seeing a wholesome play. The joylessness of "unmitigated Puritanism," he warned, filled men's minds with a "morbid excitement" and led inexorably to "secret vices, malignant sins, and horrid crimes."

Wheatley's campaign to attract "the beauty, fashion and intelligence" of Philadelphia made his theater an ideal school for young actors. John Wilkes Booth's position at the Arch promised to give him the kind of dramatic training he had yearned for during his long winters on the Harford County farm, with his sister Asia as his only teacher, and confusion his only result.

"Nothing requires more labor and untiring application than the dramatic art," Wheatley warned beginners at the Arch. "Many young men and women are attracted by the glare of the stage," the impresario said, but they soon learn it is a life of "toil, deprivation and poverty." For all but a few, the work was punishing and the wages worse than paltry—they were, in fact, insulting. In 1858, hardworking supes earned about $300 per season, about the same as unskilled laborers like farmworkers and hod carriers, the rough equivalent of $12,000 a year in twenty-first-century currency. A supe's annual pay was less than what a plumber, painter, or bricklayer might earn. For a comparison within the world of the theater, a star player easily could earn $300 in a single night. John's salary, his mother Mary Ann complained, would barely "keep [him] in cigars." The eight dollars he took home each week was not enough to cover his boardinghouse rent or the cost of new clothes, restaurant meals, train fare to Baltimore, and a daily drink or two of brandy.

A fellow actor once described John Wilkes Booth as a person who wanted "generally to fall in with the sentiment of the crowd." He was eager to belong. Yet when John started working at Wheatley's, he found it hard to shake his status as an outsider, despite his famous name. The acting troupe, John discovered, was an institution as regimented and disciplined as his old military academy, St. Timothy's Hall.

Plunged into the dizzying turnaround of rehearsals and openings, John Wilkes struggled to learn over a dozen plays during his first two weeks of work alone. The pace of work was a tough initiation for any amateur. Lessons came at John from every direction. Mr. Fredericks supervised the actors and managed rehearsals, wielding total authority. In order not to be entirely lost backstage, John needed to learn the language of Mr. Church, the stage manager. Mr. Church was the source of the cues—the soft ringing of a bell, a series of raps, a gaslight flashed in signal—that informed stagehands when to lift the curtain, when to raise or lower the backdrops or lighting, and when to produce special effects like the sound of rain or the clip-clop of horses' hoofs.

Mr. Johnson, wardrobe master, taught John the mysteries of applying makeup and of faking historically correct costumes out of material at hand. Fine points of dress were crucial to creating each play's illusion of time and place. Through 165 nights of walk-on parts, John had to master the footwear styles of two millennia: from sandals worn by a Roman centurion to slippers with cross-gartered hose from the days of King Henry VIII, peasants' sabots, medieval boots, and the bejeweled heels worn by eighteenth-century French courtiers. Wigs, mustaches, and paste-on beards were other challenges to tackle, as were the correct wearing of slashed velvet trunks, Scottish kilts, Elizabethan ruffs, togas, and a Quaker's plain garb. As one actress remembered, "all this detail was troublesome to the beginner," but once acquired, "foundation training in such matters was never forgotten."

John did not prove an apt pupil. The life he led prior to signing on with the Philadelphia troupe was no preparation for the seriousness of this kind of work. At Reverend Lamb's Quaker academy, John's reputation was that of a disruptive bully. At St. Timothy's Hall, his response to the headmaster's strict rules had been hostile disobedience. In the four years he spent on his mother's farm after his father's death, John worked little and did as he pleased. A family friend recalled, "None had influence over him . . . what he willed, he did." By the time he reached Wheatley's, submitting to an authority other than his own was a foreign experience.

There was another reason John did not shine in his first theatrical apprenticeship. A veteran of Wheatley's theater later told a newspaper reporter that as a supe, John Wilkes Booth "lacked enterprise." In a person with John's heritage, theater people expected to see serious dedication to the art of acting. For a Booth to show laziness or a lack of hustle looked like disrespect to the profession.

John was not a favorite with Mr. Fredericks. According to one company member, Fredericks "made constant complaints of Booth," calling him "a careless fellow" and opining that the son of the great Junius showed "no promise" whatsoever. Like any stage director, Fredericks expected earnestness, humility, and above all, hard work from his supernumeraries. "Wilkes Booth," recalled one Arch Street actor, "seemed too slow or indifferent" to impress his superiors.

Most actors at Wheatley's believed the young man expected good parts to come his way no matter how he behaved. The moment he arrived in Philadelphia, they claimed, John Booth appeared to be puffed with "gossamer hopes and high conceit," a novice with a deluded sense of his prospects for success. The attitude won him few friends at the Arch.

Perhaps it was Edwin Booth's homecoming that encouraged John in these assumptions. Edwin's California riches may have led John to believe it was only a matter of time before he himself would win a share of glory. After all, he was taller, stronger, and handsomer than Edwin, and much more like their father in appearance.

ALTHOUGH JOHN WILKES DID NOT EARN HIS PART IN *LUCRETIA BORGIA* through any personal merit, the newcomer did make one concession to what everyone recognized as his lack of experience: on all Wheatley's playbills and posters, Booth was billed as "J. B. Wilkes." It had been agreed among his family that John would not use "Booth" professionally until he had more acting experience. The name was a commodity in American theater. An awkward or untrained member of the clan might diminish the late star's reputation. The moment "he made his reputation as an actor," John explained to a friend, "he would take back" the name his father made great.

Most of the audience knew nevertheless who John's father was. His resemblance to the dead star was striking, and outside the margins of handbills, he always called himself Booth. Though not using the family name tonight, "J. B. Wilkes" stood onstage wearing some of the choicest pieces of his father's wardrobe. His legs were encased in silk hose and velvet shoes that once belonged to Junius Brutus Booth. The tight-fitting black tunic he now wore, called a hauberk, once served his father for a Hamlet costume. A cash-strapped Mary Ann Booth, in lieu of any other inheritance, had given the treasures from the dead actor's trunks to her favorite son.

Tonight's story, a tale of doomed love between a mother and child, must have appealed to John's feelings. The woman at the center of *Lucretia Borgia* was a tantalizing melodramatic creation, the sympathetic villainess. Borgia, a murderer, was as evil as she was beautiful. She had consolidated wealth and political power through a long career of killing. Yet when the play opens, the poisoner discovers she has one streak of human virtue left: a quality that endears her to every mother, and every mother's son, in the audience.

Twenty years before, while yet a teenager, Lucretia Borgia had a son, Gennaro. To protect him from her enemies, she sent the child into hiding and concealed the evidence of his birth. As the curtain lifts on the first scene, Gennaro has grown to manhood. Unaware of his true parentage, he is now a soldier of fortune, a wandering cavalier, pure of heart, honorable, and good—everything his mother is not. Borgia has come to Venice to find Gennaro, whom she has loved throughout twenty anguishing years of separation. She longs to be reunited with this lost child, yet she is afraid to disclose her identity to him, for fear he will reject her. If she can win Gennaro's love, if he will accept her as his mother, it will be her redemption.

John Wilkes played the part of Ascanio Petrucca, Gennaro's best friend and a fellow soldier. In the first act, Lucretia is walking the streets of Venice in a Carnival mask to search for her son. As she approaches the group of cavaliers, she hears Gennaro and Ascanio, along with four other soldiers, swearing to avenge themselves against Lucretia Borgia for her murderous deeds.

"My very name excites horror, wherever heard," Lucretia exclaims in remorse. "And all Italy hates me! Ah me! How sad my fate! I was not born to be the thing I am!"

In her distress, Lucretia's mask slips from her face, and she is recognized by the cavaliers. Torn between fear and shame, she falls to the ground at center stage as the young men, including her son, approach, prepared to confront her with a litany of the murders she and her henchmen have committed.

"No, no, no!" she cries. "Have compassion, though I merit none! O do not speak! Not before Gennaro!"

The scene is one of the best in the play: audiences relished the ensuing confrontation. Stage directions called for the leading lady to wear a low-cut gown crusted with jewels. Kneeling before her circle of accusers, Lucretia weeps and tears her hair, pleading for mercy. It was an opportunity for the star actress to pull out all the stops, pushing her emotions to the limit. She was supposed to writhe and grovel as the soldiers, drawing out their swords and pointing the blades at her throat, listed her crimes.

"Madam," thunders one, "I am Maffio Orsini, brother to the Duke of Gravinia, whom you caused to be stabbed in his dungeon!"

"Madam," declares another, "I am Jeppo Liveretto, brother of Liveretto Vittelli, whom your ruffians strangled while he slept!"

It was John Wilkes's turn to speak. He had started the play with composure, managing to deliver his first line without mishap. Now he was supposed to yank his rapier from its scabbard and stalk forward, growling these words:

"Madam, I am Ascanio Petrucca, cousin of Pandolpho Petrucco, Lord of Sienne, who was assassinated by your order, that you might seize his fair city!"

The description of what occurred next comes "fresh from the mouths of actors" present with John on the stage. Their report found its way into the pages of the *New York World*. Keyed with agitation, tormented by the Italian syllables tangling on his tongue, John Wilkes blundered. In one instant he turned this melodrama, charged with sexual tension and fear, into a farce.

"Madam," he quavered, "I am Pondolfo Pet-Pedolfio Pat-Pantuchio Ped—damn it, what am I?"

The night's elaborately constructed illusion suddenly fell in pieces. John's stumble broke the atmosphere of tragedy, and the audience burst into laughter.

It was a humiliating moment not only for John, but also for the other players, especially the star actress, whose great moment had been ruined. Trapped in a tragic posture on her knees, with the audience roaring at the mistake of a raw supe, she looked a laughingstock.

The best way to move a scene forward after a blunder like John's was for the ensemble to appear deaf to the sound of laughter from the auditorium, and carry on with the work. "We were all conscious of the audience, of course," one actress explained, "but there was a sort of dead line that separated the stage from the spectators."

Instead of following this rule, John Wilkes made things worse by breaking out of character, turning to the crowd and acknowledging their merriment. As one of Wheatley's players remembered, young Booth "though full of chagrin," started "to laugh with them." With great effort, other actors managed to pull the scene back on track, but the mood in the theater had fallen flat. The play creaked onward to its tragic climax, in which Gennaro, still ignorant of his parentage, mistakenly drinks the poisoned wine Borgia planned to give to another. As his last act on earth, the dying youth raises a knife against Lucretia.

"Fate decrees it!" bellows Gennaro, stabbing her in the heart, "You must die!"

In her death throes, Borgia shrieks the secret: *"I am your mother!"*

Hearing the revelation, Gennaro responds, according to the script, with "a scream of despair." The curtain drops while a gaggle of supes, dressed as monks, chants a funeral dirge. After John's comic disruption, the scene looked ludicrous.

The next night, Wednesday, "J. B. Wilkes" was scheduled to take to the stage once more, this time in *The Gamester*, a cautionary tale of how a husband's gambling addiction lands him in debtor's prison and impoverishes his wife and children. John would play Dawson, one of the villains who lead the main character on the road to ruin.

Setting the disaster of *Lucretia Borgia* behind him, John Wilkes spent hours fussing over his Dawson costume, making, as one Arch Street actor derisively sniffed, "abundant preparation to do himself honor." John Wilkes was so confident his appearance would win the audience's admiration, a fellow player recalled, he "invited a lady he knew to visit the theater, and witness his triumph."

Experienced members of the company disapproved. Again John Wilkes was failing to show an apprentice's proper spirit. After disrupting a production and embarrassing the star performer, low-ranking John owed the entire cast a contrite apology. Behaving as if his disgrace had never happened was unseemly. His plan to impress one particular audience member was unprofessional. According to a supe of Booth's own age working at another theater, "familiarity between the players and the public was not tolerated. I never saw our actors playing to individuals or groups in the audience." These were errors of conduct John's fellow actors chalked up to his overgrown self-importance. Theater manager John T. Ford, who knew Wilkes well, once explained that this Booth brother "was animated by a pride that contained elements of insanity."

The moment Dawson made his entrance that night, a Wheatley veteran recalled, the audience made its feelings known. At the sight of Booth, derisive sounds erupted from gallery and orchestra: hoots, laughter, "hisses and mock applause." The man who had fouled his lines in Tuesday's tragedy would not be allowed to try his luck tonight. The noise made by the crowd engulfed the cast of *The Gamester*. One actor remembered John Wilkes's face as he heard the catcalls echo across the stage: the "haughty" youth was "struck dumb" with astonishment. John had not dreamed of a hostile reception. He stood rooted on the spot, his body "rigid, with nothing to say." The uproar in the auditorium continued until "J. B. Wilkes" took himself offstage.

Wheatley's company now made a quick decision: the audience would allow the play to continue only if John's character was cut out of the story. Actors improvised the remaining scenes around Dawson's absence.

Facing his peers in the greenroom afterward was like walking a gauntlet. John's pride smarted, and he surely felt the burden of his famous name. The young actor's regular letters home to his mother, Mary Ann, from this time, have not survived. Yet in February 1858, Mrs. Booth hinted at John's bruised feelings when she sent a page of family news to her eldest son, June Booth, in San Francisco. "I think John wishes he had been something else now," Mary Ann mused, "but he won't acknowledge it."

Sleeper Clarke urged the young man to stay on in Philadelphia in spite of these disappointments, but John refused. As Mary Ann Booth explained, "He don't want to. He is for trying another City." After the last performance of the season on June 19, 1858, John packed his trunks and left. Wheatley's troupe was glad to see him go. Management, under pressure to "cut down the company," found it easy, one actor remembered, "to dispense with Wilkes Booth." He made few friends during his ten months in Philadelphia. He found no one to serve as teacher to him; indeed, at Wheatley's John seemed to resist the very idea of being taught.

The one connection John did make, he was eager to drop. In the spring, a girl living at his boardinghouse—perhaps the same young woman invited to witness John's triumph in *The Gamester*—announced she was pregnant. Local gossips whispered that John Wilkes, the putative father, was "compelled to pay a considerable sum of money . . . just as he was about to quit the city" to compensate this girl for her "shame and ruin," and to repay her parents for the "domestic insult." "It had not been a good year. After such a disastrous introduction to stage life, "J. B. Wilkes" was no closer to earning the privilege of acting under his own last name.

High summer 1858 found John on the familiar streets of east Baltimore. Charles Pope, an actor with John T. Ford's company in the city's Holliday Street Theatre, saw John for the first time during those hot months, and never forgot the encounter. They met one afternoon in a pool hall next door to an Episcopal church in downtown Baltimore. The place was well known, Pope remembered, for being managed by a burly Irishman, Michael Phelan, "then the champion of the cue." The two actors played billiards, John winning every game. "He was an expert," Pope later admitted, impressed by the twenty-year-old's "easy movements of alluring, springy grace." Most of all, Pope was astonished to see how close a copy John Wilkes was of his father. "It has been my happiness to know them all personally," Pope wrote of the Booths, "from the first, Junius Brutus, to the last and youngest." Out of all the brothers, it was John alone who possessed "the classic Booth head," he observed, "above broad shoulders and a deep chest."

Pope would not have to look far for the original version of John's features. Though the elder Booth had been dead five years, a reproduction of the star's face recently had arrived in Baltimore. A newspaper reporter at the harbor, along with a small crowd of gawkers, watched stevedores wrestling two pieces of stone off the deck of a steamship. First came a towering, four-sided obelisk of white Italian marble; next, its granite base, five feet in height, like the cornerstone of some ancient pyramid. Junius Brutus Booth's head was carved onto one side of the obelisk. A wreath of laurel leaves—the hero's crown—was chiseled around temples. Booth appeared in his youthful perfection, before the decades of drinking, fighting, and hard traveling had changed his looks. This monument—shipped at great expense from the famed Boston studio of sculptor Joseph Carew—was bound for Baltimore's Green Mount Cemetery.

The actor was to have a new grave. Groundskeepers set to work unearthing his body from Baltimore Cemetery, and that of old Richard Booth, Junius's father, who died in 1840. The two coffins were transferred to a fresh plot in the shadow of the twenty-foot-high monolith. The unveiling of this marker took place on May 1, 1858, the sixty-second anniversary of the actor's birth. Edwin Booth paid for everything. He made all the arrangements, choosing the sculptor, approving the design, and specifying that his father's face and name appear prominently. Edwin also erased his grandfather's Jewish heritage at this time. When the transfer of bodies was made, Richard Booth's original tombstone with its Hebrew inscription was discarded, replaced by a new marker decorated with a Christian cross and Latin lettering.

For the epitaph on Junius Brutus Booth's memorial, Edwin chose Mark Antony's benediction over the body of Brutus, Caesar's assassin, in *Julius Caesar*. He took lines from the speech beginning, "This was the noblest Roman of them all," delivered by Antony in honor of a killer who did not, he explains, commit his crime "in envy of great Caesar," but rather to bring "common good to all." Carved in granite over Booth's grave were the final three lines of benediction:

> HIS LIFE WAS GENTLE, AND THE ELEMENTS
> SO MIXED IN HIM, THAT NATURE MIGHT STAND UP
> AND SAY TO ALL THE WORLD—THIS WAS A MAN.

Edwin Booth, Charles Pope perceived in the summer of 1858, was bent on becoming the heir apparent. He was ready to prove himself the one who was worthy "to fill the void left by his father's death." The Booth name had been absent from the East Coast theaters for years, and during that time Americans' tastes in entertainment had changed. "The fancy of the day," Asia Booth later recalled, "was to ignore Shakespeare." Now that Edwin was home again, this monument to his father and the solemn ceremony of the actor's reinterment formed part of a campaign to reestablish his father's legacy. The obsequies and the outsize obelisk were to remind people that the dead star's crown was one worth inheriting.

John Wilkes Booth seems to have missed the May 1 unveiling of his father's impressive memorial. On that Saturday in 1858, he was in Philadelphia, appearing in a play called *The Limrick Boy*. Only after his return to Baltimore in June 1858 would he pay his respects at Green Mount Cemetery, contemplating the huge marker Edwin planted there.

One more tombstone, humble and almost hidden by clustering poplar trees in a quiet Catholic graveyard off Baltimore's Eden Street, was erected in the spring of 1858. The Booth family was acutely aware of its existence, and of the bare facts etched on its surface that could not be denied. The telltale inscription no doubt had been composed by the grave's occupant before her death on March 9, 1858:

JESUS, MARY AND JOSEPH, PRAY FOR THE SOUL OF
MARY CHRISTINE ADELAIDE DELANNOY,
WIFE OF JUNIUS BRUTUS BOOTH, TRAGEDIAN.
IT IS A HOLY AND WHOLESOME THOUGHT TO PRAY FOR THE DEAD.
MAY SHE REST IN PEACE.

Death in 1858 put an end to Adelaide's persecution of the Booths, but her gravestone remained a rebuke, proof that her husband's American-born offspring were bastards. Richard Junius Booth, Adelaide's son, continued to live in Baltimore, a teacher of languages, dour witness to what would be a prosperous, eventful new chapter in the lives of his half siblings.

UPON HIS HOMECOMING, TWENTY-THREE-YEAR-OLD EDWIN STEPPED into his father's empty place, taking full responsibility for his family, shocked to discover the meager existence they endured during his years in California. Edwin closed Tudor Hall immediately and whisked the family off the farm and back to Baltimore, installing Mary Ann, Asia, Rosalie, John Wilkes, and Joseph in a comfortable town house at 7 North High Street, in their old neighborhood. Tenant farmers took over Bel Air farm and its 150 acres. Later, Mary Ann sold the house. The Booths would never live there again.

"My poor Mother!" Edwin exclaimed in a letter to a friend, referring to the hungry winters, financial anxiety, and legal battles Mary Ann Booth had endured in five years of widowhood in Harford County. "I . . . thought my father a man of means," Edwin reproached himself. During all his time away, the actor claimed, the sufferings of his mother and four siblings were "unknown to me."

Edwin had amends to make to the family. Even as they rejoiced at his return, mother and siblings made clear he owed them a living. Edwin's money paid John Wilkes's tab at Murphy's billiard hall, covered the rent on the town house, bought new clothing for Mary Ann, Rosalie, and Asia, as well as food, books and music, writing paper, and other luxuries that had been thrown aside ever since Mrs. Booth had met a lead coffin in Cincinnati instead of the husband she was expecting to see.

A process of accommodation began as the Maryland Booths learned to know Edwin again. None of them could forget how this son had let the family breadwinner make his own way home. In a sign that Edwin was not forgiven for his past neglect, Mary Ann denied the young actor's request for what he considered his rightful inheritance: Junius's theatrical wardrobe. The heaps of satin, brocaded velvet and silk; the stage jewelry, chain mail, and weapons; the staggering assortment of shoes; the makeup case: Edwin knew each piece in the collection by heart, from his years of servitude as valet and dresser to the star. No monument Edwin could build to Booth's memory, however grandiose, would move Mary Ann to reward him with those costumes. Her husband's stage dresses, the only things to survive the actor's journey home, were for John Wilkes, the son who stayed by her side.

John Wilkes, too, struggled with the fact of his older brother's return. "When I went with my father to California," Edwin later wrote, "I left [John] a mere schoolboy . . . a rattle-pated fellow." Edwin now found his brother fully grown and a stranger to him. Since the disastrous end of their acting company, the Tripple Alley players, little love had been lost between the two. The passage of six years had done nothing to improve the relationship. John was used to being the man of the house, the sole object of his mother and sisters' care. Edwin's homecoming displaced him.

Edwin's business manager, Ben Baker, started scouting theaters for engagements the moment he arrived back "in America," as travelers from San Francisco liked to joke, in the summer of 1856. To the hordes of new theatergoers packing auditoriums from New York to New Orleans, Edwin was practically a foreigner, but to Laura Keene, who now owned a successful theater in Manhattan—Laura Keene's Varieties—he was a known quantity.

Despite their troubled romantic past, Laura was eager to hire Edwin to be leading man in her company. Between themselves, however, Edwin and Ben decided this was a bad idea. Leading men were tied to one theater by contract and drew a fixed, modest salary. The fastest route to riches, though the least secure, was to establish Edwin Booth as an independent touring star, like his father had been. Baker's job was to sell the concept of the new Booth's talent all along the eastern seaboard.

In 1886, a reporter for the *New York Star* caught up with Ben Baker, then "close on the scriptural three score years and ten," to ask about his glory days, thirty years gone, trouping the national circuit as Edwin Booth's first agent, years before the Civil War. "Money," Ben Baker said, at the thought of the gold he had struck with the skinny, raven-haired son of the great Booth. "That was what we were both after then." Between them, actor and manager were a winning combination—by the end of their eighteen months together, they had raked in well over $10,000—a sum roughly equal to $400,000 in today's currency. "Uncle Ben," as he liked to be called, reserved a cut for himself, while the rest of this river of money flowed to Mary Ann, Rosalie, and Asia; to Edwin's brother June, who was broke in California; and to John, whose pockets were empty after his single low-paid season in Philadelphia.

It was not hard to book a Booth. Edwin, unlike "J. B. Wilkes," had license to use his father's name. Most theater owners, including John T. Ford, remembered the sad-eyed boy who, trailing in Junius Brutus Booth's drunken wake, had worked supporting roles, cleaned costumes, and "imbibed most of his father's great characters by ear." Old hands in the theater profession knew which son Junius Brutus Booth had picked to be his successor. Ford invited Edwin to open at the Marshall Theater in Richmond, which he now operated, the same stage where, in 1821, a young Junius Brutus Booth gave his first American performance.

Edwin hewed close to the old Southern routes his father had followed, playing at the National Theatre in Washington, D.C., then taking his act through Wheeling, Pittsburgh, Charleston, Savannah, Montgomery, and New Orleans. It was a deliberate strategy: Edwin was claiming his father's old territory, revisiting familiar places, reviving his father's business connections, and reminding audiences that the Booth genius was marching onward. Like Junius before him, Edwin would not try his luck in New York until he felt he was ready.

Each time they rolled into a town, Baker went to a printer's shop to order up posters that shouted, in spiky black letters, praise for the amazing Edwin Booth. Edwin was "The Inheritor of his Father's Genius," the handbills said, a "Prodigy!" and a "World-Renowned Young American Tragedian!" Edwin, friends later reported, "was horrified" by this booster's tactic. It was not that he doubted the truth of Baker's boasts—no one knew better than Edwin the true extent of his own powers—but this shrewd young man did not want audiences to turn against him for showing arrogance. Audiences would like him better, he reasoned, if he approached them with humility. Edwin had "a horror of ostentation," a fellow actor remembered. The twenty-three-year-old star deliberately cultivated a "modest and unassuming" demeanor on his early tours. Asia reports that Edwin told her he did not want to seem like "a vainglorious young actor who was coming to demand rather than to deserve applause."

The circumstances of a two-man team trouping through the American South and Southwest in 1857 did not include bodily comfort. "The nomadic season," one veteran player wrote, "is a time of miserable unhappiness and utter homesickness." Even the oppressed, toiling existence of a supernumerary was "preferable to one-night stands in Oshkosh, Peoria or Skowhegan," he said. Like traveling actors before and since, the two rode for miles over the expanding network of railroads, enduring, Edwin wrote to his friend Joe Jefferson, a fellow actor, the "gut-shaking" rattle of the cars and breathing "nothing but coal smoke." They stopped at every point on the line, "athirst and mad'er'n hell," hungry for some kind of "grub," a place to perform and "a double-bedded room" for the night, where the star then suffered the awful sound of his manager's snores. "Baker sleepeth," Edwin reported, "but he giveth voice."

Ben remembered that before setting off on tour, both men hoped "the widow of old Booth" would relent and "give Edwin her husband's wardrobe." She did not, so their store of costumes was at first a makeshift and meager affair. Ben recalled, "I made most of the costumes he wore on that tour myself. After a performance, I would sit up for a couple of hours . . . and sew like a good one, while Ted sat by smoking his pipe." With "ingenious twisting," Ben even adapted his own frock coat to suit some of Edwin's characters, basting scraps of fur to collar and skirt, turning the everyday garment into an eighteenth-century prince's robe.

They hit the big towns and the small, playing where the money was and where it often was not. Barnstorming was a gamble, Edwin told Jefferson, complaining both of crowds that never showed up and of crowds that "looked as if they didn't know more than to chew tobacco and not swallow the juice." Whatever he privately thought of the people who came to see the son of Junius Brutus Booth, Edwin did his best to please them, pouring his talent out in the cold attic over a carriage shop that served Wheeling for a theater, or in the converted tobacco barn where the residents of Lee's Landing, Virginia, gathered for entertainment.

The logistical tangles of backcountry touring left Edwin unfazed. One night, he and a group of other itinerants were putting on *The Merchant of Venice* at a tiny port in tidewater Virginia. A sizable audience of tobacco planters collected for the occasion. Before Edwin could walk on for the last act, the famous trial scene, Baker grabbed his protégé's arm and whispered some unfortunate news. The steamboat they planned to leave on that night was departing ahead of schedule. If the actors and their luggage were not aboard in time, the travelers would be stranded in this out-of-the-way place, perhaps for several days, until the next boat came.

"If we explain matters," Baker said, "[the audience] will think they are being cheated, and we will have a free fight. The only thing is for you to get up some sort of impromptu ending and ring down the curtain."

Edwin had an improvisatory wit that often came to his rescue. He was playing the part of Bassanio that night, and in this role he cut short the trial scene, the climax of the play, without offending the audience. As the actors took their places before the Venetian judge, who would decide if Shylock, the moneylender, could cut a pound of flesh from his enemy as payment for a debt, Bassanio forestalled all dialogue. He turned to Shylock and asked with deadpan seriousness:

"You are bound to have the flesh, are you?"

"You bet your life," growled Shylock, gamely.

"Now I'll make you an offer," proposed Booth. "In addition to this big bag of ducats, I'll throw in two kegs of tobacco, a shotgun, and two of the best coon dogs in the state."

"I'm blarmed if I don't do it!" cried Shylock, suddenly grinning.

"And to show that there's no ill-feeling," trilled the lady playing Portia, doing her best to speed things along, "we'll wind up with a Virginny reel."

No one in the audience was fooled by this absurd finale. Virginians of the planter classes knew their Shakespeare like they knew their Bible, inside and out. Everyone in the theater had heard the steamboat's whistle and could guess the reason for the actors' haste. Yet Edwin's charm, his knack for winning an audience's goodwill, worked its usual magic. Bassanio's ridiculous offer, Baker remembered, drew roars of laughter from the crowd.

THERE WAS A POPULAR SAYING IN THE BOOTH HOUSEHOLD IN 1857, THE year Edwin paid cash to commission his father's marble obelisk: "Every man builds his own monument." The motto had a larger significance for Asia Booth as she watched her older brother setting to work building his own professional reputation—performance by performance, review by review— as if he were layering stone upon stone. The verdict of newspapers in the Northeast, particularly in Boston and New York, was crucial. Asia wrote that Edwin's debuts in those places would "decide his future." At this moment, the entrance of a writer named Adam Badeau into Edwin's world transformed the twenty-three-year-old's prospects. When Badeau became Edwin's champion in the spring of 1857, the young actor's "monument" assembled so swiftly, and on a scale so grand, that the course of his life, and that of his brother John Wilkes, would never be the same.

In years to come, Captain Adam Badeau would earn a place in history for his role as aide-de-camp to General Ulysses S. Grant during the bloodiest years of the Civil War. Badeau was at Grant's side as his private secretary throughout the Wilderness campaign, and at Appomattox, where Badeau witnessed Robert E. Lee's surrender.

In 1857 Badeau was not yet a soldier, but a fashionable man about town, a lover of the arts who might be spotted anytime, he joked, "lazily lounging in the lobbies" of Manhattan's theaters and museums. Badeau had a sizable bank account, inherited from his father, and an openness about his homosexuality that was rare in nineteenth-century New York. He was a popular presence in the city's highest circles, an acknowledged wit who penned a regular column on art, fashion, and society gossip for the *Sunday Times* under the alias of "Vagabond." "I have a connection and an influence with press," Badeau would say, smiling, "but I am independent of it as a means of support."

By May 1857, Edwin Booth and Ben Baker had traded the rough terrain of the American South for New York City. For the first time in five years, posters emblazoned with the name "Booth" could be seen on street corners near Broadway and West Third Street, where Burton's Metropolitan Theatre stood. Baker, in typical style, trumpeted Junius's son Edwin as "the Hope of the Living Drama." "I had no great expectations from such an announcement," scoffed Badeau, who could be an acid-tongued critic when displeased, and knew well the false puffery of playbills. He went into the auditorium unhopeful.

"I remember even now, after the lapse of thirty-six years," Badeau wrote in 1893, how the "whole face and form" of the man onstage "were ablaze with expression—literally transfigured . . . I never saw or heard anything more tremendous." The play was *Richard III*. He remembered Edwin was so dazzling that people could not wait for scenes to finish or the curtain to fall between acts, but spontaneously, throughout the performance, they "rose in all parts of the house and shouted with delight." As for Badeau, he was immobilized where he sat.

Badeau dashed home and wrote a review for the *Sunday Times*. "I have been several times, of late, to see the young genius who is playing at Burton's Theatre," the Vagabond began. Referring to the scarcity of native talent in his young republic, Badeau asserted, "America has yet produced no Milton, no Mozart." If people wanted to witness the emergence of a quintessential "type of American art," to discover the pure expression of their nation's unique spirit, Badeau urged them, "go to see Booth every night next week."

The gift this actor possessed was "the true development of the American mind; the result of democracy, of individuality, of the expansion of each, of the liberty allowed to all." Though he did not yet know the history of Edwin's wild and varied experiences traveling along the Mississippi and across the frontier, Badeau perceived that the young man somehow had been "inspired by the mighty forest, by the thousand miles of river, by the broad continent we call our own."

Badeau realized this new shoot of the Booth tree was attempting to change how Shakespeare was performed. He was not copying his father—far from it. Edwin was reaching for something "quieter," he said, than the "sledge-hammer style" of old-school dramatic oratory. Patrons of theaters like the Bowery, it was said, "never heard any sound short of thunder and never felt anything till it was hit with a club." Edwin was trying to perform Shakespeare in a new mode, not with the seething energy of a prizefight, as his father had done, but reasonably and deliberately, with attention to the subtleties of the poet's language.

For Badeau, Edwin's fresh approach arrived in perfect time to please "the refined and fastidious classes" now making their way to well-appointed playhouses. "Is it heresy to talk of an actor giving fuller utterance to Shakespeare's ideas?" Badeau demanded in his review. "If the human constitution is capable of passions too fleeting, too intricate, too tremendous to get entire embodiment in the language even of a Shakespeare, may not another genius incarnate those emotions in another form, which the poet has first suggested?"

In Edwin Booth, Badeau promised his readers, the future of American acting was revealed. This kind of genius, Badeau declared, appears "only in two or three men in an age. When I can see them, I throw away my books. My soul is reached through the medium of my senses."

Badeau sent a copy of his review to Edwin, along with a note offering the actor his services as a guide, adviser, and friend. "The fact that I am a young man like yourself, may make my letter seem assuming," Badeau began, "but it is induced only by the warmest and kindest feeling, and by the absolute anxiety I entertain for your future and entire success." Badeau told Edwin that as an actor, he was "uneven and fitful," yet "in every part [you] play [you] do something no other actor could rival." Edwin was on the right track, but he was a rough diamond. Between them, Badeau suggested, actor and critic could work together to make Edwin's innovative approach the new theatrical sensation.

"There are yet degrees of excellence unreached by you," Badeau urged. If Edwin would only accept his help, he assured him, "there are certainly no heights you may not attain, no distinction social or professional which may not be yours, if you please." The writer closed his letter with a plea. "It would be a positive unkindness to leave me unvisited. I beg you to write to me, and assure me that you do not misconstrue my conduct, to tell me that you will not neglect the marvelous powers with which nature has gifted you; that you appreciate the sincerity and ardor of the regard entertained for you, by, my dear Sir, your most cordial friend and admirer." Adam's offer appealed to Edwin. He, unlike his brother John Wilkes, as one family friend observed, "was not too conceited or too indifferent to learn." The actor replied immediately, agreeing to a meeting. They spent a Sunday together in June 1857, and, as Badeau later wrote, "from that time till his marriage and my entrance into the army, we were as intimate as is possible for two young men to be."

Adam felt an attachment to Edwin Booth that the actor could not return, yet "Ad" and "Ned," as they called each other, soon became inseparable. The actor knew the journalist was a useful, even invaluable, asset to his career.

Badeau proved an excellent teacher. He wanted to give a scholarly depth to Booth's pragmatic knowledge of Shakespeare. Over the summer of 1857, the two spent hours in New York's Astor Library, and in the private libraries and museums of the city's wealthiest collectors, to which the well-connected Badeau had easy access. Together they read histories of the English stage and studied facsimile editions of the First Folio. They researched the costumes and set designs used by the Lord Chamberlain's Men at the court of Queen Elizabeth, with an eye to re-creating them. Badeau pushed Edwin relentlessly, urging him to refine his interpretations of the great roles. The critic sat for hours, pen in hand, watching the actor perform, and ready to jot down ideas for improvement, while Edwin tried obsessively to perfect, as he later recalled, "every movement, every expression of face, every tone of the voice."

Adam was more than acting coach to Edwin. He wanted to mold this pipe-smoking social outsider who had left school at age twelve into a well-rounded gentleman. "Ad" forced "Ned" to learn French, and schooled him in contemporary American literature, painting, and sculpture. Moreover, he gave the onetime resident of San Francisco's hard-boozing shantytown a bracing tutorial in society manners.

"I was very anxious that Booth should receive social recognition," Badeau later remembered. "Thirty years ago, actors had not overleaped the barriers which existed for centuries, to anything like the extent we know at present, and I wanted him to meet people of distinction."

New York was then a city of one million people, but members of Manhattan's high society at the time dubbed it the city "of Four Hundred," referring to the handful of families who occupied its loftiest social precincts. Badeau launched Edwin Booth into this world, introducing the actor to artists, intellectuals, and literary men—most of whom are forgotten now, but were then the trendsetters. All clamored to meet the idol of Badeau's reviews in the weekly *Times*. Edwin's handsome face, "rare modesty and unquestionable genius," these New Yorkers remembered, helped smooth the path of his social ascent. In due time, Adam even made a successful application on Edwin's behalf to the Century Club, storied bastion of New York's wealth, talent, and privilege.

With Adam Badeau as his ally, Edwin Booth was able to rise above the sphere of his origins—born in a log cabin, the illegitimate son of a drunken, scandal-plagued tragedian—to achieve a level of acceptance no American actor had before attained. It was a leap as dramatic in its way as the one Abraham Lincoln had made by 1857, rising from menial laborer on his father's farm, to successful lawyer and prominent Illinois politician, married to the daughter of a respected Kentucky family. Like Lincoln's, Edwin's social advancement was a solo one: it would take him far away from the workaday world inhabited by the rest of his family, including John Wilkes.

While "J. B. Wilkes" trod the boards at Philadelphia's Arch Street Theatre over the 1857–58 season, Edwin and Adam made the Booth name ring. The plaudits and profits Edwin received on a national tour that season were unequaled: at the St. Charles Theatre in New Orleans, the stage where Junius Brutus Booth gave his last performance, ovations for Edwin were plentiful. He was crowned with laurel leaves by fans. A bouquet of flowers, tossed to him from a balcony, was found to be weighted by a bag of gold coins attached to the stem. A set of antique silver, whose heavy platter, pitcher, and goblets could not safely be lobbed onstage, was delivered to the star's dressing room. Edwin recorded these successes in letters to Adam, who took a share of the credit. "That's the way, Ned," Badeau would respond, "you are not yet all I want you to be, but you can be it all: you can't be more, though, than I hope for."

The good-hearted "Uncle Ben," Edwin's faithful companion and promoter on his first starring tour, had been dispensed with once Badeau came on the scene. Edwin fired Baker when he saw how useful, how influential, the New York journalist could be.

At times, Edwin's abundance of talent—dramatic genius, charm, a writer's fluent way with words—made Badeau resentful. The pupil was outshining the teacher: "I read some fifty of your letters the other day (I've got 'em all) and upon my word they made me jealous: wit and humor and felicity of language and graceful style; why should you monopolize all the gifts? Stick to your acting; I am a writer, not you."

Badeau's affection for his friend, however, always won out. "Ned," he would write, "you are a prince." Each of Adam's letters to Edwin closed with the same, simple declaration of fealty: "yours, forever and forever, Ad."

The benefits of this friendship were not all one-sided. Adam had no living family. He lost his parents at a relatively young age; since then, his had been an isolated life, its early scenes passed in the company of tutors and at an expensive boarding school. In Booth, the highly intelligent Badeau found what he had been looking for: intimacy with a mind equal to his own. The actor had given the journalist a signet ring bearing the engraved image of Edwin Booth's face. The ring was not unlike the miniature that Lord Byron presented to Junius Brutus Booth in London decades before.

As Booth's friend and champion, Badeau found he had a passport into a world where outsiders—particularly drama critics—were rarely allowed. Adam had free run of the theaters where Edwin performed. He met stock players, supernumeraries, and chorus girls; he sat in on rehearsals and shared in a backstage camaraderie only dreamed of before, in his earlier career as a lone watcher from the audience. A private box was always on reserve in Adam's name, courtesy of management, who knew what one of his columns was worth. Yet the writer inevitably could be found in the star's dressing room before a show, watching Edwin apply his makeup, marveling at the actor's process of self-transformation and reporting on it—his exclusive, behind-the-scenes scoop—for the *Sunday Times*.

Badeau discovered after less than a year of friendship that Booth's flaws were as serious as his gifts were great. The actor was subject to "fits of sadness and silence," Badeau observed, "a feeling that evil was hanging over him, that he could come to no good. These moods would pass, but would return. The depression that settled over his nature at intervals seemed a premonition of some awful future."

To cope with the moods, Edwin drank. His addiction was uncontrollable, Adam discovered, just as Laura Keene had found when she traveled with Edwin to Australia. The self-destruction of which his friend was capable, Badeau recalled, "was appalling to witness, and must have been still more appalling to endure. Doubtless he inherited it from his father."

Enduring one of Edwin's rampages through the bars of Sydney in 1855 had been enough for Laura Keene: she ended her affair with him on the spot. Adam felt differently. He accepted Edwin's drinking as the price the actor paid for his unique family history. Badeau made a joke of the episodic inebriation, and would help his friend dry out once the "fits" ran their course. "Take nothing stronger than water," Badeau would advise the actor before he departed on tour. In 1859, waiting in vain for a letter he expected to receive from Edwin, Badeau blamed alcohol for the lapse in correspondence: "Damn you. Tis just as likely as not you are on a spree; it is nearly five months since one of your performances of this sort, and since I have known you, you've never missed one in that space of time. You might have waited till I could take care of you."

Adam Badeau is the best source there is about what kind of person Edwin Booth was in private. The journalist's 1859 book *The Vagabond* is essentially a documentary history of their time together. In the hundreds of letters these two friends exchanged before, during, and after the Civil War, a portrait of the actor emerges in painful detail. Badeau's most confessional writing appeared in 1893, after Booth died. "I cannot portray him," Badeau wrote that year, "unless I make his sadness apparent; it was so strange and weird . . . this introspective, distant man, so old when he was young, so cold though gifted with every personal charm."

In the summer of 1858, soon after Edwin's monument to Junius Brutus Booth was erected in Green Mount Cemetery, the actor took Adam on a journey home, a trip into Booth history. The two young men—Edwin then twenty-four, and Badeau twenty-six—went to Baltimore together, where the actor introduced Adam to Mary Ann, Asia, Rosalie, John Wilkes, and Joseph, all living at 7 North High Street, "under Edwin's roof," Badeau wrote.

Badeau became party to all the family news, past and present. He was amazed to discover that Edwin supported not only his mother and sisters, but his brothers as well. The actor's success in drawing crowds to John T. Ford's theaters over the past year—Ford and his business partner, George Kunkel, operated playhouses in Baltimore, Washington, D.C., and Richmond—meant Edwin had been able to arrange jobs for his younger brothers in different parts of Ford's little empire. Eighteen-year-old Joseph, no talent for acting in his blood, earned four dollars a week as assistant ticket taker at Ford's Holliday Street Theatre in Baltimore. John Wilkes would go south to Richmond, to join Ford's stock company at the old Marshall Theatre for the 1858–59 season. More work as a supe awaited "J. B. Wilkes," but his wages this time would be better than in Philadelphia: $440 for the season, the same as his older brother earned in a week. Edwin supplemented his brothers' small salaries with regular loans of money—loans, Badeau later observed, that never would be repaid.

The two friends left the city at lunchtime and made the twenty-five-mile journey over dirt roads to the Bel Air farm. Badeau wrote about the excursion in *The Vagabond*, devoting an entire chapter to what he titled "A Night with the Booths." The young men hiked through the forest to reach the old log cabin, then up the path to the door of Tudor Hall. They brought a box of tapers, which they lit and placed in old shoes in lieu of candleholders, setting the improvised lamps about the abandoned, spider-infested house. As night wore on, dodging cobwebs by the flickering light, they unpacked and sorted what was left of Junius Brutus Booth's earthly possessions. Edwin told his friend the story of the dead actor's life, including some of the worst scenes from his own childhood. They rifled through what remained of Booth's wardrobe after Mary Ann gave John Wilkes his share, trying on costumes for Julius Caesar, Lear, and Shylock. When he fell asleep at last, near dawn, Badeau used "an ermine cloak that belonged to Macbeth" for a blanket.

It was a melancholy night for the journalist, who suddenly saw Edwin as the inheritor of an uncertain legacy: "I thought of the long career of triumphs the father had gone through, and wondered whether fate had in store for the youth at my side a corresponding history, as she had already showered on him corresponding gifts." Meeting John Wilkes Booth made little impression on Badeau; the young man was a minor figure in the family. "He was excessively handsome, even physically finer than Edwin," Badeau conceded, but there was no question in the journalist's mind which of the two was the "greater brother."

JOHN WILKES BOOTH ARRIVED IN RICHMOND IN LATE AUGUST 1858 TO take his place at the Marshall Theatre, still the heart of Richmond's cultural life. Its resident stock troupe of twenty-five actors and actresses, called the Dramatic Star Company, had a reputation for excellence. Manager John T. Ford and his partner George Kunkel enticed the biggest traveling stars to the Marshall's two-thousand-seat auditorium.

John arranged to share a room in a boardinghouse with another actor from his new company, Henry Langdon. "We get along very well," he said in a letter home. Kunkel gave John two speaking parts during his first week at the Marshall, to test him, but John, as usual, did not shine. Writing to Edwin what was essentially a thank-you note for finding him the job, John explained that his acting was hampered by his feeling "languid and stupid," blaming Richmond's climate. The warmth and humidity, he said, "don't agree with me. I have felt ill ever since I have been here."

Happily for John, however, he discovered that Richmond's gracious audiences could not have been more unlike the taunting critics of Philadelphia. No matter how awkward he was onstage, the residents of this city, John Wilkes told his sister Asia, "loved him for his father's sake." The son's physical resemblance to his parent created a stir of nostalgia and pride for old Junius Brutus Booth. "I like the people," John declared in a letter to Edwin on September 10, 1858, two weeks after he arrived. Though he was again billed as "J. B. Wilkes" on programs and posters, he informed Edwin proudly, "I believe everyone knows me already. I have heard my name—Booth—called for, one or two nights, and on account of the likeness [to our father] the papers deigned to mention me."

Despite his deficiencies as an actor, John was embraced by Richmond's theatergoers. They showed only warmth to the legendary star's handsome son. The belles of the city, swathed in "masses of crinoline" and accompanied by their frock-coat and cravat-wearing escorts, thronged the balconies and private boxes in the Marshall.

Best of all, this audience showed no contempt offstage for the artists who worked so hard to please. South of the Mason-Dixon Line, an actor's "social status is nine times as big as with us," one Northern theatergoer commented. "The hospitable character of the Southerner is entirely consonant with the cosmopolitanism of the stage." Where people in Northern cities "place actors outside of society, and execrate them," he explained, "the South [takes] them into affable fellowship." John Wilkes, who in Baltimore and in Harford County bore the double burden of his mother's scandalous reputation and the apartness conferred by his father's profession, was amazed to find a degree of acceptance here.

Richmond's racial hierarchy was reassuring to the twenty-year-old who had made such a mess of supervising white and black laborers on his mother's Maryland farm. In this city, John believed, he was seeing proof that slavery yielded only "the happiness of master & of man." Virginia presented a stark contrast to Harford County. As John wrote to Edwin after his first two weeks in Richmond, he liked the place: "I believe I am getting along very well," he reported.

John especially loved the culture of chivalry that characterized Richmond society. The courtly rituals and customs governing men and women's relationships imposed a structure on social interactions that was pleasing to him. He maintained a wardrobe of well-tailored clothing not for the stage, but for paying calls and promenading on the streets. He visited the parlors and dining rooms of prosperous Richmond folk and on at least one occasion signed a lady's autograph album. Polite socializing with women appealed to John's strengths. In a flirtation, he was on easy ground. His physical splendor and stock of compliments allowed him to hold his own.

John Wilkes at this time looked like "a perfect man," one actor remembered, "his chest being full and broad, his shoulders gently sloping, and his arms as white as alabaster, but hard as marble." Women greatly admired what was described as his "fine Doric face, spare at the jaws and not anywhere over-ripe," and his "lofty square forehead and square brows crowned with curling jetty hair."

Yet John's contentment did not last. A new kind of humiliation awaited him here, one that spoiled the young actor's pleasure in his work. In Richmond, something happened that never occurred when John was toiling in Philadelphia: Edwin Booth came to the Marshall to act. The different status of the two brothers was inescapable on these visits. The gulf between J. B. Wilkes, supernumerary, and Edwin Booth, star, was painfully apparent to the young men themselves, and to the public who came to see them.

Edwin arrived by train at the Seventh Street Station on September 26, 1858, one month after John started work with the Dramatic Star Company. His arrival was a citywide event. As the star, he stayed in a comfortable hotel, and was given his own dressing room at the Marshall. Edwin now traveled with a personal valet who took charge of his costumes and served his meals. It was the star's role to dictate what plays would be produced during his stay; Edwin was empowered to make casting decisions and to rehearse the company.

By all accounts, Edwin was acting the part of "the great man" offstage that autumn. Under Badeau's influence over the past year, he dispensed with the aura of modesty he previously had found useful, and now conducted himself like a famous artist. Every time he finished a performance, one supe recalled, Edwin would stagger off the stage in an attitude of drooping exhaustion. The star's valet would rush to his side, picking up the velvet train of the actor's costume, and assisting him to his private dressing room, where Edwin could be seen through the half-open door "sink[ing] into a big easy chair, almost breathless." Edwin set the Marshall's supporting actors on a demanding schedule, asking them to take their places for *Hamlet, Macbeth, Othello, Richard III, Romeo and Juliet,* and *The Merchant of Venice* in quick succession, as well as leading the cast in the rarely seen and difficult-to-perform *Henry V.*

The tour de force program drew record-breaking business to the Marshall. "Edwin Booth's engagement is one of the most successful we have ever known there," a newspaper reported. "The audiences are large and highly intelligent—the plays performed there are of the most elevated character—and the best order is maintained throughout the house. Mr. Booth's playing commands the highest mark of admiration: silence. His exhibition of that terrible passion—Remorse—so difficult to counterfeit—produced almost breathless silence: a silence which was not broken at the close of the scene."

A respected Richmond sculptor, Edward Valentine, about to leave the United States to study in Rome, begged Booth to model for a portrait bust. On October 4, the star consented to sit several hours in Valentine's studio, so the impression might be taken "from life." Edwin received adulation of this kind with an almost kingly detachment. Good looks ran in the Booth family, but no one in Richmond was clamoring to make a statue of John Wilkes. As one historian of the Marshall Theatre has written, John Wilkes Booth was "an unacclaimed member" of that company, useful only in walk-on parts, an actor whose existence was "almost totally obscured" by his brother's fame.

In a letter to his brother June in San Francisco, Edwin evaluated John Wilkes's slim chance for success onstage. "I don't think he will startle the world," he wrote with palpable condescension, but conceded John "looks beautiful on the *platform.*"

Next to his brother, John Wilkes seemed a second-rate artist. Yet it was hardly fair for the younger man to measure his modest attainments against his brother's runaway success: their backgrounds and training, their relative opportunities, even their personal abilities had been unequal from the beginning. Much of the hard labor Edwin invested in his rise to stardom was invisible to John. His years of servitude on the road with their father had looked like a holiday to Edwin's younger siblings, and the actor's five years in California and Australia seemed equally like a lark. Only his brother's meteoric ascent once he landed on the Atlantic coast, aided by Adam Badeau's worshipful reviews, appeared to John's eyes. The younger Booth may have been aggravated by his older brother's lack of interest in helping him to make similar advancements in the profession. Edwin seemed content for John Wilkes to make his way on his own.

There was one piece of advice Edwin gave to aspiring actors that he never offered to his brother John: "to get into a N.Y. theater as soon as possible." Manhattan was then, as it is now, the best place for dramatic talent to find its reward. There was more money in New York, more parts, bigger and more sophisticated audiences, and greater chances for recognition. The one thing Edwin was determined to prevent was his brother's acting in New York; that city was Edwin's domain, and no other Booth would be allowed to knock him from his pedestal there. The star wanted no competition from a younger, handsomer copy. He knew he could beat John in the realm of talent—his brother lacked a natural gift—yet Edwin could see ahead to a time when John might try his luck in New York anyway. No matter how poorly John acted, if two sons of the great tragedian were peddling Shakespeare in that city, curious crowds would go to see him, and Edwin's own business would suffer.

Edwin Booth left Richmond on October 16, 1858, leaving his brother subdued in spirit. John Wilkes wrote home to Mary Ann perturbed at his lack of prestige, complaining that he was "anxious to get on faster." Asia Booth recalled her brother complaining to her at this time how much he felt the need for a teacher or mentor to help him rise in the profession. Perhaps John Wilkes envisioned the kind of apprenticeship Edwin served with their older brother Junius in San Francisco after 1852. With the more experienced June taking the lead and casting young Edwin in good parts, those two Booth brothers had worked well together, dividing profits and taking care of each other's careers. What John didn't know was that San Francisco theatergoers had shown signs of Booth fatigue after two years of joint brotherly work.

Perhaps under pressure from Mary Ann and Asia to be more helpful to his brother, Edwin behaved differently to John the next time he acted in Richmond. When the star returned to the Marshall in April 1859, he lifted John Wilkes momentarily from a supe's obscurity. The youth was invited to play Horatio to Edwin's Hamlet, and on the last night of the star's visit, John Wilkes acted Othello to Edwin's Iago. This last performance was billed as a "benefit of J. Wilkes Booth," meaning he would be the sole recipient of the night's proceeds. Roughly four hundred dollars came to John that night. Critics were silent on his work; they had been warned in advertisements that

J. Wilkes Booth was trying out the role "for the first time." He would return to his old billing as "J. B. Wilkes" at the Marshall thereafter.

It was almost a cruel trick on Edwin's part, to force a comparison between his own ability and his brother's inexperience. A critic for the *New York Evening Post* wrote that Iago "has always, and rightfully, been considered one of Edwin Booth's masterpieces." The actor was the "incarnation of smooth, eager, supple and fathomless devilry." As Othello's murderous tormentor, Booth appeared "entirely plausible, with no hint of venomous intrigue except in soliloquies, he somehow seemed to be enveloped in an aura of evil. There was a suggestion of infernal enjoyment in the zest with which he marked each progressive step in the fabric of his plot."

Edwin owned the final scene. At the close of the play, Desdemona and John Wilkes's stiff, blockish Othello were dead at last, victims of Iago's conspiracy. Chained and manacled before representatives of the law, about to be brutally interrogated, Edwin's Iago, a critic recalled, "with a horrible gritting of clenched teeth," revealed the soul of "a callous and malignant fiend." The actor spat out Iago's famous last line: "Demand me nothing: what you know, you know. Hereafter will I never more speak word."

When the curtain rang down, the older brother apparently made a show of leading the younger by the hand out before the audience, asking in a loud and jovial voice, "I think he's done well, don't you?" Whatever applause John received must have felt patronizing.

The perceptive Adam Badeau knew well that tensions were growing between the brothers. In an 1859 letter to Edwin, he commented on John Wilkes's increasing feelings of jealousy and resentment. Learning that the sculptor Edward Valentine had finished his bust of Edwin Booth and that the resulting artwork was "superb," Adam suggested someone rescue the statue from Valentine's Richmond studio immediately, before John Wilkes did it harm. "Send word to your brother not to smash it," Badeau joked.

NINE

DESTRUCTION, DEATH, AND MASSACRE

Welcome, destruction, death, and massacre!
I see, as in a map, the end of all.

—*Richard III*, 2.4

In the five months between Abraham Lincoln's election to the presidency in November 1860 and the Confederate attack on Fort Sumter in April 1861, two hundred and fifty thousand people bought tickets to see *The Seven Sisters*, a showgirl-studded song-and-dance spectacular at Laura Keene's theater in New York City.

After the end of her affair with Edwin Booth, Keene made her way back to Manhattan, where she quickly repaired both her heart and her fortunes. Laura was nearly as much a polymath as old Junius Brutus Booth had been. Her mastery of every aspect of dramatic production—directing and playwriting, stagecraft and special-effects design—was unparalleled at the time. *Our American Cousin*, a play she substantially revised and rewrote, as well as directed and starred in, was one of the great moneymaking ventures of 1850s theater. As the first woman theater owner and producer in American history, Keene encountered her share of opposition. Pranksters broke into her playhouse, shredding canvas scenery, destroying props and costumes. Undaunted, the young impresario would raise the curtain anyway, posting advertisements in newspapers, begging the chivalrous men of New York City to come to her vandalized theater's rescue by buying tickets.

In 1857, thirty-two-year-old Keene completed construction of a huge theater on Broadway, between Bleecker and Houston streets, with her name emblazoned over the entrance. The white-and-gold building, with black marble floors, velvet seats, and a fifty-foot-high proscenium flanked by statues, carried a price tag of $75,000, roughly the equivalent of $3 million in today's currency. "The fair and talented directress," one New York newspaper observed, "seems to feel that whatever is worth doing, is worth doing *well*."

When she debuted her new play, *The Seven Sisters*, in November 1860, Keene knew it would be a hit. Critics might pronounce the show "a miracle of Rubbish," but few heeded the warning. In Miss Keene's latest eyepopper, one she described as "an operatic, spectacular, terpsichorean, musical burletta," thirty-four young women paraded the stage in nearly transparent costumes. Reviewers took note of the many pairs of "finely-shaped legs" on display. One newspaper warned that Miss Keene's beautiful dancing girls, in their "low neck dresses," would force dizzying visions of "the hidden mysteries of alabaster bosoms" on every male in the audience.

A quarter of a million tickets were sold to this show in a five-month period in New York, with its one million inhabitants. Audiences were not lining up to see half-naked chorus girls: Laura Keene was selling something besides sex and youthful beauty in this particular production. She was peddling a timely play aimed at soothing her audiences' fears. During the dark months between Lincoln's election and the attack on Fort Sumter, Americans realized that the first chapter of the Founding Fathers' great democratic experiment was coming to an end. Laura Keene had written a singing, dancing spectacle of a nation at peace with itself, a musical celebration of the enduring Union. Legions of New Yorkers, uncertain of their country's fate, flocked to Laura Keene's to drink in the reassuring fantasy.

The showstopping sequence at the heart of *The Seven Sisters* was called "Uncle Sam's Magic Lantern." Uncle Sam, clutching a bald eagle under his arm, walked onstage to give the audience glimpses of their country's past and future with his "Magic Lantern." As a cast of showgirls reenacted familiar scenes of American history and life, Uncle Sam described his ongoing search for a hero to rescue the Union from its present trouble. "The tableaux are not in the slightest degree calculated to give offense to anyone," Keene's advertisements for the new production promised, "not even the extremists in the North and South."

The opening scene was a parade of the American states. Thirty-four chorines impersonated the thirty-four states of the Union, each wearing the flag and bearing the emblem of her particular state, so audiences could tell the difference between Massachusetts and Virginia, Maryland and California. The actresses paraded arm in arm, smiling and waving, the picture of political harmony.

Viewers were then treated to a glimpse of "The Happy Plantation Home," a romanticized vision of slavery and Southern domestic life. Then showgirls in blackface acted out a scene titled "The Picture of Desolation—the Slave Market."

When the curtain lifted again to disclose another image from the magic lantern, audiences cheered. A ship in full sail plowed across the stage with the word *Constitution* painted on its prow. This was the ship of state, and though it was in rough water, with Uncle Sam's help the captain was able to steer his vessel through the billowing waves to safety, carefully avoiding the threat posed by a looming rock labeled "The Ebony Wedge," a symbol of slavery.

In the final scene of the play, President George Washington, slave owner and revered father of his country, rises from his tomb to embrace Columbia, the female embodiment of the Union. Together they ascended joyfully into the clouds, chanting "Union and Liberty Forever." The voluptuous shape of the actress playing Columbia "must be seen to be believed," Keene's playbills advised.

The Seven Sisters may have been "patriotic nonsense," as critics claimed, yet legions packed Keene's playhouse for 253 nights straight to see it. This was an unprecedented run, a full hundred nights longer even than the record-breaking *Our American Cousin*. In the lighthearted scenes of political burlesque, crowds took refuge from another series of images, sharply defined, terrifying and vivid.

A nightmare version of "Uncle Sam's Magic Lantern" had been unfolding in real time in American public life over the past decade. Unlike Laura Keene's Union-themed fairy tale, this true story carried no promise of salvation in its finale. The tableaux unfolded in Illinois, Washington, D.C., Kansas Territory, Virginia, and wherever candidates stumped on the trail of the 1860 presidential election. Many of these scenes were inflammatory and divisive, others were gruesome and violent. No latter-day George Washington appeared to rescue the nation from its impending peril; rather, the men dominating the action were the heralds and harbingers of war.

Had Laura Keene wanted to show audiences actual scenes of their country's march toward disunion, she could have opened with a tableau set in the House of Representatives in Springfield, Illinois, on an October afternoon in 1854, with forty-five-year-old Abraham Lincoln standing in his shirtsleeves at a podium before a large audience. His was a character any actor would hunger to portray. Lincoln's awkward, elongated form housed one of the greatest minds of the nineteenth century, yet his talents were often seriously underestimated, especially by educated people from the East. The twanging accents of Lincoln's frontier childhood jarred the ears of cultivated listeners. "I heerd," Lincoln always said, not "I heard."

Lincoln spoke to protest a bill crafted by a United States senator from Illinois, Stephen A. Douglas, permitting pioneers in Nebraska and Kansas Territories to decide by majority vote if slavery should be established in their region, though it lay far north of the historic 36°30' boundary line established by the Missouri Compromise. Douglas was sitting in the audience that day, and Lincoln fixed the bill's creator with a grim eye as he demanded, "Could there be a more apt invention to bring about collision and violence on the slavery question, than this Nebraska project is?"

If Senator Douglas "had literally formed a ring and placed champions within it to fight out the controversy," Lincoln cried, "the fight could be no more likely to come off than it is."

"And if this fight should begin," Lincoln warned, "will not the first drop of blood so shed, be the real knell of the Union?"

Less than two years later, Lincoln's prediction would come to pass. A second tableau, set in the Kansas wilderness on the night of May 24, 1856, could show the small group of abolitionists who rode from cabin to cabin along Pottawatomie Creek, breaking down doors and dragging proslavery farmers out of their beds to their deaths. Five farmers were hacked to pieces with swords—chests stabbed, throats slashed, hands severed, and skulls cracked wide open. The abolitionist John Brown and three of his sons committed this massacre in order, they said, to intimidate their local opponents in the Kansas battle over slavery.

Finally, in any sequence of historical images illustrating why the map of the United States by 1860 was tearing violently in two, the figure of Roger Brooke Taney, Chief Justice of the United States, would be essential. Taney had the kind of physical presence that spooked people. His body was emaciated from years of debilitating sickness. He had sunken, hungry-looking features, long hair, and dark-ringed eyes. The sight of him lurching into the courtroom reminded one witness of the forward motion of a "galvanized corpse." The abolitionist Charles Sumner despised Taney, ranking the chief justice's legal instincts second only to Pontius Pilate's.

The Maryland native was eighty years old in 1857 when he wrote the majority opinion in the Dred Scott case, rejecting a petition for freedom made by a sixty-two-year-old Virginia-born slave whose owner had taken him to Wisconsin Territory (later Minnesota), where slavery did not exist. In denying Scott's case, Taney made two momentous pronouncements: first, that no black person, whether born in freedom or slavery, could hold the right of American citizenship; second, as blacks were nonpersons under the law, no legal power could stop slavery from extending north and west across the continent and into the wilderness lying between the Rocky Mountains and the Pacific coast. This was a radical assertion of judicial power, one deserving a scene of its own: a justice hunched at his desk, eradicating the Missouri Compromise with one sweep of his pen.

Hundreds of thousands of New Yorkers could see re-creations of these and other ominous political tableaux splashed across the pages of large-circulation newspapers like *Frank Leslie's Illustrated Weekly*, which attracted readers with detailed black-and-white engravings. Faced with an avalanche of words and pictures portending war, it is no wonder a quarter million people beat a path to Keene's theater for a taste of a happier ending to this national crisis. Even after the fall of Fort Sumter, when President Lincoln summoned seventy-five thousand volunteer troops to the defense of Washington, D.C., New Yorkers continued to buy tickets to Keene's fantasy of national peace. It was not until August 1861, a few weeks after the North's defeat at the first battle of Bull Run, that Laura Keene pulled *The Seven Sisters* from the stage. The distance between her theatrical illusion and the violent reality of a country at war with itself had become too great.

John Brown's October 16, 1859, surprise attack on Harpers Ferry may have been the single most shocking and polarizing of all the spectacles that crowded the prewar period. This bloody incident, followed swiftly by the perpetrator's sensational public trial and execution, absorbed the nation and grabbed the attention of Great Britain and Europe.

It is one of the strange facts of American history that the Booths, who dominated the final act of the Civil War, should be present even in this memorable opening scene. With the magic lantern of historical hindsight, the two brothers may be observed taking their places in the story of the Union's unraveling: Edwin, because he was an intimate friend of the conspirators who helped John Brown attack Harpers Ferry; John Wilkes, because he volunteered to bring John Brown to the scaffold. In the final images of Brown's life and death, the faces of Edwin and John Wilkes hover in the background. The Booth brothers were merely extras in this stage of our national drama, but already the two young men stood on opposite sides of the developing conflict.

IN THE AUTUMN OF 1858, THE GREEN PEACE ESTATE, AN ELEGANT RESIdence in south Boston, was the picture of refinement. Lawns planted with strawberry beds and pear trees surrounded a three-story mansion. The north wing of this grand residence was a glass-walled conservatory where flowers and fruit trees grew out of season. A miniature version of the Greek Parthenon, complete with Doric columns and a carved pediment, stood nearby, doing service as a summer house.

This property belonged to a couple of the first respectability, fifty-eight-year-old Dr. Samuel Gridley Howe and his wife, Julia, twenty years his junior. The Howes' genealogy and achievements placed them at the pinnacle of the social hierarchy not only in Boston, but also in New York City and Newport, Rhode Island, where they had similarly handsome homes. Their Boston address, filled with the laughter of their five young children, was an unlikely place, perhaps, for a nest of antigovernment conspirators to take root, particularly one whose stated aim, one member testified, was to detach the South from the Union so that it might be "whip[ped] back" into place "without Slavery."

Edwin Booth made his way to Green Peace in late October 1858, an invited guest of Dr. Howe and his wife. This summons was a milestone in Edwin's life, a social triumph for the son of a scandal-ridden stage star. The Howes' teenage daughters did not forget the day of the actor's first visit. In a memoir of her mother's friendship with Edwin Booth, one Howe daughter recalled that "a maternal decree, which seemed very cruel from our point of view, forbade our appearance on the scene." Defying their mother's command, the girls hid themselves behind flowering plants in the conservatory, where they "managed to have a peep" at the twenty-four-year-old Booth. "I have always hoped that he did not notice the rustling of young folks tumbling about the shrubbery in a fever of excitement," daughter Frances Howe wrote in embarrassment. Booth's visit went well. Mrs. Howe wrote in her diary that Edwin seemed "modest, intelligent, and above all, genuine—the man as worthy of admiration as the artist." He struck her, she privately confessed, as "a beautiful youth, of heroic type." The positive impression Edwin made on the Howes that day soon deepened into an intimacy that lasted throughout the actor's life, and arguably changed the course of his career.

When John Brown made his way to Green Peace that same year, no adolescent girls gawked from the conservatory. We cannot be sure of the precise date of Brown's visit—the Howes kept their guest's arrival a secret. Even the mansion's staff of servants was dismissed so there would be no witnesses to see the man Dr. Howe described as "the one who wished to be a savior for the Negro race . . . as Christ had willingly offered his life for the salvation of mankind." Julia Howe, taking up the unaccustomed role of housemaid, waited behind the front door for the appointed time when Brown should ring the bell. "Answering it," Julia remembered, she "beheld a middle-aged, middle-sized man with beard and hair of amber color, streaked with gray. He looked a Puritan of the Puritans, forceful, concentrated and self-contained." The mistress of Green Peace then quietly conducted Brown to her husband's study, where she left the two men alone for a few hours of "confidential communication."

When he met the Howes in October 1858, Edwin Booth knew little of his wealthy hosts' other, more controversial protégé. In the short space of a year, however, a federal dragnet had produced a list of suspects in the violence than left of dozens of townspeople and antislavery insurgents dead at Harpers Ferry, Virginia. It then became clear to Edwin and the rest of the newspaper-reading public that although John Brown led the attack and fired the gun, Dr. Howe and his circle of abolitionist friends had purchased the weapon, loaded it, and helped Brown take aim.

Julia Ward Howe, Edwin Booth's lifelong friend, would later become known to the world as the writer of "The Battle Hymn of the Republic." In 1862, she would create new lyrics for the tune "John Brown's body lies a-mould' ring in the grave." The confidence and conviction infusing lines like these,

> *In the beauty of the lilies Christ was born across the sea . . .*
> *As He died to make men holy, let us die to make men free,*
> *While God is marching on*

propelled hundreds of thousands of Union soldiers through the miseries of war.

Almost from the day of her birth, Julia Howe seems to have been in training to write this lyric. It was not only the fact that John Brown had been part of her life, or that she herself had spent twenty years prior to the Civil War working as an abolitionist; she also came from a family long dedicated to revolutionary causes. Her great-grandfather was Samuel Ward, the governor of Rhode Island, who, Julia noted later in a memoir, "was one of the first men to prophesy the separation of the colonies from the mother country." Before his death early in 1776, Governor Ward was a leading participant in the First and Second Continental Congresses. Had he lived a few months longer, he would have signed the Declaration of Independence. His son, Julia's grandfather, served valiantly as a lieutenant colonel in the war for Independence. Through her mother's line, Julia, born in 1819, was a descendant of Francis Marion, the famous "Swamp Fox" of the Revolution. While still a small child, Julia was so proud of her inheritance of "military blood," she would spend hours meditating on her forefathers' involvement in the founding of the country.

From a young age, this girl was taught to see herself in fateful terms, as someone charged with carrying on the family tradition of representing American ideals. This well-learned lesson would give Julia's wartime poetry its audacious and patriotic power. Julia spent what she called her "young ladyhood" in one of the finest homes on the island of Manhattan. Her father had established a Wall Street banking firm and was a founder of New York University. His residence, a white stone edifice of splendid proportions, anchored the corner of Broadway and Bond Street.

Samuel Ward, a widower, gave his daughter every educational opportunity: lessons in a variety of ancient and modern languages; music classes; trips to hear opera, concerts, and oratorios. He even built a private art gallery inside their mansion to encourage her enjoyment of paintings. Julia was an adept pupil, motivated by an intellectual curiosity beyond her years.

Mr. Ward frowned on frivolity. He may have spent lavishly on books and artwork for his child's edification, but he deplored wasting money on fashionable clothing and barred Julia from going to the balls and parties enjoyed by other girls of her age and social class. Above all, Ward forbade his daughter to ever enter a theater. After nearly a hundred Virginians burned to death during a Christmas play at Richmond's Old Academy in 1811, ministers in pulpits across the United States used the calamity as a cautionary tale about the moral hazard of theatergoing. Young Julia Ward grew up with this event emblazoned in her imagination. In her house, she remembered, that long-ago fire was constantly "spoken of as a 'judgment' upon the wickedness of the stage and of its patrons."

"I lived much in my books," Julia recalled of these cloistered teenage years, spent confined to the library of her parents' vast house, mastering the classic texts of German, French, and Italian literature with the help of a tutor. "I seemed to myself," she confessed in a memoir, "like a young damsel of olden time, shut up within an enchanted castle. And I must say that my dear father, with all his noble generosity and overweening affection, sometimes appeared to me as my jailer." When Samuel Ward died in 1839, Julia was twenty years old. Much as she grieved, his death was a kind of liberation.

Turned loose on Manhattan's marriage market, a hefty share of her father's fortune in her pocket, Julia threw aside books, bought fine dresses, and discovered she had a "passionate fondness" for dancing. She became a favorite guest at the musicales John Jacob Astor held weekly in his mansion: the aging millionaire admired Julia's high spirits, pretty face, and beautifully trained singing voice. "I should probably have remained a frequenter of fashionable society," Julia later admitted, marrying one of the well-born bankers she encountered at Mr. Astor's social evenings, but something held her back. Julia was troubled by a restless ambition, a feeling she later described as a "sense of literary responsibility which never left me." If she ever did marry, she declared, it would be to an unusual type of man, someone who could inspire and direct her talents, giving "help and guidance toward a literary career."

In 1842, the heiress was on a driving tour of the city of Boston in the company of an old family friend, poet Henry Wadsworth Longfellow. Hoofbeats were heard, and Julia turned in her seat to behold, she later wrote, a vision of "a noble rider on a noble steed." A tall, lean man with long black hair, high cheekbones, and piercing blue eyes reined his horse to a halt beside Longfellow's carriage. Julia's heart was lost. This was forty-year-old Dr. Samuel Gridley Howe, already renowned throughout the United States and Europe, his biographer explained, as "one of the most romantic characters of our century." Though largely forgotten today, Howe was a celebrity in his own time. Florence Nightingale described him somewhat breathlessly as "one of the best and greatest men of the age."

Samuel Howe had an early start in his generation's race for glory. Born in 1801, he grew up listening to the stories told by two uncles, veterans of the Revolutionary War, who had fought at Bunker Hill and participated in the Boston Tea Party. Impulsive and idealistic, Sam Howe dreamed of the bygone days of war and adventure. While a student at Brown University and later Harvard Medical School, Howe was more interested in the works of Lord Byron than in scholarly pursuits. Awed by news that his poet hero had sailed for Greece to battle the Turks, Sam did not want to miss the chance to fight for freedom in his own time. Like his contemporary Junius Brutus Booth, young Howe made a life-altering choice because of Byron's influence. Armed with a surgeon's degree and a carbine rifle, the twenty-two-year-old left school in 1823, boarding a vessel bound for the Greek islands. His destination was Lord Byron's base at Missolonghi, where Howe planned to offer himself as a volunteer in the struggle for Greek independence.

Howe reached Greece just in time to learn the news of Byron's death by fever. Racing to the villa where the poet had spent his last days, the young doctor was able to salvage some of his dead idol's possessions, including Byron's war helmet, which Howe described as "a beautiful affair of steel inlaid with gold, with a floating plume of blue." Byron's death did nothing to weaken Sam's determination to aid the rebel forces. The young American stayed in Greece for the next decade, harassing the Turkish army in the mountains of the Peloponnesus, a soldier, as he put it, in "one of the small guerrilla bands that hung about the enemy, doing all the harm they could." Howe came of age fighting and surviving on the run in the dry, rocky Mediterranean wilderness. The experience he gained in guerrilla tactics and mountain warfare would stay with him for a lifetime.

"I could be of little or no use as a surgeon," Howe recalled of his rough initiation into manhood, "but was expected to divide my time between killing Turks, helping Greeks and taking care of my bacon." Once the war ended, Howe stayed on, coordinating American-funded relief efforts that brought food, clothing, and medical supplies to the victorious but destitute Greek people.

When Julia Ward met Sam Howe, the freedom fighter had put down his guns and taken up the work of teaching blind children to read and write. Starting with a few pupils in his Massachusetts home when he returned from Greece in 1832, Howe made plans to build a school in Boston for educating these youngsters in large numbers. "The sight of any being in human shape, left to brutish ignorance," he declared, "is always demoralizing to the beholders." By 1839, Howe had built the Perkins Institute for the Blind, complete with dormitories, classrooms, workshops, and a Braille printing press. His star pupil, a girl named Laura Bridgman, blind, deaf, and mute since infancy, was the Helen Keller of her day. Oliver Wendell Holmes celebrated Howe's educational achievement in an ode, saying the doctor had "mapped the desert of the soul, untracked by sight or sound."

Julia Ward married Sam Howe four months after first setting eyes on him. She called her suitor "Chev," short for "Chevalier," to honor his heroism in the Greek war, and to acknowledge his love for fast horses. Using a portion of Julia's inheritance, the new couple built their estate, Green Peace. There Julia bore six children and "Chev" filled a stable with horses with names like "Breeze" and "Blaze." Waking each morning at four o'clock, Dr. Howe delighted in ordering his sleepy offspring out of bed to join him in a before-breakfast gallop. The temperament that sent young Sam Howe racing across an ocean to Byron's side had not cooled by the time he married Julia Ward. The now middle-aged war veteran was still an idealist bristling with impatience to change the world.

Theirs was not an easy marriage. Green Peace was the scene of many arguments and bitter silences between husband and wife, the Howe children remembered. Julia was accustomed to luxury and the leisure time to pursue her studies. Her head was filled with the writings of "my great masters," as she called them—Kant, Spinoza, and Hegel—and with the ambition to write sonnets in English and Italian. "Chev," for all his talk of freedom, turned out to be a patriarch of the old style. He was not interested in his wife's scholarly aims. Every week, he invited a large group of famous friends—Charles Sumner, Horace Mann, Ralph Waldo Emerson, Henry Wadsworth Longfellow—for dinner, and expected Julia to cook for them. She begged to be excused, telling him truthfully she was "lamentably deficient in household skills and knowledge," unable to complete even the simplest domestic chores. Her husband demanded she learn to do the work.

This implacable assignment "cost me many unhappy hours," Julia later confessed. She wrote sadly about how little time American women had to read or to think. "The preparation of 'three square meals a day,'" she exclaimed, "the washing, baking sewing and child-bearing, fill[s] the measure of their days and exceed[s] that of their strength."

These two headstrong personalities found common ground in the antislavery cause. By 1846, when Chev and Julia were the parents of toddlers, their home had become a stop on the Underground Railroad, a way station for fugitive slaves heading north to Canada. Dr. Howe was chairman of Boston's Vigilance Committee, a citizens' group dedicated to shielding Southern runaways from slave catchers. A note he wrote at the time touts the merits of Green Peace as a secure hiding place: "I could bring anyone here and keep him secret a week," he boasted; "no person except Mrs. H and myself would know it."

Julia embraced the ideals animating the antislavery movement, and she was dazzled by the people who espoused them. "I had supposed the abolitionists to be men and women of rather coarse fiber," she exclaimed, "seeking to lay rash hands on the complex machinery of government and society," but high-born Bostonians like orator Wendell Phillips helped change her mind. "His family name was of the best," this granddaughter of a Revolutionary War hero noted approvingly. Phillips and his friend Charles Sumner came regularly to Green Peace. They were learned and deliberate, a pair of Harvard-trained lawyers. There was nothing rash about them.

By 1850, Julia recalled, Dr. Howe was impatient with "the conscience of the North." He himself had been "on fire with loathing and indignation," she said, toward the moral injustice of slavery for years. Now Southern politicians were lobbying for a legal extension of what Howe called "their persevering barbarism" into the new states soon to be carved from the western territories. Northerners, Dr. Howe complained, were not yet awake to this threat. Charles Sumner, elected to the United States Senate in 1851, was sounding the alarm from the Senate floor. The Howes, from their comfortable retreat at Green Peace, tried to jolt public opinion too. At a pair of husband-and-wife desks set before their dining room fireplace, they created the abolitionist newspaper *The Commonwealth*. Chev provided political commentary, while Julia handled cultural contributions, writing poems about the plight of the slave and giving glowing reviews to books like *Uncle Tom's Cabin*. A housekeeper was finally hired to run Green Peace on a day-to-day basis. His wife's full-time work as a writer and editor, Chev realized, took precedence now.

The contest between slave owners and "Free Soil" farmers to claim ownership of the Kansas Territory only intensified the Howes' efforts. Chev chaired a new organization called the Massachusetts Kansas Committee, charged with raising money to help people from New England uproot themselves and start new lives on the plains of Kansas. The money Howe collected sent thousands on the journey west, where he and other abolitionists hoped they would form "a living bulwark to the extension of slavery."

For a majority of families who made the trip, politics was only a secondary consideration. Most farmers were drawn by reports of the good soil that lay beyond the Mississippi. Land in the territory was going cheap. An Ohio tanner named John Brown and five of his sons—Owen, Frederick, Salmon, Jason, and John Jr.—were among the few who went to Kansas with a different mission. Following their father's orders, the brothers set out—wives and young children in tow—"to help defeat *Satan* and his legions in that direction." The Browns knew a collision over slavery would take place in Kansas, and they wanted to be in on the fight.

Groups of travelers from New England boarding Kansas-bound riverboats were met by crowds of proslavery Missouri men who carried Colt revolvers, rifles, and bowie knives. Southerners discussed their plans to fight Free Soil settlers who tried to stake land claims in Kansas. "Blow them to hell with a chunk of cold lead!" one pro-slavery politician roared. Such rhetoric was ferocious enough to turn many people back. Worse, reports came from Kansas in 1855 and 1856 of politically motivated assassinations and arson as proslavery and Free Soil neighbors clashed. Farmers from the East seemed to bear the brunt of the violence. "There is a great lack of arms here," young Salmon Brown wrote from Kansas. His brother, John Brown, Sr., agreed: "the friends of freedom are not *one-fourth* of them *half-armed*." To Sam Howe, letters of this kind read like an invitation to war.

"My father was through life subject to fits of unaccountable restlessness," one of Howe's children recalled, "during which he longed for new crusades in new places." Memories of his days fighting in the mountains of Greece were ever present. Even decades later, Howe itched to relive the experience. News that his emigrant families, the very ones he equipped with plows and seeds for farming, were being terrorized in Kansas made Howe want to pick up his gun.

Two events in the spring of 1856 spurred Dr. Howe into action. On May 22, his friend Charles Sumner was beaten on the floor of the U.S. Senate by the cane-wielding Preston Brooks of South Carolina. Sumner was dragged from the chamber after the assault, clothing soaked in blood. Coincidentally, Sam and Julia had visited Sumner in Washington, D.C., two weeks before the attack. Chev at the time urged his friend—a lightning rod for controversy—to start carrying a pistol for self-defense, but Sumner's own mother scotched the plan. "Oh doctor," the elderly woman cried, referring to her famously clumsy and absentminded son, "he would only shoot himself with it." Eerily, Julia noted in her diary, the Howes had encountered Preston Brooks at Willard's Hotel before they left Washington. He looked "a handsome man, evidently a Southerner," she wrote, "with what appeared to me an evil expression of countenance."

Only three days after Brooks's attack came news of a fresh horror from Kansas. John Brown, aided by his sons and a small group of Free Soil men, slaughtered five proslavery farmers in Pottawatomie Creek. Armed with pistols and double-edged swords that had been honed at a grindstone until exceptionally sharp, the killers dragged their prey out of bed and dismembered them. "I saw my . . . brother lying dead on the ground," said one survivor of the raid. "His fingers were cut off, and his arms were cut off; his head was cut open; there was a hole in his breast."

Word of Charles Sumner's beating in the Senate had steeled Brown's resolve to shed Southern blood. When they heard that the abolitionist had been "martyred" by a South Carolinian, one witness said, Captain Brown and his sons "went crazy—*crazy*." Brown himself said that murdering his pro-slavery neighbors was no crime. "I act from a principle," he calmly announced after the Pottawatomie incident. "My aim and object is to restore human rights."

Dr. Howe's desk in the dining room of Green Peace now became intolerable to him. As he often reminded Julia, the years in the mountains of the Peloponnesus had hardened him "to the bivouac by night, to hunger, hard fare, and constant fighting by day." His proper place was in the field. In July 1856, leaving wife and children ensconced in the Howes' summer house at Newport, Chev guided his horses onto the post roads to Kansas, driving a wagon loaded with guns and cannon through Iowa, to supply the Free Soil people of Kansas. Proslavery agitators still filled the riverboats, so Howe joined the waves of emigrants heading for the territory on this alternate overland route. The sight of men "slowly and painfully drawing their families in carts with oxen across the whole State of Iowa because Missourians block up the highway of the river" filled Howe with rage. "How long will the North eat dirt and not turn sick?" he asked in a July 31 letter to Sumner, who was still confined to bed recuperating from his injuries.

For Chev, the work of supplying abolitionist settlers with weapons was the battle for Greek freedom all over again. Howe sent home to Boston cheerful reports of "travers[ing] the whole length of the State of Iowa on horseback or in a cart, sleeping in said cart, or . . . on the floor of dirty huts." As he made his way, Dr. Howe reached out to Quaker and abolitionist communities in towns like Tabor and Iowa City. In each way station, Howe established a series of "safe houses"—usually the homes of abolitionist leaders—where guns and ammunition could be stockpiled en route to Kansas. "We have organized a pretty good line of communication between our base and the corps of emigrants who have now advanced into the territory," Chev boasted in a letter to the Massachusetts Kansas Committee, which had paid for the guns he carried.

Howe pressed on to Kansas and was charmed by the landscape he found there. He thought the grasslands and tree-lined streams were delightful to the eye, and bought several farm-sized parcels of land on the spot. Chev returned home to Boston in the fall, satisfied with the gun-running network he established, confident that Northern settlers would be able to defend themselves against proslavery forces. He would make one more trip to the territory in the summer of 1857, bringing Mrs. Howe and their daughter Florence in tow, to give the ladies a scenic tour of their new Kansas property.

THE POTTAWATOMIE MASSACRE TURNED MANY OF JOHN BROWN'S OLD ASsociates, friends, and even his children against him. The killings made him a wanted man, an exile from the peace-loving, antislavery Quaker communities of Iowa, and from his Kansas neighbors who were tired of bloodshed. These families, who once valued him as protection against proslavery harassment, now saw Brown as a sinister agitator, someone whose mission was larger than the local politics of Kansas. Brown, one settler observed, was looking "to bring on righteous and necessary war."

John Brown received a different greeting from the people Mrs. Howe referred to as "the Massachusetts aristocracy," the abolitionists in Boston and Concord to whom Brown appealed in person in 1857 for a gift of twenty thousand dollars to fund his latest project: creating, he said, a "band of 100 volunteers" to be armed and trained "for war-service against the forces of slavery." Brown addressed congregations in the city of Boston and spoke to gatherings of citizens at Concord's Town Hall.

Brown's measured, unemotional presentations about life in Kansas had a mesmerizing effect on his New England audiences. Henry David Thoreau and Ralph Waldo Emerson invited Brown into their homes, dubbing him the "perfect transcendentalist." They seemed to see in the plainspoken and resolute figure the triumph of action over rhetoric. "Our people heard him with favor," Bronson Alcott, father to Louisa May Alcott, remembered. "He did not conceal his hatred of slavery, and less his readiness to strike a blow for freedom at the fitting moment. I thought him the manliest of men."

These intellectuals saw in John Brown what they wanted to see; no one inquired too closely into the details of what had happened on May 24, 1856, at Pottawatomie Creek. Reports from Kansas were sketchy and unreliable; ugly stories of butchery might be exaggerations. People opened their purses and gave generously to Brown's vaguely worded cause of raising a regiment. "I do not expose my plans," Brown would say to prospective donors. "I will not be interrogated. If you wish to give me anything, I want you to give it freely. I have no other purpose but to serve the cause of liberty." Surprised at his money-raising success and general popularity in New England, Brown observed privately, "Nothing so charms the American people as personal bravery."

John Brown's most fateful meeting on his Boston visit was with Dr. Howe and Theodore Parker, a forty-seven-year-old graduate of Harvard who presided over the Unitarian church Mrs. Howe attended. The three men held a conference early in 1857, presumably at Dr. Howe's office in Boston. Located at 20 Bromfield Street on the top floor of a nondescript building, this meeting room was a longtime base for those of Dr. Howe's antislavery efforts that did not involve his wife. The Massachusetts Kansas Committee met here starting in 1854, and a decade earlier this was where Howe's Vigilance Committee gathered to run the Boston branch of the Underground Railroad. The window-lined space held six armchairs, a worn sofa, and a massive table strewn with maps and correspondence. "Not an inviting room," Chev's daughter remembered, "yet it drew like a magnet those who were in sorrow, need, sickness or adversity."

Howe and Parker made a confidential proposition to John Brown. They offered to establish a secret committee that would supply Brown with guns and cash to use in his future attacks on slaveholders. Dr. Howe, Reverend Parker, Thomas Wentworth Higginson, Frank B. Sanborn, and George L. Stearns formed a clandestine splinter group within the Massachusetts Kansas Committee. These five friends had a sixth supporter, Gerrit Smith, who resided in New York state. Officially, the committee's purpose was to aid Free Soil settlers in the faraway territory to obtain necessary supplies, including guns for self-defense. Arming peaceable settlers in Kansas was no crime. It was a worthy charity for any law-abiding Bostonian opposed to the spread of slavery. Yet Dr. Howe, Reverend Parker, and their allies within the committee wanted to channel its money toward a new goal. They believed that now was the time to go on the offensive against slavery outside of Kansas Territory. John Brown's desires fit the schemes of his new Boston backers. Brown told them he was finished in Kansas. "I consider it my duty," he declared, "to draw the scene of excitement to some other part of the country."

In February and March 1858, John Brown returned to Boston to meet with his friends. In a series of conversations that unfolded over several days at Dr. Howe's office on Bromfield Street and in a suite of rooms at the American House, a local hotel, Howe and the others sounded Brown for ideas about his next move. It was then that Brown disclosed his wild, even vainglorious, dream for starting a civil war: launching an attack on the arsenal at Harpers Ferry, Virginia.

Howe, Parker, and the others gave his plan their full support, offering to supply the guns and money. The immediate goal of this "experiment," as Howe and his Boston associates euphemistically termed the raid, was to sow terror and fear among slaveholders.

Brown hoped the raid would accomplish something else, a vision he appears to have discussed with Dr. Howe during their meeting at Green Peace. Once he led his force of liberators into Virginia, Brown imagined, slaves would rise up and flock to a base he planned to establish in part of the Allegheny Mountain range near Harpers Ferry. There Brown planned to start a new utopian society, well armed, well equipped, and peopled by blacks and whites living in equality.

This vision of presiding over a haven for runaway slaves in the Alleghenies was a fantasy, one that seems to have been influenced by Dr. Howe's memories of living in the mountains of the Peloponnesus with a band of Greek freedom fighters. Yet a glance at the map reveals why it could have seemed plausible. The Allegheny range, cutting a southwesterly swath from central Pennsylvania through Maryland and Virginia, was packed with sheltering forests, teeming with wildlife, and sparsely inhabited. Slaves might be guided to safety on its slopes from the Shenandoah Valley in the west, or from tidewater Virginia in the east. Bands of Northern reinforcements could rally to Brown's side if they made for his hideout from the Pennsylvania end of the mountain range. This secondary scheme, a sequel to the Harpers Ferry bloodbath, was kept quiet.

Brown does not seem to have discussed the utopian aspect of his plan with any other Boston conspirators besides Howe. Years later, Julia Howe mentioned the quixotic scenario in her memoir. "In speaking of it," she wrote, "my husband assured me that John Brown's plan had not been so impossible of realization as it appeared to have been after its failure."

After their meetings in 1858, more than a year passed in planning and preparation, all parties moving carefully. Howe, Parker, and the others took a final precaution, one historian points out, "to evade responsibility" for the carnage their protégé was sure to commit. They asked Brown not to give them any specific information about his developing strategy. They did not want to hear of the army he was recruiting, the timing of the strike, or any troublesome particulars of training, reconnaissance, and expenditure. "The little Boston group," wrote Oswald Garrison Villard, Brown's ablest biographer, "encouraged [Brown] to attack slavery in the mountains of the South, [gave] him money and arms to do it with, and sanctioned his going ahead— only they said, 'Do not tell us the details of it.'"

Having set these hidden wheels in motion, Dr. Samuel Gridley Howe was free to devote his evenings in the autumn of 1858 to the theater. Setting his carriage horses to a gallop through rainy streets, Chev took Julia to the Boston Theatre often that October, where the couple watched Edwin Booth perform Shakespeare. The Howes were impressed. "In every word and every gesture," Julia wrote in her diary, "the touch of genius made itself felt." The Howes looked at one another after first seeing Edwin perform, exclaiming "This is the real thing!"

When she married Howe, the former Miss Ward gained at least one freedom: the oppressive ban her late father set against theatergoing was gone. Most Bostonians, including her new husband, loved the theater and believed it to be a vital aspect of American culture. Far from demonizing the stage as the resort of morally corrupt lowlifes, as old Mr. Ward had done, members of "the Massachusetts aristocracy" ranked acting and playwriting among the highest of all the arts.

Edwin's great admirer Adam Badeau was a friend of Julia Howe and a frequent visitor to Boston. In his book *The Vagabond*, Badeau marveled at the absence of social prejudice against actors in that city. Bostonians, he wrote, "look upon players differently; they regard an actor of ability as a man of talent or genius, and receive him into their houses; he has shown that he has mind, and is therefore their equal; he is an artist, and they reverence art and welcome its professors."

For the blue-blooded Howes to extend a social invitation to a Booth was as shocking, in its way, as their welcoming John Brown. Brown was a known killer, a housebreaker, a horse thief, a lowly tanner by trade, yet his antislavery ideals earned him entrée into the Howes' home. By dint of his talent, a hard-drinking, uneducated, socially untutored Bohemian like Edwin Booth could make the same social ascent.

Prior to 1858, Edwin Booth cultivated an aura of humility in his dealings with the public. Craving the favor of audiences, eager to win his father's place on the American stage, the young man had not conducted himself like a famous artist. Yet after months of Adam Badeau's instruction, and the experience of being taken under the wing of a socialite like Julia Ward Howe, Edwin's head was turned. Julia threw what she called a "Booth party" that year in his honor, inviting Boston luminaries to spend an evening getting to know Edwin. Adam Badeau recounted the Ivy League guest list. His friend Edwin had never seen the inside of a college, much less worked past McGuffey's Fifth Reader in a grade school, yet "poets of European reputation, wits and scholars, critics and statesmen," Badeau wrote, "were invited solely to meet [him]." The actor was inwardly quaking with intimidation, but concealed his fear behind a pose of reticent dignity. This former Baltimore street urchin need not have worried. Julia Howe and her friends viewed Booth as a natural talent, Badeau wrote, "as a man of rare and exquisite genius, and so a most desirable acquaintance for such as these."

Not long after his first "Booth party"—Julia would throw many more for him as the years rolled by—the twenty-four-year-old wrote to his brother June Booth, still toiling away as a mediocre actor in San Francisco. Edwin, long accustomed to social exile, was overwhelmed by the experience of acceptance. He now wanted to make a permanent home in Boston.

"I have serious notions of buying a house here," Edwin informed his brother in October 1858, "and moving mother and all on to live. Mother says yes and I am sure everything would be much more pleasant than that den of corruption and oblivion Baltimore." In Boston, Edwin thought, a new beginning awaited their family. "Actors are respected [here], I observe from experience," he wrote. "The theater is nightly visited by men of standing—

families of the first class, and the profession is considered one of the first walks of art as it should be—and its favorites are treated accordingly."

Edwin advised June to leave California and make haste for Boston. "We could all be together in one house as it should be," Edwin wrote. "How delightful it would then be to have us all together in a family knot. Yourself in a comfortable and respected position—the head of the family as you should be. Even *my* back isn't strong enough to bear the weight."

June wisely ignored his brother's invitation. The future of family harmony Edwin depicted, with June as the figurehead patriarch in a household bought and paid for by his younger sibling, was practically an insult. The older actor could barely make a living out west, while Edwin, now a star, was earning more money than June Booth ever had or would. "I do hope you are doing well," the twenty-four-year-old wrote, knowing full well his older brother was in desperate need of cash. "I fear there is but little hope for our trade in California now." Edwin had won the family crown, and he knew it. His newfound social success merely confirmed that fact.

Warfare, for the Browns, was as much of a family business as act- ing was for the Booths. When John Brown, using the alias of "Mr. Smith," began moving his regiment into position to strike in the summer of 1859, five of his children—two girls and three young men—came with him. This was one of the details that Dr. Howe and his co-conspirators in Boston did not wish to know. "Mr. Smith" signed the lease on a three-story farmhouse, with attic, in Sandy Hook, Maryland. The spot was five miles distant from Harpers Ferry, on the Virginia-Maryland border. The house would be the hiding place for Brown's accomplices. These were not the one hundred men Brown originally hoped to raise, but only twenty-one volunteers, not count- ing Brown's daughter, sixteen-year-old Annie, and Martha, his seventeen- year-old daughter-in-law.

It was Annie and Martha's job to feed the men concealed in the farm- house attic, clean up after them, and stay on the alert for inquisitive neigh- bors. Brown's daughter Annie referred to her father's volunteer soldiers as "my invisibles." The men ranged in age from twenty to forty-four years, they were white and black, native and foreign-born, and their number in- cluded lawyers, a journalist, a college student, a veteran of the Mexican War, farmers, a stenographer, and a factory worker. Three of Brown's sons— Oliver, Watson, and Owen—were among them. Most were devout Chris- tians, Annie remembered, and driven by the belief that slavery countered God's will.

At nightfall on October 16, 1859, Brown made his move. His band of fighters emerged from their attic, shouldered their weapons, and proceeded along the deserted Sandy Hook road that hugged the bank of the Potomac, toward the Virginia state line.

The details of Brown's plot have been oft-told. It began behind schedule, and was perhaps incoherent, but at least he had an instinct for high drama. The spot Brown chose to stage his attack enjoyed a splendid landscape. The village of Harpers Ferry, hemmed in by steep, tree-covered mountains, was perched at the confluence of two rivers, the Potomac and the Shenandoah. This vista, Thomas Jefferson once declared, was "one of the most stupendous scenes in nature."

Brown's men moved silently across the Baltimore & Ohio Railroad bridge to reach the darkened town. He assumed, incorrectly, that the mere presence of his band of would-be liberators would impel local slaves to launch a general rebellion. Riders on a Baltimore & Ohio passenger train heading east through Harpers Ferry before dawn on October 16 were the first to take Brown's intentions seriously. A detachment of Brown's men held up the train with rifles, keeping it parked on the bridge for several hours until letting it pass at daylight. Brown wanted the word to go out that his armed rebellion had begun, and he knew trainmen had access to telegraph equipment. After the engineers sent the train steaming to the next depot on the line, the conductor tapped out a Morse code message to Baltimore; an army bent on freeing slaves, he telegraphed, had taken possession of the B & O bridge over the Potomac and was stopping trains. This message was met with disbelief. No one quite believed a warlike gang had come with that scheme in mind. The idea was too absurd.

When the spontaneous slave uprising Brown dreamed of failed to materialize, his raid quickly dissipated. Brown had plotted no escape route, and his main strategic goal, after taking possession of the arsenal, had no practical value from a military standpoint. Disastrously, Brown devoted crucial resources to kidnapping Colonel Lewis L. Washington, a descendant of President George Washington, who happened to reside in Harpers Ferry. From this victim, he would steal two historical relics: a pistol given to General Washington by the Marquis de Lafayette during the Revolutionary War, and a sword that Frederick the Great of Prussia had sent to the first president of the United States.

The fight was quickly lost. The president of the B & O railroad, notified of trouble on the tracks, alerted the governor of Virginia and President James Buchanan. Meanwhile, on the streets of Harpers Ferry, the noise of gunfire and the sight of strange figures pacing the town with weapons in the early morning light, sent local men galloping on horseback to nearby villages, where church bells tolled the emergency.

Word spread quickly through the countryside, with reports inflating Brown's twenty-one-man force to an army of seven hundred desperadoes. Hundreds of men organized themselves into militia groups and marched to the besieged arsenal from as far away as Baltimore. From Washington, D.C., dispatched by President Buchanan, came Brevet Colonel Robert E. Lee with his cavalry unit and a troop of United States Marines from the Navy Yard.

Brown, encumbered by thirty-odd hostages including George Washington's descendant, retreated to a small engine house within the arsenal where he made his last stand. Numerous townspeople, including the mayor of Harpers Ferry, were killed in the gunfire emanating from his location. As federal military units and militia converged on the scene, Brown's men were mowed down.

Watson Brown and his younger brother Oliver died in agony, the latter slowly bleeding to death as he lay on the floor in the engine house. When U.S. Marines finally stormed the building and placed John Brown under arrest, Oliver was dead. Watson lingered twenty hours longer. Among those on the scene immediately after Brown's arrest were Senator James M. Mason of Virginia and Virginia governor Henry A. Wise. Reporters from the Baltimore and New York newspapers also arrived.

Brown declined to identify those who had given him money.

Governor Wise and Senator Mason knew Brown was staying silent to protect his co-conspirators. A letter warning the government of an imminent attack on Harpers Ferry had come to light in the office of the secretary of war. This message, received months earlier and disregarded as the raving of a lunatic, urged the U.S. military to apprehend John Brown immediately. Brown was the active agent, the letter warned, "of a secret association having for its object the liberation of the slaves." The letter had apparently been sent by a number of Iowa Quakers whom Brown tried to recruit for his Harpers Ferry scheme. The Quaker men were ardent abolitionists, but they abhorred violence.

On the evening of October 17, Julia Ward Howe was sitting in the parlor at Green Peace, reading that day's issue of the *Boston Evening Transcript* by the light of a table lamp. She was seven months pregnant. By Christmas, this forty-year-old mother of five would deliver a sixth, a boy.

A startling headline in the "Telegraphic News" column of the paper caught her eyes. PROBABLE HOAX?' asked the letters in bold. "A dispatch just

received from Fredericton [*sic*] and dated this morning states that an insurrection has broken out at Harpers Ferry, where an armed band of Abolitionists have full possession of the government arsenal. The express train going
east was twice fired into, and one of the railroad hands and a negro killed
while they were endeavoring to get the train through the town. . . . The insurrectionists number about 250 whites, and are aided by a gang of negroes."
Just beneath was a brief update contradicting the report: "A later dispatch
says the affair at Harpers Ferry is much exaggerated."

As Julia wondered over this tidbit of information, her husband walked
into the room. She showed him the newspaper.

"Brown has got to work," Dr. Howe said approvingly, recognizing his protégé in action, though the bulletin mentioned no names of possible perpe-
trators. Julia noted grimly in her diary, "I had already arrived at the same
conclusion."

As dispatches continued to flow from Virginia, the situation began to
clarify. John Brown was identified as the leader of the insurrectionists. Instead of retreating to the Allegheny Mountains with his followers as he had
planned, Brown was a prisoner in the jail at Charlestown, Virginia, awaiting
trial by state court. At this news, the mood in the Howe household changed
from one of satisfaction to panic. Chev could not know what John Brown
might confess under questioning. Would the insurrectionist name him as a
co-conspirator?

Fearful he would be extradited to Virginia and tried for treason at John
Brown's side, Dr. Howe began packing his bags to flee the country. By October 25, Samuel Gridley Howe, former hero of the Greek revolution and famous teacher of the blind, was in flight like any outlaw, making for Canada.
It was not his finest hour.

Howe should have trusted John Brown. To the day of his execution,
Brown maintained he acted alone, swearing before judge and jury that he
was neither the tool nor the ally of any antislavery organization. This piece
of testimony saved Dr. Howe, Reverend Parker, and the other men involved
from prosecution.

Physical evidence told a different story. In search of clues about the raid,
Lieutenant J. E. B. Stuart led a sweep of the Maryland farmhouse where
teenage Annie and Martha Brown had cooked and cleaned for the hidden
fighters. The girls, gone to the safety of their mother's farm in Ohio, had
left their father's belongings in the house. Stuart discovered "a carpet-bag"
bursting with John Brown's correspondence, four hundred letters in all. Here
was a paper trail leading investigators to Dr. Howe's office at 20 Bromfield

Street, and to the door of Green Peace itself. Governor Wise and Senator Mason need wonder no longer the name of the man who was, as they said, "one of the chief instigators of Brown's raid."

Julia Ward Howe stayed with her children at Green Peace while Chev hid beyond the Canadian border. Howe's illicit handover to Brown of guns and money belonging to the Massachusetts Kansas Committee became public knowledge. Bostonians who had donated to the committee in good faith, believing their funds would help settlers in the West, now were dismayed to learn they unwittingly supported the raid on Harpers Ferry. It was an unsettling experience for Julia, pampered descendant of Revolutionary heroes, to have her husband classed with "murderers, *traitors,* robbers, [and] insurrectionists."

She feared that Chev might wind up on the gallows. It was a "very sad" time, Mrs. Howe later wrote. Her troubles were compounded by the physical exhaustions of pregnancy. Her nights were passed sleeplessly, she said, tossing and turning on a "pillow rough with care."

By coincidence, Edwin Booth opened at the Boston Museum in early November 1859. Trying to forget her troubles, and perhaps a bit in love with the handsome star, Mrs. Howe attended his shows nightly. She started work on a seventy-two-line poem about the feelings that came to her while watching Booth perform *Hamlet.* Her poem dwells on his physical perfection. She lingers over a description of Edwin's face, "beautiful as dreams of maidenhood," and exclaims that the smallest hint of a smile from "his fair lips magical" makes her heart leap in "strange revolution."

Julia Ward Howe's ode to Edwin Booth, "Hamlet at the Boston," was published in the *Atlantic Monthly* shortly after John Brown's execution. For a woman terrified that her husband's reputation shortly would be ruined by a charge of treason, penning a poem about Edwin Booth was a smart move. The young celebrity was wildly popular. The Howe family's reputation could not be hurt by association with such an admired figure. Also, Julia was showing her peers in Boston, New York, and Newport that she was not afraid to stand in the public spotlight. Hiding at a time like this, as Dr. Howe had done by going to Canada, looked too much like an admission of guilt.

Her husband came slinking back into Boston by the new year. He was contacted immediately by Senator Mason of Virginia, who had convened a committee to investigate the incident at Harpers Ferry. Sam Howe prepared his statement to the U.S. Senate with the help of some of Harvard Law School's most distinguished graduates, including John A. Andrew, soon to be elected governor of Massachusetts. Looking back, one historian has called

Howe's protestations of innocence to the Mason Committee an episode of "gross prevarication." By dodging some questions, and telling outright lies in answer to others, Howe evaded the blame investigators hoped to pin on him. The substantial gifts of money and guns he made to John Brown in 1858 and 1859, the doctor said, were intended "to show his sympathy." He had been entirely "without cognizance of [Brown's] purpose."

Samuel Gridley Howe walked away unscathed.

TEN

PREPARE FOR
YOUR EXECUTION

Prepare for your execution: you are condemned.
—*Coriolanus*, 5.2

AFTER SUNSET ON NOVEMBER 19, 1859, A SPECIAL TRAIN ROARED INTO Richmond's central station at Seventh and Broad streets, directly across from the Marshall Theatre. Blocks away, at the bell tower on Capitol Square, bell ringers began pulling frantically at ropes, filling the night with noise, alerting the darkened city to the arrival.

This was only a fleeting stop. Coal fires burning, the train hummed on its rails. Engineers were keeping the brakes on long enough for the city's emergency troops—over three hundred young men called into service by Governor Henry A. Wise—to crowd aboard. Members of Richmond's club-like militia companies—the Richmond Grays, the Richmond Blues, the Virginia Riflemen, the Howitzer Company, the Old Guards, and the Young Guards—struggled into uniforms and marched to the depot, throwing knap-sacks, muskets, and bedrolls into a baggage compartment at the end of the ten-car train.

Wise was not taking any chances. John Brown was locked in jail at Charlestown, Virginia. The prisoner had been tried and condemned. His sentence—death by hanging on December 2—was immutable. Yet rumors had reached the governor's ears that Brown's abolitionist supporters planned to make a second assault on Virginia soil, this time striking Charlestown. "Large forces of desperadoes from North, East and West," Wise asserted, were plotting to break their hero out of jail in the next two weeks, or would storm his scaffold on December 2 to halt his execution. Four companies of U.S. Army infantry led by Colonel Robert E. Lee, the force President Buchanan dispatched to Charlestown, were not enough, Wise decided. To meet the threat, the governor called on armed citizens' groups from across his state.

Tonight's train would rush Richmond's volunteers to the scene of Brown's execution. The mood at the station was jubilant, one newspaper noted, hundreds of young men eager to defend Virginia from her enemies were climbing into railroad cars, "in high spirits at the prospect of meeting the aides and abettors of old Brown!"

Twenty-two-year-old John Wilkes Booth, still toiling as an extra at the Marshall Theatre, heard the bells. He was getting ready for his minor part in *Timothy Toodles*, a comedy filled with gags and pratfalls, but John Wilkes never made it to the stage. He had spent his youth charging through the forests on his father's farm, a weapon from a Mexican battlefield in his hand, acting out imaginary deeds of valor. Tonight, real-life drama at the train station beckoned. Here was an avenue of escape from his unrewarding work as a supe.

Wilkes jumped to his feet, telling the other actors he was leaving. They protested. Junius Brutus Booth had been famous for pulling these stunts. It was Edwin Booth's job as a child, everyone knew, to prevent his father from running off before curtain time. But Junius had been a star; his lapses were part of his mystique. John Wilkes was no star. Members of the cast asked John what he thought his employers, John T. Ford and George Kunkel, would have to say about his last-minute desertion.

"I don't know and I don't care," John Wilkes reportedly answered, pushing his way out.

Crossing Broad Street, he dodged the crowds of uniformed men piling into the passenger cars. He headed for the back of the train, the baggage car, perhaps hoping to stow away there undetected, but he was blocked by twenty-year-old George Libby and his friend Louis F. Bossieux standing guard. Libby and Bossieux belonged to the Richmond Grays, the famous militia company whose members were sons of the city's elite. They were admired for their demonstrable skill in riding and marksmanship, and for their costumes. Billowing greatcoats adorned with shoulder capes supplemented the tight-fitting gray uniforms. Club members sported distinctive white sashes crossed over the chest in an X. Their signature gray hats, worn at a rakish tilt, were secured under the chin with a strap. Their weapon of choice was a rifle with long bayonet.

John Wilkes asked Libby and Bossieux for permission to board the train. The two Grays looked at one another doubtfully. Everyone recognized "J. B. Wilkes," as playbills called him, but the Grays' orders were clear.

"No one [is] allowed on the train but men in uniform," Libby told the actor.

John Wilkes might have been stiff and awkward when making speeches onstage, but he came alive when he stepped off the boards. In social situations, his constraints vanished. Booth had a talent for being "exceedingly companionable," one Richmond friend admitted. "He was a man of irresistible fascination by reason of his superbly handsome face . . . and a peculiar halo of romance with which he invested himself."

Smiling persuasively at the two Grays, Booth confessed he was so eager to join the Grays' expedition that he would buy a uniform if necessary—a broad hint that the actor was prepared to bribe his way onto the train. John Wilkes Booth had such a "winning personality," Libby confessed, he found it impossible to say no.

"After some consultation with [John Wilkes]," George Libby told *Confederate Veteran* magazine in 1930, when he was ninety-one years old, "Bossieux and I each gave him a portion of our uniforms, took him in the car, and carried him with us." Some money may well have changed hands, for on the ride to Charlestown John Wilkes was spotted wearing a near-complete military costume. Philip Whitlock, another Gray on the train that night, one who said he "rarely missed" a chance to see Shakespeare at the Marshall Theatre, reported being "very much surprised to see John Wilkes Booth . . . in a Richmond Gray uniform" acting like one of their company.

THE GRAYS ARRIVED IN CHARLESTOWN TO FIND THE PLACE A SWIRLING mass of uniformed bodies: students from military academies, citizen-led militia from all corners of Virginia, and a sizable detachment of U.S. Marines. A spirit of friendly competition animated the groups, even in the midst of the statewide alarm. Cadets from the Virginia Military Institute vied with their civilian rivals, showing off the complexity of their drill exercises and the speed with which they assumed battle formation. The leaders of some units make a veritable "Who's Who" of future Confederate heroes: in addition to Colonel Robert E. Lee, Turner Ashby was there and a thirty-five-year-old named Thomas Jonathan Jackson, later known as Stonewall.

The men commandeered beds and shelter in the village of Charlestown, taking over barns, schoolhouses, and churches. Space was so tight, one historian writes, "the very graveyards were invaded for washing and cooking purposes." The Grays occupied a low-lying building that once had been a tin factory. Another militia club, Turner Ashby's Black Horse Squadron, set up camp in the yard behind. Libby remembered how he, John Wilkes, and the other Grays enjoyed visiting these neighbors, who had brought with them a wagon containing "a runlet of mountain dew, which they dispensed liberally." The Virginia moonshine made the next two weeks of sleeping on mounds of straw in an abandoned factory a happier experience for all.

After sundown, when the Grays and the Black Horse Squadron were not on sentry duty, John Wilkes enlivened the hours around the campfires with performances of Shakespeare. "Nearly every night before taps," one Gray reported, "he would entertain us with dramatic plays. He was very fond of reciting." Standing before these new friends, his voice mellowed, perhaps, by swigs of Turner Ashby's home brew, John Wilkes found inspiration.

Some had scoffed at Governor Wise for summoning militia in such large numbers, but hindsight proved him right. There were in fact a number of plots unfolding in New York and Boston to spring John Brown from prison, with planning starting as soon as Brown's trial began. Dr. Howe, from Canada, contributed his own risky scheme, urging that a team of rescuers could break into the jail using volleys of "bombs and hand-grenades." More subtle strategies were proposed by abolitionist spies who came to Charlestown under pretext of visiting the prisoner or providing him with legal counsel. These men carefully observed the location of the jail, mapped the placement of Brown's cell within the building, and identified escape routes. An immense chimney stretching upward from a prison fireplace afforded one idea. "Two good Yankees could get [him] out and away *so* easily!" exclaimed a plotter, seeing this exit. Visitors urged Brown in whispers to prepare for a rescue.

In the month between his capture and his execution, John Brown became a national celebrity. Admiring stories of how the killer sat cheerfully and piously in his cell, awaiting punishment, filled Northern newspapers. Captivity did nothing to decrease his charismatic appeal. Even his jailers—Governor Wise included—admitted feeling kindly toward him. North of the Mason-Dixon boundary, this murderer was hailed as a hero, a patriot, a liberator—his death sentence was blasted as unjust. From France, Victor Hugo protested that if the state of Virginia carried out Brown's sentence, it would be martyrdom. John Brown's dying body, Hugo wrote, "would hallow the scaffold, even as the death of Christ had hallowed the cross."

Guarding this man from rescue by his supporters—especially as his prestige ballooned and his daily parade of visitors lengthened—was an around-the-clock responsibility. George Libby recalled his two weeks in Charlestown as a time of constant alertness, when the sound of a single shot sent whole companies of men running to the jailhouse to "form a hollow square around it to repel the attempt to rescue the prisoner." Libby and the Grays went through this defensive maneuver many times, but no attacks came. Jumpiness explained the false alarms: the least snap of a twig, or the unexpected hoof fall of a horse in the darkness, startled the sentries into firing off their weapons.

The day of John Brown's death, December 2, arrived, bright, crisp, and windy. The execution was scheduled for eleven-thirty in the morning. When he emerged from his jail, Brown was startled to find nearly two thousand men waiting for him in the street in silence. Arms bound tightly behind him, Brown needed help climbing into the flat bed of a wagon that was hitched to a pair of white horses. According to custom, he sat not on a proper seat, but on the coffin that had been provided for his body when the hanging finished. Thomas J. Jackson watched the scene intently, noting that the coffin was a handsome affair of dark walnut, protected by a poplar crate. Brown was conveyed a short distance out of town to an open pasture where his gallows loomed. Uniformed men flowed around the wagon, surrounding it on all sides, alert for signs of a rescue attempt.

John Wilkes had been awake since dawn, along with the other Richmond Grays. They lined up by height close to the scaffold—no more than thirty feet away—and stood at attention in the rough grass. Red-shirted VMI cadets took places nearby, some carrying flags of Virginia and the United States, others with howitzers loaded and at the ready.

Philip Whitlock, standing beside Booth in the line, noticed the actor seemed agitated. Wilkes could not take his eyes from Brown. When he ascended the platform, the abolitionist's hands were untied and he was permitted to shake hands with his executioners. John later told his sister Asia how horrible he felt at the sight of Brown "vainly" peering around the field, looking for signs of rescue. Booth watched Brown scan the tree line hemming the field. No mob armed with hand grenades made its appearance: the surrounding forest was undisturbed. Watching comprehension dawn on Brown's face, John Wilkes later said, he felt "a throb of anguish" in his chest. "He was a brave old man," John Wilkes told Asia. "His heart must have broken when he felt himself deserted." Brown may have been a villain and vigilante, but John Wilkes could not help honoring the man for his courage.

Brown was like one of the characters that John Wilkes's father so often played onstage. The elder Booth had invested his villainous characters, one reviewer claimed, with appealing qualities like "heroic courage, sublime defiance and strong affection." It was the Booth genius to present Shakespeare's evil protagonists as "fallen angels," men who were admirable and gifted in some ways, yet fatally misguided and flawed.

Indeed, it may well be that John Wilkes was thinking of his own father on that day. A story Junius Brutus Booth told Asia and John Wilkes when they were young concerned a condemned man he had witnessed being executed by guillotine in Brussels in 1814, during the Napoleonic wars. Junius had watched as the terrified convict was dragged before the large-bladed contraption. The man begged for his life, kicking and fighting each step of the way up the scaffold, clutching at the robes of his executioners. Tired of this display, the guards shoved their victim forward so that he stumbled, mid-plea, falling into the machine just as the guillotine came slicing down to sever head from shoulders.

John Brown behaved differently than this character from Booth's story. When he realized he indeed would die, he betrayed no fear. As the executioner's white bag was placed over Brown's head, and the rope about his neck, he stood quietly. Even when the man in charge of the trapdoor bungled the ropes, and ten suspenseful minutes passed while workers fumbled with the mechanism, Brown neither moved nor spoke. When the "All ready" signal was called, nothing happened. The "All ready" came again, and this time an ax chopped through the rope securing the trapdoor beneath Brown's feet, the drop released, and the hooded figure went plummeting down.

The man who would later be known as Stonewall Jackson, standing not far from John Wilkes Booth in a line of VMI cadets, sent a detailed account to his wife, Anna, of Brown's death throes: "his arms, below the elbows, flew up horizontally, his hands clinched; and his arms gradually fell, but by spasmodic motions."

Only then, Jackson wrote, did a strong wind blow "the lifeless body to and fro." Someone in the assembled crowd shouted across the stillness of the field,

"So perish all such enemies of Virginia! All such enemies of the Union! All such foes of the human race!"

Philip Whitlock turned to John Wilkes and asked in a whisper if he was all right, for the actor was trembling and looked as if he were about to be violently ill.

"He said that he felt very faint and that he would give anything for a good drink of whiskey," Whitlock reported. "Of course, he did not get it then."

For John Wilkes Booth, the hanging of John Brown was a never-to-be-forgotten episode. Thus far, he never had come close to matching the exploits of his older brothers. He had missed crossing the Isthmus of Panama and seeing the Pacific coastline. Nor could he ever claim, trapped so long on the family farm in Harford County, to have met dangers equal to those Edwin faced on his pirate-plagued voyage to Hawaii and Australia. Finally, on December 2, 1859, twenty-two-year-old Wilkes had made his way to a crossroads in history, partaking of an epic moment.

There was an edge to John Wilkes's emotions as he watched Brown die. Despite his admiration for the man's valiant showing on the scaffold, Booth had a personal stake in this criminal's punishment. Brown and his band made Maryland, John Wilkes's home state, the staging ground for their crime. And numbered among the prominent Boston abolitionists accused of encouraging Brown to attack was the new friend his brother Edwin was so proud to have made, the distinguished doctor Samuel Gridley Howe.

Late in the afternoon on Sunday, December 4, the Grays rolled back into Richmond to be greeted by crowds waiting at the Seventh Street station. "Not only the city, but the State owes the volunteers a debt of gratitude," proclaimed an editorial in the *Richmond Dispatch* the next morning, "for the promptness with which they shouldered their muskets and left their homes to defend from invasion the soil of Virginia." The Grays and the other militia were hailed as heroes.

John T. Ford and his partner Kunkel, managers of the Marshall Theatre, however, were furious. John Wilkes had flouted the rules of the Dramatic Star Company. He had left his fellow actors in the lurch, forcing them to work harder in his two-week absence. Kunkel castigated John, telling him he no longer had a place at the Marshall and that management had no obligation to pay him a salary for the period of his absence.

It is easy to imagine John Wilkes putting on a show of bravado at this news, and scoffing at his employers. Yet being fired would have been a blow. However recklessly he may have treated his obligations to Ford and Kunkel, John needed this position and the albeit meager salary that went with it, or he would be forced back home to live off Edwin's charity until he could find another job.

Discovering Booth had been fired, the Richmond Grays literally marched to his rescue. "A large contingent of the First Virginia Regiment," one Marshall actor recalled in amazement, gathered before the theater, demanding that John Wilkes Booth be restored to his former post. There was no choice but to accede. No theater owner would risk the wrath of his local audience by defying popular will. Booth must have basked in this show of soldierly fellowship. He finished out his term at the Marshall Theatre, staying on in Richmond for the remaining six months of the 1859–60 dramatic season.

• • •

When John Wilkes headed north to spend the summer of 1860 with his mother, home was no longer Tudor Hall. The Booths' farm now was occupied by tenants. Nor was home the city of Baltimore, where, since Edwin's return from California, the actor rented a residence for his mother and siblings' use. In 1860, Mary Ann Booth lived in an elegant suite of rooms in Philadelphia, having moved to a new address leased for her by Edwin, and large enough to accommodate her daughter Rosalie, her son Joseph, and any other children who chose to visit. Asia was married, living at her own home in Philadelphia with a new husband and baby.

This homecoming was not free of conflict. When John Wilkes returned from the South, his baggage stuffed with photographs and souvenirs of a moment spent in the spotlight of history, his family rebuked him for jeopardizing his relationship with theater owner Ford and for breaking his contract. Within days of his brother's dash to Charlestown, Edwin was writing friends about "the mad step John has taken." Edwin even belittled the governor of Virginia's call to arms. The Richmond Grays, he believed, were no more than a group of boys playing a war game.

"I fear the discipline is hardly severe enough to sicken [John Wilkes] immediately with 'a soldier's life,'" one of Edwin's correspondents wrote him, "'Tis a great pity he has not more sense . . . foolish boy, what can he be thinking of?" The stunt seemed the height of immaturity, a sign that John Wilkes Booth was unfit for stage work. John's desertion also seemed to his family like an unpleasant echo of Junius Brutus Booth's weird, drunken disappearances. The old star's troubling eccentricities—running away to arrange a funeral for carrier pigeons, or wandering coatless and hatless in winter, burrowing into piles of leaves—were things his family longed to forget.

Only Asia was willing to hear John Wilkes's triumphant stories of what the other Booths considered irresponsibility. She was John's main auditor, listening to his boasts of bravery, admiring his souvenir pictures and the steel-pointed pike carried all the way back from Virginia, a weapon, he said, that had belonged to John Brown. During the two weeks he spent in Charlestown, Booth met Lewis Washington, great-grandnephew to the first president of the United States. This descendant of a founding father—who survived his kidnapping by John Brown—presented young Booth with the murderous spear Brown had used when making his last stand. Asia saw the inscription, "Major Washington to J. Wilkes Booth," inked onto the weapon's wooden shaft. It was a gift that brought her young brother full circle.

The youth who played in the Maryland forests with a lance from the Mexican War now had his own memento of military service.

Asia leaves a sad account of John exaggerating the details of his service with the Grays. He let his sister believe he had been "one of the party going to search for and capture John Brown," not simply a guard at the hanging. Wilkes bragged that he and the Grays were constantly "exposed to dangers and hardships." John Wilkes told Asia "he was a scout," and brandished "a picture of himself and others in their scout and sentinel dresses."

A Richmond resident who remembered John Wilkes when he worked at the Marshall later testified that this young actor "did not like corrections." The reckoning John faced for deserting his job, coming no doubt in the form of a lecture from Edwin, probably left him on edge. The older brother was the family patriarch now, and he wielded authority coolly and confidently over the rest of his family.

EVERY HOUSE HAS ITS HERO, MEMORIALIZED IN PICTURE OR STATUE, OR IN the form of some souvenir or relic. At Richard Booth's London town house in 1796, the year his son Junius Brutus Booth was born, a portrait of George Washington had been enshrined on the wall. In the old log cabin in the Harford County woods where Edwin and John Wilkes were born, Lord Byron's miniature and his books of poetry held pride of place. At Green Peace, the Boston mansion belonging to the Howe family, Lord Byron again was the household god. The Greek war helmet Dr. Howe had rescued from a sale of the dead poet's belongings stood proudly at the top of a green metal stand in the entry hall, announcing to visitors that in the Howes' home, the crusading spirit of freedom that Byron personified, to dare anything and risk everything, held sway.

As John Wilkes settled into his mother's home in Philadelphia, he would see Edwin's face staring down at him from the drawing room wall. Around the picture's frame, Mary Ann Booth had twisted a wreath of real laurel, the traditional hero's crown. Close to Edwin's picture, perhaps on a small marble-topped table, there was a scrapbook containing all the letters of compliment and congratulations Edwin received from prominent citizens in New York, Boston, New Orleans, and Philadelphia. Edwin's correspondence from Julia Ward Howe had pride of place here. Mary Ann Booth and Edwin "prized" this fan mail, they said, from social elites. As Edwin explained, these admiring missives were worth "more than the fame or pecuniary success which has attended me." Mother and son could ask for no better proof of the change in their family's circumstances from the years of shame and poverty they weathered in the 1840s and '50s. It was Edwin's habit to show this scrapbook, he confessed, "with pride, to my brothers and sisters, who rejoice[d] with me in the enjoyment of such friendship."

This shrine to Edwin's success forced John Wilkes to realize that the long shadow his older brother cast had only become longer. Edwin's single-handed rescue of their family name and fortunes proved anything was possible in this socially mobile nation. Fortunes could be made—and lost—with astonishing rapidity. Leaps across boundaries of class could be achieved in a short span of years. Even a look at the candidate in this year's presidential race showed the scope America offered to those ambitious to rise. Abraham Lincoln climbed his way upward, freeing himself from hardscrabble obscurity and a family even more socially remote than the Booths.

Asia later wrote that by 1860 Edwin Booth "had become the most popular tragedian in the United States." Her brother was, she said, "at the acme of a fame deservedly won." The phenomenon of his celebrity was noticeable even when he walked down the street. A New Yorker remembers that whenever Edwin Booth appeared on a sidewalk in the summer of 1860, "people stopped to gaze at him" in wonder. Every time the young actor left a theater, he had to push his way through crowds of eager fans waiting by the stage door, hoping to catch sight of him.

Edwin's impressive annual income—now approaching a half million dollars in modern currency—transformed him. The "merry, cheerful and boyish" brother whom Asia welcomed home in 1856, fresh from California with a bag of gold dust in his pocket, was long gone. Edwin's pose in 1860, friends remarked, was to be "silent and aloof." In private, Edwin's mother and siblings discovered what effect new wealth had on him: The twenty-seven-year-old now directed their lives as if they were actors in a play that he was responsible for staging.

When June Booth wrote from California that his bank account was empty and his prospects dim, Edwin bailed him out. Edwin owed June for being his manager and mentor in the rough time after their father's death. In 1860, the wealthy young star sent his older brother four thousand dollars, which June promised to invest in San Francisco real estate and a gold mining operation. Joseph Booth, Mary Ann's youngest child, depended on Edwin to pay his tuition in medical school. When Joe dropped out, Edwin hired the twenty-year-old as his theatrical dresser and valet, the same job Edwin performed long ago for their father.

Even Asia allowed her life to be shaped by Edwin's wishes. In 1859 she had agreed to marry her brother's childhood friend, the comedian John

Sleeper Clarke. Booth and Clarke wanted to go into business together, dreaming of owning and operating their own playhouse like John T. Ford or Laura Keene. Marrying Asia Booth cemented Clarke's alliance with Edwin. It was an uneven match. Clarke could not equal Asia's powerful mind, nor share her literary tastes. She later wrote bitterly, "I married to please [Edwin]." Even John Wilkes, who took a break from his work at the Marshall to attend Asia's Baltimore wedding on April 28, 1859, saw the financial logic behind Clarke's proposal. He whispered disturbing words to the bride before the ceremony, warning his sister that her marriage was a sham and herself a pawn in a business transaction. "Always bear in mind that you are a professional stepping-stone," John hissed into her ear.

The Booth family's finances, including Mary Ann's lavish allowance, Rosalie's money, June's investment capital, Joe's tuition, and Asia and her husband Clarke's future assets, all depended on Edwin's continued stardom. Where John Wilkes would fit into this neatly ordered universe, in which all members of the Booth clan revolved obediently and expectantly around Edwin, was an open question.

Before he returned home in the summer of 1860, John let it be known that he was ready to launch his own career as a leading man. He had asked Edwin in February of that year for help finding an agent. John had dreams of a starring tour, perhaps a national one. He told a friend from Baltimore at this time that he was hungry "to take his initiation in the roles that made his father famous." His work as a bit player in Philadelphia and Richmond had taught him at least one lesson: that his "father's name is a power—theatrical—in the land." John knew Americans would pay eagerly to see the starring debut of another son of the great Booth.

Three frustrating years as an apprentice had done nothing to convince John Wilkes he lacked talent. A Marshall Theatre actor named John Berron, who roomed with John Wilkes in a Richmond boardinghouse, later said this younger Booth refused to accept the idea that there was any difference between him and Edwin. John Wilkes would not believe his older brother had been gifted with special abilities, while he himself had not. When John looked in a mirror, he saw a face handsomer than Edwin's. He saw features that were a perfect copy of their father's youthful face, while Edwin looked nothing like that parent. He saw a physique broader and taller than Edwin's, with musculature across the shoulders, chest, and arms that drew admiration from men and women alike.

John believed he had what he called "nature's own legacy," a share of Junius Brutus Booth's divine spark. In conversations with his sister Asia in

1860, John brushed aside his lack of theatrical training and the fact that he never had a dramatic teacher. "If I shine," he predicted confidently, "it will be in the rough." For John Wilkes, acting was a physical exercise, where the display of his impressive face and body—and the hot labor of swordfighting—was the main attraction.

John believed he had no time to lose. For actors as well as actresses, youth was the best time to strike it rich. Edwin himself planned to chase fame while his good looks lasted. His hearthrob status meant more money at the box office. "There's no home for me," he explained of his busy schedule in 1860, "until I have lost my pretties and have ceased to draw [crowds]." For John to let time tick away, delaying his hour in the spotlight, seemed a waste. Added impetus came from Mary Ann, who expected her sons to earn independent livelihoods. Much disparaging talk could be heard around the Booth table of "idlers" and "bummers," young men who lacked gumption to work and make money.

John Wilkes's homecoming to Philadelphia in the summer of 1860 was the occasion for a family conference about his future, with Edwin directing the outcome. At twenty-two, John Wilkes felt he was past due for his turn at center stage, but he could not make a move without his older brother's permission and support. "He never wanted to try to rival Edwin," Asia recorded, but everyone in the family could see that the career John Wilkes craved—a star touring nationally for profit—would set him in competition with his brother.

How to direct John Wilkes's ambition was a dilemma. Edwin was not threatened by his brother's artistic abilities, which he knew to be insignificant, but he could not afford to have another contender for the Booth crown. Two Booths on the star circuit would dampen Edwin's luster and might even fatigue audiences.

To solve this problem, Edwin split the map of the United States in two, practically along the Mason-Dixon Line as it turned out, though his intentions had everything to do with business and not politics. Each brother, Edwin said, would claim one region in which to practice his profession, with the understanding that neither would cross into the other's territory. This plan, which would shape the course of John Wilkes's future and sow lasting seeds of conflict in the Booth family, had worked before. With June Booth safely planted in California, Edwin had been free to launch his career uncontested on the East Coast.

When Edwin explained the terms of his solution, it was a blow for John Wilkes, as heavy as the news of a disinheritance. Their sister Asia later explained that John "felt it rather premature that Edwin should mark off for himself" the massive theaters, mighty populations, and rich economy of the urban Northeast, leaving the places "he no longer cared to go himself," the South, to his younger brother. As Asia relates the episode in her memoir, Edwin's fiat was ironclad. The older brother warned John Wilkes he intended to remain sole possessor of the big cities. He would not tolerate poaching or incursions. Edwin would rule uncontested in the region he had worked so hard to win.

The financial calculation behind this partition was clear. New York had one million residents in Manhattan and in the city of Brooklyn combined; Philadelphia had over a half million; greater Boston almost a quarter million. These were cities where gold-backed currency flourished, where audiences flocked to lavishly appointed theaters, and where drama critics writing for prestigious newspapers and magazines could make an actor's reputation overnight.

Banning John Wilkes from this rich theatrical territory effectively blocked him from becoming a star of his older brother's magnitude. John knew conditions for actors were much less promising in the South. Cities were smaller, populations still growing, and distances between theaters vast, requiring exhausting journeys by rail and steamboat. With 168,000 residents, New Orleans was one of the largest destinations in John Wilkes's new domain. Louisville, Kentucky, had 68,000. Other Southern cities were this size or smaller still. The populations of Richmond, Virginia, and Charleston, South Carolina, for example, did not exceed 50,000. Edwin urged John to try Chicago, St. Louis, and Cincinnati.

Reputations could not be won easily in these places, and money itself was worth less. Currencies circulating in many parts of the South and West were valued differently from those in northeastern cities. The United States had a proliferation of currencies at this time. Banknotes varied from state to state, even from city to city, acquiring their value not from one uniform national standard, but from the varying assets of the banks issuing them.

Instead of an easy chance at winning fast fame and big profits in New York, John had been sentenced to months of hard traveling, small audiences, and smaller box office receipts. He could not see the justice of Edwin's action, and privately he appears to have been enraged. It stung to submit to Edwin, who dictated his terms to John Wilkes with the firmness of a father figure, despite the mere four-year difference in their ages. "You must not think me childish," John Wilkes would later write to June Booth, "when I say that the old feeling roused by our loving brother has not yet died out."

Edwin knew what it was to crave fame; as a twelve-year-old boy, waiting backstage while Junius Brutus Booth performed, he wanted it. Their father had been a sometimes cruel teacher, shaping Edwin into an obsessive, self-critical artist by withholding praise and denying him encouragement. The elder Booth's technique was to eradicate any scrap of vanity his gifted son might have possessed. Later, a teenage Edwin earned a living entertaining the miners, prostitutes, adventurers, and gamblers in the wildcat settlements of 1850s California. By the time he was John Wilkes's age, Edwin had drudged in every backstage job, swallowed some unfriendly reviews, and done more and harder traveling than most Americans ever had, even in this age of pioneers.

To Edwin's mind, giving John Wilkes half the United States in which to launch his career was an undeserved gift. Edwin's younger brother had not yet displayed the focus or discipline necessary for real advancement. John had squandered his past opportunities and alienated potential teachers. In three years as an apprentice, he had not proved himself worthy of a field as great as the one Edwin was giving him. The cities of New Orleans, Savannah, Charleston, St. Louis, and Chicago, though smaller than New York, were civilized places: someone with the Booth name could make a living and achieve a reputation there. This vast territory was far more than Edwin had to work with in California, where he made his beginning as a star.

Parke Godwin, a New York writer who knew the Booth brothers, later explained that Edwin was proud he had not made his "leap to the top at once—nobody ever does." The strange story of how Edwin "had to climb to it," Godwin observed, "through thickets and thorns," became part of the actor's personal legend. If Edwin could make this difficult ascent alone, why should the path be any easier for John Wilkes?

THERE WAS ONE CHINK IN EDWIN'S EXTERIOR PERFECTION. EVEN IN THE summer of 1860, after Junius Brutus Booth had been dead seven years, the son was still haunted by the father's memory. Years spent at the famous actor's side had twisted Edwin's character, filling him with what friends described as "silent bitterness" and instilling in him a habit of "abnormal self-containment."

Playing watchdog to hard-drinking Junius, Edwin wrote, "rendered me prematurely old," and left him with a legacy of alcoholism. The actor could function normally for weeks at a time before slipping, but once he had started on a binge, no one had the power to keep Edwin sober. Mary Ann and Asia called Edwin's sickness "his unfortunate failing." The women consulted doctors only to be told that Edwin's condition was "an hereditary disease." Asia remembered how her brother, after every slip, promised his family "never to drink again," only to succumb to temptation the next time. "Alas, the fallacy of human vows," she observed.

Theater critics could not help but notice, as one wrote, that Edwin Booth was "beginning to show some of the eccentric habits that marred the career of his great father." The young star, like his father before him, was using alcohol to fire his passions before a performance. Trying to explain his bouts of drinking, Edwin told a friend, "but could you read the history of my blighted youth, you'd wonder at my being above the sod." His coldness, his episodic cruelty to friends, his "gloomy soul" that drove him to seek oblivion in drink, all were the result, he argued, of his "dark" and "wretched" past. Adam Badeau tried to keep the actor from damaging himself, but Edwin was too often alone or away on tour for his friend's influence to be of any use.

There was one person Edwin Booth believed could be the remedy. He first met her in November 1856, when he returned from California. She was only sixteen years old, playing Juliet to his Romeo at the Marshall Theatre in Richmond. Her name was Mary Devlin. Like Edwin, she started acting at age twelve, and like him was driven by a powerful ambition. She had dark hair and eyes like his, and a mind that was equally lively and intelligent. Few people could resist Mary, describing her "exquisite personality" and "ineffable charm of manner." Like Edwin, she was a gifted musician, singing and playing the guitar with skill. Mary Devlin came from a large family of Irish immigrants, and since childhood had needed to make her own way in the world. Her father, a tailor and costume maker to the theatrical trade, had used his connections to help his daughter find the theater work she craved. In a few short years, Mary had made a name for herself as an ingénue, playing Juliet and Ophelia to the Romeos and Hamlets of big stars. She had acted in the best theaters in New York, Boston, Baltimore, and Washington, D.C.

The one crucial difference between Mary Devlin and Edwin Booth was that her youth was, and continued to be, a happy one. Everyone in the business who knew her testified to her sunny temperament and affectionate nature. Mary's appealing personality earned her a place as a welcome presence in the household of Joseph Jefferson and his wife. Jefferson, a well-to-do comic actor, worked for many years in the company of Laura Keene.

When Edwin met Mary Devlin in 1856, he wrote home to his mother announcing, "I [have] lost my heart. I [have] found a resting place." Her fellow actors wanted to protect Mary from the attentions of the older star.

Edwin's drinking was notorious, and so, too, was his history as a sexual adventurer. His love affair with Laura Keene was no secret, and neither were his dalliances with stagestruck chambermaids, aspiring actresses, and assorted other females met on the road. Edwin already had a case of what he called "the glorious clap"—gonorrhea—something he contracted while enjoying the freedoms of a traveling star. He was no fit match for sheltered Mary Devlin. To his credit, Edwin backed away from the relationship with the sixteen-year-old. "I loved her," he recalled, "but felt like a villain [when] I pictured to myself the wretched life hers would be if linked to mine. I at once endeavored to break off all further connection with her, for the sake of her reputation."

Two years later, *Romeo and Juliet* brought Edwin and Mary together once again, this time before audiences in Boston. Word had gotten out that Edwin was smitten with his young co-star. The news drew crowds of Bostonians to the theater eager to see Booth showing his real emotions onstage, not counterfeit feeling. Julia Ward Howe, perhaps with twinges of jealousy, never forgot this couple's portrayal of the doomed lovers of Shakespeare's tragedy. "For once," Julia Howe wrote, "the mimic scene bodied forth the truth."

Edwin's resolve to protect the actress from his own damaged temperament melted in 1858. She now was eighteen. Edwin, as one friend put it, felt free to "lay desperate siege to the susceptible Mary." If he could make this warmhearted actress his wife and constant companion, Edwin believed, she might charm him away from his addiction.

For her part, Mary Devlin had idolized Edwin Booth since her childhood. His physical attractions were undeniable, but it was his combination of genius and misery that made him so appealing. It was his spiritual torment, the tragic story of his boyhood, and his plea that she alone could rescue him from his misery that Mary could not resist. The pair exchanged hundreds of letters during their courtship. In a typical passage, she tries to parse the riddle of why their two opposite natures—hers so bright and his so dark—are drawn together. "You have ever seemed to me like what Shelley says of himself—'a phantom among men'—'companionless as the last cloud of the expiring storm'—and yet my spirit seems lighter and more joyous when with you. This I can only account for by believing that a mission has been given to me to fulfill, and that I shall be rewarded by seeing you rise to be great and happy," Mary wrote. "Let me hope to be the sunshine to follow so close, as to cause all traces of recent darkness to pass away."

The lovestruck teenager was ready to devote her life to the challenge of redeeming Edwin Booth from alcohol. "Think over the future, and all the good things I am going to do, to soothe and comfort you, in your tired moments," she promised. "Then, the foot-lights will fade, the cares of your profession be forgotten—and the 'great artist' become a man! Ah, Edwin, I shall so strive to make you happy—I love you too fondly to do aught else—and if I succeed, 'mine the joy, mine the bliss.' In the night, when no one sees, or can reach our souls, save He who joined them, you will tell to me, your heart's sad story of the past; I will kiss your pale cheek, dearer to me for the trouble that has robbed it of its hue—and persuade you into forgetfulness." In her most fanciful flights of imagination, Mary confessed to Edwin, she almost could hear the spirit of Junius Brutus Booth speaking to her, "guiding me," she said, "to see the true nature of his son."

Adam Badeau was now "entirely given up," Asia reported. Edwin's loyal champion, the writer who introduced him to high society and taught him the manners of a gentleman, felt the anguish of rejection. After Mary Devlin arrived on the scene, Edwin's old friend began to "wander forlorn and brokenhearted," a Booth family member wrote. Edwin received unhappy letters from the journalist that mourned the new place Mary occupied in the actor's life. "I have seen for some time evidence enough not only of her growing importance," Adam wrote to Edwin, "but of my own eclipse. I wish to God I'd never seen you. It's a frightful thing to live out of one's self, to be buried alive in somebody else." The worst suspense Adam felt involved when the wedding would be. "Damnation, damnation, damnation. Hell. I've asked three or four times when you meant to be married," Adam wrote, "but never a word in reply, damn you."

The matter of marriage was a difficult point with social-climbing Edwin. He never doubted Mary was the wife he wanted, but there was one problem. "I had almost vowed I would never marry—had resolved never to marry an actress," Edwin explained, "that was the only striking flaw in the whole catalogue of the long list of good on Mary's part." Every step he took was calculated to elevate the Booth name. "It cost me many sleepless nights," he confessed, "tossing and troubling of brains and bedclothes." The degree of prejudice against female performers in nineteenth-century America is almost impossible to comprehend today. The contempt for actresses was intense, on par with social attitudes toward prostitutes. Hypocritical as it may seem, Edwin, the bastard son of a drunken actor, could only reconcile himself to Mary's low status by insisting she withdraw from the stage for a full year before they married, and in that time devote herself to polishing her manners and studying genteel subjects like French and literature. After this period of seclusion, they would marry.

It is a measure of Mary Devlin's attachment to Edwin that she turned her back on the work she loved. She gave her last performance in New York in July 1859, then moved to a small cottage in Hoboken, New Jersey, with a staff of servants and a pet greyhound for her companions. Over the next year, a parade of tutors hired by Edwin descended on the house, shaping Mary into an accomplished lady, teaching her to be the kind of person Edwin might take with him into the highest social circles—to Julia Ward Howe's Boston "Booth parties," or to formal dress balls at Manhattan's Century Club. This was a transformation similar to the one Edwin experienced at the hands of Adam Badeau. Mary, despite loneliness and boredom, bravely opened her books of French grammar and tackled the works of Victor Hugo. She studied poetry, practiced on her guitar and the piano, and wrote reports to Edwin of her progress toward the goal of social refinement. "My darling Edwin," she wrote. "Forget, if possible, as I shall, that the Stage ever claimed me as its votary—and any love I may have had for the Art I transfer to you."

Mary was true to her word. Edwin's career, the furtherance of his fame, would be her focus now. "Ah, you do not know how close a *critic* I will be of your 'Genius,'" she laughingly warned him. Her letters were full of plans for improving Edwin's work. This pair discussed the new "naturalness" in performing Shakespeare that Edwin was trying to introduce to American audiences. The couple deplored the old-fashioned stage bellowing of Junius Brutus Booth's generation. "You can, if you will, change the perverted taste of the public, by your truth and sublimity, and you must study for this!" nineteen-year-old Mary urged. "Dear Edwin, I will never allow you to droop for a single moment—for I know the power that dwells within you—and my ambition is to see you surrounded by greatness."

Adam Badeau was a frequent visitor at the cottage. He first came out of curiosity to know better the woman he believed had parted him from Edwin, and later he returned out of a sincere affection for Mary and an impulse to be a part of their new life. As the months of her isolation wore by, Badeau spent hours telling Mary his own history with the star. She soon came to value Badeau, for this friend could tell her things about Edwin she herself had yet to experience. "Waywardness and melancholy," Badeau once told her, are "inherent with genius." He informed the bride-to-be that Edwin's bad spells came upon him suddenly and without warning, "bursting forth," Adam said, "volcano-like."

On the afternoon of July 7, 1860, Adam Badeau and John Wilkes Booth proceeded solemnly, with Edwin Booth between them, to the house of a clergyman in New York City. "My head is full of 'Marry Mary-marry-marriage,'" Edwin exclaimed. "This is a panorama of my brain a present—wandering about from 'nix' to nothing." His inward emotions were jumbled, he said, a mix of "fear, hope, regret, bliss, love, etc." Mary Devlin was waiting for him calmly, one of her sisters serving as matron of honor.

It was "a simple ceremony," Badeau remembered, with few guests in attendance. "After it was over," Badeau noted, "Wilkes threw his arms about Edwin's neck and kissed him." The anger John Wilkes felt over Edwin's partition of the national map, he kept to himself. He was the only member of the Booth family to witness the wedding.

Asia Booth Clarke had boycotted the affair. Her brother's marriage to an actress seemed to dredge up memories of the humiliation and shame she had experienced in Baltimore years before, when her mother, Mary Ann Booth, had been castigated in the streets as a whore. Asia splashed a stream of venomous words across paper, calling Mary Devlin "a deep designing artful actress," and declaring that "nothing can induce me to condescend to her level." Asia told Edwin she would never agree to meet her new sister-in-law face-to-face. "I cannot stoop to that which I despise," Asia wrote. She was furious at her brother for damaging the Booth name by marrying "a bold-faced woman who can strut before a nightly audience." The fact that Asia's own husband was a slapstick comedian seemed to have no bearing on her attitude.

The bride's being Irish was another mark against her in Asia's mind, who nursed a palpable hatred for this newly arrived contingent. "Her family are of the lowest Irish class," she wrote to a friend. "Ned, I presume . . . will have them to support."

However, the strongest reason for the Booth clan to give Mary Devlin a hostile reception was neither her Irish heritage nor her successful stage career. As Edwin's wife, this young woman now had first claim on the river of money the star had been producing for his family's benefit since 1856. "She wants his money and his name," Asia wrote, "a grand position for a poor obscure girl." Mary Ann Booth did not express her daughter's open fury. While she did not attend the wedding, Edwin's mother accompanied the newlyweds to a cottage they rented for the summer on the Canadian side of Niagara Falls. Twenty-year-old Joe Booth, Edwin's youngest brother, also joined them there.

Mary and Edwin soon wrote to Adam Badeau, inviting him to spend two weeks with them in Canada. Edwin's membership in Manhattan's Century Club was secure, and Julia Ward Howe remained a warm friend, but perhaps this couple, stung by Asia's fury, wanted to safeguard their entrée into New York society. Badeau later remembered of this honeymoon visit with Mr. and Mrs. Booth, "he was most anxious to show me that his marriage had made no difference in his feeling toward me, and his wife was quite as anxious that I should perceive none."

JOHN WILKES SPENT THE SUMMER OF 1860 MEMORIZING HIS SHAKE-speare. The twenty-two-year-old actor had been taken on by an agent, Matthew Canning, a onetime Philadelphia lawyer now turned show business impresario. Canning cut a dashing figure—he dressed in expensive suits, shined his boots to a gleaming brightness, sported a well-groomed goatee and stuck diamond studs in his cravat. He planned to take young Booth down south to headline the new theater being built at Alabama's capital, Montgomery. Canning knew that John Wilkes, despite his famous last name, was inexperienced in leading roles; perhaps as insurance, the agent added another leading man to the roster of his small touring company, Baltimore stage veteran John W. Albaugh. Throughout the month of August, presumably, John Wilkes practiced his fencing moves and learned the lines for the title parts in *Hamlet, Richard III, Romeo and Juliet,* and other pieces Canning wished to stage for Montgomery audiences.

Never had John Wilkes traveled so far south. In October, Canning and his company stopped in Columbus, Georgia. There the young actor suffered perhaps one of the most inauspicious precurtain disasters imaginable. On October 12, one hour before he was supposed to open in *Hamlet,* John Wilkes and Canning were joking around backstage, probably drinking. The agent was holding a revolver in one hand. While carelessly pointing the gun in Booth's direction, one witness remembered, Canning "touched the trigger and it exploded."

News reports notified the public of this "unfortunate occurrence" in different ways. One paper delicately explained that a bullet had hit John Wilkes Booth "in the fleshy part of the thigh." Another, sparing no reader's sensibility, stated the actor "was accidentally shot in the rear." The lead ball penetrated so deeply into the flesh it could not be removed surgically. Even three months later, after the actor cut short this ill-fated tour and returned to his mother's home in Philadelphia to recuperate, family members noted that the wound was unhealed and John Wilkes "still carrie[d] the ball in him." The alternate leading man, Albaugh, took Booth's place that night, newspapers reported, after "an hour's notice and without the least study."

On October 21 or 22, a feeble and subdued Booth departed Columbus aboard the westbound cars of the Montgomery & West Point Railroad. John Wilkes, no doubt, remained standing for the duration of the hundred-mile ride through rolling countryside, a landscape blanketed with cotton fields and acres of corn. He had been unable to act since October 12; the gymnastic work of stage fighting was impossible with a bullet wound. He planned to try again in Montgomery. Yet even in this next town, Matthew Canning's instincts as a manager would prove no better than his caution in handling firearms. John Wilkes Booth's first tour as a star would be marred by more mishap than a stray gunshot.

The Alabama State House, adorned with six white pillars and a big clock dial, overshadowed all other buildings visible from the train depot. Montgomery was a small place: less than nine thousand people lived here, half of whom were slaves. The richness of the state's cotton crop showed in the Italianate residences that graced the streets, in the magnificent size of the Exchange Hotel, where cotton growers and merchants gathered for meetings, and in the huge fireproofed warehouses at the wharves where a million bales of cotton rested every harvest before shipment down the Alabama River. A number of well-appointed brothels did a brisk trade among the business travelers who arrived by steamboat and railroad. Slave auctions took place on a regular schedule in Montgomery's Market Square, where a decorative fountain surrounded by gas lanterns formed a convenient setting. Each night, when the illuminated clock face on the capital indicated nine o'clock, bells rang in the streets, signaling all slaves to go indoors for curfew.

Presidential campaigns were bad for theater business: this was a fact familiar to any experienced manager. Nineteenth-century political events unfolded dramatically in the streets. Rallies, torchlit parades, and open-air speeches transformed cities into backdrops for civic drama. "On quiet nights the houses are great," one actress recalled of her ticket sales during a presidential race, "but on political nights they are bad." In 1860, perhaps more than any other year, this old theatrical wisdom held true. This was no ordinary election, but one of the most convulsive in American history. The future allegiance of the cotton states waited on the outcome of this election: firebrand secessionists in Alabama, Georgia, and elsewhere were ready to leave the Union if a Republican president was elected on November 6. In Montgomery, as this day approached, excitement seemed to be everywhere but inside the new brick theater with seating for four hundred that had opened at the corner of Monroe and Perry streets.

In a February 27 speech at New York's Cooper Union, candidate Abraham Lincoln accused leaders in the South of being beyond the reach of reasonable argument. "If they would listen—as I suppose they will not—I would address a few words to the Southern people," he said. "Your purpose, then, plainly stated, is that you will destroy the Government, unless you be allowed to construe and enforce the Constitution as you please." Further, Lincoln said, "you will not abide the election of a Republican president! In that supposed event, you say, you will destroy the Union; and then, you say, the great crime of having destroyed it will be upon us! That is cool. A high-wayman holds a pistol to my ear, and mutters through his teeth, 'Stand and deliver, or I shall kill you, and then you will be a murderer!' . . . What will satisfy them? . . . This, and this only: cease to call slavery *wrong*, and join them in calling it *right*."

John Brown failed to ignite a statewide uprising of Virginia's slaves when he attacked Harpers Ferry. But his violent deed succeeded as planned in one important respect. It awakened a storm of fury in the South and hastened the onset of war. "The universal chorus of applause" for Brown echoing from Northern cities, where many newspapers celebrated the bloody abolition-ist as a hero, incensed Southern leaders. "The Harpers Ferry Invasion has advanced the cause of Disunion more than any other event that has hap-pened since the formation of the Government," a Richmond newspaper asserted. Eighteen sixty was the year, one historian has written, when "the conviction became common in the South that John Brown differed from the majority of Northerners merely in the boldness and desperation of his methods."

When his train pulled into the depot at Montgomery two weeks before the election, John Wilkes Booth arrived at an epicenter of Southern anger and indignation. A local lawyer named William Lowndes Yancey, widely known as the "Apostle of Secession," had whipped emotions in Montgom-ery to fever pitch. Books advocating the common humanity of blacks and whites were being burned at demonstrations in the town square. Militia groups were arming, drilling, and preparing for war in Montgomery's streets. One local moderate, alarmed at the temper of his fellow citizens and fearful of what the future might bring, wrote a letter to Democratic friends in the North, warning, "We are here in the midst almost of a revolution."

The future of slavery in the western territories was the heart of the matter. The Supreme Court's Dred Scott decision, by defining black Americans as property, cleared a legal path for slave owners to carry human chattel all the way to the Pacific. The Republican candidate argued the Dred Scott decision was unconstitutional. "Can we, while our votes will prevent it, allow [slavery] to spread into the National Territories, and to overrun us here in these Free States?" Lincoln asked. "If our sense of duty forbids this, then let us stand by our duty, fearlessly and effectively." The time for compromise with the South was over, he said. Lincoln's Democratic opponent, Senator Stephen A. Douglas, author of the policy that created "Bleeding Kansas," advocated popular sovereignty, that is, local decision, as a solution to slavery's status in the territories.

Secessionists castigated Douglas as "an itinerant peddler of Yankee notions" and urged everyone to fall in line behind the third-party candidacy of John Breckinridge, who represented the new Southern Democratic Party. By entering the race, Breckinridge split the Democratic vote, ensuring Lincoln's victory. This outcome was exactly what men like Yancey craved: Lincoln's election, he said, would be the trigger for Alabama and other cotton states to leave the Union. Did the South want to submit "to the rule of a party whose avowed purpose is the abolition, not the restriction, of slavery," Yancey demanded, or would she rather fight the North to win "a glorious career of uninterrupted prosperity as a separate nationality"?

The paint was only recently dry on the Montgomery Theater when Canning's Dramatic Company took up residence there for the season. John Wilkes, still hobbled, spent a week of enforced leisure in the town. He would not attempt acting until October 29. In the meantime, as high-profile speakers were speeding to Montgomery to address the secession issue, the town fathers commandeered Canning's stage as a venue for political meetings.

When Georgia senator Robert Toombs arrived on October 25, supporters welcomed him at the train depot with torches and a marching band, then paraded with him to the Exchange Hotel. Only four months later, Jefferson Davis would stand on the grand balcony of this same hotel while William Lowndes Yancey introduced him to cheering thousands as the new president of the Confederate States of America.

On October 26, Toombs was the starring attraction at the Montgomery Theatre, thundering to a packed auditorium that now was the time to end the Union. His warlike words, one auditor remembered, spared "no form of appeal or invective" to achieve his purpose, which was to "urge on the masses to secession and if necessary civil war."

Sidelined by his injury, Booth had nothing to do but listen to the locals talk politics and to visit Montgomery's brothels and saloons, finding himself once more a witness to history. Unlike at John Brown's hanging, where the young actor had slipped into the costume of a Richmond Gray, in Montgomery John Wilkes had a difficult time choosing sides. There was a dissenting view in the town, a minority position to be sure, but one that was clearly advanced during John Wilkes's time there.

Presidential candidate Stephen A. Douglas arrived by steamboat on the night of November 1. He appeared in Montgomery despite death threats from Yancey's supporters and a warning from Robert Toombs that no one in Georgia would be answerable for the Democratic candidate's safety. Five days remained until the election, and this midwestern orator hoped to tame the furor that had seized hold of the citizens of Alabama. Douglas would try to persuade them to abandon the idea of secession.

Douglas indeed seemed "the leader of a forlorn hope," as one historian has dubbed him, for undertaking this eleventh-hour mission. The Illinoisan was in poor health; he had less than a year to live. Yet when he divined by state races in October that a Republican victory was coming, Douglas declared, "We must try to save the Union. I will go South." The forty-seven-year-old brought his wife, twenty-five-year-old Adele Cutts Douglas, with him on the trip. As the couple walked swiftly from Montgomery's steamboat landing to the Exchange Hotel, they knew they were in hostile territory: a gauntlet of townspeople threw rotten eggs and tomatoes in their direction. Douglas was hit in the head by the garbage, while a spray of stinking yolk ruined Adele's dress.

Booth had gone back to work on October 29, three days before Douglas arrived. Reviews of his six-night run were tepid. Critics supposed the twenty-two-year-old star was still suffering the effects of his "late accident." It is likely John Wilkes made his way with the rest of Montgomery's residents at noon on November 2 to the muddy lawn before the capitol. Here, the Democratic presidential candidate delivered an impassioned four-hour defense of the Union. Key phrases and ideas from Douglas's speech do crop up in John Wilkes's later writing, evidence that the young actor listened closely to what Douglas had to say, or at least read the text of the address as it was printed in the next day's newspaper.

Stephen A. Douglas's speech was hard to resist—one plantation owner, after listening to the address, said resignedly, "Well, if Lincoln is elected, *perhaps* we can stand it for four years." The senator's words seem to have fired John Wilkes Booth's imagination, staying with him for days afterward. Douglas painted a grim picture of the ruin that war would bring. This "most prosperous" land, he predicted, would be torn to pieces by "the horrors of revolution, anarchy and bankruptcy." Douglas blamed the "wild frenzy of fanaticism" shown both by abolitionists in the North and fire-eaters in the South for forcing the present crisis. "I regard this Union as the greatest blessing ever conferred upon a free people," the Democratic candidate said. Douglas begged his listeners to "rally round" and oppose "sectional strife and agitation." Together, he promised, "we will crush out Northern abolitionism and Southern disunion."

If ever a listener were primed to absorb Douglas's message, it was John Wilkes Booth. He was the son and grandson of men who had idolized the Union. The elder Booth had solemnly observed the traditional July Fourth ritual: every year after his and Mary Ann's arrival in America, he made the customary toast to "the Union—no cement stronger than the mutual interest which binds us together," and "the United States—may she continue until time shall be no more." The compact of the states, inextricable from the text of the Constitution itself, was the cherished creation of the Founding Fathers, a body of men the elder Booth had taught all his sons to venerate. The blessings of Union—shared commerce, shared connections, shared culture—were tangible, permeating every aspect of American life. The kind of upheaval that disunion would bring was too shocking to contemplate. It would not be out of character, therefore, for John Wilkes Booth to try to push back against the war-hungry attitude of local secessionists and seek to find a middle ground.

The twenty-two-year-old had a public disagreement with Montgomery's fire-eaters, perhaps ones he encountered in a bar or brothel. Tone-deaf to the temper of the people, and perhaps forgetting the threats that had been made against Senator Douglas's life, Booth apparently proclaimed his allegiance to the Union in an exchange with some allies of Yancey. A fragment of John Wilkes's private writing, dated late December 1860, gives a hint of what language he may have used.

"Now Yancy [*sic*] says if his state goes out of the union he must go with her, of course he means if she's right or wrong," John Wilkes wrote. "Now I believe in country right or wrong! . . . We should love the whole Union and not only the state in which we were born. Will you, my brothers, destroy this Union. Can you tear down this great temple of civilation [*sic*]. This Monument of our father's greatness."

He continued, "I will not fight for cesession [*sic*]. No I will not fight for disunion." John had watched his own mother's struggles during the lean, impoverished years after Junius Brutus Booth's death. He feared what worse suffering a civil war would bring. "Famine will range around," he wrote. "Banks will fail. Familys [*sic*] ruined. Poor widow's who want their little mite to rear their children, will point to the famished stricken forms of their dear infants."

These sentiments provoked anger in Montgomery. John A. Ellsler, an actor who knew John Wilkes well, said that the young man's "sympathy for and utterances on behalf of the Union were so unguarded in their expression that his life was in jeopardy." The same citizens, perhaps, who threw garbage at Senator Douglas and his wife now planned a reprisal for Booth. Matthew Canning, realizing it was dangerous for the actor to remain in Montgomery, decided to smuggle him out of town to protect him from vigilante action.

Alabama native Louise Catherine Wooster—a "strikingly handsome" eighteen-year-old prostitute who worked in a Montgomery brothel during the 1860 election season—tells a similar story. She describes John Wilkes Booth hightailing out of town after becoming unpopular with local secessionists. In her 1911 memoir *Autobiography of a Magdalen*, Wooster explains how she became a prostitute at fifteen, when her mother died leaving six daughters with no means of support. A Montgomery madam quickly hired the teenager. "I was young, rather pretty and had a sweet disposition. Soon, I became quite a favorite," Wooster said, with "the higher class of men who visited our house." She claimed John Wilkes was more to her than a loyal customer during the six weeks he spent in Montgomery. He was going to be her rescuer, she wrote, the man who would save her from the sex trade and launch her career onstage.

"Oh! How I loved him," she recalled. "We were never to part, he said. He had advised me to adopt a theatrical career. Then we would always be together." Promising a girl a shot at stardom was standard seduction practice for the Booth men. Before he married, Edwin Booth reported how easily he charmed a "singing chambermaid" with promises of a stage career, then admitted, "I can't brag on her acting so much as what we do in secret." Louise Wooster seems to have fared no differently with John Wilkes. "I had considerable stage talent," Wooster recalled. She and Booth "would have our little rehearsals and he would encourage me and for a time I was truly happy." "But alas," the girl who called herself "Lou" exclaimed, "this castle in the air was soon to be shattered."

"Poor Wilkes had foolishly expressed himself in regard to the rebellion," she remembered. "I felt very uneasy about him." John shared with Wooster the opinions he vented in Montgomery's barrooms. During their meetings, he told her that he "loved the union," and that "he was as bitter against secession as he was against abolition."

Late one night, sometime in the first week of December 1860, the actor burst into Louise's room, declaring, "I must go home or I cannot get away at all." Of the war that was coming, John told her, "This thing cannot last longer than a few weeks or a few months. . . . Such a glorious country as ours cannot be broken up by a few fanatics. All will be over in a few weeks."

"Then," the actor promised, "you shall come to me and my little girl shall have a new life opened for her."

Louise Wooster never saw John Wilkes Booth again. She continued to work in brothels for the duration of the war. In time, Wooster would start her own house of prostitution in Birmingham. She operated this successful establishment for twenty years, retiring a wealthy woman in 1901. To the end of her life, one Birmingham newspaper reported, Wooster guarded carefully "a drawer filled with letters, notes, pictures, valuable presents and trinkets that [Booth] gave her" during their brief association. Because her early history with Lincoln's assassin was known to many Alabama residents, Louise would find herself bothered by proposals of marriage from enthusiastic Booth admirers. Wooster politely declined them all. "I know men only too well," she wrote in her reminiscences. "Very little now could be taught me about [them]."

John's northward journey must have been an uncomfortable experience. The lead ball was still embedded in his flesh. Whether traveling by steamboat or rail, the actor would have been subjected to painful bumping and rattling along his route. One imagines him curled awkwardly to one side, his haunch lifted off the seat. The thoughts running through his mind could not have been happy ones. It was Edwin's edict that had banished him to the Southern circuit this disastrous season. Alabama's residents, too busy parading, speechifying, and preparing for war to pay much attention to shows, seemed only to take note of John Wilkes Booth when he defended the Union. Having to flee for his life at the end of such a disappointing debut was a final indignity.

When he arrived in Philadelphia, John Wilkes found his brother Edwin, his brother-in-law John Sleeper Clarke, and his former employer William Wheatley, manager of the Arch Street Theatre, intent on a lucrative new venture. These three richly dressed gentlemen were making great strides in the managerial game. Clarke and Wheatley planned to produce a ten-night series of Shakespeare's plays at the Academy of Music in Philadelphia over Christmas, starring Edwin Booth. The men would make good money with this scheme.

A wide gulf separated John Wilkes from these polished professionals. Edwin, who always maintained John Wilkes was "irresponsible," could not have had better proof of this opinion than the sight of his younger brother home unexpectedly from the South with a bullet in his tail and his pockets empty. John Wilkes tried to explain what he had experienced firsthand of Montgomery politics, but the older brother only "laughed at John for his patriotic froth," Edwin later recalled. There was no question of the three business partners inviting impecunious, unreliable John Wilkes to take a share in their Academy of Music speculation. This wounded young man—almost, to their eyes, the embodiment of a joke—had been given the South and the West to tour in, and so had no reason to complain. John Wilkes was on his own.

Edwin did not understand who his brother had become during those fatherless years in rural Maryland after Junius Brutus Booth died. Edwin, thousands of miles away on the California frontier, had not endured with John Wilkes the social isolation, the ugly conflicts with field laborers and neighbors, or the outright hunger that drove the Booth children to poach food from adjoining Bel Air farms. Nor, as an itinerant artist, could Edwin begin to gauge what it meant for John Wilkes to spend his formative years in a slave-owning community thirty miles from the Pennsylvania state line in the 1850s. Coming of age in a crucible of racial tensions helped to make John a political being. By contrast, Edwin's single-minded focus on the stage excluded all else: it was almost as if he had become a citizen solely of the theater's world, rather than of any state or region.

Largely ignored by his brother and brother-in-law—Edwin and Clarke were intent on producing and publicizing their ambitious program at the Academy of Music—John Wilkes appears to have spent the last weeks of December 1860 at his mother's home in Philadelphia, mulling politics. In Alabama, John had disagreed with the fiery, war-hungry supporters of William Lowndes Yancey. Now, returned to the North, neither could he fall in line with his family's complacent Republican views. During his time in Philadelphia, John's opinions on secession underwent a change. The direction of his thoughts showed in the draft of a speech he composed in his hours of solitude that Christmas holiday.

Scrawling in the pages of a notebook, he imagined he was addressing a crowd of Northern men. He told this audience to appease all Southern demands. Abolitionists must "throw away their principles," John Wilkes exclaimed, and "be hushed forever." Slave owners must be allowed to bring their slaves into all western territories. Only these remedies would save the Union, John Wilkes argued, "from the fearful brink of self-destruction."

"Say that you [Northerners] will be rich and prosper in everything, and the South be weak & poor, that she would crawl in the dust before you," John wrote. "Is that a cause you should deny her equal rights & justice. Is that a cause for her to be trod upon." In his conclusion, John's anger at the political situation seems to merge with his feelings of being disregarded by his family. The dishonorable conduct of Northern men, John cried, "makes me hate my brothers in the north. It severs all our bonds of friendship. It induces our brothers in the north to deny us our rights, to plunder us, to rob us! . . . It misrepresents me to the whole world."

PART THREE

1861–1865

ELEVEN

MY BROTHER,
MY COMPETITOR

Let me lament,
With tears as sovereign as the blood of hearts,
That thou, my brother, my competitor . . . should divide
Our equalness to this.

—*Antony and Cleopatra*, 5.1

RESIDENTS OF NEW YORK STATE DIVIDED THEIR VOTES FAIRLY EVENLY between the Republican candidate for president in 1860 and his Northern Democratic opponent, Stephen A. Douglas. Though the people of Albany voted in greater numbers for the Democrat, they nonetheless displayed a unified enthusiasm when told an eastbound train carrying Abraham Lincoln to Washington, D.C., would stop in their city on February 18, 1861. Since December, South Carolina, Mississippi, Florida, Alabama, Georgia, Louisiana, and Texas had seceded from the Union. The United States was balanced precariously on the edge of the unknown. As an Albany resident remembered, New Yorkers of all political persuasions were determined to unite behind Lincoln, the man chosen "to stand at the helm of the ship of state, in this her hour of deadly peril."

Inside Fort Sumter, the thick-walled garrison in the harbor of rebel-controlled Charleston, South Carolina, close to a hundred U.S. soldiers had retreated to safety with a dwindling supply of food. The small federal force was commanded by Kentucky-born Major Robert Anderson, a veteran of the Mexican War. Anderson hoped to hold his position until after the inauguration, when the new president might devise an end to the standoff. Lincoln had two choices: provide Major Anderson the supplies he needed to defend the fort, or order him to surrender it to the Carolinians. Either way, war seemed a certainty.

Everyone's "blood was at fever heat," one New Yorker recalled: men walked the streets of Albany in suspense, "faces . . . pale with anticipation of what was about to come." To prove their spirit was warlike, their hearts "true blue" and their politics pure Union, a committee of Albany's citizens readied a banner to greet the president-elect: "Welcome to the Capital of the Empire State—No More Compromise!"

John Wilkes Booth was eating breakfast at Albany's Stanwix Hotel on the morning of February 11, 1861. As he ate, Lincoln's train was leaving Springfield for Washington. Newspaper headlines described the recent rebel congress at Montgomery, Alabama, where the seven seceded states met to declare themselves a new nation. This representative body ratified a constitution and named Jefferson Davis of Mississippi president of the Confederate States of America.

The unsettled state of political affairs had forced Edwin Booth to relax the rules he had earlier set on his younger brother's touring: the national map was not what it had been. Edwin now encouraged John Wilkes to try provincial stops on the Northern circuit like Albany and Portland, Maine, and to turn his attention to points west. Although Edwin had to make these concessions, it seemed unfair to John that even as war loomed, Edwin's exclusive claim on New York City—with its one million people, plentiful theaters, and secure currency—remained in effect. According to Asia, John was "devastatingly ambitious" to shine in his father's profession.

The twenty-two-year-old actor had changed his position since clashing with Montgomery's fire-eaters. His political opinions suddenly had crystallized over the Christmas holiday he spent with his brother Edwin and the rest of the Booth family in Philadelphia.

Contrary to his family's Union feelings, and to the professions of loyalty he made in Montgomery, John Wilkes now "expressed his sentiments in public," witnesses reported, as "a violent secessionist." Once more, John Wilkes misjudged the mood of a locality. Staff and guests at the Stanwix Hotel glowered at the young man who, in loud tones and "with the greatest freedom," one listener testified, celebrated the Confederate news from the South.

John was not an anonymous figure in Albany. Though it was the first day of his visit, word of his engagement at the local Gayety Theatre had generated advance excitement. His father, Junius Brutus Booth, had been a favorite here in the 1840s.

The box office manager of the Gayety, notified of Booth's unwise outburst in the hotel dining room, worried it would dampen ticket sales. He rushed to the Stanwix to tell the actor that his disloyal talk "not only would kill his engagement, but endanger his person."

Offended, John Wilkes demanded, "Is this a democratic city?"

The treasurer, puzzled by the actor's inability to understand the currents of his time and place, answered impatiently, "Democratic, yes, but disunion, no!"

John Wilkes said nothing further in Albany that would jeopardize his profits there, and in truth, he could not afford to do so. The unraveling of the Union sent scores of traveling entertainers northward, cutting short their Southern engagements out of fear of the approaching war. Players' competition for engagements was fiercer than ever before.

The novice's attempt at a starring tour in the South had been a fiasco. Every night John Wilkes performed in Alabama, the bullet wound from Matthew Canning's gun held him back. Albany was a new beginning. Here, a newspaper noted, the youth's recovery "from the effects of a pistol shot" was evident. John gave the audience of the Gayety on February 12 a series of realistic combat scenes. Playing Pescara, "a bloody villain of the deepest red" in *The Apostate*, one of his father's favorite plays, John moved with frenzied energy, slashing, brawling, and roaring for over two hours. As was becoming his habit, he delivered lines loudly and in a disjointed, staccato rhythm. The Albany audience applauded with enthusiasm. John had managed to capture something of this father's furor in fighting. He lost control of himself only in the final act. Carried away by his death scene, he fell onto his sword. The blade thrust deep into the flesh of one armpit, newspapers reported, "inflicting a severe muscular wound under his right arm." The novice star found himself consigned to bed rest for the next five nights.

Booth returned to the Gayety's stage on February 18 for a reprisal of *The Apostate*, his appearance coinciding with Abraham Lincoln's arrival in Albany aboard a New York Central Railroad car. Thousands of spectators waited for the train that afternoon, as did New York's Twenty-fifth Regiment, in full uniform with rifles loaded. When the report of a twenty-one-gun salute in honor of the president-elect momentarily silenced the crowd, a man was heard to mutter "that negro-lover will never get to the Executive Mansion." Witnesses reported that the disgruntled man was punched in the face and kicked to the ground by a strapping Lincoln supporter standing in earshot.

After riding in an open carriage to Albany's statehouse, Lincoln spoke to a gathering that included the governor and members of the state legislature. "It is true that while I hold myself without mock modesty, the humblest of all individuals that have ever been elevated to the presidency," he told his listeners, "I have a more difficult task to perform than any one of them."

John Wilkes Booth kept his thoughts to himself on this historic day. Locals remembered that while Mr. and Mrs. Lincoln welcomed crowds of well-wishers at the Delavan House hotel in the evening, Booth was going through Pescara's paces at the theater only blocks away, his injured right arm bound in a sling, "but fencing with his left, like a demon."

WHEN JULIA WARD HOWE RECEIVED A WEDDING ANNOUNCEMENT FROM the stars who portrayed Romeo and Juliet at the Boston Museum, she was delighted. She wrote to Edwin Booth instantly, congratulating him on his choice of Mary Devlin as a wife, and hailing the new couple as "Great B" and "Little B."

In the early months of 1861, letters from Julia Howe and other well-wishers reached Mr. and Mrs. Edwin Booth in New York City at a spot many Americans considered to be "the exact center of the universe." The newlyweds occupied a suite of rooms in the Fifth Avenue Hotel, a gleaming palace of cream-colored marble at the junction of Broadway, Fifth Avenue, and Twenty-third Street. The city's most expensive retail shops lined these thoroughfares and noisy traffic—omnibuses, carriages, wagons, pedestrians—flowed in all directions. Captains of Wall Street built their tall mansions here, on tree-filled Madison Square. Constructed in 1859 to overlook the square, the Fifth Avenue Hotel was said to be "one of the largest and most elegant buildings of its kind in the world." With room for a thousand guests, the hotel was equipped with a magnificent rotunda, a library, rooms for dances and social events, a dining hall, and a mirrored, mahogany-trimmed bar famous for the quality and rarity of its liquors. Residents ascended and descended the hotel's six stories by stepping aboard a strange contraption called "a vertical railway": the hotel was the first in New York City to install a passenger elevator.

The Booths were resident celebrities. Porters carrying luggage for other long-term guests would point out the location of the young couple's apartment. At times, a half-opened door permitted the curious to glimpse a book-lined parlor decorated with framed theatrical pictures and a collection of sheet music and guitars. Gawkers noted other Bohemian touches: a bearskin and large pillows had been artfully arranged before the fireplace, for lounging.

The "Prince," as the reclusive Edwin Booth was called by hotel denizens, was not often seen. But his "Princess" was unmistakable. "Slight in figure, but with lovely lines; honest, straightforward eyes, brown and tender; years that counted nineteen; an ineffable grace that made strangers love her," is how one neighbor at the hotel remembered Mary Booth. The former actress dressed dramatically in eye-catching dresses of a single color—red, purple, or emerald green—and wore her hair down over her shoulders, contrary to prevailing fashion. Even Mary's pet dog, a greyhound that followed her everywhere, was striking. Whenever this pair appeared in the hotel's restaurant for a meal, other diners stared.

Edwin's marriage was everything he hoped it would be. Mary's companionship absorbed him completely. His existence dwindled to two spaces—the apartment he and Mary shared, and the hundred-foot-wide stage of Broadway's Winter Garden Theatre. Edwin never consulted a newspaper except to read reviews of his own performances. He never entered the Fifth Avenue Hotel's bar, where antique American brandies, ryes, and whiskeys—some costing as much as a dollar per shot—flowed freely. Mary shared his isolation. With her own career as a star behind her, she devoted herself to the work of being Edwin's full-time companion, acting coach, and informal critic.

Friends remarked on the couple's obliviousness to the impending war. "No hermit in his cell, no nun in her cloister, was more secluded from the world than this happy pair," observed a resident of the hotel. Every afternoon found "the Prince lying on the black bearskin rug, face downward, going over his cues for the evening," this neighbor recalled, while Mary sat nearby, checking his accuracy against a promptbook.

Husband and wife rode to the theater each night in a cab. While Edwin put on his makeup, Mary took her place in a private box. From the audience, she watched his work with attention. Playgoers spying Mrs. Booth noticed that throughout the performance her lips moved in time with her husband's, mouthing every word he spoke. Mary's fixation on her spouse did not appear one-sided to anyone. "So subtle and close was the tie between them," one audience member recalled, Edwin often directed his lines to the corner of the theater where he knew she was sitting. "The play for him was all for that sweet girl-wife."

The hours after a show were thirsty ones for Edwin, and his wife always had a place reserved for him by the fireplace at home, a new song ready to perform on her guitar, or an absorbing topic in mind to talk over until morning if need be. Edwin had done the same years before to distract his own father from the taverns. Relentless work also helped the actor bury his craving for alcohol. The hardest evenings were those that found Edwin dissatisfied with his acting. He would mull over his mistakes, saying "Kick me! I haven't done decently. I ought to be thrashed." Patiently, Mary talked him out of his irritation.

Only once in her diary did the new wife confess to the loneliness she felt when Edwin failed to reciprocate the attention she so devotedly provided him. "At times I feel I am required to stand alone," Mary wrote. "At first this affected me as I imagine a drowning sensation would do—I looked around for something to grasp—but now I find a resting place when driven to this strait; his nature craves my patience and fortitude, and twill strengthen me."

The Booths' marriage reminded many people of the connection shared by doomed lovers in the pages of Shakespeare. Reports of the couple from 1861 are filled with references to Romeo and Juliet, Othello and Desdemona, Hamlet and Ophelia—in each tragic pairing, the hero, however much he adores the heroine, always ends by destroying her. Within Edwin's circle of friends, it was privately observed that Mary Booth's life was not an easy one. While she kept her husband sober, she could not banish his memories of his past. Edwin's was an unpredictable personality, happy one day and melancholy the next. Beside this troubled man, lighthearted Mary seemed threatened by the touch of his shadow.

Whatever his private struggles cost him and his wife, Edwin Booth cast a spell over New York during his 1861 engagement at the Winter Garden playhouse. Jefferson Davis assuming the presidency of the Confederate States of America on February 9, 1861, intensified the standoff between federal and rebel forces in Charleston harbor, but three days later the *New York Evening Post* found room for a column on Edwin's extraordinary achievement. "Mr. Edwin Booth," the article announced, "seems to share with Fort Sumter the sensation of the hour."

There was little room for politics in the artistic idyll Mary and Edwin enjoyed through the spring of 1861. The couple was too engrossed in their joint project of advancing Booth's career. They had no financial worries: earning $5,000 in two weeks was now a typical feat for the young star. To put this income in perspective, after his swearing-in on March 4, President Abraham Lincoln would receive a check for $2,083.33 from the United States Treasury on the fifth of every month.

"Money is not what I want," Edwin Booth explained to Richard Cary, a twenty-five-year-old Harvard graduate he had befriended at the Howe mansion in Boston. "Unless I aim at a larger circumference than the rim of the 'almighty dollar' (which one can't help in America) I'll go down eye-deep in the quicksand of popular favor." Edwin was determined not to let his reputation suffer as his father's had, either by becoming complacent or by acting the drunken fool. The son wanted to outpace Junius Brutus Booth's legacy, to build an even bigger monument to the Booth talent. Edwin believed his success was incomplete until he had conquered London, where his father had debuted at the Drury Lane theater, and where his mother once sold flowers in Covent Garden.

"All American actors seek for an English confirmation of their title to distinction," one New York journalist noted at the time, "the ambition to shine in the land of Shakespeare constantly asserts itself." As Edwin's own manager at the Winter Garden Theatre reported, "there was an impression existing in theatrical circles here at the time that no actor's position was established until he had the endorsement of a London audience." More than other American actors, perhaps, Edwin Booth had a unique claim on such a dream. There seemed no better time than now to try.

ON APRIL 12, 1861, WORD FLASHED ACROSS THE NATION'S TELEGRAPH wires that Confederate guns were blasting at the walls of Fort Sumter. News of the siege reached the seaside town of Portland, Maine. The next night, as John Wilkes Booth performed in Portland's Deering Hall, hundreds streamed to a Union rally in Market Square, directly outside the theater. This gathering of Maine men, like so many others that convened in towns and cities across the North and West in days to come, raised "one great Eagle-scream" for war.

John Wilkes Booth had been playing in Portland for a month. During his stay, he charmed local shopkeepers into extending him generous lines of credit, and began a flirtation with a nineteen-year-old actress named Helen Western, stepdaughter of the man who managed the local theater. And in the end, he did make a lasting impression on Portland's theatergoers, though not of the kind any actor would relish.

In addition to the tragedies of Shakespeare, John Wilkes added a physically demanding and gimmick-laden play, *The Corsican Brothers*, to his repertoire. This was a spooky tale of twin brothers, Fabien and Louis, swordsmen who share a telepathic bond. When one twin dies in a duel, the other sees an apparition of his brother's bleeding ghost and races to avenge the crime. The play was a favorite, not only for its special effects, but because the same actor was supposed to play both brothers. There was a thrill in the sight of one man speeding through costume changes, using tricks of stage machinery to make lightning-fast entrances and exits, popping up where least expected, and dropping out of sight in an instant. John was perfectly suited to this part. His sword arm and ability to dash and leap served him well in the dual role.

For his special performance at Deering Hall, carpenters turned the stage into a wooden puzzle, complete with trapdoors, sliding floor panels, wooden ramps, and wheeled platforms. The best moment in the play was the corpse's entrance, when the slain brother's spirit emerged from beneath the stage, rising upward and hurtling toward the audience in a swift, unbroken movement, while violins in the orchestra scraped away like banshees.

To achieve this effect, John Wilkes crouched beneath the stage on a contraption similar to a modern-day skateboard, with a rope hitched to the front. He was supposed to be dragged up a hidden ramp while balancing on the moving plank. At the same time, a panel opened above him in the stage floor, disclosing his rising form to the audience. Before a crowded house, the mechanism jammed. Portland resident Nathan Goold relayed what the audience saw John Wilkes do instead:

"He was dressed in a loose white shirt and black pants. He stood with a rapier in his right hand raised up, and his left arm about the same position. He was to be slid across the stage under an illumination of red fire. I suppose he stood on a plank which had not been properly greased, for it would stop, then start, with a sympathetic movement of the head and shirt each time, which destroyed the scene." The risible sight of a much-annoyed Booth being "unwillingly jerked along" became part of Portland's local lore for decades. "I shall never forget it while I remember such things," laughed a member of the audience.

John left Portland in a foul mood after Fort Sumter surrendered, quitting the town without paying off his local creditors. The *Portland Advertiser* printed an irate notice: "Our experience with him shows he lacks the requisites of a gentleman. He was extremely liberal in his offers, and not sparing of promises. Just before his departure we called on him for the amount of his indebtedness, but were referred to his agent, who referred us to his principal . . . to cut the story short, we have not seen the color of the gentleman's money."

John hastened back to Albany, to appear again at the Gayety in late April. Once again, injury cut short his performance, but this time a woman was responsible. Henrietta Irving, a young Albany actress, had become emotionally entangled with John Wilkes. Angered by a report of John's infidelity, Henrietta burst into his room at the Stanwix Hotel and drove a knife into his neck. His injury was not life-threatening, but it disabled him from acting.

Booth canceled the rest of his engagement. Theatrical agents in Albany complained the young man was behaving like "a soured cynic," and asserting he appeared "sullen and morose." Armed regiments of volunteer soldiers from all corners of the Union, in answer to President Lincoln's urgent April 15 summons, were hastening to the defense of Washington, D.C. At this unsettled moment in history, Booth sought familiar ground. He boarded a train bound for the familiar streets of his childhood, in Baltimore.

THE BROTHERS BOOTH, DISTRACTED BY THEIR RESPECTIVE ROMANCES and by the demands of touring, did not focus on the opening events of the Civil War. In Boston, however, at the home of the Howe family, matters were different. Early in the day on April 13, as Confederate mortars rained on Fort Sumter, Samuel Gridley Howe fired off a letter to Massachusetts governor John A. Andrew:

"Since they will have it so, in the name of God, Amen!" Howe wrote, referring to South Carolina's rebel leaders. "Now let all the governors and chief men of the people see to it that war shall not cease until Emancipation is secure." This sixty-year-old veteran of the Greek fight for independence added in a bold postscript, "If I can be any use, anywhere, in any capacity (save that of spy) command me."

On April 15, President Lincoln issued an emergency call for seventy-five thousand men to serve as volunteer soldiers for a three-month term. Their task, the president explained, was "to repossess the forts, places and property which have been seized from the Union." Northern enthusiasm was so great, many states sent more regiments than the government requested. The number of volunteers accelerated as word arrived that Virginia, Arkansas, North Carolina, and Tennessee were joining the seven states that had seceded.

No state answered Lincoln's summons more quickly than Massachusetts. Years of funneling money, guns, and provisions to antislavery settlers in Kansas had been a dress rehearsal for this moment. Four thousand Massachusetts men—the Third, Fourth, and Sixth regiments—boarded southbound trains to Washington, D.C., on April 17. Two Boston steamships, paid for by cash donations from local families, were fitted with cannon and filled with foodstuffs collected for the entrained troops, who had packed their rucksacks hastily and lightly.

Dr. Howe followed in the ships' wake, dispatched by Governor Andrew to Washington to survey the health and well-being of Massachusetts's new volunteers and report on their needs. As he toured soldiers' encampments around the capital, Howe was astonished by the change in the appearance and bearing of his fellow New Englanders. "It seemed but yesterday that they were mechanics, citizens, traders, clad in varied but plain dress, going soberly about with most unmartial looks, and busy with their various callings in shops or factories," Chev wrote. "Today, they are all armed, uniformed in martial array, five hundred miles from home and ready to go a thousand more."

Dr. Howe noted the drawbacks of billeting a new army in the open air on short notice. There was a plague of lice, a total absence of soap and washing facilities, a shortage of blankets and tents, and an unhealthful diet of hardtack and salt pork. But these hardships looked puny next to the privations Dr. Howe had endured in the mountains of Greece in 1821. "Had [they] perchance, been so sharp set with hunger as to find relish in boiled sorrel and raw snails?" he asked. Howe expressed special disgust for the unmanly cosseting the militia seemed to receive when the two steamships sent by the people of Boston finally unloaded their cargo: boxes of oolong tea, sacks of fine white sugar, and large blocks of ice had been sent by doting parents for the comfort of beloved sons.

"The breaking in of a soldier to campaign life seems a rough and hard process, but it is not a killing one," Dr. Howe observed acidly in his report. "You may depend upon it that when our boys come back, they will laugh heartily at the recital of fears and sorrows excited among their papas and mammas by the stories of their privations and sufferings on their first march to Washington."

Howe's wife, Julia, was not so cavalier. She had no humor to summon to her aid when watching the opening act of what to her was a national tragedy. The volunteers Massachusetts sent to defend the capital were among the first to die. When the men reached Baltimore's President Street Station on April 19, they detrained to walk to Camden Station on the other side of the city, where cars of another railroad line waited to take them to Washington. A mob of rebel sympathizers harried the soldiers as they marched, first shouting epithets, then lobbing bricks and firing bullets. Four Massachusetts men died in the clash.

Mrs. Howe and her family were present for the burial of the four coffins, which arrived in Boston by returning train. At King's Chapel, these first casualties of the Civil War were interred. Exhausted by weeping at the funerals, Julia sat down to write an ode of mourning, one of many she would produce in the next four years:

> *Weave no more silks, ye Lyons looms,*
> *to deck our girls for gay delights.*
> *The crimson flower of battle blooms,*
> *and solemn marches fill the night.*

Weave but the flag whose bar today
drooped heavy over our early dead,
and homely garments, coarse and gray,
for orphans who must earn their bread.

Julia realized that this war would "fasten its cruel fangs upon the very heart of Boston, and [take] from us our best and bravest." On April 21, her friend the antislavery orator Wendell Phillips addressed a war-impassioned crowd at Boston's Music Hall. Like an oracle, Phillips foretold the terrible suffering Northern armies would rain on the Southern people. He hurled a quotation from the Old Testament book of Jeremiah at his audience. "Therefore thus saith the Lord: Ye have not hearkened unto me proclaiming liberty every one to his brother," Phillips roared. "Behold, I proclaim liberty for you, saith the Lord, to the sword, to the pestilence, and to the famine."

EVERYWHERE IN THE SPRING OF 1861, AMERICANS WERE CHOOSING SIDES. In a letter to Adam Badeau soon after Fort Sumter fell, Edwin inquired which of their friends were "true blue," loyal to the Union, and which of them were not. Even gangs of children in city streets echoed the conversation of parents and family members by demanding of their playfellows, "Are you Union?"

Twenty-nine-year-old Badeau, with his large family fortune, established career in journalism, and no previous military experience, proved "true blue" indeed, putting away his evening clothes to join the staff of Brigadier General Thomas W. Sherman. This first posting would take Adam to Louisiana. Edwin's twenty-five-year-old Boston friend Harvard-educated Richard Cary signed up as a captain in the Second Massachusetts Infantry, answering Lincoln's May 17, 1861, call for three-year volunteers. Cary's tour of Virginia battlefields would encompass the October 1861 slaughter at Ball's Bluff and the Battle of Cedar Mountain in the summer of 1862. Even the bookish, physically unfit child of Charles Francis Adams, President Lincoln's ambassador to England, volunteered for a Massachusetts's cavalry regiment. "I have feared this," the father wrote grimly, "because of all my sons" young Charles "is less suited [for war] than for literature."

Service in the military would be the defining life experience for many young men of their generation, but neither Edwin nor John Wilkes Booth chose to enlist. In Edwin's case, theater was the overriding passion of his existence. His single-minded focus excluded all else: he was an artist, a creature of the stage. "Cold steel & my warm blood don't mingle well," he wrote sheepishly to Captain Badeau. "If it was not for the fear of doing my country more harm than good, I'd be a soldier too—a coward always has an 'if' to shrink behind you know; those cursed bullets are awkward things & very uncivil at times too, and as for a bayonet charge," Edwin said, he would run in the opposite direction like a rabbit. "I'd be cashiered or 'broke' in two after the first day's roll call." The actor joked that even when performing the stylized battle scene at the end of *Richard III,* "I feel sick at the stomach."

Edwin brushed aside the seriousness of the mounting crisis, viewing secession and the mobilization for war through his own scrim of artistic detachment. He seemed untouched by the emotions that spurred his friends into action. In a letter to his old mentor, San Francisco actor David Anderson, Edwin expressed confidence that the national conflict would be short and insignificant. Winfield Scott, general in chief of the Union Army, the actor wrote, was "a mighty man." "Old Scott," Booth predicted, "will make but one battle of it—and wipe away secession with a bloodless sword." Confederate president Jefferson Davis "will die in battle," Booth cheerfully continued, "then peace will come like an untrained virgin to her wedding bed, coy & bashful, but she'll warm."

Perhaps Edwin assuaged a lingering guilt by imagining the war would be only temporary. In early May, his longed-for summons from the land of Shakespeare appeared in the gilded letterbox of his suite at the Fifth Avenue Hotel. The proprietors of London's Haymarket Theatre wrote to invite the son of Junius Brutus Booth to be the star of their fall season. Accepting the offer immediately, Edwin did not hesitate to leave his country in its hour of mortal danger.

"It is the grand turning point of my career," Edwin wrote happily to Captain Richard Cary, who, underfed and lice-ridden, was encamped with the U.S. Army outside Washington. "Though it pains me to leave my country at this time, I look forward with a heart full of hope that I may achieve abroad all that you may desire for me." Before crossing the Atlantic, Edwin told Cary, he would spend a few summer weeks at a vacation resort in the White Mountains of New Hampshire. He was exhausted from his recent work at the Winter Garden, Edwin said, and needed rest before meeting the scrutiny of discriminating London critics.

The actor was not completely tone-deaf; he had enough sense to realize the difference between his and Cary's respective enterprises. "Here I have been egotistically scribbling 'I,' 'I,' 'I,'" Edwin wrote remorsefully, "and not a word of you. You know I am not so selfish as all that, don't you?" The star closed with a prayer for the soldier's safety on the battlefield and a pledge of eternal friendship. "I sincerely hope, that 'ere the fight be o'er, your name may be among the proudest of your country's saviors."

On August 7, 1861, Mr. and Mrs. Booth loaded a mountain of trunks packed with costumes, stage swords, promptbooks, wigs, hats, and makeup onto the steamship *Arabia* in Boston harbor. At the time, Mary knew she was going to have a baby. Her pregnancy, by August, was four months advanced. The couple's child would be born abroad: Edwin did not plan to return to America for over a year.

Unlike his older brother, John Wilkes Booth would never cite cowardice as a reason for staying out of the war. John was physically brave, even daring. By the time Fort Sumter surrendered, the young man made the point, his fellow actors reported, of "express[ing] himself as very strongly Southern." George Wren, a stage manager at Laura Keene's theater in Manhattan, spoke of having "a little spat" with John Wilkes about Fort Sumter. When Wren announced he was going to join up and fight for the Union, Booth responded with anger, saying "he did not doubt but what the South would gain what they were fighting for." Wren walked away from the argument with the impression, he later testified, that Booth planned to "go into the Southern service."

John Wilkes Booth seemed a natural candidate for recruitment into the Confederate Army. According to William A. Howell, an actor at John T. Ford's Holliday Street Theatre, when Booth arrived in Baltimore in late April 1861, the city was still "ablaze with excitement" over the blood spilled in its streets when rebel gangs fought federal soldiers trying to reach Washington. Howell and Booth shared a room at a boardinghouse on High Street on the east side, in what had been John's old neighborhood as a boy. John was unemployed, spending his days soaking up the heated talk in local saloons. "He would come round to the theater and wait for me until the play was over," Howell said, "when we would go home together . . . [and] talk for hours."

The young men had much to discuss. Baltimore's brief rebel ferment met resistance among loyal residents. The Union men of the city—thousands of clerks, mechanics, teachers, and lawyers—organized themselves to police the streets and oversee enlistment to the First Maryland Infantry, U.S.A. In defiance, some Confederate sympathizers, including several of John Wilkes's former classmates from St. Timothy's Hall, were stealing across the state line into Virginia to pledge their names to the First Maryland Infantry, C.S.A.

Howell later recalled that Confederate recruiters were active in Baltimore, promising one hundred dollars in gold to any youth who would sign a muster roll, offering ten dollars down, the balance to be paid in Richmond. He and John briefly flirted with this idea. "J. Wilkes proposed that he would go to Harford County, Maryland . . . and get up a company to take to Richmond," Howell remembered. "I was to have commission as a lieutenant." Nothing came of these plans.

John Wilkes Booth would later say he never enlisted in the Confederate ranks because of a promise made to Mary Ann Booth. His mother already had suffered too much grief; she could not bear the anxiety of a son taking part in the war. It is undeniable John was devoted to Mary Ann, but it is equally true that since his father's death he always had his way in anything he chose to do. No one, not even Mary Ann, could turn John Wilkes from a purpose once his mind fixed on a plan. The young actor had other reasons for staying out of the fight in 1861, reasons apparent to many around him.

One member of the theatrical community wrote that he could hardly imagine the self-aggrandizing John Wilkes Booth "fancying conscription into the Southern service." The actor's admiration for the Confederate cause was heartfelt, even passionate, but his personality would not submit to the indignities of a soldier's life. As a cadet at St. Timothy's Hall, John Wilkes tasted regimentation, discipline, and inflexible authority, and hated the experience. Even the work of a walk-on extra was abhorrent to him because it meant surrendering to a rigid hierarchy. The life of a Confederate infantryman would be no different. As one historian has written, "those in uniform have made the greater sacrifice by losing the man in the soldier—the warrior's abnegation [is] his renunciation of thought and action." John Wilkes was incapable of submerging himself in the anonymous, gray-clad regiments of the Confederate Army. He had no desire to give up his identity as an actor, or as a son of the great Junius Brutus Booth, by donning what one writer has called the soldier's "crown of thorns, among its spikes none more painful than passive obedience."

The crown John Wilkes dreamed of wearing was an actor's. In conversations with Howell at their High Street boardinghouse over the summer of 1861, Booth disclosed his plans to launch a starring tour in the fall. "He would crayon out for me his hopes and desires in a way that was irresistibly fascinating," Howell remembered. John knew his older brother was committed to a long engagement in London: Edwin planned to spend the entire 1861–62 season overseas. For the first time in John's life, an empty field lay open to his dramatic ambition. With Edwin an ocean away, American audiences lacked a Booth to play for them. This was a unique opportunity, his sister Asia realized, for the twenty-three-year-old to "prove himself in the cities of the North and East." Asia would later write that though "Wilkes expressed himself bitterly against the North," now, this first year of the war, was his time to "act North and travel among Northerners indiscriminately," uncontested by his older brother's superior claims.

Comedian Joseph Jefferson—the actor who first introduced Mary Devlin to Edwin Booth at John T. Ford's theater in Richmond in 1857—was in Baltimore when the rebel mob attacked the Sixth Massachusetts Regiment. His reaction to the first outburst of violence illustrates the dilemma some American actors faced at the moment of disunion. Traveling stars like Jefferson and Edwin Booth were an itinerant breed. Born on the road, to theatrical parents, they were not rooted in any one section of the country. They felt most at home in a theater, whatever its location, embraced by the clannish subculture of their profession. Expressing political opinions always was bad for business: most stars were accustomed by long habit to claiming neutrality. "I am neither a Northerner or a Southerner," Jefferson said. "I cannot bring myself to engage in bloodshed or to take sides." In an emotional conversation with John T. Ford in late April 1861, Jefferson declared "he would have no part or share in [the war]; he would not fight brother against brother." The entertainer packed his trunks for Australia. Jefferson was determined, he said, "to go abroad and remain there as long as the fratricidal conflict lasted."

Thirty-two-year-old John T. Ford took a different view. Though he felt pulled by loyalties to both sides of the national conflict, Ford was a businessman above all else. He did not want to miss the golden investment opportunity the war presented. Tens of thousands of soldiers were massing in Washington, D.C. As the federal government mobilized for the fight, there was no doubt other varieties of traffic soon would follow: "politicians of every grade, adventurers of either sex, inventors of all sorts of military appliances, and simple citizens, good and bad." The headquarters of the Northern war effort drew journalists and foreign correspondents, religious leaders, volunteer nurses, bankers, businessmen, philanthropists, prostitutes, sightseers, and spies. These milling additions to the city's population meant big profits for the dramatic trade. Ford, who already operated playhouses in Baltimore and Richmond, now turned his eyes to Washington. It looked a likely place to start a new theatrical venture.

EARLY IN NOVEMBER 1861, A SMALL PARTY OF TRAVELERS FROM BOSTON watched the outlines of Washington, D.C., come into view through the windows of an evening train. Julia Ward Howe, sitting beside her husband in the heated compartment, peered through the glass at light shining from dozens of fires alongside the railroad tracks. The blazes were tended by soldiers guarding the rail lines from rebel saboteurs. An autumnal chill had descended on Washington, turning leaves yellow and red. Those on picket duty in the cold nights now wrote home for wool socks and flannel drawers to wear beneath their uniforms, and for heavy blankets to outfit their tents over the coming winter.

The regiments that poured into Washington over the spring and summer of 1861 now encircled the city like a shield. The Army of the Potomac was immense. General Winfield Scott had retired and newly appointed general in chief George B. McClellan now commanded 175,000 men. "Our army gathered for the defense of the Union," Secretary of State William H. Seward had declared on November 11, is "as large as any monarch on the face of the earth has ever, in the tide of time, brought into the field, as brave as any; and yet it is an army that contains not a single conscript. Every soldier is a volunteer, and nearly every volunteer is a citizen . . . come here to defend an experiment [in self-government]." Surveying these soldiers, Samuel Howe was troubled by the difference between their vast numbers and the modesty of the goals they were pledged to fight for. In the fall of 1861, subduing a defiant South and restoring the Union to its original boundaries were the official missions of the war; liberating the slaves was not yet a military objective.

Howe was visiting Washington to fulfill his duties as an officer of the U.S. Sanitary Commission, a group responsible for overseeing the health of Union soldiers in the field and in hospitals. Though it meant leaving her two-year-old son behind in Boston, Julia Howe had been eager to join her husband on this trip. She wanted to see the war front, tour the camps and medical facilities at Chev's side, and accompany a group of radical Republicans to a private audience that had been scheduled with President Lincoln.

Before leaving Boston, Dr. Howe called a meeting in his office at 20 Bromfield Street, the discreet space that served for decades as a war room in the campaign against slavery. Frank Sanborn and George Stearns, veterans of the Kansas struggle and the Harpers Ferry conspiracy, were present at the table, as was William Lloyd Garrison, founder of the abolitionist journal the *Liberator*, and Wendell Phillips, the antislavery agitator. The topic of discussion: how to make emancipation the central policy of the Lincoln administration.

Howe and his friends believed freedom must be the overriding aim of the

Union forces assembled at Washington. These men, the Bostonians believed, required a greater cause to fight for than the one currently being offered to them. Despite the Union's setback at Bull Run, Dr. Howe did not doubt the outcome of the war. He believed the Northern states were too populous not to prevail. Because victory was guaranteed, Howe argued, "we *must* raise the moral standard of our war if we would have our country come out of it with honor, instead of conquering by dint of greater numbers and greater strength." The doctor packed his bags for Washington with the intent of spurring Lincoln to action on emancipation. He would remind the president his soldiers "lacked noble watchwords and inspiriting ideas such as are worth fighting and dying for."

Arriving, the Howes rode by carriage down dusty, gaslit avenues jammed with teams of horses pulling ambulances and supply wagons. Checking in to Willard's Hotel on Pennsylvania Avenue and Fourteenth Street, Mrs. Howe discovered with dismay that her room overlooked a grim prospect: a large billboard outside the window advertised cheap embalming services for the Union dead. At bargain rates, the sign proclaimed, bodies of fallen heroes could be expertly preserved from putrefaction before being shipped to the wives, mothers, and children hungry for a last look at their loved one.

The Howes' November 1861 meeting with President Lincoln did not go well. Massachusetts governor John A. Andrew accompanied the couple, as did Unitarian minister James Freeman Clarke. Taking a chair across from President Lincoln's in one of the White House drawing rooms, Mrs. Howe could not help but compare the noble visage of George Washington, whose famous portrait by Stuart hung on a nearby wall, with the homely, harassed countenance of Lincoln. "I remember well the sad expression of Mr. Lincoln's deep blue eyes," she wrote, "the only feature of his face which could be called other than plain."

The president was distracted and tired. The conversation proceeded in a desultory way, unsatisfying to the Bostonians, who were shocked by the chief executive's unstatesmanlike demeanor. He evidently was not a member of their own class: the self-educated Lincoln lacked a gentleman's deportment, and what women of Julia Ward Howe's generation called "breeding." Perhaps without these signs to guide them, the Howes missed sight of Lincoln's abilities—his mental powers, his gift for language, his deep political craft. They left the room with sinking hearts, convinced the president was a bumbling incompetent, a simple man, overwhelmed by circumstances, who was profoundly unequal to his task. "We have seen it in his face," Reverend Clarke sighed in despair; "hopeless honesty; that is all."

"None of us knew then," Julia later wrote, the true nature of Lincoln's greatness. "How could we have known?" she asked. "At the moment few people praised or trusted him. 'Why did he not do this, that or the other? He, a President, indeed! Look at this war, dragging on so slowly. Look at our many defeats and rare victories.' Such was the talk one constantly heard regarding him."

Dr. Howe continued to press Lincoln on the issue of slavery, coming to know the president better after successive meetings. Chev would write excitedly to a friend in Boston of his discovery, in private conversation with Lincoln, that the president "considers slavery to be a great stumbling-block in the way of human progress, and especially of this country. He feels that whoever has a hand in its removal will stand out before posterity as a benefactor of his race." What Howe could not understand was Lincoln's refusal to act immediately on his beliefs. "Why in the world then, does he not speak out?" demanded Chev. This hotheaded abolitionist who once helped John Brown to attack Virginia now compared Abraham Lincoln to a man who knows he must take a bath, but who hesitates outside the tub because he is afraid of how cold the water will be. "He puts off and puts off the evil day of effort," Howe cried, "and stands shivering with his hand on the string of the shower-bath."

A mood "of discouragement" settled over her and her husband, Julia Howe remembered, for the duration of their stay in Washington. One last activity was attending a review of General George B. McClellan's troops in company with the Reverend James Freeman Clarke. Riding home from the military exercise in a carriage, the sightseers found their road blocked by columns of infantryman leaving the parade ground. Trying to lighten each other's spirits, Julia and the Unitarian minister passed the time in traffic by singing. They belted out the popular fighting song, "John Brown's body lies a-mould'ring in the grave." Julia's trained soprano soared over the heads of the soldiers filling the road. At the sound, the marching men cheered her along, shouting "Good for you!"

Turning suddenly to her in the carriage, Reverend Clarke demanded, "Mrs. Howe, why do you not write some good words for that stirring tune?"

After spending the night at Willard's, in the room with a view of the sign advertising mortuary services for the war dead, Julia Howe was struck by what she called an "attack of versification" an hour before dawn. The whole shape of "The Battle Hymn of the Republic" came to her in a flood, new words fitting themselves neatly and rapidly to the tune of "John Brown's Body." She crept out of bed, not wanting to wake Chev, and scrambled for pen and paper in the darkness. Her hands seized a scrap of stationery embossed with the letterhead of the U.S. Sanitary Commission. Julia jotted blindly, in a slanting script, *"Mine eyes have seen the glory of the coming of the Lord: he is trampling out the vintage where the grapes of wrath are stored; He hath loosed the fateful lightning of His terrible swift sword: His truth is marching on."* Four more stanzas poured out, including lines that would add their share to the store of "noble watchwords" and "inspiriting ideas" soon to transform the rhetoric of the war. Three months later, in February 1862, the poem appeared in the *Atlantic Monthly*.

"In the beauty of the lilies Christ was born across the sea, With a glory in His bosom that transfigures you and me," this granddaughter of revolutionaries had written. *"As He died to make men holy, let us die to make men free, While God is marching on."*

WHEN EDWIN AND MARY DEVLIN BOOTH MADE THEIR ARRIVAL AT LONdon in September 1861, they rented an elegant flat in Bloomsbury Square. The last time a Booth had performed in London was the year 1835, when Junius Brutus Booth and Mary Ann Holmes made an ill-fated excursion to the city of their birth. Their five children—June, Rosalie, Henry Byron, Edwin, and Asia—sailed with them. Fifty years later, Mary Ann would look back on this trip as an interlude in her life that "cast a gloom over everything." "It was nothing but Misfortune & Death," she recalled, for her beloved son Henry Byron caught smallpox in the city and died. Junius Brutus Booth attempted suicide soon after Henry's burial.

While pregnant Mary spent her days sightseeing at Westminster Abbey and Buckingham Palace, Edwin started rehearsals at the Haymarket theater. The actor felt an "over anxiety," he later confessed, "to set the Thames on fire." His dream was to do what his father had done in 1817: create a sensation with the power of his genius. After a month of performances, a crushed and crestfallen Booth wrote to a friend in New York, "the Thames is as wet as ever." Edwin had failed. For the first time in his life, he neither became a popular favorite nor received the admiration of local critics.

Disasters plagued the young American from the first. Actors in the Haymarket company showed the "long-haired Yankee" nothing but hostility. The star at the time wore his black hair in curls to his shoulders, the better to play Hamlet without a wig. This Romantic look had been much admired in New York, but in London the affectation was met with sneers. Edwin's co-stars showed disdain for his American origins. They made him feel, Edwin later exclaimed, as if he were "a d___d tobacco-chewing, expectorating Yankee" who was "capable of nothing more refined than spitting on the carpet, and whittling a stick." British players hissed him in rehearsal; during performances, they tried to sabotage his scenes.

To make matters worse, a royal death and a spell of unseasonably warm weather combined to empty London theaters. "Good weather is death to the theatricals here—I pray continually for the fogs to set in!" Edwin entreated. "The fashionable [people] . . . are at the sea-side yet." When Queen Victoria's husband, forty-two-year-old Prince Albert, succumbed to illness, sympathy for the widowed queen kept many Londoners indoors, mourning. Night after night, Edwin played to sparse houses.

An initial blow to the actor's hopes came on November 8, 1861, when a political crisis erupted between Great Britain and the Lincoln administration. The Confederacy, eager to win recognition from European powers as an independent nation, sent two emissaries to make diplomatic overtures in London and Paris. James Mason, the former U.S. senator of Virginia who had questioned Dr. Howe on his ties to John Brown, would represent the Confederacy to the British; John Slidell, former senator of Louisiana, would visit the French. These agents, each in their mid-sixties, embarked from Charleston aboard a Confederate privateer. Slipping through the Union blockade, they transferred to a British steamer the *Trent*, bound for Liverpool. An officer of the U.S. Navy, Charles Wilkes, acting on his own authority, put a halt to their journey. Captain Wilkes steered his steam frigate, the USS *San Jacinto*, into the path of the *Trent*, boarded the British vessel in defiance of international law, and took Mason and Slidell prisoner.

News of American aggression against a British ship on the high seas filled London with wrath. "The people here are now all lashed up into hostility," Charles Francis Adams, Lincoln's minister to London, observed in his diary. "The newspapers are more and more ferocious." The British considered the incident an act of war, and insisted the North make reparation for the insult as well as set the Confederate travelers at liberty. Adams, a third-generation diplomat, managed to hold a lid on emotions in London while Lincoln and his secretary of state found their way to a resolution. Nevertheless, until the captive Mason and Slidell were released on January 6, 1862, the Union came perilously close to fighting a second war.

"The feeling against Americans is very bitter," Mary Booth wrote at the height of agitation to Richard Cary's sister in Boston. "My game in London is blocked," Edwin declared. "What I came for—Justice—I shall never get . . . [this] will be my last visit to these inhospitable shores."

The patriotism that Booth had been too distracted by his own fame to feel in New York that past spring, now burst forth with intensity. American newspapers, arriving by steamship in London two weeks after their publication dates, were scanned anxiously by husband and wife for war news. "The seeming standstill of McClellan's armies tortures us; we await the arrival of every steamer to hear the cry of victory, and each week disappoints us," Mary exclaimed. Edwin posted letters to Captain Richard Cary, tucking photographs of himself into the envelopes and asking the officer to "cheer me with glorious news of yourself in particular and of the whole army in general." When Mary Booth finally went into labor on December 8, the frantic father-to-be draped a "Star Spangled Banner" over the backboard of her bed to ensure that the latest addition to the Booth clan would be born under American colors.

Childbirth, the new mother wrote, was "the most trying period my life has ever known." Listening to Mary's screams, Edwin described his mental state as being "on the verge of agony." When it was all over, the exhausted star wrote to a fellow member of the Century Club, New York artist Thomas Hicks, about the baby: "I shan't tell you what it is—but if you feel disposed to try your hand again at painting portraits—paint my babe, and you'll hit it no doubt so long as you paint it very red and don't make it a boy." The letter Edwin mailed to his mother in Philadelphia at this time has not survived, but his sister Asia's waspish response to the news was preserved. She still seethed with irrational dislike for Edwin's Irish-American wife. "They are going to call the child Edwina," Asia scoffed. "Did you ever hear anything to beat that?"

By all accounts, Edwin was struggling to cope with his first professional failure and his first exposure to the challenges of raising a child. Mary Booth's letters to friends at home betrayed "an undertone of sadness," one correspondent noted. "He has borne up bravely under his disappointment," Mary reported of her husband, but it was clear this wife could no longer devote her full attention to the needy artist she married. The watchful, almost obsessive care Mary gave to Edwin came to an abrupt end with motherhood.

Booth's celebrity in his home country had not faded during this period overseas. Notices of the great actor's doings abroad appeared often in newspapers from Manhattan to Baltimore. Captain Cary, stationed in Maryland, commented to his wife early in 1862, "I see by the papers that Mrs. Booth has a daughter & as there is nothing contrary said, I presume she is doing well. I trust so with all my heart," the soldier earnestly wrote, "for it would be very difficult to say what result any such misfortune as her death might have on [Edwin]."

Eager to take the sting out of his London defeat, the star moved his little family to Paris. The Booths rented an apartment on the right bank of the Seine, in the second arrondissement, near the Rue de la Paix, and hired a French nurse for baby Edwina. Without nightly performances to absorb his attention, Edwin began falling prey to the rare vintages poured in sidewalk cafés, succumbing to the flavors of never-before-tasted brandies and chartreuses. Mary Booth, fearing the worst, encouraged her husband to pursue other diversions offered by Parisian life.

"We've been through the Louvre and the Luxembourg—the Bois du Boulogne, and a few other pleasures," Edwin wrote to Captain Adam Badeau, who was then stationed with his company at Port Royal, South Carolina, a position recently captured by Union warships. Art was a useful distraction. Edwin told Badeau he was losing himself in happy contemplation of the elaborate costumes on display at the Louvre. The actor paid many visits to couturiers in Paris, commissioning robes and vestments in the seventeenth-century style to be worn in future productions. Edwin spent a great deal of money very quickly, more than was wise after his embattled fall season in London. It was a sign that he had started to drink again.

By the spring of 1862, the star was nearly penniless. He was forced to write Captain Badeau for a cash loan, and sent urgent messages to Junius Brutus Booth, Jr., in California, requesting funds. Before leaving for Europe, Edwin had entrusted two thousand dollars to his older brother, asking him to place the money safely in a San Francisco bank. June wrote back with profuse apologies, telling Edwin he had gambled away the entire sum on gold-mining stocks that tumbled in value as soon as purchased. Every last dollar was gone. "I need not tell you my dear brother how bad I [feel]," Junius wailed, "to know you [are] in a foreign land & no money." Cursing his "unlucky mining stock," June apologized for the "unbusinesslike proceeding of using your money without asking." In self-defense, June said he never imagined the day would arrive when Edwin's genius could not raise a cent onstage. Fearful that Edwin would be angry with him for losing the sum, June confessed "my anxiety was relieved when Mother informed me that John had sent the money you needed."

Humiliatingly for Edwin, long accustomed to being the family breadwinner, his rescuer proved none other than John Wilkes Booth. John had found steady work in the North as an actor during Edwin's trial in London. The younger brother made the most of the elder's absence, scooping up bookings even in New York City, Edwin's private kingdom, the one place John had been forbidden to play. John Wilkes "acted a short engagement" in New

York City, Asia remembered, from March 17 through April 5, 1862. The sister did not deny the grave consequences of this unexpected move, admitting in her memoir that John Wilkes's defiance of his brother's edict had a lasting effect, causing, she wrote, "the first wearing away of family affection." By appearing on Broadway, John signaled his willingness "to place himself in opposition to Edwin."

The challenge could not have been more pointed. John Wilkes sought the Broadway booking even though he had had less than a full season's experience in starring roles, his gunshot wound and stabbing having cut short his previous engagements. At the time of his Broadway appearance, Wilkes had been onstage for only twelve weeks in the new season, working mostly in such western cities as Detroit, Cincinnati, and St. Louis. Nonetheless, he was "determined upon a debut in New York," one fellow actor later reported, because that was the place where "his brother Edwin achiev[ed] a decided success."

John Wilkes's audacity was unmistakable. Instead of offering a light bill of swashbuckling entertainment that played to his physical strengths, he tackled the three most difficult parts of all: his father's favorite role of Richard III, and the two characters his brother Edwin was famous for playing, Shylock in *The Merchant of Venice* and Hamlet.

Edwin, in Paris, learned of John's trespass onto his New York territory in the most surprising of ways. In the first week of April, a frantic letter arrived for him in Paris from his mother. Mary Ann was distraught: her youngest child, twenty-one-year-old Joseph Adrian Booth, had disappeared. Joe, a sensitive, unhappy young man, had been traveling with his brother John Wilkes and working as his valet and assistant. Joe ran away from John's care, leaving a note that said he was going to enlist in the Union Army. "We can find no trace of him," the mother despaired.

"No news yet of Joe have hunted every place I can think of," John Wilkes reported. "I can't tell what to do poor Mother will take it so hard."

In early May, the lost boy materialized on Edwin's Parisian doorstep. Joe had not joined the U.S. Army, but instead jumped a steamship to London, then made his way Paris, propelled by a desperate need to reach Edwin's side. As Joe told the story, he ran off because he and John Wilkes had a terrible fight. Their argument was so upsetting, the younger man said, he had no choice but to leave the country. "I was troubled in mind and worried," Joe explained. "[I] had money and left . . . to see my brother Edwin."

The relationship between Joe and John Wilkes had never been the same since a fight on the Booth farm in 1853 left Joe so battered that Mary Ann sent the younger child to a boarding school for his own safety. No letter or diary reveals precisely what was at the heart of the brothers' explosive 1862 dispute. They may have started by trading words about the war. Joe Booth sided staunchly with the North. Given the timing of their fight, however, it is also possible that the political tensions between the brothers mingled with a larger conflict about the family business. Their quarrel fell on the eve of John Wilkes Booth's debut in New York City. The path of Joe's impetuous flight out of the country—straight to Edwin's side—suggests John Wilkes's decision to disobey Edwin's ruling was partially at issue.

Reunited with Edwin in Paris, Joe Booth poured out his heart in a long conversation with the older brother he "dearly loved." During a long walk in the Bois de Boulogne, the two siblings traded stories of the hardships they faced growing up in the Booth household. Joe claimed he was "the only ill-used being in the world," and repeated the common belief in the family that Edwin's existence had long been "a golden holiday." To set Joe straight, Edwin later wrote, he confessed to him "all the hideousness of my past life— all the remorse of my present," explaining how he had suffered at their father's hands, and why he now found himself drinking again.

When she learned Joe was safe with Edwin in France, their mother was overjoyed. "I wish you were all worth millions so that you could travel and see everything," Mary Ann wrote to her sons in May 1862. "I have no doubt [Joe] will be delighted with Paris." She also sent a bundle of newspapers "that Joe might see how we are going on with the war—the last battle, which took place 8 or 10 days since, was at Fair Oaks, near Richmond—loss on our side, 5739." Of the staggering Union casualty count, Mary Ann wrote, "it's shocking." "They have not taken Richmond yet," she reported. "Before they do there will be another tremendous fight."

Her words were a reminder that while the Booth brothers were absorbed in their personal dramas, the national conflict was assuming a terrifying new aspect. The federal victory on May 31 at Fair Oaks, Virginia, came at the cost of 11,000 casualties on both sides. Weeks earlier, on April 7, Union forces prevailed at the Battle of Shiloh but left 20,000 men dead or wounded. These kinds of battlefield numbers had never before been seen, or even imagined, by military leaders on either side. After a year of war, the intransigence of the rebellion now stood revealed. The North would not triumph easily, as many had assumed. Looking back, Ulysses S. Grant later said the Battle of Shiloh was the instant when, for him, the goal of the fighting changed. From that moment, Grant remembered, he "gave up all idea of saving the Union except by complete conquest."

For his part, Edwin Booth was an ocean away from home, powerless to rein in his brother John Wilkes's brazen expectations. Worse, he needed John's money, a portion of the income the inexperienced youth had earned by his performances in New York and elsewhere. The younger brother sent the necessary cash to help Edwin buy tickets for himself, Mary, and Edwina on a passenger steamer, the *Great Eastern*, bound homeward to New York City. The brothers' relationship, which Edwin formerly had ruled, seemed topsy-turvy now. John Wilkes Booth had the upper hand.

TWELVE

THE WORKING
OF THE HEART

Glory grows guilty of detested crimes,
When, for fame's sake, for praise, an outward part,
We bend to that the working of the heart
—*Love's Labour's Lost,* 4.1

THE GOLD RUSH OF 1849 HAD BEEN A BONANZA FOR AMERICAN ACTORS, drawing fortune seekers on the perilous journey by sea and through the Panamanian jungle to theaters in California. The Northern home front now presented actors with a similar opportunity. "It was the harvest time for theaters, the years of that disastrous war," John Wilkes's sister Asia remembered. Her younger brother skimmed a generous share of these profits in what would prove the peak years of his work as an actor, from November 1861 through June 1863. "He made great sums of money," Asia said, "and so did other theatrical men."

This period may have been the happiest of the young man's life. The North was for the moment entirely his. He could play on stages from New York to St. Louis, from Boston to Chicago, free from Edwin's authority and far from the shadow of his talent. "John Wilkes is off on his travels," Asia wrote on November 16, 1861. Recovered from his injuries, the actor packed his trunks and launched himself westward, riding trains across Michigan and over the prairies of Illinois at the furious speed of thirty-five miles per hour.

"His face has fortune for him," a newspaper observed of John Wilkes Booth at this time. John's features, a close copy of his dead father's, were indeed his strongest advertisement. Unlike Edwin, John Wilkes possessed the face, one critic testified, that "called up afresh to the memory of men of the last generation the presence . . . of his father."

John's excitement when he first rode a train to Chicago in January 1862 can only be imagined. He was booked for a two-week engagement at McVicker's Theatre, a three-story edifice at 24 West Madison Street, not far from Lake Michigan. The auditorium held 2,500 patrons and had been erected at the eyepopping cost of eighty-five thousand dollars. McVicker's was one of the largest, most profitable venues John Wilkes Booth would ever play, as he made three separate visits to the city over the course of this year.

News of Booth's performances packed McVicker's to the brim. Many of his patrons visited the next-door saloon, the Green Room, which specialized in cream ales and German lager beer, prior to buying tickets. A disgruntled critic observed that the people coming to see Booth appeared to be so drunk they could have "turn[ed] a somersault." The excited crowd made a constant "noise of boots upon the stairs, in the lobby and down the aisles," he complained. "The first acts are completely lost by the eternal tramp, tramp, tramp. At the same time a little police authority to put a stop to the loud talking would be wholesome."

These particular Chicagoans were less concerned with hearing Booth's dialogue than watching what he did with his sword. They bought tickets to see Shakespeare's villains served up raw, in blood-and-thunder style, with purposeful swordplay and plenty of noise, and certainly received their money's worth.

Reporters from local papers strained their ears through the mob's din, trying to take Booth's measure as an artist. What they heard disappointed them: the young man unloaded "a severe dose of rant" on his listeners, reviewers said. His "careless" delivery of Shakespeare's blank verse gave the impression that he was "too young to perceive the intention of the great dramatist." One writer for the *Chicago Evening Journal* saw trouble ahead for this new star. Booth's "future lies with himself," the critic warned. Rigorous professional training was required if this novice wished to advance "to the head and front of the American stage"; without help, the Chicago reviewer predicted, John Wilkes Booth would "add another name to the list of victims of a fatal appetite, upon whose breakers so many of his profession have perished."

John left Chicago in early February 1862, a month before his first appearance in New York City. Between these two engagements, this "scion of the House of Booth," as reviewers had started to call him, performed for eighteen nights at the Holliday Street Theatre in his hometown, Baltimore. John T. Ford, who managed the Holliday, knew John Wilkes Booth to be "a shouter," yet Ford was eager to book him. "Trust to my energy in the matter,"

Ford declared. "I am going to make all my stars successes"—his implication being, whether they had talent or not.

The playbills John T. Ford and John Wilkes Booth devised to boost excitement for his three-week run at the Holliday succeeded in grabbing instant attention. John's father had performed at the Holliday more than a hundred times between 1830 and 1852, and even managed the theater for a spell, but it was not Junius Brutus Booth whom the young actor invoked in his advertisements. Rather, he alerted Baltimore of his ambition to steal the absent Edwin's spotlight. His posters proclaimed: "I have no brother. I am no brother . . . I am myself alone!"

One night between February 17 and March 8, 1862, Edwin's friend Captain Richard Cary made his way to the 1,200-seat theater four blocks from the harbor to see John Wilkes perform. Inside the Holliday, ninety jets of gas, each flame fitted with a metal reflector to enhance its brightness, ran across the edge of the stage, illuminating John's posturing form. Cary sat through John's performance for "an hour or so," he reported to his wife, before walking out of the theater. "Did not like him at all," the soldier wrote. "He rants & his face has no more expression than a board fence."

The theater where John made his New York debut also had a long association with his father. Known variously as Wallack's Theatre, the National, or the Broadway over the years, located near the corner of Broadway and Broome Street, had hosted the elder Booth many times. Few New York managers seemed willing to risk Edwin's ire by booking his younger brother. Only Mary Provost, an actress who was renting Wallack's Theatre for a short time in 1862, signed John Wilkes to a short contract.

New York journalists were no kinder to the twenty-three-year-old than Richard Cary had been. While it was acknowledged that in battle scenes John "wielded his two-handed sword with such vim and vigor as to astonish the audience," his bid to shine in his father's and brother's signature parts before Manhattan crowds unsurprisingly "failed." Summing up the junior brother's record, the *New York Herald* declared, "youth might be an excuse for his errors, but there was no excuse for presenting them to a metropolitan audience." Another critic groaned, "I found coming upon myself, a sensation of dullness" as he watched John Wilkes labor through *Hamlet*. Such boredom was relieved only by the mayhem the actor improvised whenever a scene called for fighting. Playing Richard one night, he reportedly alarmed New Yorkers by attacking his co-star, an actor named Tilton, "so violently as to knock him into the orchestra, nearly breaking his arm."

The final summit John Wilkes tackled was the city that had awarded

Edwin Booth the highest compliment an actor could receive: social acceptance. In Boston, Edwin dined with statesmen and Harvard professors. Here
a wealthy socialite had written an ode to his artistry. The public crammed the
Boston Museum to catch a glimpse of John Wilkes, but critics were quick to
spot an imposter. The truth, an anonymous reviewer explained in the *Boston Daily Advertiser* on May 19, 1862, was that John Wilkes Booth was no
actor. Aside from good looks and an athletic ability, he had little to recom-
mend him to audiences. It was evident this Booth had never been trained
to breathe, to project his voice, or to speak in a way that conveyed emotion.
Shakespeare was a foreign language to him.

"In what does he fail?" the reviewer asked before plunging into a list of
complaints that included mention of the star's "proclivity to a nasal quality."
"He is apparently entirely ignorant of the main principles of elocution. We
do not mean by this word merely enunciation, but the nature and proper
treatment of the voice as well. He ignores the fundamental principles of
all vocal study and exercise—that the chest, and not the throat or mouth,
should supply the sound necessary for singing or speaking. When Mr. Booth
wishes to be forcible or impressive, he produces a mongrel sound in the back
of the mouth or top of the throat, which by itself would be unintelligible and
without effect . . . [but when paired with speech, gives] no hint of the emotion to be thereby conveyed."

Even more embarrassing, the critic continued, this son of a British actor
spoke his lines in an accent that reeked of Baltimore's east side, revealing
a childhood spent utterly free from the study of Shakespeare. "He mispro-
nounces many words which he articulates distinctly," the writer exclaimed
in surprise. "There is no possible excuse to be found for his saying <u>toe</u> for <u>to</u>,
<u>oll</u> for <u>all</u>, <u>entruls</u> for <u>entrails</u>, <u>saw</u> for <u>soar</u>, <u>humanuty</u> for <u>humanity</u>, for turn-
ing <u>Henry</u> into <u>Hen-er-y</u>, and dropping the letter <u>h</u> like a Cockney, saying
<u>w'ip</u> and <u>w'at</u> for <u>whip</u> and <u>what</u>." These errors in style were compounded
by John's tendency to emphasize the most bloodthirsty or striking word in a
sentence, at the expense of the line's overall sense.

"These are not trivial faults," the review concluded. "We have no place for
a professed vocalist who should be false in intonation, wrong in accent and
in rhythm, inaccurate in phrasing, imperfect in vocal method and deficient in
quality of tone, though his person and action might be pleasing to the eye."

The verdict of criticism had little impact on John's box office success in
Chicago, St. Louis, and Boston. His effect was perhaps akin to that of a
novelty act. His fencing was never simply for show. "When he fought," one
of John's co-stars testified, "if his antagonist did not strain his nerve and skill,

he would either be forced over the stage into the orchestra . . . or [be] cut and hurt, as almost always happened."

Cheered lustily by half-drunk spectators, John's bouts of combat forced his actor-opponents to struggle for their safety. Crowds who came first to see a simulacrum of the dead Junius Brutus Booth's face and form often returned for a second look at the brutality of John's fight scenes, or, in the case of many young women whose husbands and sweethearts had marched off to war, of John himself.

"It is scarcely an exaggeration to say the sex was in love with John Booth," reported Clara Morris, a Cleveland-based actress. Though "rather lacking in height," she recalled, John was "truly beautiful. His coloring was unusual, the ivory pallor of his skin, the inky blackness of his densely thick hair, the heavy lids of his glowing eyes, were all Oriental, and they gave a touch of mystery to his face."

When he traveled from theater to theater, these striking looks worked a powerful effect. Morris wrote that many of the hardworking maids and waitresses Booth met on tour fell victim to his charms, proving their infatuation by catering attentively to the actor's needs. In restaurants, Morris said, female servers who normally dumped plates of food unceremoniously onto tables or took customers' orders with impatience, made a favorite of John Wilkes Booth, presenting to him "swift and gentle offerings of hot steaks, hot biscuits, hot coffee, crowding around him like doves about a grain basket, leaving other travelers to wait upon themselves or to go without refreshment."

The situation, according to Morris, became even more pronounced in hotels, where housekeepers hovered outside John's room, opening the door in his absence to fuss over the condition of linens and bedclothes, often "tear[ing] asunder the already made-up bed, that the 'turn over' might be broader by a thread or two, and both pillows slant at the perfectly correct angle." The star drank up this female attention, allowing himself to be "spoiled and petted." These same women, and thousands of others like them, bought tickets to his evening shows, where their "faces, smiling, turned to him" from the audience, Morris wrote, "as the sunflowers turn upon their stalks to follow the beloved sun."

Another source of John's attraction for both male and female audiences was the wary nervousness that stock company actors displayed when sharing a stage with him. By wandering off script, John Wilkes kept everyone guessing during a performance, most of all his co-stars. "In truth," recalled James Shettel, a friend of John Wilkes, "he would not study . . . but he would skim over a part and improvise, and that would cause a confusion on the stage, because the other actors would miss their cues."

John Wilkes left a particularly bad impression on the tight-knit company of players at the Boston Museum, where he played for two weeks in May 1862. Catherine Reignolds was the leading lady at the Museum. A London-born actress, granddaughter of a British soldier slain at the Battle of Waterloo, she had made her way to New York as a teenager in the 1850s, where she was groomed for the stage by Laura Keene, the exacting "directress," producer, and star. Reignolds cut her teeth as a chorus girl at Keene's theater in New York, and by 1862 was a consummate professional. When John Wilkes Booth arrived for his engagement, Reignolds was apprehensive.

"The necessity of ordinary study had not been borne in upon him," she recalled. The actress knew she would have to play Desdemona and Juliet to John Booth's Othello and Romeo, and worried it would be physically dangerous to work opposite "this boy," she said, who "was as undisciplined on stage as off." Weapons were involved in several of their scenes together. Having heard tales of John's cutting himself by accident onstage, and harming other actors, Catherine decided to take precaution. "The sharp dagger seemed so dangerous an implement in the hands of such a desperado that I lent him my own—a spring dagger, with a blunt edge, which is forced back into its handle if it is actually struck against an object." Yet even this measure did not save Reignolds from nightly injury.

"How he threw me about!" she recalled of scenes where John Wilkes played the angry, aggressive hero to her fainting heroine. "Once [he] even knocked me down, picking me up again with regret as quick as his dramatic impulse had been vehement." She was terrified of the spastic convulsions John performed as Othello, to convey his remorse for strangling his wife. When "he rushed to the bed of Desdemona after the murder," Reignolds wrote, "I used to gather myself together and hold my breath, lest the bang his scimitar gave when he threw himself at me should force me back to life with a shriek."

In her memoirs, Reignolds described a particularly painful encounter with John while they performed the double-suicide scene in *Romeo and Juliet.* One night, the buttons on the sleeve of John's costume became tangled in Catherine's long hair as he cradled the actress's inert body. John, as Romeo, ripped his arm free, pulling her tresses out by the roots. He then shook and flung Juliet's supposedly unconscious form around the set, dragging her with such force, Catherine said, that she ripped her dress and lost the slippers off both her feet.

Whatever complaints John Wilkes received from his co-stars, whatever warning and slights the critics tossed his way, such blows seemed to glance off this twenty-four-year-old during the season of his brother's absence from the country. The money he earned at this time does much to explain why.

Though his New York debut failed, John Wilkes amassed more cash from audiences in Boston, Chicago, and St. Louis than he had ever earned in his life. Booth operated without an agent now; Matthew Canning and his handy pistol belonged to the past. He made arrangements with theater managers directly, writing to solicit bookings for himself, and planning his touring schedule on his own. The independence suited him. John's only help came from twenty-three-year-old Joseph H. Simonds, who worked as a clerk in a Boston bank and who agreed to function as an informal accountant and business adviser.

In the 1861–62 season, Booth made more in a single week as a leading man than he had in an entire year as a supernumerary at the Arch Street or Marshall theaters. While he never came close to matching his brother Edwin's haul of $5,000 from a two-week engagement, John could write to a friend at the close of 1862, "My goose does indeed hang high (long may she wave) I have picked up on average this season over $650 per week." The key to his phrase was "on average": after a week of work in Detroit, for example, John was able to bank only $117. His best week, in Chicago, brought him $900. A touring star's returns were always uneven. St. Louis, a city where John spent six weeks acting in 1862, had the drawback of paying him only in a locally issued currency that was valueless outside Missouri. "Don't you pity me?" John demanded of his friend Simonds. "I can get nothing but St. Louis money here," he complained, "and they won't take that East."

There was euphoria for John Wilkes in making money. For the first time, he was free to indulge his love for fine clothing. His choice of attire, friends said, reflected the young man's "rare perception of what was becoming to his figure and complexion." He purchased a gray wool coat with a chinchilla collar. He bought tailored walking suits with satin-edged lapels; patterned vests; fine leather gloves; a gentleman's cane; silk ties printed in colorful patterns; a black beaver hat. John also paid to be photographed at different studios, spending money on reprints of the portraits he liked best, so he could distribute them, in the form of *cartes de visites*, to young women who caught his fancy. John was decidedly a "man of fashion," his fellow actors claimed, who paid particular attention to the trimming and upkeep of what would remain a signature affectation, "his silky moustache."

The figure John Wilkes cut on the streets advertised his prosperity and his class pretensions. James Shettel, Booth's former classmate, used a slang term to describe what his friend had become by 1862. "He was, what was designated before the War of 1861, a *spad*," the elderly Shettel recalled in 1916. "We call them dudes or mashers now."

By EARLY SEPTEMBER 1862, MR. AND MRS. EDWIN BOOTH HAD RETURNED to New York City and resumed life in the Fifth Avenue Hotel. The actor hired the same suite of rooms in which the familiar furnishings—the books and pictures, Mary's guitar—were unpacked and arranged as before. The difference now was that ten-month-old Edwina played with blocks and wooden animals on the bearskin rug, tended by Mary Booth's new French maid, Marie Fournier. Marie had agreed to accompany the Booths on their steamship ride across the Atlantic. During her stay in Paris, Mrs. Booth started to complain of weakness and ill health: help taking care of her child was now essential.

Critics and the public embraced Edwin like a returning hero. The actor's hostile reception in London, so devastating to his ego and expectations, here counted for nothing. The stage of Broadway's Winter Garden Theatre awaited his convenience: the star was booked immediately to play a run of seven weeks. Tens of thousands of New Yorkers, hungry for escape from the "seething . . . indescribable excitement of the war," lined up to see Edwin perform, recalled Lillian Woodman, a friend of the family. "Crowded and brilliant audiences nightly sat enthralled by the masterly rendering of Shakespeare's verse." The Winter Garden was filled with "men and women anxious to forget in the mimic world the realities of the actual one in which they lived." Ticket sales soared. "My affairs are flourishing," Edwin rejoiced. "I've made more money than I thought I should." Presumably he earned enough to repay his outstanding debt to his brother John Wilkes.

The Prince and Princess, as the Booths were affectionately known, had seemed glamorous to New Yorkers before their sojourn in Europe. Now, friends remarked, the couple appeared even more exotic, dressing in the latest Paris fashions and carrying themselves with a new veneer of sophistication. The Booths were swept up in the lively culture of New York's wartime literary world.

A poet and his novelist wife, Richard and Elizabeth Stoddard, presided over a salon of artists and intellectuals in their second-floor apartment on Tenth Street, at Fourth Avenue. The eclectic guest list for the Stoddards' near-nightly gatherings encompassed, one habitué recalled, "authors, actors, artists, musicians, mathematicians, professors, journalists, critics and essayists." Besides the Century Club—and a particular saloon on Broadway, Pfaff's, favored by hashish-smoking intellectuals—the Stoddards' house had the reputation of being the place in this city of one million where conversation flowed with the most wit, felicity, and charm. At their dining table, lit by candelabra, one might encounter landscape painter Albert Bierstadt; *New York Tribune* writer Bayard Taylor; war correspondent Edmund Clarence Stedman; Thomas Bailey Aldrich, a popular poet and journalist; sculptor Launt Thompson; or Parke Godwin, a writer whose father-in-law, the powerful William Cullen Bryant, owned the *New York Evening Post*.

Edwin Booth and his wife soon were favorites of this glittering group. On some nights, the dinner party moved from the Stoddards' apartment to Bierstadt's spacious studio, where his giant canvases were the subject of debate and praise. Other times, Mrs. Stoddard's guests adjourned from dinner to reserved seats in Mary Devlin Booth's private box at the Winter Garden. After the curtain fell on Edwin's performance, members of the salon trooped with the star back to the Fifth Avenue Hotel, where they talked into the morning hours.

Edwin's triumph in New York was absolute. Surrounded by new allies—including representatives of some of the most influential papers in the city—his performances received breathtaking reviews. It was as if London and its disappointments had never happened. Mary Devlin Booth had struck up a friendship with Captain Richard Cary's sister, Mary Felton, whose husband had been appointed to the presidency of Harvard University in 1860. She sent long letters to the Cambridge socialite, marveling at the current state of affairs in Manhattan. "Judging from the appearance of this city one would scarcely believe in the existence of such a thing as war," Mrs. Booth exclaimed. There was, she said, "as much gaiety and extravagance [here] as in happier times."

Yet the tragedies of war managed to touch the Booths, even in their cosseted spot at the center of the city's art scene. When their steamship from Liverpool docked in New York, sad news awaited the couple. Sorting through a bundle of correspondence, Mary Booth learned that in mid-August, Edwin's friend Captain Richard Cary had been killed in Virginia, dying in the summer heat at the Battle of Cedar Mountain. When she broke the news to Edwin, Mary reported, the actor "wept like a child."

On Captain Cary's body, recovered by his comrades, an unfinished letter to Edwin Booth was found in an inner pocket. Cary's family sent the pages to Edwin in New York. "The sad, sweet relic he has left me—the letter signed with his death—will forever be to me a source of consolation,"

Edwin wrote to Richard's sister, Mrs. Felton. "It will keep forever fresh the truth of him who thought of his friend even on the field of battle. That our friendship was so well appreciated by his family, and your assurance that this friendship was a source of happiness to him, are, and ever will be, as a glimpse of heaven in the dark void his untimely death has caused."

Cary's death appears to have wrought a change in the actor, bringing an awareness of the gravity of this war and the comparative frivolousness of his own endeavors onstage. To Captain Adam Badeau, Edwin wrote, "myself and my profession . . . are themes unworthy to be thought or talked of now when everyone's brain and heart should be fixed upon the glorious cause for which you are struggling." "May the God of Battles guard you, Ad," the actor prayed on September 14, 1862. "God grant . . . that the traitors may be squelched . . . before they get back to their nest of damnation."

Edwin was referring to the confrontation about to take place in Maryland between General McClellan's 75,000 blue-clad troops and a smaller invading force of 40,000 gray-coats, led by Robert E. Lee. On September 17, the armies clashed outside Sharpsburg, along Antietam Creek, a battle site not many miles away from Harpers Ferry. Many hoped this fight would crush Lee's strength once and for all. In a horrific day of slaughter, Union forces repulsed the Confederate advance into Maryland, but McClellan held his troops back from following and destroying the retreating enemy. Before sunset, more than twenty thousand had fallen on the field, wounded or dead.

Adam Badeau sent Edwin graphic descriptions of the "heavy firing" that decimated Union and rebel ranks alike on what he called "the terrible 17th of September." Badeau had not seen this fight with his own eyes, but as he told Edwin, his information came from a new source. He had met a man— Union cavalry officer James H. Wilson—who now took Edwin's former place in Badeau's affections. Badeau told Edwin that Wilson "found time on the eve of the Battle of Antietam to send me [a] long letter" ending with the words, "God bless you my true heart. I go at once to the front." Miraculously, Wilson survived the day's carnage. Adam had found a "Left Arm," as he called Wilson, to replace the "Right Arm" he once hoped Edwin might be to him. The matter of Adam's new friendship was a profound secret. "Ned," he wrote urgently, "tis out of my confidence that I tell you this . . . I can't tell more than one or two in the world of it. You are one of these."

The Union's victory at Antietam, though it fell short of annihilating Lee, gave Lincoln the opportunity he wanted. For several months, the president had been resolved to emancipate all slaves living within the boundaries of the rebelling states. Men and women held to bondage in the Confederacy,

Lincoln had told members of his cabinet in July, "were undeniably an element of strength to those who had their service." Liberating these workers was an urgent measure of war. "We must free the slaves," Lincoln asserted, "or be ourselves subdued." His counselors in the cabinet advised the president to key his announcement to a showing of federal military strength.

Less than one week after Antietam, on the morning of September 22, Lincoln dropped what Samuel Gridley Howe gleefully hailed as "a bombshell." The president notified the citizens of the Union and residents of states at war with the federal government that unless hostilities ceased by January 1, 1863, slaves in rebel territory would be immediately, and in perpetuity, free.

Hearing this news in New York City on September 22, Mary Devlin Booth composed an emotional letter to Richard Cary's grieving sister. "Such men as your brother we cannot replace," Mrs. Booth wrote. "The proclamation of the President this morning is a most important one. God grant it may put an end to this vile rebellion. I should be very sorry to see anything short of an entire demolition of the Southern Confederacy. Too much brave blood has been split for anything save a complete restoration of the Union."

"Patriotism [was] rampant" in the North after Antietam, remembered Lillian Woodman, a friend of Edwin and Mary. Edwin Booth in New York City, and Dr. Howe in Boston, were mobilized to new action by Lincoln's proclamation. Edwin, after consulting with Julia Ward Howe and the actress Charlotte Cushman, planned a series of plays to benefit the U.S. Sanitary Commission. Money raised would buy medical supplies for hospitals, and provide food and clothing for the indigent wives and children of Union war dead. "In my poor way I am endeavoring to do some little good towards relieving those who suffer most—the orphans of those who have fallen," Edwin announced to Adam Badeau in an October 26 letter. "Colonel Cushman of the Federal Dramatic Corps and Corporal Booth of ditto," he joked, would rush into battle their own way, with a charity performance of *Macbeth*. On the first night alone of this experiment, Cushman and Booth collected $1,300 for the Union cause—roughly $52,000 in modern currency.

For his part, Samuel Gridley Howe launched a one-man fact-finding investigation into the numbers of slaves who had already escaped Confederate lines. Howe wanted to understand the challenges facing the people about to be freed on January 1, 1863. "It seems to me," Howe told a fellow abolitionist, "that what we want now is a knowledge of the actual condition of the freedmen. We must be able to present, as early as possible, a general and reliable [report] of the actual condition of those who are actually out of the house of bondage; their wants and capacities. We must collect facts." The lives of millions of people were about to change, Dr. Howe argued. A new government bureau must be established when Lincoln's proclamation took effect, dedicated to helping the newly liberated. "Everything now depends on the people backing up the President," Howe concluded, "and insisting upon his coming up to scratch on the first of January."

JOHN WILKES BOOTH SPENT THE FALL MONTHS OF 1862–63 IN TWO TOWNS accessible by steamboat on the Ohio River where, decades before, his father had been a favorite: Louisville and Cincinnati. The first of December 1862, however, found the star once again on the shores of Lake Michigan, in Chicago. By inviting Booth back for a third appearance, James H. McVicker, owner-manager of the immense playhouse on Madison Street, was catering less to critics than to the boot-stomping hordes who enjoyed Booth's swordplay. John spent three weeks at McVicker's, giving eighteen performances in all.

Talk in Chicago concerned the approaching deadline of January 1 that President Lincoln had set for emancipation. Only three summers before, Chicago had hosted the 1860 Republican National Convention that launched a fifty-one-year-old Illinois lawyer toward the White House. Chicago had its share of Democrats and fierce critics of the administration, but it was a city with much loyalty to its home-state candidate, Abraham Lincoln.

Displaying his characteristic blindness to local moods and allegiances, and to the enormous Union flag rippling over the roof of McVicker's Theatre, John Booth freely expressed his Southern sympathies. Over drinks one afternoon in December 1862, probably in the saloon next door to McVicker's where so many actors congregated, John was heard arguing angrily with a group of "theatrical gentlemen," as a newspaper account later described them. His tongue loosened by drink, Booth mused aloud, "What a glorious opportunity there is for a man to immortalize himself by killing Lincoln!"

His incredulous auditors challenged John Wilkes to explain his meaning. The young man answered with a line from a version of *Richard III* that had been adapted to fit popular tastes by the eighteenth-century English author Colley Cibber. These particular lines were not written by Shakespeare, but they figured prominently in Act 3 of Cibber's abridged version of *Richard III*, one John Wilkes Booth always performed.

"The ambitious youth who fired the Ephesian dome outlives in fame the pious fool who reared it," Booth intoned.

The Ephesian dome, a temple built in 550 B.C. at Ephesus, in present-day

Turkey, was one of the marvels of the ancient world. Dedicated to the goddess Artemis, the structure was said to be equal in splendor to the pyramids of Egypt. It stood for two centuries until a deranged Ephesian set it on fire, reducing it to ruins. The arsonist claimed he wished to be remembered through the ages for his act of destruction.

"Well, who was that ambitious youth—what was his name?" one of the Chicagoans in the saloon asked John Wilkes Booth.

"That I don't know," the actor answered.

"Then where's the fame you speak of?" objected a listener.

At this rejoinder, John Wilkes seemed to be "nonplussed," a witness later stated.

No one reported the young man's threat to any federal authority. Booth was from out of town. People in the dramatic profession who either claimed neutrality in the war, or tacitly favored secession, were so numerous, one actor recalled, that John's rebel opinions "gave him no particular notoriety." His good looks, and the widespread respect for his famous father's memory, earned John Booth indulgence as well. As John G. Nicolay and John M. Hay, private secretaries to President Lincoln, would later write of their employer's assassin, John Wilkes Booth "was the pet of his little world." It is true, however, that the actor was not welcomed back to Chicago after this particular engagement. Five months later, when John Booth wrote to McVicker requesting another booking, he was denied.

In December 1862, Edwin Booth was making a fortune in Boston. Mary Devlin Booth and their daughter, Edwina, were with him, staying in a hotel. In regular letters to Elizabeth Stoddard, Mary tried to give a picture of the "immense crowds" packing the Boston Museum to see Edwin every night. His share of the profits in December 1862 exceeded $600 per night, Mary reported. The actor earned over $7,000 in just twelve days.

The Howe family closed up Green Peace, their secluded country house, for the duration of the war. Julia moved her children—and the family's prized possession, Lord Byron's Greek war helmet—to 13 Chestnut Street, a mansion on Beacon Hill. In this house, on December 6, 1862, the Howes hosted the first of several Booth parties they would hold for Edwin that winter. Henry Ward Beecher, brother of Harriet Beecher Stowe, was among the guests. Julia Howe's daughter later recalled that her mother's "drawing rooms were filled with literary, artistic and fashionable folk, all anxious and glad to meet the celebrated actor." No less a personage than United States senator Charles Sumner had been invited to attend. Julia promised the glum abolitionist "that he would find Mr. Booth a most interesting person."

"The truth is," Sumner replied, "I have got beyond taking an interest in individuals." Julia Howe looked at him archly, but did not argue. Later that evening, she wrote in her diary: "Charles Sumner has got beyond taking an interest in individuals. Even God Almighty has not got so far."

Mary Devlin Booth attended this gala affair at her husband's side, wearing a Parisian silk dress and a large opal brooch—a gift from her husband. She reported to Elizabeth Stoddard that the night's event "was a real ovation to Edwin. All Beacon St was invited and all Beacon St was there," but confessed that the gathering felt "heartless" to her. For every Harvard president's wife, such as Richard Cary's sister, Mrs. Felton, who warmly embraced the actors, there was a Charles Sumner who rejected the acquaintance with condescension.

Several of the literary men she met that night, Mary wrote, showed her with a private leer or a lightly contemptuous manner what they really thought of the Irish actress's background and origins. Even worse, the twenty-two-year-old complained, the very guests who professed their "amazement" at Edwin's acting and who claimed to be "thunderstruck by his power" were the same ones who traded poisonous gossip about the Booths behind their backs. Edwin's struggles with alcoholism furnished fascinating material for the Beacon Hill crowd.

Subtle slights from well-born Bostonians hurt her very little, Mary claimed: Edwin was a "genius," she said, and anyone who scorned him, or by extension her, was a "d___d fool." "I love Mrs. Howe, though," the actress added. Julia Howe's admiration for Edwin and his work was free of hypocrisy. What wore painfully on Mary's peace of mind was the rumormongering. "I think New York is the only place, away from Paris, for liberal-minded people to abide!" she wrote in frustration. "Boston is a fearful place for small talk. They pay attention to everyone's business but their own. I have heard since I have been here the most ridiculous stories about us.... They have divorced us & had our darling baby dead a dozen times. As for me—I am according to [them] living in a state of conjugal misery the like of which is unparalleled in modern times."

The tales circulating in Boston about Mr. and Mrs. Booth had some foundation in fact. Since Paris, Edwin's drinking had become relentless. There were nights during his seven-week New York engagement when Mary spent the hours between midnight and dawn pacing the room at her husband's side, her arm across his shoulders, trying to talk him out of the impulse to leave their apartment. If he eluded her, Edwin would be seen in the corridors of the Fifth Avenue Hotel the next morning, his eyes unusually bright, his shoulders hunched forward, his manner intense and overly animated, just as his own father had appeared when drunk in the old days. "You will have to suffer the most poignant grief on our account at times," Mary wrote to her friend Elizabeth Stoddard. "Well you know the demon that pursues [Edwin]."

Mary's ability to charm the actor away from temptation no longer worked. Asia Booth Clarke observed that Mary's "wonderful influence had wonderfully ebbed away of late," leaving Edwin to "his old wild ways again." Perhaps the young wife was simply not strong enough for the task. Two years of marriage and a pregnancy had made an invalid of her. Guests at Mrs. Howe's sparkling soiree at 13 Chestnut Street commented on Mrs. Booth's fragile physical appearance, and noted an ominous detail: she wore a bad-luck stone on her dress. Opals, to the superstitious, Mrs. Howe's daughter explained, "boded the early death of the wearer."

Mary's illness would have been easily cured today. But American medicine was barely a science in 1862, with no knowledge of the bacterial organisms that could infect the body and cause systemic diseases. It was not until the 1870s that doctors in the United States began to ask the question posed by cases like hers: "why [do] so many healthy, blooming young girls begin to suffer and fail as soon as they enter the bonds of marriage?" The answer was gonorrhea, or, as Edwin Booth called the sickness he first contracted from a hotel maid in 1856, "the glorious clap." "Glorious," because clap was seen in those days as a sign of sexual prowess: doctors hypothesized that an overindulgence in sex caused the problem.

In men, gonorrhea might exist as a latent infection for years, producing the occasional inflammation of the urethra, or, in the worst case, a painful twisting of the reproductive organ that some midcentury physicians would treat by laying the misshapen body part "on a table and [striking it] a violent blow with a book . . . and so flattening it."

Women faced an appalling array of gonorrhea symptoms that were made worse by pregnancy and childbirth. Having a baby, as Mary Booth did on December 9, 1861, caused bacteria initially localized to the cervix to spread through the entire body—infecting not only the uterus, but damaging the tissues of the heart, inflaming the abdominal cavity, and invading the joints. Many women became sterile from this infection; others were permanently weakened.

"For months past," Mary Booth wrote to a friend on December 13, 1862,

"I have been suffering where almost all women suffer." She felt "ill & weary" every day, and, Mary confided, "lately, I have felt ... heating in the abdomen." "My case," she wrote sadly, "is serious."

"Before I was eighteen I was a drunkard," Edwin once remarked, "by twenty, a libertine." Mary Devlin Booth paid a price for her husband's roistering past.

Her illness put an end to the Booths' luxurious sojourn at the Fifth Avenue Hotel. Mary had heard of a doctor named Miller in the Boston area who specialized in her kind of gynecological problem. In mid-December, less than a week after Mrs. Howe's great party, the Booths rented a two-story house near the doctor's practice in Dorchester. The back windows of this bungalow, at 386 Washington Street, offered a panoramic view of Boston harbor. The horse car line to and from the city stopped at their door. "I think the conductors all know now where Mr. Booth lives," Mary remarked.

Dr. Miller prescribed isolation and total rest for Mary Booth: no more parties, no more dinners with friends, and no more late nights at the theater. He visited her once every ten days to perform an unspecified treatment on his unhappy patient. Miller's visits left Mary in a state of shock. She dreaded them, writing to a friend after he took his leave, "all my courage is gone—I pass half my time in tears." We do not know what method Miller advocated, but as Julia Ward Howe later observed, his practices seemed "too heroic" for young Mrs. Booth. One American physician in this decade recommended pouring scalding-hot water into the afflicted orifice "until 'sometime after the point of toleration has been reached.'"

John Wilkes Booth, fresh from Chicago, opened at the Boston Museum on January 19, 1863. He was booked for a three-week engagement, and would spend many off-hours at the little house in Dorchester, meeting his one-year-old niece Edwina, and spending time with Edwin and his wife. "I have had several letters from John Wilkes," Mary Ann Booth wrote happily from Philadelphia to Edwin in Boston, "and he tells me he has seen you often. . . . Wilkes tells me his houses are good, I am very glad of it."

Making the trip from Dorchester to Boston to watch John Wilkes act was a milestone for Edwin, and an occasion for his wife to break her doctor's strict order against late-night outings. John Wilkes Booth had been working as an actor since 1857: he had spent six years onstage. "I saw last night—for the first time—my brother act," Edwin wrote to Richard Stoddard on January 22, 1863. The star, so utterly detached from his brother's career, had kept his distance for a very long time. Sitting in the audience now, he could take no credit or blame for the quality or folly of his brother's appearance.

"He played Pescara—a bloody villain of the deepest red, you know, an admiral of the red, as twas, and he presented him—not underdone—but rare enough for the most fastidious beef-eater; John Bull himself, Esquire, never looked so savagely at us poor 'mudsills' than did J. Wilkes himself, Esquire," Edwin observed. Edwin had watched their father, Junius Brutus Booth, play Pescara dozens of times. John Wilkes had never seen their parent act the role. Evidently John had pushed his voice and body to the hilt, shouting, jumping, and slashing his way through the old-fashioned melodrama, making up with energy for what he lacked in craft. "When time and study round his rough edges he'll bid them all 'stand apart,'" Edwin concluded.

Mary Devlin Booth took a more jaundiced view than Edwin. She wrote on January 22, 1863, that her brother-in-law "has a great deal to learn and unlearn," but that his audience seemed not to mind the errors. After watching a second performance on February 12—Edwin only attended one—Mary commented, John "looked badly: for although he had a good costume & was made up well for the part—yet he lacked character. That is one great draw-back to his success, I think—he can't transform himself. The combat was strictly gladiatorial—the muscles of his arms—for his sleeves were rolled up—eclipsing everything else besides. 'Look at his arm,' everyone exclaimed—and highly delighted the audience seemed at this exhibition. He was . . . no better—if quite so good—as a host of others I have seen in the same part."

The family name that Junius Brutus Booth and Edwin together had made great now was lifting into prominence a novice whose training was not equal to his task. Edwin and Mary grudgingly saw the wisdom of John's decision to go onstage despite his lack of talent: the younger brother could not act, but Boston crowds still roared their approval.

Edwin Booth left Boston in the first week of February 1863, before his brother's engagement was over. The elder brother, booked for another six-week run at the Winter Garden, was heading down a dangerous path. He left his wife behind, telling her to follow the doctor's orders, though Mary begged Edwin to let her accompany him. The actor would later say of this decision, "I had not yet got control of my devil."

Arriving in New York, Edwin started on an epic drinking spree. "He was ill alike in mind and body," a friend recalls of this fateful engagement: "unnerved and depressed." Mary had tried to explain to the Stoddards in a letter what was afflicting Edwin: "You know I live with a genius," the young woman wrote, "and am forced to bear the ills & restlessness of his untaught mind, his undefined purposes; & I know how it is to suffer as . . . Edwin suffer[s]." For the first time in several years, his wife was not at Edwin's side.

The Stoddards and other members of their famous salon tried to take Mary's place. "When Mr. Booth was not at the theater," Lillian Woodman wrote, "he could always be found at Mrs. Stoddard's rooms on Tenth Street. Many were the councils held there, sub rosa, as to the mode of procedure that could protect him." The sculptor Launt Thompson and the young newspaper editor Thomas Bailey Aldrich were deputized to watch Edwin constantly, preventing him from visiting a bar or ordering a bottle of brandy. They did not always succeed, and New York audiences, expecting the return of their artful Prince, were treated to the sight of a fool.

One ticket holder remembers seeing Edwin play Hamlet at this low point: "It was played as never Hamlet was played before or since. Booth began the play by bouncing right on with the words 'To be or not to be—that is the question,' then quoting the line, 'Tis not my inky cloak, dear mother.' Then quoting some other line from some other part of the play and mixing up quotations generally, in a way that would have driven William Shakespeare crazy, but which made the audience almost crazy with delight at the fun and queerness of the thing." What a novelty to see the dignified tragedian cutting up like a comic, stumbling across the stage, doing slapstick gags from his old California days, when he used to star in minstrel shows and farces.

William Stuart, manager of the Winter Garden, "at first was dumbfounded with wonder, then was petrified with fear for the consequences, and then finally was electrified with laughter." Stuart let Edwin rampage drunkenly through the theater for hours. "Altogether it was a very rich scene," one patron recalled, "and it got into the papers, and this fact caused a great deal of serious trouble."

Elizabeth Stoddard declared an emergency. The actor's reputation was at stake. She sent an urgent letter to Mary Booth at Dorchester, saying, "Sick or well, you must come. Mr. Booth has lost all restraint or hold on himself. Last night there was the grave question of ringing down the curtain before the performance was half over. Lose no time. Come."

But it was John Wilkes Booth who, on February 14, took the train to New York and came to the Stoddards' apartment on Tenth Street. He brought the news that Mary was very sick. On Thursday, February 11, she had been in fine health, going to see John act in *The Corsican Brothers*. This was one of the severest winters Boston had seen in years, and Mary, with no private carriage to take her home to Dorchester, planned to ride the horsecars. But a snowstorm stopped the drivers on the route. She waited for hours in the wind, wool skirts icing over, feet damp, her body chilled to the bone. John Wilkes reported that after taking this exposure in the cold, Edwin's wife remained in bed, "suffering intensely."

Edwin was in a sustained state of intoxication similar to his escapade in Sydney, Australia, in 1855, when Laura Keene had broken off their relationship in disgust. Letters and telegrams arrived daily at the theater, informing him of Mary's worsening status. These communications did not spur Edwin to action, if they were read at all. "She is very weak & feeble & easily excited," Dr. Miller telegrammed on February 18. "She wishes me to express to you the hope that soon she may be able to write a few lines & in the mean time to accept her love."

Mary's physician apparently could not bring himself to order the star to cut short a Broadway appearance—where he stood to earn thousands of dollars—to be at his wife's bedside: "I hope you will not give yourself any undue anxiety in regard to the actual condition of Mrs. B. . . . I congratulate you on the success of your engagement." (Dr. Miller was not the only one whose judgment was perhaps distorted by Edwin's fame. An intrusive operator at the American Telegraph Company offices on lower Broadway, who deciphered incoming Morse code messages from Miller, added his own illtimed request to the bottom of a report stating Mrs. Booth was "improving slowly." "P.S.," scrawled the telegrapher, "Mr. Booth cannot you oblige me with 2 tickets for tomorrow night?")

Early in the day on February 19, Miller wrote that Mary "would of course be perfectly delighted could you be with her, but [she] says . . . were you here you could do nothing to relieve her physically." Miller concluded, "Mrs. Booth looks upon it philosophically & will waive her own feelings for your good." By nightfall, the patient was so debilitated she had difficulty moving and breathing. Her form was emaciated, her eyes lacked focus, her skin drained frighteningly of color. There was no question Mary was dying.

"Dr. Miller thinks you had better come on," a family friend telegraphed Edwin at the Winter Garden. By this time, Miller was unable to leave Mary's side, even to send a message to Booth. Two more urgent cables were fired off by friends, imploring the actor to interrupt his performance and board a train straightaway. The final communication demanded, "Why does not Mr. Booth answer? He must come at once."

Finally, while Edwin was stumbling in a haze before an amused crowd at the Winter Garden late at night on February 19, a week into Mary's sickness, a Boston friend sent a telegram to William Stuart, the theater's manager, "stating that Edwin Booth must come right on, his wife was dying."

Edwin reacted at last. The night train to Boston by that time had pulled out of the station. The next was at seven o'clock in the morning. He spent a sleepless night at the Stoddards' apartment on Tenth Street, prowling their dining room, drinking huge drafts of coffee to sober up. At dawn on February 21, Stoddard bundled a stricken Booth onto the Boston train. Lulled to a state of calm by the rhythm of wheels on track, Edwin pressed his face to the cold glass of the window. He later recalled being blind to the passing scenery. "O God, I have an ill-divining soul!" Mary Devlin, playing Juliet to Edwin's Romeo, once had said. "Methinks I see thee now, thou art so low, as one dead in the bottom of a tomb." Now Edwin had the same vision. The image of his wife's corpse in a rectangular box, the jaw bound shut with cotton strips to inhibit rigor mortis, blotted out everything else. The actress was breathing her last, Booth learned afterward, just as his train cleared New York City.

At four o'clock that afternoon, a small group of Boston friends met Edwin at the station. Speech was unnecessary. The long ride to Dorchester was made in silence. When the carriage stopped at 386 Washington Street, Edwin's body uncoiled with sudden energy. He pushed his way out, ignoring his friends' entreaties, and ran into the house, locking himself inside the second-floor bedroom where Mary's body awaited burial. Deaf to the sounds of his toddler daughter, Edwina, in the hall outside, Edwin did not open the door again until the next day.

During their careers onstage, Edwin and Mary Booth, independently or together, had rehearsed and performed countless times the climactic scene in the Capulets' tomb, when Romeo discovers what he believes to be the lifeless body of Juliet. The actor used to hunch over Juliet's inert form, curling his fingers through her unresisting ones, touching her face and hair, pledging that "here, here I will remain, with worms that are thy chambermaids," and "seal[ing] with a righteous kiss, a dateless bargain to engrossing death." Edwin Booth did not kill himself at his wife's bedside, as many feared he would do, but when the actor left the bedroom, he was transfigured, obsessed with the idea that Mary's ghost was at his side, and filled with morbid fantasies of his own dying day.

Writing to Adam Badeau the news that he had "place[d] my darling in the ground," Edwin said "my own grave is dug beside hers—I jumped into it, and wondered how long it would be (and prayed it might be soon) before I should be laid there."

Some of Massachusetts's foremost statesmen, artists, and scholars purchased burial plots at the Mount Auburn Cemetery in Cambridge. Members of such families as the Cabots and the Lowells would take their final rest no place else, sleeping comfortably alongside members of their class. On February 23, 1863, an odd assortment of people gathered in Mount Auburn's chapel for the funeral of Mary Devlin Booth, the enterprising daughter of an impecunious Irish tailor, who started onstage at the age of twelve, in Troy, New York, billed as a "Trojan danseuse."

Edwin was present, of course. "Such an image of sorrow I have never seen," a spectator reported. "His wonderfully expressive features mirrored the grief within . . . while his long, black hair seemed a fitting frame for the dark, melancholy face." Julia Ward Howe sat in a nearby pew, wearing a black dress and a veil, her eyes on the open casket. The body of the twenty-two-year-old actress "was a most pathetic figure," Julia Howe later wrote. Mary looked "serene and lovely, surrounded with flowers." Edwin's portrait—an oval miniature of the actor's face—was visible to all, pinned to the bodice of the dead woman's dress.

Mrs. Howe experienced a jarring moment of déjà vu watching Booth walk solemnly behind his wife's coffin as it was carried from the church. "I could not but remember how often I had seen him enact the part of Hamlet at the stage burial of Ophelia," Mrs. Howe exclaimed.

"Behind or beside [Edwin,]" she noted, was "a young man of remarkable beauty," walking with head bowed. This youth, Mrs. Howe observed in her 1909 memoir, would "be sadly known at a later date as Wilkes Booth, the assassin of Lincoln." John Wilkes Booth, booked to play in Philadelphia, had "postponed [his] engagement for a few nights," Asia records, "and went on to the funeral." Edwin's mother was also there. Reticent, black-garbed Mary Ann Booth sat unobtrusively amid the socialites and Harvard intellectuals in the chapel.

Mary's sudden death, and the abrupt end it brought to Edwin's drunken performances at the Winter Garden, became the talk of New York. It was widely understood that the actor had no immediate plans to return to the stage. Edwin now was "contemplating," one drama critic reported, "a long seclusion from public life." In a letter to the clergyman who had performed his and Mary's wedding ceremony two years before, the actor supplied his reasons for quitting. "When I was happy my art was a source of infinite delight and pride to me, because she delighted in my success and encouraged me in all I did; I had then an incentive . . . to achieve something great," Edwin wrote. "But my ambition is gone with her; it can give me no pleasure to paint a picture of my grief and hold it up as a show for applause again." To Adam Badeau, Edwin confessed that the mere thought of speaking Shakespeare's words made him choke.

Staying in Dorchester with baby Edwina was out of the question. The very sight of Mary's child, even of her guitar "hanging on the wall, mute and tuneless now," Edwin said, drove him to floods of tears. Mary's presence haunted him so vividly, the actor wrote, "I think she is somewhere near me now; I see her, feel her, hear her, every minute of the day . . . I lie awake at night, and look for her in the darkness; I hold my breath and listen, and sometimes fancy I can *feel* her speak away in somewhere—in my soul, perhaps."

His brother John Wilkes and mother, Mary Ann, provided Edwin comfort in the days immediately after the funeral. They had survived a similar blow in 1852, when Junius Brutus Booth died far from home and his sealed coffin was returned to them. As they helped Edwin pack away his wife's possessions, the talk was of ghosts and apparitions and the lingering presence of the dead. "My mother says she saw my father standing by her bedside twice during the first month of his decease," Edwin recorded. "She declared he was awake, and saw him; but he vanished before she had time to speak to him."

His family's soothing presence made Edwin realize what he owed them. In the decade since his father died, Edwin had never bestowed a permanent home on Mary Ann Booth and his siblings, never established a family haven to replace the abandoned Tudor Hall. Instead he had paid rent on a succession of suites and apartments in different cities for their use. Edwin declared he "felt ashamed" for neglecting this responsibility, letting his mother for years past "grope along as best she could." Now the star envisioned buying one house for all the Booths to live in. This future home must be in Manhattan, in a place large enough to accommodate him, his mother, the baby Edwina, his unmarried sister Rosalie, and the rest of the family. The residence also would "be a home for John and my other brothers," Edwin vowed in March 1863. His long-suffering mother at last deserved to "have all her children about her."

The book publisher George Palmer Putnam agreed to sublet his exquisitely furnished town house at 107 East Seventeenth Street, near Manhattan's Gramercy Park, to the Booths for the spring and summer of 1863. By mid-April, the family was in residence at No. 107, actively searching the neighborhood for a home of their own to buy.

The actor's loyal circle of friends clamored to welcome him back to the city. Plans were devised to fill Edwin's dark hours with distractions and company. Several older actors, avuncular types, well established in the profession, arranged to pay daily visits to the star's home, as one later explained, "to occupy [Edwin's] mind . . . and save him from his despairing sorrow." In gentle conversations, they tried to reawaken the twenty-nine-year-old's dormant ambitions, reminding him that Hamlet's throne stood empty and that the people of New York still hungered for the gift of his greatness.

Launt Thompson, the sculptor whose studio on Tenth Street had been a gathering place for Edwin and Mary's Bohemian circle in happier times, had the best solution. He proposed that Edwin visit his studio daily, to sit for his portrait, first to be modeled in clay, then cast in bronze. No better diversion could be imagined. Edwin donned his Hamlet robes—the portrait Thompson wanted to make was of Edwin Booth in character as Shakespeare's tortured hero—then sat immobile in a chair for hours, his hair brushed over his shoulders, while the artist worked at capturing his features.

Launt Thompson sculpting Edwin Booth became a performance in itself. As the months of May and June 1863 wore away, curious New Yorkers stopped by the studio to watch the progression of the artwork and to catch a glimpse of the famous sitter. Also in the same studio towered a life-size statue of General Winfield Scott, one Thompson was close to finishing. The sculpted war hero and the flesh-and-blood dramatic star, together in the same room, were a sight to see. The project proved a brilliant success. "All pronounce it great!" Edwin informed Badeau; the finished product "is worthy of Mike Angelo." In time, this bust would grace the main hall of The Players club in Manhattan.

It was obvious to everyone who visited Thompson's studio that the actor was now sober. Instead of brandy and wine, he consumed tobacco. When he was not eating, sleeping, or sitting for Thompson's portrait, Booth puffed on his pipe ceaselessly. Mary's death had worked a change on him: Edwin Booth could not touch alcohol now. The actor's self-reproach for what he believed he had done to his wife was bottomless. He ate little, and spent his days in a bitter lethargy, wallowing in feelings of guilt, hoping involuntary death might put an end to his suffering. Edwin stopped reading newspapers and evinced no interest in the events of the war. He was content, he said, "to be wrapped in my grief as in a shroud, alone with her."

The alluring promise of Spiritualism—then a national mania in a country facing staggering loss of life—drew Edwin irresistibly. He found a medium in the city, a Miss Edwards, who claimed she was in touch with two spirits desirous of communicating with the actor. During weekly séances, Booth—

no stranger to stage illusions—allowed himself to be beguiled by the raps on the table, the eerie noises and cryptic messages scratched by the medium's left hand. "Surely there is something marvelous in this mysterious business," he wrote to Badeau. "My Father and Mary have both been with me there & have written and spoken through Miss E, in a curious manner." The idea that Mary came to the medium's table, a passionate ghost from the world beyond who was eager to tell her husband "she is still mine forever," was balm to his unquiet mind. "It may be all air," Edwin wrote Adam defiantly, "but as Coleridge says, if it's a dream, why wake me from it."

Edwin was unmoved by casualty reports from the war, freely confessing the extremity of his self-absorption. "Forgive me, I am so selfish still that other's woes seem nothing to mine," he warned Badeau by letter; "you must put up with my 'selfishness'—I'm ten times worse than ever you knew me in the days that have passed away." Edwin explained that he was engrossed not only in the depth of his mourning, but in winning his battle against alcohol. He believed the fate of his immortal soul, his hope of being reunited with Mary in heaven, depended on achieving a daily victory over his craving. "There is a revolution going on within me more terrible than the one you are engaged in quieting," the actor wrote to the Union officer. "My cause is more desperate than yours . . . for souls, not bodies, are at stake."

Even the news, in June 1863, that Badeau had been wounded in battle failed to puncture Edwin's self-obsession. Sitting at a small writing desk—one that his landlord said had belonged to Washington Irving—the actor dashed off a letter to the injured man, then lying in the summer heat of a New Orleans military hospital. "Whose wound is deeper, Ad?" Edwin demanded. "My scar is hidden. I can show no mark to prove what I have done—what I have lost." Presumably, reading this line required some degree of forbearance on Badeau's part.

A sense of the reality of his friend's trouble gradually emerged in Edwin's letters. Badeau had been shot in the leg, and needed to be immobilized in bed while bones and flesh knit together. "The agony of keeping your foot in one position, to say nothing of the pain of the wound, is next to hell, if not greater," Edwin conceded and extended an invitation to the wounded soldier to stay at the house on East Seventeenth Street over the month of July, while he recuperated. Edwin looked forward to Badeau's company. What better time than now, when both were laid low by adverse fortune, for the two old friends to spend time together. "God bless you, Ad," Edwin said after their plans had been fixed, "and bring you safely home to us all who love you."

• • •

AFTER ATTENDING HIS SISTER-IN-LAW'S FUNERAL, JOHN WILKES HAStened back to Philadelphia to make his appearance at the Arch Street Theatre, where years before he had been an unhappy supernumerary. Management booked John on very unfavorable terms: the young actor's reputation for rough improvisation and undisciplined work preceded him. John did not anticipate earnings in Philadelphia to match his Boston success. "I don't expect to do much," he wrote his business agent, Joe Simonds, the night before his opening. "The theaters here seemed filled nightly with empty benches." Mary Ann Booth was disappointed at the stringent terms of her son's Arch Street contract, complaining that he received a share of box office receipts only after management cleared a profit of $175 each evening— "and it will be sent," she sniffed, as opposed to being paid to him on the spot. Nevertheless, Asia Clarke reported her brother seemed happy during his Philadelphia visit.

John Wilkes had a new project: gambling his theatrical earnings on stock and real estate opportunities. Five days after Mary's funeral, on February 28, he directed his agent, Simonds, to buy $1,500 worth of shares in the Boston Water Power Company. John placed a bank draft for this sum in an envelope with the message "Invest it for me at once dear Joe. I think I will have to make you my banker and give you an interest in my speculations, so that if we are lucky you may be able in a few years to throw aside those musty ledgers." The actor was on fire to turn his income into greater profits. Pressing Simonds for more information on a possible real estate deal, he enthused, "find out all about it and let us invest at once . . . I would like to risk about $2000 on it." Little more than a month later, on April 3, John decided to spend $8,000 on a lot of land in Boston's Back Bay neighborhood, hoping to make a profit by resale when property values increased.

April 11, 1863, found the actor opening for the first time in Washington, D.C., at Grover's National Theatre on Pennsylvania Avenue. His debut was heralded by advertising that strove for factuality: posters trumpeted the twenty-four-year-old Booth as "The Youngest Tragedian in the World . . . Son of the Great Junius Brutus Booth and Brother and Artistic Rival of Edwin Booth." The engagement was a brief seven nights, and it would not be renewed.

Bodily discomfort plagued John Wilkes during his first appearance in the capital. On one side of his neck, possibly in the same place Henrietta Irving's knife inflicted its damage, an unsightly lump was growing. The actor needed to display his neck: many costumes revealed that part of his anatomy. The blemish, steadily increasing in size, had become visible to audiences. Dr. John Frederick May, a respected surgeon in the city, removed the lump—he called it "a large fibroid tumor"—with a scalpel. The procedure left a bloody cavity in John's neck requiring stitches, or, as he described the state of his health in a letter to his friend Simonds, "[I] have a hole in my neck you could run your fist in."

As he was laid up recuperating for a week after the surgery, John's head whirled with schemes for making more money. He wanted to return to McVicker's Theatre in Chicago and tried to solicit another engagement, but was turned down. With typical energy, however, John hired an old performance space in an unfashionable part of Washington, where, for two weeks, he mounted a series of productions with a hastily assembled supporting cast.

The ambitious enterprise, scheduled to run from April 27 to May 9, was poorly timed. The Battle of Chancellorsville, fought in Virginia over five days during the first week of May, crushed Union spirits. General Robert E. Lee brilliantly deployed his smaller force of men against the Army of the Potomac's superior numbers. Lee's victory stunned the North. Very few Unionists in Washington had the heart to attend the theater that week, while Confederate sympathizers in the city were in a state of tense excitement.

Those citizens who did buy tickets were treated to the sight of an ill-looking John Wilkes, drinking heavily to mask the pain of the surgical gash in his neck, struggling through his usual repertoire—*Richard III, Romeo and Juliet, Macbeth,* and *Othello*. "Booth was inflamed with brandy," a witness reported one night. "He ranted and leaped for three acts." Before the play ended, an audience member told a reporter, the star's strength simply gave out: "he could not articulate at all . . . the most he could do was speak in a whisper."

John Wilkes Booth left Washington, D.C., in a state of exhaustion. Dr. May later testified the actor had come to see him a second time, seeking treatment for his neck incision that stubbornly refused to close. John had constantly strained and reopened the injury during stage fights, causing it to bleed. The depleted Booth managed to reach his final engagements of the season. At the end of June 1863, the actor spent ten nights in St. Louis, with its devalued local money, then played for four nights in Cleveland. Early July found John heading home to New York City.

His arrival would put to the test Edwin's plans to reunite the Booth family beneath one roof. John would join his mother, his older brother, his niece Edwina, and the Union officer Adam Badeau in the rented mansion on East Seventeenth Street.

• • •

SAMUEL GRIDLEY HOWE AND HIS WIFE, JULIA, VISITED WASHINGTON, D.C., during John Wilkes Booth's stay in the city. The secretary of war, Edwin M. Stanton, appointed Dr. Howe to a small investigative body, the Freedmen's Inquiry Commission, ordering him to research the condition of former slaves who had found their way to Washington. Chev and Julia planned to visit the camps the government had established for these fugitives, also called contrabands, on the outskirts of the city. On April 19, 1863, the Howes' hired carriage rattled forth on an expedition to find, as the doctor recorded the next morning, "four long low buildings enacting a quadrangle with doors opening on the center square—they call them houses but they are merely long sheds." Each shelter was filled with women and children, who struck Dr. Howe as being "happy." Julia and her husband listened to a program of songs given by the children and young women.

The doctor strode in smiling his excitement through the milling scene, joking with the singers. "I asked them," he later recalled with a laugh, "how they could be so cruel as to abandon their old masters and mistresses."

One woman's answer, "They are a very damn good way off!" pleased the doctor enormously.

Ten thousand refugees had passed through this "Contraband Camp," Howe discovered. "All have now found employment," he reported, "except about one thousand who are waiting to find places." The sight of these women and children, uprooted from their places of former enslavement, and facing a new future, filled Dr. Howe with jubilation. This was the moment he had longed for since the 1840s, when he and Julia joined the Underground Railroad network and founded their abolitionist journal. This was the outcome John Brown purported to dream of but did not live to see. While Chev talked and mingled with the occupants of the camp, Julia felt weighed down by dread and premonitions. As usual, she could take no part of her husband's light spirits.

She poured a torrent of words onto the page of her diary at the end of that visit. "Would it were all at an end!" Julia wrote. "The dead wept and buried, the living justified before God." In the displaced women and children at the contraband camp Julia Howe saw the first result of freedom's mandate, but she worried how her country would come to terms with this new reality. Not everyone in the North had seen, or could even imagine, what she had seen today. How would her countrymen respond? "The deep and terrible secret of the divine idea still lies buried in the burning bosom of the contest," she observed; "it has not as yet leapt to light in the sight of all."

The drama of the war was unfinished, Julia wrote. The Northern audience had yet to apprehend the full meaning of this play, and had yet to deliver a verdict. "This direful tragedy, in whose third weary act we are, hangs all upon a great thought," she wrote. "This terrible development of moral causes and effects will enchain the wonder of the world until the crisis of poetical justice which must end it shall have won the acquiescence of mankind, carrying its irresistible lesson into the minds of the critics, into the heart of the multitude."

THIRTEEN

BEAT DOWN THESE REBELS HERE AT HOME

March on, March on, since we are up in arms;
If not to fight with foreign enemies,
Yet to beat down these rebels here at home.

—*Richard III*, 4.4

THE FOURTH OF JULY, 1863, MARKED A MILESTONE IN THE RESPECTIVE military fortunes of the Union and the Confederate governments. By that date, the Battle of Gettysburg had blocked Robert E. Lee from advancing into the North, while Vicksburg had strengthened Grant's hold on the West. "Although the war would continue for almost two more years," one historian has observed, "these twin Confederate defeats foretokened ultimate Union victory."

The battles depleted both armies. Gettysburg alone drained the North of at least a quarter of its active soldiers. Regular enlistments could not replace such losses. By the summer of 1863, volunteer fighters had become increasingly rare. Few Northerners held the illusion anymore that the war would be short. Staggering numbers of casualties made fathers and husbands think twice about leaving families behind to sign up. Anticipating the need for more soldiers, the Lincoln administration in March 1863 outlined a policy—the first of its kind in the history of the United States—for drafting men into the ranks of the army.

Under the new rule, every male citizen between twenty and forty-five years old was liable for conscription. A system of lotteries held in each congressional district would be used to select names. Men who had enough money to pay the government a lump sum of three hundred dollars, or who could afford to hire a substitute, would be excused.

Draft officials did not anticipate trouble as the date of the first lottery,

July 11, 1863, approached. The good news from Gettysburg and Vicksburg, it was believed, had softened the mood of the people toward conscription. In the public euphoria greeting these Independence Day triumphs, one New Yorker predicted, "the lot in the impending draft will fall as noiselessly as a snowflake." He was wrong.

On Monday, July 13, 1863, the Union faced an unexpected new battlefield: the streets of New York. For five days, as large segments of the city's Irish population rose to resist the draft, Edwin and John Wilkes Booth found themselves closer to actual combat than at any prior point in their lives. The actor's residence at 107 East Seventeenth Street stood near the epicenter of what one historian has called "the worst urban violence in American history." Men were lynched and their bodies burned within earshot of the Booths' front steps; ashes and stench from dozens of flaming buildings seeped through the windows of the town house. On Second Avenue, only blocks away, five thousand people armed with stones and clubs clashed with police who shot a howitzer into their midst. The Booths heard this, as well as the staccato sound of snipers hitting Union cavalry at Third Avenue and Twenty-second Street. They may also have seen the two cannon dragged into position beneath the elm trees of Gramercy Park, long barrels aimed eastward at the rioters' stronghold.

Those who endured the mayhem, arson, and bloodshed of the Draft Riots later recalled that all thoughts of the outside world, all ideas of the existence of any place other than the island of Manhattan, were erased by the terror and suspense of those five days. As carnage overtook the city, the scenes of the Civil War itself—of the massive armies at work in Virginia, in Mississippi, and elsewhere—receded from mind. "The war at the door," one witness to the riots explained, "drowned the battle afar off."

After John Wilkes Booth closed his theatrical season at Cleveland's Academy of Music on July 3, he headed to Edwin's New York City home to spend the summer holiday. John seemed to be in a good mood. The young actor found it not unpleasant, perhaps, to see his once-high-handed older brother reduced to a humble, even pathetic, state by bereavement. In any case, the death of Mary Booth seems to have created a rare mood of goodwill between the brothers. Edwin's relentless professional drive had stilled. Sunk in melancholy, the star no longer looked like a rival. When Mary died, Edwin swore he never wanted to return to the stage. Writing to Adam Badeau in June 1863, Edwin confessed he craved "quiet time" and said the very thought of acting was "hateful" to him—it was no longer an art in his eyes, but a tiresome means to the "nightly . . . accumulation of money."

Edwin had offered to house and care for Adam Badeau after the officer was wounded in southern Louisiana. Adam, though he had been discharged from a New Orleans military hospital, could not yet walk, and would not be able return to active duty for months. "My home is at your service & you know it," the actor wrote. "Mother is there, and John will be on hand." The officer, his injured leg tightly bandaged, arrived at the Booths' town house on Saturday, July 11, the same day the provost marshal's office in Manhattan commenced picking names for the draft.

Because Adam could not move on his own, Edwin and John Wilkes together lifted the officer from his carriage and carried him into the house to Edwin's room, which the actor "gave up for me," Adam later recalled. A "negro servant" accompanied him to the Booths' residence. The officer's wound was bad enough to require the regular attention of this nurse, who cleaned the injury and applied fresh bandages daily.

Badeau later recalled that John Wilkes Booth showed sympathy and compassion for his wounded state. During the first day of his visit, he remembered, the brothers sat by his bedside and talked to him. John Wilkes was "very captivating," while Edwin, hollow-eyed, could speak of nothing but his lost wife, and the sensation besetting him that he was haunted by the dead woman's benevolent spirit. The city was blanketed with sultry, oppressive heat, which the Booths endured by pulling down window blinds against the sun, and sipping liquid cooled by the ice delivered daily to their door.

Around lunchtime on Monday, July 13, people in the Booths' neighborhood first became aware something had gone wrong. All the ordinary street noises—typical sounds produced by the horse-drawn trolleys on Third and Fourth avenues; the rattle of carts, hacks, or wagons; the bustle of pedestrian footsteps and voices—came to a halt. Streets and sidewalks emptied of traffic. A young woman living not far from the Booth home remembered how, in that unaccustomed quiet, "a great roaring burst upon our ears—a howling." Running to the window, she saw "thousands of infuriated creatures, yelling, screaming and swearing in the most frantic manner," as they raced through the street outside. There were "bareheaded men . . . brandishing sticks and clubs, or carrying heavy poles and beams," she reported, "and boys, women and children hurrying on and joining with them in [a] mad chase up the avenue, like a company of raging fiends." Equally alarming was the tang of smoke in the air, and, issuing from all directions, the clanging of fire bells.

As Badeau remembers, John Wilkes was the only male in the Booth household mentally and physically equal to the job of going out and discovering what was happening. Adam retained a vivid memory of the young man setting forth, as he wrote, "to inquire the news." Edwin and the others probably read the complete story in the next morning's newspaper, but what John would have been able to glean on that first day of rioting must have been sobering enough.

Early that morning, thousands of men—some firefighters, some railroad workers and carpenters together with large numbers of Irish-born factory employees and street laborers—did not report to work. They had organized themselves in a body to visit the draft office at Third Avenue and Forty-seventh Street, with signs proclaiming "No Draft!" Their driving emotion—anger at the high price set by the government for purchasing exemption from the draft—had risen to fever pitch over the weekend. The Lincoln administration appeared to be shoving the burden of the war onto people at the bottom of the income scale. "[We] are to give up [our] lives and let rich men pay $300 in order to stay at home?" was the incredulous refrain.

When the provost marshal ignored these demonstrators and started pulling names out of the lottery wheel, the crowd's behavior spun out of control. They stormed the draft office with clubs and pistols, setting a fire that in a short time reduced the building to a pile of smoking rubble. As the timber burned, a Confederate sympathizer stoked the rioters' fury. In a tirade delivered from a nearby roof, the orator compared President Lincoln to ancient Roman despots like Nero and Caligula. "Resist the draft!" he shouted, decrying Lincoln and the Republicans for decreeing that "the poor man [be] dragged from his family and sent to war to fight for the negro!" His listeners screamed in response, "To hell with old Abe!"

Looting hardware stores to arm themselves with axes and crowbars, the mob—swelled by the addition of thousands of women and youths—fanned out across the city. People felled telegraph poles, pried up the rails of streetcar lines, and pushed trolleys off the tracks. Many rioters made for Lexington Avenue, where numerous rich Republicans kept mansions. As resident families practically flew out the back doors and windows of their homes, axe-wielding men and women broke down front doors, smashed the contents of parlors and dining rooms, and tore up curtains. Another mob congregated before the stone façades of the Republican-leaning *Times* and *Tribune* buildings downtown in Printing House Square, shouting threats to burn the newspapers' presses and to lynch and "to cut" out "the heart[s]" of the newspapers' "abolitionist" editors.

Police officers trying to put a brake on this chaos found themselves outnumbered. Men in uniform unlucky enough to be captured by the crowds were stabbed with knives, or beaten so ferociously that face and torso became a bloody pulp. Arsonists began attacking houses where policemen's families were known to live.

New Yorkers then at work in stores, offices, and schools fled for the safety of home. The number of rioters grew as the afternoon progressed. Abandoned saloons were pillaged for barrels of alcohol, jewelry and furniture shops were emptied of goods, even the tailoring company Brooks Brothers was stripped of its stock of men's clothing.

Author Herman Melville marveled at how swiftly the lawlessness spread, overwhelming the city in the space of a single day. "The town is taken by its rats," he exclaimed, watching from a rooftop as red and orange fires of arson blossomed across the island of Manhattan. All controls usually imposed on human behavior seemed to have melted away. It was an unprecedented experience, Melville reflected, when civic order itself "like a dream, dissolves, [and] Man rebounds whole aeons back in nature."

The information John Wilkes Booth could gather in the confusion of the riot's first day probably left him and his family worried for their personal safety. There was logic to the violence: mobs were targeting the homes and offices of well-known Republican leaders, wealthy and prominent abolitionists, blacks of all ages, newspapermen, draft officials, and the police. These facts did not bode well for Edwin Booth's security. The actor's support for the Lincoln administration's war effort was public knowledge, Edwin having raised thousands of dollars by his sold-out charity performances for the widows and orphans of the Union dead. He was himself a rich man, and his friendly connections to scores of New York journalists were well known. Booth was also a member of the Century Club, a bastion of Republican sentiment. His comfortable home stood blocks away from that stretch of Second Avenue between Fourteenth and Thirty-fourth streets where the fiercest rioters—mainly Irish immigrant families—were making a stand.

By Monday evening, when plumes of smoke, gunfire, and deafening shrieks issued from the direction of a rifle factory on Twenty-first Street, the Booths proceeded as if they were under siege. John Wilkes took on the job of scouting and provisioning, the same work he had done long ago for the Richmond Grays in Charlestown, Virginia. He may even have relished the job of reconnaissance. Once again history was giving him a chance to play a part on a different kind of stage. "He went out daily," Badeau remembered of John at this time, "and was indignant at the outrages he reported." Adam and Edwin stayed safely indoors with Mary Ann, Rosalie, and Edwina.

The editors and reporters guarding the *Times* and *Tribune* presses through the night with rifles and a Gatling gun ensured that fresh editions of the newspapers hit New York's streets on Tuesday morning, July 14. If John obtained a paper, he and the family could have read the mayor's proclamation canceling the draft lottery. This news had no effect on the mob and, as the mayor acknowledged, the entire city remained "in a state of insurrection." An editorial in the *New York Times* observed that the true motives of the rioters had now come to light. " 'Resistance to the draft' was the flimsiest of veils to cover the wholesale plundering [of shops and businesses]," the author declared. "Pillage was the prime incentive of the majority."

All regular services that New York residents relied on day-to-day had ceased. There were no dairy wagons making deliveries of milk, butter, or cheese. In the stupefying heat, ice wagons were nowhere to be seen. Grocers and butchers did not open shop; produce markets stopped operating.

Supplies in the Booth household, as in so many other homes in the neighborhood, started running low. At least two of the seven people in residence at 107 East Seventeenth Street relied on special provisions—the invalid Badeau, and baby Edwina. Obtaining sufficient food for everyone would be a challenge during the riots. A foreign and unpredictable landscape awaited those who ventured beyond their front door. Rioters were building barricades and bonfires in the streets. People could be seen running haphazardly in all directions, weapons or plunder in hand. Every time John Wilkes walked abroad in search of information and supplies, it was impossible for him to tell which people passing him by were merely seeking news and food, as he was doing, and which were intent on perpetrating violence.

Ever-protective Mary Ann Booth no doubt was terrified by John's daily missions. Augustus Saint-Gaudens, a sculptor who decades later would become a member of The Players, lived with his family at Fourth Avenue and Twenty-third Street at the time of the riots. Saint-Gaudens never forgot how his mother endured "a paroxysm of fear" the day he first braved the chaos of the riots. He long remembered how she clutched him "wildly into her arms" the minute he returned safely home.

Such qualms were not unfounded. People were dying at the hands of the mob, Tuesday's newspapers stated. Reports of murderous acts committed by gangs of rioters against black adults and children poured in from all corners of the city. On Monday night, a group of Irish men and women burned down an orphan asylum for black children. Before the mob had finished its work, the teachers at the orphanage managed to evacuate their pupils to a police station. In other neighborhoods, black men, chased down in the streets, were shot or lynched by white men who called their victims "Lincoln." Some of these attackers, one witness reported, could be heard "rav[ing] fiercely for

Jeff Davis and the Southern Confederacy" as they killed. Additional reports described black adults and children being dragged from their homes by white neighbors and beaten.

The Booths paid close attention to these accounts. Rioters reportedly were burning the homes of some white people who sheltered blacks. On Tuesday, the family decided to hide Badeau's attendant nurse. If the man were glimpsed through the windows of the house, the Booths might be punished by the mob. "For nearly a week," Adam Badeau recounted, John Wilkes "assisted to shield my negro servant . . . in the cellar." The Booths created a secure place for the man belowstairs where food, water, and other necessities could be conveyed to him in secret for the duration of the riots. The brothers then took over the job of cleaning and bandaging Adam's injured leg, believing it too dangerous for the servant to leave the basement, even at night. For the next four days, Badeau later explained, "both [Edwin] and his brother dressed my wounds and tended me with the greatest care."

The largest group of rioters operating near the Booths' home, a force of five thousand people, was trying to break into a warehouse on Second Avenue and Twenty-second Street that held a large stockpile of guns. The battle over this building and its dangerous contents raged between police and Irish immigrants for hours on Tuesday afternoon. The sounds of gunfire, including shots from a six-pound police howitzer, would have been audible to the Booths. The uniformed forces lost the fight, which ended with the mob setting fire to the warehouse and the police station. In a grotesque victory celebration, the local people tortured a policeman to death and suspended his body from a lamppost. Events like this filled the neighborhood with panic.

By Wednesday morning, July 15, it was clear to the Booths that Adam Badeau himself now posed a threat to their security. After killing the police officer, rioters on the East Side started making house-to-house searches, looking for policemen, Union soldiers, and city officials to harass. Gangs threatened families found to be shielding these representatives of civic and military authority. Even though Badeau was not wearing his uniform, he had a gunshot wound and an educated Northern accent, two attributes likely to mark him as a Union officer. For the rest of his life, Badeau would express gratitude to the Booths for standing by him during the riots. "I can never forget," he declared years later in an emotional letter to Edwin, "the protection you gave me from [the] mob."

The Booths had no choice. There was no way to smuggle the officer out of the city. From the moment the riots began, the Booths were virtually trapped with the officer and his servant. No cart, carriage, or other conveyance could move through the streets at this time without attracting the attention of gangs. For the Booths, whether motivated by self-interest or compassion, protecting Captain Badeau and his servant was the safest course of action they could take.

At dawn on Thursday, July 16, help arrived at last. New York's Seventh Regiment—hastily summoned from the field of Gettysburg—roared into the city by train along with five thousand other troops. The federal soldiers worked quickly to wrest control from "the riotous assemblages," as the mayor called them, who had ruled the city since Monday. The sound of bluecoats firing muskets at mobs on the East Side elicited "loud cheers," one New Yorker remembered, from the weary residents of Third and Fourth avenues.

After the rest of the city was pacified, the Booths' neighborhood remained a trouble spot. For two more days, in areas south and east of Gramercy Park, there were fatal encounters between the army and the last holdouts of the insurgency. While police worked to clear the avenues of makeshift barricades, teams of infantry and U.S. cavalry searched houses along Second Avenue for snipers and hidden weapons. Slowly, the Booths began to feel secure. They might have taken comfort, as Saint-Gaudens remembered doing, from the sight of the cannon planted by U.S. forces on the lush lawn of Gramercy Park.

By close of day on Friday, July 17, the mayor was able to announce to his citizens that "business is running in its usual channels. The various lines of omnibus, railway and telegraph have resumed their ordinary operations. Few symptoms of the disorder remain." As soon as it was safe to do so, John Wilkes carried Captain Badeau down the front steps of the house to the street, where, with Edwin's help, he hoisted the invalid into a carriage. The officer and his nurse spent the rest of the summer in a seaside hotel at Newport, Rhode Island.

It was not until 1893, after three decades had passed and Edwin Booth himself was dead, that Adam Badeau told that story, of how John Wilkes Booth had protected a Union officer and a black man during the New York Draft Riots. For whatever reason, no Booth family member ever alluded publicly to this terrifying interlude, though other New Yorkers who witnessed the riots later claimed the bloody week of July 1863 was the most vivid and startling incident of the Civil War—equal only, in their memories, to the shock of Lincoln's assassination.

Edwin had hoped that by living with Mary Ann and his siblings under one roof after so many years apart, he could make amends for past selfishness. He had retreated from his career and now wished to devote attention to helping his family. But after the riots, Edwin's intentions changed. His hunger for work returned. Perhaps the powerlessness Edwin Booth felt—trapped with his young daughter in a house unprotected and vulnerable to attack, as buildings went up in flames around them and policemen and civilians died in the streets—was partly responsible. "My baby, my little girl, must be cared for," Edwin wrote to Badeau after the riots; "for her I shall do all that I can." The actor now wanted "a pile [of money] sufficient to hide behind."

The riots affected John Wilkes as well. Badeau later expressed amazement that, "in all the exciting period of the riot," the future assassin of President Lincoln "said no word that indicated sympathy with the South." Badeau remembered that John seemed happy at that time to take care of "a soldier wounded for the cause he should have hated." It may have been the rare interval of amity between the brothers—enabled by Edwin's temporarily crushed ambition—that made it easier for John to behave charitably toward the Union officer.

Toward the end of the summer, as Edwin resumed his career, John gave his sister Asia a truer picture of his attitudes and allegiances. Asia remembered the young man's anger as he described carrying Captain Badeau in his arms.

"Imagine me," John spat, "helping that wounded soldier with my rebel sinews!"

Just as her brother once regaled Asia with his adventures at John Brown's hanging, he now told her tales of the "fierce scenes of terror and bloodshed, of riots and raids," she wrote, that filled the streets of New York that July. John Wilkes's graphic descriptions of the atrocities committed by rioters, Asia wrote, "distressed and surprised me."

It also was upsetting for her to be reminded of how passionate her brother's identification with the South had become. John told Asia he abhorred the Lincoln administration for imposing the draft. The new federal policy, he said, implicitly relied on the high rates of immigration from Ireland "to swell their armies." John was not concerned about the well-being of the draftees; he opposed conscription because it gave the Union Army numerical superiority on the battlefield.

"Nothing grated this fierce Southern partisan more," Asia observed, than the "enlistment of Irishmen."

John would become overwrought, she recalled, when explaining how dishonorable it was for the North to rely on an endless supply of "hordes of ignorant foreigners . . . [to win] their battles for them."

"The time will come," John predicted, "when the braggart North will groan at not being able to swear they fought the South man for man. If the North conquers us, it will be by numbers only, not by native grit, not pluck, not by devotion."

"We are of the North," Asia told her brother.

"Not I, not I!" John answered. "So help me, holy God!"

Watching Irish immigrants violently resist a government policy he himself opposed did not give John any new sympathy for them. The Draft Riots appeared to reinforce in his mind the conviction that the Civil War was a contest between mismatched adversaries, a conflict in which one side wielded a permanent but unfair advantage over the other.

In the months following the riots, there would be a noticeable change in John's demeanor. His moods became darker and more intense. His displays of political belligerence increased, even manifesting a physical component, as when John would end some conversations about the war by pulling out a gun or attempting to choke his interlocutor. During the 1863–64 theatrical season, he would become known for playing ugly pranks backstage, starting fights, and defying representatives of Union authority.

Watching a city fall into chaos may have helped free John to act on his aggressive impulses. It is also true, however, that after the summer of 1863, as the tide of war turned against the South, John's brother Edwin— now fully sober, his ambition once again on fire, his mind free of paralyzing melancholy—aimed for and achieved unprecedented heights of stardom and profit. In addition to making a triumphant return to the stage in New York, he would soon give a command performance for President Lincoln and launch a phenomenally lucrative new business venture from which John Wilkes, quite pointedly, was excluded.

WHEN AUTUMN ARRIVED IN 1863, THERE WERE BLOCKS OF NEW YORK City, especially on the East Side, that testified to the extent of the riots' destruction. Where houses or offices once had stood were bare patches blackened by fire and strewn with debris, the façades of many buildings pockmarked with bullet holes. Pedestrians walked past these sights with a quickened step, intent on resuming the normal rounds of life. The Booth family, too, moved to put July's grim events behind them. By September they were preparing to leave publisher George P. Putnam's Seventeenth Street house. Mary Ann, Rosalie, John Wilkes, and Edwina would take up residence in a splendid home at 28 East Nineteenth Street—close to Broadway and Gramercy Park—that Edwin Booth recently found for them.

"Mother is on the go all day," he happily wrote, "buying 'fixins' for my house." Mary Ann was encouraged to spend money with a free hand. She chose carpets, curtains, loads of furniture, and other necessities to beautify her son's new residence. Edwin had made a comfortable living before, but now that he had launched on his new "mighty undertakings," as he called them, the actor believed he would become wealthier than any Booth had ever been. On September 26, a proud and excited Edwin told Adam Badeau that he was so busy with his "tremendous speculations" he "scarce had time to eat."

Fifteen years earlier, in Baltimore, teenage Edwin Booth, a young John Wilkes, and their neighbor Sleepy Clarke together had scraped and leveled the earthen floor of a hotel basement to create a stage for their amateur troupe, the Tripple Alley players. In the weeks following the New York Draft Riots, Edwin and Clarke, now brothers-in-law and approaching thirty years of age, revisited this boyhood dream. The two actors became "enthused," Edwin explained, "with the idea of establishing ourselves in the Metropolis as permanent stars in a theater of our own." The partnership they wished to form would be like a grown-up version of the Tripple Alley players, except this time the impresarios would buy theaters in New York, Philadelphia, and Boston.

By the spring of 1863, John Wilkes Booth had invested roughly $10,000 of his acting income in real estate and utility stocks in the city of Boston, but these had yielded him little in the way of profit. The fall of the same year saw Edwin and Clarke together investing $20,000 of their cash savings to buy Philadelphia's Walnut Street Theatre, a beautiful playhouse that had graced the city for more than fifty years.

The Walnut cost $100,000: Edwin and Clarke took out a bank loan to cover the difference. Borrowing a sum roughly equivalent to $4 million in modern currency might have given some people pause, but not Edwin Booth. "My popularity and reputation were such that I did not hesitate a moment," he said. The star felt "perfectly secure," he claimed, "[that] I alone could do it & with Clarke's aid (who was already immensely popular wherever he acted) I 'went in' without fear."

Edwin's newfound abstinence from drink made him a different person. In the star's dressing room at Manhattan's Winter Garden Theatre, where Edwin was booked to open in late September 1863, the only liquids on hand were coffee and cold water. "I could not take another cup of wine," he told a friend, for "it would seem as if I killed Mary all over again." This was the first time since his teenage years that Edwin had been completely sober.

Edwin's confidence in his and Clarke's investment was justified. The Walnut proved hugely profitable for its new owners: wartime crowds turned the ticket office into a geyser of cash. Less than a year after purchasing the theater, Edwin and Clarke were able to retire fifty thousand dollars of their original loan. At the same time, the two partners earned enough additional money to buy the lease to the Winter Garden and begin the expensive process of restoring the old building to its original splendor.

By 1864, Edwin and Clarke would be the resident stars and owner-managers of two of the most popular playhouses in the two largest cities of the Union. By the time they added the Boston Theatre to their holdings in 1866, the brothers-in-law dominated the theatrical scene in the urban Northeast. Describing these maneuvers to Adam Badeau, Booth crowed that he expected to earn so much money, his baby daughter Edwina "will be an heiress!"

John Wilkes would not share in his brother and brother-in-law's good fortune. Even though Booth and Clarke needed help renovating these old theaters, supervising the companies of actors, designing new productions, and running the box offices, they did not ask him to take part in the speculation or share the profits.

Personal antipathy shut John out. Edwin still considered his brother erratic and troublesome, unfit to work in the profession. Clarke did not like him, either. "As for Clarke," John Wilkes Booth once told Asia, "we are as the Antipodes." The two were sick of hearing John Wilkes's belligerent views on the war. "My brother Edwin and brother-in-law Clarke would not argue with him," June Booth later remembered, "for they considered him a monomaniac on the subject [of the South] and not worth while arguing with."

The same week that Edwin Booth bought a hundred-thousand-dollar theater, a telegram from the impresario John T. Ford arrived at Edwin's home in New York, addressed to John Wilkes. Ford, who had been a close friend of John's father, inquired if the twenty-five-year-old was available to spend two weeks of the fall season starring at his new theater in Washington, D.C. Ford had profited handsomely from the first theater he leased in that city, the Athenaeum on Tenth between E and F streets, but a fire started by a faulty gas meter belowstage had consumed the building in December 1862. To begin the work of rebuilding, Ford hired James Gifford, the same Baltimore architect who, more than a decade before, had built Tudor Hall to the specifications of Junius Brutus Booth.

Early in 1863, Gifford started sketching plans. His design was simple but handsome. High brick walls enclosed a spacious auditorium painted white and gold. The new theater's five arching doorways fronted on Tenth Street, and ten windows glittered in the building's upper stories. Gifford made the stage larger than usual, to accommodate big casts, and allowed enough space in orchestra and balcony to seat 1,600 people. In a bid to attract Washington's status-conscious residents, Ford asked Gifford to add eight private boxes, their interior walls papered red to contrast with the whiteness of the rest of the theater, close to the stage. The new building, called Ford's Theatre and completed at a cost of seventy-five thousand dollars, opened on August 24, 1863.

On September 17, 1863, John telegraphed his assent. "All right," he wrote. "Book me for Nov 2nd for two weeks I will be there." The actor cleared his schedule for the rest of the month so Ford might extend the engagement, if he wished. "I will keep the two following weeks open a time longer," John Wilkes promised. "You may want to keep me in Washington." Ford, it turned out, did not want to do so.

The actor filled the weeks prior to his Ford's engagement with a stint in Boston, followed by one- and two-night stands at Providence, Hartford, and New Haven. Playing the Brooklyn Academy of Music for two nights in October, John disappointed critics. The young actor's work in a popular melodrama, *The Marble Heart*, was only "second-rate," the *New York Clipper* decreed. John appeared to be aiming beyond his natural abilities, the reviewer wrote, by trying to play roles his father and older brother were better equipped to handle. One can only wonder about John's feelings upon reading the following: "It is to be regretted that his ambition to excel should lead him to attempt higher flights than his age and experience, if not his capacity, should warrant him in attempting, and we think he does this when he strives to equal his father in his renditions of the leading characters of Shakespeare."

On or about the first day of November, John Wilkes arrived in the Union's capital. Conditions were dry and blustery in the city. Winds whipped small cyclones of dust into the air above Washington's streets, filling pedestrians' eyes and nostrils with grit. John appeared to be in an unsettled mood. Billy Ferguson, a callboy who worked backstage at Ford's New Theatre, remembered his visit chiefly for the malicious pranks Booth played against Ford's employees.

"I saw him deliberately create . . . a sudden riot," Ferguson recalled in his memoir, "[that] flared into violence in a billiard hall across the street from the theater." This gaming room was packed every afternoon with actors and orchestra musicians enjoying time off from Ford's. When a disagreement erupted between two pool players, John Wilkes picked up a heavy book from the bar—perhaps a hardbound *Washington City Directory*—took aim at one of the arguers, and hurled the tome "square in the middle of the man's back." The injured man whirled around, fists at the ready, accusing a bystander of hurting him. The resulting fight filled the hall with struggling, shouting forms. Meanwhile, John Wilkes slipped away laughing, Ferguson marveled, "entirely unsuspected of having started the melee."

During one of his performances of *Richard III*—either on November 7, two nights before President Lincoln visited Ford's to see him, or on November 13, the second-to-last night of his engagement—John Wilkes almost lacerated a man who worked as prompter at Ford's. According to Ferguson, the actor became angry when the prompter failed to provide him with an exit cue on time. The script called for Richard to leave the stage in "a flourish of trumpets," Ferguson explained. When these expected notes did not sound, John was left standing awkwardly midstage, waiting. In the moments that followed, the callboy saw Booth seize a carpenter's wedge from the floor of the set, "and with a quick jerk of the arm, send it flying against a wall a fraction of an inch above the prompter's head as he stood at the prompt box." The target of Booth's rage collapsed in fright, and from a cowering position on the ground, signaled the trumpets. Afterward, Ferguson said, the prompter seemed as terrified "as if he had actually been hit." Wedges were sharp, heavy objects used to stabilize pieces of scenery: the thick chunks of wood tapered on one end to a bladelike thinness, like the edge of an axe. A direct blow to the head from one would have resulted in serious injury.

Gossip spread swiftly from theater to theater, traveling with actors themselves. The tale of John's treatment of the prompter added to other stories in circulation about him, and helped fix his reputation as a hot-tempered, undisciplined man with a vicious streak. Edwin Forrest, playing Othello at Ford's Holliday Street Theatre in Baltimore, outright refused to accept John as a last-minute substitute when the actor originally playing Iago canceled.

Despite the actor's penchant for "deviltry," and his lack of popularity with seasoned performers, Ferguson admitted that he and other lower-status employees at Ford's were dazzled by Booth. The star liked to show off his athletic ability to the stagehands, entertaining a small circle of these men by setting up a high obstacle at the edge of the stage—for example, a five-foot-tall scenic flat—then leaping over it in a single jump and landing on his feet in the orchestra, to general applause.

Abraham Lincoln, his wife, and four guests visited Ford's on November 9, 1863, the night John Wilkes Booth acted *The Marble Heart*. This time-traveling love story compares the lives of two sculptors—Phidias, of ancient

Athens; and Raphael, of present-day Europe—who become obsessed with two different objects of affection. Phidias loses his heart to his own creation, a marble statue of flawless beauty, while Raphael is ensnared by a cruel woman, Marco, a flesh-and-blood temptress incapable of real human attachment. Twenty-one-year-old Edwin Booth had been the first to popularize this play to America, playing Raphael before enraptured San Francisco audiences in 1855.

Brooklyn audiences had disliked John Wilkes in the role when he attempted it two weeks before, and President Lincoln and his party were similarly unimpressed. "Rather tame than otherwise," John Hay, Lincoln's private secretary, opined in his diary that night. The *Washington Evening Star* gently concurred, refraining from reviewing the performance because "it would be unjust to institute a comparison between [John Wilkes] and his sire." Years later, when Hay penned his ten-volume record of Lincoln's life, he stated that the sole source of John Wilkes Booth's appeal seemed to "lay rather in his romantic beauty of person, than in any talent or industry he possessed." The president did not return to Ford's at any other time during John's engagement, nor did John T. Ford extend John's contract beyond November 14.

Cleveland, Ohio, was the next stop on the actor's tour, where he had a ten-night engagement at that city's Academy of Music beginning November 25. By early the next year, John was finally convinced to find another way to earn his living. The 1863–64 theatrical season would be his last as a full-time performer.

The residents of Cleveland had formed an "unfavorable" impression of Booth on his first visit, and thereafter did not crowd the local playhouse to see him. The *Cleveland Herald* blamed the population's seeming lack of enthusiasm on bad weather, "the wretched condition of the streets," and competition from "the Opera at Brainerd's Hall and the gloom thrown over the city by the sad tidings from the Seventh Regiment." John Wilkes made some bold choices in terms of his program here, tackling the part of Iago and appearing in a melodrama called *The Stranger*. The latter show particularly displeased the local press. One reviewer urged the actor never again to perform the play, calling it "unsatisfactory, unnatural and unfinished." Once again the energy and effort Booth put into his work was not compensated with comparable financial return or critical praise.

One of John Wilkes Booth's promptbooks—the palm-sized, paperbound scripts that actors used in rehearsals—still survives, a testament to the labor he expended on learning his most effective role, Richard III. The pages of this little pamphlet are heavily scrawled over with John's jagged handwriting. In some spots, he marked the timing of his cues, specifying the intervals when "a distant trumpet" or the "low tolling of bell" from the orchestra signaled his entrances. In others, he reminded himself of stage directions. At Richard's line, "I'll to my couch, and once more try to sleep," John wrote in the margin, "Groan when near couch." On the script's inner cover, and on several blank pages toward the end, John wrote his stage name, J. WILKES BOOTH, over and over again in large, calligraphic capitals, laboriously outlining the letters with a double layer of pen strokes to achieve a bold effect. His repetitive tracing of his own name is a sad reminder of how fierce was his determination to succeed in a profession in which few things came easily to him.

John's engagement in Cleveland ended December 5, but having no other work scheduled until the end of the month, he stayed on in his room at the American Hotel. A kind editorial appeared in the *Plain Dealer* on December 9, predicting the young man's acting would improve as he grew older. "Time, the Great Corrector, will smooth the uneven precipices and level all difficulties, great or small, that mar his portraiture," the newspaper said. Yet a great deal of time already had passed since John Wilkes's 1860 debut. Critics had been making this prediction for years, and no improvement was yet discernible. Time was running out on his bankability as a star.

It was at this moment that a new plan for making money took hold. On December 11, 1863, the actor—in company with his friends John A. Ellsler, manager of the Cleveland Academy of Music, and Thomas Mears, a professional card player and retired boxer—boarded a train to Venango County, Pennsylvania, where the rolling landscape of the Allegheny River valley, visitors testified, presented "some of the most beautiful scenery to be found in the United States."

Lush forests of beech and hemlock had thrived for centuries in this region bounded by the shores of Lake Erie and the western slopes of the Allegheny range. Sandstone rock formations along the banks of the waterways were riddled with the fossilized imprints of primordial plants and animals—the fanning leaves of ancient ferns, the spiral and curving traces left by innumerable species of snail and shellfish.

In this valley in 1859, a prospector working near the town of Franklin struck a rich deposit of crude oil. The galvanizing effect of this discovery on the public was comparable to the finding of gold ten years before in the river bottoms of northern California. Petroleum was prized, experts of the time noted, for "furnishing the best and cheapest artificial light yet known." Americans had illuminated their houses and buildings for decades with lamps that burned whale oil. When news came that "black gold" was bubbling from the soil of western Pennsylvania, newspapers carried cartoons of sperm whales, dressed in tuxedoes and ball gowns, dancing jubilantly and drinking glasses of champagne to celebrate their reprieve.

In a reenactment of the Gold Rush, thousands of fortune seekers came to the region now referred to as "Oil Dorado," or "Petrolia." "I never saw such excitement," a prospector later remembered. "Merchants abandoned their storehouses, farmers dropped their plows, lawyers deserted their offices and preachers their pulpits." Pennsylvanians, and those living nearby in Ohio and New York, "went wild." "Never before, in all the history of civilization," one newspaper observed, "had a more tempting bait been offered to the cupidity of man."

Stepping off the train at Franklin, the entry point to the oil country, John Booth, Ellsler, and Mears must have experienced the very same "tingling in the blood" a *New York Times* scribe felt when he set foot on the spot. The knowledge that a vast treasure lay only a few hundred feet below the surface, waiting to be tapped, was irresistibly alluring.

Booth and his friends made a tour of the area and liked what they saw. Oil derricks fifty feet high and shaped like narrow pyramids loomed along the banks of Oil Creek, the small river running through the town. Visitors to active wells reported watching in fascination as "the oil, of a beautiful, dark olive green, was dashed into spray against the side of the huge receiving tank[s], forming a prism of colors, rainbow in hue, resplendent in the sun's rays." Men swarmed busily around every site, tending engine houses or loading barrels of crude onto barges for transport on Oil Creek.

At night the scene was especially dramatic. As soon as the sun set, prospectors set fire to the gas fumes pouring from the peak of each derrick. "One after another, with a dull exploding boom, heavy sheets of flame leap roaring and glaring about," witnesses reported, "and by the light of these, among the woods, men work as easily as at noon-day."

During their short visit, the three friends would observe that drilling for petroleum did not require distinctive knowledge, talent, or training. "The chances of success were equal for all," one oilman testified. With an up-front investment of two to three thousand dollars, anyone could try their luck at sinking a well. Everywhere they went, Booth, Ellsler, and Mears would have encountered other parties of men who, just like themselves, were exploring Franklin's oil works, hiking the surrounding forests and rocky embankments, surveying the scene before deciding whether to join the rush.

The venturesome attitude needed for prospecting came naturally to John

Wilkes Booth. It had been a disappointment for him as a teenager to miss the chance of traveling to San Francisco in 1851 with his father and older brothers. Petrolia promised a comparable opportunity for adventure. It also promised profit. John left the oil country in time to fulfill a nine-night engagement at Leavenworth, Kansas, that began December 22, 1863. When he and his friends parted ways, they agreed to consider forming a company to start drilling.

If John Wilkes Booth had any doubt that now was the time to leave the theater business and start speculating in oil, his physical suffering over the next four weeks on tour settled the question in Petrolia's favor. John had agreed to travel across the Kansas prairie at the height of winter to play Shakespeare for the people of Leavenworth. Curiosity to see a place where John Brown once lived may have drawn him to that remote place. Whatever his reason, the trip from Kansas to St. Louis nearly broke John down. "It was hard to get to Leavenworth," the actor said, "but coming back it was a hundred times worse." Describing the experience to his friend Ellsler, John Wilkes exclaimed, "I will say this I never knew what hardship was until then."

Temperatures plummeted far below zero as the actor set forth from Kansas, trying to reach Ben DeBar's Theatre in St. Louis. When a blizzard stopped trains from running, John found himself stranded for the first week of January 1864 in a town in northern Missouri. "It seems to me that some of my old luck has returned to hunt me down," he wrote to a friend, shivering with cold and exhaustion. "[I have] an ear frost-bitten." John said he felt like "a dead man."

The only way to leave the snowbound region and reach a functioning railroad line was to cross sixty miles of snowfields by horse-drawn cutter. This was a mode of transport that John, who had earned little money in Leavenworth, could not afford. Local citizens agreed to speed the actor on his way with a fund-raising benefit. In a hall so cold he could see his own breath, John rasped out "The Charge of the Light Brigade" and other poems, to the loud accompaniment of the audience stomping their icy feet to restore circulation and chafing their hands for warmth. The hired cutter, John later reported, carried him for "four days and nights in the largest snowdrifts I ever saw." When he finally reached St. Louis on January 12, he was eight days late for his performance, and sick with a severe cold, his chest and limbs racked by aches and pains.

At the next stop on his tour, Louisville, Kentucky, a startled audience never forgot the sight of John Wilkes Booth slumping over in a deep sleep on stage, midperformance. Whether he was prostrated by drink or illness, they could not discern. Sick and exhausted, John could think only of Petrolia and the salvation it seemed to promise him from the rigors of the touring life. From his Louisville hotel room, he wrote to Ellsler and Mears, urging his friends to prepare the documents necessary to establish their oil prospecting company. John had five hundred dollars in start-up money to contribute. "Every day I have thought of writing you, for I am as anxious for bus[iness] to go on, as you can be," the actor wrote. "Let us push this thing through."

Thirty years of life on the road had destroyed the mental and physical health of Junius Brutus Booth. After drinking for decades, he ultimately died of an illness contracted on a Mississippi River steamboat. It is a small miracle that as a child Edwin Booth survived accompanying his father on the repeated journey from Albany to New Orleans. British actor Charles Kean died immediately after he completed a tour of the western United States in the last year of the Civil War—the overwork, bad food, sleepless nights, and exposure to harsh weather combined to finish him off. After spending nearly three years at the same work, John Wilkes's body showed the ravages of theatrical touring. He had been shot by his manager, he had endured stabbings—both intentional and accidental—as well as chilblains, frostbite, and sickness. The grueling slog over the snowy western landscape may have been the final straw.

All actors knew the risks of national tours. Edwin Booth and John Sleeper Clarke avoided those perils by creating permanent fiefdoms in New York and Philadelphia, and were looking to expand their monopoly farther, to Boston. The stars, comfortably situated in their urban settings, knew that the Walnut and Winter Garden theaters would bring them wealth for years to come. Edwin's beautifully furnished town house near Gramercy Park—even the exquisite four-wheeled coupé he purchased to carry his daughter Edwina through the streets of New York—could not but remind John Wilkes of the difference in their fortunes, and of the fact that there was no place for him in the rising edifice of the Booth family business. Trying his luck in Petrolia would be a means of escape from the toil and uncertainty of being an itinerant star. Oil was the best chance for John Wilkes Booth to launch a big-time speculation of his own.

On February 14, 1864, Edwin arrived in Washington, D.C., and checked into a room at Willard's Hotel. Not atypically, he found himself accosted by adoring fans, including a Union general, as he sat perusing a newspaper in Willard's reading room. Managers as far away as Ohio had promised Edwin five thousand dollars per week to play their theaters, and usually it was his policy to decline. Yet this month the star made a rare exception, agreeing to leave New York City for Leonard Grover, manager of the New National Theatre in Washington, D.C.

Theatrical managers Grover and John T. Ford vied constantly to surpass one another, each striving to place his playhouse first in the estimation of Washington's fashionable audiences. When Ford built his new theater in 1863 Grover renovated his own house, trying to outdo his rival in every particular of design. Where Ford's New Theatre provided cane-bottomed chairs and wooden pews for the comfort of his audience, Grover's New National offered padded armchairs in the orchestra and long velvet sofas in the balconies. When Ford painted the interior walls of his theater white, with gold trim and wainscoting, Grover hired the same fresco artists who beautified the interior of the U.S. Capitol to decorate the ceilings and walls of his theater with scenes from Shakespeare. And when Ford offered the talents of John Wilkes Booth to the public, Grover brought Edwin Booth to Washington.

Grover was an abolitionist and a strong supporter of Lincoln's administration. He hailed from Auburn, New York, the hometown of Lincoln's secretary of state, William H. Seward. Seward and Grover had known one another since childhood: the secretary, in fact, started his political career at an Auburn law firm belonging to Grover's family. President and Mrs. Lincoln and their son Tad were fond of visiting the New National. Grover was ever eager to gratify the president's well-known love for Shakespeare, and decided that inviting Edwin Booth to perform Shakespeare on the third anniversary of Lincoln's inaugural would be a fitting way to celebrate the special day. He arranged to invite the president's family and members of his cabinet to the series.

On February 26, 1864, the morning after President Lincoln came to see him act the title role in *Brutus, or The Fall of Tarquin*, a play Booth's father made popular, Edwin dashed off an excited report to Adam Badeau. "Father Abraham visited Rome with me last eve to see the Tarquin's face," the star boasted, "and tonight he & Seward and their et ceteras will join [me again]. . . . My trade is good—may yours prosper likewise."

Edwin addressed the letter to General Grant's headquarters in Nashville, Tennessee. Colonel Badeau was fully healed now, enjoying a prestigious new appointment as General Grant's aide-de-camp. The two old friends no doubt relished the thought of how each, in his own capacity, had drawn close to the highest circles of power. "I congratulate you, Ad," Edwin had written. "If honors make you happy, God knows I wish you a sea of them."

President and Mrs. Lincoln paid six visits to Grover's theater to see Edwin perform. The president made a special request for the actor to portray Hamlet on March 2. This was a gala occasion. "By previous arrangement with the President and Mrs. Lincoln, Mr. Booth will give his splendid rendition of Shakespeare's Hamlet," the *National Republican* reported. "The President, Mrs. Lincoln and family will occupy their accustomed double box this evening, and Secretary Seward has secured for himself a private box directly opposite." Grover, thrilled at the public excitement Edwin's appearance generated, had extra chairs brought into the theater and hired additional ushers to help seat the throng of ticket holders. He ordered his orchestra to prepare special musical numbers to enhance the grandeur of the evening.

The *National Republican* ran out of superlatives when reporting, over the course of three weeks, the nightly event of Edwin's acting. An auditorium overflowing with members of the Lincoln administration and their families carried its own complement. Nothing in the actor's experience thus far had more closely approximated a coronation, both of himself as the reigning actor of his time and of theater as a high-status art. "It really seems that the dreams of my past life, so far as my profession is concerned, are being realized," he wrote happily to a friend from his room at Willard's Hotel.

On March 4, as Grover had planned, the president and his wife took their usual seats moments after the curtain rose on Edwin Booth in *Richelieu*. Secretary of State Seward and his family were also present. In honor of "the third anniversary of our President's inauguration," the *National Republican* reported, the auditorium had been specially decorated with bunting and flags. The Lincolns were cheered by the enthusiastic crowd, and then the gaze turned to Edwin Booth.

Acting for a president of the United States was something Edwin's father had done on many occasions, usually when well lubricated with alcohol. The experience was new to Edwin. The perfectionist actor strove to give Lincoln the best performances he could muster. "I was perhaps nearer to a mad house than I could ever go again without entering and having the door locked upon me," Edwin wrote to Badeau, describing how he had drained himself of energy in the effort to please.

Badeau's new employer, Ulysses S. Grant, arrived at Willard's Hotel on March 8, 1864, for what would be his first meeting with President Lincoln. Booth glimpsed the soldier in Willard's lobby, and wrote Badeau about the sighting: "Grant looks like the man he is—solid, true and honest."

"On March 10, Edwin's second-to-last night in Washington, *Richard III* was on the bill. Grover alerted Edwin that Mrs. Lincoln had planned a

Shakespeare-themed evening in Grant's honor, first hosting a formal dinner at the White House for her husband and Grant, later transferring the party to their box at the National in time for Edwin's performance. The star immediately prepared for the double honor of entertaining both Lincoln and Grant, but when the play began, Edwin saw only the president and his wife seated in their familiar box. Grant, who could be ill at ease in formal settings, had departed earlier in the day for his headquarters in Tennessee, saying to Lincoln, "Mr. President, I believe I have had enough of the 'show' business!"

The pinnacle of Edwin's success came on March 11, 1864, when Secretary of State Seward invited the actor to share dinner with his family at their mansion on Lafayette Square. Leonard Grover was also invited, and it was left open that President Lincoln might make an appearance. On this day, Edwin Booth crossed the last invisible barrier that separated him—the illegitimate son of a drunken actor—from full acceptance into high society. Secretary Seward's invitation was more significant in this respect than the "Booth parties" that Julia Ward Howe had thrown at her mansion. Julia Howe was a patron of the stage, a radical, a woman. Seward, by contrast, was a statesman of international reputation. Many believed that this former U.S. senator and governor of New York was, after the president himself, the second most powerful man in the country.

Edwin Booth had been born into another world than that of his hosts. By inviting the actor into his home, and by introducing him to his young daughter Fanny and his daughter-in-law Anna, Secretary Seward was declaring Edwin Booth to be a gentleman, a person fit to associate with the sheltered, gently bred females of the American upper class.

Fanny Seward was nineteen years old when the actor came to her father's house. She was a pensive, retiring girl who spoke few words in public, but her exterior concealed a precocious, wide-ranging intellect, as her voluminous Civil War–era diary attests. Fanny kept a faithful record of the parade of famous people who passed through Washington. She was a sharp observer of men and women, but of all the figures she encountered—President Lincoln, the generals Grant and Sherman, Prince Napoleon of France, and a score of dashing and heroic Union officers near her own age—none occupied more space in her diary than Edwin Booth.

There "is so much worthy of admiration and esteem in Edwin Booth," Fanny wrote, "that I am unwilling to leave it all to memory—and unrecorded." Fanny had gone to see Edwin at the New National Theatre as many times as President Lincoln. To meet him out of character, in the parlor of their home was startling. She saw "a small, slight gentleman, with a melancholy face betraying an intensely sensitive nature, and such a quick apprehension!" The actor wore his "dark, long silky hair" loose to his shoulders, Fanny noted. His face seemed to her "handsome more from its intellect" than any other quality.

Booth in person looked nothing like the characters he transformed into onstage, she felt. Even his eyes seemed to alter their shape and color with the different costumes he wore. "Those wonderful eyes," she wrote, "how can they be the same, they are black points in Shylock, in Richelieu they command—in Richard they hate—in Hamlet they are so full of tenderness & sadness, that one's heart aches at the sight." Now, seeing the actor in repose, in the role of himself, Fanny decided that "Booth's eyes are Hamlet's eyes, in their sad expression."

In the Seward dining room, as servants poured wine into glasses and began serving the courses of the evening meal, "there was a good deal of conversation about Richard." The family asked Edwin what his inner feelings and thoughts were as he acted the part of this villain. Richard commits criminal deeds and says scandalous things. He is lewd, he murders people, he tells lies and connives his way to the top of the kingdom. The Sewards' question cut to the heart of the social prejudice against actors, and of the stories told about Edwin's roistering past, and about his eccentric father, who was believed to descend into a state of insanity while acting. Edwin answered them carefully, explaining how his own mind remained calm at all times onstage, critically detached from the work of performing a character.

"Booth spoke of a peculiar feeling which sometimes seized him in the midst of [*Richard III*]," Fanny recorded, "a sort of vision rises in his mind, he seems to see the little show of Punch and Judy, which makes the part at once ridiculous & difficult to play."

Fanny appreciated his response, assuring Booth that "however thoroughly he may depict crime & vice, no words he speaks, whatever they may be, sound low or vulgar, because he says them gravely."

The Sewards asked their guest to name the greatest living actors. Edwin spoke only one name, that of the tragedienne Charlotte Cushman, the one performer other than himself who had been recognized socially by the Sewards. Then Edwin complained, "the great difficulty with actors was that they were not content to play parts best suited to their capacities." Too often, he said, untalented men who were not satisfied with the minor positions available to them in the companies of large theaters instead "would go out West & there play Hamlet," to the detriment of the profession as a whole.

After dinner, Booth rose and said he must go to the theater to dress for the night's performance of *Hamlet,* his last in Washington. "He bade us good-evening with dignified bows, grave & in his manner," Fanny remembered. "An hour later we saw him again, not changed to another character as on previous play nights—but, though wearing stage dress & though fully realizing, explaining, adorning the character of Hamlet, the same sad, sensitive and dignified gentleman who had just been our guest." Before Edwin left Seward's home, the secretary of state suggested that he and the actor should plan to see one another more often, socially.

THROUGHOUT THE SPRING OF 1864, THE MEMBERS OF THE DRAMATIC OIL Company—this was the auspicious name that Booth, Ellsler, and Mears decided to give to their newfound enterprise—corresponded busily. It was agreed among the partners that Booth and Ellsler should work to the end of the theatrical season, earning enough cash to get the business off the ground. Mears would go to Franklin to do the advance work: looking at land for sale; reckoning supplies they would need; researching the costs of lumber, pulleys, rope, steel bars, and iron drills.

It seems fitting that Thomas Mears had spent part of his career earning a living by gambling. The card player was the member of the Dramatic Oil Company to spend the most time in Venango County, arriving before Booth and Ellsler made their appearance. Mears seems to have disregarded the many signs abounding in "Oil Dorado" that success in this business was risky, uncertain, and, as one experienced oilman warned, "speculative in the extreme."

The landscape around Franklin was crowded with oil wells that had been abandoned by their owners after never pumping a single drop. Derelict shanties, discarded equipment, and hordes of disappointed men paid testament to the hazard of drilling: no one really knew where the rich deposits lay beneath the Pennsylvania farmland.

Reporters visiting Petrolia expressed amazement that the waves of prospectors did not see how the odds were stacked against them. Oil seeking, one traveler to the region warned, "is the purest gambling that was ever adopted wholesale by any mercantile community. If it were done with cards, nine-tenths of those engaged in it would draw off." Sinking a well was an act as random as throwing a dart blindfolded. Sheer luck decided the outcome.

Ironically, it was because this wager was made with tools, machinery, and hard labor—instead of with a pair of dice—that people expected a more positive outcome. Why would anyone waste sweat and muscle on boring holes five hundred feet through solid sandstone, if the odds of striking crude were tiny? As he embarked for work at the St. Charles Theatre in New Orleans at the end of February 1864, John Wilkes Booth was unaware that he and his friends had chosen the one moneymaking game where the chances for success were even worse than in the theatrical business.

There is no record of how John Wilkes Booth made his journey south, but a husband-and-wife team of touring British actors, Charles and Ellen Kean, traveled to the same theater in New Orleans several months after he did and kept a grim record of the wreckage of war they glimpsed from the windows of trains. A three-year record of military maneuvers was written on the landscape; devastation was everywhere. Even the pro-Union Keans were horrified. "Poor New Orleans undone," the actors exclaimed. "Mobile in ruins. Charleston but a name. Vicksburg battered to pieces." They sadly took note of "torn-up railroad track" and "shattered bridges" along their route.

For John Wilkes Booth, staunchly on the Confederate side, such sights would have filled him with anger. Here was more proof, he would say, of "the braggart North" inflicting "cruelty and injustice" on its weaker foe. "*Even should we allow, they* [the South] *were wrong* at the beginning of the contest," John wrote less than a year later, "*cruelty and injustice* have made the wrong become the *right.*" In an open letter to the people of the North, written after his journey through the south, John would exclaim, "O my countrymen, could you all but see the reality or effects of this horrid war, as I have seen them . . . I know you would think like me."

The first St. Charles Theatre—erected in 1835 at the cost of three hundred thousand dollars—was the pride of New Orleans. Where Ford's Theatre in Washington had eight private boxes, the St. Charles boasted forty-seven, each with its own bathroom. A high dome soared over the auditorium, with a two-ton crystal chandelier suspended from its apex. Each of the twenty thousand glass droplets on this light had been faceted by jewelers in London. The first St. Charles and its legendary chandelier burned to the ground in 1845; the second St. Charles, built on the site of the old, was nowhere near as grand. Yet the memory of the old theater's lost magnificence remained, proof of how well the people of the Crescent City loved the dramatic arts.

When Fort Sumter fell to rebel fire in April 1861 and Louisianans mobilized for war, the second St. Charles closed its doors. Only in 1864, well after the city came into the possession of federal troops, did life and light return to the stage. Ben DeBar, manager of the St. Louis theater where John Wilkes Booth so often played, dispatched a company of actors to the occupied city, with John Wilkes as one of the big attractions. The young star, counting the days until the start of his new career as an oil prospector, agreed to head the St. Charles playbill from mid-March through early April 1864.

John's family name was sacred in New Orleans, the place, where, in 1852, Junius Brutus Booth acted his last piece before dying. In 1857, when the young Edwin Booth revived old memories of his father's lost genius, New Orleans audiences had showered him with crowns of laurel and purses filled with gold. The arrival of another son of the Booth family filled the entertainment-starved city with anticipation.

After John Wilkes Booth's death, some people would claim he was forced to abandon his acting career because he suffered from laryngitis or another throat problem. "The statement that his voice had failed had no valid foundation," John's fellow actors informed a journalist. Rather, they explained, the myth originated with New Orleans dramatic critics, who, unwilling to tarnish the silver-tongued reputations of John Wilkes's father and older brother, politely insisted that only a serious vocal malady could explain his dismal articulation.

The *New Orleans Times* refrained from printing a review of John's opening night, claiming "the late hour to which Mr. Booth's rendition detained us, precludes any specific comment we would otherwise make." After a week spent stifling its dismay at his lack of skill, one New Orleans newspaper finally wrote, "we do not pretend that Mr. Booth is the greatest actor on the stage." Another found a glimmer of poignancy in the young man's untutored efforts, saying they managed to "win a strange, unwitting sympathy from the observer."

It was offstage that John Wilkes made his most vivid impression on the people of New Orleans. After the curtain fell, he would take to the streets in search of amusements with an entourage of new friends. The actor's antics as he drank his way through a succession of bars and billiard halls, one friend remembered, "interested and amused hundreds of people who, perhaps, never thought of going to see Booth at the theater."

Ed Curtis, one of Booth's New Orleans friends, later recalled the actor was restless and unhappy in social situations "unless he occupied a conspicuous position." Similarly, Curtis reported, any time a bowling match or game of pool was at stake, Booth "was not content unless he was winning." When John hit a losing streak at the Phoenix Bowling Hall one evening, he refused to let his victorious opponents leave. Instead the actor stubbornly challenged them to play him over and over again for hours, until finally, near dawn, he won the game.

Curtis observed another pronounced feature of his friend's behavior. At bars, after John "had imbibed more than his custom, his mind was haunted by strange ideas." Gripped with moroseness, the actor informed his drinking companions "that he was the victim of conspiracies." John's aggressively competitive edge and his descents into peculiar moods did not alienate the young men who gathered nightly to carouse with him. Curtis could only explain the phenomenon by saying that John Wilkes Booth "had a way about him which could not be resisted, the way which permits a man to overstep the boundaries . . . and do things for which other people would be punished."

A forcible illustration of the actor's charisma came one night in a sidewalk clash between the actor and some Union soldiers who were patrolling to enforce the laws of occupation. By order of General Benjamin Butler, residents of New Orleans were forbidden to sing or even whistle Confederate anthems in public. High on the list of prohibited music was "The Bonnie Blue Flag," a stirring tune from 1861 that celebrated Southern independence and blamed "Northern treachery" for starting the war.

John Wilkes and his friends were walking home, presumably drunk, after a long night spent playing pool. One of the number dared Booth to sing "The Bonnie Blue Flag" in the street. "Without a moment's hesitation," Curtis remembered, John "broke into . . . song."

His companions fled the scene. Imprisonment, Curtis said, was a penalty for such shows of defiance. The lyrics to "The Bonnie Blue Flag" were incendiary, with such lines as "Here's to our Confederacy, strong we are and brave—like patriots of old we'll fight, our heritage to save!"

Booth ignored his fleeing friends, and sang louder than ever. As federal soldiers came running from various directions, they may have heard him ring out the chorus, "Hurrah! Hurrah! For Southern rights, hurrah!"

The actor, Curtis said, stopped singing only when he was "surrounded."

Creeping back to see what punishment John Wilkes would receive, Booth's associates were amazed to find him smiling and talking with the Union men, an expression of perfect innocence on his face. "He made the soldiers believe he did not know anything about a law against a song of that kind, and he sang it just because he heard it on the streets of this city, and liked the words and the tune," Curtis later stated. Miraculously, the troops accepted Booth's explanation and sent him on his way. Curtis chalked up Booth's escape to "his marvelous power of fascination." In later years, Curtis would tell interviewers that he did not believe John was at that moment "particularly interested in the cause of the South." Booth's act of defiance preceded more "from a spirit of dare-deviltry," Curtis believed, "to show his contempt for authority in general and for that of the military in particular."

One person, presumably, who approved of Booth's spirited gesture was his host in New Orleans, George W. Miller. John spent the three weeks of his visit boarding at Miller's house near the corner of Felicity and Dryades streets. Miller was a rebel sympathizer, his close ties to high-ranking members of the Confederate government in Richmond an open secret among New Orleans residents. Miller's proclivities were so marked, locals claimed, that soldiers at the federal garrison kept his household "under suspicion." The friendship that started between Booth and his landlord outlasted the young actor's stay in New Orleans. John Wilkes, Curtis said, "kept up a correspondence with Miller some time after his departure."

The inner workings of the Confederate Secret Service are difficult to determine. By the end of the summer of 1864, John Wilkes was in active contact with Confederate agents and had been shown how to operate their cipher system. How precisely John Wilkes Booth came to the attention of Confederate authorities, and was identified as a candidate for recruitment, is unclear. It is tempting to speculate that George W. Miller might have been John's entrée into that world. Another friend John acquired during his short time in New Orleans, a blockade runner named Hiram Martin, also may have been a bridge to officials in Richmond. Booth and Martin were seen "very much together" at the Phoenix Bowling Hall, Curtis remembered, the actor and the sailor being "very chummy."

AFTER LEAVING NEW ORLEANS IN THE SPRING OF 1864, JOHN WILKES Booth made his way to what would be the last starring engagement of his life: a thirty-night run at the Boston Museum, near the corner of Tremont and School streets, blocks from the Massachusetts State House. Here, Booth entertained Boston crowds for five weeks straight, from late April through the end of May 1864—resting only on Sundays. A schedule like this would be physically draining for any actor, but John Wilkes doggedly endured. He needed the cash to fund his oil venture. The actor had pinned his hopes for the future on the success of the Petrolia scheme. In this final season of his acting career, John's friends remembered, the young man's obsession with wealth emerged as "a marked trait in his character." Booth was "exceedingly fond of money," theater manager Ben DeBar recalled, to the point that his fellow players described John as "avaricious."

The proprietor of the Boston Museum decked the front of his theater in three dozen gas lamps, each encased in a white glass globe. These beacons shone with a blinding light after sunset, luring crowds to the Museum's entrance. On the final night of his Boston run, John Wilkes Booth seemed to make a symbolic farewell to his theatrical career. He chose to act a rarely seen tragedy, *Ugolino,* which his father, Junius Brutus Booth, had written thirty years before. The play is a bloodbath: Ugolino, the main character, kills the woman he loves as well as his archenemy, then, in the final scene, commits suicide. Angry Venetians demand that Ugolino tell them why he is so evil. "Accursed wretch," they cry, "What moved thee to act?"

In answer, John Wilkes's character steps forward, his sword upraised, ready to plunge the blade into his chest, and shouts:

> *What mov'd me to it? To murder him who sacrificed my peace?*
> *This was the crowning crime! This was Hell's greatest triumph!*
> *. . . Dost thou not know me? Tis Despair*
> *From the abyss of ever-burning Hell,*
> *Where on the footstool of the great fiend's throne,*
> *I sit and form dark snares for wavering souls!*

FOURTEEN

MY THOUGHTS
BE BLOODY

O, from this time forth, my thoughts be bloody, or be nothing worth.
—*Hamlet*, 4.4

JUNIUS BRUTUS BOOTH, JR., ARRIVED BY STEAMSHIP IN BOSTON ON MAY 26, 1864, the night before John Wilkes acted *Ugolino* in that city. These two brothers had last met at Tudor Hall in 1854, when John was fifteen years old and still grieving over their father's death.

Now the eastward steamship journey from San Francisco to the Atlantic states was swift and easy, comparatively free of danger. A new railroad spanned the Isthmus of Panama. From Panama City on the Pacific coast to the port of Aspinwall on the Atlantic side, June Booth sped through the jungle in the comfort of a glassed-in train carriage. The weeklong trek on foot and by mule through the rain forest's fever-ridden undergrowth was a thing of the past.

Junius must have felt like Rip Van Winkle, returning to discover that in his ten years of absence in California, the American cities he once knew had grown and changed almost beyond recognition. From Boston, Junius made his way to New York City by June 2, 1864, to take part in a family gathering at Edwin's home. The returning traveler found all the Booths transformed, but Edwin, perhaps, was the most changed. What a contrast the thirty-one-year-old star made, in the summer of 1864, to the bedraggled youth Junius once rescued in 1852. Half crazed by the news of their father's death, Edwin had crashed through the door of his older brother's shanty on Telegraph Hill, ill and starving after his march across the Sierra Nevada. Junius had carefully restored his younger brother to health, found him a job at a San Francisco theater, and helped the teenager start his career onstage.

Now Edwin was a renowned artist with an air of command. He was richly dressed, conscious of his standing in society, the proprietor of two great theaters, owner of a valuable town house. All his enterprises were thriving, while Junius, aged forty-two, was yet an itinerant player forced to watch every penny he spent. The cost of shipping his trunks of costumes from San Francisco alone had been almost beyond his means. Junius's diary from this year makes a painful record of how he spent his dwindling funds on new "street clothes," shoes, and other small items. This was an uneasy reunion, as Junius took the measure of his younger brother's wealth and saw how far he himself now fell short.

The tension among all three brothers—Junius, Edwin, and John Wilkes—was apparent to William Stuart, longtime manager of the Winter Garden Theatre. Observing the siblings interact, Stuart concluded that Edwin's success had poisoned his brothers against him. John Wilkes "had—indeed the two brothers had—considerable jealousy and suspicion, both, it seemed to me unwarranted, of Edwin," Stuart later told an interviewer. He first made these observations on June 4, 1864, the day the entire Booth family made a formal tour of Edwin's playhouse on Broadway.

Approaching the Winter Garden, visitors that summer saw advertisements for Edwin Booth everywhere. Stuart, charged with promoting the star and his new theater, papered fences and the sides of buildings along Broadway with huge posters—many of them "big enough for a circus," one New Yorker remembered—all carrying Edwin's name. Manhattan photography studios displaying the star's portrait in their windows did a brisk business selling prints of his face, "shaded by dark flowing locks," to a female clientele. "Public excitement about the actor was then at fever heat," one journalist observed.

During the tour, Edwin showed Junius and John Wilkes the progress his teams of carpenters, set designers, and artists had made in beautifying the building for the start of the 1864 fall dramatic season. Hoping to realize his dream of staging a perfect production of *Hamlet,* Edwin hired the best scenic painter and the most skilled wardrobe mistress in the city to supervise preparations. The backstage area was filled with "rich stuffs," visitors to the Winter Garden then remembered. Antique furniture, exquisite rugs, silver goblets, and candelabra packed the property rooms. In Edwin's private dressing chamber, there were chairs, a couch, a makeup table, and a small cookstove for brewing coffee. A servant perpetually stood on hand to assist the star. Edwin's enormous wardrobe—satin robes tailored in Paris, bejeweled crowns, dresses trimmed with "Venetian and Spanish lace"—contained several of their father's prized possessions, including the elder Booth's stage sword.

Stuart remembered watching that day as Junius and John Wilkes picked up some swords and began sparring on the empty stage of the Winter Garden. He approached the pair with a proposition: would they like to act with Edwin in a one-night performance of *Julius Caesar*? The Booth brothers could divide the principal roles, Stuart suggested, Junius playing Cassius, Edwin playing Brutus, and John Wilkes playing the part of Mark Antony. Junius agreed at once. He was planning to tour East Coast theaters that fall; early publicity generated by a Winter Garden performance could only help him. John Wilkes's reaction to the idea, however, was initially hostile. Stuart remembered the young man showing a marked distrust of his older brother's motives.

"Is this some trick of Edwin's?" John Wilkes demanded, ordering Stuart to show him the script so he could read Mark Antony's scenes.

"I brought it to him," Stuart later testified, "and after looking it over for some ten minutes, he said grudgingly, 'I will play that fellow.' "

John's surly reaction made an impression on Stuart. The manager also was surprised at how ignorant John Wilkes was of this classic dramatic work. He later told an interviewer it was evident that "John's early education had been entirely neglected, and he really had no conception of the character."

In the end, the brothers agreed to bring *Julius Caesar* to the Winter Garden's stage in late July or early August, after John Wilkes returned from a planned trip to Petrolia. As of June 17, 1864, Edwin wrote a friend, "My brother W[ilkes] is here for the summer, and we intend taking advantage of our thus being brought together, with nothing to do, and will, in the course of a week or two, give a performance of Julius Caesar . . . for the benefit of the statue we wish to erect in Central Park." To commemorate the three-hundredth anniversary of Shakespeare's birth, a fund was started to place a statue in his honor in the heart of New York City.

In a sense, John Wilkes Booth's instincts were correct: the *Julius Caesar* plan was indeed a "trick of Edwin's." The star knew his brothers wanted money: neither of their earnings came close to matching his own income. Yet they would not be paid for their work in *Julius Caesar*. Rather, all money from the joint appearance would go to the Shakespeare fund. After taking over one of the most popular theaters on Broadway, Edwin Booth would not share the opportunity with his less fortunate brothers. Going forward, they were invited to join him onstage only for the benefit of a charity. The Winter Garden and the Walnut Street Theatre would remain the exclusive domains of Edwin and his partner, Clarke. Junius and John Wilkes would have to earn their own way.

Edwin's brothers were treated to one last proof of his high place in Manhattan society that first week of June 1864. The star took them both on a visit to the Tenth Street studio of sculptor Launt Thompson, where the artist's workroom was decorated for a party. Vases of flowers stood on tables by pots of coffee and bowls of punch. A collection of writers, painters, journalists, and Union officers filled the space, admiring Thompson's latest works: the bronze bust of Edwin Booth, life-size, in character as Hamlet, and a towering sculpture of General Winfield Scott in full military dress. The talk at this party, one guest remembered, concerned the war and art: soldiers and literary men discussed "the latest news from the front" while considering the merits of Thompson's new creations.

In the short time they spent together at Edwin's house, a friendship kindled between John Wilkes and Junius, who previously had been strangers. "June," as his family called him, was privately dismayed at how Edwin neglected John Wilkes. The young man was obviously unhappy, Junius later would recall, and it troubled him to see his own brother "so strongly sympathizing with the Southern cause." Knowing Edwin had forbidden John Wilkes to vent his rebel opinions in the house, Junius now made it his project to take the younger man aside and quietly, patiently, reason with him about the war.

"I felt it my duty as an elder brother," Junius later explained, "to do all I could & prove to John that the government was doing its duty . . . I told him the Civil War was but a large family quarrel & would in a few years be made up and peace restored." Junius begged John to stay away from the conflict for the sake of the family. He later said he received on many occasions John's earnest "promise" that he would do so.

John Wilkes did not change his opinions after talks with Junius, but he was moved by the protective, almost fatherly concern this long-absent older brother showed for him. June Booth, a onetime speculator in California gold, was curious to learn more about John's oil venture; the two even considered traveling together to Pennsylvania. Every time they shared such conversations, Junius later remembered, John would "express much gratitude for the interest I took in his welfare." In the young man's appreciative response, Junius read a record of Edwin's coldness and lack of care. Ostensibly the head of the family, Edwin had abandoned the idea of making this younger sibling his responsibility. Having genial, even-tempered Junius pay attention to him was a new experience for John. This older brother was the mentor, perhaps,

John had needed since their father's death. No personal animosity troubled their relationship; they were not competitors.

THE MORNING OF JUNE 8, 1864, FOUND JOHN WILKES BOOTH AND HIS friend Joseph Simonds en route by train from New York City to Franklin, Pennsylvania, erstwhile capital of Petrolia. The sea of mud that greeted the young men as they descended from their railway car, other travelers attested, was "deep and indescribably disgusting." This sticky ooze was unique to Oil Dorado. It was a combination of rain, eroded soil, and glistening rivulets of petroleum, and would "ever be fresh," one prospector wrote, "in the memory of those who saw and were compelled to wade through it."

The town of Franklin was an eyesore. Its various hotels, banks, bars, houses of prostitution, and prospectors' shanties had been built hastily and haphazardly on streets that in early summer, residents said, were "liquid lakes or lanes" of evil-smelling muck. Garbage was everywhere—food leavings, broken barrels, discarded clothing and equipment. A thin film of oil burnished the surface of the river flowing past the town; grease-coated barges and ferries crowded the wharves. Groups of men in overalls and knee-high boots could be seen puffing away at pipes and cigarillos, ignoring the "No Smoking" warnings posted near every working oil derrick. Petroleum fumes were combustible, but as locals allowed, "men will smoke, regardless of its too probable consequences." A newspaper article describing this unlovely place acknowledged that there were more attractive corners of the United States in which to start a career, but none besides Franklin offered "a better chance to make one's first million in, and thus start favorably on the road to comfortable affluence."

John Wilkes had a rough start in Franklin. According to Albert Smiley, who met Booth when they were forced to share a room at the overbooked United States Hotel, the actor was "very stylish in his dress" and "cold in manner toward strangers," qualities that did not win favor in the eyes of longtime residents. One night soon after his arrival, John donned his typically exquisite clothing to attend a dance at a local hall. Booth's "dudish appearance" and lofty behavior, Smiley recalled, offended the rougher guests at the gathering. A sizable gang of "deckhands from the steamboats and freshwater sailors from the lumber fleets," Smiley wrote, fell on Booth and bloodied his nose. The dandy was tossed out the door "with orders not to return." As a parting insult, Booth's attackers made sure his finely dressed body was smeared with some of the ubiquitous local sludge. Smiley did not escape, either, sharing Booth's fate in the mud. Humiliated, John wanted to keep the story of the episode from spreading through the town, but he failed. "It leaked out," Smiley recalled, "and we were often nagged by our friends."

John would not make the same mistake again. He quickly traded his gentleman's garments for the local uniform of "slouched hat, flannel shirt, overalls and boots," one friend recalled, and abandoned his superior attitude. When Thomas Mears, one of Booth's partners in the Dramatic Oil Company, took him to meet the mechanic chosen to operate their drill, the actor shook hands with the laborer energetically. Seeing his palm come away streaked with oil from the other man's skin, John smiled and said, "Never mind, that's what we're after."

Smiley remembered that just as Booth made an effort to avoid offending Petrolia's working men, the actor concealed his passionate feelings about the war. "During the short time I knew Booth," the young clerk later testified, "I never heard him talk a word of politics . . . or make any reference whatever to either the North or the South." John's partner Mears was an abolitionist. Many other oil seekers in the Allegheny River valley were vocal supporters of the Union cause. The profit-minded young actor was not going to let his pro-Southern sentiments complicate, or risk ruining, his opportunity to earn a fortune.

By June 11, 1864, Booth and Mears had settled on a piece of land and were busy acquiring the last bits of equipment necessary to raise a derrick and begin drilling. The start-up expenses were steep. After buying the land, Booth and his friends planned to sink three separate wells, each costing over a thousand dollars to build. On average, drillers expected to tunnel five hundred feet down through alternating layers of soil and rock before hitting any kind of deposit. Filled with optimism, Booth watched work begin on his site.

The site seemed promising. Part of an old farm, the property was a half mile from Franklin, a place where many wells already had struck oil. The land was bordered on one side by the Allegheny River, giving the Dramatic Oil Company easy access to water transportation—an important consideration once petroleum started spouting out of the ground. On June 11, Booth wrote a frantic letter to his third partner, John Ellsler, in Cleveland, begging him to contribute extra cash to their project. "I have as little money and as much use for that little as any man can have," John Wilkes wrote. "We can do nothing without [your] money," Booth urged Ellsler. "So meet it, John, it will be the last big PULL. . . . I am sure we will be pumping oil in less than a month."

By June 17, 1864, the actor's mood was completely changed. On June 15, he had left his oil claim and spent two days traveling the mountains around Franklin on foot, asking questions of the oil prospectors who were working on sites at higher elevations. As John Wilkes walked for nearly fifty miles across the region, the stories of failure he encountered were alarming. His tour of the mountains revealed that hundreds of abandoned derricks littered the forest, proof of how many people, in the grip of "oil fever," had been made to look like fools. In truth, the majority of oil prospectors who made a bid for riches ended the experiment in acute embarrassment and, often, poverty. One prospector wrote an article on the scores of men "who had taken leases and opened oil wells," only to "retire from the trade disgusted with their enterprise" a few weeks later. These disappointed gamblers returned home to be greeted with ridicule by family and friends who demanded to know why so many thousands of dollars had been thrown away, and who blamed the hapless speculator for not realizing that his "undertaking would prove a failure." The unlikely odds of the oil game dawned on John Wilkes during his two-day hike, leaving him with a sense of foreboding just at the moment he was making his own roll of the dice.

Gripped with panic after returning from this excursion, Booth dashed off a letter to Ellsler in Cleveland. "I want to see you here bad," the actor wrote from Franklin on June 17, 1864. "This may be a big thing for us, or it may be *nothing*. . . . I must see you. I have seen all the oil regions. I got back the other day from a two days *walk* of 48 miles. And I know more about these things than anyone can tell me. Make it your business to come at once." Ellsler answered the summons, arriving in Franklin to find a highly nervous Booth dressed like a mechanic and living in a shanty room bare of all furnishings except for a bed, a rifle, and "photographs of [the actor's] family decorat[ing] the wall."

As the days elapsed and Booth waited anxiously for news from the drilling site, he became increasingly somber. With Ellsler, he joined a circle of men who formed a club to pass the summer nights in lighthearted amusement. The members, Ellsler remembered, all "had come to Franklin to have a tussle with this new way of making fortunes." To enliven the tedium of the oil town, they gathered nightly in a private room over a saloon, drinking, singing comic songs, telling jokes, and acting, in an amateurish way, scenes from popular plays. Though he went to the club's meetings, Booth did not share the freewheeling, raucous mood of the rest of party. Indeed, his withdrawn, taciturn demeanor made him conspicuous at the gatherings. "[John Wilkes Booth] never indulged in a hearty laugh," Ellsler remembered. Those belonging to the Franklin fraternity later marveled at how "nothing more than a smile could be brought to [Booth's] face by the most amusing of actions or utterances."

Booth had reason to be dour. Using an engine to drive an iron bit down through solid rock, the driller hired by the Dramatic Oil Company had bored to a depth of five hundred feet in two locations on the riverfront property. These wells apparently did not yield a drop of petroleum, and were pronounced dry. A third well, sunk to the unusual depth of eight hundred feet, did not gush oil, but gave forth a meager amount, around a dozen barrels per day. At ten dollars per barrel, split three ways among the partners, the profit was not worth the price of pumping such a thin stream from the ground.

John's great speculation—the ambitious scheme to which he had devoted $5,000 of his own cash—approximately $200,000 in today's currency—as well as six months of work, planning, and anticipation—came to nothing. The venture, freighted with so many hopes, turned out a fiasco. In a last bid for success, John Wilkes put down an additional thousand dollars on a share in a new oil claim being started by a different company outside of Franklin. This, too, proved worthless.

On July 6, 1864, his plans dashed, John Wilkes returned to Edwin's town house at 28 East Nineteenth Street in New York City. Edwin and Junius were there, the former absorbed in supervising renovations at the Winter Garden Theatre, the latter, as he recorded in his diary, "doing nothing but loafing, reading and smoking." John told his family not a word of his disappointments in Petrolia, giving them instead the impression that his oil investments were thriving. When Edwin wrote a letter to Adam Badeau later that year, he announced what he supposed was his younger brother's newfound career. "J. Wilkes is up to his knees in an ile well," the actor joked. The Booths' joint performance of *Julius Caesar* did not occur in July as originally planned. The renovation of the Winter Garden was not yet complete, and John Wilkes was ill. The play would be postponed until the fall season.

"I am tired and sick," John complained in a letter to a friend on July 14, 1864. As usual when in Edwin's house, he had to keep his political sentiments muzzled. Now he saddled himself with the extra burden of lying about his Petrolia venture. The failure of these business schemes meant the twenty-five-year-old actor now was thrown back into the life that had become hateful to him. Booth's harrowing winter trek through Kansas and Missouri in January 1864 had drained his finances and injured his health. Future seasons of similarly hard traveling on the western theatrical circuit for little reward now loomed before him. Perhaps even more oppressive was the thought of continuing to be a petitioner for shelter and largesse from his famous older brother, the one who banished him to a career in the provinces in the first place.

On July 26, 1864, John Wilkes's prospects for the future changed. On that day, representatives from the Confederate Secret Service summoned him to a meeting at a hotel in Boston, the Parker House. According to Louisiana resident Ed Curtis, John Wilkes Booth had "kept up a correspondence with [George W.] Miller"—his Confederate landlord in New Orleans—"for some time" after leaving that city. It may be the case that either Miller or Booth's other New Orleans connection, the blockade-runner Hiram Martin, brought John Wilkes to the attention of Richmond authorities, identifying him as a promising recruit for conspiracy. However he found his way to the meeting, John discovered that an entirely new kind of speculation was open to him. A job—not that of actor or oilman, but of conspirator against the Lincoln administration—appears to have been offered to Booth on this occasion, and he accepted it.

Years before, at Richmond, Virginia, in November 1859, John had run out of the Marshall Theatre and talked his way onto a train bearing volunteer militiamen to Charlestown, the site of John Brown's hanging. For two weeks he wore the uniform of the Richmond Grays, reveled in his temporary association with that respected group, and performed guard and sentry duties mandated by the governor of Virginia. The Grays conferred on John Wilkes, so long an outsider, the gratifying feeling of belonging, and—perhaps for the first time in his life—the sense of fulfilling an important duty. Now, on July 26, 1864, John Wilkes Booth appears to have been given the chance to trade his membership in the brotherhood of actors and the world of the theater—sources to him of so little comparative success and so much frustration—for a vital mission on behalf of the Southern cause he loved. He joined a new brotherhood: the network of active conspirators against the Lincoln administration.

On August 1, less than a week after meeting with Confederate agents, John Wilkes met Edwin, June, and other members of his family at a summer cottage on Long Island Sound, acting as if nothing had changed. "Fine time sunning and rowing," Junius observed in his diary. John would have no trouble concealing his new employment from the Booth family. Whatever traveling this work entailed, or whatever income it accrued, John would ascribe to "my coal and oil lands [that] I have bought near Cleveland." The failed Petrolia enterprise provided a helpful cover for the novice agent. Yet there was one thing John Wilkes could not hide. Contact with rebel authorities and involvement in their cause seem to have freed him from feeling a need to acknowledge Edwin Booth's authority. After his July 26 meeting in Boston, John Wilkes began making gestures of defiance toward his Union-sympathizing family, his hostility bursting out forcefully. August 1864 opened a volatile chapter in the record of the brothers' relationships.

On the surface, life in the Booth family had never been better. "Dear mother is happy with her children about her, thank God!" Edwin wrote at this time. Though Mary Ann Booth yearned for her youngest son, Joe, who now was living in San Francisco, it was a joy for her to have her oldest son, Junius, with her for the first time in a decade. The Booth matriarch had all her grandchildren with her as well: besides little Edwina and Asia's two young children in Philadelphia, Junius had brought his ten-year-old daughter, Molly, with him from California, a girl whom Asia described as "the wildest hoyden that ever skipped." The family finances were booming. The Winter Garden and Walnut Street theaters poured record profits into John Sleeper Clarke's and Edwin Booth's bank accounts. Private carriages, vacations by the seaside, sumptuous clothes, and elegantly furnished homes now were regular features of Mary Ann and Asia's everyday lives. The privations this mother and daughter had endured during their hungry years at Tudor Hall in the 1850s were a long way away.

Edwin and Clarke were busy throughout August readying their two theaters for grand openings in the fall. "I've been in the scene-room and wardrobe night and day lately," Edwin said to a friend. "Everything looks fair and prosperous for the coming season." The star was planning another revival of *Hamlet*, this time with backdrops, costumes, and furniture perfectly reproducing the interior of a tenth-century castle in Denmark. "Every scene, every dress, every chair and table and nearly all the actors will be new," Edwin said. His promoter, William Stuart, hoping to build public excitement, invited reporters to daily lunches at the Winter Garden to watch scene painters at work and see actors in rehearsals. Junius was occupied as well. "Busy getting my phys[ique] ready," the forty-two-year-old actor announced in his diary, referring to the fencing and stage-fighting techniques he must practice prior to barnstorming theaters in Boston, Baltimore, and Washington, D.C., in the fall.

John Wilkes Booth's anger intruded on this hum of theatrical preparation, reminding his family of the war still being fought beyond the footlights. One memorable episode most likely occurred August 7, 1864, when John Sleeper Clarke, Edwin, and John Wilkes rode the cars together from New York City to Philadelphia. On this train ride, Clarke apparently referred to Jefferson

Davis in an insulting manner. The instant Clarke spoke, John dove for him, seizing him by the neck and choking him. "He swung [me] from side to side with maniac strength while his grip tightened," Clarke later remembered. John's face, he said, appeared "twisted with rage." Witnesses shouted and made attempts to stop the attack, but John Wilkes ended it himself, shoving Clarke back into his seat with the words, "Never, if you value your life . . . speak in that way to me again of a man and a cause I hold sacred."

Stunned by this display of aggression, the Booth family seems to have construed John's behavior as a temporary derangement brought on by high fever. The twenty-six-year-old returned to Edwin's house in New York, where he collapsed. For the next three weeks, John was confined to a sickroom, his right arm inflamed with erysipelas, a streptococcal infection of the skin. In the days before penicillin, the condition could be fatal. Sufferers were racked with nausea, chills, headaches, exhaustion, and pain as their bodies battled the disease. A doctor visited John Wilkes, who remained bedridden through the final days of August.

President Lincoln's standing in the North, and Republican morale in general, had never been lower than at the end of this month in 1864. Union forces appeared to be at a standstill. General Grant was halted outside Richmond; Sherman's divisions were massed around Atlanta, their progress, for the moment, obstructed. Feeding off Northern frustration, a resurgent Democratic Party castigated Lincoln for his emancipation policy and called for an immediate end to the war and the restoration of the Union with slavery intact. When Democrats convened in Chicago that summer, they nominated former general George B. McClellan to challenge Lincoln in the November presidential elections. Campaign posters for the Democratic candidate warned voters that reelecting Lincoln would not only bring on the horrors of "Universal Anarchy and Ultimate RUIN!" but also the threats of "Negro Equality, More Debt, Harder Times and another Draft." A McClellan victory, on the other hand, promised to "defeat Negro equality, restore prosperity, and re-establish the Union in an honorable, permanent and happy peace." Abraham Lincoln gauged the mood of his war-weary countrymen and predicted a grim electoral future. "I am going to be beaten," the president said, "and unless some great change takes place, badly beaten."

Sick as he was, John Wilkes could not resist arguing politics with his brother Edwin. On August 29, a shouting match broke out between them that even Junius, always eager to smooth over family quarrels, called "severe." The specific words the two brothers traded are unknown, but Adam Badeau later testified that Edwin, in a terrible voice, at the end of a "long and violent" exchange with his brother, threatened to expel John Wilkes from the Booth home. After John had ranted and stormed, "wish[ing]," Badeau reported, "for the success of the Rebellion," Edwin shot back that "he should go elsewhere to make such sentiments known; that he was not at liberty to express them in the house of a Union man."

This was not an insignificant warning. Whatever differences divided the clan, their commitment to protecting Mary Ann Booth's happiness had always been paramount. These sons "were greatly attached to their mother," a Booth family friend observed. Keeping the family united was a goal to which all the Booth children dedicated themselves. The point was not only to spare their long-suffering mother any further sadness, but to guard their privacy, to advance their professional reputation, and to raise their social standing. A split in this family's famously united front would be noticed by the press. The suggestion that politics had broken the Booth brothers apart would be news indeed.

Asia Booth Clarke later credited Edwin and John's argument to the dangerous topic of Abraham Lincoln. She notes in her memoir that John Wilkes was obsessed with the president's reelection, spouting dire predictions that the Republican was planning on "making himself a king" come November. "His success, I tell you—will be a reign!" John thundered at Asia. He said Lincoln was trying "to crush out slavery" with foul play, resorting to "robbery, rapine, slaughter and bought armies" to achieve his ends. With somewhat confused logic, Wilkes held that Lincoln's tactics were shameful compared to the liberating crusade "of old John Brown . . . that rugged old hero." "Great God!" John Wilkes cried, "John Brown was a man inspired, the grandest character of the century." Next to Brown, the young actor said, Lincoln was "coarse," "vulgar," and "a disgrace." Listening to her brother's words, Asia worried his mind had been strained by his recent illness and too much hard work.

Edwin Booth afterward referred to his fight with John Wilkes as "a disgusting quarrel." The argument gave him "the blues," he said. When it was over, Edwin composed a letter to Adam Badeau, then stationed outside Richmond with General Grant. Edwin asked his friend to "send me Jeff Davis's head" as a present, and talked about his plans to support President Lincoln in the fall elections. "I go in for cursing every damned rebel out and waving the old 'stars and stripes' all over," he told Badeau. Lincoln "is what is called right." A second term in office for the Republican leader would be "glorious." Edwin had marked the celebrations of the third anniversary of Lincoln's inaugural with a command performance for the president. Badeau was at Grant's side as that general besieged the Confederate capital, Richmond. Edwin counted Secretary of State William H. Seward among his friends. Thus Edwin Booth's loyalty to the Lincoln administration was more than abstract patriotism—it was personal.

Fortunately for the sake of family peace—and particularly for the feelings of Mary Ann Booth, who was distressed by any strife among her children—Edwin, Edwina, and Junius packed their bags for Philadelphia on September 1, where Edwin was due to perform at the Walnut Street Theatre. A day after his departure, Atlanta fell to General Sherman's army. This long-sought victory turned the fortunes of war in Lincoln's favor at last. The public mood in Northern cities was jubilant. Patriotic demonstrations celebrated Sherman's advance through Georgia. From September 2 onward, Lincoln's reelection seemed assured.

"Whenever I would mention any success of the federal arms," Junius later recalled, John Wilkes "would say that he had not heard it—or that it was a false report & and soon would be corrected." There was no denying, however, that bluecoats had captured Atlanta, the city the *New York Times* referred to as a "rebel stronghold." This news compounded John Wilkes's already powerful feelings of anger and alienation. He was ready to drop all association with his clan; it was only his attachment to his mother and sister that kept him within the family's orbit. John declared to Asia, "if it were not for mother I would not enter Edwin's house." The young man added, "I would never darken [Clarke's] door, but for you."

Edwin Booth put all thoughts of John Wilkes behind. Family troubles were easily forgotten in the adulation greeting the star at the start of his new season. "My trade," Edwin announced to Colonel Badeau in September 1864, "has been great in every sense." Money poured into the ticket office of the Walnut Street Theatre: "If no crashes come, I shall make out to have a snug little home to leave behind me," the actor crowed.

The people of Philadelphia even presented the star "with a fine portrait of my father," Edwin noted, as a token of their admiration. "The face is beautiful," he informed Badeau, "it was taken when he was 30. I think more of it than of the fame and money I have made during this engagement." Yet Booth had a further ambition in view. The anticipation for his *Julius Caesar*, scheduled for November 25, was surpassed only by the news that the actor, on the night following his joint performance with his brothers, would debut a new production of *Hamlet* and proceed to play the part for one hundred nights running, a feat never before attempted by any actor, even in Shakespeare's time.

John Wilkes Booth left New York City after the infection in his arm had cleared. In the last week of September, he made a final visit to Franklin, Pennsylvania, where he filed documents officially ending his stake in the failed claim of the Dramatic Oil Company. With the help of his friend Joe Simonds, John transferred ownership of the nonproductive oil wells to his brother Junius. Though the property itself was virtually worthless, John's gesture acknowledged the one male member of the Booth family he held to be his friend.

Franklin's streets were alive with talk of the approaching elections. People were animated as well by reports of General Philip Sheridan's string of victories in northern Virginia. The Army of the Shenandoah was sweeping the gray-coats southward. As they crossed the landscape, United States soldiers either burned or commandeered the rich produce of Virginia's autumn harvest: crops, the contents of storehouses, and livestock fell alike into their hands. On orders from Ulysses S. Grant, Sheridan had vowed to render "the Shenandoah Valley a barren waste."

Whether it was because of the news of the rebel defeats in Virginia, or the sting of contemplating his own losses in Petrolia, John Wilkes spent most of his time in Franklin drinking, witnesses said, the "strongest brandy." On more than one occasion he was seen weaving his way through town, "as drunk as he could possibly get," once even stopping on the sidewalk in a half stupor, roaring out a monologue from *Richard III* while slashing the air before him with a tree branch instead of with a sword.

It is likely John Wilkes was drunk for most of his stay in Franklin, for on at least two occasions the actor threatened unarmed men in the town with a loaded gun. Only the quick action of bystanders prevented bloodshed. James Lawson, a local barber, reported that Booth almost shot a man while waiting his turn for a haircut. The trouble started when Caleb Marshall, a black resident of Franklin, entered the shop and "began to rejoice loudly over the news of a great victory for the Union army." Booth challenged Marshall to be silent, "pointing his finger" and saying in a threatening voice, "Is that the way you talk among gentlemen, and with your hat on, too?"

Marshall stood his ground, calmly replying that he only removed his hat when entering a parlor where ladies were present. "When I go into a barroom or a barber shop or any other public place," Marshall said, "I keep my hat on."

At this juncture, Lawson recalled, "Booth's face turned white" and his hand gripped the butt of the pistol he carried in his coat pocket. Men sitting next to Booth grabbed him by the arms and shoulders, immobilizing his upper body and dragging him out the door and down the street before the situation turned violent.

Another episode—one that mirrored John Wilkes's earlier attempt to choke his brother-in-law Clarke on a train car—occurred while Booth was riding the ferryboat from Franklin. He took offense when a man on board disparaged Southerners and spoke admiringly of Abraham Lincoln. John disagreed vehemently, brandishing his pistol. The Lincoln supporter—a carpenter—countered by thrusting a steel-tipped barge pike at John's face and threatening to "run him through." Fellow passengers restrained the men, and peace was restored.

Booth left Franklin at the end of September, planning never to return. He spent the early part of October in New York City, once again staying in Edwin's house. The two managed to get along this time without an explosion. On October 14, Edwin penned a peaceful letter to Adam Badeau, remarking that as he wrote John Wilkes "is on the sofa at this juncture in t'other room."

During this visit, John told Edwin and their friends in the theater world that he had grown wealthy by his investment in oil. Fellow actors later reported that John said he had no intention of returning to work onstage, "petroleum," he bragged, "being more profitable than the profession." Booth claimed his oil wells "netted within six months between $50,000 and $75,000," a sum resembling Edwin and Clarke's profits from their New York and Philadelphia theaters. As this description of his oil riches spread through acting circles, John's longtime friend Joe Simonds sounded a note of warning. "I hardly know what to make of you," Simonds wrote. "Don't get offended with me John but . . . you must not tell such extravagant stories." Simonds knew better than anyone how much cash Booth had lost on his risky Petrolia speculation. He admonished the actor for telling lies. "We have not got rich yet, John," he said. Simonds probably believed John spread the falsehoods to escape being teased as a failure. He had no knowledge of the actor's real reason for using Petrolia as a smoke screen.

John Wilkes traveled to Montreal, in the third week of October 1864. Here he attended a meeting of high-ranking Confederate spies who outlined in greater detail their plans for the abduction of President Lincoln. Booth apparently received a large sum of money from these agents—in excess of $1,500—with which to launch the conspiracy.

In the clearest sign yet that John had committed himself fully to this fateful course of action, he carried with him into Canada the trunk of costumes that once had belonged to his father. An actor's wardrobe was his passport. Without the requisite garments in which to play Macbeth, Richard III,

Hamlet, or Romeo, a traveling actor could not work. In Montreal, Booth entrusted these precious tools of his profession to a man named Martin. John Wilkes later told a friend that Martin would bring the trunk on board his vessel when he ran the Union blockade of Southern ports. This was a drastic measure. By shipping his best means of earning a living across Southern lines, John was turning his back on any future as an actor he might have had in the North and West. John's action indicated he was preparing to leave his home and his family permanently behind.

Booth stayed in Montreal through October 27, when he left for Washington, D.C. In that city, one week after President Abraham Lincoln won re-election to a second term by a landslide of four hundred thousand votes over George B. McClellan, John Wilkes Booth deposited the operating funds paid him by Confederate authorities in a local bank.

"**I** wish you [would] send me stirring news of what's going on in the world," Edwin pleaded in a letter to Colonel Badeau during that election season. "I never read the papers," he confessed. The star felt like a prisoner of the stage. "I live in a world bounded by a few painted tents and trees, outside of which I know nothing," he explained. "Isn't my life a strange one? I only just begin to realize its unreality."

For all his protests of ignorance, Edwin Booth paid enough attention to the world beyond his theater's walls to make his way to a polling station on November 8 to vote for Abraham Lincoln. "The first vote I ever cast," he cried. For this son of Junius Brutus Booth, who always had followed his father's example of staying clear of political affiliations, Edwin's gesture was significant. "I suppose I am now an American citizen all over," he mused, "as I have ever been in heart."

Edwin Booth might only have skimmed the headlines for war news, but he read all theatrical notices avidly. Rave reviews following his brother Junius's performances at John T. Ford's theaters in Baltimore and Washington, D.C., filled Edwin with trepidation. After carefully positioning himself as the reigning Booth in New York City, Edwin did not wish to be outshone on his own stage the night *Julius Caesar* came to the Winter Garden. "According to the papers," Edwin wrote to a friend, "*he* [Junius] is *the Booth* of the family; so I must brush up, or lose my laurels." For Edwin to feel threatened by Junius seems almost absurd. At this stage in Edwin's career, Junius was hardly a rival. A competitive edge was ever present in the relationships among the brothers.

. . .

JUNIUS, EDWIN, AND JOHN WILKES GATHERED IN NEW YORK CITY ON November 23, 1864, to rehearse for *Julius Caesar*. Promoter William Stuart had done his publicity work well. Posters in the streets and advertisements in newspapers invited audiences to see THE THREE SONS OF THE GREAT BOOTH walk the same stage together. Edwin's team of carpenters and artists had exerted themselves to produce gorgeous backdrops that evoked the interior and exterior scenes of ancient Rome and its stately Forum.

While Edwin and Junius, playing Brutus and Cassius, respectively, would wear togas that swept to their ankles, Mrs. Bohmer, wardrobe mistress at the Winter Garden, fitted John Wilkes in a different costume. He donned a pair of white hose, an embroidered tunic cut above the knee to show his muscular legs, and leather sandals whose straps wound tightly up his calves. She apparently ordered John to shave his face clean before the performance: Mark Antony could not sport a drooping mustache.

The audience that promenaded through the wrought-iron gates of the Winter Garden on Friday, November 25, was spectacular both in size and distinction. Every private box was filled, the balcony level was densely packed, and every seat in the orchestra had been taken. "The theater was crowded to suffocation," Asia remembered, "people standing in every available place. The greatest excitement prevailed." Mary Ann Booth, in her handsomest dress, sat beside Asia in a private box. John Sleeper Clarke and eleven-year-old Molly, Junius's daughter, were with them. The next morning, the *New York Herald* cataloged those present in the glittering assembly as "Boothites, Shakespeare men, artists, authors, actors, the men of taste in the city generally, and Bohemians, of course, without number."

The curtain rose, and the audience waited breathlessly for the opening of the play's second scene, the moment when Brutus, Cassius, and Mark Antony make their first entrance. The sight of the Booth brothers dashing onstage in a group, one witness remembered, "fairly carried the house by storm." Applause and roars of approbation greeted the actors—Junius was the tallest and broadest of the three; John Wilkes, the youngest, had the most perfect features; Edwin, the smallest, nonetheless commanded the most attention. As the characters began to speak, the audience saw the unequal distribution of talent and training in the Booth family. Edwin's superiority was evident. Stuart later recalled that while John Wilkes "was physically the handsomest," Edwin "was head and shoulders, as an actor, above the other two." Drama critics taking notes that night agreed. One asserted after the show that "as an actor, J. Wilkes could not compare with either of his brothers, although his resemblance to them in form, feature, voice and manner was remarkable." The *New York Herald* was kinder to John. After heaping praise on Edwin and Junius, the *Herald* reviewer stated that if the audience noticed the youngest Booth brought "less of a real personality to Mark Antony, the fault was rather in the part than in the actor."

At the moment the second act began, the doors leading into the auditorium burst open and firefighters poured into the theater dragging hoses, and a small fire engine behind them. The audience leaped out of their seats, ready to run for an exit. It had been almost half a century since the Richmond Theatre burned to the ground during a performance, killing nearly a hundred people, but the memory of that death trap lingered in the popular mind. Edwin and William Stuart were able to calm the crowd. As it turned out, no smoke or flames had touched the Winter Garden. A fire at the LaFarge Hotel next door, soon extinguished, was responsible for the interruption. The firefighters departed, the doors closed behind them, and the play continued to its end, when the three brothers were called onstage "side by side, again and again," Asia remembered, "to receive the lavish applause of the audience, mingled with waving handkerchiefs and every mark of enthusiasm."

The box office at the Winter Garden sold $3,500 worth of tickets that night—the approximate equivalent of $140,000 in modern currency. As Edwin had decreed, the entire sum would be given to benefit the Shakespeare fund. A repetition of this kind of performance, with profits divided three ways among the Booth brothers, would have made every difference in the cash-strapped lives of Junius and John Wilkes. Edwin never offered to make such an arrangement, however, and his siblings never brought themselves to ask.

No one could doubt who owned the lion's share of genius in the Booth family. The attention of the city now was trained on the Winter Garden as Edwin prepared to unveil the greatest achievement of his career. On Saturday, November 26, he would walk onstage, this time alone, to begin a record-breaking marathon—acting *Hamlet* one hundred nights in a row "with a magnificence," critics would enthuse, "unknown in the history of the American stage."

ON THE MORNING OF NOVEMBER 26, ASIA AND HER HUSBAND, CLARKE, returned to their home in Philadelphia by train, taking Junius's daughter, Molly, with them. Edwin hastened to the Winter Garden, where he rehearsed with his stock company for the night's gala opening of *Hamlet*. It was not until Sunday, November 27, that Mary Ann, Junius, Edwin, and

John Wilkes were able to gather around the breakfast table to discuss the terrifying report that was sending waves of shock through the residents of the metropolis. At exactly nine o'clock on Friday night, a network of Confederate conspirators, stationed at points across Manhattan, set fire to major buildings. Their goal was to touch off a massive fire, burning the city to the ground. The firefighters who had burst into the Winter Garden as the Booth brothers started the second act of *Julius Caesar* were responding to a blaze Confederates had lit inside the LaFarge Hotel next door.

Newspapers passed on the intelligence that this "Vast Rebel Conspiracy" was inspired in part by the work of arsonists during the Draft Riots the previous summer, when fires, proliferating across the city, had thrown New York into confusion and chaos. "The original plan of the marauders," the *New York Herald* reported, "was to have simultaneously fired the hotels at the lower and upper part of the city, and while the Fire Department and Police had their attention distracted to these remote portions of New York, to fire the hotels and other public buildings in the central points."

Investigators quickly discovered that dozens of Confederate agents— many of them "importations from Richmond and Canada," the *Herald* informed its readers—had descended on the city Friday morning, carrying carpetbags filled with jars of turpentine and phosphorus. These men had checked into rooms at the Metropolitan, the St. James, the Gramercy Park, the LaFarge, and other hotels, where they soaked the beds and blankets with turpentine. At the stroke of nine o'clock, the agents then broke open their jars of phosphorus and hurled the contents around the rooms.

The quick response by teams of volunteer fire companies foiled the scheme. None of the blazes set by Confederate arsonists ever reached the point of raging out of control. New York, however, had been given a reminder of the horrifying days of the Draft Riots. Fire alarms sounding across the city, more than a year later, still had the power to fill residents with special dread.

The Confederate motive for launching this incendiary attack, the *New York Herald* reported, "was retaliation for General Sheridan's operations in the Shenandoah Valley." As Union armies carried the war to Southern civilians, rebel conspirators now sought "to carry destruction into our Northern cities." A lead editorial suggested the attack was evidence the South had realized it was losing the war. Richmond's leaders were "steeped to their necks in blood," the *Herald* accused; their only wish now was "to inflict vengeance upon us for their disappointments."

The Booths, like nearly every other newspaper-reading household in the city, could not avoid talking about this startling development. As might be imagined, the discussion among the brothers turned ugly. Junius seems to have touched off the argument. He was furious that the rebel arsonists now in custody would receive due process of law. After a long residence in California, this oldest Booth brother was attracted to frontier-style vigilante justice. Had the same attack been made against the city of San Francisco, June cried, "the whole pack of incendiaries would have been caught and hanged from the window of the Vigilante headquarters on Sacramento Street."

John Wilkes disagreed. He apparently defended the arsonists, describing their work as a legitimate "act of war," honorable payback for General Sheridan's wanton destruction of civilian property in Virginia. Confederate agents had no choice but to wage war on the people of New York, he said.

Listening to John Wilkes's words, Edwin lost control. He had experienced, as John Wilkes also had, the lawlessness of the Draft Riots. During that bloody week in 1863 both brothers had lived in fear that violent gangs would break into their house, discover the Union officer and the black man concealed within it, and burn the place in retaliation. The lives of their mother, their sister Rosalie, and Edwin's daughter, Edwina, had been in peril. For John Booth now to advocate acts of terror against the city where the Booth family made its home, Edwin decided, was going too far.

In a towering rage, one witness later recalled, Edwin shouted that John was "a rank secessionist." He ordered his brother "to cease his treasonable language, telling him he could not stay in the house if he persisted." John refused to back down. At this point, the witness said, Edwin "peremptorily expelled his brother from his residence," no doubt seizing John and forcing him out the front door and into the street.

John was enraged and humiliated. Once again, as during his last fight with Edwin in August, he was suffering from a physical illness. One side of John's neck, Junius noted in his diary, had erupted in large, painful "boils," or "carbuncles." On November 28, Junius, ever the peacemaker, helped "the rank secessionist" pack his bags. Too sick to stay in a hotel, John Wilkes was compelled to seek shelter under Asia's roof in Philadelphia. Junius accompanied his brother there on the train, where Asia put John to bed and summoned a doctor to drain the abscesses on his neck.

Scholars of Lincoln's assassination agree that it was at the home of his sister Asia in the month of November 1864 that John Wilkes Booth composed two important letters. In these rambling, emotional screeds, he attempts to explain first to his mother and then to a national audience his firm resolve to plot against the president of the United States.

The first missive is addressed to "Dearest beloved Mother." Mary Ann Booth had lived with social ostracism for decades. Now, just as she was achieving a measure of peace and security, the deed John Wilkes planned to commit would renew her misery. The son justified his action to the mother by reminding her of the strife troubling their family since the war began. "For four years I have lived (I may say) A *slave* in the north," John writes, "not daring to express my thoughts or sentiments, even in my own home. Constantly hearing every principle, dear to my heart, denounced as treasonable . . . For four years I have borne it mostly for your dear sake . . . but it seems that uncontrollable fate, moving me for its ends, takes me from you, dear Mother, to do what work I can."

In his second letter, addressed "To Whom It May Concern" and no doubt intended for publication in national newspapers, John Wilkes acknowledges "how foolish I shall be deemed, for undertaking such a step as this." He describes the North as his home, the place, he writes, where "I have many friends, and everything to make me happy." With some exaggeration, John claims that in the North "my profession alone has gained me an income of more than twenty thousand dollars a year. And where my great personal ambition in my profession has such a great field of labor."

Booth grants that it "seems insane . . . to give up" this comfortable Northern world in favor of "the South . . . where I have no friends . . . a place, where I must either become a private soldier or a beggar." Yet, he declares, it is the abject oppression of the Southern people by the armies and government of the North that has won him over to their side. His last lines in the letter: "My love (as things stand today) is for the South alone. They say she has found that 'last ditch' which the North have . . . been endeavoring to force her in, forgetting they are our brothers, and that it is impolitic to goad an enemy to madness. Should I reach her in safety and find it true, I will proudly beg permission to triumph or die in that same 'ditch' by her side."

In early December, John Wilkes Booth went to Washington, D.C. His family was relieved to see the troublesome young man depart. John Sleeper Clarke abominated Wilkes and did not care to have him stay long in Philadelphia. Junius, engaged to star in Boston theaters for the entire month, was too busy to devote much attention to him. Edwin had thrown John Wilkes out of his house. The conspirator took his leave without fanfare, speeding onward toward his then inscrutable purpose. As Junius Booth later testified to a federal investigator, John Wilkes told them on his departure that "he was forming an oil co. in Washington & could do better by it than acting & we all believed him."

• • •

Edwin Booth's one hundred consecutive performances of *Hamlet* at the Winter Garden Theatre between November 26, 1864, and March 22, 1865, was a feat never attempted before that date. In this marathon of artistic endurance, the star gave the people of New York an astonishing display of his virtuosity. Endlessly inventive, ever improvising, the actor managed to make each successive performance seem somehow different from the one before. He dug deep into himself, layering fresh inflections on Shakespeare's language, finding new interpretations of familiar passages. William Stuart, the Winter Garden's seasoned showman, knew the stunt was box office gold. When Edwin's energies flagged, and he felt "heartily sick and wearied of the monotonous work," he begged his manager to end the run. Stuart always refused, urging the star onward with the words "No, not at all, my dear boy! Keep it up, keep it up! If it goes a year, keep it up!"

The critics of New York were transfixed by Edwin's feat, and so was the nation as a whole. Decades later, the episode was remembered for how it took up space on the pages of newspapers that otherwise would have been devoted to General Grant as he closed in on Richmond. Part of Edwin's genius, the *New York Sun* marveled, was his ability to "challenge attention even in the midst of the trouble, excitements and anxieties of the war."

On March 27, 1865, Adam Badeau was stationed with General Grant at his headquarters in City Point, Virginia. The president and Mrs. Lincoln were also present, having made a special visit to the front. It was not an easy period for Badeau. Mrs. Lincoln was his special charge, and her easily wounded temper and unrestrained outbursts made her presence at Grant's headquarters difficult and upsetting for everyone.

Badeau, who had read the newspaper accounts of his old friend's latest success, took time away from his duties playing host to the first lady to write a word of congratulation to Edwin Booth. "Your triumph has realized all I ever hoped you would accomplish," he exclaimed, "and will certainly be historical in the annals of your art." Badeau informed Edwin that Grant was preparing to march on Richmond immediately. "We start tomorrow night or early next morning, according to present orders." Drawing a parallel between the soldier's life and the actor's, Badeau joked, "Just as your campaign is over, ours begins. I hope we shall be as successful as you have been." At the close of this letter, Badeau mentioned "Generals Sherman and Sheridan are both here in person today. Also the President."

Laurence Olivier, a twentieth-century actor who spent a great deal of his time playing Hamlet, noted that after a certain number of nights the performance of this character becomes a self-portrait of the actor who is playing him. "Hamlet," Olivier said, "has to be you in all the facets you can muster." Edwin Booth brought the experiences of his own life to bear on his work that season—his understanding of a son's relationship to his father and his mother; the uneasy boundary that exists between genius and madness; the lure of fame; when it is best to take bold action, and when it is better simply to "let be." Audiences thought they perceived a special intensity in the scenes Edwin played with the ghost of Hamlet's father. Every night, the actor wore a medallion portrait of his own parent, Junius Brutus Booth, on a heavy gold chain around his neck, an integral part of his costume.

While Edwin's hundred nights were drawing to a close, the Century Club made plans to honor the record-breaking star. A committee of distinguished men, including the governor of New York and the assistant secretary of war, Charles A. Dana, wished to present Booth with a "Hamlet Medal," an oval, cast in solid gold, designed by Louis Comfort Tiffany. Tiffany announced that his creation would bear "in the center, Booth's head as Hamlet, sur-rounded by a serpent, the skull of Yorick, two foils crossed and a raven." The inscription on the opposite side would read, "To Edwin Booth, in commem-oration of the unprecedented run of Hamlet as enacted by him in New-York City for one hundred nights."

In February 1864, the president of the United States and his secretary of state both had honored Edwin Booth with proofs of their sincere regard. After he completed one hundred nights of *Hamlet* in March 1865, Booth would arrive at yet another pinnacle of his career. Any greater laurel an actor might receive beyond these rewards would be difficult to imagine.

But that did not stop Edwin Booth from trying. Though "the terrible suc-cess of 'Hamlet' seems to swallow up everything," Edwin confessed he was preoccupied with thoughts of how to "follow it up with something still bet-ter done, if it can be, in the way of costumes and scenery." One idea was to summon his brothers, John Wilkes and Junius, back to the Winter Gar-den on the next anniversary of Shakespeare's birthday—April 23, 1865—for another charity performance. This time, Edwin thought, the brothers could share the leading parts in *Romeo and Juliet*: Edwin taking Mercutio; Junius, Friar Lawrence; and John Wilkes, Romeo. Looking ahead to winning his next accolade, Edwin said, "keeps me far off in fairy-land, day and night, in my dreams and in my days."

John Wilkes rarely replied to the mail his family sent him that winter. His visits to New York were infrequent: Edwin's antipathy made brotherly meetings difficult. Finally, on January 17, 1865, in answer to an anxious letter from Junius demanding to know what John was doing in Washington and why he refused to write, the twenty-six-year-old sent this response: "You ask me what I am doing. Well a thousand things. Yet no more, hardly than what I could attend to if I was at home. But dear brother you must not think me childish when I say that the old feeling aroused by our loving brother has not yet died out. I am sure he thinks I live upon him. And its only for dear Mother that I have gone there at all when in New York, and as I cannot live in that city without him at home and as this season I would be home all the time, I thought it best not to be in the City at all, and as I like this place next, and my bus[iness] at present calls me here. I thought I would here make my stand."

Onstage with Edwin Booth throughout the marathon run of *Hamlet* was a man who did have an idea of what kind of stand John Wilkes Booth was planning to make. Samuel Knapp Chester was a member of the Winter Garden's stock company, listed on playbills as S. K. Chester. He acted Claudius to Edwin's Hamlet during the hundred-night run, and his wife played a supporting role in the production. Beginning in November 1864, Chester had been the recipient of a number of disturbing visits and letters from Edwin Booth's younger brother.

Chester had known John Wilkes for years, and shared the stage with him on November 25, 1864, during *Julius Caesar*. It was in rehearsals for this performance that John first intimated he had a scheme afoot in Washington. As Chester later told a federal court, he overheard some Winter Garden actors teasing John Wilkes "about his oil speculations," questioning whether his profits were as big as he represented them to be. After the men departed, Booth whispered to Chester "he had a better speculation than that on hand, and one they wouldn't laugh at."

A month later, Chester claimed, in late December 1864, Booth appeared at his door in Manhattan one cold night and asked Chester to go for a walk. On a deserted stretch of Fourth Street, where there were few other pedestrians, Chester recalled, Booth spilled the entirety of his plot against the Lincoln administration. "He stopped and told me he was in a large conspiracy to capture the heads of the Government, including the President, and take them to Richmond," Chester reported. Chester was terrified, and his fear increased when Booth demanded he join him in the plan.

"I told him I could not do it; that it was an impossibility; and asked him to think of my family," Chester remembered, but Booth refused to accept this answer and began badgering him, promising several thousand dollars in payment to Chester's wife if anything should happen to the actor.

"He told me the affair was to take place at Ford's Theatre in Washington, and the part he wished me to play in carrying out this conspiracy, was to open the back door of the theater at a signal."

When the actor still declined to help, Booth became angry, threatening to "ruin" Chester and to send Confederate agents after him, who would "hunt [him] down through life." Trembling and protesting, Chester begged to be left alone. Finally, Booth relented and took his leave, muttering that if Chester breathed a word of the affair to anyone, Booth would punish him.

For three months, while John Wilkes continued to hound him with letters and demands to join the conspiracy, Samuel Chester acted in *Hamlet* at the Winter Garden with Edwin Booth, divulging nothing of the secret plot to his employer and co-star. Chester seemed sincerely to believe John Wilkes Booth's threats to kill him.

EVEN AT THE PEAK OF HIS FAME, EDWIN BOOTH HAD THE PRICKING FEELING that bad luck would soon befall him. This sense of impending disaster often troubled him, Edwin admitted, perhaps a legacy from his early years of traveling with the chaotic and unpredictable Junius Brutus Booth. This anxious tendency was exacerbated by the shock of his wife Mary's sudden demise.

"All my life has been passed on picket duty, as it were," the actor wrote. "I have been on guard, on the look-out, for disasters—for which, when they come, I am prepared. Therefore, I have seemed, to those who do not really know me, callous to the many blows that have been dealt me. Why do you not look at this miserable little life, with all its ups and downs, as I do? At the very worst, tis but a scratch, a temporary ill, soon to be cured by that dear old doctor, Death."

Edwin's words, as bitter as they seem, were an echo of Hamlet's austere philosophy. It is a philosophy perfectly expressed in the moment before the play's bloody denouement. Throughout his life, Edwin Booth would refer to these lines, ones Hamlet delivers in the last act, as his favorite in all of Shakespeare:

> *There is a special providence in the fall of a sparrow.*
> *If it be now, tis not to come;*
> *If it be not to come, it will be now;*
> *If it be not now, yet it will come—the readiness is all.*

FIFTEEN

THIS PLAY IS THE IMAGE OF A MURDER

—This play is the image of a murther . . . You shall see anon.
'Tis a knavish piece of work.

—*Hamlet*, 3.2

COLONEL ADAM BADEAU, AIDE-DE-CAMP TO GENERAL ULYSSES S. GRANT, was one of only a few present at Appomattox Court House on April 9, 1865, when Generals Lee and Grant met to negotiate an end to the war. Badeau never forgot, he later wrote, the impressive sight of Robert E. Lee and his brother officers as they made their solemn entrance into the room. General Sheridan, in recent battle with Lee's army, had captured and destroyed many of the trunks and stores in the Confederate general's supply train. Lee had been able to save only a few pieces of his dress uniform, including a ceremonial sword awarded him by the citizens of Virginia. This weapon Lee carefully donned for the meeting with his opponent.

Grant—who, Badeau recalled, was similarly "battle-stained, in a common soldier's coat"—took note of the Virginian's sword while composing the terms of Confederate surrender. "Each officer and man will be allowed to return to his home, *not to be disturbed by United States authority*, so long as they observe their paroles and the laws in force wherever they reside," Grant wrote. To this clause Grant then added a key provision. While the Confederate rank and file were required to give up their arms, Grant wrote an order "permitting *officers* to retain their side-arms, horses and personal effects." Many of the Confederates affected by this exemption, Badeau noted, had been Grant's "comrades at West Point, in the Mexican war, or on the Indian frontier." The Union general would not impose on these fellow officers the same conditions he levied on the lower ranks.

After General Lee departed, Adam Badeau was the first to speak in the silence that followed. "I stood near [Grant] as Lee left the room," Badeau later remembered, "and thus happened to be the first to congratulate him upon the result. I said something about the event being one that would live forever in history." Grant was startled by Badeau's prediction that the scene just enacted would endure in memory. His only thought, the general sternly replied to his aide-de-camp, was "of the captured soldiery returning home without their weapons to work their farms; of a destitute country, ravaged by law, but now to be restored."

Grant was an insomniac. He remained awake late that night, Badeau reported, pondering "the terms he had granted Lee." The general anticipated objections from Union officers and some members of the Lincoln administration who believed high-ranking Confederates should stand trial, but Grant resolved to preserve the agreement as it stood. "Lincoln," Grant declared, "was certain to be on his side." As the general made preparations to depart for Washington, he ordered Colonel Badeau to travel to Richmond, and there help General Edward Ord and other Union officials lead the city's transition from Confederate back to federal authority.

Adam Badeau communicated with Robert E. Lee one last time. Arriving in Richmond and finding the city in ruins and much of the population "destitute," he recalled, Badeau "sent at once to [General Lee] and inquired if I could furnish him and his staff with supplies." A reply came from Lee's secretary, "that he was greatly obliged, and did not know what he should have done had the offer not been made." Badeau sent the general and his staff military ration cards that enabled them to obtain food for their horses, and other supplies.

No one wanted to sit inside Ford's Theatre on Thursday, April 13, 1865. Something extraordinary was going to happen outside at sunset, and many of Washington's eighty thousand inhabitants would take to the streets to see it. Any other day, the coming of night plunged the city into near total blackness. Gaslights along Pennsylvania Avenue could not hold back the shadows; streets off the main thoroughfares had no public lighting at all. Candles and lamp oil, so costly in wartime, were used sparingly. People retired indoors at day's end, shuttering their windows against the dark. But on April 13, 1865, darkness did not fall as usual. The news of Lee's surrender at Appomattox had arrived five days earlier. When the Morse code operator at Grant's headquarters pressed his ivory key, sparks raced over thousands of miles of cable and caused, by one newspaper's estimate, "twenty millions to rejoice in the honor and glory of our common country." Scores of cities made plans to celebrate the peace, but the capital's scheme was the grandest of all.

When the bells of firehouses and churches tolled seven, Washington seemed to burst into flames. Light blazed from thousands of windows, torches and bonfires roared to life along the avenues, and rockets filled the sky. All the households in the city—from the stone mansions of Lafayette Square to the shanties along Ohio Avenue—lit wax tapers, gas jets, and oil lamps. Every shop and business within the city limits did the same: restaurants, hotels, banks, and bookstores vied to outshine one another. The branches and departments of the federal government were illuminated, too, their granite buildings glowing like giant lanterns. By eight o'clock, the streets were bright as noonday.

Before electric lighting, illuminating a metropolis was nearly impossible: only cooperation on a vast scale could bring it off. The coming of peace proved the perfect impetus. Washington's city government, the Lincoln administration, and private residents eagerly prepared for the largest illumination in the city's history. Now that the appointed hour had arrived, people poured outside to enjoy the results. Over the sidewalks, "Union flags burst out like Spring flowers, the red, white and blue dancing and tossing in the air." Onlookers wept with joy and relief, strangers clasped hands and laughed, and voices in the milling crowds were heard exclaiming, as after previous Union victories, "God be thanked!" and "We are safe, we are safe!"

The actress Laura Keene never liked being upstaged, but tonight may have been an exception. From her windowless dressing room in Ford's Theatre, two blocks north of Pennsylvania Avenue on Tenth Street, the thirty-eight-year-old star could not see the illumination but she would have heard it. Tens of thousands turned out to see night change into day, shouting with excitement as the first flashes appeared. Marching bands played. Fireworks whined and popped. As Laura dressed for her night's performance in a low-cut costume of white silk she must have shared the crowd's elation.

Laura Keene remained a national favorite. For more than a decade, she had captivated crowds from New York to San Francisco. Audiences loved her looks—she was described by one admirer as "tall, slender and exceptionally handsome"—but this star's greatest attraction was her voice. Critics raved over her "clear, copious, musical tones." She had arrived in Washington on April 1 to fulfill a two-week engagement at Ford's. It was her own bad luck that the city of Richmond fell to Union forces two days later. The rush of events ending the war played havoc with her box office returns. Some nights Ford's auditorium was packed with crowds; others it stood empty while revelers gathered in saloons and hotel lobbies to celebrate the latest news bulletins. April 13 was the night of Laura's second-to-last performance; the comedy on the bill was called *Peggy the Actress*.

John T. Ford's competitor, Grover's National Theatre on E Street, shut its doors early because of the illumination. Leonard Grover had strong ties to President Lincoln and his family: closing so as not to compete with the victory celebration was a patriotic gesture and a practical one. Ford might have done the same had he been in Washington, but the impresario was in Richmond. He had rushed to Virginia days earlier to salvage his family's Richmond properties from the chaos of a collapsing Confederate government and the incoming Union army. His brothers, Henry and James Ford, stayed behind in Washington, D.C., to manage the box office, but they lacked authority to change set schedules.

Laura Keene, of course, was a theater manager herself, long accustomed to command. A New York journalist accused this star who "looked like an angel" of being "in fact, a martinet." The actress had not made a fortune and established her famous playhouse on Broadway, Laura Keene's Varieties, by being weak-willed. Yet in the spring of 1863, Laura had decided to sell her Broadway playhouse and take her productions on the road. The actress was struggling to overcome a sickness known then as consumption—today, we call it tuberculosis—which was a product of her impoverished childhood. The stress and strain of devising new shows, starring in productions night after night, and managing her stock company—bills, payroll, contracts, hiring new members—seemed to exacerbate her symptoms. For the past two years, after selling her theater, Laura had been traveling across the Union entertaining home-front audiences, largely women and children who missed husbands, fathers, brothers, and who were glad of the diversion.

As difficult as her work was, the theatrical business had given Laura a scope for her creative talents, a way of involving herself in the political and social issues of the time, and a measure of freedom that seemed astonishing compared to the circumscribed lives led by other women of her day. She was at liberty to earn money and invest it as she chose, to write and perform whatever plays she wanted. Laura also was free to conduct her personal life according to her whims.

She had been free to fall in love with Edwin Booth in California in 1855. Though their affair ended badly, with Laura walking out on Booth in Sydney, Australia, their initial voyage across the Pacific had been an idyll. In the ten years since they last met, however, Edwin had taken his revenge on Laura. All stars were rivals for audiences, critical attention, and box office returns, but in the case of these two former lovers, alcoholism was not the only crime Laura Keene could set against Edwin Booth.

For years she had been locked in an expensive copyright lawsuit against Booth's business partner and brother-in-law, John Sleeper Clarke. She accused Clarke, and by extension, Booth, of stealing the script of her copyrighted play *Our American Cousin* and producing it without her permission.

Courts in Massachusetts and New York had heard the case. At issue was the question of whether a piece performed nightly by actors—by necessity fleeting and partially improvisatory—could be protected under copyright. Laura had bought the American rights to an original script by the British author Tom Taylor, but she had restaged and rewritten certain key scenes herself. It was her adapted version that became a hit on Broadway. Clarke stole a copy of Keene's altered and improved script and used it to mount his own rival production. Laura's lawsuit, an attempt to keep control of profits stemming from her version of the play, lost in court in part because of Edwin Booth's interference. Booth told Clarke's lawyers a fact about Laura Keene that only he was privileged to know. It was a detail he gleaned during their passage to Australia: the actress had never divorced her first husband, an abusive London tavern keeper she had run away from as a girl. The man currently residing at her home address, John Lutz, who was her business partner, seeming husband, and guardian to her daughters, had no legal relationship to her whatsoever.

Questioned about this illicit relationship in a sealed court proceeding, Keene, fearful of risking her reputation, decided not to contest the copyright issue further. To have her adultery exposed before a jury would cost her more in scandal than what she currently was losing in income due to Clarke's theft of her play. For this and other private reasons, Edwin Booth's success still had the power to sting Laura Keene.

On the night of April 13, as she prepared to go onstage, Laura Keene probably heard the jubilee fireworks through her dressing room walls. Ford and Keene had planned her performance schedule in Washington long before they knew about the plans for the capital's victory illumination. She had saved her two best roles for the final two nights of her engagement in the city. By arranging to play Peggy the Actress on April 13, and the leading part of Florence Trenchard in *Our American Cousin* on April 14, Laura hoped to end her Washington run with shows guaranteed to bring down the house.

FORD'S RED VELVET CURTAIN FELL ON *PEGGY THE ACTRESS* AT ELEVEN o'clock on the night of April 13. Some actors collapsed in exhaustion after a

night's work; others remained full of energy until the euphoria of performing receded. Laura reportedly belonged to the second category: a tour of the
victory illumination would have suited her temperament exactly. She was not
required to return to the theater until six o'clock the following evening, April
14, when she would perform *Our American Cousin.* The actress could easily
afford to spend an hour driving through streets where people still roamed in
a holiday mood, drinking in sights the next day's newspapers called "grand
beyond all powers of description."

In the seventy-five years since its founding, the nation's capital had not
earned a reputation for beauty. One writer dismissed the city in 1861 as "a
congeries of hovels, inharmoniously strewn with temples." Four years of civil
war had transformed Washington, but the place remained an eyesore. By
1865 it was a heavily fortified military outpost on the border between Union
and Confederacy. Hovels and temples competed for room with military hospitals, army barracks, boardinghouses, refugee camps, saloons, and slaughter
yards. Tonight these features disappeared behind the lights of victory.

Gas jets blazing from rooftops along Pennsylvania Avenue caused pedestrians to stop and point upward. The words *Union* and *Victory* sparkled over
the U.S. Patent Office. The names LINCOLN and GRANT towered nearby in
oversize letters of flame. Huge portraits of the president, his generals, and
the secretary of war hung from balconies and porticoes. A department store
near Ford's Theatre displayed a picture of the national eagle, outlined in gaslight, clutching the word *Richmond* in its talons.

Ulysses S. Grant was in Washington this night, accompanied by his wife.
The general had received a strange invitation from Mary Lincoln for the
evening. "Mr. Lincoln is indisposed with quite a severe headache," the first
lady announced, "& I want you to drive around with us to see the illumination." By "us," Mrs. Lincoln appeared to mean herself alone. The president
would not join them, and, as Badeau later noted in dismay, Mrs. Lincoln
"did not ask Mrs. Grant" to come along. It would have been an uncomfortable ride for the general. He disliked publicity, and the sight of his name on
banners and in fiery signs would have pained him.

Worse, Grant still retained "shocked and horrified" memories, Badeau
reported, of Mary Lincoln's paranoid outbursts during her recent visit with
President Lincoln to City Point. Seeming to find insults and slights leveled
at her from every side during the trip, Mrs. Lincoln had "stormed till she was
tired," Badeau reported, calling Union officers and their wives "vile names"
in retaliation for a series of imagined offenses. Among other rude exclamations, the president's wife had attacked Mrs. Grant for harboring political

ambitions, demanding of the shy, self-effacing woman, "I suppose you think you'll get to the White House yourself, don't you?"

The tributes to General Grant to be seen everywhere in the illumination would hardly have quieted Mrs. Lincoln's temper. A bank located next door to Grant's hotel hoisted a banner that read, "Glory to God, Who Hath to US Grant'd the Victory." The hotel itself, Willard's, was covered in red, white, and blue Chinese lanterns. Masses of people gathered under the colored lights, eagerly waiting to glimpse the military hero.

The Capitol building was the illumination's crowning glory. It blazed at the lower end of Pennsylvania Avenue, a mass of white stone glowing from base to peak with lights. People later recalled how fireworks exploded over its dome, "displaying the national colors far over the clouds, flashing like lightning across the whole city."

Tomorrow would be the performance of *Our American Cousin*. Uneven ticket sales had made Laura's tour less rewarding than expected. Only by selling out this last show could the actress hope to make a clear gain. April 14 was her benefit night. By prior agreement with John T. Ford, all of tomorrow's box office returns would go to her alone. If she could fill Ford's 1,600-seat auditorium, Laura Keene would reap a tidy sum.

The only obstacle in her way was Leonard Grover, whose National Theatre was poised to steal her audience. April 14, 1865, was a significant anniversary: four years ago to the day, U.S. soldiers surrendered Fort Sumter to Confederate forces in Charleston, South Carolina, after a two-day siege, the action that had started the Civil War. Grover planned to mark the anniversary by staging a reenactment of the 1861 rebel bombardment, followed by a scene of Union forces recapturing the fort and pulling down a Confederate flag. Mr. Strong, the National Theatre's scenic artist, was painting a panoramic backdrop of Charleston's harbor for the occasion. Grover's advertisement for the Sumter reenactment shone from the roof of his theater: a banner in the shape of a tombstone for the Confederacy, backlit by lamps. The glowing sign read: "April 14, 1861: The Cradle. April 14, 1865: The Grave."

Laura Keene and the Ford brothers made the reasonable assumption that President Lincoln planned to attend Grover's reenactment. The president's young son, Tad Lincoln, practically lived at the National; he would not dream of missing the thrill of Sumter's bombardment and recapture.

A year earlier, Laura herself had been the star attraction at Grover's theater. On the nights of February 6 and 7, 1864, President and Mrs. Lincoln came to see the actress in two shows at the National: a special effects extravaganza called *The Sea of Ice,* and *Our American Cousin.* Mary Lincoln and little Tad must have gasped at the climax of *The Sea of Ice,* in which a ship's captain and his family, set adrift by mutineers on an Arctic ice floe, are threatened with doom. "Suddenly a storm arises," advertisements for the play proclaimed, "and then occurs the awful, the sublime spectacle of the breaking up of the immense sea of ice. Amid the deafening crash of its icy fragments, towering icebergs disappear and the entire stage is filled with a raging sea of boiling foam. The Captain and his wife cling to the fragments, but are engulfed in the furious waters, while their child, tossed about on a single block of ice, is left in the hands of an omnipotent power for succor." The stage machinery producing this mind-boggling spectacle was the most sophisticated of its day.

Memories of this triumph perhaps inspired Ford's management to invite the Lincolns to the theater on April 14, 1865, disregarding the fact that the couple had seen Laura in *Our American Cousin* only last year. Even John T. Ford considered the long-running play somewhat stale. John Sleeper Clarke had produced it endlessly, compounding audience fatigue. "Of late years it has not been a strong card," Ford opined, "but only a fair attraction." Laura Keene herself could have little hope the Lincolns would accept.

On April 13, John Wilkes Booth happened to be walking about Washington, D.C., seeing the sights of the blazing city. He penned a letter to his mother at 2 A.M., after the last of the victory lights went dark. "The illumination," John wrote. "Everything was bright and splendid. More so in my eyes if it had been a display in a nobler cause. But so goes the world. Might makes right."

CAPTAIN CHARLES LEALE RUSHED INTO FORD'S WHITE AND GOLD LOBBY at ten minutes past eight o'clock on the evening of April 14, 1865. The room was empty: *Our American Cousin* started on the hour. Leale, a surgeon at one of the larger military hospitals in the city, normally had no time for theatergoing. Only news that Abraham Lincoln would be at Ford's tonight had dragged the twenty-three-year-old doctor away from his duties. His shift over, he came from the hospital campus on the National Mall, hoping for a glimpse of the president.

Henry C. Ford manned the ticket window, tallying receipts. Ford told Leale he was out of luck: over a thousand people had packed into the theater before curtain time. All six hundred seats in the orchestra—the section with the best view of the stage and the president's box—were occupied. The cheap benches in the third-floor balcony were also full. Openings remained in the second-floor balcony, the seating area on the same level with the private compartment favored by Mrs. Lincoln. Thinking he might spot his hero during intermission or after the curtain, Leale paid Ford and pushed aside the draperies leading to the theater's dark interior. The doctor climbed a stairway to the second floor to reach his place in the balcony, forty feet from the Lincolns' box.

Other ticket seekers fared better. Jason Knox, a Princeton undergraduate, arrived early with one of his classmates. The two students bought seats at the front of the orchestra. Knox's parents, worried their son would encounter prostitutes or fall under dangerous influences, forbade him going to theaters during his trip to the capital. The boy told them later, "I could not resist the temptation to see . . . the President." Young Helen DuBarry and her older brother also bought tickets because of Lincoln. The siblings' seats were in the orchestra, next to debutante Julia Shepherd, who had hastened to Ford's with a party of friends, eager, she said, to bask in the presence of "Father Abraham." All were settled comfortably, rejoicing in a clear view of the presidential box.

By eight-fifteen the audience was in an uproar over the first scene's comic stunts. Laura Keene waited for her cue in the wings, stage right. From this place, the star was able to see directly into the Lincolns' balcony compartment. The "State Box" at Ford's was a three-walled chamber with a low balcony overlooking stage left. Lit by its own small chandelier, the box was opulent: red velvet lined its walls and yellow silk curtains framed the sides. A pair of gold-fringed regimental flags—on loan from the Treasury Department for this special occasion—adorned the balcony. An upholstered rocking chair, armchairs, and a sofa set in place to receive the Lincolns stood empty: the honored guests were expected any minute. Anticipation coursed through actors and audience, giving a pleasant charge to the performance.

The White House messenger who arrived at Ford's Theatre that morning bore fortunate news: the first lady's request for a set of tickets to *Our American Cousin*. Mrs. Lincoln's note came at ten-thirty, in plenty of time for James Ford to notify the afternoon newspapers that "Lieutenant General Grant, President Lincoln and lady, and other distinguished personages, are to visit the theater this evening, on the occasion of Laura Keene's farewell benefit." Ford's advertisement produced an overwhelming response.

At the last moment, the Grants declined the Lincolns' invitation to the theater. The antipathy Mrs. Grant felt toward the president's erratic wife was too strong. Mrs. Lincoln had included Secretary of War Edwin M. Stanton and his wife in her invitation for the evening's entertainment. Knowing this,

Julia Grant had a hasty conference with Mrs. Stanton about whether or not they should attend. "Unless you accept the invitation I shall refuse," the wife of the secretary of war told Mrs. Grant. "I will not sit without you in the box with Mrs. Lincoln." To escape what was to her an unpleasant social obligation, Mrs. Grant declared she and her husband must leave Washington that evening to visit their children, who were attending a boarding school in Burlington, New Jersey. Mrs. Stanton also begged to be excused.

Even without General Grant and Secretary Stanton, Laura's benefit night looked like it would be a triumph, for Leonard Grover's Fort Sumter re-enactment now lacked its star attraction. Only one member of the Lincoln family sat in the National Theatre: twelve-year-old Tad, accompanied by his tutor instead of his parents. Why this change in plans by the White House? Mrs. Lincoln had a habit of supporting the work of professional women. She admired and sought to meet many of the female novelists, artists, journalists, and aid workers passing through Washington during the war years. The impulsively generous first lady may not have hesitated to throw the star power of the White House behind the pioneering Laura Keene.

More importantly, however, *Our American Cousin* held a unique appeal for Mary Lincoln and her husband. The play drew much of its humor from clashes between raw Yankee manners and the ossified conventions and social prejudice of the British upper class. The collision of high-born and low-born people never failed to amuse Mrs. Lincoln's husband; he himself had enacted many such scenes during his long ascent from farm hand to president. But the first lady probably had another reason for throwing aside Grover's tickets in favor of Laura's: her sentimental attachment to certain love scenes from Act 2 of *Our American Cousin*.

In theatrical parlance, *Our American Cousin* was a "plain play," so called because it did not require many props or stage machinery. Simple painted backdrops depicted the walls and gardens of an English country estate. A few chairs and benches completed the setting. Rather than special effects and sets, the actors' comic dialogue and rich clothing anchored the story. Costumes for the play were so elaborate that Ford's stage manager was forced to widen all the stage entrances to accommodate the women's skirts. The script called for Laura's character, young aristocrat Florence Trenchard, to make her entrance at a sprint, "tearing across the stage like a three-year-old colt." Laura's dress made the maneuver difficult: her hoops were nearly four feet in diameter. When Florence Trenchard's cue came at 8:20, she managed to dash onstage with energy.

Ten minutes after Laura's entrance, a wave of applause drowned out all dialogue. Lord Dundreary, a caricature of a bumbling British peer, was winding up a speech. The actor whispered to Laura as he brushed past her in the scene, "That line went well. Hear my applause?"

"Don't flatter yourself," Laura hissed as she turned toward the audience and curtsied. "The president has just entered."

The cast stopped the play to acknowledge the Lincolns' arrival. Their gesture was both respectful and necessary: a cheering audience forced the action to a standstill. The house rose in a body, shouting its approval of the tall man shouldering his way past the columns of the second-floor balcony.

Jason Knox remembered breaking into "deafening cheers" at the sight of the president. Helen DuBarry, well-bred young lady that she was, contented herself with clapping as she "followed him with [her] eyes." Laura Keene directed the lighting technician to turn up the house lights so the Lincolns and their guests could navigate the aisles. The house lights also let young Dr. Leale realize his wish. He had a perfect view of the president and Mrs. Lincoln as they followed an usher to their seats.

Leale saw the first lady smile at the crowd's welcome. He later recalled, "she gracefully curtsied several times and seemed to be overflowing with good cheer and thankfulness." The president bowed to acknowledge the ovation. The doctor never forgot Lincoln's expression when receiving this tribute, writing that though "the audience seemed to be enthusiastically cheerful, he alone looked peculiarly sorrowful." Lincoln then turned and walked down a hallway to his private compartment. Once the guests were settled, the usher exited the box, closing its inner and outer doors behind him. The play should have started up at this point, but Leale noted "there was difficulty quieting the audience." Only when the president motioned to the actors to continue did the furor subside. The theater went dark, a hush descended, and Lord Dundreary repeated his lines.

A different mood pervaded Ford's now. The actors, keyed in anticipation of this moment, competed for the president's approval. Audience attention wandered from the stage to the Lincolns. Though he was partly concealed by drapery hanging on the left side of the box, people craned to catch a glimpse of Lincoln's profile and the first lady's rounded white arm. The cast of *Our American Cousin* played to this divided attention. At the end of Act 1, Dundreary is wooing a beautiful young lady in the gardens of the Trenchard estate. Chilled by a gust of wind, the girl begs her suitor to warm her, exclaiming "I am afraid of the draft!" The actor playing Dundreary pounced on this opportunity to score points with Lincoln. He stretched his arm toward the president's box and cried, "Nonsense! Don't you know there is no more draft?" A roar of laughter greeted this reference to the end of the war.

Julia Shepherd knew the reason for the audience's buoyant mood. "Everyone has been so jubilant for days, since the surrender of Lee," the girl wrote the next morning to her mother, "that they laugh and shout at every clowning witticism." With "Father Abraham here," she continued, "how sociable it seems, like one family sitting around their parlor fire." Lincoln's presence charmed the audience. "How differently this is from the pomp and show of monarchial Europe," Julia observed. For her, the scene in the theater exemplified America's egalitarian spirit. Where else could a president and his people share the experience of sitting together and laughing, she wondered, with "everyone's attention fastened upon the stage"?

Our American Cousin aimed to please a Yankee crowd. It begins as Asa Trenchard, a "rough-spun and honest-hearted" American frontiersman according to the script, crosses the Atlantic to England, with the aim of introducing himself to the British branch of his family. The log cabin dweller arrives at his cousin Florence Trenchard's country mansion during a party. Asa bursts onto the scene in boots and a straw hat, horrifying the aristocratic guests with his American slang and sloppy garments.

Grinning broadly, the actor Harry Hawk proclaimed: "I'm Asa Trenchard, born in Vermont, suckled on the banks of Muddy Creek, and just about the tallest gunner, slickest dancer and generally the loudest critter in the state!" Comedy ensues as the Yankee hayseed ruffles the feathers of his hoity-toity British relations. The plot involves courting couples, an inheritance of half a million dollars, and a villain bent on robbing Florence of her estate.

The audience laughed at Asa Trenchard's unpolished ways, but beneath his backwoods manner and folksy speech they recognized the hero of the play. Asa rescues Florence from disaster, captures the villain, restores the inheritance to its owner, and wins the girl of his dreams. Much of the play's enduring popularity was due to the yokel's heroism: Americans loved watching a tobacco-chewing Yankee triumph over British snobs to win a lady for his wife.

When Asa meets a beautiful, refined English girl named Mary, played that night by actress Effie Germon, things take a romantic turn. A love affair between the uncivilized boy and the genteel girl dominates Act 2. Watching Harry Hawk and Effie Germon perform, Laura Keene may have understood why Mary Lincoln was eager to see *Our American Cousin* for a second time.

Scenes of a frontier hero wooing a young woman high above him in birth, fortune, and education mirrored the real-life romance of President Lincoln and his wife. More than twenty years earlier, Abe Lincoln sought to win the hand of Mary Todd, the belle of Springfield, Illinois, society. From Miss Todd's point of view, Lincoln was a " 'bottomland' Kentuck' native" better suited to farm work than the social gatherings of her blue-blooded "carriage" set.

In *Our American Cousin*, Asa Trenchard "slicked his hair down and gave his boots a lick of grease" before going off to court his lady love. In 1830s Springfield, Abe Lincoln had been no different. He showed up at dances in countrified clothing with rough manners on display. According to one Springfield old-timer, Lincoln was made a laughingstock for "bursting into an evening party in rough Conestoga boots" and exclaiming, "Oh boy, how clean these girls look!" The thirty-year-old lawyer was a terrible dresser who could barely move around on a dance floor. Even loyal friends admitted Lincoln's "lack of social graces made him unfit to talk to women." In *Our American Cousin*, the character Mary sees past Asa's roughness to the noble nature underneath. Similarly, a young Mary Todd had perceived the gold beneath her suitor's unpolished exterior: after meeting Abe Lincoln, the Springfield beauty declared that she found all other men "uninteresting."

Our American Cousin must have revived memories of the Lincolns' long-ago courtship. Mary Lincoln's appreciation of the night's romantic theme was reflected in the guests she chose to replace the absent General and Mrs. Grant: Miss Harris, daughter of Senator Ira Harris of New York, and her fiancé, Major Rathbone. The newly engaged couple could be counted on to enjoy the marriage subplot.

Years later, Mary Lincoln recalled that she leaned close to her husband during the romantic passages of Act 2. She even risked impropriety by half embracing the president during one love scene when Asa tells Mary about his life in the wilderness.

"Don't you know I've listened to your stories till I'm half a backwoodsman's wife already?" Mary says.

Turning to the audience, Asa exclaims wistfully, "Wouldn't I like to make her one!"

Mary Lincoln sat hugging her husband's arm in appreciation. The first lady later remembered whispering to the president in a flirtatious tone, "What will Miss Harris think of my hanging on to you so?"

His words of reply, "She won't think anything about it," were the last he ever spoke.

At ten o'clock that night, Laura Keene stood stage right in the four-foot-wide space between the gas box and the prompter's desk. She only needed to look across at the Lincolns sitting contentedly in their box to know her last show in Washington was a success. A stagehand named

Billy Ferguson stood near her holding a script. The gas technician sat behind them, his hands at the gears, ready to cut the lights at the end of the scene. Laura would have had a clear view of Mrs. Lincoln as she pressed close to the president. The couple, along with everyone else in the theater, was engaged by the scene passing onstage. When all the elements of a performance came together, a play could seem almost real. During the first two acts of *Our American Cousin,* the audience shed sentimental tears, gasped in surprise, laughed, and found their hearts racing and palms sweating in suspense. After a night of such powerful illusions, they would leave the theater awakening to their own identities as if from a dream.

It was the top of Act 3. Harry Hawk, as Asa Trenchard, stood alone at center stage, delivering a comic rant. Behind the scenes, Billy Ferguson raised a hand, signaling Laura to prepare for her entrance. The actress heard a crescendo of laughter, then an explosion. She may have thought the sound was a stray firework from last night's victory celebration. The theater went quiet. A figure in a dark suit materialized on the rim of the president's balcony. Arms flung wide, the man sprang from his perch into the air. Landing unevenly, he lost his balance and stumbled backward. Then, with deliberate calmness, the jumper righted himself before the footlights. He held a long, double-edged knife in one hand, which he pointed upward for all to see. The stranger stalked forward, his torso turned to the audience, knife angled in a warlike pose. The crowd, uncomprehending, watched in silence. One onlooker marveled at the man's "statuesque beauty." Another was struck by the glare of his eyes, like those of a "mad animal." Reaching center stage, the stranger shouted something incomprehensible and made a stabbing motion with his blade. Then he turned and ran for the stage right exit, straight at Laura Keene.

The figure reached the actress where she stood behind the proscenium. He shoved her out of the way, smelling of sweat and alcohol, and disappeared backstage to the exit. What had Laura just seen? As another witness in the theater recalled, "the whole occurrence, the shot, the leap, the escape—was done while you could count eight." It was difficult for anyone in Ford's Theatre that night to sort fact from fiction. Many confessed later that they believed the interruption "to be part of the play." The source of their confusion was obvious: the man's fiendish look and crouching walk were the well-known tricks of a theatrical villain, stage business familiar to anyone who had sat through a melodrama. But the man's dagger was not a prop.

There was a silence. Though half the people in the auditorium jumped to their feet when the man leaped out of the box, they all stood motionless in their places after he disappeared. Helen DuBarry huddled next to her brother in the darkness of the orchestra until she heard a man's cry break the stillness.

"Our president! Our president is shot!"

Then the crowd erupted. From all parts of the theater, voices took up the alarm:

"Kill the murderer! Shoot him! Catch him! Stop that man!"

A middle-aged lawyer in the front row left his seat and scrambled over the footlights, bent on chasing down the apparition. Jason Knox and his classmate joined the pursuit. Blundering over piles of scenery in the dark, the two young men found neither the knife-wielding stranger nor the door he used to escape. They gave up the search and returned, drawn by shouts from the auditorium.

When Knox stepped back in front of the proscenium, he remembered, a scene from "some horrible carnival" met his eyes. Men were shouting profanities while they smashed wooden seats and broke balcony railings in fits of impotent rage. Others, gripped by fear, fell to the ground screaming or ran in panicked circles. Out of the noise and confusion, the growing chant of "Kill him! Kill him!" could be discerned. Helen DuBarry heard someone shout, "Take out the ladies and hang him here on the spot!" Fearing a lynch mob, her brother dragged her to the lobby. Julia Shepherd stayed in her seat, gazing upward at the Lincolns' box. She perceived no movement within, only wisps of smoke from the intruder's pistol curling beneath the small chandelier.

Laura Keene watched orderly rows of people devolve into what she later called "a chaos of disorder beyond control." Her ears rang, she later said, with the sound of "women screaming, men hallooing and children crying, as if a fire panic had taken place." The sight of some trying to climb onstage moved her to action. The woman who once ruled her New York theater with an iron hand walked to the footlights and stopped the riot. She bellowed, "For God's sake have presence of mind and keep your places! Order, gentlemen! Order, gentlemen!" Years of training made her voice a formidable instrument.

Everyone heard her. Clara Harris, in the Lincolns' box, remembered how Keene "momentarily arrested the panic." All eyes turned to the actress. Florence Trenchard's fancy costume sat strangely on her now that she was no longer playing an ingénue. Festive ringlets and rouged cheeks did not fit the stern presence onstage. There was a moment of silence in the theater. In it, Clara Harris's voice called from the president's box: "Miss Keene, bring some water!"

A full pitcher and glass were obtained backstage and pressed into Laura's hands. Billy Ferguson accompanied her down from the stage and into the orchestra. They forced a way through the mob, heading for the stairs to the second floor. Laura's progress was not helped by the technician at the gas box. He was busy raising and lowering the house lights, a signal to clear the auditorium.

To reach the president, she had to follow a hallway off the main balcony. As Laura stepped into this corridor, she encountered the group of men now guarding the entrance to the box. They parted to let her pass into a small, empty antechamber. There she found a second door, which opened into the actual box. Through the thin wooden partition, the sounds of a woman crying and a man issuing commands were audible. Laura reached for the door's handle and pushed it open.

The president was sprawled on his back on the floor. To Laura's eyes, she later stated, he looked dead already. All clothing had been cut away from Lincoln's chest. Three men held his body. One grasped his left arm, another his right, while a third knelt at his head, searching for signs of response in the unconscious face. Two of the men manipulated the president's outstretched arms in a slow rhythm. After every third movement, Leale later wrote, one of the rescuers bent forward and blew air into the president's mouth and nostrils.

Observing this scene, Laura later recalled, "the thought passed through her mind how much [it] resembled a picture of 'The Dead Christ.'" On childhood visits to London's National Gallery, she had seen Rembrandt's famous painting of mourners surrounding the dead body of Jesus. The red carpet beneath Lincoln glowed in the chandelier light. The box's canary yellow draperies pooled to the floor beside the body like a painter's backdrop. Two women standing nearby completed the composition, their faces pale and tense. As Laura turned to Mary Lincoln and Clara Harris, all notions of biblical imagery must have faded. These women were not mourners yet: the body on the floor was still alive.

Captain Leale reached the Lincolns before any other doctor. He went to Mrs. Lincoln first. After the gunshot, she had wrapped her arms around Lincoln's body and braced her feet against the floor, preventing him from collapsing out of the chair. Leale was amazed that she succeeded. "By Mrs. Lincoln's courage, strength and energy," he wrote, "the President was maintained in his upright position."

Mrs. Lincoln appealed to the officer: "Oh Doctor! Is he dead? Can he recover? Will you take charge of him? Do what you can for him? Oh my dear husband!" Methodically, Leale initiated the standard steps of battlefield triage. Feeling for a pulse in Lincoln's right wrist and finding nothing, he shifted the body from Mary Lincoln's arms and eased it to the carpet. He stripped Lincoln's chest and upper arms, but found no wounds beneath the evening clothes. Only when he lifted the president's eyelids did Leale find the cause of injury: fixed, dilated pupils indicated damage to the brain.

The doctor discovered a bullet hole behind the left ear. He noted the wound was "within two inches of the physiological point of selection when instant death is required." Leale later wrote of the sinking feeling that came over him when he realized that "the history of surgery fails to record a recovery from such a fearful injury to the brain." Laura Keene, listening to the doctor tell Mary Lincoln her husband would not survive, froze at the sound of the first lady's screams. When Leale went to consult with two physicians who had entered the box, he left Lincoln unattended on the floor.

Mary Lincoln writhed in misery on a sofa. Both Laura and Clara Harris tried to calm her, but the woman's cries did not stop. Like any veteran actress, Laura had played most of Shakespeare's tragic heroines. Acting Lady Macbeth, Queen Gertrude, Juliet, or Cleopatra, she could produce an impressive catalog of wails, howls, and shrieks. Mrs. Lincoln's screams were different. They were, Laura later said, "the most piteous" she had ever heard. Powerless to comfort the first lady, Laura turned to where the president lay. Laura Keene asked Leale, "May I hold his head?" The doctor gave the actress his permission.

Sitting down beside the dying man and taking his head onto her lap, Laura placed her palms on either side of his face. Leale reached down at intervals to scrape at the president's bullet wound with his fingers: he wanted the blood to flow so pressure would not build on the brain. Each time Leale did this, wetness seeped through the layers of Laura's costume. As Keene's daughter later reported, when her mother showed her "the stage clothes she had worn, not only her dress, but even her underskirts were bespattered with blood."

Any actor's memory could supply a barrage of lines to fit the role Laura found herself playing. A monologue from *Richard II* was grotesquely appropriate: "For God's sake let us sit upon the ground and tell sad stories of the death of kings. How some have been deposed, some slain in war, some sleeping killed . . . all murdered!" Many Washington newspapers, unable to express the magnitude of the night's tragedy in their own words, also turned to Shakespeare. "Confusion now hath made his masterpiece!" proclaimed one April 15, 1865, headline, quoting *Macbeth*. "Most sacrilegious murder hath broke ope the Lord's anointed temple, and stole thence the life of the building!"

Like the other people who worked at Ford's, Laura Keene had recognized the murderer the instant he started his premeditated march across the stage. A member of her own profession, the brother of a man she once loved, had committed the crime. His moment in the limelight, which struck one on-looker as having been crafted entirely "for the glorification of the actor," succeeded brilliantly. His performance would not be forgotten.

Laura Keene supported Lincoln for twenty minutes while Leale organized volunteers to carry the president out of the theater. The actress crawled aside when many pairs of hands reached down to lift the man's body onto an improvised stretcher. The team carried him feet-first through the doors of the box and down the hallway. As the procession moved away, Laura covered her face with her hands, then rose and followed.

Keene was disoriented enough to lean against the wall as she crossed the length of the main balcony to the stairs. Dressed for her part in a comedy, the actress now looked like Lady Macbeth after Duncan's murder. People who saw her shrank back from her gory appearance. Seaton Munroe, a man who ran to Ford's at the first news of the shooting, accosted Keene on the stairs, demanding a report of the president. She could hardly answer. "The memory of that apparition will never leave me," Munroe later wrote of his meeting with the stunned actress. Keene's "hair and dress were in disorder," he said, "and not only was her gown soaked in Lincoln's blood, but her hands and even her cheeks where her fingers had strayed, were bedaubed with the sorry stains!"

According to her daughter, Laura Keene passed the rest of the night in self-recrimination. The pleasant spell cast by her play had smoothed a path for Lincoln's assassin. A visitor to the actress's hotel the next morning found her "shaking all over like a leaf." Like Mary Lincoln, Laura Keene was past comfort. "I tried to give her courage," recalled Laura's visitor, "but the frightful calamity of the night before was too much, and it seemed as if grief was breaking her heart."

Years after she broke with Edwin Booth, Laura Keene could still agree with Adam Badeau, who wrote of Edwin's genius: "he has made me know what tragedy is. He has displayed to my eyes an entirely new field; he has opened to me the door to another and exquisite delight; he has shown me the possibilities of tragedy." Now Edwin's brother had unleashed his own brand of tragedy, destroying the boundary between stage and reality to bring his inner drama to life.

A stage actor once reflected on the temporal limitations of his art. Acting, he explained, was all the more precious for being impermanent: "We actors are born at the rise of a curtain, and we die with its fall, and every night in the presence of our patrons we write our new creation, and every night it is blotted out forever." After April 14, 1865, these words no longer held true. John Wilkes Booth's "new creation" never would be expunged from memory.

ON THE MORNING OF APRIL 15, JULIA HOWE AND HER CHILDREN WERE sleeping in the upper story of their home on Boston's Beacon Hill. They were not yet out of bed when frantic shouting from Samuel Gridley Howe belowstairs roused them in alarm. "Our father's face of tragedy, the anguish in his voice, as he called us down to hear the news," Howe's daughters later recalled, was "one of the clearest impressions of our youth."

Julia Howe, in a daze of grief, stumbled to her desk to record her feelings in the moment. "Nothing has happened that has given me so much personal pain as this event," she wrote in her diary with a shaking pen. "President Lincoln was assassinated in his box at the theater, last evening, by J. Wilkes Booth. This act, which was consummated in a most theatrical manner, is enough to ruin not the Booth family only, but the theatrical profession."

Feeling like "a weary ghost," as she put it, Julia left her home and made her way onto the streets of Boston. "The city is paralyzed," she observed, "but we can only work on, and trust in God." Like so many other Americans that Saturday, Julia seemed to take comfort in a simple mission: she went to a shop and purchased black gloves, black ribbons, and yards of black crepe. Across the North and South, people draped themselves, their homes, and their places of work in the color of mourning.

For his part, Dr. Howe claimed the inside of his head was "a humbly-bumbly of confusion"; the reports from Washington, D.C., read like "a chapter of horrors." Not only Ford's Theatre but William H. Seward's mansion on Lafayette Square had been spattered with blood. John Wilkes Booth sent an accomplice, Lewis Powell, armed with a long-bladed knife to the house where Edwin Booth had enjoyed dinner with the secretary of state a year before. Fighting his way through the front door and upstairs to Seward's bedroom, Powell stabbed the sixty-three-year-old politician in the face and neck. The secretary's son, Frederick, was bludgeoned into unconsciousness with the butt of a gun when he tried to stop the intruder. Fanny Seward, who had been spellbound by the handsome face of Edwin Booth, was battered and shoved aside when Powell burst into her father's room. Shrieking in fear, she stood a helpless witness to the unfolding violence. None of these attacks proved fatal, but the members of Seward's family would bear the mental and physical scars of this night for the rest of their lives.

Edwin Booth slept late on Saturday. He had been awake past midnight the night before, acting to a crowded auditorium at the Boston Museum. When a servant ran to his room and shook him awake on the morning of the 15th Edwin was so infuriated at the intrusion he threw a small object—a teacup or a clock—into the man's face. His anger turned to dazed understanding, however, once he heard the message the servant had to impart. "[My] mind accepted the fact at once," Edwin said. "[I] thought to [myself] that [my] brother was capable of just such a wild and foolish action. It was just as if I was struck on the forehead by a hammer."

Unlike Julia Howe, Edwin Booth did not keep a diary. He wrote a record of his feelings on that fateful day, however, to Adam Badeau, addressing the letter to General Grant's headquarters. "You know, Ad, how I have labored," Edwin began, "to establish a name that my child and all my friends were proud of; you know how I have always toiled for the comfort and welfare of my family—though in vain, as well you know, how loyal I have been from the first moment of this damned rebellion, and you must feel deeply the agony I bear in being thus blasted in all my hopes by a villain."

The actor included one piece of cheering news, informing Badeau that the people of Boston were rallying to his side, refusing to blame Edwin for his brother's murderous act. "You will be pleased to know," the star wrote to Badeau in closing, "that the deepest sympathy is expressed for me here—and by none more sincerely than dear old Gov. Andrew of Massachusetts."

The wartime governor, John A. Andrew, was also a longtime friend of Dr. and Mrs. Howe. Julia and her husband walked in their mourning garb with crowds of other Bostonians to the State House, where the governor delivered a speech about Abraham Lincoln's assassination. Andrew touched on the shame some might see in the circumstances of the murder—thinking it morally unseemly, or beneath the dignity of a leader of the American people, to be shot in a theater, his bleeding head cradled in the lap of a lowly actress. Andrew quoted Shakespeare, speaking with emotion some lines from *Macbeth*: Lincoln, like the murdered King Duncan, the governor of Massachusetts proclaimed, "hath borne his faculties so meek, hath been so clear in his great office, that his virtues will plead like angels, trumpet-tongued, against the deep damnation of his taking off."

A sweeping federal investigation, Secretary of War Edwin M. Stanton leading the charge, had already begun. With John Wilkes Booth at large, the War Department was tracking every lead to unravel the assassination conspiracy, identifying masses of people for questioning. Governor Andrew personally assured Edwin Booth that he stood beyond suspicion in the eyes of local authorities. The affectionate letters the actor had exchanged with Boston-born Richard Cary—the officer from the Second Massachusetts Infantry who died on a Virginia battlefield in 1862—were only part of a large body of evidence testifying to the loyalty of this member of the killer's family. Edwin's public association with the abolitionist Julia Ward Howe, and his many charity performances on behalf of the U.S. Sanitary Commission, helped. The assurance of goodwill from Governor Andrew lessened the humiliation when federal agents searched Edwin's trunks for clues. This cursory examination occurred before the actor was allowed to climb on board the midnight train to New York City on April 16. The actor wished to join his family in the town house on East Nineteenth Street.

Before Edwin reached Boston, his fellow members of the Century Club had rushed to the aid of Mary Ann Booth, Edwin's sister Rosalie, and his daughter, Edwina. The actor's close friend poet and journalist Thomas Bailey Aldrich gained admittance to the Booth home and found the women huddled together, "stricken and stunned with grief." The sound of boys hawking newspapers outside echoed in the parlor; their shouted refrain that Lincoln was dead, and that a Booth had killed him, tortured Mary Ann. In mental agony, she cried in Aldrich's presence, "Oh God, if this be true, let him shoot himself, let him not live to be hung! Spare him, spare us, spare the name that dreadful disgrace!"

"Poor Mother, who can condole her?" Junius Booth asked Edwin by letter. "I am afraid she can never be brought to look calmly upon this dreadful calamity." June had been acting at a Cincinnati theater when the news came. He raced to board a train for Clarke and Asia's house in Philadelphia, where husband and wife showed him a packet of letters and papers John Wilkes had left in their care. June discovered that his younger brother had given him a share in the Pennsylvania oil property: a sealed envelope, addressed to Junius in the assassin's hand, contained a deed of ownership to the wells in Franklin. Additional papers named Mary Ann Booth and Rosalie Booth the beneficiaries of John Wilkes's remaining investments. To his other siblings—the wealthy Edwin; Asia, wife of the rich Clarke; Joe, whose loyalty always had been to Edwin—the killer left nothing.

Joe Booth, after saying good-bye to Edwin and his wife, Mary, in Paris in 1862, had wandered the world for the past three years—first working on a ranch in Australia, then later as a letter carrier in San Francisco for Wells Fargo & Company, a job his brother Junius had secured for him. Missing his family after so long a separation, Joe Booth started the trans-isthmian journey homeward on April 13, 1865. Retracing the route his father traveled in 1852, Joe left San Francisco by steamship heading south down the coast of Mexico. When he reached Panama, Joe saw telegraphic bulletins posted on every street corner, stating that a man named Booth had shot President Lincoln. No other details were available. Though well aware the world contained many families named Booth, Joe later confessed to federal investigators, "then was the first moment I could imagine it was a brother of mine done it." He did not need to specify which of the three—June, Edwin, or John Wilkes—occurred to him as the likely culprit.

In suspense, twenty-five-year-old Joe rode the train across the Isthmus to Aspinwall, the port on the Caribbean Sea where steamers departed for the United States. Here American newspapers carried by inbound ships confirmed his fears. "I saw the papers, full particulars," he recounted. "That news made me insane." He was three days out at sea, bound for New York City, Joe Booth recalled, "before I began to get my thinking faculties [back]."

June Booth's pragmatic, even-keeled temperament sustained him through the first few desperate days after Lincoln's killing. "Human pride must always be liable to fall—but our fall has been heavy," he wrote calmly and philosophically to Edwin, while the rest of the family descended into panic. "Time is the only cure for our ills—& I feel sure Time will bring all things right—that is, as right as we have any right to expect."

ON THE MORNING OF APRIL 17, A CARRIAGE DELIVERED EDWIN BOOTH TO the doorstep of 28 East Nineteenth Street. Century Club members, still in attendance at the Booth home, remembered watching the actor's "spectral" form descend from the vehicle. "His eyes were the only ones without tears," a witness said, as a reunion of the bereaved family took place on the doorstep. "Wrapped in a long cloak, with a soft hat drawn over [his] face," Edwin had disguised himself to make the journey from Boston, uncertain of the temper of New Yorkers. All the Booths feared attacks of retribution. Crowds had gathered angrily outside the Philadelphia home of the Clarkes. Poison-pen letters came to Edwin's house. "Revolvers are already loaded with which to shoot you down," one warned. "We hate the name of Booth."

"Mother is very much broken," Edwin reported in a letter to a friend. "She seems to have a still lingering hope in her heart that all this will prove a dream." Indeed, the days following Edwin's return passed in a nightmarish haze. The sleepless family sat up together through the nights, with Aldrich, Launt Thompson, and a few other trusted friends for company. During this period of self-imposed confinement, as the Booths awaited news of the assassin's pursuit and capture, their eyes turned irresistibly to a picture of John Wilkes Booth hanging on one wall of the house. At night, light from streetlamps and passing cabs played across the picture's surface, revealing, then obscuring, John's face. For the melancholy people keeping vigil, Aldrich later wrote, these erratic glimpses of the haphazardly lit portrait brought to mind John Wilkes himself, moving through the farmlands and woods of northern Virginia, on the run in the darkness, as indistinct as a ghost. Everyone dreaded that the killer would be taken alive—his trial, his inevitable execution, were scenes none of the family, least of all Edwin, wished to endure.

Bad news arrived each day by telegram, letter, and newspaper. On April 18, John T. Ford—a faithful friend to the Booth family since the days of Junius Brutus Booth, Sr.—was arrested and confined in Washington's Old Capitol Prison. Matthew Canning, the pistol-wielding theatrical agent who conducted John Wilkes on his first tour of the South in 1860, was placed in the same cell. "No chair, no table, no convenience whatever save a slop bucket and a stone pitcher," Ford later reported to his family. "When I wanted to sit down straw was the only accommodation." Ford's two brothers, who worked the box office the night of the shooting, were imprisoned as well.

The secretary of war's dragnet gathered up others believed to have close ties with the assassin. Military police imprisoned three of John Wilkes Booth's siblings on suspicion of conspiring to kill the president: his eldest brother Junius, his brother-in-law John Sleeper Clarke, and his sister Asia. Junius and Clarke were taken under armed escort to Washington, D.C. On April 26, June was confined in the Old Capitol. The following day, Clarke was locked in with him. Both men, June recorded in his diary, were kept "like malefactor[s] in a small room on prison fare, forbid[den] to speak to anyone or see a paper." For more than a week, the two were denied fresh air and daylight. Only in early May were they permitted to take exercise under guard in the Old Capitol's yard.

"Bugs and roaches in abundance," June observed of his living conditions. His cell, No. 14, he said, was "very hot, intolerably hot." Clarke was jailed for a month; June would spend twice that time in prison. His many letters to John Wilkes, discovered by detectives in the assassin's trunk, were the cause of the older brother's detention. The kindly missives June Booth had sent to his younger brother charted the beginnings of what might have been a mentorship. The interest he expressed in John Wilkes's plans, along with his detailed questions about the actor's investments in Pennsylvania oil, made him look like a co-conspirator.

Asia Booth Clarke, five months pregnant with twins, submitted to house arrest at her Philadelphia residence. The sheaf of papers and documents John Wilkes left behind in his sister's house incriminated both Asia and Clarke in the eyes of investigators. Being accused of complicity in her brother's crime, and the humiliating circumstances of her captivity, filled the thirty-year-old woman with rage. Federal guards never left her unattended. "I would not object to have back for my private uses all the money squandered in sanitary commissions, hospital endowments, relief of soldiers' widows and the like," she spat, "for the good done by them as actors and citizens [has been] good for nothing towards proving loyalty."

With so many family members in government hands, it seems miraculous that Edwin Booth remained at liberty after his brother's crime. It was no miracle, but rather the star's network of powerful friends and his social connections in the Lincoln administration that kept him out of jail and free from any imputation of guilt by association. Members of the Century Club closed ranks around him, making statements of support. Assistant Secretary of War Charles A. Dana, one of the committee who had nominated Edwin Booth for the Hamlet Medal, questioned the actor informally about his brother. Dana declared himself satisfied after this private interview that Edwin Booth was innocent.

Colonel Adam Badeau also did his part. Armed with hundreds of letters from Edwin dating from 1858 through 1865, many of them containing proofs of the actor's political beliefs, Badeau petitioned General Grant and others in the War Department on his friend's behalf. "I lose no chance," Badeau wrote Edwin from Grant's headquarters in Washington, "to tell officials and others how staunch I know your loyalty is and has been from the very outset of the Rebellion." Adam tried to reassure Edwin that all would be well. "I hear great sympathy expressed for you, especially here where the fullest confidence is expressed in your patriotism." Yet Badeau, like many others, puzzled over John Wilkes Booth's motivations. "Your brother never in any hearing spoke a word that seemed like sympathy with the rebellion," he wrote to Edwin in perplexity. "I cannot understand it."

Editorial writers in New York newspapers had hunted in vain to explain the motives of the Confederate agents who tried to burn New York City on November 25, 1864, the night the Booth brothers made their joint performance of *Julius Caesar*. The timing of the attack made little sense to anyone. Abraham Lincoln already had won reelection to the presidency; the outcome of the war would not be changed by the attack. One writer suggested that "the folly of the late rebel attempt" at arson was inspired by the certainty of the South's approaching defeat. Setting fire to a dozen hotels across the city, he wrote, was a way for Confederates "to inflict vengeance upon us for their disappointments."

Many journalists and friends in the wake of Lincoln's assassination applied a similar line of reasoning to John Wilkes Booth, claiming that despair must have driven the killer to commit his inexplicable act, for Lincoln's death in no way aided Southern interests. "He who could lend himself to such a dark and damnable enterprise, could have, at least," one journalist wrote, "pleaded [it] would be favorable to the Southern cause." Yet the assassination occurred "when the loss of no one, or a dozen men, could, in so much as a hair, affect the result [of the war]; when, indeed, all being given up as lost to the rebellion, the insurgents themselves looking forward to peace, and placing their trust in the clemency and large-hearted magnanimity of the Executive for terms as little humiliating and penal in their character as it was his power to grant."

One writer said, "those who know [John Wilkes Booth] best feel confident that he has committed suicide" by the act. Asia Booth Clarke appeared to agree. "Already people are asserting that it is [a] political affair, the work of a bloody rebellion, the enthusiast's love of country, etc.," she wrote in exasperation to a friend, weary of these insufficient explanations. "I am afraid to us it will always be a crime. . . . Some terrible oath hurried him to the wretched end, God help him."

On April 24, 1865, while John Wilkes Booth was yet at large, actors who had been working at Ford's Theatre the night of Lincoln's murder published a notice in the pages of the *National Republican* urging the citizens of Washington, D.C., not to blame actors as a class for a crime committed by one of their number. Many feared that mobs would attack theaters or harm actors themselves in retribution for what had been done to the president.

"John Wilkes Booth," the players wrote, "has used our profession as an instrument to the accomplishment of his horrible and inhuman design. . . . Disloyalty, under any guise, has not nor ever will be countenanced by our noble profession." The advertisement concluded with the observation that actors especially had reason to mourn the loss of Mr. Lincoln, "a good and kindly man of liberal mind," whose love for actors and acting was widely known, and whose frequent attendance at playhouses like Ford's "was refining and popularizing the dramatic art."

On April 26, 1865, after a long chase through the Virginia countryside, the actor had been discovered hiding in a tobacco barn. His pursuers set fire to the structure to force him out alive, but a Union cavalry officer fatally shot him in the neck against orders. A friend of Edwin Booth's wrote to congratulate him on this desired outcome. "John is dead, not by the rope, which he could not have escaped (and by which I would not have had him die, for your sake, and your mother's and the fame of your great dead father) but fighting for his life. Because it is all over with him, I write you rejoicing, though with tears, for your sake and his own."

Mary Ann Booth was alone when she learned her son was dead. She was traveling from Edwin's town house in New York to join Asia in Philadelphia: a telegram notifying Mary Ann that Asia's pregnancy was not progressing well prompted her to pack her bags in haste. As she arrived at the train station, Mrs. Booth heard news vendors shouting and a shocked murmur from the waiting passengers. Obtaining a paper, Mrs. Booth took her seat in the car and began to scan the front page. A Booth family friend recalled how, "on the moving train, surrounded by strangers, the poor mother sat alone in her misery, while everyone about her, unconscious of her presence, was reading and talking, with burning indignation, of her son, the assassin of the President. Before the train reached its journey's end, Mrs. Booth, with wonderful fortitude and self-restraint, had read the pitiful story of her misguided boy's wanderings, capture and death."

Not long afterward, John T. Ford, released from the Old Capitol Prison after a month's detainment, attempted to open for business the theater where John Wilkes Booth had made his stand. On July 10, 1865, the company of actors at Ford's Theatre stood ready to perform a play for the Washington public, but three dozen heavily armed soldiers appeared before curtain time and stopped the show. The secretary of war, Edwin M. Stanton, wished to block Ford from what seemed like an attempt, he said, "to make money from the tragedy by drawing crowds to the place where Lincoln was slain." An angry editorial put it more graphically, asserting that "the re-opening of Ford's Theatre for the mimicries of the stage . . . would be dancing in the scarcely dried blood of the nation's noblest martyr. The theater is and must be a monument to Mr. Lincoln." Congress immediately took steps to buy Ford's Theatre from its unhappy owner, claiming the property in perpetuity for the American people.

Though no official body connected him to the tragedy, Edwin Booth vowed to leave the theatrical profession forever. The star declared that his own retirement was the worst penance he could impose on himself for his brother's heinous deed. This was a serious pledge indeed. By abandoning the stage, Edwin not only renounced the exercise of his abilities, but cut himself and the rest of the Booth family off from the income won by his art. Baring his soul in a letter to the American public that appeared in major newspapers over the summer of 1865, Edwin Booth explained: "It has pleased God to afflict my family as none other was ever afflicted. The nature, manner and extent of the crime which has been laid at our door have crushed me to the very earth. My detestation and abhorrence of the act in all its attributes, are inexpressible; my grief is unutterable. . . . I shall struggle on in my retirement, bearing a heavy heart, an oppressed memory and wounded name—heavy burdens—to my too welcome grave."

EPILOGUE

THE CURTAIN FALLS

Nature cast me for the part she found me best fitted for,
and I have to play it, and must play it, till the curtain falls.

—Edwin Booth
April 14, 1890

EDWIN BOOTH DID NOT KEEP HIS PROMISE. NOT ONLY WOULD HE AN-
nounce his plan to return to the stage little more than six months after
Lincoln's body was laid in its tomb at Springfield, but the star and his
brother-in-law, John Sleeper Clarke, brought *Our American Cousin* to the
Winter Garden in September 1865.

William Stuart, the impresario who ran the Winter Garden in partnership with Booth and Clarke, well knew that any publicity was good publicity.
What better way to draw crowds and money to the theater than to produce
the play that killed a president? And who better to star in this comedy than
John Sleeper Clarke, fresh from a jail cell at the Old Capitol Prison, where
he had been held on suspicion of conspiring against Lincoln?

It was a bold move. Edwin was supposed to be living in mournful retirement from the public eye, but, as he wrote to Julia Ward Howe on September 24, 1865, nothing could be more uplifting to his depressed spirits than
the "bustling and interesting character" of planning shows for the Winter
Garden Theatre.

Laura Keene wrote a letter to John Sleeper Clarke expressing her anger
at him, and at the profiteering Booth family he had married into. Her statement was published in the *New York Herald* on October 2, 1865. Keene already had sued Clarke for stealing her unique version of the play, but in this
letter her contempt is directed to Edwin Booth as well. *Our American Cousin*,
Laura Keene wrote, "[is] my personal, private property, and should have been
held sacred to me by every respectable member of our profession. The bad
taste of seeking to deprive me of the use of this play is only equaled by your

ever appearing in a comedy which ought to have only a memory of shame and horror for you and every member of your family. You cannot lift the cloud which has fallen upon our whole profession by acts which set at naught all regard for principle and right." Laura's was one of only a few voices raised against Clarke and Booth's willingness to profit from *Our American Cousin*'s post-assassination notoriety. These businessmen knew the value of sensation, and seemed to trust in the short memories of the theatergoing public if their venture backfired.

If Abraham Lincoln's ambition for the presidency was, as his law partner William Herndon said, an "engine that knew no rest," Edwin Booth's desire to excel in the work his father raised him to do was equally insatiable. "My art," he said, "[is] the world to me. Out of [its] influence I am dead." Staging *Our American Cousin* was only the first step in Booth's larger plan for a comeback. Returning to the stage as a star once more was a matter of personal survival, Edwin explained to Julia Ward Howe in his September letter: only the thought of acting, he said, "keeps my mind from dwelling too intensely on things past."

Booth also felt he needed to repair the damage his brother had done to the family name. Almost immediately after Lincoln's assassination, the old charge of bastardy against the Booth children was dredged up in newspapers. Mary Ann Booth was named once more a scarlet woman who had conceived her children out of wedlock. An editorial in a Philadelphia newspaper went so far as to demand that Edwin Booth change his name, claiming "the American people will not tolerate him under his hated family title."

The thirty-two-year-old actor had spent twenty years of his life onstage. His genius, and his single-minded pursuit of success, had lifted his mother and siblings out of poverty and raised the Booth name to heights greater than his father could have imagined. He was not about to let John Wilkes's crime undo those accomplishments. Encouraged by high-placed friends and an unshakable confidence in his ability to captivate audiences, Edwin announced the end of his retirement that fall. "I am sure that the unanimity of public sentiment [will] uphold me in any action I might take," he predicted calmly.

When word spread that Edwin Booth was planning to appear at the Winter Garden on January 3, 1866, a volcano of editorial commentary erupted in city papers, but the theatergoing public championed Edwin's decision. The day that a *New York Herald* headline spitefully inquired of Edwin's plans, "Is the Assassination of Caesar to Be Performed?," an angry mob stormed the offices of that newspaper, terrorizing its editor into silence.

Most of the other newspapers boosted Edwin's debut, absolving the actor for breaking his pledge. "It is not of his own seeking now that the actor is about to appear again in a public capacity," declared the *New York Tribune*. "Some of our most influential and high-minded citizens have urged him to resume the duties of his profession."

"Long before the doors were opened," recalled a ticket holder of the day of Edwin's return, "Broadway was so blocked up with ladies and gentlemen that the casual passer-by was not only struck with amazement to see such a thing, but in order to pass up or down that wide thoroughfare, was obliged to cross the street." Cordons of police held back crowds. The enthusiasm for Booth was "so strange and unique," commented one journalist on the scene, "it amounts to a positive psychological phenomenon—the niche in which his country's heart has enshrined him was never filled before by mortal man."

Edwin wisely chose not to play Julius Caesar, but instead Hamlet. When the actor made his entrance, his face molded in Hamlet's expression of pensive melancholy, there was total silence. A reporter recorded what happened next:

> Then succeeded such a storm, such a tempest, such a persistent hurricane of applause as was never paralleled. It was a full four minutes before he was permitted to go on with the play. The audience rose to their feet, the women waved their handkerchiefs, the men swung their hats, and all cheered to their very utmost, from the women, too, came the sound of many a sob, and I saw tears rolling down some cheeks whereon whiskers are wont to grow. There was no repressing the cheers till the house had fairly cheered itself out of breath. . . . "Nine cheers," "six cheers," "three cheers," "nine more cheers," were the repeated calls that were responded to with all the tremendous vigor of thousands of enthusiastic voices, as time after time the artist attempted to speak the words set down for him in the text. He was himself much agitated at the opening of the scene, and the overwhelming enthusiasm of his reception still further disturbed his equanimity, and he did not fully regain his accustomed tranquility until the second act.

At the end of every act, patrons in the balcony tossed armfuls of "bouquets and wreaths" onto the stage. At intermission, while "the audience amused themselves by indulging in three groans for the New York *Herald*," the newspaper that objected to Edwin return, distinguished men visited the star backstage. In his dressing room, Edwin reportedly shook hands with officers of the New York Police Department, the grand master of the Free Ma-sons of the State of New York, the historian and California explorer George Bancroft, and "Dr. Charles D. Brown, embalmer of President Lincoln's remains," among many others. Edwin's acting that night exceeded anything he had done before, witnesses claimed; some privately observed that his work never again would be as spectacular as it was on this night. "Booth," one newspaper stated simply, "had reached his zenith."

On January 22, 1867, a procession of prominent New Yorkers—including Admiral David G. Farragut, Major General Robert Anderson, and other Union Army veterans—walked onstage after a show to present him with his Hamlet Medal. This prize, commemorating the hundred nights of *Hamlet* he acted in the last months of Lincoln's life, now had an added significance. Before Edwin bowed forward to allow the gold pendant to be hung about his neck, the presenter of the prize faced the audience.

"Mr. Booth," he said, ". . . it is not alone your success as an actor which has attracted public attention and called forth this demonstration. You have won alike the applause and respect of your fellow men . . . [who] desire to present you with some evidence of their appreciation of your genius as an actor, and their respect for you as a man, more substantial and enduring than the fleeting though hearty plaudits nightly heard within these walls. To that end they have instructed me to present you with this medal . . . as a token of the regard of your fellow-citizens, it possesses a significance far more valuable than the gold of which it is composed, or the artistic skill—Louis Comfort Tiffany's—which beautified it." Today, this medal is housed in the archives of The Players in Gramercy Park.

After such a triumphal return, Edwin Booth began laying plans to build a temple to the Booth family name in midtown Manhattan. Completed in 1869, his Booth Theatre, occupying nearly an entire city block at the corner of Sixth Avenue and Twenty-third Street, put Laura Keene's former playhouse to shame. This gigantic theater boasted the latest in stage machinery, a façade of white Italian marble, and a domed interior decorated with floor-to-ceiling murals and mammoth chandeliers. A steam engine in the basement sent cooled or heated air wafting through the auditorium as the season required. Busts of Shakespeare and Junius Brutus Booth loomed in the lobby. Here Edwin reigned supreme as director and star, working to stage Shakespeare's plays as magnificently as possible, even *Julius Caesar*. But the actor aimed too high: he was never able to recoup the cost of the building itself. The Booth Theatre went dark in 1874, a victim of an economic recession. Its bankrupt former proprietor hit the road like his father before him, traveling the country as a touring star. In a few years, Edwin easily recovered his fortune.

Americans hungered to see Edwin's genius onstage, not only for the thrill of witnessing his virtuosity, but to experience the sense of connection he gave to the martyred Lincoln. This actor was a living touchstone to the tragedy that marked the end of the Civil War. As the leading expositor of Shakespeare for nearly three decades in America, and as the foremost actor of his generation, Edwin offered himself as an expiator of his brother's crime. William Shakespeare's works exposed the passions of war, the fight of brother against brother, the plight of families split by rival allegiances, and the trauma of nations rocked to their foundations by greed, ambition, violence, and assassination. Such themes struck a chord with shell-shocked audiences, helping people make sense of what had happened to them and their country during the crucible years of 1861 to 1865.

Audiences were tantalized, too, by Edwin's fondness for playing villains. His genius as an actor was bound up in his ability to plumb the depths of human nature, to present Macbeth, Iago, and Richard III as flawed yet sympathetic beings. While Edwin Booth had a gift for humanizing Shakespeare's murderers, those watching could never forget the real-life villain who had authored a crime as epic in stature and as tragic in its implications as any plot Shakespeare wrote. Because Edwin's features brought the face of his dead brother vividly to mind, his performances always possessed a heightened tension, a sensational charge. After April 14, 1865, any appearance by Edwin Booth would be great theater.

The star was rarely tested by public allusions to his brother's crime. Friends and fans maintained a respectful silence on the topic of John Wilkes, and never referred to Abraham Lincoln in Edwin's presence. In 1879, one member of the audience at McVicker's Theatre in Chicago fired two shots at Edwin Booth during a sold-out performance of *Richard III*. The actor did not even flinch. He walked to the footlights and pointed to where the shots had come from, while other patrons subdued the culprit, a deranged young man who worked as a clerk in a Chicago clothing store. Edwin was unscathed. Later he set one of the spent bullets in a gold brooch engraved with the motto "From Mark Gray to Edwin Booth, April 23, 1879," his would-be assassin's name and the date of the attempt on his life. He certainly did not miss the significance of the attack's coming on Shakespeare's birthday. Booth wore this souvenir constantly thereafter, a reminder of his brush with an assassin.

In 1880, Edwin toured his parents' native England with nineteen-year-old Edwina, the daughter born to him and Mary Devlin Booth in London during the Civil War. It was an artistic homecoming, his every performance met with jubilation and praise. The poets Robert Browning and Alfred, Lord

Tennyson invited him to dinner, and Booth even took tea with members of the royal family at Buckingham Palace. Edwina, for much of her life, fulfilled the role her mother had done before her. She was her father's constant companion, his faithful admirer, and after his death, a guardian of his legacy.

When he retired from the stage at last, in 1888, Edwin Booth was an international icon and an extremely wealthy man. The idea for The Players, at once a monument to his achievements and a gathering place for America's greatest minds, was conceived while Edwin was yachting with his millionaire friends. He hoped this living institution, more so than his lost Booth Theatre, would immortalize his name and elevate the reputation of the dramatic profession, as well as lay the troublesome ghost of John Wilkes to rest. President Grover Cleveland, Mark Twain, and General William T. Sherman, among other greats, were founding members. The club was a resounding success, and survives to this day.

Laura Keene was never able to outrun the events of April 14, 1865. Unlike Edwin Booth, who seemed to derive new inspiration and an infusion of popular glamour from his brother's crime, Laura was tarnished by her presence on the scene. After Lincoln's murder, instead of buying tickets to her shows to enjoy a night of comedy, audiences came to gaze in morbid fascination at a woman who had been smeared with Abraham Lincoln's blood. The comedienne's performances fell flat. Harder still for Keene to bear was the moral condemnation that surrounded her: many Americans disapproved of her coming to Lincoln's aid. They felt it unseemly for an actress, a woman whose reputation was on par with a prostitute's, to have come in physical contact with the dying president. "It desecrated his idea to have his end come in a devil's den—a theatre," Asia Booth Clarke wrote in a memoir of her brother John Wilkes; equally desecrating, she implied, was the embrace of a Jezebel like Keene.

In 1869, after spending four years on national tours, Laura retreated to Philadelphia to take over the management of the Chestnut Street Theatre. Here she tried to weave the old stage magic that once made her queen of Broadway. Somehow she had lost her touch. In 1871, desperate to try a new kind of creative effort, the actress established a magazine, *Fine Arts*. This lavishly illustrated journal of American poetry, music, playwriting, and literature was a labor of love: Laura never earned back the cost of publishing the volumes. Supporting herself and her two daughters soon became difficult. Increasingly weakened by tuberculosis, she could no longer deliver her lines onstage. Keene died of a tubercular hemorrhage in 1873, at age forty-six. She left a legacy of debts.

The course of Julia Ward Howe's life changed after Lincoln's murder. Stricken with grief, she spent days after the shooting in a white heat of creative energy, writing poems about the assassination. On the morning of April 23, 1865, Julia selected her best composition, and was preparing to read it at a public event that afternoon, when her husband, Samuel Gridley Howe, confronted her in the parlor of their Beacon Hill mansion, forbidding her to leave the house.

"He attacked me with the utmost vehemence and temper, called my undertaking a mere display, a mere courting of publicity, would not argue or hear me at all," Julia wrote in her diary that day. Dr. Howe was outraged by Julia's writing about Lincoln. The success of "The Battle Hymn of the Republic" had made hers a household name. For his wife now to come forward with a poem for the martyred president, the husband said, was unseemly, outside the bounds of woman's proper sphere. "Chev said among other things," Julia recorded, "that if he had been engaged to Florence Nightingale and loved her ever so dearly, he would have given her up as soon as she commenced her career as a public woman. This phrase needs no comment." The ensuing fight was terrible. Chev moved out of the house, vowing to take control of their children and of the fortune Julia had inherited from her father.

In that moment, Julia later recalled, she had a flash of inspiration. Her husband was wrong to silence her tribute to Lincoln. She realized, Julia wrote, that she now was "a free agent, fully sharing with man every human right and every human responsibility." This thought, which suddenly illuminated the grief of her mourning for Lincoln, "was like the addition of a new continent to the map of the world, or of a new testament to the old ordinances." Gripped at once by excitement and distress, Julia ran to her desk, she later remembered, and "wrote to Edwin Booth." Booth belonged, she said, to the "wonder-world" of the theater, an entirely different realm where women could write and perform with comparative freedom, leading lives that were less circumscribed—though far less comfortable—than Julia's. She had found a new cause. In time, this granddaughter of Revolutionary War heroes would be elected to the presidency of the American Association for the Advancement of Women, and to the vice presidency of the National American Woman Suffrage Association.

Samuel Gridley Howe never made peace with his wife embracing the cause of rights for women. To his mind, Julia's battle to win the vote and open the doors of American colleges and universities to female students was insane. He could not comprehend her crusade, any more than his own father had been able to understand why young Sam Howe wanted to run away from home to join Lord Byron's fight for Greek independence in 1821. "It jarred on [my] traditions," Chev complained, but his wife would not be turned back. Even into her seventies and eighties, Julia Howe traveled by railroad and steamship on business for the organizations she represented, visiting almost every state in the Union, as well as many nations in Europe, to address gatherings of suffragettes.

To the end of his days, Edwin Booth remained a friend of Julia Howe. She wrote a poem for the actor when he died in 1893. Though she lived a long life, she did not live to see women vote in national elections. It was not until 1920 that the Nineteenth Amendment would be ratified; Julia died in 1910, at ninety. Before her death, she wrote proudly, "I have had the honor of pleading for the slave when he was a slave, of helping to initiate the woman's movement . . . and of standing with the illustrious champions of justice and freedom, for woman suffrage, when to do so was a thankless office, involving public ridicule and private avoidance." Looking back on her life, she concluded, "We acted, one and all, under the powerful stimulus of hope."

After Lincoln's assassination, a chill settled over Adam Badeau's friendship with Edwin Booth. Grant's aide-de-camp had done everything in his power to defend Edwin's patriotism before the War Department in April 1865, and he was deeply hurt when the actor claimed to be too busy that summer to pay a visit to his old friend. By the fall of 1865, when Edwin and his brother-in-law Clarke were preparing to mount *Our American Cousin* at the Winter Garden, Badeau declared he was finished with Edwin Booth. Edwin himself was unperturbed by the soldier's anger. He wrote to Julia Ward Howe to explain the break in his friendship with Badeau: "We can't love everyone so passionately as they love us."

Captain Badeau never entirely left the employ of Grant, whom he called "my chief, my general, my friend." He remained an official member of Grant's staff for four years after the Civil War. During the 1868 presidential campaign, Badeau traveled with Grant as an adviser on his whistle-stop tour. When the general moved into the White House the following year, Badeau was given his own office in the Executive Mansion. This one-time drama critic, now a brigadier general, had stood witness to some of the most extraordinary scenes of Grant's career, and he would see many more.

As a historian, Badeau first set pen to paper in his White House office, beginning a three-volume *Military History of Ulysses S. Grant*. In 1870, to reward Badeau for his years of service, and to give him financial support while he labored on this project, Grant appointed Badeau consul general in London, a post he would hold for more than a decade. Diplomacy was Adam's forte, but he dropped the duties of this office in 1878 to join the fifty-six-year-old ex-president Grant on a whirlwind tour of the world. With Mrs. Grant in tow, the pair of friends climbed Mont Blanc in the Alps, visited the composer Richard Wagner at Heidelberg, and galloped through the art galleries of the Vatican. The Grants pressed onward to the Far East alone, but sent thick envelopes to Badeau care of the embassy in London, filled with their enthusiastic impressions of Bombay, Peking, Canton, Singapore, and Tokyo.

This friendship, renewed by Adam's frequent visits to the Grants' home in Galena, Illinois, deepened in the final year of Grant's life, when financial catastrophe and cancer struck simultaneously. The bank holding all his assets, and in which his son was a partner, failed through mismanagement. Everything the Grants owned—their mansion in New York, their savings, their furniture, even the general's collection of weapons and battlefield memorabilia—was forfeited to creditors. Grant himself—crippled by the pain of his cancer, unable to swallow solid food, and walking only with the help of crutches—seemed to have lost the desire to live. Badeau was summoned to help.

The writer occupied a room in the Grant home for the next seven months, conducting intense interviews with the suffering invalid. Every day, Badeau remembered, he urged Grant to galvanize his memory and muster his will "to tell the story of his motives and purposes and plans." With the help of his former aide-de-camp, Grant finished his *Personal Memoirs* before dying on July 23, 1885. Scholars have called the book "one of the clearest and most powerful military memoirs ever written."

Badeau, who lived until 1895, won acclaim as Grant's historian and as an authority on the life of Edwin Booth. When Edwin was dying, Adam made a few quiet visits to The Players on Gramercy Park, where the actor told his old friend stories and details, insights and observations, which he shared with few others. Badeau would have loved to have been elected a member of The Players. Despite sterling qualifications for admission, his wish was never granted. Edwin had written into the rules of his club that no drama critic—current or former—would ever be allowed the privilege of belonging.

Lincoln's assassination pushed Asia Booth Clarke into the role of Booth family historian. The young woman wasted no time trying to repair the damage John Wilkes had done to their father's name. Her first work of biography, she tells us, was born in the toils of anguish, anger, and fear she experienced in the weeks after the president was shot. She started work on her *Memoir of Booth the Elder* while pregnant and under house arrest in the summer of 1865. "It was ready for the press by the 20th of August, 1865," Asia remembered, "on which day the sad writer gave birth to two babies."

Telling the story of her father, Junius Brutus Booth, was an imperative for Asia. Published in 1866, her memoir was a rebuke to the storm of denunciation that threatened to engulf her family's record of achievement. Writing also was an avenue of escape from the wreck of her marriage. John Sleeper Clarke never forgave Asia for involving him in John Wilkes's troubles. When he was released from prison, Clarke ordered her to grant him a divorce. Asia, a stickler for social conventions, refused to comply. Enmity ruled between this husband and wife, the parents of seven children, as the decades of their marriage dragged miserably onward. "There is no solidity in love, no truth in friendship, no steadiness in marital faith," Asia wrote in her later years. "I think I am getting like poor mother, hardened to sorrow."

In 1868, the Clarkes left the United States to make a new home in London. The coarse Yankee antics that were the comedian's specialty proved enduringly popular with Londoners, making Clarke even richer. Little though she liked England—the British "are such a prejudiced, self-conceited people," she sniffed—Asia embraced her isolation there, confining herself to her London residence, a recluse. "I shall never recross that perilous sea," Asia promised a childhood friend by letter in 1869, and she never did. This decision meant that Asia would never see her mother again. America was too full of hurtful memories for Asia; she called it a place of "gloomy scenes." Despite the lifelong pain this separation caused her, Asia declared she only wished to return home in her coffin, arranging to be buried with her father, her mother, and her brother John Wilkes in the Booth family plot at Green Mount Cemetery, Baltimore.

Homesick until the day of her death in 1888, Asia never failed to celebrate the Fourth of July, decorating her house in red, white, and blue for the holiday. Her free time she devoted to writing further histories of the Booths, composing, among others, a memoir of her girlhood and lengthy chronicles of the lives and adventures of her brothers Edwin and John Wilkes. Much of her writing is tinged with unhappiness. The foreknowledge of John Wilkes's crime seems to touch even the earliest scenes of her family sagas, yet she strove to defend the Booth name, and her beloved John Wilkes, from criticism.

"So many tongues are free to calumniate us," she explained, "I am urged to complete my work in the belief that it will serve in all honest minds to confute the aspersions of evil men." For Asia, her brother's crime was not the act of a madman, nor was it, she claimed, "a political affair." Committing her memories to paper, Asia encouraged others to see John Wilkes's act as she herself saw it: something incomprehensible outside the context of the Booth family saga.

Junius Brutus Booth, Jr., perhaps the least remarkable of all of Mary Ann and Junius Brutus Booth's children, settled into a quiet career as a small-time actor. June, greatly fond of female company, acquired two wives and a common-law spouse in the course of his life. He was a doting father, and seemed embroiled in constant financial trouble. June liked to joke that his money worries were caused by that classic combination of circumstances, "small means and a large family." Working sometimes as an actor, sometimes as a theater manager, and finally as the proprietor of a seaside resort at Manchester, Massachusetts, he often was forced to ask his younger brother for help paying bills.

June maintained an uneasy truce with the great Edwin Booth. "The old feeling"—a mixture, perhaps, of jealousy, resentment, and awe—that Edwin had inspired in both June and John Wilkes during the war years never seemed to dissipate. Humiliatingly, even as late as 1878, June was forced to ask his younger brother's permission before performing in East Coast theaters so as not to disturb Edwin's box office prerogatives. He did this, June explained, "to regulate their business without clashing"—a seemingly unnecessary courtesy, given the enormous disparity between the brothers' incomes.

Mary Ann Holmes Booth died in New York City in the autumn of 1885, at age eighty-three. For nearly thirty years, ever since his 1856 return from California with a bag of gold on his belt, Edwin Booth had lavished upon his mother every material comfort his money could secure. Letters exchanged between them well into the 1870s reveal Mary Ann's laughing in protest at the immense checks her son enjoyed making out in her name. She followed Edwin's achievements avidly.

Yet as much as she enjoyed Edwin's success, it is safe to guess that not a day passed in Mary Ann's life when she did not dwell on what her surviving children referred to as "the miseries of her great sorrow." John Wilkes's crime and death on the lam were, Edwin firmly believed, "subjects too much talked of by the rest of the world," and perhaps too often mulled over in private by the Booths themselves. Inwardly tormented by thoughts about John Wilkes, Mary Ann nonetheless made a show of fortitude. "None see so plainly as I the depth of her sorrow," Edwin confessed to Julia Ward Howe, "for she bears up bravely and conceals the pain she feels." Certainly Mary Ann could not afford to break under the weight of her feelings. She had five adult children, as well as Edwin's motherless daughter, Edwina, who needed her care in various ways.

Joe and Ann Hall, the former slaves who had lived with Mary Ann, Junius, and their children on the Booth farm from 1822 through 1852, never left Bel Air. While a succession of different tenants and owners occupied the Booths' old log cabin and Tudor Hall itself, Joe, Ann, and many of their children remained in the area. By the end of the Civil War, Joe and Ann were able to purchase their own house and three dozen acres of farmland in Bel Air with the savings they had accumulated over the years. When an interviewer made his way to Harford County in 1935, he met Joe Edwin Hall, the couple's youngest son, who conducted the visitor to his mother's grave. Ann Hall had died in 1904, at the age of ninety-two.

On February 15, 1869, President Andrew Johnson granted Edwin Booth's petition to release the remains of John Wilkes Booth into his family's care. "What a consolation it would be," the actor had written in his appeal, for the assassin's mother finally "to have the privilege of visiting the grave of her child." John's coffin was unearthed from the federal arsenal in Washington, D.C., and transferred to a vault in Baltimore.

When she learned that her son's body would be returned to her, Mary Ann Booth wrote at once to her former neighbor in Harford County, Mrs. Elijah Rogers. This was the woman who had known the Booths since 1822. As Mrs. Rogers reported, Mary Ann asked her "to get the children" out of the ground of the old farm at Bel Air, meaning the bodies of young Mary, Frederick, and Elizabeth Booth, the little ones who had died in the cholera epidemic of 1833. It was their deaths that first sent Junius Brutus Booth spiraling out of control.

Mrs. Rogers obligingly "took up the children's little bones and brought them to Baltimore . . . and they were put in a casket." Mary Ann's wish was for these three siblings to be interred with their brother John Wilkes, so all four of them, she said, "could sleep there together." The body of her other child, Henry Byron, remained in its London graveyard.

At the Baltimore mortuary where the bodies were placed in new caskets, Mrs. Rogers saw the moldy, government-issue blankets and battered pine box that had encased John Wilkes's form for four years. As his remains were transferred to their new container—a very "elegant" box, Mrs. Rogers observed—this thoughtful neighbor clipped "a piece of John's hair for the family," observing that "it was not so black and shiny as it was long ago."

Mrs. Rogers also noted that John's body was poorly clad, "one boot on one foot and a slipper on the other—his leg was broken square off below the knee, and the bones had passed each other and one was protruding out of the flesh." She was moved to tears at the sight, writing in a flood of emotion that she was "sorry full, for such a handsome boy he was, to let the enemy of souls cheat him out of so much pleasure, as he could have done so much good in this world. Dear boy, good boy, I loved all the dear children so much."

President Johnson had ruled that no marker would be allowed to indicate the precise location of John Wilkes Booth's body in a cemetery. He wanted to discourage demonstrations of support for Lincoln's killer. To comply with this order, the Booths rearranged their existing plot at Green Mount Cemetery in Baltimore. They purchased an enlarged lot to hold all the new bodies awaiting reburial, and commissioned stonemasons to carve a fresh inscription on the blank side of Junius Brutus Booth's twenty-foot-high marble monument. "To the memory of the children of Junius Booth and Mary Ann Booth," it read. "John Wilkes, Frederick, Elizabeth, Mary Ann, Henry Byron."

Before the two caskets holding Mary Ann's four children could be buried alongside this towering marker—the funeral had been set for June 26, 1869—one last change was made. By Edwin's decree, the epitaph from *Julius Caesar* that had been carved on one side of the obelisk in 1858 was covered. The lines, spoken by Mark Antony to the body of Brutus, Caesar's assassin, violated the terms of discreet burial that Edwin had negotiated. A marble plaque awaiting the day when Mary Ann Booth would join her husband in the ground appears to have been used to conceal the offending inscription.

Rosalie Booth spent most of her sixty-six years at her mother's side. Their fierce bond of companionship and mutual devotion remained unbroken until Mary Ann's death. This close tie had been formed, perhaps, in the dark weeks of 1833 when cholera killed so many of Mary Ann's children and drove Junius Brutus Booth to acts of desperation. Rosalie had been a survivor of, and witness to, the hardest years of her parents' lives.

Mrs. Rogers told an interviewer in 1886 that Rosalie Booth had for years supported two children, a brother and sister named "Alonso" and "Ogretia," whom she believed to be the illegitimate offspring of her brother John Wilkes. "None of the family takes any account of John Wilkes's children but Rosalie," wrote Mrs. Rogers to a Booth biographer in 1886. "She is very kind to them; does not visit them but sends them money every spring and fall. Calls them her children." Ogretia, Mrs. Rogers noted, "was beautiful," while Alonso "was very much like old Mr. Richard Booth." Rosalie died in

1889. Joseph Adrian Booth, youngest of the Booth children, outlived all his family, dying in New York City in 1902.

Edwin Booth's tombstone stands within the stately precincts of Mount Auburn Cemetery in Cambridge, Massachusetts. He did not wish to lie in death in Baltimore, in the shadow of his father's monolith and his brother's name, but in Boston, the city where he first entered high society, and where Mary Devlin Booth had died. Mount Auburn was a special place, enclosing the bones of some of the oldest, most respected families in the United States. Charles Sumner is buried there, as well as Henry Wadsworth Longfellow and Julia Ward Howe. Over the years, Edwin's grave has been largely forgotten, as has his transcendent talent and the majestic trajectory of his career. The long shadow he cast over nineteenth-century American life proved to be just that—a penumbra.

Out of respect for the actor during his lifetime, many members of the Northern press observed an unofficial ban on discussions of John Wilkes Booth. Only after Edwin's death in 1893 did popular interest in his younger brother flourish. John Wilkes's admirers stoked a legend of the assassin's great acting abilities. The unhappy youth was cast as the inheritor of his father's genius. In generations of mythmaking about Lincoln's killer, Edwin's own name and story were lost, leaving John Wilkes to stand alone on the stage of national memory, as he no doubt would have wished.

NOTES

ABBREVIATIONS

ALPLM   Abraham Lincoln Presidential Library and Museum, Springfield, Illinois
BA   Boston Athenaeum, Boston, Massachusetts
BAMA   Beth Ahabah Museum and Archives, Richmond, Virginia
BRTD, NYPL   Billy Rose Theatre Division at the Performing Arts Research Center, New York Public Library, New York, New York
CHM   Research Center, Chicago History Museum, Chicago, Illinois
EB   Edwin Booth
FLP   Free Library of Philadelphia, Philadelphia, Pennsylvania
FSL   Folger Shakespeare Library, Washington, D.C.
H-BTL   Hampden-Booth Theatre Library, New York, New York
HL   Houghton Library, Harvard University, Cambridge, Massachusetts
JBB   Junius Brutus Booth
JWB   John Wilkes Booth
LC   Manuscript Division, Library of Congress, Washington, D.C.
KC   Stanley Kimmel Collection, Macdonald-Kelce Library, University of Tampa, Tampa, Florida
MHS   Baldwin Library, Maryland Historical Society, Baltimore, Maryland
PL   Department of Rare Books and Special Collections, Princeton University Library, Princeton, New Jersey
RB   Richard Booth
RRL   Special Collections, Rush Rhees Library, University of Rochester, Rochester, New York
SCRC, UCL   Special Collections Research Center, University of Chicago Library, Chicago, Illinois
UIUC   Rare Book and Manuscript Library, University Library, University of Illinois at Urbana-Champaign, Urbana, Illinois
SHM   Surratt House Museum, Clinton, Maryland
UCL   University of Chicago Library, Chicago, Illinois
WL   Widener Library, Harvard University, Cambridge, Massachusetts

PROLOGUE: THE PLAYERS

Page
1 *tempest hit Manhattan:* "The New Year's Storm," *New York Tribune*, January 1, 1893; Allan Nevins, *Grover Cleveland: A Study in Courage* (New York: Dodd, Mead, 1933), 449, 457.
1 *"as something between a black art":* Edith Wharton, *A Backward Glance* (New York: Simon & Schuster, 1998), 69; "Edwin Booth," *New York Daily Tribune*, June 16, 1890; John Tebbel, *A Certain Club: One Hundred Years of The Players* (New York: Wieser & Wieser, 1989), 63.
2 *Cleveland agreed to deliver the night's keynote:* Grover Cleveland to Albert F. Simmons, March 7, 1903, private collection; Eric Foner and John Garraty, eds., *The Reader's Companion to American History* (Boston: Houghton Mifflin, 1991), 191.
2 *"What shall be done with our ex-presidents?":* Grover Cleveland, *Letters of Grover Cleveland,*

1850–1908, Allan Nevins, ed. (New York: Houghton Mifflin, 1933), 449; Hermione Lee, *Edith Wharton* (New York: Vintage, 2007), 24; George Frederick Howe, *Chester A. Arthur: A Quarter-Century of Machine Politics* (New York: Dodd, Mead, 1934), 34; Tebbel, *A Certain Club*, 20; John B. Pine, "Gramercy Park," in Henry Collins Brown, ed., *Valentine's Manual of Old New York, No. 4* (New York: Valentine's Manual, 1920), 213–15, 227–28; Eric Homberger, *Mrs. Astor's New York: Money and Social Power in a Gilded Age* (New Haven, Conn.: Yale University Press, 2002), 76–80; George Edward Montgomery, "The Players," *Cosmopolitan*, June 1889, in EB Scrapbook B.7.5, 65, FSL.

3 *Over a lunch at Delmonico's:* Tebbel, *A Certain Club*, 13–14; John S. Phillips, *The Players: Occasional Pieces* (private printing at the behest of the board of directors of The Players, 1936), 4–15; The Players, *Minutes of the First Meeting, December 28, 1888, Together with the Deed of Gift from Edwin Booth* (New York: Devinne, 1908), 4–12.

3 *"all the world's a stage":* Walter Oettel, *Walter's Sketchbook of The Players* (New York: Gotham, 1943), 5–6; Tebbel, *A Certain Club*, 17; "An Actor King," *Illustrated American*, June 24, 1893, in EB newspaper clippings, Theatre Collection, HL.

3 *fifth anniversary of The Players':* Laurence Hutton, *Edwin Booth* (New York: Harper & Brothers, 1893), 8; Tebbel, *A Certain Club*, 24; "Honors to Edwin Booth: Founder's Night Celebration at The Players Club," *New York Times*, January 1, 1893.

3–4 *"the Beast of Buffalo":* John Garraty, ed., *Encyclopedia of American Biography*, 202–4; Phillips, *The Players: Occasional Pieces*, 8–9; Oettel, *Walter's Sketchbook of The Players*, 82; "Paintings, Art Treasures, Relics in Safes," in Roy Day, ed., *Catalogue of the Paintings and the Art Treasures of The Players*, 1–93 (New York: privately printed, 1925).

4 *Yellow and gold:* Montgomery, "The Players"; Tebbel, *A Certain Club*, 342; Brander Matthews, "The Player's," *Century Illustrated Magazine*, November 1891, 28.

4 *Grill Room:* Montgomery, "The Players," 143; Oettel, *Walter's Sketchbook of The Players*, 83; "Interior of The Players," illustration by E. K. Meeker, *Harper's Weekly*, January 19, 1889, 44; interview and guided tour with Raymond Wemmlinger, curator and librarian of the Hampden-Booth Theatre Library, New York, March 28, 2008.

5 *Not only William T. Sherman and Grover Cleveland:* "List of Members," in Tebbel, *A Certain Club*, 285–348.

5 *Bish, Bnkr, CP, Expl, Lyr:* Tebbel, *A Certain Club*, 284; Oettel, *Walter's Sketchbook of The Players*, 17.

6 *Refined people disapproved of theaters:* Adam Badeau, "Edwin Booth On and Off the Stage," *McClure's Magazine*, August 1893, 260; Arthur Bloom, *Joseph Jefferson: Dean of the American Theater* (Savannah, Ga.: Frederic C. Beil, 2000), 2–4, 207.

6 *"We actors do not mingle enough":* Katherine M. Goodale, *Behind the Scenes with Edwin Booth* (Boston: Houghton Mifflin, 1931), 256; Tebbel, *A Certain Club*, 24; William Winter, *Life and Art of Edwin Booth* (New York: Macmillan, 1893), 133–34.

6 *"the attempts of vulgar persons":* Edith Wharton, *Old New York: Four Novellas* (New York: Simon & Schuster, 1995), 210; "The Actor King," *Illustrated American Magazine*, June 24, 1893, EB clippings, Theatre Collection, HL; EB to Horace H. Furness, March 13, 1887, in Edwina Booth Grossman, *Edwin Booth: Recollections by His Daughter* (New York: Century, 1894), 271; William Winter, "Incidents in the Life of Edwin Booth," T.B.5 (9), FSL; "Edwin Booth," EB Scrapbook B.7.6, FSL; Thomas Bailey Aldrich to [unknown], February 14, 1873, in "The Theatrical Scrapbook of Adelaide Neilson," W.b.59, FSL.

7 *"the most shameful period":* George Wheeler, *Pierpont Morgan and Friends* (Englewood Cliffs, N.J.: Prentice-Hall, 1973), 90–91; Vernon Louis Parrington, *Main Currents in American Thought*, vol. 3, *The Beginnings of Critical Realism in America 1860–1920* (New York: Harcourt, Brace, 1930), 23–24.

7 *stealing chickens when hungry:* J. J. McCloskey, "Edwin Booth in Old California Days,"

Green Book Album, June 1911, 1324–26, EB clippings, Theatre Collection, HL; Description of EB's California poverty, in Asia Booth Clarke, *The Elder and the Younger Booth* (Boston: James R. Osgood, 1882), extra-illustrated ed., October 29, 1885, UIUC; John Ford Sollers, "The Theatrical Career of John T. Ford," Ph.D. diss., Stanford University, 1962, 438–40; Otis Skinner, *Footlights and Spotlights: Recollections of My Life on the Stage* (1925; reprint, Westport, Conn.: Greenwood, 1972), 177–78; Goodale, *Behind the Scenes with EB*, 96.

7 *refused to set foot in the nation's capital:* "Booth Kept His Vow," *Boston Herald*, June 7, 1893; "Book of Autograph-letters to Edwin Booth, 1885, from President Chester A. Arthur, members of his Cabinet, and members of the Senate and House of Representatives," in Day, ed., *Catalogue of the Paintings and the Art Treasures of The Players*, 90 (Item # 669); Goodale, *Behind the Scenes with EB*, 94.

8 *"How many brothers and sisters":* Goodale, *Behind the Scenes with Edwin Booth*, 95–96.

8 *"extreme prejudice and wild excitement":* William Stump Forwood, "Manuscript of a biography of Junius Brutus Booth," Maryland Historical Society, 26; Skinner, *Footlights and Spotlights*, 178; "The Career of Edwin Booth," EB Scrapbook B.7.6, FSL; "Resolutions of the Theatrical Profession Respecting the Assassination," *(Washington, D.C.) Daily National Republican*, April 24, 1865, SCRC, UCL.

8 *"loved, honored and respected for his transcendent talents":* Montgomery, "The Players."

8 *"the dark time of our national indifference":* Wharton, *Old New York*, 202, 204.

8 *"no hired assassin":* Charles Pope, "The Eccentric Booths: Their Peculiarities Described by One Who Knew Them, or, An Old Actor's Reminiscences," *New York Sun*, March 27, 1897, in EB Scrapbook B 7.6, FSL.

9 *"The fiend in human shape":* Diary of Annie G. Dudley Davis, April 20, 1865, Huntington Library.

9 *The Founder's Night feast:* "Honors to Edwin Booth: Founder's Night Celebration at The Players Club," *New York Times*, January 1, 1893; Nevins, *Grover Cleveland*, 4–5, 245, 347, 442; Henry F. Graff, *Grover Cleveland* (New York: Times Books, 2002), 133; Rosamund Gilder, ed., *Letters of Richard Watson Gilder* (New York: Houghton Mifflin, 1916), 162, 295.

10 *"bright lights":* Cleveland, *The Letters of Grover Cleveland*, 561; Nevins, *Grover Cleveland*, 455; Richard Watson Gilder, *Grover Cleveland: A Record of Friendship* (New York: Century 1910), 49.

10 *Edwin Booth and Grover Cleveland:* "Edwin Booth: Recollections of Commodore E. C. Benedict," in Henry Collins Brown, ed., *Valentine's Manual of Old New York*, No. 6 (New York: Valentine's Manual, 1922), 179–80; Gilder, ed., *Letters of Richard Watson Gilder*, 162, 295–96; The Players, *Minutes of the First Meeting, December 31, 1888*, 3; Nevins, *Grover Cleveland*, 443, 449, 495; Phillips, *The Players: Occasional Pieces*, 5–6; Grover Cleveland to Albert F. Simmons, March 7, 1903, private collection.

10 *"sunning and rowing":* Junius Brutus Booth Jr., diary, August 1 and June 7, 1864, Y.d.374, FSL; Commodore E. C. Benedict, " 'Friendship Grove' and its Memories," in Henry Collins Brown, ed., *Valentine's Manual of Old New York, No. 5* (New York: Valentine's Manual, 1921), 23–24.

10 *The marble mantel, heavily carved:* Interview and guided tour with Raymond Wemmlinger, curator and librarian, H-BTL, March 28, 2008.

10 *"lock yourself in a dark room and sandpaper your soul":* Tebbel, *A Certain Club*, 194–95; Thomas Bailey Aldrich, "Sargent's Portrait of Edwin Booth," *Harper's New Monthly Magazine*, February 1891, 329.

11 *He looked a decade older:* Badeau, "Edwin Booth On and Off the Stage," 266–67; Tebbel, *A Certain Club*, 68; William Winter, *Life and Art of Edwin Booth*, 134–35; EB to David C. Anderson, May 1, 1879, in Grossman, *EB: Recollections by His Daughter*, 198–99; Hutton, *Edwin Booth*, 53–54.

NOTES

11 *"You drink tonight to my health"*: Oettel, *Walter's Sketchbook of The Players*, 18; "William Warren's Loving-Cup . . . Used on the night of the opening of The Players, December 31, 1888. It is used every Founder's Night by members, in drinking to the memory of Edwin Booth and 'The Perpetual Prosperity of The Players'," in Day, ed., *Catalogue of the Paintings and the Art Treasures of The Players*, 94.

11 *"Gentlemen, this is one of the occasions"*: "Honors to Edwin Booth: Founder's Night Celebration at the Players Club," *New York Times*, January 1, 1893.

12 *"the chill at the heart"*: James Clarence Harvey, "The Players" (1893), EB Scrapbook B.7.6, FSL, 584; interview and guided tour with Raymond Wemmlinger, curator and librarian, H-BTL, March 28, 2008; Tebbel, *A Certain Club*, 31.

12 *"Now blessings light on him that first invented sleep"*: Interview and guided tour with Raymond Wemmlinger, curator and librarian, H-BTL, March 28, 2008; Oettel, *Walter's Sketchbook of The Players*, 101; Goodale, *Behind the Scenes with Edwin Booth*, 149–50.

12 *"in the aching gloom"*: EB to Emma F. Cary, December 20, 1865, and EB to Edwina Booth Grossman, April 14, 1890, in Grossman, *Edwin Booth: Recollections by His Daughter*, 174–75, 109–10; Winter, *Life and Art of Edwin Booth*, 154–56.

13 *"Good friend, for Jesus' sake forbear"*: Interview and guided tour with Raymond Wemmlinger, curator and librarian, H-BTL, March 28, 2008; Badeau, "Edwin Booth On and Off the Stage," 263; "Painting of Mary Devlin Booth," "Rubbing of the inscription over the tomb of Shakespeare," and "Junius Brutus Booth—colored photograph," in Day, ed., *Catalogue of the Paintings and the Art Treasures of The Players*, 26, 72, 75; Oettel, *Walter's Sketchbook of The Players*, 102.

14 *Ford had seen John Wilkes make the same jump*: "Testimony of John T. Ford, Witness for the Defense, May 31, 1865," in Benn Pittman, ed., *The Assassination of President Lincoln and the Trial of the Conspirators: The Courtroom Testimony* (New York: Moore, Wilstach, & Baldwin, 1865), 101–2; Badeau, "Edwin Booth On and Off the Stage," 264.

14 *"a kingless kingdom"*: Goodale, *Behind the Scenes with Edwin Booth*, 97; Clarke, *The Elder and the Younger Booth*, 124; EB to Adam Badeau, September 13 and October 14, 1864, FSL; Junius Brutus Booth, Jr., diary, October–November 1864, FSL.

15 *"Oh where has my glory gone?"*: EB to John E. Russell, January 23 and June 22, 1884, Special Collections, Rush Rhees Library, University of Rochester.

15 *"Edwin Booth was devoured with a thirst"*: "Howard's Letter: Stories about Booth from Stuart, His Old Manager," *New York Record* (n.d.), printed material in extra-illustrated ed. of Matthews and Hutton, eds., *Actors and Actresses of Great Britain and the United States*, TS931.2, Theatre Collection, HL; Parke Godwin, "Commemorative Address," Program of the Memorial Celebration of the Sixtieth Anniversary of the Birth of Edwin Booth, Madison Square Garden Concert Hall, New York, November 13, 1893, 33.

15 *"I am glad I have not sons"*: Goodale, *Behind the Scenes with Edwin Booth*, 152.

16 *"took a flower from his button hole"*: Phillips, *The Players: Occasional Pieces*, 16–17.

16 "And when the smoke ascends": Interview and guided tour with Raymond Wemmlinger, curator and librarian, H-BTL, March 28, 2008; JBB, *Memoirs of Junius Brutus Booth, From His Birth to the Present Time: With an Appendix Containing Original Letters from Persons of Rank and Celebrity* (London: Chapple, Miller, Rowden & Wilson, 1817), 25, SCRC, UCL; Stanley Kimmel, *The Mad Booths of Maryland* (New York: Bobbs Merrill, 1940).

CHAPTER ONE: A FAMOUS REBEL

Page

21 *On June 30, 1821*: Asia Booth Clarke, *Booth Memorials: Passages, Incidents and Anecdotes in the Life of Junius Brutus Booth (the Elder) by His Daughter* (New York: Henry L. Hinton, 1870), 65–66; Clarke, *The Elder and the Younger Booth*, 53–54.

21 *Bound from Madeira:* William S. Forrest, *Historical and descriptive sketches of Norfolk and vicinity: Including Portsmouth and the adjacent counties, during a period of two hundred years; also sketches of Williamsburg, Hampton, Suffolk, Smithfield, and other places, with descriptions of some of the principal objects of interest in eastern Virginia* (Philadelphia: Lindsay & Blakiston, 1853), 160; Clarke, *Booth Memorials,* 64.

21 *smallest class of freighters:* Virginia Steele Wood, *Live Oaking: Southern Timber for Tall Ships* (Annapolis, Md.: Naval Institute Press, 1981), 55; Clarke, *The Elder and Younger Booth,* 53–54; Clarke, *Booth Memorials,* 66.

21 *pay for their passage in gold:* Anon., *The Actor, Or, A Peep Behind the Curtain: Being Passages in the Lives of Booth and Some of His Contemporaries* (New York: W. H. Graham, 1846), 14; JBB to Richard Booth, March 1, 1826, H-BTL.

21 *"Actors":* Richmond *(Va.) Enquirer,* July 3, 1821, UCL; Stanley Kimmel, *The Mad Booths of Maryland* (New York: Bobbs-Merrill, 1940), 32.

21 *husband and wife:* Clarke, *Booth Memorials,* 64; Anon., *The Actor,* 63; Clarke, *The Elder and the Younger Booth,* 55; JBB to Madame Delannoy, May 30, 1815, Taper Collection, ALPLM; Frank A. Burr, "Junius Brutus Booth's Wife Adelaide: The Elopement, Marriage and Divorce of the Famous Actor Told through his Wife's Letters," *New York Press,* August 9, 1891, JBB family collection, 1828–1953, Manuscript Division, LC; Archer, *Junius Brutus Booth: Theatrical Prometheus,* 18, 66–67.

22 *mountain of trunks:* "Recollections of an Interesting Character of Booth," from the *Petersburg (Va.) Express,* JBB Scrapbook W.a.67, FSL.

22 *costly wardrobe:* Costume list in JBB Scrapbook, W.a.67, FSL; JBB to J. Sefton, March 8, 1850, H-BTL; Otis Skinner, *The Last Tragedian: Booth Tells His Own Story* (New York: Dodd, Mead, 1939), 146; Archer, "Recorded Engagements, 1821–1822" in *Theatrical Prometheus,* 254–56.

22 *playbills:* Asia Booth Clarke, *Personal Recollections of the Elder Booth* (London: privately printed, 1902), 37; Edwin Booth, "Junius Brutus Booth: Some Words about My Father," in Brander Matthews and Laurence Hutton, eds., *Actors and Actresses of Great Britain and the United States: Kean and Booth; and their Contemporaries,* vol. 3 (New York: Cassell, 1886), 107–8; Adam Badeau, *The Vagabond* (New York: Rudd & Carleton, 1859), 347, 350.

22 *"like a child's toy":* Charles Dickens, *American Notes for General Circulation* (New York: Penguin, 1987), 76.

22 *The town clung:* Thomas J. Wertenbaker, *Norfolk: Historic Southern Port* (Durham, N.C.: Duke University Press, 1931), 28.

22 *"tuskers":* Wood, *Live Oaking,* 134, 5–6; Wertenbaker, *Norfolk,* 4, 94.

22 *coffee, sugar:* Wertenbaker, *Norfolk,* 47, 96, 138.

23 *Eyewitnesses remembered:* Richmond *(Va.) Enquirer,* July 3, 1821, UCL; Wertenbaker, *Norfolk,* 130; Anon., *The Actor,* 64–65.

23 *Booth was small:* James Freeman Clarke, *Memorial and Biographical Sketches* (Boston: Houghton, Osgood, 1878), 269; Thomas R. Gould, *The Tragedian: An Essay on the Historic Genius of Junius Brutus Booth* (New York: Hurd & Houghton, 1868), 6, 18–19.

23 *arresting features:* JBB Scrapbook, W.a.67, FSL; Skinner, *Mad Folk of the Theatre,* 264.

23 *gold hoops dangled:* Clarke, *Personal Recollections of the Elder Booth,* 7.

23 *"exceedingly beautiful":* "A Scandalous Story about the Booth Family," *Baltimore American,* April 22, 1865, Booth-Grossman family papers, 1840–1953, BRTD, NYPL.

23 *"handsomest woman":* William Stump Forwood, "Manuscript of a biography of Junius Brutus Booth" (unpublished, May 1887), 112, MHS.

23 *"Forty doses as usual":* "The Experiments on the Exhilarating Gas," *(Norfolk, Va.) American Beacon,* June 21, 1820, UCL.

23 *ten million people:* United States Census Office, *Aggregate Amount of each description of per-*

sons within the United States of America, and the territories thereof, in the year 1810 (New York: Norman Ross, 1990), 1; United States Census Office, *Abstract of the Fifth Census of the United States, 1830* (Washington, D.C.: F. P. Blair, 1832), 42–43.

23 *"a wonder-working mind":* JBB, diary, May 1, 1839, H-BTL; EB, "Some Words About My Father," in *Actors and Actresses*, vol. 3, 93, 122.

23 *a highly educated clan:* Clarke, *Memorial and Biographical Sketches*, 279; Archer, *Theatrical Prometheus*, 4–5.

23 *a startling facility for language:* Clarke, *Personal Recollections of the Elder Booth*, 26, 37; Archer, *Theatrical Prometheus*, 105, 162–63; Matthews and Hutton, eds., *Actors and Actresses*, vol. 3, 101.

24 *like a seasoned poet:* JBB, diary, May 1, 1839, H-BTL; Anon., *The Actor*, 5–6; Archer, *Theatrical Prometheus*, 8; JBB, *Memoirs of Junius Brutus Booth, From His Birth to the Present Time* (London: Chapple, Miller, Rowden & Wilson), 11–12.

24 *enlist in the British navy:* Clarke, *The Elder and the Younger Booth*, 8.

24 *"any and all things appertaining to America":* JBB, diary, May 1, 1839, H-BTL; Clarke, *Booth Memorials*, 16.

24 *Finally, in 1813:* Clarke, *The Elder and the Younger Booth*, 9; JBB, Memoirs of Junius Brutus Booth, vi–vii, SCRC, UCL.

24 *"like reading Shakespeare by flashes":* Jean Raimond and J. R. Watson, eds., *A Handbook to English Romanticism* (New York: St. Martin's, 1992), 95–96.

24 *"a sort of convulsive fit":* Leslie A. Marchand, *Byron: A Biography* (New York: Knopf, 1957), 451.

25 *August 1814:* JBB, diary, 1814–15, of a tour of Belgium and the Netherlands, 1–4, 9, 18, H-BTL; JBB to Richard Booth, March 17, 1815, FSL.

25 *"two interesting mademoiselles":* Anon., *The Actor*, 61–62; Archer, *Theatrical Prometheus*, 25.

25 *"the god-damnedest":* Skinner, *Mad Folk of the Theatre*, 279; Gould, *The Tragedian*, 7; Anon., *The Actor*, 10.

26 *disrupt Booth's performances at Covent Garden:* Scrapbook of the 1817 Booth-Kean theatrical fracas, 10–11, 20–21; FSL; Clarke, *The Elder and the Younger Booth*, 23–24, 32–33, 37.

26 *"the highest pinnacle of fame":* Anon., *The Actor*, 57; Archer, *Theatrical Prometheus*, 46.

26 *"some passages of his life":* JBB, *Memoirs of Junius Brutus Booth, from his birth to the present time; with an appendix, containing original letters, from persons of rank and celebrity; and copious extracts from the journal kept by Mr. Booth, during his theatrical tour of the continent* (London: Chapple, Miller, Rowden & E. Wilson, 1817), 1–3, SCRC, UCL.

26 *radical British artists:* Kenneth Neill Cameron, *Romantic Rebels: Essays on Shelley and His Circle* (Cambridge, Mass.: Harvard University Press, 1973), v–vi; John Mullan, ed., *Lives of the Great Romantics by Their Contemporaries*, vol. 1, *Shelley* (London: William Pickering, 1996), 24–25, 337.

27 *"was nearly twenty-five":* Forrest, *Historical and Descriptive Sketches of Norfolk and Vicinity*, 160.

27 *slum of brothels and taverns:* Wertenbaker, *Norfolk*, 138; James Oakes, *Slavery and Freedom: An Interpretation of the Old South* (New York: Vintage, 1991), 70–72.

27 *greater crime than killing:* Dickens, *American Notes for General Circulation*, 183; Winthrop D. Jordan, *White Over Black: American Attitudes Toward the Negro, 1550–1812* (New York: Norton, 1977), 109–13, 399.

27 *"tea wagons":* Wertenbaker, *Norfolk*, 148, 141.

27 *pronounced* cow *as "kyow":* Theodosia Walton, "New Booth Diary: Additional Light on the Erratic Character of Junius Brutus, Edwin's Father," *New York Times*, June 12, 1921.

27 *Exchange Coffee House:* John C. Emmerson, *The Steam-Boat Comes to Norfolk Harbor, and the Log of the First Ten Years, 1815–1825* (Portsmouth, Va., 1947), 123; "Reading Room," *(Norfolk, Va.) American Beacon,* June 26, 1820, UCL.

28 *"All the news":* Samuel Mordecai, *Virginia, Especially Richmond, In By-Gone Days; With a Glance at the Present* (Richmond, Va.: West & Johnson, 1860), 62–63; "Laborers Wanted," *(Norfolk, Va.) American Beacon,* June 27, 1820, UCL.

28 steamboat Powhatan: Emmerson, *The Steam-Boat Comes to Norfolk Harbor,* 205, 287.

28 *"the terrible effects":* JBB, diary, 1814–15, of a tour of Belgium and the Netherlands, H-BTL, 16, 4; JBB, memorandum and account books, 1822–47 and undated, H-BTL; "Four pages from Junius Brutus Booth's account book," reproduced in Archer, *Theatrical Prometheus,* 82–91.

29 *Marsh Gate:* Archer, *Theatrical Prometheus,* 66; Clarke, *Personal Recollections of the Elder Booth,* 37–38.

29 *selling bouquets to the audiences:* "A Scandalous Story about the Booth Family," *Baltimore American,* April 22, 1865, BRTD, NYPL.

29 *In 1820:* Anon., *The Actor,* 52–54, 56; Clarke, *Personal Recollections of the Elder Booth,* 24; Archer, *Theatrical Prometheus,* 66.

29 *"my own soul":* JBB to Mary Ann Holmes, July 9, 1846, H-BTL; Archer, *Theatrical Prometheus,* 66, 163.

29 *in January 1821:* Clarke, *The Elder and the Younger Booth,* 52.

29 *"very religious":* Clarke, *Personal Recollections of the Elder Booth,* 37–38; JBB to Madame Delannoy, May 30, 1815, Taper Collection, ALPLM.

30 *"a gentlewoman":* Burr, "Junius Brutus Booth's Wife Adelaide," *New York Press,* August 9, 1891, JBB family collection, LC.

30 *"not pretty":* Forwood, "Manuscript of a biography of Junius Brutus Booth," 112, MHS; Archer, *Theatrical Prometheus,* 286.

30 *declared war on the institution of marriage:* Raimond and Watson, eds., *A Handbook of English Romanticism,* 12, 26, 59.

30 *Byron's one-man campaign of free love:* Leslie A. Marchand, *Byron: A Portrait* (Chicago: University of Chicago Press, 1970), 117–18, 126.

30 *ten thousand copies:* Marchand, *Byron,* 162.

30 *his half sister:* Marchand, *Byron,* 222–25, 232, 248, 260; Raimond and Watson, eds., *A Handbook to English Romanticism,* 27, 62; Betty T. Bennett, ed., *Lives of the Great Romantics III, Mary Shelley* (London: Pickering & Chatto, 1999), x–xi; R. Glynn Grylls, *Mary Shelley: A Biography* (New York: Oxford University Press, 1938), 152; Cameron, *Romantic Rebels,* v.

31 *"In the cold, formal English world":* Mullan, ed., *Lives of the Great Romantics,* vol. 1, 160.

31 *"These are my companions":* Archer, *Theatrical Prometheus,* 123.

31 *Adulterers wore their brand:* Bennett, ed., *Lives of the Great Romantics,* vol. 3, xii–xiii; Marchand, *Byron,* 373, 466–68, 476; Mullan, ed., *Lives of the Great Romantics,* vol. 1, 24, 106.

31 *"get up at night and read":* Clarke, *Personal Recollections of the Elder Booth,* 37–38.

31 *"There has been an eleventh":* Marchand, *Byron,* 315–16.

32 *Byron's poem "The Giaour":* Asia Booth Clarke, *The Unlocked Book: A Memoir of John Wilkes Booth by his Sister* (New York: Putnam's, 1938), 41.

32 *Byron had sat:* Marchand, *Byron,* 532, 534, 541; Benita Eisler, *Byron: Child of Passion, Fool of Fortune* (New York: Knopf, 1999), 469.

32 *"backed in gold":* Clarke, *Personal Recollections of the Elder Booth,* 39.

32 *Lord's Byron's cameo:* Clarke, *Personal Recollections of the Elder Booth,* 39; daguerreotype of Mary Ann Holmes, LC, LC-USZ6-2065.

32 *"ninety-three letters":* Archer, *Theatrical Prometheus,* 66.

32 *"the worst of all laws"*: William Godwin, "On Marriage," in Duncan Wu, ed., *Romanticism: An Anthology* (Malden, Mass.: Blackwell, 1998), 49–50.

33 *"the brutal outcry"*: Clarke, *The Elder and the Younger Booth*, 44–45; Brander Matthews and Laurence Hutton, eds. *Actors and Actresses of Great Britain and the United States*, vol. 3, *Kean and Booth* (New York: Cassell, 1886), 107–08.

33 *"rather have a nod from an American"*: Marchand, *Byron*, 376.

33 *"Never creature"*: Frank A. Burr, "Junius Brutus Booth's Wife Adelaide," *New York Press*, August 9, 1891, JBB family collection, LC.

33 *Richard Booth paid a visit*: Archer, *Theatrical Prometheus*, 66; Clarke, *Personal Recollections of the Elder Booth*, 37–39.

CHAPTER TWO: O BRAVE NEW WORLD

Page

35 *After two days listening*: Emmerson, *The Steam-Boat Comes to Norfolk Harbor*, 205, 287.

35 *Close to a hundred passengers*: Eliza Ripley, *Social Life in Old New Orleans* (New York: Appleton, 1912), 131–32, 136; A. O. Hall, *The Manhattaner in New Orleans* (New York: J. S. Redfield, 1851), 180.

35 *"fancy work"*: Ripley, *Social Life*, 136; Hall, *The Manhattaner*, 179.

35 *melancholy tears*: JBB to RB, April 7, 1833, H-BTL; JBB, diary, May 1, 1839, H-BTL; James Freeman Clarke, "My Odd Adventure with Junius Brutus Booth," *Atlantic Monthly*, September 1861, KC; Clarke, *Personal Recollections of the Elder Booth*, 25.

36 *Like Percy Shelley*: Mullan, ed., *Lives of the Great Romantics*, vol. 1, 107; JBB to RB, April 7, 1833.

36 *sacred responsibility*: Clarke, *The Elder and the Younger Booth*, 89; JBB to RB, April 7, 1833, H-BTL.

36 *"Murderer! Murderer!"*: "Some Personal Reminiscences of Junius Brutus Booth," undated newspaper clipping, KC.

36 *"the eye was pained"*: Dickens, *American Notes*, 199; Clarke, *The Elder and the Younger Booth*, 70; Clarke, *Memorial and Biographical Sketches*, 271–74.

36 *a range of steep hills*: Dickens, *American Notes*, 181; Samuel Mordecai, *Virginia, Especially Richmond*, 46.

36 *Parades by local militia*: "Celebration of Independence," in *Richmond (Va.) Enquirer*, July 6 and 10, 1821, UCL; Archer, *Theatrical Prometheus*, 69; Clarke, *Booth Memorials*, 66.

37 *"There is something"*: JBB to RB, June 15, 1825, H-BTL; Maurice Duke and Daniel P. Jordan, eds., *A Richmond Reader: 1733–1983* (Chapel Hill: University of North Carolina Press, 1983), 53.

37 *the Old Academy*: Mordecai, *Virginia, Especially Richmond*, 211–12; Duke and Jordan, eds., *A Richmond Reader*, 51–52.

37 *hesitated to flee*: Mordecai, *Virginia, Especially Richmond*, 213–14; Duke and Jordan, eds., *A Richmond Reader*, 53; Sol Smith, *Theatrical Management in the West and South for Thirty Years* (New York: B. Blom, 1968), 199.

38 *"the most horrid disaster"*: Mordecai, *Virginia, Especially Richmond*, 216; "Junius Booth of the London Theatre," *Richmond (Va.) Enquirer*, July 20, 1821, UCL.

38 *uncomfortable silence*: Walt Whitman, *Prose Works 1892*, vol. 2, *Collect and Other Prose*, Floyd Stovall, ed. (New York: New York University Press, 1964), 596; Clarke, *The Elder and the Younger Booth*, 57; Anon. *The Actor*, 64.

38 *"a shudder [go] through"*: Whitman, *Prose Works 1892*, vol. 2, 596; Smith, *Theatrical Management*, 229–30; "Edwin Booth: Notes and Anecdotes," *New York Dramatic Mirror*, June 24, 1893, EB clippings, Theatre Collection, HL; Anon., *The Actor*, 64–65; Clarke, *The Elder and the Younger Booth*, 60.

39 *"his face the ashy hue"*: Matthews and Hutton, eds., *Actors and Actresses*, vol. 3, 116; *Richmond (Va.) Enquirer*, July 20, 1821, UCL.

39 *"anxious desire"*: *Richmond (Va.) Enquirer*, July 20, 1821, UCL; "Passengers—Steamboat Powhatan—Sept. 29 [1821]," in Emmerson, *The Steam-Boat Comes to Norfolk Harbor*, 184, 205; "Mr. Booth," *New York Evening Post*, October 3, 1821, UCL.

39 *"an immense hive teeming"*: James Grant Wilson, *The Memorial History of the City of New-York from Its First Settlement to the year 1892*, vol. 3 (New York: New York History Company, 1893), 298; Isaac S. Lyon, *Recollections of an Old Cartman, or, Old New York Street Life* (Newark, N.J.: Daily Journal Office, 1872), 10.

39 *The metropolis then covered:* Lyon, *Recollections*, 6, 10; Wilson, *Memorial History of the City*, 337.

40 *Park Theatre:* Wilson, *Memorial History of the City*, 304; Eric Homberger, *The Historical Atlas of New York City* (New York: Henry Holt, 2005), 64, 75; Lyon, *Recollections*, 9.

40 *nemesis Edmund Kean:* John W. Francis, *New York During the last Half Century: A Discourse* (New York: John F. Trow, 1857), 152; Lyon, *Recollections*, 7.

40 *"vexations"*: Burr, "Junius Brutus Booth's Wife Adelaide," *New York Press*, August 9, 1891, JBB family collection, LC; "Mr. Booth," *New York Evening Post*, October 3, 4, 8, and 13, 1821, UCL.

41 *topped one hundred dollars per night:* Clarke, *Booth Memorials*, 71, 74.

41 *"dear darling child"*: Junius Brutus Booth, Jr., to Mary Ann Holmes Booth, n.d., 1863, HL; Forwood, "Manuscript of a Biography of Junius Brutus Booth," 95–97, MHS.

41 *"No city in the world"*: J. Thomas Scharf, *The Chronicles of Baltimore: Being a Complete History of Baltimore Town and Baltimore City* (Baltimore: Turnbull Brothers, 1874), 405; Badeau, *The Vagabond*, 347.

41 *"thick growth of trees"*: Badeau, *The Vagabond*, 348; Clarke, *The Elder and the Younger Booth*, 66; "Records of the Booth Property in the Belair Courthouse," KC; Forwood, "Manuscript of a Biography of Junius Brutus Booth," 133–34, MHS.

41 *"the social world, and the amusements"*: Walton, "New Booth Diary," *New York Times*, June 12, 1921; Clarke, *The Elder and the Younger Booth*, 68.

42 *tracking the actor's movements:* "Mr. Junius Booth of Covent Garden ... and Lady," in Emmerson, *The Steam-boat Comes to Norfolk Harbor*, 205; "Mr. Booth's Benefit," *New York Evening Post*, October 15, 1821, UCL; "Theatre," *Baltimore Patriot & Advertiser*, November 6, 1821, and "Mr. Booth Leaves," *Baltimore Patriot & Advertiser*, November 10, 1821, UCL.

42 *"object in moving to our county"*: Mrs. Elijah Rogers to William Stump Forwood, August 16, 1886, JBB family collection, LC; Forwood, "Manuscript of a Biography of Junius Brutus Booth," 119, MHS; Clarke, *The Elder and the Younger Booth*, 68.

42 *"Big Woods"*: Clarke, *The Elder and the Younger Booth*, 66; Archer, *Theatrical Prometheus*, 96.

43 *Booth had to travel thousands of miles:* See "Recorded Engagements, 1821–1852," in Archer, *Theatrical Prometheus*, 255ff.; S. Augustus Mitchell, *Mitchell's Traveler's Guide Through the United States: A map of the Roads, Distances, Steamboats and Canal Routes* (Philadelphia: S. Augustus Mitchell, 1832); Benjamin Tanner, *United States of America* (Philadelphia: Carey & Lea, 1827) Map Collection, UCL.

43 *"What could he do else?"*: Burr, "Junius Brutus Booth's Wife Adelaide," *New York Press*, August 9, 1891, JBB family collection, LC.

43 *three huge Newfoundland dogs:* Clarke, *Memorial and Biographical Sketches*, 273; Benita Eisler, *Byron: Child of Passion, Fool of Fame* (New York: Knopf, 1999), 160–61.

43 *She chained them close:* JBB to RB, April 7, 1833, H-BTL; Forwood, "Manuscript of a Biography of Junius Brutus Booth," 106, MHS.

43 *"did not visit"*: Mrs. Elijah Rogers to William Stump Forwood, August 11, 1886, JBB family collection, LC.

43 *The elder Booth agreed:* JBB to RB, December 1, 1822, H-BTL; Edward V. Valentine, "My Recollections of Booth," October 6, 1891, original manuscript in the Valentine Museum, Richmond, facsimile copy, KC.

43 *"Robinson Crusoe's Island":* Asia Booth Clarke, *The Unlocked Book: A Memoir of John Wilkes Booth* (New York: Putnam's, 1938), 88; Clarke, *The Elder and the Younger Booth,* 71.

43 *crops in abundance:* Scharf, *The Chronicles of Baltimore,* 402–4; JBB to RB, May 2, 1832; JBB to RD, October 26, 1834; JBB to RB, "Instructions for Plowing and Planting," n.d., H-BTL.

44 *"I have witnessed often with regret":* Archer, *Theatrical Prometheus,* 93.

44 *Junius had leased:* Archer, *Theatrical Prometheus,* 79–80; JBB to RB, September 22, 1825; JBB to RB, February 15, 1826; JBB to RB, April 14, 1826; JBB to RB, January 28, 1837, H-BTL.

44 *Ann Hall:* Ella V. Mahoney, *Sketches of Tudor Hall and the Booth Family* (Belair, Md., 1925), 8–10.

44 *built a barn:* JBB to RB, June 15, 1825; JBB to RB, April 7, 1833; JBB diary, August 27, 1832, H-BTL.

44 *"Joe had best":* JBB to RB, October 26, 1834; JBB to RB, December 15, 1824, H-BTL.

44 *"Madagascan Prince":* Clarke, *The Elder and the Younger Booth,* 70; JBB to RB, April 7, 1833, H-BTL.

45 *"Nearly all the children":* Mrs. Elijah Rogers to William Stump Forwood, n.d. (1886–87), JBB family collection, LC.

45 *Enemas of salt:* Philip K. Wilson, ed., *Midwifery Theory and Practice* (New York: Garland, 1996), 420–22.

45 *Mary Ann's firstborn son:* Kimmel, *The Mad Booths of Maryland,* 340.

45 *"Let nothing be neglected to keep them in health":* JBB to RB, February 15, 1826, H-BTL.

46 *a wealth of skills:* Robert Palmer, *Deep Blues: A Musical and Cultural History* (New York: Penguin, 1982), 31, 33–34; Clarke, *The Elder and the Younger Booth,* 70.

46 *"I have seen him act Richard":* Smith, *Theatrical Management,* 229–30.

46 *portrait of Mary Ann Holmes:* Thomas Sully, *Portrait of Mary Ann Holmes (Mrs. Junius Brutus Booth),* oil on panel, 18.5 x 15 inches, private collection, details courtesy of Skinner, Inc., Boston, and Marlborough, Mass.; Monroe H. Fabian, *Mr. Sully, Portrait Painter* (Washington, D.C.: Smithsonian Institution Press, 1983), 15–17; "Mr Sully Has Returned from Monticello," *Richmond (Va.) Enquirer,* July 20, 1821, UCL; John Clubbe, *Byron, Sully and the Power of Portraiture* (Aldershot, England: Ashgate, 2005), 163–64; Archer, *Theatrical Prometheus,* 93–94.

46 *"my greatest ambition":* Burr, "Junius Brutus Booth's Wife Adelaide," *New York Press,* August 9, 1891, JBB family collection, LC; Archer, *Theatrical Prometheus,* 100.

47 *The actor was terrified:* JBB to RB, February 15, 1826, H-BTL.

48 *"until he fell into bad company":* Smith, *Theatrical Management,* 229–30.

CHAPTER THREE: THIS BE MADNESS

Page

49 *In 1823 . . . "industriously circulating the bottle":* Archer, *Theatrical Prometheus,* 256–57; Marquis James, *The Raven: A Biography of Sam Houston* (New York: Blue Ribbon, 1929), 53, 206.

49 *surviving an arrow shot:* C. E. Lester, *The Life of Sam Houston: The Only Authentic Memoir of Him* (New York: J. C. Derby, 1855), 31, 38; P. G. Williams, "Houston, Sam," in Foner and Garraty, eds., *The Reader's Companion to American History,* 523–24; James, *The Raven,* 20.

49 *"professed chagrin":* James, *The Raven,* 53.

50 *"Now Booth, let's have a speech":* James, *The Raven,* 206, 170.

50 *chief among the "bad company":* Smith, *Theatrical Management,* 229; Charles Pope, "The

Eccentric Booths, Their Peculiarities Described by One Who Knew Them," *New York Sun*, March 27, 1897, EB Scrapbook B.7.6, FSL.

50 *"the hero of so many of his father's anecdotes"*: James, "Interview with Mrs. Nettie Houston Bringhurst," in *The Raven*, 445.

50 *"magnificent barbarian"*: Oliver Dyer, *Great Senators of the United States Forty Years Ago* (New York: R. Bonner's Sons, 1889), 116; Clarke, *The Elder and the Younger Booth* (Boston: James R. Osgood, 1882), extra-illustrated ed., October 29, 1885, printed insertion describing JBB's friendships, UIUC.

50 *Nashville's New Theatre:* James, *The Raven*, 69–70; Archer, *Theatrical Prometheus*, 258; Pope, "The Eccentric Booths."

51 *on three major rivers:* Leland Baldwin, *The Keelboat Age on Western Waters* (Pittsburgh: University of Pittsburgh Press, 1941), 59–61, 66; Emerson W. Gould, *Fifty Years on the Mississippi; or, Gould's History of River Navigation* (St. Louis: Nixon-Jones 1889), 538; Mark Twain, *Life on the Mississippi* (New York: Random House, 2007), 10.

51 *nineteen-year-old Abraham Lincoln:* David Herbert Donald, *Lincoln* (New York: Simon & Schuster, 1995), 34; Baldwin, *The Keelboat Age*, 87.

51 *but Junius Brutus Booth:* "Floating Down the River, the Ohio: A Song by J. B. Booth, Tragedian Puissant,'" scrapbook of material relating to JBB, W.A.67, FSL; Gould, *Fifty Years on the Mississippi*, 538.

51 *"ungainly water buildings"*: Hall, *The Manhattaner*, 5–6; Gould, *Fifty Years on the Mississippi*, 214.

51 *Cherokee ceremonial regalia:* Archer, *Theatrical Prometheus*, 133; Pope, "The Eccentric Booths."

52 *"intoxicating liquor"*: Roy P. Basler, ed., *Abraham Lincoln: His Speeches and Writings* (New York: Da Capo, 1990), 135.

52 *highly intelligent young men:* Basler, ed., *Abraham Lincoln: His Speeches and Writings*, 139.

52 *gesture to the forehead:* JBB, diary, May 1, 1839, H-BTL; William Winter, "Memories of The Players," *Colliers Weekly* (1913), in EB clippings, Theatre Collection, HL; "Lunacy of a Tragedian," EB Scrapbook B.7.5, FSL.

52 *Booth learned nearly a dozen ancient and modern languages:* JBB Scrapbook, W.a.67, FSL.

52 *"thoroughly acquire the Cherokee language"*: Alfred M. Williams, *Sam Houston and the War of Independence in Texas* (Boston: Houghton Mifflin, 1895), 7.

52 *"those gigantic heroes"*: Lester, *The Life of Sam Houston*, 21.

52 *"was strongly tempted"*: James, *The Raven*, 85.

53 *"bury sorrow in the flowing bowl"*: William Carey Crane, *Life and Select Literary Remains of Sam Houston* (Dallas: William G. Scarff, 1884), 254; James, *The Raven*, 157.

53 *According to his onetime manager:* Noah Ludlow, *Dramatic Life as I Found It: A Record of Personal Experience* (St. Louis: G. I. Jones, 1880), 237; Hall, *The Manhattaner*, 19; Clarke, *Memorial and Biographical Sketches*, 270–71.

53 *Booth gave in to the brotherhood:* Joe Cowell, *Thirty Years Passed Among the Players in England and America* (New York: Harper & Brothers, 1844), 72–73; JBB to RB, n.d., H-BTL.

53 *"whilst he was drunk"*: Adelaide Delannoy Booth to Therese Delannoy, December 17, 1846, in Burr, "Junius Brutus Booth's Wife Adelaide," *New York Press*, August 9, 1891, JBB family collection, LC.

53 *"I must have been insane"*: JBB to David Brown, May 24, 1834, H-BTL; JBB to Francis Wemyss, n.d., Theatre Collection, HL.

54 *"Lunacy of a Tragedian"*: EB Scrapbook B.7.5, FSL; Skinner, *Mad Folk of the Theatre*, 278.

54 *"take me to the Lunatic Hospital"*: William W. Clapp, *A Record of the Boston Stage* (Cambridge, Mass.: J. Munroe, 1853), 278, 280.

54 *"I never believed"*: Smith, *Theatrical Management*, 229.

54 *a nasty prank:* JBB to Thomas Hamblin, February 14, 1833, FSL.

54 *"a messenger covered with dust":* "A Startling Story Concerning the Elder Booth and His Dead Child," EB Scrapbook B.7.5, FSL.

55 *"had been buried a week":* Mrs. Elijah Rogers to William Stump Forwood, August 11, 1886, JBB family collection, LC.

55 *"gibbering in idiotic madness":* "A Startling Story Concerning the Elder Booth."

55 *His son Frederick and daughter Elizabeth died:* JBB to Thomas Hamblin, April 15, 1833, H-BTL; Archer, *Theatrical Prometheus*, 124, 127.

55 *Ground was cleared:* Clarke, *The Elder and the Younger Booth*, 68; Clarke, *The Unlocked Book*, 32; Forwood, "Manuscript of a Biography of Junius Brutus Booth," 112, MHS; Clarke, *The Elder and the Younger Booth*, extra-illustrated ed., October 29, 1885, printed insertion between 91 and 92, UIUC.

55 *A lapse in his vegetarian principles:* JBB to RB, April 7, 1833, H-BTL.

56 *When trade vessels from London:* Joseph Brevitt to RB, October 9, 1832, H-BTL; JBB, diary, July 4, 1832, H-BTL.

56 *Sixty thousand people bought their food:* William Wirt to Catharine Wirt, November 24, 1822, in Scharf, *The Chronicles of Baltimore*, 402.

56 *When the Booths ordered bushels of herring:* JBB to RB, April 7, 1833, H-BTL.

56 *"penance":* Clarke, *Personal Recollections of the Elder Booth*, 32.

56 *His manager was irate:* JBB to Thomas Hamblin, February 14, 1833, FSL; JBB to [unknown], August 26, 1847, H-BTL; JBB to J. Pennington, February 6, 1851, FSL; JBB to Richard Booth, April 7, 1833, H-BTL.

56 *Returning to the stage:* Mrs. Elijah Rogers to William Stump Forwood, March 30, 1887, JBB family collection, LC.

57 *"his fellow-actors were afraid":* Clarke, *Memorial and Biographical Sketches*, 277.

57 *"more than twenty-two hundred millions":* Clarke, *Memorial and Biographical Sketches*, 274–75; John James Audubon, *Ornithological Biography* (Philadelphia: Carey & Hart, 1832), 323–24.

57 *"brutal Americans":* Archer, *Theatrical Prometheus*, 129; JBB to James Freeman Clarke, January 4 and 13, 1834, Autograph File, HL.

57 *bushels of dead birds:* Clarke, *Memorial and Biographical Sketches*, 273–75.

58 *"I heard, in a day or two":* Clarke, *Memorial and Biographical Sketches*, 276.

58 *"What Rage, what Fury and Madness":* JBB, Argument against killing animals for food, [1834], H-BTL.

58 *Christ had been nailed to the cross:* JBB to Joseph Cowell, "Exterior of Louisville Jail. Year of the Christ Feb. 3, 1834, of the Planet 5994. Praise be to Allah!" reproduced in Skinner, *Mad Folk of the Theatre*, 282.

58 *"Ah Junius, Junius":* Charles H. Eaton, "Junius Brutus Booth," n.d., KC.

58 *labor pangs started November 13, 1833:* Mary Ann Holmes Booth to EB, May 10, 1862, H-BTL; Adam Badeau, "Boyhood of Booth: Good Childhood Stories of America's Great Actor," BRTD, NYPL; Scharf, *The Chronicles of Baltimore*, 465–67.

59 *transparent layer of skin:* Clarke, *The Elder and the Younger Booth*, 119; G. Blakemore Evans, ed., *The Riverside Shakespeare* (Boston: Houghton Mifflin, 1974), 1148.

59 *saved the bit of membrane:* Goodale, *Behind the Scenes with Edwin Booth*, 107–8; Brander Matthews and Laurence Hutton, eds., *Life and Art of Edwin Booth* (Boston: L. C. Page 1886), 59.

59 *His old drinking partner had found his destiny at last:* JBB, diary, October 20, 1836, reproduced in Clarke, *Booth Memorials*, 127–28

59 *"you damned old scoundrel":* JBB to Andrew Jackson, July 4, 1835, in Archer, *Theatrical Prometheus*, 135; "Junius Brutus Booth in Poore's *Reminiscences*," KC.

59 *entire Booth family boarded:* JBB to RB, January 28, 1837, H-BTL; John Schwartz, "Soldier's Smallpox Inoculation Sickens Son," *New York Times*, May 18, 2007.

60 *"So proud as I was of him":* JBB to RB, January 28, 1837; JBB to RB, February 15, 1826, H-BTL.

60 *"not pretty, but a noble girl":* Mrs. Elijah Rogers to William Stump Forwood, August 11, 1886, JBB family papers, LC; JBB to RB, January 28, 1837, H-BTL.

60 *"Oh, even in spite of death":* Clarke, *The Elder and the Younger Booth*, 95.

60 *"cost me the price of a Son's life":* JBB to Francis Wemyss, March 25, 1837, Theatre Collection, HL; Burr, "Junius Brutus Booth's Wife Adelaide."

61 *On March 7, 1838:* "Junius Brutus Booth," JBB Scrapbook W.a.67, FSL.

61 *"We consider him":* Editorial in the *Charleston (S.C.) Mercury*, March 19, 1838, reproduced in Archer, *Theatrical Prometheus*, 153–54.

61 *Edwin Booth later claimed:* Badeau, "Edwin Booth On and Off the Stage: Personal Recollections," *McClure's Magazine*, August 1, 1893, 255.

61 *"had finally to go with him":* Mrs. Elijah Rogers to William Stump Forwood, March 30, 1887, JBB family papers, LC; Badeau, "Edwin Booth On and Off the Stage," 255.

62 *"misery" and "fear":* Clarke, *The Elder and the Younger Booth*, 93–94; Sol Smith to Noah Ludlow, April 11, 1838, in Archer, *Theatrical Prometheus*, 155; Noah Ludlow to Mary Ann Holmes Booth, December 6, 1852, HL.

62 *John Wilkes Booth was born:* Clarke, *The Unlocked Book*, 41; Kimmel, *The Mad Booths of Maryland*, 66, 340; Matthews and Hutton, eds., *Actors and Actresses*, vol. 3, 97.

62 *Richard Booth, then in his seventy-fifth year:* Clarke, *Booth Memorials*, 15–16, 157; Clarke, *Personal Recollections of the Elder Booth*, 38.

62 *claimed the politician John Wilkes:* RB to John Wilkes, October 28, 1777, in Clarke, *The Elder and the Younger Booth*, 4–6; Kimmel, *The Mad Booths of Maryland*, 16; Owen A. Sherrard, *A Life of John Wilkes* (London: George Allen & Unwin, 1930), 301, 309; JBB, *Memoirs of Junius Brutus Booth, from His Birth to the Present Time*, 10.

63 *"the Americans will rise to independence":* Sherrard, *A Life of John Wilkes*, 274, 309.

63 *The original John Wilkes was not born a gentleman:* Sherrard, *A Life of John Wilkes*, 14–18.

63 *"as grand as his private life was intemperate and eccentric":* Benjamin Perley Poore, *Perley's Reminiscences, of Sixty Years in the National Metropolis*, vol. 1 (Philadelphia: Hubbard Brothers, 1886), 125.

63 *"Absalom":* Clarke, *Booth Memorials*, vii.

CHAPTER FOUR: A POPULOUS CITY

Page

64 *Locals called the cabin "unattractive":* Ella V. Mahoney, *Sketches of Tudor Hall and the Booth Family* (Belair, Md., 1925), 7; Clarke, *The Elder and the Younger Booth*, 69–70.

64 *"straight-backed, hard":* Clarke, *Personal Recollections of the Elder Booth*, 15; Mahoney, *Sketches of Tudor Hall*, 7; Badeau, *The Vagabond*, 347–50.

64 *the tree was the favorite haunt:* Mahoney, *Sketches of Tudor Hall*, 13; Clarke, *The Elder and the Younger Booth*, 67–68.

65 *"how, from the crotch of the tree":* Mahoney, *Sketches of Tudor Hall*, 12.

65 *spoke Shakespeare aloud all day:* JBB Scrapbook W.a.67, FSL; Eldridge Henderson to Stanley Kimmel, April 5, 1940, KC.

65 Coriolanus *and* King John: Clarke, *Personal Recollections of the Elder Booth*, 15.

66 *"In the youth of his children":* EB, "Some Words about My Father," in Matthews and Hutton, eds., *Actors and Actresses*, vol. 3, 120–21.

66 *He also feared what would happen:* According to EB, his father often warned his sons that the stage was "a troublous sea, where [those] without talent would either sink, or, buoyed by vanity alone, flounder in its uncertain waves." See EB, "Some Words about My Father," in Matthews and Hutton, eds., *Actors and Actresses*, vol. 3, 98.

66 *Costumes were everywhere:* Badeau, *The Vagabond*, 347, 353.

66 *Mary Ann was constantly employed:* JBB to Mary Ann Holmes, June 23, 1840, H-BTL; "Tombs of the Booths," unidentified newspaper clipping, July 26, 1891, EB Scrapbook B.7.6, FSL.

66 *Piles of playbills were scattered:* Badeau, *The Vagabond*, 347, 350; Booth family playbills, Taper Collection, ALPLM.

67 *Books in Latin and Greek:* Badeau, *The Vagabond*, 349.

67 *bloodbath of seduction and murder:* Excerpts from *Ugolino* by JBB, in Booth Family Scrapbook B.9.1, FSL.

67 *His daughter Asia:* Mrs. Elijah Rogers to William Stump Forwood, August 11, 1886, JBB family papers, LC; Clarke, *Personal Recollections of the Elder Booth*, 16; Asia Booth Clarke to Jean Anderson, May 22, 1855, copy courtesy of Michael W. Kauffman, author of *American Brutus: John Wilkes Booth and the Lincoln Conspiracies*, and Laurie Verge, director, Surratt House Museum; "The Mother's Vision, 2 June 1854" in Clarke, *The Unlocked Book*, 42–43.

67 *"were as wide apart as points of the compass":* John M. Berron, "With John Wilkes Booth in His Days as an Actor," newspaper clipping, March 17, 1907, KC.

67 *"to be a lawyer or a doctor":* Mrs. Elijah Rogers to William Stump Forwood, August 13, 1886, JBB family papers, LC.

68 *"fairly good":* Berron, "With John Wilkes Booth in His Days as an Actor," KC.

68 *"June would make a better merchant than an actor":* John Carboy, "Theatrical Reminiscences: Edwin Booth," Booth Scrapbook B.7.5, 55, FSL.

68 *"Of dramatic fire Joe had not one spark":* Berron, "With John Wilkes Booth in His Days as an Actor."

68 *"but which one will excel":* Carboy, "Theatrical Reminiscences: Edwin Booth."

68 *John Wilkes's face:* Typescript of Booth reminiscences from the collections of the Baltimore Municipal Museum, KC.

68 *Edwin claimed that John Wilkes:* EB to Nahum Capen, July 28, 1881, in Edwina Booth Grossman, *Edwin Booth: Recollections by His Daughter . . . and Letters to Her and to His Friends* (New York: Century, 1894), 227; Berron, "With John Wilkes Booth in His Days as an Actor" Clarke, *The Unlocked Book*, 59.

68 *"I do not remember a father":* "Booth As Man and Artist: The Long and Checkered Career of America's Most Honored Artist," EB clippings, Theatre Collection, HL; "The Career of Edwin Booth," EB Scrapbook B.7.6, FSL; Barton Hill, "Personal Recollections of Edwin Booth," *New York Dramatic Mirror*, EB clippings, Theatre Collection, HL.

69 *"other children were more vivacious":* EB, "Some Words about My Father," in Matthews and Hutton, eds., *Actors and actresses*, vol. 3, 96.

69 *"Robinson Crusoe's Island":* Clarke, *The Unlocked Book*, 88.

69 *talked of friendships:* Marquis James, "Interview with Mrs. Nettie Houston Bringhurst," in *The Raven*, 445; Clarke, *Personal Recollections of the Elder Booth*, 26.

69 *"grotesque" appearance:* Clarke, *Personal Recollections of the Elder Booth*, 19–20.

70 *"bootblack and knife-scourer":* Mrs. Elijah Rogers to William Stump Forwood, August 11, 1886, JBB family collection, LC.

70 *"they could have starved":* Clarke, *The Elder and the Younger Booth*, 19; Mrs. Elijah Rogers to William Stump Forwood, August 11, 1886, JBB family papers, LC.

70 *threatened Booth with blackmail:* Kimmel, *The Mad Booths of Maryland*, 55–56; Burr, "Junius Brutus Booth's Wife Adelaide."

71 *"to assist and wait upon her sickly":* Clarke, *Personal Recollections of the Elder Booth,* 19; Mrs. Elijah Rogers to William Stump Forwood, August 11, 1886, JBB family collection, LC.

71 *"clever, self-taught negro musician":* Clarke, *The Elder and the Younger Booth,* 122; "Edwin's Booth's Boyhood: Stories of His Early Life Told by his Brother-in-Law," *New York Tribune,* October 8, 1892, EB Scrapbook B.7.6, FSL.

71 *"run over the farm together":* Stanley Kimmel, notes from an interview with Harriet Kennett, KC; see also Kimmel, *The Mad Booths of Maryland,* 60.

71 *"depicting the passions of hate, fear, terror":* "Junius Brutus Booth" and excerpt from *Ugolino,* in Booth Family Scrapbook B.9.1, FSL.

72 *"Mrs. Booth was a handsome woman":* Kimmel, *The Mad Booths of Maryland,* 60.

72 *The "peculiar" Mr. Booth:* Eldridge Henderson to Stanley Kimmel, April 5, 1940, KC; Mahoney, *Sketches of Tudor Hall,* 8, 10.

73 *"I don't think he ever spoke":* Mrs. Elijah Rogers to W. S. Forwood, August 11, 1886, JBB family collection, LC; Clarke, *Personal Recollections of the Elder Booth,* 36–37; Archer, *Theatrical Prometheus,* 160.

73 *he watched Booth entertain U.S. presidents:* Poore, *Perley's Reminiscences of Sixty Years in the National Metropolis,* vol. 1, 125–26, 281.

73 *"collect her husband's salary":* "Edwin Booth's Real Self, by an Intimate for Twenty-Five Years," *New York Theatre,* December 1916, in EB clippings, Theatre Collection, HL; JBB to Mary Ann Holmes, July 9, 1846, H-BTL.

74 *By the fall of 1840, Mary Ann:* Baltimore City Directory entries for "JBB, Tragedian," 1841–52, typescript record, KC.

74 *six-block walk to the inner harbor:* "Map of the Business Section of Baltimore" in Sollers, "The Theatrical Career of John T. Ford," 643; Clarke, *Personal Recollections of the Elder Booth,* 10, 30–31.

74 *In 1840, Baltimore:* Clayton Colman Hall, ed., *Baltimore: Its History and People,* vol. 1 (New York: Lewis Historical, 1912), 64; Sherry H. Olson, *Baltimore: The Building of an American City* (Baltimore: Johns Hopkins University Press, 1997), 139; Marion E. Warren and Mame Warren, *Baltimore—When She Was What She Used to Be, 1850–1930* (Baltimore: Johns Hopkins University Press, 1983), 57; for a general survey of how the city grew, see Baltimore Municipal Journal, *Baltimore, 200th Anniversary, 1729–1929* (Baltimore: Fleet-McGinley, 1929), 51, 55, 112–13, 129.

74 *hum of steam-powered machinery:* Olson, *Baltimore,* 84–85, 103, 111; Warren and Warren, eds., *Baltimore,* 27, 52.

75 *Marble-fronted mansions:* Olson, *Baltimore,* 112, 62.

75 *"filthy vagabonds":* Olson, *Baltimore,* 140; *Baltimore Sun,* December 12, 1898, EB clippings, Theatre Collection, HL; "Edwin Booth: His Boyhood Days," *The Figaro,* n.d., EB clippings, Theatre Collection, HL.

76 *Franklin stove:* Clarke, *Personal Recollections of the Elder Booth,* 26, 9.

76 *terminus of a railroad line:* "Map of the Business Section of Baltimore," in Sollers, "The Theatrical Career of John T. Ford," 643; Olson, *Baltimore,* 105; Clarke, *Personal Recollections of the Elder Booth,* 5–7, 17.

76 *washing dirt from wagonloads of potatoes:* "John Cassard's Reminiscences," typescript, KC.

76 *French dancing master:* "Statement of J. R. Codet: A transcript of the May Manuscript at the Peale Museum, Baltimore," KC; Terry Alford, ed., *John Wilkes Booth: A Sister's Memoir* (Jackson: University Press of Mississippi, 1996), 34; Clarke, *Personal Recollections of the Elder Booth,* 30, 24.

77 *Charles Dickens visited Barnum's Hotel:* Warren and Warren, eds., *Baltimore,* 61; Hall, ed., *Baltimore,* vol. 1, 131, 135–36, 242; "Edgar Allan Poe," in Foner and Garraty, eds., *The Reader's Companion to American History,* 846.

77 *The temples of entertainment:* Hall, ed., *Baltimore*, vol. 1, 139; Baltimore Municipal Journal, *Baltimore: 200th Anniversary*, 285, 204.

77 *Wherever they went with their father:* Clarke, *Personal Recollections of the Elder Booth*, 7; EB, "Some Words about My Father," in Matthews and Hutton, eds., *Actors and Actresses*, vol. 3, 96.

77 *"Actors in those days":* Clarke, *Personal Recollections of the Elder Booth*, 6; "Map of the Business Section of Baltimore" in Sollers, "The Theatrical Career of John T. Ford," 643; Clarke, *The Unlocked Book*, 58.

78 *"set apart":* "Statement of J. R. Codet," KC.

78 *"horrible, flat, hard, glazed cap":* Clarke, *Personal Recollections of the Elder Booth*, 24.

78 *"intuitive intelligence":* Clarke, *The Unlocked Book*, 43–45.

78 *dominated by mobs of children:* Olson, *Baltimore*, 100–1; Warren and Warren, eds., *Baltimore*, 48.

79 *"fighters of our little neighborhood":* Clarke, *The Unlocked Book*, 45.

79 *"Wilkes Booth was always ready for a fight":* George L. Stout, "Recollections of Tripple Alley," unidentified newspaper clipping, KC; JBB to RB, February 15, 1826, H-BTL.

79 *"a short Italian cloak":* "Edwin Booth's Boyhood: Stories of His Early Life Told by His Brother-in-law," *New York Tribune*, October 8, 1892, EB Scrapbook B.7.6, FSL.

79 *"I did [Edwin's] fighting for him":* Stout, "Recollections of Tripple Alley."

80 *But in March 1847:* Burr, "Junius Brutus Booth's Wife Adelaide," *New York Press*, August 9, 1891, JBB family collection, LC.

80 *Young Richard had been raised:* "Tombs of the Booths," unidentified newspaper clipping, July 26, 1891, in Booth Family Scrapbook B.9.1, FSL.

81 *"The Holmes residence":* Burr, "Junius Brutus Booth's Wife Adelaide."

81 *the star's weeklong engagement:* "JBB Recorded Engagements," in Archer, *Theatrical Prometheus*, 273; Baltimore Municipal Journal, *Baltimore: 200th Anniversary*, 204.

82 *Before an audience:* Burr, "Junius Brutus Booth's Wife Adelaide"; JBB to J. Pennington, Esq., February 6, 1851, FSL; J. Pennington, Esq., to JBB, February 7, 1851, FSL; JBB to Mary Ann Holmes, July 9, 1846, H-BTL.

82 *"reticent and singular, profound and sensitive":* "Edwin Booth," *Baltimore American*, June 10, 1893, EB clippings, Theatre Collection, HL; "Booth," *New York Herald*, June 7, 1893.

83 *The chosen one "was envied":* Clarke, *The Elder and the Younger Booth*, 122; EB to Richard Henry Stoddard, January 13, 1863, H-BTL; JBB to RB, February 15, 1826, H-BTL.

84 *"my punishment":* EB to Edwina Booth, April 23, 1876, in Grossman, *Edwin Booth: Recollections by His Daughter*, 49; EB to Richard Henry Stoddard, January 13, 1863, H-BTL.

84 *Mitchell, his wife, and eight children:* Mrs. Elijah Rogers to William Stump Forwood, August 13, 1886, JBB family collection, LC.

84 *"grotesque":* EB, "Some Words about My Father," in Matthews and Hutton, eds., *Actors and Actresses*, vol. 3, 94; EB to Richard Henry Stoddard, January 13, 1863, H-BTL.

CHAPTER FIVE: STAND UP FOR BASTARDS

Page

85 *"the broadest and brightest in the city":* Alvin F. Harlow, *Old Bowery Days: The Chronicles of a Famous Street* (New York: Appleton, 1931), 216–19, 230.

85 *"every second door":* Harlow, *Old Bowery Days*, 230–32.

85 *"tableaux vivants":* Jack W. McCullough, *Living Pictures on the New York Stage* (Ann Arbor, Mich.: UMI Research Press, 1983), 16–17, 20.

85 *Edwin came to this part of Manhattan:* Menken Collection of playbills showing joint appearances by JBB and EB, 1847–52, H-BTL; "JBB Recorded Engagements," in Archer, *Theatrical Prometheus*, 273–77.

86 *Booth's "genius":* Walt Whitman, "The Old Bowery: A Reminiscence of New York Plays and Acting Fifty Years Ago," in *Prose Works 1892*, vol. 2, *Collect and Other Prose*, 597, 595.

86 *"Bowery B'hoys":* Harlow, *Old Bowery Days*, 196–97, 276; Whitman, "The Old Bowery," 595.

86 *velvet curtain parted:* Harlow, *Old Bowery Days*, 241, 277–78.

86 *The workaday men and women:* Harlow, *Old Bowery Days*, 275.

86 *"mimic scene seemed really to have happened":* Archer, *Theatrical Prometheus*, 193; Harlow, *Old Bowery Days*, 246–47; Clarke, *The Elder and the Younger Booth*, 123.

87 *his son waited with a bottle of brandy:* Badeau, "Boyhood of Booth," EB clippings, Theatre Collection, HL.

87 *"a peculiar gesture, sawing the air":* William Winter, "Memories of the Players," *Collier's Weekly*, April 12, 1913, EB clippings, Theatre Collection, HL.

88 *"jig, double shuffle":* Rufus R. Wilson, "Booth's Young Days—Stories of Varied Adventures," *New York Advertiser*, June 3, 1894, EB clippings, Theatre Collection, HL.

88 *"I could do more with him than anybody":* Winter, "Memories of the Players," *Collier's Weekly*, April 12, 1913, Theatre Collection, HL.

88 *"how splendidly":* Wilson, "Booth's Young Days."

88 *an excitable, nervously-organized youth":* Clarke, *The Elder and the Younger Booth*, 122.

88 *"The boy lived almost a servant's life":* "Edwin Booth," EB Scrapbook B.7.6, FSL; Badeau, "Boyhood of Booth."

88 *One night, Junius sprinted through the streets of Louisville:* B. O. Flower, "Edwin Booth: A Sketch of the Life of America's Great Tragedian," *American Spectator*, October 1888, 1, EB clippings, Theatre Collection, HL.

89 *"You shall not!":* "Edwin Booth: Notes and Anecdotes," *New York Dramatic Mirror*, June 24, 1893, UCL.

89 *"It was an odd and dangerous way to bring up a boy":* "Edwin Booth," EB Scrapbook B.7.6, FSL.

89 *"oddities":* EB, "Some Words about My Father," in Matthews and Hutton, eds., *Actors and Actresses*, vol. 3, 94.

89 *"would engage in some more healthful work":* EB, "Some Words about My Father," 98–99.

90 *a complete kit for self-transformation:* Booth family makeup case containing powder, pigment, charcoal, brushes, wigs, paste-on eyebrows, scissors, apron, hare's foot and other items, Taper Collection, ALPLM.

90 *"seemed to put the character on with it":* EB, "Some Words about My Father," in Matthews and Hutton, eds., *Actors and Actresses*, vol. 3, 100.

91 *"in the full sunlight":* EB, "Some Words about My Father," 100.

91 *Whatever Joe Hall harvested :* "John Cassard's Reminiscences," typescript, KC. Cassard gives this description of one of the Booth family's produce stands: "In 1844 Junius Brutus Booth presided over a vegetable stall in the Marsh Market. I cannot tell why, whether from a business standpoint, or because he so elected. His stand was a few stalls removed from that of my father, Mr. Gilbert Cassard, a York butcher."

91 *market vending was "a family affair":* Warren and Warren, eds., *Baltimore*, 46.

91 *Lexington market was the most crowded:* "Map of the Business Section of Baltimore" in Sollers, "The Theatrical Career of John T. Ford," 643; Warren and Warren, eds., *Baltimore*, 47–48; "John Cassard's Reminiscences," KC.

92 *Baltimore attorneys had assured her:* Burr, "Junius Brutus Booth's Wife Adelaide," *New York Press*, August 9, 1891, JBB family collection, LC; "Tombs of the Booths," unidentified newspaper clipping, July 26, 1891, in Booth Family Scrapbook B.9.1, FSL.

92 *"It was a custom with [Adelaide]":* "A Scandalous Story About the Booth Family," *Baltimore American*, April 22, 1865, KC.

93 *"a frequent victim of the bottle":* Harlow, *Old Bowery Days*, 244; "A Scandalous Story About the Booth Family," *Baltimore American*; "The Booth Family: A Liberal Article from a Radical Newspaper," *Albany Evening Journal*, April 27, 1865, Booth-Grossman family papers, BRTD, NYPL.

93 *"was a bad boy":* James W. Shettel, "J. Wilkes Booth at School: Recollections of a Retired Army Officer Who Knew Him Then," *New York Dramatic Mirror*, February 26, 1916, UCL; Clarke, *The Unlocked Book*, 46.

93 *world's first telegraphic message:* Baltimore Municipal Journal, *Baltimore: 200th Anniversary*, p. 17; Clarke, *The Unlocked Book*, 46–47.

94 *serious acts of juvenile delinquency:* Olson, *Baltimore*, 100–1, 139; Warren and Warren, eds., *Baltimore*, 48.

94 *Old Watch-House on North Street:* Baltimore Municipal Journal, *Baltimore: 200th Anniversary*, 43, 91; Clarke, *The Unlocked Book*, 47–49.

94 *Junius and Edwin traveled down the Mississippi:* Archer, *Theatrical Prometheus*, 186–88, 274; JBB diaries of Mississippi River steamboat travel, 1845–47 and undated, H-BTL; Menken Collection of Booth playbills, 1847–52, H-BTL.

94 *"Of all the places in the world":* Hall, *The Manhattaner*, 185–86.

95 *Edwin was a born observer:* "Edwin Booth," EB Scrapbook B.7.6, FSL.

95 *500 million pounds of cotton each year:* "Cotton," in Foner and Garraty, *The Reader's Companion to American History*, 240–41; Henry C. Castellanos, *New Orleans as It Was: Episodes of Louisiana Life* (Baton Rouge: Louisiana State University Press, 1978), 16; Hall, *The Manhattaner in New Orleans*, 5–6, 26–27; Smith, *Theatrical Management*, 79–80.

96 *The St. Charles Hotel:* "Menu of a Dinner at the St. Charles Hotel, 22 December 1846," *New Orleans Daily Picayune*, December 23, 1946, in Martin Siegel, *New Orleans: A Chronological and Documentary History* (New York: Oceana, 1975), 82.

96 *dropped like flies from "yellow jack":* Chronology showing yellow fever epidemics in Siegel, *New Orleans*, 7, 16, 20; Hall, *The Manhattaner*, 9–11; Smith, *Theatrical Management*, 211–12.

96 *indispensable to him while he was working:* EB, "Some Words about My Father," in Matthews and Hutton, eds., *Actors and Actresses*, vol. 3, 94; JBB to [?], requesting theatrical contract, August 26, 1847, H-BTL.

96 *"Those long wanderings by night and day":* Laurence Hutton, "Edwin Booth," *Harper's Weekly*, June 17, 1893, 577–78.

97 *"rapidly learn[ing] things":* "Edwin Booth," EB Scrapbook B.7.6, FSL.

97 *"Sometimes one boy will influence the taste":* Celia Logan, "The Youth of Eminent Actors—Forrest and Logan's First Appearance—Edwin Booth's Early Ambition," EB clippings, Theatre Collection, HL.

97 *"Oh, it seems very long ago":* "Booth's First Play: *Richard III* in Stolen Armor in a Baltimore Cellar," EB clippings, Theatre Collection, HL.

98 *The boys lacked a space to perform in:* George L. Stout, "Recollections of Tripple Alley," KC.

98 *"of distinguishing ourselves":* "Booth's First Play: *Richard III* in Stolen Armor in a Baltimore Cellar."

98 *When Kilmiste Garden:* Stout, "Recollections of Tripple Alley."

99 Allessandro Massaroni: Stuart Robson, "As a Boy with Edwin and John Wilkes Booth," KC.

99 *"jealousy developed in the company":* Stout, "Recollections of Tripple Alley," and Robson, "As a Boy with Edwin and John Wilkes Booth."

100 *a "predilection" for monopolizing:* Stout, "Recollections of Tripple Alley."

101 *"broke into" the basement:* Logan, "The Youth of Eminent Actors."

101 *"Of course we went after it":* Stout, "Recollections of Tripple Alley."

101 *"was torn to shreds":* Logan, "The Youth of Eminent Actors."

101 *Milton Academy:* John Rhodehamel and Louise Taper, *"Right or Wrong, God Judge Me":* *The Writings of John Wilkes Booth* (Urbana: University of Illinois Press, 2001), 37; Clarke, *The Unlocked Book,* 51.

102 *"I attended that school":* Shettel, "J. Wilkes Booth at School."

102 *"to excite in [John Wilkes] a love of mechanical pursuits":* Matthews and Hutton, eds., *Actors and Actresses,* vol. 3, 120–21.

102 *"a home and occupation":* Clarke, *The Unlocked Book,* 50.

102 *"elated":* Clarke, *The Elder and the Younger Booth,* 126.

103 *"Who was Tressel?":* "Edwin Booth: Notes and Anecdotes of the Great Tragedian's Life," printed material in Matthews and Hutton, eds., *Actors and Actresses of Great Britain and the United States,* extra-illustrated ed., TS931.2, Theatre Collection, HL.

103 *For the next three years:* Menken Collection of playbills showing joint appearances by JBB and EB, 1847–52, H-BTL.

103 *"the monotony of school life":* Clarke, *The Elder and the Younger Booth,* 122.

103 *In 1850, Mary Ann Holmes:* Barton Hill, "Personal Recollections of Edwin Booth," *New York Dramatic Mirror,* n.d., EB clippings, Theatre Collection, HL.

104 *three years at Milton Academy cost:* Rhodehamel and Taper, eds., *"Right or Wrong, God Judge Me,"* 37.

104 *In February 1851:* JBB to J. Pennington, Esq., February 6, 1851, and J. Pennington, Esq., to JBB, February 7, 1851, FSL; full text of the Bill of Divorce sent to the Judge of the Baltimore County Court by Adelaide Delannoy Booth, including her 1815 marriage license to JBB, may be found in Kimmel, *The Mad Booths of Maryland,* 340–41.

104 *"the vindication of her own rights":* Kimmel, *The Mad Booths of Maryland,* 341.

105 *"the facts as stated":* Archer, *Theatrical Prometheus,* 197.

105 *"He announced that he was too ill":* Wilson, "Booth's Young Days," *New York Advertiser,* June 3, 1894, EB clippings, Theatre Collection, HL.

105 *"Upon which of your sons":* Badeau, "Edwin Booth On and Off the Stage: Personal Recollections," *McClure's,* August 1893, 257.

CHAPTER SIX: IN THE DUST

Page

109 *On February 22, 1847:* K. Jack Bauer, *The Mexican War: 1846–1848* (New York: Macmillan, 1974), 212–17; Robert W. Johannsen, *To the Halls of the Montezumas: The Mexican War in the American Imagination* (New York: Oxford University Press, 1985), 92–93, 115.

109 *Vera Cruz, Cerro Gordo, and Mexico City:* Foner and Garraty, eds., *The Reader's Companion to American History,* 723; Johannsen, *To the Halls of the Montezumas,* 6.

110 *"the hero of so many of [my] father's anecdotes":* James, *The Raven,* 445; Skinner, *The Last Tragedian: Booth Tells His Own Story* (New York: Dodd, Mead, 1939), 147.

110 *Santa Anna's cavalry officers:* Johannsen, *To the Halls of the Montezumas,* 94; EB to Nahum Capen, July 28, 1881, in Grossman, *Edwin Booth: Recollections by His Daughter,* 227–28.

110 *"Who thundering comes":* "The Giaour," in Mathilde Blind, ed., *The Poetical Works of Lord Byron* (London: Walter Scott, 1886), 49.

110 *"rattle-pated":* EB to Nahum Capen, July 28, 1881, in Grossman, *Edwin Booth: Recollections by His Daughter,* 227.

110 *"the country was filled with would-be great men":* Hubert Howe Bancroft, *The Works of Hubert Howe Bancroft: California Inter Pocula,* vol. 35 (San Francisco: History Company, 1888), 266; Clarke, *The Unlocked Book,* 76.

111 *On June 21, 1852:* Clarke, *The Elder and the Younger Booth,* 102, extra-illustrated ed., printed insertion at 130, UIUC; "Record of Booth Performances in San Francisco," Ferdinand C. Ewer to EB, October 16, 1877, 28, FSL; Bancroft, *California Inter Pocula,* 123–24.

111 *"the banks and bottoms":* Thomas O Larkin to James Buchanan, July 20, 1848, in George P. Hammond, ed., "Letters of the Gold Discovery," *Book Club of California Keepsakes Series* (private printing, May 1948), SCRC, UCL.

111 *"the gold or yellow fever":* Thomas O. Larkin to R. B. Mason, May 25, 1848, in Hammond, ed., "Letters of the Gold Discovery."

111 *"each ravenous to be in at the rich harvest":* Bancroft, *California Inter Pocula*, 126.

111 *scooping and sifting "until they die[d]":* Larkin to James Buchanan, July 20, 1848, in Hammond, ed., "Letters of the Gold Discovery."

112 *"the yellow fever":* Bancroft, *California Inter Pocula*, 122.

112 *arduous overland route:* John Haskell Kemble, ed., "Clipper Ships of the California Line," *Book Club of California Keepsake Series*, SCRC, UCL; Charles A. Dana, *The Life of Ulysses S. Grant* (Springfield, Mass.: Gurdon Bill, 1868), 34; Bancroft, *California Inter Pocula*, 124.

112 *"to protect the growing settlements":* Dana, *Life of Ulysses S. Grant*, 34; Albert D. Richardson, *A Personal History of Ulysses S. Grant* (Hartford, Conn.: American, 1868), 139, 142–43.

113 *"had been caught in the toils of matrimony":* Charles Pope, "The Eccentric Booths," March 27, 1897, EB Scrapbook B.7.6, FSL.

113 *"an absolute and unmitigated wonder":* Bancroft, *California Inter Pocula*, 264; Walter Leman, *Memories of an Old Actor* (San Francisco: A. Roman, 1886), 272; George MacMinn, *The Theater of the Golden Era in California* (Caldwell, Idaho: Caxton, 1941), 38; "Reminiscences of Edwin Booth's Early Days," n.d., in EB clippings, Theatre Collection, HL; Helen Throop Purdy, "Portsmouth Square," *California Historical Society Quarterly*, April 1924, 36.

113 *"The Booth Face":* EB to David C. Anderson, May 13, 1880, in Skinner, *The Last Tragedian*, 41; J. J. McCloskey, "Edwin Booth in Old California," *Green Book Album*, June 1911, 1322, EB clippings, Theatre Collection, HL; "Performances of Junius Brutus Booth, Jr.," *Sacramento Union*, August 21–22, 1851, KC.

114 *"The craving for excitement":* Bancroft, *California Inter Pocula*, 268; "Edwin Booth: End of a Notable Career," *San Francisco Examiner*, June 7, 1893, EB clippings, Theatre Collection, HL; Clarke, *The Elder and the Younger Booth*, extra-illustrated ed., printed insertion describing California journey, UIUC.

114 *The couple chose May 10:* "Tombs of the Booths," July 26, 1891, in Booth Family Scrapbook B.9.1, FSL; Clarke, *The Elder and the Younger Booth*, extra-illustrated ed., printed insertion at 113, UIUC; JBB to John Rogers, October 21, 1851, reproduced in Archer, *Theatrical Prometheus*, 198.

115 *the same man to design Ford's Theatre:* Sollers, "The Theatrical Career of John T. Ford," 44, 127; Archer, *Theatrical Prometheus*, 324.

115 *St. Timothy's Hall:* J. Appleton Wilson, "St. Timothy's Hall," *Baltimore Sun*, March 29, 1925, KC; Clarke, *The Unlocked Book*, 58.

115 *fencing and boxing "with skill and power":* Leman, *Memories of an Old Actor*, 273.

115 *"left me at home, in compliance":* EB, "Some Words about My Father," in Matthews and Hutton, eds., *Actors and Actresses*, vol. 3, 97; "Edwin Booth: End of a Notable Career," *San Francisco Examiner*.

116 *"While not [my father's] favorite":* EB, "Some Words about My Father," 97; Clarke, *The Elder and the Younger Booth*, extra-illustrated ed., 130–31, UIUC; "Record of Booth Performances in San Francisco," a list enclosed in Ferdinand C. Ewer to EB, October 16, 1877, FSL.

116 *"nursery of heroes":* Johannsen, *To the Halls of the Montezumas*, 44; Clarke, *The Unlocked Book*, 58.

116 *three-story brick edifice:* "St. Timothy's: An etching of the buildings and grounds," unidentified artist, n.d., KC; Wilson, "St. Timothy's Hall."

116 *"Something is rotten in the State of Denmark":* Clarke, *The Unlocked Book*, 60; Rhodehamel and Taper, eds., *The Writings of John Wilkes Booth*, 88.

117 *an uprising at St. Timothy's:* Clarke, *The Unlocked Book,* 60.

117 *The 1,250-ton behemoth:* Bancroft, *California Inter Pocula,* 124–25, 145; Leman, *Memories of an Old Actor,* 226–27; Richardson, *A Personal History of Ulysses S. Grant,* 139; Robert O'Brien, ed., "Bill of Fare for Pacific Mail Steamship, November 23, 1851," *Book Club of California Keepsake Series,* SCRC, UCL.

117 *calibrated scales:* Leman, *Memories of an Old Actor,* 231; Bancroft, *California Inter Pocula,* 144, 146.

118 *revived in a vat of ice:* Bancroft, *California Inter Pocula,* 144; Leman, *Memories of an Old Actor,* 228.

118 *A castle dating from the days of the conquistadors:* Bancroft, *California Inter Pocula,* 158, 155.

118 *Dumped unceremoniously:* Clarke, *The Elder and the Younger Booth,* extra-illustrated ed., printed insertion at 130, UIUC; Bancroft, *California Inter Pocula,* 172.

118 *upriver for two days and nights:* Richardson, *A Personal History of Ulysses S. Grant,* 140.

119 *local men armed with machetes:* Clarke, *The Elder and the Younger Booth,* extra-illustrated ed., printed insertion at 130, UIUC; Bancroft, *California Inter Pocula,* 175–76.

119 *"the comparative safety of Panama City":* Clarke, *The Elder and the Younger Booth,* extra-illustrated ed., printed insertion at 130, UIUC; description of Panama City in Bancroft, *California Inter Pocula,* 178–81.

119 *A typical dinner included fresh salmon:* Robert O'Brien, ed., "Bill of Fare for Pacific Mail Steamship," *Book Club of California Keepsake Series,* SCRC, UCL.

119 *On July 28, 1852:* "Record of Booth Performances in San Francisco," in Ferdinand C. Ewer to EB, October 16, 1877, FSL; "Reminiscences of Edwin Booth's Early Days," EB clippings, Theatre Collection, HL; McCloskey, "Edwin Booth in Old California," *Green Book Album,* June 1911, 1323–24, EB clippings, Theatre Collection, HL; Leman, *Memories of an Old Actor,* 239–40.

120 *"We all recognized the father":* McCloskey, "Edwin Booth in Old California," 1323.

120 *"No matter what happened":* MacMinn, *The Theater of the Golden Era in California,* 38.

120 *monstrosity of pink stone:* Lois Foster Rodecape, "Tom Maguire, Napoleon of the Stage," *California Historical Society Quarterly,* December 1941, 296.

120 *plans already had been made:* Barton Hill, "Personal Recollections of Edwin Booth," *New York Dramatic Mirror,* EB clippings, Theatre Collection, HL; Rodecape, "Tom Maguire, Napoleon of the Stage," 297.

120 *on July 29, 1852:* "Record of Booth Performances in San Francisco," in Ferdinand C. Ewer to EB, October 16, 1877, FSL; McCloskey, "Edwin Booth in Old California," 1323–24.

121 *"performed nightly":* "Record of Booth Performances in San Francisco"; Rodecape, "Tom Maguire, Napoleon of the Stage," 296.

121 *"seeming indifference":* EB, "Some Words about My Father," in Matthews and Hutton, eds., *Actors and Actresses,* vol. 3, 99; MacMinn, *The Theater of the Golden Era in California,* 38–39; Laurence Hutton, "Edwin Booth," *Harper's Weekly,* June 17, 1893, 578, EB clippings, HL.

121 *"seemed harsh":* Clarke, *The Elder and the Younger Booth,* extra-illustrated ed., insertion between 130–31, 132, UIUC.

122 *"a worn-out hat, short monkey-jacket":* "Reminiscences of Edwin Booth's Early Days"; Rodney Blake, "How Success First Came to Edwin Booth," *New York Theatre Magazine,* February 1913, EB clippings, Theatre Collection, HL; Clarke, *The Elder and the Younger Booth,* extra-illustrated ed., printed insertion at 132, UIUC.

122 *On October 1, 1852:* Hill, "Personal Recollections of Edwin Booth"; Clarke, *The Elder and the Younger Booth,* 104.

122 *Junius Brutus Booth was robbed:* "Tombs of the Booths," July 26, 1891, in Booth Family Scrapbook B.9.1, FSL.

123 *Booth performed at the St. Charles Theatre:* James H. Simpson, "Driftwood: The Story of the Death of the Elder Booth," *New York Dramatic Mirror,* July 31, 1880, UCL; Noah Ludlow to Mary Ann Holmes Booth, December 6, 1852, HL; "Mr. Booth," *New Orleans Times Picayune,* November 20, 1852, KC.

123 *"walking back and forth in the saloon":* Simpson, "Driftwood."

123 *On November 30, 1852:* Clarke, *The Elder and the Younger Booth,* 106.

124 *kept vigil by Booth's remains:* Clarke, *Personal Recollections of the Elder Booth,* 33, 35.

124 *"once seized with sickness":* Bancroft, *California Inter Pocula,* 186.

124 *"Recounting the circumstances":* Clarke, *Personal Recollections of the Elder Booth,* 32.

124 *"broken up forever":* Asia Booth Clarke to Jean Anderson, [n.d.] 1852 or 1853, copy courtesy of M. Kauffman, and L. Verge, director, SHM; "Inventory of the Estate of Junius Brutus Booth. December 30, 1852," KC; "Tombs of the Booths"; EB to Laurence Barrett, January 13, 1860, in Skinner, *The Last Tragedian,* 132–33.

125 *The pair sued Mary Ann for everything:* "Tombs of the Booths"; EB to Barrett, January 13, 1860, in Skinner, *The Last Tragedian,* 32; Clarke, *Personal Recollections of the Elder Booth,* 39.

125 *"with her own hands":* "Tombs of the Booths."

125 *"black-beaded Hamlet hauberk":* Skinner, *The Last Tragedian,* 146–47; "Costume Inventory," JBB Scrapbook, W.a.67, FSL.

125 *Though a crunching carpet of ice:* "Funeral of Mr. Booth," in JBB Scrapbook W.a.67, FSL; Clarke, *The Elder and the Younger Booth,* 107; telephone interview, December 7, 2009, with Tim Burke, superintendent of Baltimore Cemetery, to verify the lot card for the burial of the body of JBB in a plot next to his father, RB.

125 *the "matchless Booth":* Clarke, *Personal Recollections of the Elder Booth,* 32; "Tombs of the Booths"; "Mr. Booth," *New Orleans Times Picayune,* November 20, 1852, KC.

126 *Sixty thousand pieces of mail:* Bancroft, *California Inter Pocula,* 279, 272; Helen Throop Purdy, "Portsmouth Square," *California Historical Society Quarterly,* April 1924, 38.

126 *Mary Ann had one command:* "Early Wanderings," EB Scrapbook B.7.7, 20, FSL; Clarke, *The Elder and the Younger Booth,* 135.

126 *"on horseback, on muleback and sometimes on footback":* "Speech by David Anderson at Booth's Theatre, 1872," in Skinner, *The Last Tragedian,* 15; "Booth in California," *Boston Journal,* n.d., EB clippings, Theatre Collection, HL.

126 *"the audience":* William Cushing Bamburgh, *Tributes, Sketches, Souvenirs, Portraits, Memorials and Programmes of Edwin Thomas Booth, 1833–1893* (1905), extra-illustrated vol., 132, Theatre Collection, HL.

127 *Red Dog:* Rufus R. Wilson, "Booth's Young Days," *New York Advertiser,* June 3, 1894, EB clippings, Theatre Collection, HL; Blake, "How Success First Came to Edwin Booth"; Hutton, "Edwin Booth," *Harper's Weekly,* June 7, 1893, 578, EB clippings, Theatre Collection, HL.

127 *"What news is there?":* Hutton, "Edwin Booth," 578; Clarke, *The Elder and the Younger Booth,* 134.

127 *fifty miles through deep snow to Marysville:* Wilson, "Booth's Young Days"; EB to Adam Badeau, October 21, 1866, H-BTL.

127 *"I feel the deadness of an outcast soul":* EB to Adam Badeau, June 6, 1863, H-BTL.

127 *"considerably the worse for wear":* Wilson, "Booth's Young Days"; "Reminiscences of Edwin Booth's Early Days," n.d., EB clippings, Theatre Collection, HL.

128 *"power to win love":* Clara Morris, *Life on the Stage: My Personal Experience and Recollections* (London: Ibister, 1902), 162; Charles Pope, "The Eccentric Booths," March 27, 1897, EB Scrapbook B.7.6, FSL; McCloskey, "Edwin Booth in Old California," 1322.

128 *June's cottage overlooked Portsmouth Square:* Purdy, "Portsmouth Square," 36, 38–39; Clarke, *The Elder and the Younger Booth,* 134.

128 *"The native Indian":* Bancroft, *California Inter Pocula,* 234–35.

128 *thousands congregated in Portsmouth Square:* Purdy, "Portsmouth Square," 39; McCloskey, "Edwin Booth in Old California," 1325.

128 *He signed his younger brother on as a bit player:* "Reminiscences of Edwin Booth's Early Days"; Blake, "How Success First Came to Edwin Booth."

129 *"courteous and considerate":* McCloskey, "Edwin Booth in Old California," 1324; Wilson, "Booth's Young Days"; Clarke, *The Elder and the Younger Booth,* extra-illustrated ed., printed insertion at 138, UIUC; EB to David C. Anderson, "Doggerel Verse," n.d., H-BTL.

129 *his jeweled crown:* Clarke, *The Elder and the Younger Booth,* 101; "Notes on Edwin Booth's Early Professional Doings in California," in Ferdinand C. Ewer to EB, October 16, 1877, 6, FSL.

129 *Ferdinand Ewer, a Harvard-educated drama critic:* Charles H. Shattuck, "Edwin Booth's First Critic," *Theatre Survey,* May 1966, 2–3; Ferdinand C. Ewer to EB, October 16, 1877, 6, FSL.

130 *Ewer could be seen at work in a saloon:* Ferdinand C. Ewer to EB, October 16, 1877, 13, FSL.

130 *"blaze of genius":* Ferdinand C. Ewer to EB, October 16, 1877, 11, 20, FSL.

130 *"worthy to receive the mantle of the father":* Ferdinand C. Ewer to EB, October 16, 1877, 11, FSL.

CHAPTER SEVEN: BROTHER, YOU HAVE DONE ME WRONG

Page

131 *made the twenty-five-mile journey:* Badeau, *The Vagabond,* 348; Asia Booth Clarke to Jean Anderson, [n.d.] 1852, copy courtesy of M. Kauffman, and L. Verge, director, SHM; Clarke, *Personal Recollections of the Elder Booth,* 15, 26, 38–39; Clarke, *The Elder and the Younger Booth,* 106.

131 *line of telegraph poles:* JWB to T. William O'Laughlen, April 30, 1854 in Rhodehamel and Taper, eds., *The Writings of John Wilkes Booth,* 38.

131 *"Love is terrible":* Asia Booth Clarke to Jean Anderson, May 18, 1856, SHM.

132 *"some rock to break her heart upon":* Asia Booth Clarke to Jean Anderson, [n.d.] 1852, SHM.

132 *"sudden . . . dreadful affliction":* Mary Ann Holmes Booth to Noah Ludlow, December 24, 1852, HL; Clarke, *The Unlocked Book,* 70; Clarke, *The Elder and the Younger Booth,* 107.

132 *"monetary affairs":* Clarke, *The Unlocked Book,* 51.

132 *"painful":* Mary Ann Holmes Booth to Noah Ludlow, December 24, 1852, HL; EB to Laurence Barrett, January 13, 1860, reproduced in Skinner, *The Last Tragedian,* 132; JBB to RB, April 14, 1826, H-BTL; Clarke, *The Unlocked Book,* 74.

132 *Mary Ann found tenants:* "Inventory of the Estate of Junius Brutus Booth. December 30, 1852," KC; Asia Booth Clarke to Jean Anderson, [n.d.] 1852, SHM; Archer, *Theatrical Prometheus,* 78.

132 *metropolis of 170,000:* Barbara Jeanne Fields, *Slavery and Freedom on the Middle Ground: Maryland During the Nineteenth Century* (New Haven, Conn.: Yale University Press, 1985), 8–9; JBB to RB, December 1, 1822, H-BTL; Mrs. Elijah Rogers to William Stump Forwood, August 11, 1886, JBB family collection, LC.

133 *A formal dining room:* "Tudor Hall (undated engraving)," JBB Scrapbook, W.a.67, FSL; Clarke, *The Elder and the Younger Booth,* 113.

133 *dark moods predominated:* JBB to John Rogers, October 21, 1851, in Archer, *Theatrical Prometheus,* 198; Asia Booth Clarke to Jean Anderson, May 22, 1855, SHM; Clarke, *The Unlocked Book,* 70; "Examination of Joseph Adrian Booth Before Maj. Gen. [John A.] Dix, May 12, 1865," reproduced in Alford, ed., *John Wilkes Booth: A Sister's Memoir,* 138.

133 *nail a picture of Job:* Asia Booth Clarke to Jean Anderson, September 10, 1856, SHM; "Examination of Joseph Adrian Booth," in Alford, ed., *John Wilkes Booth: A Sister's Memoir*, 138.

133 *inhale the woodsy smells:* Clarke, *The Unlocked Book*, 73, 77, 60.

134 *"broken up forever":* Asia Booth Clarke to Jean Anderson, [n.d.] 1852, SHM.

134 *"When I was a little boy":* EB to Edwina Booth, February 5, 1872, in Edwina Booth Grossman, *Edwin Booth: Recollections by His Daughter*, 34; Clarke, *The Unlocked Book*, 60–61.

134 *cereal crops:* JBB to RB, June 15, 1825, and October 26, 1834, H-BTL; JBB, diary, July 14, 1832, H-BTL.

134 *The boys decided to build a cabin:* Clarke, *The Unlocked Book*, 61–62.

135 *Joseph, by contrast:* Photograph of Joseph Adrian Booth, Taper Collection, ALPLM; "Examination of Joseph Adrian Booth" in Alford, ed., *John Wilkes Booth: A Sister's Memoir*, 137–38; EB to David Anderson, September 9, 1877, H-BTL.

135 *a fast horse:* Clarke, *The Unlocked Book*, 106, 72.

135 *"engage in prayer for your conversion":* Clarke, *Personal Recollections of the Elder Booth*, 34–35.

136 *Many residents:* Mrs. Elijah Rogers to William Stump Forwood, August 11, 13, and 16, 1886, JBB family papers, LC; Cowell, *Thirty Years Passed Among the Players in England and America*, 73.

136 *"funny anecdotes":* Clarke, *The Unlocked Book*, 68; Clarke, *The Elder and the Younger Booth*, extra-illustrated ed., printed insertion at 92, UIUC.

136 *"only lies":* Clarke, *The Unlocked Book*, 68; Asia Booth Clarke to Jean Anderson, [n.d.] 1855, SHM.

137 *"salad[s] of beets and potatoes:* Asia Booth Clarke to Jean Anderson, September 10, 1856, SHM.

137 *"we have never owned a slave":* Clarke, *Personal Recollections of the Elder Booth*, 34–35, 14.

137 *"He delighted to seek out the destitute":* "Junius Brutus Booth," in Matthews and Hutton, eds. *Actors and Actresses*, vol. 3, 120, 122; Cowell, *Thirty Years Passed Among the Players in England and America*, 72–73.

137 *He offered the freezing men glasses of Madeira:* Clarke, *Personal Recollections of the Elder Booth*, 26.

137 *"little deeds of kindness":* "Junius Brutus Booth," in Matthews and Hutton, eds. *Actors and Actresses*, vol. 3, 119–20.

137 *"Please excuse me, Eliza":* Clarke, *Personal Recollections of the Elder Booth*, 14, 18.

138 *The actor officiated at the burials:* Clarke, *The Elder and the Younger Booth*, 68.

138 *full measure of a "Master's" due:* Clarke, *The Unlocked Book*, 63.

138 *"there were two Marylands":* Fields, *Slavery and Freedom on the Middle Ground*, 6.

138 *Conditions supporting slavery:* Fields, *Slavery and Freedom on the Middle Ground*, 5, 12.

138 *new source of cheap white labor:* Tyler Anbinder, *Nativism and Slavery: The Northern Know Nothings and the Politics of the 1850s* (New York: Oxford University Press, 1992), 3, 6–7.

138 *"If the ladies thought themselves too mighty good":* Clarke, *The Unlocked Book*, 63–64.

139 *"dirty British blood":* Clarke, *The Unlocked Book*, 65.

139 *a free black farmer named Stephen Hooper:* Clarke, *The Unlocked Book*, 96–97.

139 *Tensions between whites and blacks ran high:* Fields, *Slavery and Freedom on the Middle Ground*, 16, 24–26.

139 *"my bosom friend" and "my playmate":* JWB [Draft of a Speech, December 1860], in Rhodehamel and Taper, eds., *The Writings of John Wilkes Booth*, 64, 68.

139 *Gorsuch and his men approached the farmhouse:* Junius P. Rodriguez, ed., *Slavery in the United States: A Social, Political and Historical Encyclopedia*, vol. 1 (Santa Barbara, Calif.: ABC-CLIO, 2007), 222.

140 *"the agony of slavery's slow death, but not the deliverance":* Fields, *Slavery and Freedom on the Middle Ground*, 24.

140 *The Halls faced an impossible situation:* Stanley Kimmel, "Notes from two interviews with Joseph Edwin Hall, son of Joseph and Ann Hall, conducted November 3 & 19, 1935, in Bel Air, Maryland," KC; Mahoney, *Sketches of Tudor Hall*, 8, 10.

141 *In the spring of 1854:* JWB to T. William O'Laughlen, August 8, 1854, in Rhodehamel and Taper, eds., *The Writings of John Wilkes Booth*, 38.

141 *"very insolent":* Clarke, *The Unlocked Book*, 99–100.

141 *"I knocked him down":* JWB to T. William O'Laughlen, August 8, 1854, in Rhodehamel and Taper, eds., *The Writings of John Wilkes Booth*, 38.

141 *"he was killed and murdered":* Clarke, *The Unlocked Book*, 101–2.

142 *"gun, ride, sleep and eat":* JWB to T. William O'Laughlen, June 18, 1855, in Rhodehamel and Taper, eds., *The Writings of John Wilkes Booth*, 41.

142 *"with and without a saddle":* Clarke, *The Unlocked Book*, 76; Asia Booth Clarke to Jean Anderson, April 4, 1854, SHM; JWB to T. William O'Laughlen, June 18, 1855, in Rhodehamel and Taper, eds., *The Writings of John Wilkes Booth*, 41.

142 *Know-Nothing Party:* Anbinder, *Nativism and Slavery*, iv, xi; Clarke, *The Unlocked Book*, 105.

142 *Four hundred thousand émigrés landed:* Anbinder, *Nativism and Slavery*, 3, 8.

142 *"filth" that must be "washed":* Asia Booth Clarke to Jean Anderson, September 10, 1856, SHM; Anbinder, *Nativism and Slavery*, xiii.

143 *"the most monstrous and fatal":* Anbinder, *Nativism and Slavery*, 18.

143 *people settling Kansas:* Oswald Garrison Villard, *John Brown: A Biography Fifty Years After* (Boston: Houghton Mifflin, 1910), 265, 199, 90.

143 *paling into boredom:* JWB to T. William O'Laughlen, September 14, 1855, in Rhodehamel and Taper, eds., *The Writings of John Wilkes Booth*, 42; Anbinder, *Nativism and Slavery*, 23.

143 *a rally in November 1854:* JWB to T. William O'Laughlen, November 8, 1854, in Rhodehamel and Taper, eds., *The Writings of John Wilkes Booth*, 40; Clarke, *The Unlocked Book*, 106.

144 *"a man of letters":* Clarke, *The Unlocked Book*, 68, 70.

144 *"Truly we delved and worked like moles":* Clarke, *The Unlocked Book*, 70; Badeau, *The Vagabond*, 350.

145 *"morbid grief":* Clarke, *The Unlocked Book*, 69–70.

145 *"for the benefit of the Fund":* JBB playbill, January 27, 1824, Philadelphia Theatre, "The celebrated tragedy of Hamlet, Prince of Denmark, by Mr. Booth, who has volunteered his services on this occasion for the benefit of the Fund in Aid of the Greeks," JBB Scrapbook, W.a. 67, FSL.

145 *"spent many hours . . . reading aloud from Byron's poems":* Clarke, *The Unlocked Book*, 91; Marchand, *Byron*, 452–58.

145 *"crape [sic] on his arm thirty days for this poet":* Clarke, *Personal Recollections of the Elder Booth*, 39; Clarke, *The Unlocked Book*, 91, 76.

146 *"Mind happily belongs":* JBB, diary, May 1, 1839, H-BTL.

146 *"Our childhood was waning fast":* Clarke, *The Unlocked Book*, 92; Asia Booth Clarke to Jean Anderson, n.d. [1860], beginning "To think that my brother, the best beloved of all, should occasion these bitter tears," in Paul Amelia, "Highlights of Asia Booth Clarke's Letters to Jean Anderson," typescript (compiled September 5, 1979, from originals at the Peale Museum, Baltimore), H-BTL.

146 *a more immediate plan:* Clarke, *The Unlocked Book*, 107–8.

146 *"toggeries":* Badeau, *The Vagabond*, 353; "Costume Inventory," JBB Scrapbook, W.a.67, FSL; JBB costume jewelry and weaponry, H-BTL; EB costumes and Booth family makeup cases, Taper Collection, ALPLM.

147 *"my slow student":* Clarke, *The Unlocked Book*, 108; Badeau, "Edwin Booth On and Off the Stage: Personal Recollections," *McClure's Magazine*, August 1893, 262.

147 *"imbibed" all the works of Shakespeare:* Charles Pope, "The Eccentric Booths," March 27, 1897, EB Scrapbook B.7.6, FSL; EB performance of "Most Potent Grave and Reverend Signiors," *Othello* (1.3), in *Great Historical Shakespeare Recordings*, audio CD (Naxos, 2000).

148 *"Whether wrong or right":* Clarke, *The Unlocked Book*, 66.

148 *"intuitively made clear":* Clarke, *The Elder and the Younger Booth*, extra-illustrated ed., printed insertion at 130, UIUC.

149 *"How shall I ever have a chance on stage?":* Clarke, *The Unlocked Book*, 66; Asia Booth Clarke to Jean Anderson, [n.d.] March 1855, SHM.

149 *"at a time when $19 was thought ruinous":* "Reminiscences of Edwin Booth's Early Days," n.d., EB clippings, Theatre Collection, HL; "Edwin Booth: Experience of the Famous Actor in his Prentice Days," *Inter Ocean*, May 21, 1893, EB clippings, Theatre Collection, HL.

149 *famous British actress Laura Keene:* Vernanne Bryan, *Laura Keene: A British Actress on the American Stage* (Jefferson, N.C.: McFarland, 1997), 9, 14, 42, 71–72; Ben Graf Henneke, *Laura Keene: Actress, Innovator and Impresario: A Biography* (Tulsa, Okla.: Council Oak, 1990), 12, 16.

150 *"tall graceful body":* Eleanor McClatchy, ed., "Sacramento Theatre Benefit to Laura Keene: Pioneer Playbills," *Book Club of California Keepsake Series*, SCRC, UCL; Bryan, *Laura Keene*, 45–46; Constance Rourke, *Troupers of the Gold Coast* (New York: Harcourt, Brace, 1928), 59.

150 *"one of the handsomest fellows in the world":* McCloskey, "Edwin Booth in Old California," *Green Book Album*, June 1911, 1323, EB clippings, Theatre Collection, HL; Bryan, *Laura Keene*, 52–55.

150 *The seventy-two-day voyage:* William Stuart, "Reminiscences of the Early Days of Edwin Booth: Why Laura Keene's Trip to Australia Was a Failure," n.d., EB clippings, Theatre Collection, HL.

150 *Pirates attacked:* Clarke, *The Elder and the Younger Booth*, extra-illustrated ed., printed insertion at 140, UIUC.

151 *"lively and oblivious condition":* "Reminiscences of the Early Days of Edwin Booth: Why Laura Keene's Trip to Australia Was a Failure"; Bryan, *Laura Keene*, 57; "Miss Laura Keene, Mr. E. Booth and Mr. D. C. Anderson will make their first appearance Monday, October 23, 1854 at the Royal Victoria Theatre [Sydney, Australia]," EB playbills, H-BTL.

151 *"Edwin Booth and Laura Keene were never friends again":* "Reminiscences of the Early Days of Edwin Booth: Why Laura Keene's Trip to Australia Was a Failure"; Henneke, *Laura Keene*, 32.

151 *On Oahu, Edwin spent eight weeks:* "Speech by David Anderson, Booth's Theatre, 1872," in Skinner, *The Last Tragedian*, 16; Clarke, *The Elder and the Younger Booth*, 141.

151 *"their jet-black tresses":* Gay Wilson Allen, *Melville and His World* (New York: Viking, 1971), 61.

152 *"promises soon to be home":* Asia Booth Clarke to Jean Anderson, [n.d.] March 1855, SHM; Pope, "The Eccentric Booths."

152 *"take the position that should be his":* Clarke, *The Elder and the Younger Booth*, 143.

152 *"We came near to sickness through want":* Clarke, *The Unlocked Book*, 104, 103.

152 *Edwin Booth arrived:* Benjamin Baker, "Some Stories of Booth by His Old Manager," *Star*, September 5, 1886, printed material in Matthews and Hutton, eds., *Actors and Actresses*, extra-illustrated ed., TS931.2, Theatre Collection, HL; Clarke, *The Elder and the Younger Booth*, 145.

152 *a huge diamond pin:* Clarke, *The Elder and the Younger Booth*, 144; "Edwin Thomas Booth," unidentified newspaper, n.d., 1857, in Matthews and Hutton, eds., *Actors and Ac-*

tresses, extra-illustrated ed., TS931.2, Theatre Collection, HL; EB, "A Letter of Thanks to the Citizens of San Francisco," *Daily Alta California,* September 2, 1856, KC.

153 *"the esteem in which you are held":* "Resolution of the California State Legislature on the Departure of Edwin Thomas Booth," September 1, 1856, original at the California State Library in Sacramento, typescript at KC.

153 *the equivalent of twenty thousand dollars:* "Farewell Benefit for Edwin Booth . . . Positively His Last Appearance in San Francisco," *Daily Alta California,* September 3, 1856, KC; Clarke, *The Elder and the Younger Booth,* 144–45; Pope, "The Eccentric Booths."

154 *On August 14, 1855:* Gordon Samples, *Lust for Fame: The Stage Career of John Wilkes Booth* (Jefferson, N.C.: McFarland, 1982), 16; Sollers, "The Theatrical Career of John T. Ford," 50, 643–45.

154 *"worthy of wearing the mantle of his father":* Ferdinand C. Ewer to EB, October 16, 1877, 25, FSL; Clarke, *The Unlocked Book,* 107.

154 *"affectionate . . . toward his mother":* George Allen Townsend, *The Life, Crime and Capture of John Wilkes Booth* (New York: Dick & Fitzgerald, 1865), 20–21, SCRC, UCL.

CHAPTER EIGHT: A DELICATE AND TENDER PRINCE

Page

155 *William Wheatley's Arch Street Theatre: Wheatley's Gift: A neat and very attractive sheet furnishing playgoers at the Arch with something to read between acts,* January 1857, 1–4, Theatrical Periodicals, SCRC, UCL; "Our Theaters," *The Play-Goer and Theatrical Recorder,* February 4, 1858, Theatrical Periodicals, SCRC, UCL; Samples, *Lust for Fame,* 225.

155 *"Beauty, Grandeur and Great Acting":* "Advertisement to the Public," *Wheatley's Gift,* January 1857, 4, SCRC, UCL; J. M. Weston, *Lucretia Borgia, A Drama In Three Acts, adapted from the French of Victor Hugo* (Boston: W. V. Spencer, 1856), 1–5, 9, 10, SCRC, UCL.

156 *John Sleeper Clarke:* Mary Ann Holmes Booth to JBB, Jr., February 3, [1858], HL.

156 *"Wilkes induced J. S. Clarke":* Townsend, *The Life, Crime and Capture,* 21, SCRC, UCL.

157 *appeared in 165 performances:* "A Chronology of the Theatrical Performances of John Wilkes Booth," in Samples, *Lust for Fame,* 196–201.

157 *Supernumeraries, as a rule:* Kate Ryan, *Old Boston Museum Days* (Boston: Little, Brown, 1915), 62–65.

157 *tonight he would play Ascanio Petrucca:* "Cast of Characters," in Weston, *Lucretia Borgia,* n.p., SCRC, UCL; Edward Moore, *The Foundling: A Comedy; and The Gamester: A Tragedy,* A. Amberg, ed. (Newark: University of Delaware Press, 1996), 206, 256; Townsend, *The Life, Crime and Capture,* 21; Samples, *Lust for Fame,* 200.

157 *"studied faithfully":* Townsend, *The Life, Crime and Capture,* 21; Ryan, *Old Boston Museum Days,* 92.

157 *"a sure card":* Weston, *Lucretia Borgia,* 4; "Our Theatres," *The Play-Goer and Theatrical Recorder,* February 4, 1858, Theatrical Periodicals, SCRC, UCL.

158 *rival Walnut Street Theatre:* Howard Shapiro, "An Icon Unbowed: The Walnut Street Theatre's 200th Anniversary," *Philadelphia Inquirer,* February 1, 2009, clipping courtesy of Judith Callard; "Sour Grapes: The new drama *White Lies,*" *The Play-Goer and Theatrical Recorder,* February 4, 1858, Theatrical Periodicals, SCRC, UCL.

158 *threw out lures:* Samples, *Lust for Fame,* 196–201; *Wheatley's Gift,* January 1857, Theatrical Periodicals, SCRC, UCL.

158 *as vulgar as* Mazeppa: "Mazeppa at the Bowery," *The Play-Goer and Theatrical Recorder,* January 1, 1858, and William Wheatley, "A Hearty Laugh" and "Theatrical Amusements and Our Rigid Moralists," in *Wheatley's Gift,* January and February 1857, Theatrical Periodicals, SCRC, UCL; "Adah Isaacs Menken in Mazeppa, or, The Wild Horse of Tartary," collection of pioneer playbills, *Book Club of California Keepsake Series,* SCRC, UCL.

159 *"Nothing requires more labor":* William Wheatley, "Aspirations for the Stage," *Wheatley's Gift,* January 1857, Theatrical Periodicals, SCRC, UCL.

159 *supes earned about $300 per season:* Townsend, *The Life, Crime and Capture,* 22; Scott Derks, *The Value of a Dollar: Prices and Incomes in the United States, 1860–2004* (Millerton, N.Y.: Grey House, 2004), 9; Mary Ann Holmes Booth to JBB, Jr., Taper Collection, ALPLM.

159 *"generally to fall in with the sentiment of the crowd":* Townsend, *The Life, Crime and Capture,* 20–21; Handbill for Wheatley's Arch Street Theatre, Philadelphia [August 15, 1857], reproduced in Samples, *Lust for Fame,* 225; Ryan, *Old Boston Museum Days,* 21, 23, 136, 171.

160 *"all this detail was troublesome to the beginner":* Ryan, *Old Boston Museum Days,* 171; Townsend, *The Life, Crime and Capture,* 20.

160 *"lacked enterprise":* Townsend, *The Life, Crime and Capture,* 20–22.

161 *The moment "he made his reputation":* George Crutchfield to Edward V. Valentine, July 5, 1909, original at the Valentine Museum, Richmond, Va. transcript in KC; Charles F. Fuller, "Edwin and John Wilkes Booth: Actors at the Old Marshall Theatre in Richmond," *Virginia Magazine of History and Biography,* October 1971, 481, 483.

161 *"J. B. Wilkes":* Samples, *Lust for Fame,* 23, 200; "Properties and Costumes," in Weston, *Lucretia Borgia,* 6, 7; Skinner, *The Last Tragedian,* 146–47; Benjamin Baker, "Some Stories of Booth by His Old Manager," *Star,* September 5, 1886, printed material in Matthews and Hutton, eds., *Actors and Actresses of Great Britain and the United States,* extra-illustrated ed., TS931.2, Theatre Collection, HL.

162 *"My very name excites horror":* Weston, *Lucretia Borgia,* 17, 19, 24–26.

163 *"fresh from the mouths of actors":* Townsend, *The Life Crime and Capture,* 21.

163 *"We were all conscious of the audience":* Ryan, *Old Boston Museum Days,* 242; Townsend, *The Life, Crime and Capture,* 21.

163 *"Fate decrees it!":* Weston, *Lucretia Borgia,* 60.

164 *The next night, Wednesday:* Samples, *Lust for Fame,* 200; Moore, *The Foundling: A Comedy; and the Gamester: A Tragedy,* 204–5.

164 *"invited a lady he knew":* Townsend, *The Life, Crime and Capture,* 21; Ryan, *Old Boston Museum Days,* 242.

164 *"was animated by a pride":* John T. Ford, "Behind the Curtain of a Conspiracy," *North American Review,* April 1889, 485.

164 *"hisses and mock applause":* Townsend, *The Life, Crime and Capture,* 21.

165 *"I think John wishes he had been something else":* Mary Ann Holmes Booth to JBB, Jr., February 3, [1858], HL.

165 *"cut down the company":* Townsend, *The Life, Crime and Capture,* 24–25.

165 *"then the champion of the cue":* Pope, "The Eccentric Booths," *New York Sun,* March 27, 1897, EB Scrapbook B.7.6, FSL.

166 *two pieces of stone off the deck:* "A Monument Erected to the Memory of Junius Brutus Booth," newspaper clipping [1858], KC; Badeau, *The Vagabond,* 354.

166 *two coffins were transferred to a fresh plot:* Clarke, *The Elder and the Younger Booth,* 107–8; dates of interment, description of lot cards for the transfer of Booth bodies, and multiple photographs of the Booth obelisk and family grave markers provided by Dan Monahan, superintendent of the Greenmount Cemetery, Baltimore, in a telephone interview on September 16, 2009, and via e-mail on September 17, 2009; Archer, *Theatrical Prometheus,* 160.

166 *For the epitaph:* Badeau, *The Vagabond,* 354.

166 *"to fill the void":* Pope, "The Eccentric Booths"; Clarke, *The Elder and the Younger Booth,* 147.

167 *her death on March 9, 1858:* Burr, "Junius Brutus Booth's Wife Adelaide," *New York Press,* August 9, 1891, JBB family collection, LC; "Tombs of the Booths," newspaper clipping, July 26, 1891, in Booth Family Scrapbook B.9.1, FSL.

167 *7 North High Street:* to David C. Anderson, n.d., 1857, H-BTL; EB to JBB, Jr., October 31, 1858, HL; Mahoney, *Sketches of Tudor Hall*, 5.

168 *"My poor Mother!":* EB to Laurence Barrett, January 13, 1860, reproduced in Skinner, *The Last Tragedian*, 132–33.

168 *Edwin's money paid:* Badeau, "Edwin Booth On and Off the Stage: Personal Recollections," *McClure's Magazine*, August 1893, 261; EB to Laurence Barrett, January 13, 1860, in Skinner, *The Last Tragedian*, 132–33.

168 *Mary Ann denied the young actor's request:* Baker, "Some Stories of Booth by His Old Manager," *Star*, September 5, 1886, printed material in Matthews and Hutton, eds., *Actors and Actresses of Great Britain and the United States*, extra-illustrated ed., TS931.2, Theatre Collection, HL; EB to Nahum Capen, July 28, 1881, in Grossman, *Edwin Booth: Recollections by His Daughter*, 227–28.

169 *Laura was eager to hire Edwin:* Clarke, *The Elder and the Younger Booth*, 147; Baker, "Some Stories of Booth by His Old Manager," *Star*, September 5, 1886, printed material in Matthews and Hutton, eds., *Actors and Actresses of Great Britain and the United States*, extra-illustrated ed., TS931.2, Theatre Collection, HL.

169 *raked in well over $10,000:* EB to Laurence Barrett, January 13, 1860, reproduced in Skinner, *The Last Tragedian*, 132–33; Pope, "The Eccentric Booths," *New York Sun*, March 27, 1897, EB Scrapbook B.7.6, FSL.

169 *"The Inheritor of his Father's Genius":* Barton Hill, "Personal Recollections of Edwin Booth," *New York Dramatic Mirror*, n.d., EB clippings, Theatre Collection, HL; Clarke, *The Elder and the Younger Booth*, 150.

170 *"The nomadic season":* Ryan, *Old Boston Museum Days*, 28.

170 *"gut-shaking":* EB to Joseph Jefferson, April 26, 1857, reproduced in Bloom, *Joseph Jefferson: Dean of the American Theatre*, 67–68.

170 *"the widow of old Booth":* Baker, "Some Stories of Booth by His Old Manager."

170 *"not swallow the juice":* EB to Joseph Jefferson, April 26, 1857, in Bloom, *Joseph Jefferson*, 67; "Edwin Booth: An Early 'Barn-Storming' Expedition in Virginia and What Came of It," *Buffalo (N.Y.) Times*, n.d., EB clippings, Theatre Collection, HL.

171 *"Every man builds":* Clarke, *The Elder and the Younger Booth*, 149.

172 *Captain Adam Badeau:* James Grant Wilson and John Fiske, eds., *Appleton's Cyclopaedia of American Biography*, vol. 1 (New York: Appleton, 1888), 132; Allen Johnson, ed., *Dictionary of American Biography*, vol. 1 (New York: Charles Scribner's Sons, 1928) 485.

172 *"lazily lounging in the lobbies":* Badeau, *The Vagabond*, 28, 14, x; Adam Badeau to EB, June 15, 1857, H-BTL.

172 *Burton's Metropolitan:* Winter, *The Life and Art of Edwin Booth*, 21; Clarke, *The Elder and the Younger Booth*, 149–50; Badeau, "Edwin Booth On and Off the Stage."

173 *"I have been several times, of late":* Badeau, *The Vagabond*, 120, 122, 124.

173 *"never heard any sound short of thunder":* William Winter, *Shadows of the Stage* (New York: Macmillan, 1893), 67; Badeau, *The Vagabond*, 292.

174 *"The fact that I am a young man":* Adam Badeau to EB, June 15, 1857, H-BTL.

174 *"was not too conceited or too indifferent to learn":* Parke Godwin, "Commemorative Address," Program from the 60th Anniversary, 27; Badeau, "Edwin Booth On and Off the Stage," 256.

174 *"Ad" and "Ned":* Booth-Badeau correspondence, 1857–66, H-BTL; Badeau, "Edwin Booth On and Off the Stage," 259.

174 *Over the summer of 1857:* Badeau, "Edwin Booth On and Off the Stage," 259; Godwin, "Commemorative Address," 27.

175 *forced "Ned" to learn French:* Adam Badeau to EB, August 25, 1859, H-BTL; Badeau, "Edwin Booth On and Off the Stage," 260.

175 *the city "of Four Hundred"*: Hermione Lee, *Edith Wharton* (New York: Vintage, 2008), 24; Godwin, "Commemorative Address," 27; Badeau, "Edwin Booth On and Off the Stage," 260.

176 *crowned with laurel leaves:* Clarke, *The Elder and the Younger Booth*, 150; Adam Badeau to EB, October 7, 1858, H-BTL.

176 *Edwin fired Baker:* EB to JBB, Jr., October 31, 1858, HL; Adam Badeau to EB, October 7, 1858, H-BTL.

176 *"Ned, you are a prince":* Adam Badeau to EB, April 22, 1860, H-BTL; Adam Badeau to EB, October 7, 1858, H-BTL.

176 *a signet ring:* Adam Badeau to EB, January 18, [1860], H-BTL.

176 *Adam had free run:* Badeau, *The Vagabond*, 189–93; Badeau, "Edwin Booth On and Off the Stage," 259; EB to Adam Badeau, August 18, 1864, FSL.

177 *"fits of sadness":* Badeau, "Edwin Booth On and Off the Stage," 261.

177 *"Take nothing stronger than water":* Adam Badeau to EB, April 14, [no year], H-BTL; Adam Badeau to EB, April 21, 1859, H-BTL.

177 *"I cannot portray him":* Badeau, "Edwin Booth On and Off the Stage," 261.

177 *In the summer of 1858:* "A Night with the Booths," in Badeau, *The Vagabond*, 347–54; EB to David C. Anderson, [January 1857], H-BTL; Badeau, "Edwin Booth On and Off the Stage," 264.

178 *Ford and . . . Kunkel operated playhouses:* Sollers, "The Theatrical Career of John T. Ford," 2, 42; Charles F. Fuller, Jr., "Edwin Booth and John Wilkes Booth," *Virginia Magazine of History and Biography*, October 1971, 477.

178 *earned four dollars a week:* EB to JBB, Jr., December 12, 1858, HL; Mary Ann Holmes Booth to JBB, Jr., October 2, 1858, Taper Collection, ALPLM.

178 *"an ermine cloak that belonged to Macbeth":* Badeau, *The Vagabond*, 352, 351.

178 *"He was excessively handsome":* Badeau, "Edwin Booth On and Off the Stage," 264.

179 *John Wilkes Booth arrived in Richmond:* Fuller, "Edwin Booth and John Wilkes Booth," 481; Sollers, "The Theatrical Career of John T. Ford," 42.

179 *"We get along very well":* JWB to EB, September 10, 1858, reproduced in Rhodehamel and Taper, *The Writings of John Wilkes Booth*, 45.

179 *"loved him for his father's sake":* Clarke, *The Unlocked Book*, 11; Rhodehamel and Taper, *The Writings of John Wilkes Booth*, 45.

179 *"masses of crinoline":* Badeau, *The Vagabond*, 29; Townsend, *The Life, Crime and Capture*, 22.

180 *"happiness of master & of man":* Rhodehamel and Taper, *The Writings of John Wilkes Booth*, 62, 45.

180 *signed a lady's autograph album:* Ibid., 45–47; Townsend, *The Life, Crime and Capture*, 26.

180 *Edwin arrived by train:* "Newspaper notices [from the Richmond *Dispatch* and the Richmond *Whig*] for the 1858 engagements of Edwin Booth at the Marshall Theatre," in Fuller, "Edwin Booth and John Wilkes Booth," 479; Adam Badeau to EB, August 15, 1859, H-BTL; Ryan, *Old Boston Museum Days*, 180.

181 *"The audiences are large":* Mary Ann Holmes Booth to JBB, Jr., October 2, 1858, Taper Collection, ALPLM; Fuller, "Edwin Booth and John Wilkes Booth," 480, 483.

181 *"I don't think he will startle the world":* Francis Wilson, *Fact and Fiction of Lincoln's Assassination* (Boston: Houghton Mifflin, 1929), 17, SCRC, UCL.

182 *"to get into a N.Y. theater as soon as possible":* EB to Laurence Barrett, December 23, 1860, reproduced in Skinner, *The Last Tragedian*, 136–37; Clarke, *The Unlocked Book*, 111–12.

182 *Edwin Booth left Richmond:* Fuller, "Edwin Booth and John Wilkes Booth," 479; Wilson, *Fact and Fiction of Lincoln's Assassination*, 18.

182 *"benefit of J. Wilkes Booth":* "Announcement of John Wilkes and Edwin Booth in Othello,

Richmond Theatre," *Richmond Dispatch*, May 2, 1859, reproduced in Samples, *Lust for Fame*, 33.

183 *"one of Edwin Booth's masterpieces":* John Ranken Towse, *Sixty Years of the Theater: An Old Critic's Memories* (New York: Funk & Wagnalls, 1916), 190–91.

183 *"I think he's done well, don't you?":* Fuller, "Edwin Booth and John Wilkes Booth," 481.

183 *"Send word to your brother not to smash it":* Adam Badeau to EB, November 12, 1859, H-BTL.

CHAPTER NINE: DESTRUCTION, DEATH, AND MASSACRE

Page

184 *two hundred and fifty thousand people:* Henneke, *Laura Keene*, 144.

184 *Her mastery of every aspect:* John Creahan, *The Life of Laura Keene: Actress, Artist, Manager and Scholar* (Philadelphia: Rodgers, 1897), 102–03, 128–34; Henneke, *Laura Keene*, 89–91; Bryan, *Laura Keene*, 83–84.

184 *Pranksters broke into her playhouse:* Bryan, *Laura Keene*, 64, 71–72; Henneke, *Laura Keene*, 60, 64–65.

185 *"The fair and talented directress":* "Laura Keene's Varieties," *The Programme: A Journal of the Drama, Music, Literature and Art*, December 10, 1860, Z.e.24, FSL.

185 *"a miracle of Rubbish":* Bryan, *Laura Keene*, 74; "Laura Keene's Varieties," *The Programme*, November 26, 1860, Z.e.24, FSL.

185 *"finely-shaped legs":* Henneke, *Laura Keene*, 157.

185 *"Uncle Sam's Magic Lantern":* "Laura Keene's Varieties," *The Programme*, February 16, 1861, Z.e.24, FSL.

185 *parade of the American states:* Playbill for *The Seven Sisters*, with "A Synopsis of Scenery and Incidents," May 16, 1861, reproduced in Henneke, *Laura Keene*, 144.

186 *"must be seen to be believed":* Playbill for *The Seven Sisters*; Henneke, *Laura Keene*, 157.

186 *October afternoon in 1854:* Abraham Lincoln, *Abraham Lincoln: His Speeches and Writings*, Roy P. Basler, ed. (New York: Da Capo, 1990), 324–25; Julia Ward Howe, *Reminiscences, 1819–1899* (New York: Negro Universities Press, 1969), 272.

187 *Douglas was sitting in the audience:* Lincoln, *His Speeches and Writings*, 324, 310.

187 *the night of May 24, 1856:* Oswald Garrison Villard, *John Brown: 1800–1859; A Biography Fifty Years After* (Boston: Houghton Mifflin, 1910), 155–63.

187 *"galvanized corpse":* Shelby Foote, *The Civil War: Fort Sumter to Perryville* (New York: Vintage, 1986), 40; John A. Garraty and Jerome L. Sternstein, eds., *Encyclopedia of American Biography* (New York: Harper & Row, 1974), 1077.

187 *the Dred Scott case:* Garraty and Sternstein, eds., *Encyclopedia of American Biography*, 974, 1077–78.

188 *It was not until August 1861:* Henneke, *Laura Keene*, 146; Villard, *John Brown*, 426.

188 *Green Peace estate:* "Residence of Dr. S. G. Howe," in Laura E. Richards, *Stepping Westwards* (New York: Appleton, 1931), illustration facing 48; Laura E. Richards, *Samuel Gridley Howe* (New York: Appleton, 1935), 182–83.

189 *Dr. Samuel Gridley Howe and his wife, Julia:* Richards, *Samuel Gridley Howe*, 134; Julia Ward Howe, *Reminiscences*, 3, 13, 81, 84; Villard, *John Brown*, 56.

189 *Edwin Booth made his way to Green Peace:* EB to JBB, Jr., October 31, 1858, HL; Florence Marion Howe Hall, "The Friendship of Edwin Booth and Julia Ward Howe," *New England Magazine*, November 1893, 316, EB clippings, HL.

189 *"modest, intelligent, and above all, genuine":* Howe, *Reminiscences*, 237, 241.

189 *"the one who wished to be a savior":* Howe, *Reminiscences*, 253–54; Julia Ward Howe, *Memoir of Dr. Samuel Gridley Howe* (Boston: Albert J. Wright, 1876), 44–45.

190 *"In the beauty of the lilies":* "The Battle Hymn of the Republic," facsimile of first draft, in Howe, *Reminiscences,* 276–77.

190 *"was one of the first men to prophesy":* Howe, *Reminiscences,* 3–4.

191 *"young ladyhood":* Howe, *Reminiscences,* 44–46, 15–16.

191 *"I lived much in my books":* Howe, *Reminiscences,* 48–49.

191 *"passionate fondness":* Ibid., 78, 60.

192 *"a noble rider on a noble steed":* Richards, *Samuel Gridley Howe,* 134, 146; Howe, *Reminiscences,* 83.

192 *Samuel Howe had an early start:* Richards, *Samuel Gridley Howe,* 1, 5, 7, 9; Maud Howe Elliott, *Lord Byron's Helmet* (Boston: Houghton Mifflin, 1927), 10–13, 23–26.

192 *"one of the small guerrilla bands":* Richards, *Samuel Gridley Howe,* 13.

193 *"The sight of any being in human shape":* Richards, *Samuel Gridley Howe,* 144, 88.

193 *short for "Chevalier":* Richards, *Samuel Gridley Howe,* 180–81, 185–86.

193 *not an easy marriage:* Richards, *Samuel Gridley Howe,* 178–79, 135; Howe, *Reminiscences,* 169–70, 213–14; Julia Ward Howe, diary, April 23, 1865, bMS Am 2119 (1107), HL.

194 *"lamentably deficient in household skills":* Howe, *Reminiscences,* 213–14, 216–17.

194 *chairman of Boston's Vigilance Committee:* Richards, *Samuel Gridley Howe,* 193–94.

194 *"I had supposed the abolitionists":* Howe, *Reminiscences,* 152, 154.

194 *"the conscience of the North":* Ibid., 252–53; Howe, *Memoir of Dr. Samuel Gridley Howe,* 43–44.

195 *Massachusetts Kansas Committee:* Richards, *Samuel Gridley Howe,* 209; Villard, *John Brown,* 80.

195 *Brown and five of his sons:* Villard, *John Brown,* 79, 81.

195 *"Blow them to hell":* Villard, *John Brown,* 145, 82, 83.

195 *"My father was":* Richards, *Samuel Gridley Howe,* 130; Howe, *Reminiscences,* 177, 179.

196 *"I saw my . . . brother lying dead":* Villard, *John Brown,* 160, 154, 358.

196 *"to the bivouac by night":* Howe, *Reminiscences,* 85; Samuel Gridley Howe to Charles Sumner, July 31, 1865, in Richards, *Samuel Gridley Howe,* 211–12.

197 *"travers[ing] the whole length of the State of Iowa":* Richards, *Samuel Gridley Howe,* 210.

197 *He would make one more trip:* Ibid., 212; Laura E. Richards and Maud Howe Elliott, *Julia Ward Howe, 1819–1910,* vol. 1 (Boston: Houghton Mifflin, 1916), 168–69.

197 *"to bring on righteous and necessary war":* Villard, *John Brown,* 180, 166–67; Howe, *Reminiscences,* 218.

198 *"band of 100 volunteers":* Villard, *John Brown,* 268.

198 *"perfect transcendentalist":* Ibid., 273, 398, 275, 51.

198 *The three men held a conference:* Richards, *Samuel Gridley Howe,* 214, 242–43; Villard, *John Brown,* 271–76.

198 *establish a secret committee:* Frank B. Sanborn to Thomas Wentworth Higginson, September 11, 1857, in Villard, *John Brown,* 303, 272, 528–31.

199 *"I consider it my duty":* Villard, *John Brown,* 375, 303.

199 *In February and March 1858:* Ibid., 531, 324–25, 340, 396.

199 *Brown hoped the raid would accomplish:* Ibid., 332; Howe, *Memoir of Dr. Samuel Gridley Howe,* 10; Howe, *Reminiscences,* 255; Richards, *Samuel Gridley Howe,* 12–17, 23, 31–32, 214, 226.

199 *The Allegheny range:* Saul B. Cohen, ed., *The Columbia Gazetteer of the World,* vol. 1 (New York: Columbia University Press, 1998), 72, 376; "Map of Harper's Ferry," in United States Army Corps of Engineers, *Military Maps Illustrating the Operations of the Armies of the Potomac and the James, May 4, 1864 to May 9, 1865,* David Rumsey Historical Map Collection, Harvard Library; G. L. Gillespie, *Upper Potomac from McCoy's Ferry to Conrad's Ferry and Adjacent portions of Maryland and Virginia* (NY: Julius Bien, 1865), David Rumsey Historical Map Collection, Harvard Library; Howe, *Reminiscences,* 255.

200 *"to evade responsibility":* Villard, *John Brown,* 341–42.

200 *"In every word and every gesture":* Howe, *Reminiscences,* 237; Florence Marion Howe Hall, "The Friendship of Edwin Booth and Julia Ward Howe," *New England Magazine,* November 1893, 316–17, EB clippings, HL.

200 *Adam Badeau was a friend of Julia Howe:* EB to Julia Ward Howe, September 24, 1865, bMS AM 2119 (65), HL; EB to Adam Badeau [concerning Badeau's friendship with Julia Ward Howe], September 26 and November 1, 1863, H-BTL; Badeau, *The Vagabond,* 332.

201 *"Booth party":* Richards and Elliott, *Julia Ward Howe,* 205; Howe, *Reminiscences,* 174; Badeau, *The Vagabond,* 332; Mary Devlin Booth to Elizabeth Stoddard, December 13, 1862, in L. Terry Oggel, ed., *The Letters and Notebooks of Mary Devlin Booth* (New York: Greenwood, 1987), 86–87.

201 *"I have serious notions":* EB to JBB, Jr., October 31, 1858, HL.

202 *Brown, using the alias of "Mr. Smith":* Villard, *John Brown,* 402, 404–5, 418.

202 *"my invisibles":* "Recollections of Mrs. Annie Brown Adams" and "John Brown's Men-at-Arms," in Villard, *John Brown,* 417–49, 678–87.

203 *"one of the most stupendous scenes":* Villard, *John Brown,* 426–28.

203 *Morse code message to Baltimore:* Ibid., 434, 431.

204 *Hundreds of men organized themselves:* Ibid., 444, 449–50.

204 *"a secret association":* Ibid., 410.

204 *On the evening of October 17:* Howe, *Reminiscences,* 255; Richards and Elliott, *Julia Ward Howe,* 178; "Probable Hoax?," *Boston Evening Transcript,* October 17, 1859, WL.

205 *"Brown has got to work":* Howe, *Reminiscences,* 255.

205 *By October 25, Samuel Gridley Howe:* Villard, *John Brown,* 530–32; Richards, *Samuel Gridley Howe,* 216–17; Julia Ward Howe to [her sister Anna], November 6, 1859, reproduced in Richards and Elliott, *Julia Ward Howe,* 176–77.

205 *Stuart discovered "a carpet-bag":* Villard, *John Brown,* 467; Richards, *Samuel Gridley Howe,* 215.

206 *Julia Ward Howe stayed with her children:* Richards and Elliott, *Julia Ward Howe,* 176–77; Villard, *John Brown,* 465.

206 *It was a "very sad" time:* Howe, *Reminiscences,* 256; Julia Ward Howe, "Hamlet at The Boston," *Atlantic Monthly,* February 1860, 173.

206 *Booth opened at the Boston Museum:* Richards and Elliott, *Julia Ward Howe,* 177; Howe, "Hamlet at The Boston," 172–74.

206 *with the help of some of Harvard:* Villard, *John Brown,* 532, 341.

CHAPTER TEN: PREPARE FOR YOUR EXECUTION

Page

208 *After sunset on November 19, 1859:* "Affairs at Charlestown," *Richmond (Va.) Dispatch,* November 23, 1859, KC; "The Life of Philip Whitlock, Written by Himself," unpublished MS, 36, BAMA; George W. Libby, "John Brown and John Wilkes Booth," *Confederate Veteran,* April 1930, 138–39, SCRC, UCL.

208 *the Richmond Grays, the Richmond Blues:* "Affairs at Charlestown," *Richmond (Va.) Dispatch,* November 23, 1859, KC; Libby, "John Brown and John Wilkes Booth," 138–39.

208 *"Large forces of desperadoes from North":* Villard, *John Brown,* 524–25; "Affairs at Charlestown," *Richmond (Va.) Dispatch.*

209 *his minor part in* Timothy Toodles: Samples, *Lust for Fame,* 208; George Crutchfield to Edward V. Valentine, July 5, 1909, original at the Valentine Museum, Richmond, Va., copy in KC.

209 *Crossing Broad Street:* Libby, "John Brown and John Wilkes Booth," 138–39.

210 *"exceedingly companionable":* John M. Berron, "John Wilkes Booth in His Days as an

Actor: Reminiscences," newspaper clipping, March 17, 1907, KC; Edward M. Alfriend, "Recollections of John Wilkes Booth," newspaper clipping, KC.

210 *a "winning personality":* Libby, "John Brown and John Wilkes Booth," 138–39.

210 *"rarely missed" a chance to see Shakespeare:* "The Life of Philip Whitlock, Written By Himself," 38, 37.

210 *detachment of U.S. Marines:* Glenn Tucker, "John Wilkes Booth at the John Brown Hanging," *Lincoln Herald*, Spring 1976, 5; Libby, "John Brown and John Wilkes Booth," 138–39.

210 *"the very graveyards were invaded":* Villard, *John Brown*, 547; Libby, "John Brown and John Wilkes Booth," 138–39.

211 *"Nearly every night before taps":* Alfriend, "Recollections of John Wilkes Booth."

211 *volleys of "bombs and hand-grenades":* Villard, *John Brown*, 517, 512.

211 *admitted feeling kindly toward him:* Ibid., 547–49; Howe, *Reminiscences*, 256.

212 *"form a hollow square":* Libby, "John Brown and John Wilkes Booth," 138–39.

212 *December 2, arrived:* Frank E. Vandiver, *Mighty Stonewall* (New York: McGraw-Hill, 1957), 125.

212 *had been awake since dawn:* Villard, *John Brown*, 553–54; "The Life of Philip Whitlock, Written By Himself," 37.

212 *the sight of Brown "vainly" peering:* Clarke, *The Unlocked Book*, 113.

212 *"heroic courage, sublime defiance":* Godwin, "Commemorative Address," Program from the 60th Anniversary, November 13, 1893, 35.

213 *A story Junius Brutus Booth told:* JBB, entry for August 17, 1814, in 1814–15 travel journal, H-BTL; Clarke, *The Elder and the Younger Booth*, extra-illustrated ed., insertion between 8 and 9, UIUC.

213 *John Brown behaved differently:* Vandiver, *Mighty Stonewall*, 126.

213 *"So perish all such enemies of Virginia!":* Villard, *John Brown*, 557; "The Life of Philip Whitlock, Written By Himself," 37–38.

214 *December 4, the Grays rolled back:* "Soldiers Returned—The Richmond Grays and Company F Returned from Charlestown," *Richmond (Va.) Dispatch*, December 5, 1859, KC.

214 *Kunkel castigated John:* Alfriend, "Recollections of John Wilkes Booth."

214 *"A large contingent of the First Virginia Regiment":* Alfriend, "Recollections of John Wilkes Booth"; Samples, *Lust for Fame*, 43.

215 *home was no longer Tudor Hall:* Asia Booth Clarke to Jean Anderson, October 28, 1860, copy courtesy of M. Kauffman, and L. Verge, director, SHM.

215 *his baggage stuffed with photographs and souvenirs:* Clarke, *The Unlocked Book*, 113–14; Mary Devlin to EB, November 28, 1859, in Oggel, ed., *The Letters and Notebooks of Mary Devlin Booth*, 22.

215 *"I fear the discipline is hardly severe enough":* Mary Devlin to EB, November 28, 1859, in Oggel, ed., *The Letters and Notebooks of Mary Devlin Booth*, 22.

215 *Only Asia was willing to hear:* Clarke, *The Unlocked Book*, 113–14; Villard, *John Brown*, 467.

216 *"one of the party going to search for":* Clarke, *The Unlocked Book*, 113; Valentine, "My Recollections of Booth," October 6, 1891, MS, facsimile copy, KC.

216 *a portrait of George Washington:* Clarke, Booth Memorials, 16; Clarke, *Personal Recollections of the Elder Booth*, 37–39; Maud Howe Elliott, *Lord Byron's Helmet*, 24–25.

216 *Around the picture's frame:* "The wreath of laurel you crowned me with is hanging above a portrait of myself, as green and fresh-looking as it was when you placed it on my brow," EB wrote from his mother's house to an admirer, "I have placed your letter, with others I prize highly, in a book I have for the purpose." See EB to Madame [?], June 18, 1859, bMS Thr 467, Theater Collection, HL.

216 *"more than the fame or pecuniary success":* EB to Madame [?], June 18, 1859, bMS Thr 467, HL.

217 *"had become the most popular tragedian":* Clarke, *The Elder and the Younger Booth*, 152; Mrs. Thomas Bailey Aldrich, *Crowding Memories* (Boston: Houghton Mifflin, 1920), 6.

217 *"merry, cheerful and boyish":* Clarke, *The Elder and the Younger Booth*, 145; Aldrich, *Crowding Memories*, 5.

217 *sent his older brother four thousand dollars:* EB to Laurence Barrett, January 13, 1860, in Skinner, *The Last Tragedian*, 133; JBB, Jr., to EB, October 20, 1862, H-BTL; William A. Howell, "Memories of Wilkes Booth: An Old Associate's Recollections of the Trying Days of '60 and '61," *Baltimore Sun*, n.d., KC; "Examination of Joseph Adrian Booth Before Major Gen. John A. Dix," in Alford, ed., *John Wilkes Booth: A Sister's Memoir*, 135; Clarke, *The Elder and the Younger Booth*, extra-illustrated ed., insertion at 146, UIUC.

218 *"I married to please [Edwin]":* Asia Booth Clarke to Jean Anderson, n.d., 1860, copy courtesy of M. Kauffman and L. Verge, director, SHM; "Married. On the 28th ultimo at St. Paul's Church . . . Miss Asia Booth, daughter of the late Junius B. Booth," *Baltimore American*, May 2, 1859, KC; Clarke, *The Unlocked Book*, 110.

218 *He had asked Edwin in February:* Mary Devlin to EB, March 1, 1860, in Oggel, ed., *The Letters and Notebooks of Mary Devlin Booth*, 44.

218 *"to take his initiation":* Pope, "The Eccentric Booths," *New York Sun*, March 27, 1897, EB Scrapbook B.7.6, FSL; Clarke, *The Unlocked Book*, 110–11.

218 *Booth refused to accept the idea:* John M. Berron, "John Wilkes Booth in His Days as an Actor: Reminiscences," newspaper clipping, March 17, 1907, KC.

218 *"nature's own legacy":* Clarke, *The Unlocked Book*, 111.

219 *"There's no home for me":* EB to JBB, Jr., October 31, 1858, HL; JBB, Jr., to EB, October 20, 1862, H-BTL.

219 *"He never wanted to try to rival Edwin":* Clarke, *The Unlocked Book*, 107.

220 *"felt it rather premature that Edwin":* Ibid., 111–12, 122.

220 *Reputations could not be won easily:* EB to Laurence Barrett, December 23, 1860, reproduced in Skinner, *The Last Tragedian*, 136–37; John Ripley, " 'We Are Not in Little England Now': Charles and Ellen Kean in Civil War America," *Theatre Notebook*, 61, no. 2 (2007), 83; Arthur Nussbaum, *A History of the Dollar* (New York: Columbia University Press, 1957), 88–89, 97–101, 123; Derks, *The Value of a Dollar: Prices and Incomes in the United States, 1860–2004*, 379.

220 *"You must not think me childish":* JWB to JBB, Jr., January 17, 1865, in Rhodehamel and Taper, *The Writings of John Wilkes Booth*, 132.

221 *giving John Wilkes half the United States:* Clarke, *The Unlocked Book*, 112; Godwin, "Commemorative Address," 26–27.

221 *"silent bitterness":* "Edwin Booth's Real Self, by An Intimate for Twenty-Five Years," *New York Theatre Magazine*, December 1916, EB clippings, Theater Collection, HL.

221 *"rendered me prematurely old":* EB to Walter [Brackett], September 12, [1859], HL; Asia Booth Clarke to Jean Anderson, n.d., 1860, in Paul Amelia, "Highlights of Asia Booth Clarke's Letters to Jean Anderson," typescript (compiled September 5, 1979, from originals at the Peale Museum, Baltimore), H-BTL.

222 *"beginning to show some of the eccentric habits":* Pope, "The Eccentric Booths," *New York Sun*, March 27, 1897, EB Scrapbook B.7.6, FSL; EB to Walter [Brackett], September 12, [1859], HL.

222 *"exquisite personality":* Florence Marion Howe Hall, "The Friendship of Edwin Booth and Julia Ward Howe," *New England Magazine*, November 1893, 317, EB clippings, Theater Collection, HL.

222 *large family of Irish immigrants:* "The Devlin Family" in Oggel, ed., *The Letters and Notebooks of Mary Devlin Booth*, xxi–xxii; Bloom, *Joseph Jefferson*, 57, 62.

223 *"I [have] lost my heart":* EB to Walter [Brackett], September 12, [1859], HL; EB to JBB, Jr., December 12, 1858, HL.

223 *"For once the mimic scene":* Hall, "The Friendship of Edwin Booth and Julia Ward Howe," 317.

223 *"lay desperate siege":* Pope, "The Eccentric Booths"; Mary Devlin to EB, October 11 and 13, 1859, BRTD, NYPL.

224 *"Think over the future":* Mary Devlin to EB, August 24, 1859, BRTD, NYPL.

224 *"entirely given up":* Asia Booth Clarke to Jean Anderson, October 28, 1860, in Amelia, "Highlights of Asia Booth Clarke's Letters to Jean Anderson."

224 *"I have seen for some time":* Adam Badeau to EB, April 22, 1860, H-BTL.

224 *"I had almost vowed I would never marry . . . an actress":* EB to Walter [Brackett], September 12, [1859], HL.

225 *She gave her last performance:* "Mary Devlin Booth Chronology," in Oggel, *The Letters and Notebooks of Mary Devlin Booth*, x; Mary Devlin to EB, n.d. [letter beginning, "The door has but closed upon you, and I have hastened to my room, to write what Mr. Badeau's presence forbade me speaking . . ."], BRTD, NYPL.

225 *"Ah, you do not know how close a* critic": Mary Devlin to EB, January 24, 1860, in Oggel, *The Letters and Notebooks of Mary Devlin Booth*, 31.

225 *Adam Badeau was a frequent visitor:* Mary Devlin to EB, December 28, 1859, in Oggel, *The Letters and Notebooks of Mary Devlin Booth*, 27–29.

225 *On the afternoon of July 7, 1860:* William Winter, *Life and Art of Edwin Booth* (New York: Macmillan, 1893), 22.

226 *"My head is full of 'Marry Mary-marry-marriage' ":* EB to Richard F. Cary, June 30, 1860, in Grossman, *Edwin Booth: Recollections by His Daughter*, 131.

226 *"a simple ceremony":* Badeau, "Edwin Booth On and Off the Stage: Personal Recollections," *McClure's*, August 1893, 263.

226 *Asia Booth Clarke had boycotted:* Asia Booth Clarke to Jean Anderson, letters beginning "Thursday 1860 [n.d.]" and "To think that my brother, the best beloved of all, should occasion these bitter tears," in Amelia, "Highlights of Asia Booth Clarke's Letters to Jean Anderson."

226 *"Her family are of the lowest Irish class":* Asia Booth Clarke to Jean Anderson, [n.d.] letter beginning, "To think that my brother, the best beloved of all, should occasion these bitter tears," in Amelia, "Highlights of Asia Booth Clarke's Letters to Jean Anderson."

227 *"he was most anxious to show me":* Badeau, "Edwin Booth On and Off the Stage," 263.

227 *Matthew Canning:* Townsend, *The Life, Crime and Capture*, 23; Pope, "The Eccentric Booths," March 27, 1897; William Warren Rogers, Jr., *Confederate Home Front: Montgomery During the Civil War* (Tuscaloosa: University of Alabama Press, 1999), 6–7.

227 *"touched the trigger and it exploded":* Samples, *Lust for Fame*, 47; John M. Berron, "John Wilkes Booth in His Days as an Actor: Reminiscences," newspaper, March 17, 1907, KC; "John Wilkes Booth's 1860–1861 Starring Tour," *New York Clipper*, April 22, 1865, KC; newspaper accounts of JWB at Columbus, Georgia, in October 1860, the Alonzo May MS, transcript (original at the Peale Museum, Baltimore), KC.

227 *"still carrie[d] the ball in him":* Asia Booth Clarke to Jean Anderson, December 16, 1860, in Amelia, "Highlights of Asia Booth Clarke's Letters to Jean Anderson"; newspaper accounts of JWB at Columbus, Georgia, in October 1860, KC.

227 *On October 21 or 22:* Samples, *Lust for Fame*, 47, 211–12; Rogers, *Confederate Home Front*, 49, 10.

228 *The Alabama State House: Market Street scene, looking toward the capitol from the Artesian Basin, 1861*, reproduced in Rogers, *Confederate Home Front*, 2; see also Rogers, *Confederate Home Front*, 3, 9, 10, 8.

228 *"On quiet nights the houses are great":* Ripley, "We Are Not in Little England Now," *Theatre Notebook* 61, no. 2 (2007), 93; Rogers, *Confederate Home Front*, 16–18, 6–7.

229 *"If they would listen":* Lincoln, *His Speeches and Writings,* 524, 532, 533–34, 535.

229 *But his violent deed succeeded:* Lincoln, *His Speeches and Writings,* 529; Villard, *John Brown,* 475–76.

229 *William Lowndes Yancey:* David R. Barbee and Milledge L. Bonham, Jr., "The Montgomery Address of Stephen Douglas," *Journal of Southern History* (November 1939), 527; Rogers, *Confederate Home Front,* 11–12, 15.

229 *Dred Scott decision:* Foner and Garraty, eds., *The Reader's Companion to American History,* 295–96; Lincoln, *His Speeches and Writings,* 536.

230 *"itinerant peddler of Yankee notions":* Robert W. Johannsen, *Stephen A. Douglas* (New York: Oxford University Press, 1973), 798, 799.

230 *He would not attempt acting until October 29:* Kimmel, *The Mad Booths of Maryland,* 157; Samples, *Lust for Fame,* 212; Rogers, *Confederate Home Front,* 17.

230 *"no form of appeal or invective":* Johannsen, *Stephen Douglas,* 800.

231 *Douglas arrived by steamboat:* Barbee and Bonham, Jr., "The Montgomery Address of Stephen Douglas," 527; Johannsen, *Stephen Douglas,* 798, 801.

231 *townspeople hurled rotten eggs and tomatoes:* Barbee and Bonham, Jr., "The Montgomery Address of Stephen Douglas," 527; Johannsen, *Stephen Douglas,* 800.

231 *Reviews of his six-night run were tepid:* Samples, *Lust for Fame,* 49.

231 *at noon on November 2:* Barbee and Bonham, Jr., "The Montgomery Address of Stephen Douglas," 528–29, 536, 548–49, 551–52; JWB, "[Draft of a Speech] Philadelphia, late December 1860," in Rhodehamel and Taper, *The Writings of John Wilkes Booth,* 55, 59.

231 *"Well, if Lincoln is elected":* Johannsen, *Stephen Douglas,* 801.

231 *"the horrors of revolution, anarchy and bankruptcy":* Ibid., 807; Barbee and Bonham, Jr., "The Montgomery Address of Stephen Douglas," 536, 529, 551.

232 *son and grandson of men who had idolized the Union:* Clarke, *Booth Memorials,* 15–16, 80; "Independence Day Toasts," *Richmond (Va.) Enquirer,* July 10, 1821, UCL.

232 *"Now Yancy [sic] says if his state goes out":* JWB, "[Draft of a Speech] Philadelphia, late December 1860," in Rhodehamel and Taper, *The Writings of John Wilkes Booth,* 56, 57, 58, 55, 61.

233 *These sentiments provoked anger:* Effie Ellser Weston, ed., *The Stage Memories of John A. Ellsler* (Cleveland: Rowfant Club, 1950), reproduced in Rhodehamel and Taper, *The Writings of John Wilkes Booth,* p. 66.

233 *Louise Catherine Wooster:* Louise Wooster, *The Autobiography of a Magdalen* (Birmingham, Ala.: Birmingham, 1911) 50–53, 56; James L. Baggett, ed., *A Woman of the Town: Louise Wooster, Birmingham's Magdalen* (Birmingham, Ala.: Birmingham Public Library Press, 2005), 61–62.

233 *"I was young, rather pretty":* Baggett, ed., *A Woman of the Town,* 59; Wooster, *The Autobiography of a Magdalen,* 50.

233 *"Oh! How I loved him":* Baggett, ed., *A Woman of the Town,* 61; EB to JBB, Jr., October 31, 1858, HL.

233 *"I had considerable stage talent":* Baggett, ed., *A Woman of the Town,* 61–62, 64.

234 *"a drawer filled with letters, notes, pictures":* Baggett, ed., *A Woman of the Town,* 146; Wooster, *The Autobiography of a Magdalen,* 59.

234 *When he arrived in Philadelphia:* Asia Booth Clarke to Jean Anderson, December 16, 1860, SHM.

234 *always maintained John Wilkes was "irresponsible":* "Edwin Booth's Real Self, by An Intimate for Twenty-Five Years," *New York Theatre Magazine,* December 1916, EB clippings, Theater Collection, HL; EB to Nahum Capen, July 28, 1881, in Grossman, *Edwin Booth: Recollections by His Daughter,* 227.

235 *"throw away their principles":* JWB, "[Draft of a Speech] Philadelphia, late December 1860," *The Writings of John Wilkes Booth,* 60, 58.

235 *"Say that you [Northerners]"*: JWB, "[Draft of a Speech] Philadelphia, late December 1860," 61.
236 *"makes me hate my brothers in the north"*: JWB, "[Draft of a Speech] Philadelphia, late December 1860," 63.

CHAPTER ELEVEN: MY BROTHER, MY COMPETITOR

Page
239 *people of Albany:* William Kennedy, *O Albany! Improbable City of Political Wizards* (New York: Penguin, 1983), 68; James M. McPherson, *Battle Cry of Freedom: The Civil War Era* (New York: Ballantine, 1988), 235; H. P. Phelps, *Players of a Century: A Record of the Albany Stage* (Albany, N.Y.: Joseph McDonough, 1880), 324, SCRC, UCL.
240 *"blood was at fever heat"*: Phelps, *Players of a Century*, 324; EB to Adam Badeau, September 14, 1862, FSL; Kennedy, *O Albany!*, 68.
240 *rebel congress at Montgomery:* Rogers, Jr., *Confederate Home Front*, 25; "Interview with George Wren," April 18, 1865, Records of the Office of the Judge Advocate General, National Archives, copy at KC; Phelps, *Players of a Century*, 325–26.
241 *"not only would kill his engagement"*: Phelps, *Players of a Century*, 326.
241 *scores of traveling entertainers northward:* "Theatricals are very dull throughout the entire South," *Wilkes' Spirit of the Times* (New York), January 26, 1861, KC; "Sketch of JWB," Booth Family Scrapbook B.9.1, 91, FSL; Herbert Adams, "JWB Won Hearts in Portland," in Donald W. Beattie and Rodney M. Cole, eds., *A Distant War Comes Home: Maine in the Civil War Era* (Camden, Maine: Down East, 1996), 35; Clarke, *The Unlocked Book*, 111.
241 *"from the effects of a pistol shot"*: "J. Wilkes Booth . . . at the Gayety Theatre," *Wilkes' Spirit of the Times*, February 23, 1861, KC; Phelps, *Players of a Century*, 325; EB to Richard Henry Stoddard, January 22, 1863, H-BTL.
241 *a reprisal of* The Apostate: Samples, *Lust for Fame*, 212; Phelps, *Players of a Century*, 324; "February 18, 1861," in Earl Schenck Miers, ed., *Lincoln Day by Day: A Chronology, 1809–1865* (Dayton, Ohio: Morningside House, 1991), 17; Kennedy, *O Albany!*, 68.
241 *"It is true"*: "February 18, 1861," in Miers, ed., *Lincoln Day by Day*, 17; Phelps, *Players of a Century*, 326.
242 *"Great B" and "Little B"*: Hall, "The Friendship of Edwin Booth and Julia Ward Howe," *New England Magazine*, November 1893, EB clippings, Theatre Collection, HL; Arthur Butler Maurice, *Fifth Avenue* (New York: Dodd, Mead, 1918), 86; William Leete Stone, *History of New York City from the Discovery to the Present Day* (New York: Virtue & Yorston, 1872), 513–14; Maurice, *Fifth Avenue*, 88; Aldrich, *Crowding Memories*, 3.
242 *"Slight in figure"*: Aldrich, *Crowding Memories*, 4; Mary Devlin to EB, August 16 and 20, 1859, H-BTL; Mary Devlin Booth to Julia Nash, n.d., 1860–61, in Oggel, ed., *The Letters and Notebooks of Mary Devlin Booth*, 50.
243 *Fifth Avenue Hotel's bar:* William F. Munhall, "The Golden Age of Booze," in Henry Collins Brown, ed., *Valentine's Manual of Old New York, No. 7* (New York: Valentine's Manual, 1923), 132–33; Aldrich, *Crowding Memories*, 6, 8.
243 *"So subtle and close was the tie"*: Aldrich, *Crowding Memories*, 8; "Booth's First Manager: A Talk with a Man Who Has Been Forty Years in a Theatre," May 11, 1879, Booth Scrapbook B.7.5, 56, FSL; Mary Devlin Booth, diary, November 11, 1860, in Oggel, ed., *The Letters and Notebooks of Mary Devlin Booth*, 114.
244 *The Booths' marriage reminded many:* Aldrich, *Crowding Memories*, 6; Skinner, *The Last Tragedian*, 80, 83–84, 101–2.
244 *"Mr. Edwin Booth"*: "Mr. Edwin Booth as Shylock," *New York Evening Post*, February 12, 1861, loose clipping in Clarke, *The Elder and the Younger Booth*, Q.927.92 H97, UIUC

(thanks to RBML imaging expert Dennis Sears for bringing this newspaper fragment to the attention of the author).

244 *earning $5,000 in two weeks:* Mary Devlin Booth to Elizabeth Stoddard, December 7, 1862, in Oggel, ed., *The Letters and Notebooks of Mary Devlin Booth,* 86; "April 5, 1861," in Miers, ed., *Lincoln Day by Day,* 33; EB to Richard F. Cary, n.d., 1860, in Grossman, *Edwin Booth: Recollections by his Daughter,* 132–33.

245 *"All American actors seek":* E. H. House, "Edwin Booth in London," *Century Magazine,* December 1897, 269, EB, printed matter, Theatre Collection, HL; EB to Thomas Hicks, October 13, 1861, Booth-Grossman family papers, BRTD, NYPL; "Howard's Letter: Stories about Booth from Stuart, His Old Manager," *New York Record* (n.d.), printed material in Matthews and Hutton, eds., *Actors and Actresses of Great Britain and the United States,* extra-illustrated ed., TS931.2, Theatre Collection, HL.

245 *in Portland's Deering Hall:* Adams, "JWB Won Hearts in Portland," in Beattie and Cole, eds., *A Distant War Comes Home,* 36–37; McPherson, *Battle Cry of Freedom,* 274.

245 The Corsican Brothers: E. Grangé and X. de Montépin, *The Corsican Brothers* (New York: Samuel French, 186-), 10–16, 57, 60, Atkinson Collection, SCRC, UCL.

245 *tricks of stage machinery:* J. Steinmeyer, *Hiding the Elephant: How Magicians Invented the Impossible* (New York: Carroll & Graf, 2003), 23–24; Adams, in Beattie and Cole, eds., *A Distant War Comes Home,* 36–38. For these citations, the author is greatly indebted to the kindness of Maine state representative Herbert Adams.

246 *drove a knife into his neck:* Phelps, *Players of a Century,* 326–27; William A. Howell, "Memories of Wilkes Booth," *Baltimore Sun,* n.d., KC.

247 *"Since they will have it so":* Richards, *Samuel Gridley Howe,* 221–22.

247 *"It seemed but yesterday":* Richards, ed., *The Letters and Journals of Samuel Gridley Howe* (Boston: Dana Estes, 1909), 483–84.

248 *Julia, was not so cavalier:* Julia Ward Howe, *Reminiscences,* 262, 257.

249 *"Therefore thus saith the Lord":* Fields, *Slavery and Freedom on the Middle Ground,* 106.

249 *Edwin inquired which of their friends were "true blue":* EB to Adam Badeau, September 14, 1862, FSL; Ripley, " 'We Are Not in Little England Now,' " *Theatre Notebook* 61, no. 2 (2007), 95.

249 *join the staff of Brigadier General Thomas W. Sherman:* James Grant Wilson and John Fiske, eds., *Appleton's Cyclopedia of American Biography,* vol. 1 (New York: Appleton, 1888), 132; EB to Richard Cary, [April] 30 and August 4, 1861, in Grossman, *Edwin Booth: Recollections by his Daughter,* 134–36; Charles Francis Adams, diary, December 9, 1861, microfilm of the Adams Papers (Boston: Massachusetts Historical Society, 1954–58), reels 75–76, consulted at Lamont Library, Harvard University.

249 *"Cold steel & my warm blood":* EB to Adam Badeau, June 15, 1863, H-BTL.

250 *"Old Scott will make but one battle":* David C. Anderson to EB, June 13, 1865 (enclosing excerpt from EB to David C. Anderson, May 1861), H-BTL.

250 *"It is the grand turning point of my career":* EB to Richard Cary, August 4, 1861, in Grossman, *Edwin Booth: Recollections by His Daughter,* 135–36; EB to Thomas Hicks, December 9, 1861, Booth-Grossman family papers, BRTD, NYPL.

251 *"express[ing] himself as very strongly Southern":* "Interview with George Wren," April 18, 1865, Records of the Office of the JAG, National Archives, copy at KC.

251 *"ablaze with excitement":* Howell, "Memories of Wilkes Booth"; Kevin Conley Ruffner, *Maryland's Blue and Gray: A Border State's Union and Confederate Junior Officer Corps* (Baton Rouge: LSU Press, 1997), 60–61, 68; Clarke, *The Unlocked Book,* 58.

252 *"J. Wilkes proposed that he would go":* Howell, "Memories of Wilkes Booth"; "Statement of J. B. Booth, 5 May 1865," in Alford, ed., *John Wilkes Booth: A Sister's Memoir,* 118.

252 *"fancying conscription into the Southern service":* "JWB," in Booth Family Scrapbook B.9.1,

141, FSL; Anthony Powell, *A Dance to the Music of Time: 3rd Movement* (Chicago: University of Chicago Press, 1995), 107–8.

252 *"He would crayon out for me his hopes and desires":* Howell, "Memories of Wilkes Booth"; Clarke, *The Unlocked Book,* 112, 114.

253 *"I am neither a Northerner nor a Southerner":* Bloom, *Joseph Jefferson,* 94.

253 *"politicians of every grade, adventurers of either sex":* Howe, *Reminiscences,* 269; Sollers, "The Theatrical Career of John T. Ford," 121.

254 *light shining from dozens of fires:* Howe, *Reminiscences,* 269; "Correspondence from Washington, December 2, 1861," *Iowa State Register,* December 11, 1861, microfilm loaned by University of Iowa Library.

254 *McClellan now commanded 175,000 men:* Shelby Foote, *The Civil War: A Narrative, Fort Sumter to Perryville* (New York: Random House, 1986), 396; "Governor Seward's Speech," *(Washington, D.C.), Daily National Republican* November 14, 1861, SCRC, UCL.

254 *leaving her two-year-old son behind:* Richards, ed., *Letters and Journals of Samuel Gridley Howe,* 503, 500, 497–98.

255 *cheap embalming services:* Howe, *Reminiscences,* 269, 271–72.

256 *"considers slavery to be a great stumbling-block":* Samuel Gridley Howe to F. W. Bird, March 5, 1852, in Richards, ed., *Letters and Journals of Samuel Gridley Howe,* 501.

256 *A mood "of discouragement":* Howe, *Reminiscences,* 273, 274–75, and facsimile of "First draft of the 'Battle Hymn of the Republic,' by Julia Ward Howe, November 1861," insert between 276 and 277.

257 *flat in Bloomsbury Square:* EB to Thomas Hicks, October 13, 1861, Booth-Grossman family papers, BRTD, NYPL.

257 *"cast a gloom over everything":* Mary Ann Holmes Booth to Edwina Booth, April 21, 1881, Taper Collection, ALPLM.

257 *"long-haired Yankee":* Clarke, *The Elder and the Younger Booth,* extra-illustrated ed., insertion beginning "Booth allowed his hair to grow long . . . rendered him a conspicuous object in London," UIUC; EB to Thomas Hicks, December 9, 1861, Booth-Grossman family papers, BRTD, NYPL.

258 *"Good weather is death to the theatricals":* EB to Thomas Hicks, October 13, 1861, Booth-Grossman family papers, BRTD, NYPL; Charles Francis Adams, diary, and December 19 and 22, 1861, January 8, 1862, microfilm of the Adams Papers, reels 75–76, Lamont Library, Harvard University; McPherson, *Battle Cry of Freedom,* 390–91.

258 *"The feeling against Americans is very bitter":* Mary Devlin Booth to Mary L. Felton, February 14, 1862, Booth-Grossman family papers, BRTD, NYPL; EB to Thomas Hicks, December 9, 1861, Booth-Grossman family papers, BRTD, NYPL.

259 *"The seeming standstill of McClellan's armies":* Mary Devlin Booth to Mary L. Felton, February 14, 1862, Booth-Grossman family papers, BRTD, NYPL; EB to Richard Cary, March 20, 1862, in Grossman, *Edwin Booth: Recollections by His Daughter,* 136–37; EB to Thomas Hicks, December 9, 1861, Booth-Grossman family papers, BRTD, NYPL.

259 *"the most trying period":* Mary Devlin Booth to Mary L. Felton, February 14, 1862, Booth-Grossman family papers, BRTD, NYPL; EB to Thomas Hicks, December 9, 1861, Booth-Grossman family papers, BRTD, NYPL; Asia Booth Clarke to Jean Anderson, February 28, 1862, in Paul Amelia, "Highlights of Asia Booth Clarke's Letters to Jean Anderson," typescript (compiled September 5, 1979, from originals at the Peale Museum, Baltimore), H-BTL.

259 *"an undertone of sadness":* Aldrich, *Crowding Memories,* 12; Mary Devlin Booth to Mary L. Felton, May 13, 1862, in Oggel, ed., *The Letters and Notebooks of Mary Devlin Booth,* 79; Richard Cary to his wife, January 1, 1862, original in the Richard Cary Letters, Massachusetts Historical Society, copy courtesy of Megan Kate Nelson.

260 *near the Rue de la Paix:* EB to Adam Badeau, April 8, 1862, FSL; Clarke, *The Elder and the Younger Booth*, extra-illustrated ed., insertion beginning "At the termination of these engagements, he went to Paris with his family," UIUC.

260 *write Captain Badeau for a cash loan:* EB to Adam Badeau, April 8, 1862, FSL; JBB, Jr., to EB, October 20, 1862, H-BTL.

260 *"acted a short engagement":* Clarke, *The Unlocked Book*, 111; Samples, *Lust for Fame*, 215–16.

261 *Detroit, Cincinnati, and St. Louis:* Samples, *Lust for Fame*, 213–16; "Sketch of JWB, the Murderer of the President," in Booth Family Scrapbook B.9.1, 91, FSL.

261 *Joseph Adrian Booth, had disappeared:* "Examination of Joseph Adrian Booth, 12 May 1865," in Alford, ed., *John Wilkes Booth: A Sister's Memoir*, 135; EB to Adam Badeau, April 8, 1862, FSL; JWB to Joseph H. Simonds, March 22, 1862, in Rhodehamel and Taper, ed., *The Writings of John Wilkes Booth*, 78.

261 *"I was troubled in mind":* "Examination of Joseph Adrian Booth, 12 May 1865," 134; EB to Richard Henry Stoddard, January 13, 1863, H-BTL.

262 *"I wish you were all worth millions":* Mary Ann Holmes Booth to EB, May 10, 1862, H-BTL.

262 *victory on May 31 at Fair Oaks, Virginia:* McPherson, *Battle Cry of Freedom*, 461, 411, 414; Clarke, *The Elder and the Younger Booth*, 157.

CHAPTER TWELVE: THE WORKING OF THE HEART

Page

264 *"It was the harvest time for theaters":* Clarke, *The Unlocked Book*, 114; Asia Booth Clarke to Jean Anderson, November 16, 1861, original at the Peale Museum, Baltimore, copy courtesy of M. Kauffman and L. Verge, director, SHM.

264 *"His face has fortune":* "Local Matters: Dramatic & etc., JWB," *Boston Daily Advertiser*, May 19, 1862, clipping in KC; "JWB," Booth Scrapbook B.9.1, 141, FSL; Richard Christiansen, *A Theater of Our Own: A History and a Memoir of 1001 Nights in Chicago* (Evanston, Ill.: Northwestern University Press, 2004), 11–12.

265 *"turn[ed] a somersault":* "That Critic Again," *Chicago Evening Journal*, December 8, 1862, Research Center, Chicago History Museum; "A Nuisance . . . in McVicker's Theatre," *Chicago Evening Journal*, June 9, 1862, CHM.

265 *"a severe dose of rant":* "That Critic Again," *Chicago Evening Journal*; "Amusements: To-night Mr. J. Wilkes Booth takes his farewell of Chicago," *Chicago Evening Journal*, February 1, 1862, CHM.

265 *"scion of the House of Booth":* *Buffalo Courier*, November 4, 1861, in Rhodehamel and Taper, eds., *The Writings of John Wilkes Booth*, 75; Sollers, "The Theatrical Career of John T. Ford," 143, 155.

266 *"I have no brother":* Playbill cited in Rhodehamel and Taper, eds., *The Writings of John Wilkes Booth*, 77–78; Sollers, "The Theatrical Career of John T. Ford," 44–46, 58; Richard Cary to his wife, March 14, 1862, original in the Richard Cary Letters, Massachusetts Historical Society, copy courtesy of Megan Kate Nelson.

266 *Wallack's Theatre:* Joseph N. Ireland, *Records of the New York Stage, from 1750 to 1860*, vol. 2 (New York: T. H. Morrell, 1866–67), 610–11; Archer, *Theatrical Prometheus*, 264, 268; "Sketch of JWB, the Murderer of the President," Booth Family Scrapbook B.9.1, 91, FSL; Samples, *Lust for Fame*, 83.

267 *"In what does he fail?":* "Local Matters: Dramatic & etc., John Wilkes Booth," *Boston Daily Advertiser*, May 19, 1862, clipping in KC.

267 *"When he fought":* Catherine Mary Reignolds-Winslow, *Yesterdays with Actors* (Boston:

Cupples & Hurd, 1887), 140; Clara Morris, *Life on the Stage: My Personal Experience and Recollections* (London: Ibister, 1902), 98–99.

268 *"In truth, he would not study":* James W. Shettel, "J. Wilkes Booth at School: Recollections of a Retired Army Officer Who Knew Him Then," *New York Dramatic Mirror*, February 26, 1916, UCL; Reignolds-Wilson, *Yesterdays with Actors*, 71, 141.

270 *He made arrangements with theater managers directly:* JWB to various correspondents, 1862–63, in Rhodehamel and Taper, eds. *The Writings of John Wilkes Booth*, 80–91.

270 *"My goose does indeed hang high":* JWB to Edwin Frank Keach, December 8, 1862; JWB to Joseph H. Simonds, December 6, April 13, and January 10, 1862; in Rhodehamel and Taper, eds., *The Writings of John Wilkes Booth*, 83, 82, 79, 76.

270 *"rare perception of what was becoming to his figure":* "John Wilkes Booth," Booth Family Scrapbook B.9.1, 141, FSL; William J. Ferguson, *I Saw Booth Shoot Lincoln* (Boston: Houghton Mifflin, 1930), 49; carte-de-visite photographs of JWB in various poses, Theatre Collection, HL; Rhodehamel and Taper, eds., *The Writings of John Wilkes Booth*, 76, 103; Morris, *Life on the Stage*, 98.

271 *"He was, what was designated":* Shettel, "J. Wilkes Booth at School."

271 *Marie Fournier:* Aldrich, *Crowding Memories*, 27, 25–26; EB to Adam Badeau, October 26, 1862, H-BTL.

271 *"authors, actors, artists":* Aldrich, *Crowding Memories*, 14–15, 25; Ferris Greenslet, *The Life of Thomas Bailey Aldrich* (Boston: Houghton Mifflin, 1908), 55–56, 63, 67.

272 *"Judging from the appearance of this city":* Mary Devlin Booth to Mary L. Felton, October 31, 1862, in Oggel, ed., *The Letters and Notebooks of Mary Devlin Booth*, 83; Mary Devlin Booth to Mary L. Felton, September 10, 1862, Booth-Grossman family papers, BRTD, NYPL; EB to Mary L. Felton, September 11, 1862, in Grossman, *Edwin Booth: Recollections by His Daughter*, 138–39.

273 *"myself and my profession":* EB to Adam Badeau, October 26, 1862, H-BTL; EB to Adam Badeau, September 14, 1862, FSL.

273 *more than twenty thousand had fallen:* McPherson, *Battle Cry of Freedom*, 544; Adam Badeau to EB, December 4, 1862, H-BTL.

274 *"were undeniably an element of strength":* McPherson, *Battle Cry of Freedom*, 504, 557; Richards, ed., *Letters and Papers of Samuel Gridley Howe*, 500; Mary Devlin Booth to Mary L. Felton, September 22, 1862, in Oggel, ed., *The Letters and Notebooks of Mary Devlin Booth*, 81.

274 *"Patriotism [was] rampant":* Aldrich, *Crowding Memories*, 20; EB to Adam Badeau, October 26, 1862, H-BTL; EB to Adam Badeau, August 6, 1863, FSL; Clarke, *The Elder and the Younger Booth*, 157.

274 *"It seems to me":* Samuel Gridley Howe to F. W. Bird, September 17, 1862, in Richards, ed., *Letters and Papers of Samuel Gridley Howe*, 501.

275 *fall months of 1862–63:* Samples, *Lust for Fame*, 217–18; Mary Cochran, Reference Librarian, Cincinnati Public Library, to Stanley Kimmel, September 23, 1936, enclosing local newspaper accounts of JWB's appearances, KC; "Amusements—Booth," *Chicago Evening Journal*, November 29, and December 1, 4, and 5, 1862, CHM.

275 *Displaying his characteristic blindness:* Christiansen, *A Theater of Our Own*, 12; "Booth's Idea of Immortal Fame," *Cleveland Leader*, April 17, 1865, in Booth Family Scrapbook B.9.1, 87, FSL.

276 *John's rebel opinions:* "Sketch of JWB, the Murderer of the President," Booth Family Scrapbook B.9.1, 91, FSL; John G. Nicolay and John Hay, *Abraham Lincoln: A History*, vol. 10 (New York: Century, 1914), 295; JWB to Joseph H. Simonds, April 19, 1863, in Rhodehamel and Taper, eds., *The Writings of John Wilkes Booth*, 88; Samples, *Lust for Fame*, 219–20.

276 *"immense crowds":* Mary Devlin Booth to Elizabeth Stoddard, December 13, 1862, in Oggel, ed., *The Letters and Notebooks of Mary Devlin Booth*, 88; Laura E. Richards and Maud

Howe Elliott, *Julia Ward Howe, 1819–1910*, vol. 1 (Boston: Houghton Mifflin, 1916), 194–95; Hall, "The Friendship of Edwin Booth and Julia Ward Howe," *New England Magazine*, November 1893, 318, EB clippings, Theatre Collection, HL.

277 *"that he would find Mr. Booth a most interesting":* Hall, "The Friendship of Edwin Booth and Julia Ward Howe," 318.

277 *"was a real ovation to Edwin":* Mary Devlin Booth to Elizabeth Stoddard, December 13 and 24, 1862, in Oggel, ed., *The Letters and Notebooks of Mary Devlin Booth*, 87, 94.

277 *"d___d fool":* Mary Devlin Booth to Elizabeth Stoddard, December 7 and 13, 1862, January 7, 1863; Mary Devlin Booth to Matilda Woodman, January 29, 1863, in Oggel, ed., *The Letters and Notebooks of Mary Devlin Booth*, 86, 87, 96, 103–4.

277 *pacing the room at her husband's side:* Aldrich, *Crowding Memories*, 27–28; Mary Devlin Booth to Elizabeth Stoddard, December 30, 1862, January 19, 1863, in Oggel, ed., *The Letters and Notebooks of Mary Devlin Booth*, 95, 99.

278 *"wonderful influence had wonderfully ebbed away":* Asia Booth Clarke to Jean Anderson, March 3, 1863, original at the Peale Museum, Baltimore, copy courtesy of M. Kauffman and L. Verge, director, SHM; Hall, "The Friendship of Edwin Booth and Julia Ward Howe," 318.

278 *"why [do] so many healthy":* Allan M. Brandt, *No Magic Bullet: A Social History of Venereal Disease in the United States* (New York: Oxford University Press, 1987), 11, 12; EB to JBB Jr., December 12, 1858, Theatre Collection, HL.

278 *infecting not only the uterus:* Brandt, *No Magic Bullet*, 10, 15; Mary Devlin Booth to Emma Cushman, December 13, 1862; Mary Devlin Booth to Elizabeth Stoddard, December 13 and 24, 1862, in Oggel, ed., *The Letters and Notebooks of Mary Devlin Booth*, 88, 87, 94.

279 *"Before I was eighteen I was a drunkard":* EB to Elizabeth Stoddard, n.d. [1863], in Skinner, *The Last Tragedian*, 84; "Edwin Booth's House in Dorchester," *Boston Transcript*, September 13, 1919, EB clippings, Theatre Collection, HL; Mary Devlin Booth to Mary L. Felton, January 7, 1863, in Oggel, ed., *The Letters and Notebooks of Mary Devlin Booth*, 97.

279 *"all my courage is gone":* Mary Devlin Booth to Elizabeth Stoddard, December 30, 1862, in Oggel, ed., *The Letters and Notebooks of Mary Devlin Booth*, 95; Hall, "The Friendship of Edwin Booth and Julia Ward Howe," 318; Brandt, *No Magic Bullet*, 12.

279 *John Wilkes Booth, fresh:* Samples, *Lust for Fame*, 218; Mary Ann Holmes Booth to EB, January 29, 1863, H-BTL; EB to Richard Henry Stoddard, January 22, 1863, H-BTL.

280 *"has a great deal to learn and unlearn":* Mary Devlin Booth to Emma Cushman, January 22, 1863; Mary Devlin Booth to EB, February 12, 1863, in Oggel, ed., *The Letters and Notebooks of Mary Devlin Booth*, 101, 105.

280 *"I had not yet got control of my devil":* William Winter, *Life and Art of Edwin Booth* (New York: Macmillan, 1893), 27–28; Mary Devlin Booth to Elizabeth Stoddard, December 30, 1862, in Oggel, ed., *The Letters and Notebooks of Mary Devlin Booth*, 95.

281 *"When Mr. Booth was not at the theater":* Aldrich, *Crowding Memories*, 31; William Stuart, "Reminiscences of the Early Days of EB—Tragedy Played as Farce at the Old Winter Garden—The Death of Mary Devlin," n.d., EB clippings, Theatre Collection, HL.

281 *"Sick or well, you must come":* Aldrich, *Crowding Memories*, 34–35; Samples, *Lust for Fame*, 219; Hall, "The Friendship of Edwin Booth and Julia Ward Howe," 318–19.

282 *"She is very weak":* Erasmus Miller to EB, telegram, February 18, 1863; Orlando Tompkins to EB, telegram, February 18, 1862; Erasmus Miller to EB, telegram, February 19, 1862; Orlando Tompkins to EB, telegram, in "Telegrams and letters from Dr. Erasmus Miller and Orlando Tompkins concerning Mary Devlin Booth's last illness," Booth-Grossman family papers, BRTD, NYPL.

282 *"Why does not Mr. Booth answer":* Aldrich, *Crowding Memories*, 37–38; William Stuart, "Reminiscences of the Early Days of EB"; EB to Adam Badeau, March 3, 1863, in Grossman, *Edwin Booth: Recollections by His Daughter*, 144.

283 *"place[d] my darling in the ground"*: EB to Adam Badeau, July 3, 1863, FSL; Hall, "The Friendship of Edwin Booth and Julia Ward Howe," 319; Howe, *Reminiscences*, 242.

284 *"postponed [his] engagement"*: Asia Booth Clarke to Jean Anderson, March 3, 1863, original at the Peale Museum, Baltimore, copy courtesy of M. Kauffman and L. Verge, director, SHM; Clarke, *The Elder and the Younger Booth*, extra-illustrated ed., insertion between 156 and 157, UIUC.

284 *"contemplating a long seclusion"*: Winter, *Life and Art of Edwin Booth*, 29–30; EB to Adam Badeau, March 3, 1863, in Grossman, *Edwin Booth: Recollections by His Daughter*, 145.

285 *"hanging on the wall, mute"*: EB to Adam Badeau, March 3, 1863, in Grossman, *Edwin Booth: Recollections by His Daughter*, 145, 141, 143–44.

285 *"felt ashamed"*: EB to Elizabeth Stoddard, March 24, 1863, reprinted in "The Life Tragedy of Edwin Booth," printed material in extra-illustrated edition of Matthews and Hutton, eds., *Actors and Actresses of Great Britain and the United States*, TS931.2, HL; EB to Adam Badeau, May 18, 1863, H-BTL.

286 *"to occupy [Edwin's] mind"*: Barton Hill, "Personal Recollections of Edwin Booth," in *New York Dramatic Mirror*, December 1896, EB, printed matter, Theatre Collection, HL; EB to Adam Badeau, May 18, 1863, H-BTL.

287 *"Surely there is something marvelous"*: EB to Adam Badeau, June 15, 1863, H-BTL; EB to Adam Badeau, July 3, 1863, FSL.

287 *"Forgive me, I am so selfish"*: EB to Adam Badeau, June 15, 1863, H-BTL; EB to Adam Badeau, May 18, 1863, H-BTL; EB to Adam Badeau, July 3, 1863, FSL.

287 *"The agony of keeping your foot"*: EB to Adam Badeau, July 3, 1863, FSL.

288 *John Wilkes hastened back to Philadelphia*: Asia Booth Clarke to Jean Anderson, March 3, 1863, SHM; JWB to Joseph H. Simonds, March 1, 1863, in Rhodehamel and Taper, eds., *The Writings of John Wilkes Booth*, 85; Mary Ann Holmes Booth to EB, January 15, 1863, H-BTL.

288 *$1,500 worth of shares in the Boston Water Power Company*: JWB to Joseph H. Simonds, February 28 and April 3, 1863, in Rhodehamel and Taper, eds., *The Writings of John Wilkes Booth*, 84–85, 86–87.

288 *"The Youngest Tragedian in the World"*: Rhodehamel and Taper, eds., *The Writings of John Wilkes Booth*, 87–88; Samples, *Lust for Fame*, 107, 110.

289 *from April 27 to May 9, was poorly timed*: McPherson, *Battle Cry of Freedom*, 645; Samples, *Lust for Fame*, 112–13, 107.

289 *ten nights in St. Louis*: Samples, *Lust for Fame*, 220; Rhodehamel and Taper, eds., *The Writings of John Wilkes Booth*, 89.

290 *On April 19, 1863*: Samuel Gridley Howe to Laura Elizabeth (Howe) Richards, April 20, 1863, bMS Am2214 (183), HL; Richards, *Letters & Papers of Samuel Gridley Howe*, 503.

290 *"Would it were all at an end!"*: Richards and Elliott, *Julia Ward Howe*, 192–93.

CHAPTER THIRTEEN: BEAT DOWN THESE REBELS HERE AT HOME

Page

292 *"Although the war"*: James M. McPherson, ed., *The Most Fearful Ordeal: Original Coverage of the Civil War by the Writers and Reporters of the New York Times* (New York: St. Martin's, 2004), 244; Iver Bernstein, *The New York City Draft Riots: Their Significance for American Society and Politics in an Age of Civil War* (New York: Oxford University Press, 1990), 7–8.

292 *first lottery, July 11, 1863*: Adrian Cook, *The Armies of the Streets: The New York City Draft Riots of 1863* (Lexington: University Press of Kentucky, 1974), 54; McPherson, ed., *The Most Fearful Ordeal*, 261, 259.

293 *On Second Avenue*: John B. Pine, "Gramercy Park and the Draft Riots, 1863," in Henry

Collins Brown, ed., *Valentine's Manual of Old New York*, vol. 4 (New York: Valentine's Manual, 1920), 236–40; Homer Saint-Gaudens, ed., *The Reminiscences of Augustus Saint-Gaudens* (New York: Century, 1913), 51; Ellen Leonard, "Three Days of Terror," *Harper's New Monthly Magazine*, January 1867, 228.

293 *"quiet time":* EB to Adam Badeau, June 15, 1863, H-BTL; EB to Adam Badeau, June 6, 1863, H-BTL.

294 *"My home is at your service":* EB to Adam Badeau, [n.d., 1863] Y.c.215 (12b), FSL; EB to Adam Badeau, July 3, 1863, FSL; Badeau, "Edwin Booth On and Off the Stage: Personal Recollections," *McClure's Magazine*, August 1893, 264.

294 *Edwin and John Wilkes together:* Badeau, "Edwin Booth On and Off the Stage," 264; EB to Adam Badeau, June 15, and September 26, 1863, H-BTL; EB to Adam Badeau, August 6, 1863, FSL.

294 *Monday, July 13:* Cook, *The Armies of the Streets*, 63, 69–70; Saint-Gaudens, ed., *The Reminiscences of August Saint-Gaudens*, 50–51; Leonard, "Three Days of Terror," 225.

295 *"to inquire the news":* Badeau, "Edwin Booth On and Off the Stage," 264; Bernstein, *The New York City Draft Riots*, 18; Cook, *The Armies of the Streets*, 55.

295 *"Resist the draft!":* Cook, *The Armies of the Streets*, 60–61, 66.

295 *People felled telegraph poles:* "The Reign of the Rabble," *New York Times*, July 15, 1863, in McPherson, ed., *The Most Fearful Ordeal*, 261, 264–65; Bernstein, *The New York Draft Riots*, 21, 25; Cook, *The Armies of the Streets*, 88.

296 *a bloody pulp:* "The Death of Colonel O'Brien," *New York Times*, July 15, 1863, in McPherson, ed., *The Most Fearful Ordeal*, 262; Cook, *The Armies of the Streets*, 130–31; Herman Melville, "The House-top. A Night Piece, July, 1863," in Nina Baym et al., eds., *The Norton Anthology of American Literature*, vol. 1 (New York: Norton, 1989), 2292.

296 *mobs were targeting:* Bernstein, *The New York City Draft Riots*, 40–41, 37–38; Leonard, "Three Days of Terror," 225; "Eighteen Persons Reported Killed," *New York Times*, July 15, 1865, in McPherson, ed., *The Most Fearful Ordeal*, 261; Badeau, "Edwin Booth On and Off the Stage," 264.

297 *"in a state of insurrection":* Bernstein, *The New York City Draft Riots*, 51; "The Reign of the Rabble," *New York Times*, July 15, 1863, in McPherson, ed., *The Most Fearful Ordeal*, 260; Leonard, "Three Days of Terror," 226.

297 *"a paroxysm of fear":* Saint-Gaudens, ed., *The Reminiscences of Augustus Saint-Gaudens*, 50–51; Leonard, "Three Days of Terror," 226; Bernstein, *The New York City Draft Riots*, 20–21, 27, and "The Geography of Racial Murders, July 13–17, 1863," 282; Cook, *The Armies of the Streets*, 83, 135.

298 *"assisted to shield my negro servant":* Badeau, "Edwin Booth On and Off the Stage," 264; Bernstein, *The New York City Draft Riots*, 36; Cook, *The Armies of the Streets*, 100; "The Death of Colonel O'Brien," *New York Times*, July 15, 1865, in McPherson, ed., *The Most Fearful Ordeal*, 262; Leonard, "Three Days of Terror," 229–30.

298 *"I can never forget":* Adam Badeau to EB, October 23, 1866, H-BTL; Leonard, "Three Days of Terror," 227, 233; Cook, *The Armies of the Streets*, 162–63, 164.

299 *as Saint-Gaudens remembered:* Saint-Gaudens, ed., *The Reminiscences of Augustus Saint-Gaudens*, 51; Pine, "Gramercy Park and the Draft Riots, 1863," in Brown, ed., *Valentine's Manual of Old New York*, vol. 4, 239; Cook, *The Armies of the Streets*, 164; EB to Adam Badeau, [n.d.] 1863, Y.c.215 (12b), FSL.

300 *"My baby, my little girl":* EB to Adam Badeau, September 13, 1863, FSL; Badeau, "Edwin Booth On and Off the Stage," 264.

300 *"Imagine me":* Clarke, *The Unlocked Book*, 118, 123, 114–15.

301 *28 East Nineteenth Street:* EB to Adam Badeau, June 15, 1863, and February 26, 1864, H-BTL; EB to Adam Badeau, September 26, 1863, H-BTL.

302 *"permanent stars in a theater of our own"*: EB to Harry [Magonigle], November 14, 1874, T.b.5 (1), FSL; EB to Adam Badeau, September 26, [1864], Y.c.215 (15b), FSL.

302 *In the star's dressing room:* "Reminiscences of EB Backstage at the Garden," unidentified newspaper article, EB clippings, Theatre Collection, HL; Diary of Fanny Seward, March 1864, in *The Papers of William H. Seward* (Woodbridge, Conn.: Research Publications, 1983), consulted at Lamont Library, Harvard University.

303 *The Walnut proved hugely profitable:* Charles H. Shattuck, "The Theatrical Management of Edwin Booth," in *The Theatrical Manager in England and America: Player of a Perilous Game* (Princeton, N.J.: Princeton University Press, 1971), 144–46; EB to Adam Badeau, September 26, [1864], Y.c.215 (15b), FSL; EB to Adam Badeau, October 14, 1864, FSL.

303 *"As for Clarke":* Clarke, *The Unlocked Book,* 118; "Statement of Junius Brutus Booth, Jr., 5 May 1865," in Alford, ed., *John Wilkes Booth: A Sister's Memoir,* 118.

303 *Atheneum on Tenth:* Sollers, "The Theatrical Career of John T. Ford," 124–25, 129–34.

304 *"Book me for Nov 2nd for two weeks":* JWB to John T. Ford, September 17, 1863, in Rhodehamel and Taper, eds., *The Writings of John Wilkes Booth,* 90; Samples, *Lust for Fame,* 220; "John Wilkes Booth . . . at the Brooklyn Academy," *New York Clipper,* October 31, 1863, KC.

304 *cyclones of dust into the air:* "Weather," *Washington Evening Star,* November 3 and 9, 1863, KC; Ferguson, *I Saw Booth Shoot Lincoln,* 19, 16–17.

305 *refused to accept John:* James W. Shettel, "J. Wilkes Booth at School: Recollections of a Retired Army Officer Who Knew Him Then," *New York Dramatic Mirror,* February 26, 1916, UCL; Ferguson, *I Saw Booth Shoot Lincoln,* 19, 13, 16.

305 *visited Ford's on November 9:* Tyler Dennett, ed., *Lincoln and the Civil War In the Diaries and Letters of John Hay* (New York: Dodd, Mead, 1939), 118; "November 9, 1863," in Miers, ed., *Lincoln Day by Day,* 218; Rodney Blake, "How Success First Came to Edwin Booth," *New York Theatre Magazine,* February 1913, 60.

306 *"Rather tame than otherwise":* Dennett, ed., *Lincoln and the Civil War in the Diaries and Letters of John Hay,* 118; "J. Wilkes Booth," *Washington Evening Star,* November 3, 1863, KC; Nicolay and Hay, *Abraham Lincoln: A History,* Vol. 10, (New York: The Century Co., 1914), 289; Samples, *Lust for Fame,* 221.

306 *"unfavorable" impression of Booth:* "Booth," *Cleveland Herald,* December 3 and 4, 1864; "The Stranger," *Cleveland Plain Dealer,* December 4, 1864; KC.

306 *One of John Wilkes Booth's promptbooks:* "Promptbook for Shakespeare's King Richard the Third," Arch Street Theatre, Philadelphia, n.d., belonging to JWB, with his defacements, stage directions and notes, TS Promptbooks Sh154.313-335, #322, HL. The author is grateful to Fredric Woodbridge Wilson, late curator of the Harvard Theatre Collection, for bringing this artifact to her attention.

307 *"Time, the Great Corrector":* "J. Wilkes Booth," *Cleveland Plain Dealer,* December 9, 1863, KC.

307 *On December 11, 1863:* Rhodehamel and Taper, eds., *The Writings of John Wilkes Booth,* 93, 97; "Petrolia," *Leisure Hour,* May 1866, 295.

307 *Lush forests of beech and hemlock:* John S. Schooley, "The Petroleum Region of America," *Harper's New Monthly Magazine,* April 1865, 563; William Wright, *The Oil Regions of Pennsylvania* (New York: Harper & Brothers, 1865), 16–17; Brian Black, *Petrolia* (Baltimore: Johns Hopkins University Press, 2000), 45, 59.

307 *"furnishing the best and cheapest artificial light":* Andrew Cone and Walter R. Johns, *Petrolia* (New York: Appleton, 1870), 10; Black, *Petrolia,* 17–18.

308 *"I never saw such excitement":* Black, *Petrolia,* 59; Cone and Johns, *Petrolia,* 70.

308 *"tingling in the blood":* Black, *Petrolia,* 64; Cone and Johns, *Petrolia,* 16–17.

308 *"One after another, with a dull exploding boom"*: "Petrolia," *Leisure Hour*, May 1866, 299.

308 *"The chances of success were equal for all"*: Cone and Johns, *Petrolia*, 15; Schooley, "The Petroleum Region of America," 571.

309 *a nine-night engagement*: Rhodehamel and Taper, eds., *The Writings of John Wilkes Booth*, 94, 96.

309 *"It was hard to get to Leavenworth"*: JWB to John A. Ellsler, January 23, 1864, in Rhodehamel and Taper, eds., *The Writings of John Wilkes Booth*, 96.

309 *"It seems to me that some of my old luck"*: JWB to Moses Kimball, January 2, 1864, in Rhodehamel and Taper, eds., *The Writings of John Wilkes Booth*, 93.

309 *"four days and nights"*: Rhodehamel and Taper, eds., *The Writings of John Wilkes Booth*, 95–96, 101; Samples, *Lust for Fame*, 139.

310 *"Every day I have thought of writing"*: JWB to John A. Ellsler, January 23, 1864, in Rhodehamel and Taper, eds., *The Writings of John Wilkes Booth*, 96.

310 *British actor Charles Kean died*: John Ripley, " 'We Are Not in Little England Now,' " *Theatre Notebook* 61, no. 2 (2007), 80, 90, 92.

310 *Walnut and Winter Garden theaters*: Shattuck, "The Theatrical Management of Edwin Booth," 150–51; EB to Harry [Magonigle], November 14, 1874, T.b.5 (1), FSL; EB to Adam Badeau, October 14, 1864, FSL.

310 *checked into a room at Willard's*: EB to Adam Badeau, February 26, 1864, H-BTL; EB to Emma F. Cary, February 14, 1864, in Grossman, *Edwin Booth: Recollections by His Daughter*, 157.

311 *Grover and John T. Ford vied constantly*: Sollers, "The Theatrical Career of John T. Ford," 136–40.

311 *Grover was an abolitionist*: Leonard Grover, "Lincoln's Interest in the Theatre," *Century Magazine*, April 1909, 943, 946.

311 *"Father Abraham visited Rome with me"*: EB to Adam Badeau, February 26, 1864, H-BTL.

311 *new appointment as General Grant's aide-de-camp*: EB to Adam Badeau, April 2, [1864], Y.c.215 (14b), FSL.

312 *President and Mrs. Lincoln paid six visits*: "February 25 and 26; March 2, 4, 7 and 10 1864," in Miers, ed., *Lincoln Day by Day*, 242–45; "The President at Grover's Theater," *(Washington, D.C.) Daily National Republican*, March 1 and 2, 1864, SCRC, UCL.

312 *The* National Republican *ran out of superlatives*: "The President at Grover's Theater," *(Washington, D.C.) Daily National Republican*, March 3, 5, and 10, 1864, SCRC, UCL; EB to Emma F. Cary, February 14, 1864, in Grossman, ed. *Edwin Booth: Recollections by His Daughter*, 157.

312 *"the third anniversary"*: "The President at Grover's Theater," *(Washington, D.C.) Daily National Republican*, March 5, 1864, SCRC, UCL.

312 *"I was perhaps nearer to a mad house"*: EB to Adam Badeau, April 2, [1864], Y.c.215 (14b), FSL.

312 *On March 10*: "A Gala Night at Grover's Theater: The President and family, the Secretary of State and family, and Lieutenant General Grant and staff will be present," *(Washington, D.C.) Daily National Republican*, March 10, 1864, SCRC, UCL; Francis B. Carpenter, *Six Months at the White House* (New York: Hurd & Houghton, 1866), 57.

313 *The pinnacle of Edwin's success*: Diary of Fanny Seward, March 1864, in *The Papers of William H. Seward*, consulted at Lamont Library, Harvard University.

315 *Dramatic Oil Company*: Rhodehamel and Tapers, eds., *The Writings of John Wilkes Booth*, 112–13; "Petrolia," *Leisure Hour*, May 1866, 299.

315 *"is the purest gambling"*: "Petrolia," *Leisure Hour*, May 1866, 299.

316 *embarked for work at St. Charles Theatre*: John S. Kendall, *The Golden Age of the New Or-*

leans Theatre (Baton Rouge: Louisiana State University Press, 1952), 497; Samples, *Lust for Fame*, 222; Ripley, " 'We Are Not in Little England Now,' " 93, 91.

316 *"the braggart North":* Clarke, *The Unlocked Book*, 115; JWB, "To Whom It May Concern [Philadelphia, November] 1864," in Rhodehamel and Taper, eds., *The Writings of John Wilkes Booth*, 125–26.

316 *The first St. Charles Theatre:* Kendall, *The Golden Age of the New Orleans Theatre*, 114–16, 184–85, 495; Samples, *Lust for Fame*, 222–23.

317 *"The statement that his voice":* Townsend, *The Life, Crime and Capture of John Wilkes Booth*, 27, SCRC, UCL; New Orleans *Daily Picayune*, April 3, 1864, in Samples, *Lust for Fame*, 147; Kendall, *The Golden Age of the New Orleans Theater*, 497.

317 *"the late hour":* "Mr. Booth as Richard III," *New Orleans Times*, March 15, 1864, KC; *(New Orleans) Daily True Delta*, April 3, 1864, in Samples, *Lust for Fame*, 147.

317 *"interested and amused hundreds of people":* Kendall, *The Golden Age of the New Orleans Theater*, 499.

317 *"unless he occupied a conspicuous":* Ibid., 499, 498.

318 *"Without a moment's hesitation":* Ibid., 498, 500.

319 *contact with Confederate agents:* Rhodehamel and Taper, eds., *The Writings of John Wilkes Booth*, 119; Clarke, *The Unlocked Book*, 125; Kendall, *The Golden Age of the New Orleans Theater*, 499–500.

319 *the last starring engagement:* Samples, *Lust for Fame*, 223; JWB to John A. Ellsler, June 11, 1864, Theatre Collection, HL; "Interview with Ben De Bar and Blanche Booth, Saint Louis, Missouri," April 24, 1865, transcript, Provost Marshal General Report, KC.

319 *three dozen gas lamps:* "The Boston Museum in 1876," illustration opposite page 4 in Ryan, *Old Boston Museum Days*; JBB "Ugolino: A Tragedy," in Booth Family Scrapbook, B.9.1, FSL.

CHAPTER FOURTEEN: MY THOUGHTS BE BLOODY

Page

321 *Junius Brutus Booth, Jr., arrived by steamship:* JBB, Jr., diary, April 11, May 26, 1864, Y.d. 374, FSL; Samples, *Lust for Fame*, 223; Asia Booth Clarke to Jean Anderson, January 8, 1854, original in the Peale Museum, Baltimore, copy courtesy of M. Kauffman and L. Verge, director, SHM.

321 *to New York City by June 2:* JBB, Jr., diary, June 2, 1864, Y.d. 374, FSL.

322 *proprietor of two great theaters:* EB to Harry [Magonigle], November 14, 1874, T.b.5 (1), FSL; ED to Adam Badeau, June 15, 1863, H-BTL; JBB, Jr., diary, September 18, 1864, FSL.

322 *The tension among all three brothers:* "Howard's Letter: Stories about Booth from Stuart, His Old Manager," *New York Record* (n.d.), printed material in extra-illustrated ed. of Matthews and Hutton, eds., *Actors and Actresses*, TS931.2, Theatre Collection, HL; JBB, Jr., diary, June 4, 1864, FSL.

322 *"big enough for a circus":* "The Career of Edwin Booth: The Long Run of Hamlet," in EB Scrapbook B.7.6, FSL.

322 *teams of carpenters:* EB to Adam Badeau, October 14, 1864, FSL; "Reminiscences of Edwin Booth Backstage at the Garden," unidentified newspaper article, EB clippings, Theatre Collection, HL; Booth family sword collection, Reading Room display case, first floor, The Players, 16 Gramercy Park South, New York.

323 *"Is this some trick of Edwin's?":* "Howard's Letter."

323 *"My brother W[ilkes] is here":* EB to Emma F. Cary, June 17, 1864, in Grossman, *Edwin Booth: Recollections by His Daughter*, 153.

323 *Yet they would not be paid:* JBB, Jr., diary, November 25, 1864, FSL; EB to Emma F. Cary,

November 11, 1864; EB to Mrs. Richard F. Cary, March 10, 1865, in Grossman *Edwin Booth: Recollections by His Daughter*, 154, 171; "John Wilkes Booth," Booth Family Scrapbook B.9.1, 141, FSL (article states that JWB "was to have played with Edwin Booth again at the same theatre [Winter Garden] on the 22nd of this month [April 1865] for the benefit of the same fund [Shakespeare Monument Fund]. The play selected was *Romeo and Juliet*, the cast of the Booths being—John Wilkes as Romeo, Edwin as Mercutio, and Junius as Friar Lawrence"); Clarke, *The Unlocked Book*, 122.

324 *visit to the Tenth Street studio:* Aldrich, *Crowding Memories*, 55–57.

324 *"so strongly sympathizing":* "Statement of Junius Brutus Booth, Jr., 5 May 1865," in Alford, ed., *John Wilkes Booth: A Sister's Memoir*, 118–19.

325 *The morning of June 8, 1864:* JWB to Isabel Sumner, June 7, 1864, in Rhodehamel and Taper, eds., *The Writings of John Wilkes Booth*, 110; Cone and Johns, *Petrolia*, 100, 99.

325 *"liquid lakes or lanes":* Cone and Johns, *Petrolia*, 100, 19; "Petrolia," *Leisure Hour*, May 1866, 296.

325 *"very stylish in his dress":* Alfred Wilson Smiley, *A Few Scraps, Oily and Otherwise* (Oil City, Pa.: Derrick, 1907), 78, 80–81.

326 *"slouched hat, flannel shirt":* Samples, *Lust for Fame*, 156; Ernest C. Miller, *John Wilkes Booth—Oilman* (New York: Exposition, 1947), 28.

326 *"During the short time I knew Booth":* Smiley, *A Few Scraps*, 81; Miller, *John Wilkes Booth—Oilman*, 32.

326 *By June 11, 1864:* Cone and Johns, *Petrolia*, 214; Miller, *John Wilkes Booth—Oilman*, 51.

326 *three separate wells:* Black, *Petrolia*, 48; "Petrolia," *Leisure Hour*, May 1866, 299; JWB to John A. Ellsler, June 11, 1864, Theatre Collection, HL.

326 *By June 17, 1864:* JWB to Isabel Sumner, June 17, 1864, in Rhodehamel and Taper, eds., *The Writings of John Wilkes Booth*, 113–14; John S. Schooley, "The Petroleum Region of America," *Harper's New Monthly Magazine*, April 1865, 567.

327 *"I want to see you here bad":* JWB to John A. Ellsler, June 17, 1864, in Rhodehamel and Taper, eds., *The Writings of John Wilkes Booth*, 113; Samples, *Lust for Fame*, 156.

327 *"had come to Franklin to have a tussle":* Samples, *Lust for Fame*, 157.

328 *Using an engine to drive an iron bit:* Black, *Petrolia*, 60; Cone and Johns, *Petrolia*, 214; Miller, *John Wilkes Booth—Oilman*, 35, 51.

328 *John's great speculation:* "Joseph H. Simonds [Testimony] for the Prosecution," May 13, 1865, in Benn Pittman, ed., *The Assassination of President Lincoln and the Trial of the Conspirators* (New York: Moore, Wilstach & Baldwin, 1865), 45; Cone and Johns, *Petrolia*, 214.

328 *On July 6, 1864:* JBB, Jr., diary, June 7 and July 6, 1864, FSL; EB to Adam Badeau, October 14, 1864, FSL; EB to Emma F. Cary, June 17 and November 11, 1864, in Grossman, *Edwin Booth: Recollections by His Daughter*, 153–54.

328 *"I am tired and sick":* JWB to Isabel Sumner, July 14, 1864, in Rhodehamel and Taper, eds., *The Writings of John Wilkes Booth*, 115; Joseph Simonds to JWB, [n.d.] February 1865, excerpted in Miller, *John Wilkes Booth—Oilman*, 57–58; Clarke, *The Unlocked Book*, 111–12, 122.

329 *Confederate Secret Service summoned him:* Rhodehamel and Taper, eds., *The Writings of John Wilkes Booth*, 119; Kendall, *The Golden Age of the New Orleans Theater*, 597, 500.

329 *"Fine time sunning and rowing":* JBB, Jr., diary, August 1, 1864, FSL; Charles Pope, "The Eccentric Booths: Their Peculiarities Described by One Who Knew Them: An Old Actor's Reminiscences," in EB Scrapbook B.7.6, FSL.

330 *"Dear mother is happy with her children":* EB to Emma F. Cary, August 26, 1864, in Grossman, *Edwin Booth: Recollections of His Daughter*, 164; Asia Booth Clarke to Jean Anderson, December 1, 1864, in Paul Amelia, "Highlights of Asia Booth Clarke's Letters to Jean

Anderson," typescript (compiled September 5, 1979, from originals at the Peale Museum, Baltimore), H-BTL; EB to Adam Badeau, October 14, 1864, FSL.

330 *"I've been in the scene-room":* EB to Emma F. Cary, August 26, 1864, in Grossman, *Edwin Booth: Recollections of His Daughter*, 164; EB to Adam Badeau, October 14, 1864, FSL; JBB, Jr., diary, September 18, 1864, FSL.

330 *most likely occurred August 7, 1864:* JBB, Jr., diary, August 7, 1864, FSL, reads "Clarke, Edwin and John left for Phila."; Rhodehamel and Taper, eds., *The Writings of John Wilkes Booth*, 128.

331 *returned to Edwin's house:* JBB, Jr., diary, August 28–29, 1864, FSL, reads "John Booth ill 3 weeks with Erysipelas in the Right Elbow. Had Dr. Smith"; Asia Booth Clarke to Jean Anderson, August 15, 1864, original in the Peale Museum, Baltimore, copy courtesy of M. Kauffman and L. Verge, director, SHM; Clarke, *The Unlocked Book*, 118.

331 *morale in general, had never been lower:* McPherson, ed., *The Most Fearful Ordeal*, 292; Election Broadsides, 1864 U.S. presidential campaign of George Brinton McClellan, SCRC, UCL; McPherson, *Battle Cry of Freedom*, 756, 760, 771.

331 *On August 29, a shouting match:* Adam Badeau, "Dramatic Reminiscences," n.d., EB clippings, Theatre Collection, HL; JBB, Jr., diary, September 2 and 18, 1864, FSL; EB to Adam Badeau, September 13, 1864, FSL.

332 *"were greatly attached to their mother":* "A Scandalous Story About the Booth Family," *Baltimore American*, April 22, 1865, KC; Winter, "Memories of the Players," *Colliers Weekly*, April 12, 1913.

332 *"making himself a king":* Clarke, *The Unlocked Book*, 124–25.

332 *"a disgusting quarrel":* EB to Adam Badeau, September 13, 1864, FSL; EB to Adam Badeau, September 26, 1864, FSL; EB to Adam Badeau, October 14, 1864, FSL.

333 *packed their bags for Philadelphia:* JBB, Jr., diary, September 2, 1864, FSL; McPherson, ed., *The Most Fearful Ordeal*, 292.

333 *"Whenever I would mention any success":* "Statement of Junius Brutus Booth, Jr., 5 May 1865," in Alford, ed., *John Wilkes Booth: A Sister's Memoir*, 121; McPherson, ed., *The Most Fearful Ordeal*, 292; Clarke, *The Unlocked Book*, 118.

333 *"My trade":* EB to Adam Badeau, September 13, 1864, FSL.

333 *"with a fine portrait of my father":* EB to Adam Badeau, September 26, 1864, FSL; "Souvenir Programme of the Hundredth Night of Edwin Booth's Hamlet, Winter Garden Theatre," March 22, 1865, in EB Scrapbook B.7.6, FSL.

334 *a final visit to Franklin:* Smiley, *A Few Scraps*, 81; Miller, *John Wilkes Booth—Oilman*, 35–36.

334 *talk of the approaching elections:* Miller, *John Wilkes Booth—Oilman*, 32; Smiley, *A Few Scraps*, 81, McPherson, *Battle Cry of Freedom*, 778.

334 *"strongest brandy":* Miller, *John Wilkes Booth—Oilman*, 40, 36.

335 *"run him through":* Miller, *John Wilkes Booth—Oilman*, 33; EB to Adam Badeau, October 14, 1864, FSL.

335 *"petroleum being more profitable than the profession":* "John Wilkes Booth," Booth Family Scrapbook B.9.1, 141, FSL; EB to Harry [Magonigle], November 14, 1874, T.b.5 (1), FSL; EB to Adam Badeau, September 26, 1864, FSL.

335 *"I hardly know what to make of you":* Joseph Simonds to JWB, [n.d.] February 1865, excerpted in Miller, *John Wilkes Booth—Oilman*, 57–58.

335 *traveled to Montreal:* Rhodehamel and Taper, eds., *The Writings of John Wilkes Booth*, 119; "Statement of Junius Brutus Booth, Jr., 5 May 1865," in Alford, ed., *John Wilkes Booth: A Sister's Memoir*, 119–20; Otis Skinner, *Footlights and Spotlights: Recollections of My Life on the Stage* (1924; reprint, Westport, Conn.: Greenwood, 1972), 180–84.

336 *a second term by a landslide:* McPherson, *Battle Cry of Freedom*, 805; Rhodehamel and Taper, eds., *The Writings of John Wilkes Booth*, 119.

336 *"I wish you [would] send me":* EB to Adam Badeau, September 26, 1864, FSL; EB to Emma F. Cary, November 11, 1864, in Grossman, *Edwin Booth: Recollections of His Daughter*, 154.

336 *Edwin did not wish to be outshone:* Clarke, *The Unlocked Book*, 122; EB to Emma F. Cary, November 11, 1864, in Grossman, *Edwin Booth: Recollections of His Daughter*, 154; "Howard's Letter: Stories about Booth from Stuart, His Old Manager," *New York Record* [n.d.], printed material in extra-illustrated ed. of Matthews and Hutton, eds., *Actors and Actresses*, TS931.2, Theatre Collection, HL.

337 *"The Three Sons of the Great Booth":* Charles H. Shattuck, "The Theatrical Management of EB," in *The Theatrical Manager in England and America: Player of a Perilous Game*, 152; EB to Harry [Magonigle], November 14, 1874, T.b.5 (1), FSI; Jeremiah Gurney, *John, Edwin & Junius Booth* (albumen silverprint, 1864), National Portrait Gallery, Smithsonian Institution.

337 *"The theater was crowded to suffocation":* Clarke, *The Elder and the Younger Booth*, 159; JBB, Jr., diary, November 25 and 26, 1864, FSL; "Winter Garden Shakespeare Benefit," *New York Herald*, November 26, 1864.

337 *"fairly carried the house by storm":* "Winter Garden Shakespeare Benefit," *New York Herald*, November 26, 1864; "Howard's Letter: Stories about Booth from Stuart, His Old Manager," *New York Record* [n.d.], printed material in extra-illustrated ed. of Matthews and Hutton, eds., *Actors and Actresses*, TS931.2, Theatre Collection, HL; "Sketch of John Wilkes Booth, the Murderer of the President," Booth Family Scrapbook B.9.1, 91, FSL.

338 *doors leading into the auditorium:* "Winter Garden Shakespeare Benefit," *New York Herald*, November 26, 1864; Clarke, *The Elder and the Younger Booth*, 159.

338 *$3,500 worth of tickets:* JBB, Jr., diary, November 25, to December 31, 1864, FSL; EB to David C. Anderson, October 23, 1878, H-BTL; Clarke, *The Unlocked Book*, 122; Laurence Hutton, "Edwin Booth," *Harper's Weekly*, June 17, 1893, 579.

338 *On the morning of November 26:* JBB, Jr., diary, November 26 and 28, 1864, FSL; Kimmel, *The Mad Booths of Maryland*, 192; "Conspiracy to Burn Hotels," *New York Herald*, November 26, 1864.

339 *"Vast Rebel Conspiracy":* "Attempt to Burn the City," *New York Herald*, November 27, 1864.

339 *"importations from Richmond and Canada":* "Conspiracy to Burn Hotels," *New York Herald*, November 26, 1864; "Attempt to Burn the City," *New York Herald*, November 27, 1864.

339 *The Confederate motive:* "Folly of the Late Rebel Attempt and Its Reactionary Effect," and "Late Incendiary Plot," *New York Herald*, November 28, 1864.

340 *"the whole pack of incendiaries":* Kimmel, *The Mad Booths of Maryland*, 192–93.

340 *"a rank secessionist":* " 'J. Wilkes Booth': Correspondence from the *Boston Journal*—The following communication comes to us from a reliable source," *(Washington, D.C.) Daily National Republican*, April 18, 1865, SCRC, UCL. This article begins: "His brother Edwin, now in this city, not long since turned J. Wilkes out of his house for talking treason. . . . We mention this in justice to Edwin, who is loyal."

340 *large, painful "boils," or "carbuncles":* JBB, Jr., diary, November 28, 29, and 30, 1864, FSL; Clarke, *The Unlocked Book*, 119.

341 *"Dearest beloved Mother":* JWB to Mary Ann Holmes Booth [Philadelphia, November] 1864, in Rhodehamel and Taper, eds., *The Writings of John Wilkes Booth*, 130–31.

341 *"To Whom It May Concern":* JWB to "To Whom It May Concern" [Philadelphia, November] 1864, in Rhodehamel and Taper, eds., *The Writings of John Wilkes Booth*, 124–27.

341 *In early December:* Asia Booth Clarke to Jean Anderson, December 1, 1864, original in the Peale Museum, Baltimore, copy courtesy of M. Kauffman and L. Verge, director, SHM; "Statement of Junius Brutus Booth, Jr., 5 May 1865," in Alford, ed., *John Wilkes Booth: A Sister's Memoir*, 118–19.

342 *"heartily sick and wearied":* EB to Harry [Magonigle], November 14, 1874, T.b.5 (1), FSL.

342 *Decades later, the episode was remembered:* Winter, *Life and Art of Edwin Booth*, 33–36; Laurence Hutton, "Edwin Booth," *Harper's Weekly*, June 17, 1893, 579; "Life of Edwin Booth: The Great Tragedian as a Man and an Actor," *New York Evening Sun*, June 7, 1893, EB clippings, Theatre Collection, HL.

342 *On March 27, 1865:* Adam Badeau, *Grant in Peace: From Appomattox to Mount McGregor, A Personal Memoir* (Hartford, Conn.: S. S. Scranton, 1887), 356–60.

342 *"Your triumph has realized all I ever hoped":* Adam Badeau to EB, March 27 and 28, 1865, H-BTL.

343 *"Hamlet has to be you":* Interview with Laurence Olivier, in Trevor Nunn, *The Great Hamlets*, video directed by Derke Eailey (New York: ABC Wide World of Learning, 1985); Badeau, *The Vagabond*, 288; costume medallion, with oval portrait of JBB, worn by EB in "Hamlet," Booth-Grossman family papers, BRTD, NYPL; Adam Badeau to EB, November 12, 1859, H-BTL; Skinner, *The Last Tragedian*, 7–8.

343 *A committee of distinguished men:* Winter, *Life and Art of Edwin Booth*, 42–43; EB to Emma F. Cary, January 10, 1865, and EB to Mrs. Richard Cary, February 9 and March 10, 1865, in Grossman, *Edwin Booth: Recollections by His Daughter*, 167–71; Richard Lockridge, *Darling of Misfortune: Edwin Booth, 1833–1893* (New York: Century, 1932), 143–44.

343 *"terrible success of 'Hamlet' ":* EB to Emma F. Cary, January 10, 1865, and to Mrs. Richard F. Cary, March 10, 1865, in Grossman, *Edwin Booth: Recollections by His Daughter*, 167, 171–72; "John Wilkes Booth," Booth Family Scrapbook B.9.1, 141, FSL.

344 *"You ask me what I am doing":* JWB to JBB, Jr., January 17, 1865, in Rhodehamel and Taper, eds., *The Writings of John Wilkes Booth*, 132.

344 *Onstage with Edwin Booth:* Sollers, "The Theatrical Career of John T. Ford," 80; Cast List, including "S. K. Chester as Claudius, King of Denmark" and "Mrs. S. K. Chester as Actress (The Player Queen)," in "Souvenir Programme of the Hundredth Night of Edwin Booth's *Hamlet*, Winter Garden Theatre," March 22, 1865, EB Scrapbook B.7.6, FSL.

344 *"about his oil speculations":* "Samuel Knapp Chester, [Testimony] for the Prosecution," May 12, 1865, in Pittman, ed., *The Assassination of President Lincoln*, 44–45.

345 *"All my life has been passed on picket duty":* Skinner, *The Last Tragedian*, 211.

CHAPTER FIFTEEN: THIS PLAY IS THE IMAGE OF A MURDER

Page

346 *Colonel Adam Badeau, aide-de-camp:* Badeau, *Grant in Peace*, 18, 20.

346 *"Each officer and man":* Badeau, *Grant in Peace*, 19, 21.

347 *"I stood near [Grant] as Lee left":* Badeau, *Grant in Peace*, 20–21, 22–23.

347 *No one wanted to sit inside Ford's Theatre:* "The Illumination Tomorrow Night," *(Washington, D.C.), Daily National Republican*, April 12, 1865, SCRC, UCL; A. Roger Ekirch, *At Day's Close: Night in Times Past* (New York: Norton, 2005), 110; "The Grand Illumination Last Night: Scenes and Incidents," *(Washington, D.C.) Daily National Republican*, April 14, 1865, SCRC, UCL.

348 *When the bells of firehouses and churches:* "Preparations for Tonight," *(Washington, D.C.) Daily National Republican*, April 13, 1865; "The Illumination Tomorrow Night," *(Washington, D.C.) Daily National Republican*, April 12, 1865.

348 *Before electric lighting:* Ekirch, *At Day's Close*, 69–73; "The Grand Illumination Last Night: Scenes and Incidents," *(Washington, D.C.) Daily National Republican*, April 14, 1865; "Correspondence from Washington," *(Des Moines) Iowa State Register*, March 5, 1862.

348 *The actress Laura Keene:* "Amusements Tonight: Ford's Theater," *(Washington, D.C.) Daily National Republican*, April 13, 1865; Tom Taylor and Charles Reade, "Masks and Faces:

A Comedy in Two Acts," *French's Standard Drama: The Acting Edition, #240* (New York: Samuel French, n.d.), 60, UCL.

348 *"tall, slender and exceptionally handsome":* MacMinn, *The Theater of the Golden Era in California*, 93; "Amusements Tonight: Ford's Theater," *(Washington, D.C.) Daily National Republican*, April 6 and 13, 1865; Creahan, *The Life of Laura Keene*, 23, 26; McPherson, *Battle Cry of Freedom*, 845–48.

349 *Grover's National Theatre on E Street:* "Grover's New Theater," *(Washington, D.C.) Daily National Republican* April 5 and 13, 1865; Leonard Grover, "Lincoln's Interest in the Theater," *Century Magazine*, April 1909, 944–45, 948; Sollers, "The Theatrical Career of John T. Ford," 196; "Testimony of John T. Ford," and "Testimony of H. Clay Ford," in Pittman, ed., *The Assassination of President Lincoln*, 102, 99–100.

349 *"looked like an angel":* MacMinn, *The Theater of the Golden Era in California*, 94; Henneke, *Laura Keene*, 175–76; Bryan, *Laura Keene*, 109–11.

350 *expensive copyright lawsuit:* Henneke, *Laura Keene*, 129–43; "Ford's New Theater," *(Washington, D.C.) Daily National Republican*, April 13 and 14, 1865.

351 *"grand beyond all powers of description":* "The Grand Illumination Last Night," *(Washington, D.C.) Daily National Republican*, April 14, 1865; Michael Burlingame, ed., *Lincoln's Journalist: John Hay's Anonymous Writing for the Press, 1860–1864* (Carbondale: Southern Illinois University Press, 1998), 48; William O. Stoddard, *Inside the White House in War Times* (New York: Webster, 1890), 97.

351 Union *and* Victory *sparkled:* "Local Affairs," *(Washington, D.C.) Daily National Republican*, April 12, 1865; "The Grand Illumination Last Night," *(Washington, D.C.) Daily National Republican*, April 14, 1865, SCRC, UCL.

351 *Ulysses S. Grant was in Washington:* Badeau, *Grant in Peace*, 361–62.

351 *"shocked and horrified":* Badeau, *Grant in Peace*, 359, 358.

352 *"Glory to God, Who Hath to US Grant'd":* "The Grand Illumination Last Night," *(Washington, D.C.) Daily National Republican*, April 14, 1865, SCRC, UCL.

352 *April 14 was her benefit:* "Benefit and Last Appearance of Miss Laura Keene," *(Washington, D.C.) Daily National Republican*, April 14, 1865, SCRC, UCL; Sollers, "The Theatrical Career of John T. Ford," 130–31.

352 *The only obstacle:* "Grover's New Theater: The Anniversary of Sumter's Fall," *(Washington, D.C.) Daily National Republican*, April 14, 1865, SCRC, UCL; "Statement of Roeliff Brinkerhoff," in Timothy S. Good, ed., *We Saw Lincoln Shot: One Hundred Eye Witness Accounts* (Jackson: University Press of Mississippi, 1995), 109.

352 *made the reasonable assumption:* Grover, "Lincoln's Interest in the Theater," 938–40, 948.

353 The Sea of Ice: "Amusements," *(Washington, D.C.) Daily National Republican*, February 6, 8, and 9, 1864; Allen C. Clark, *Abraham Lincoln in the National Capital* (Washington, D.C.: W. F. Roberts, 1925), 95, SCRC, UCL.

353 *invite the Lincolns to the theater:* Clark, *Abraham Lincoln in the National Capital*, 95; "Testimony of John T. Ford," in Pittman, ed., *The Assassination of Abraham Lincoln*, 104.

353 *"The illumination":* Clark, *Abraham Lincoln in the National Capital*, 95.

353 *Captain Charles Leale rushed into Ford's:* Charles A. Leale, *Lincoln's Last Hours: An Address Delivered Before the State of New York Military Order of the Loyal Legion, in the City of New York* (private printing, 1909), 2–3, SCRC, UCL.

353 *Henry C. Ford manned:* "Testimony of Henry C. Ford," in Pittman, ed., *The Assassination of Abraham Lincoln*, 100; Leale, *Lincoln's Last Hours*, 3; Ferguson, *I Saw Booth Shoot Lincoln*, 9.

354 *"I could not resist the temptation":* Good, ed., *We Saw Lincoln Shot*, 40, 53, 55.

354 *Laura Keene waited for her cue:* Ferguson, *I Saw Booth Shoot Lincoln*, 24–26, 33–34; Tom Taylor, *Our American Cousin: A Drama in Three Acts* (1869), 3, SCRC, UCL; "Testimony of Henry C. Ford," 99–100.

354 *Mrs. Lincoln's note came:* "Testimony of James R. Ford," in Pittman, ed., *The Assassination of Abraham Lincoln*, 100–101; "Ford's Theater," *(Washington, D.C.) Daily National Republican*, April 14, 1865; Clark, *Abraham Lincoln in the National Capital*, 97.

354 *the Grants declined the Lincolns' invitation:* Badeau, *Grant in Peace*, 362.

355 *Grover's Fort Sumter reenactment now lacked:* Grover, "Lincoln's Interest in the Theater," 944–47; Ruth Painter Randall, *Mary Lincoln: Biography of a Marriage* (Boston: Little, Brown, 1953), 358.

355 Our American Cousin *held a unique appeal:* Taylor, *Our American Cousin*, 10–11, SCRC, UCL.

355 *"plain play":* "Testimony of John T. Ford," 102; Taylor, *Our American Cousin*, 4.

355 *a wave of applause drowned out:* Ferguson, *I Saw Booth Shoot Lincoln*, 28; Leale, *Lincoln's Last Hours*, 3.

356 *"deafening cheers":* Good, ed., *We Saw Lincoln Shot*, 40; Leale, *Lincoln's Last Hours*, 3.

356 *"she gracefully curtsied":* Leale, *Lincoln's Last Hours*, 3; Ferguson, *I Saw Booth Shoot Lincoln*, 28.

356 *A different mood pervaded Ford's:* Creahan, *The Life of Laura Keene*, 7; Good, ed., *We Saw Lincoln Shot*, 56; Taylor, *Our American Cousin*, 28.

357 *"Everyone has been so jubilant":* Good, ed., *We Saw Lincoln Shot*, 56.

357 *aimed to please a Yankee crowd:* Taylor, *Our American Cousin*, 6, 10, 38; Clark, *Abraham Lincoln in the National Capital*, [cast list for *Our American Cousin*, Ford's Theatre, April 14, 1865, illustration facing 97].

357 *A love affair between:* Taylor, *Our American Cousin*, 32–35.

357 *" 'bottomland' Kentuck' native":* Jean H. Baker, *Mary Todd Lincoln* (New York: Norton, 1987), 83–85, 89–91; Taylor, *Our American Cousin*, 12.

358 *"Don't you know I've listened":* Taylor, *Our American Cousin*, 32; Leale, *Lincoln's Last Hours*, 3; Randall, *Mary Lincoln*, 344.

358 *At ten o'clock that night:* Ferguson, *I Saw Booth Shoot Lincoln*, 33–34; Randall, *Mary Lincoln*, 343; Leale, *Lincoln's Last Hours*, 3; Good, ed., *We Saw Lincoln Shot*, 53.

359 *It was the top of Act 3:* Taylor, *Our American Cousin*, 37; "Miss Laura Keene's Statement," in Creahan, *The Life of Laura Keene*, 27; Good, ed., *We Saw Lincoln Shot*, 53, 111; Clark, *Abraham Lincoln in the National Capital*, 106.

359 *"the whole occurrence, the shot, the leap":* "Miss Laura Keene's Statement," 27; Good, ed., *We Saw Lincoln Shot*, 38, 48.

360 *"Our president!":* Clark, *Abraham Lincoln in the National Capital*, 104–5; Good, ed., *We Saw Lincoln Shot*, 40, 48, 53.

360 *"some horrible carnival":* Clark, *Abraham Lincoln in the National Capital*, 105–6; Good, ed., *We Saw Lincoln Shot*, 40, 53; "The Assassination: The Depositions of Major Rathbone and Miss Harris," *(Washington, D.C.) Daily National Republican*, April 18, 1865, SCRC, UCL.

360 *a chaos of disorder beyond control":* "Miss Laura Keene's Statement," 27; Seaton Munroe, "Recollections of Lincoln's Assassination," *North American Review*, April 1896, 424–25; "The Assassination: The Depositions of Major Rathbone and Miss Harris," *(Washington, D.C.) Daily National Republican*, April 18, 1865, SCRC, UCL.

361 *They forced a way through:* Ferguson, *I Saw Booth Shoot Lincoln*, 52.

361 *a hallway off the main balcony:* "Testimony of Henry C. Ford," 99; Leale, *Lincoln's Last Hours*, 4–5.

361 *The president was sprawled:* Creahan, *The Life of Laura Keene*, 25; Leale, *Lincoln's Last Hours*, 6.

361 *"the thought passed through her mind":* Creahan, *The Life of Laura Keene*, 25; Bryan, *Laura Keene*, 10; "The Assassination: The Depositions of Major Rathbone and Miss Harris," *(Washington, D.C.) Daily National Republican*, April 18, 1865, SCRC, UCL.

361 *"By Mrs. Lincoln's courage, strength"*: Leale, *Lincoln's Last Hours*, 4–6; "Miss Laura Keene's Statement," 27.

362 *"the most piteous"*: "Miss Laura Keene's Statement," 27; Henneke, *Laura Keene*, 214; Munroe, "Recollections of Lincoln's Assassination," 424–26.

362 *"For God's sake let us sit"*: William Shakespeare, *Richard II*, in G. Blakemore Evans, ed., *The Riverside Shakespeare* (Boston: Houghton Mifflin, 1972), 822–23; "The Awful Murder," *(Washington, D.C.) Daily National Republican*, April 15, 1865, SCRC, UCL.

363 *"for the glorification of the actor"*: Good, ed., *We Saw Lincoln Shot*, 112; Leale, *Lincoln's Last Hours*, 5–6.

363 *"The memory of that apparition"*: Munroe, "Recollections of Lincoln's Assassination," 424–26; Creahan, *The Life of Laura Keene*, 25.

363 *"he has made me know what tragedy is"*: Badeau, *The Vagabond*, 287; Micheál MacLiammoir,, "Hamlet in Elsinore," in *The Best from The Bell": Great Irish Writing*, Sean McMahon, ed. (Totowa, New Jersey: Rowan A. Littlefield, 1979), 172.

364 *"Our father's face of tragedy"*: Laura E. Richards and Maud Howe Elliott, *Julia Ward Howe, 1819–1910*, vol. 1 (Boston: Houghton Mifflin, 1916), 220.

364 *"Nothing has happened"*: Julia Ward Howe, diary, April 15, 1865, bMS Am 2119 (1107), HL.

364 *"a weary ghost"*: Julia Ward Howe, diary, April 15–19, 1865, bMS Am 2119 (1107), HL.

364 *"a humbly-bumbly of confusion"*: Samuel Gridley Howe to Laura Howe, July 3, 1865, bMS 2214 (184), HL; "The Awful Murder," *(Washington, D.C.) Daily National Republican*, April 15, 1865.

365 *he threw a small object*: Skinner, *The Last Tragedian*, 114; Anon., "Edwin Booth and Lincoln," *Century Magazine*, April 1909, 919–20.

365 *"You know, Ad, how I have labored"*: EB to Adam Badeau, April 16, 1865, in Alford, ed., *John Wilkes Booth: A Sister's Memoir*, 112–13.

365 *"You will be pleased"*: EB to Adam Badeau, April 16, 1865, in Skinner, *The Last Tragedian*, 139–40; Julia Ward Howe, *Reminiscences*, 258–59.

365 *Julia and her husband walked*: Richards and Elliott, *Julia Ward Howe*, 220.

366 *Governor Andrew personally*: Julia Ward Howe, diary, April 18, 1865, bMS Am 2119 (1107); EB to Adam Badeau, April 16, 1865, in Alford, ed., *John Wilkes Booth: A Sister's Memoir*, 112–13; Skinner, *The Last Tragedian*, 139; Aldrich, *Crowding Memories*, 72–73.

366 *"stricken and stunned with grief"*: Aldrich, *Crowding Memories*, 72–73.

366 *"Poor Mother, who can condole her?"*: JBB, Jr., to EB, [n.d.] April 1865, H-BTL; Clarke, *The Unlocked Book*, 127–28.

366 *Joe Booth*: Mary Ann Holmes Booth to EB, May 10, 1862, H-BTL; JBB, Jr., diary, June 2, and December 27, 1864, FSL; "Examination of Joseph Adrian Booth Before Major General [John A.] Dix," May 12, 1865, in Alford, ed., *John Wilkes Booth: A Sister's Memoir*, 133, 139, 138.

367 *"Human pride must always be liable"*: JBB, Jr., to EB, [n.d.] April 1865, H-BTL.

367 *"spectral" form*: Aldrich, *Crowding Memories*, 73; Anon. to EB, May 1, 1865, in Skinner, *The Last Tragedian*, 142.

367 *"Mother is very much broken"*: EB to Emma F. Cary, November 24, and May 6, 1865, in Grossman, *Edwin Booth: Recollections by His Daughter*, 174, 172–73; Aldrich, *Crowding Memories*, 74.

368 *On April 18, John T. Ford*: Sollers, "The Theatrical Career of John T. Ford," 203–5.

368 *On April 26, June*: JBB, Jr., diary, April–June 1865, in Alford, ed., *John Wilkes Booth: A Sister's Memoir*, 124–25.

369 *submitted to house arrest*: Asia Booth Clarke to Jean Anderson, May 22, 1865, original in the Peale Museum, Baltimore, copy courtesy of M. Kauffman and L. Verge, director, SHM.

369 *powerful friends:* William Stuart, EB's manager at the Winter Garden Theatre, was a friend of Charles A. Dana. In an interview given after EB's death, Stuart claimed Dana had secured the actor's freedom: "There was a warrant, however, issued for [EB's] arrest, a necessity of such an hour," Stuart said. "But . . . through the kind intervention of Mr. Dana, who was the Under Secretary of War, it was withdrawn. His brother Junius, however, and his brother-in-law Mr. Clarke, were confined in the Washington prison for some time." Stuart's statement is in "Howard's Letter: Stories about Booth from Stuart, His Old Manager," *New York Record* (n.d.), printed material in extra-illustrated ed. of Matthews and Hutton, eds., *Actors and Actresses*, TS931.2, Theatre Collection, HL. The following sources corroborate Stuart's claim: JBB Jr. diary, June 22, 1865, in Alford, ed., *John Wilkes Booth: A Sister's Memoir*, 125; Winter, *Life and Art of Edwin Booth*, 42.

369 *"I lose no chance":* Adam Badeau to EB, April 29, 1865, H-BTL; Adam Badeau to EB, April 19, 1865, H-BTL.

370 *"to inflict vengeance upon us":* "The Folly of the Late Rebel Attempt and Its Reactionary Effects," *New York Herald*, November 28, 1864.

370 *"He who could lend himself to such a dark and damnable":* "The Assassin of the President," Booth Family Scrapbook B.9.1, 141, FSL.

370 *"those who know [John Wilkes Booth] best feel confident":* "The Assassination," Booth Family Scrapbook, B.9.1, 99, FSL; Asia Booth Clarke to Jean Anderson, May 22, 1865, original in the Peale Museum, Baltimore, copy courtesy of M. Kauffman and L. Verge, director, SHM.

370 *feared that mobs would attack theaters or harm actors:* Skinner, *Footlights and Spotlights*, 178; "Resolutions of the Theatrical Profession Respecting the Assassination," *(Washington, D.C.) Daily National Republican*, April 24, 1865, SCRC, UCL.

371 *"John is dead, not by the rope":* Richard Henry Stoddard to EB, April 27, 1865, reproduced in "The Life Tragedy of Edwin Booth," EB clippings, Theatre Collection, HL.

371 *Mary Ann Booth was alone:* Asia Booth Clarke to Jean Anderson, May 22, 1865, original in the Peale Museum, Baltimore, copy courtesy of M. Kauffman and L. Verge, director, SHM; Aldrich, *Crowding Memories*, 75–76.

371 *On July 10, 1865, the company:* Sollers, "The Theatrical Career of John T. Ford," 216, 218, 221.

372 *"It has pleased God to afflict my family":* "Letter from Edwin Booth: The members of the New York Lodge of Freemasons, No. 330, having addressed a letter of greeting to Mr. Edwin Booth, expressive of their sympathy in the hour of his deep affliction, the following answer was returned: 'No. 28 East Nineteenth Street, Dear Brothers . . .'"; [n.d.] May 1865, EB clippings, Theatre Collection, HL.

EPILOGUE: THE CURTAIN FALLS

Page

373 *brought* Our American Cousin *to the Winter Garden:* Shattuck, "The Theatrical Management of EB," 162, 146–48; Henneke, *Laura Keene*, 221–23; EB to Julia Ward Howe, September 24, 1865, bMS Am 2119 (63), HL.

373 *"[is] my personal, private property":* "Card from Laura Keene to J. S. Clarke, Lessee of Winter Garden, Sept. 29, 1865: "Sir—I see by your advertisement in the HERALD that you purpose playing Our American Cousin . . ."; in Booth Family Scrapbook, B.9.1, 153; Henneke, *Laura Keene*, 222–23.

374 *"engine that knew no rest":* William H. Herndon and Jesse W. Weik, *Herndon's Life of Lincoln*, Paul M. Angle, ed. (Cleveland: World, 1942), 304; EB to Julia Ward Howe, September 24, 1865, bMS Am 2119 (63), HL.

374 *old charge of bastardy:* Clarke, *The Unlocked Book,* 131; "The Booth Family: A Liberal Article from a Radical Newspaper," *Albany (N.Y.) Evening Journal,* April 27, 1865, Booth-Grossman family papers, BRTD, NYPL.

374 *"I am sure that the unanimity":* EB to [?], December 26, 1865, bMS Thr 467, HL; EB to Mrs. Richard F. Cary, December 20, 1865, in Grossman, *Edwin Booth: Recollections by His Daughter,* 174–75; Winter, *Life and Art of Edwin Booth,* 37.

374 *volcano of editorial commentary:* Undated material, including articles titled "Infamous," "The Old Man Impotent," "Edwin Booth," and "A Heartless Pact: People of New York to the Rescue," from a collection of New York newspaper clippings (December 1865–January 1866) covering the return of EB to the stage after Lincoln's assassination, in the Booth-Grossman family papers, BRTD, NYPL; "The Career of Edwin Booth," in EB Scrapbook B.7.6, FSL.

375 *"It is not of his own seeking":* "A Heartless Act—People of New York to the Rescue," "Edwin Booth at the Winter Garden—Brilliant Reception," "Edwin Booth's Rentree at the Winter Garden," articles from New York newspapers on the return of EB to the stage, January 1866, Booth-Grossman family papers, BRTD, NYPL.

376 *"reached his zenith":* "The Career of Edwin Booth," EB Scrapbook B.7.6, FSL; Laurence Hutton, "Edwin Booth," *Harper's Weekly Magazine,* June 17, 1893, 579; Winter, *Life and Art of Edwin Booth,* 42–43.

376 *Booth Theatre went dark in 1874:* EB to John E. Russell, January 24, March 21, August 17, 1868, and February 12, 1869, in EB correspondence, RRL; "Opening Night at Booth's Theater," *New York Tribune,* February 4, 1869, Booth Scrapbook B.9.1, FSL; Winter, *Life and Art of Edwin Booth,* 73–78, 272–73; Shattuck, "The Theatrical Management of Edwin Booth," 168–72.

377 *Americans hungered to see Edwin's genius:* "Receipt received by Edwin Booth from De Bar's Opera House, St. Louis, 10 October 1870, for the sum of six thousand and ninety-five dollars, his share for five nights of performances," bMS Thr 467, HL; William Winter, "Incidents in the Life of Edwin Booth," T.B.5 (9), FSL; Godwin, "Commemorative Address," Program from the 60th Anniversary, November 13, 1893, 30–39.

377 *allusions to his brother's crime:* Skinner, *Footlights and Spotlights,* 177–78; Goodale, *Behind the Scenes with Edwin Booth,* 96; EB to David C. Anderson, May 1, 1879, in Grossman, *Edwin Booth: Recollections by His Daughter,* 198–99; Mary Ann Holmes Booth to EB, April 28, 1879, H-BTL; Winter, *Life and Art of EB,* 127–28.

377 *In 1880, Edwin toured:* EB to Adam Badeau, June 3, 1881, Y.c.215 (22–25), FSL; Lockridge, *Darling of Misfortune,* 265.

378 *The idea for The Players:* Phillips, *The Players: Occasional Pieces,* 4–15; "List of Members, 1888–1988," in Tebbel, *A Certain Club,* appendix.

378 *Laura Keene was never able:* Creahan, *Life of Laura Keene,* 24–25, 78–79; Skinner, *Footlights and Spotlights,* 178; Clarke, *The Unlocked Book,* 139; Henneke, *Laura Keene,* 250, 268, 272.

379 *"He attacked me with the utmost vehemence":* Julia Ward Howe, diary, April 22, 23, and 24, 1865, bMS Am 2119 (1107), HL; Julia Ward Howe, "Poems: Lincoln," bMS Am 2214 (321), HL.

379 *"a free agent":* Julia Ward Howe, *Reminiscences,* 372–73, 393; Julia Ward Howe, diary, April 23, 1865, bMS Am 2119 (1107), HL; Julia Ward Howe, "Poem: Edwin Booth, June 9, 1893," bMS Am 2119 (1059), HL; Richards and Elliott, *Julia Ward Howe,* 365.

380 *"I have had the honor of pleading":* Julia Ward Howe, *Reminiscences,* 444, 378.

380 *a chill settled over Adam Badeau's friendship:* EB to Adam Badeau, July 27, 1865, bMS Thr 467, HL; Adam Badeau to EB, March 24, 1882; EB to Julia Ward Howe, September 24, 1865, bMS Am 2119 (63), HL.

380 *Captain Badeau never entirely left the employ:* Badeau, *Grant in Peace*, 11–14, 177–79, 299, 304–5, 409, 420–25, 462–65.

381 *"to tell the story of his motives and purposes":* Badeau, *Grant in Peace*, 428; Foner and Garraty, eds., *The Reader's Companion to American History*, 466.

381 *Badeau, who lived until 1895:* "Adam Badeau" in Johnson, ed., *Dictionary of American Biography*, 485; Tebbel, *A Certain Club*, 25–26; Badeau, "Edwin Booth, On and Off the Stage," *McClure's Magazine*, August 1893, 265–67.

382 *"It was ready for the press by the 20th of August":* Clarke, *The Unlocked Book*, 137, 132; Asia Booth Clarke to Jean Anderson, April 16, 1866, in Paul Amelia, "Highlights of Asia Booth Clarke's Letters to Jean Anderson," typescript (compiled September 5, 1979, from originals at the Peale Museum, Baltimore), H-BTL.

382 *"are such a prejudiced, self-conceited":* Asia Booth Clarke to Jean Anderson, January 28, 1869, February 23, 1868, and December 6, 1874, in Amelia, "Highlights of Asia Booth Clarke's Letters to Jean Anderson."

382 *devoted to writing further histories of the Booths:* Only with her family's approval did Asia publish her biographies of JBB and EB. She wrote her memoir of JWB in secret, giving the manuscript to a close family friend at her death. During their lifetimes, neither EB nor John Sleeper Clarke knew of the memoir's existence. See EB to David C. Anderson, December 17, 1880, in Grossman, *Edwin Booth: Recollections of His Daughter*, 217; and Eleanor Farjeon's "Foreword" to Clarke, *The Unlocked Book*, 15–16, 20–24.

382 *"So many tongues are free to calumniate us":* Clarke, *Booth Memorials*, viii; Asia Booth Clarke to Jean Anderson, May 22, 1865, original in the Peale Museum, Baltimore, copy courtesy of M. Kauffman and L. Verge, director, SHM.

383 *"small means and a large family":* JBB, Jr., to EB, November 4, 1870, "Booth's Theater—Manager's Office," [n.d., 187?], and March 4, 1874, H-BTL; EB to David C. Anderson, October 23, 1878, H-BTL.

383 *Mary Ann Holmes Booth died:* EB to Edwina Booth Grossman, October 22, 1885, in Grossman, *Edwin Booth: Recollections by His Daughter*, 65; Mary Ann Holmes Booth to EB, May 8, 1877, H-BTL.

383 *"the miseries of her great sorrow":* EB to David C. Anderson, May 1, 1879, in Grossman, *Edwin Booth: Recollections by His Daughter*, 199; EB to Julia Ward Howe, September 24, 1865, bMS Am 2119 (63), HL.

384 *Joe and Ann Hall:* Stanley Kimmel, "Notes from two interviews with Joseph Edwin Hall, son of Joseph and Ann Hall, conducted November 3 & 19, 1935, in Bel Air, Maryland," KC.

384 *"What a consolation it would be":* EB to Ulysses S. Grant, [n.d.] September 1867, in Kimmel, *The Mad Booths of Maryland*, 279–80; Mrs. Elijah Rogers to William Stump Forwood, August 16, 1886, JBB family collection, Manuscript Division, LC.

384 *a very "elegant" box:* Mrs. Elijah Rogers to William Stump Forwood, August 16, 1886, JBB family collection, Manuscript Division, LC; Kimmel, *The Mad Booths of Maryland*, 281.

385 *"To the memory of the children":* Badeau, *The Vagabond*, 354; Kimmel, *The Mad Booths of Maryland*, 282; dates of interment, description of lot cards for the transfer of six Booth bodies, and multiple photographs of the Booth obelisk and family grave markers were provided by Dan Monahan, superintendent of the Greenmount Cemetery, Baltimore, on September 17, 2009.

385 *Rosalie Booth spent:* EB to Edwina Booth Grossman, October 22, 1885, in Grossman, *Edwin Booth: Recollections by His Daughter*, 66; Mrs. Elijah Rogers to William Stump Forwood, August 16, 1886, JBB family collection, Manuscript Division, LC; Thomas Bailey Aldrich to William Winter, [n.d.] 1893, "We reached Mount Auburn a few minutes before sunset," in Skinner, *The Last Tragedian*, 212–13.

BIBLIOGRAPHY

MANUSCRIPT SOURCES

RARE BOOK AND MANUSCRIPT ARCHIVES

Abraham Lincoln Presidential Library and Museum, Springfield, Illinois

Baldwin Library, Maryland Historical Society, Baltimore, Maryland

Beth Ahabah Museum and Archives, Richmond, Virginia

Billy Rose Theatre Division at the Performing Arts Research Center, New York Public Library, New York, New York

Boston Athenaeum, Boston, Massachusetts

Department of Rare Books and Special Collections, Princeton University Library, Princeton, New Jersey

Folger Shakespeare Library, Washington, D.C.

Free Library of Philadelphia, Philadelphia, Pennsylvania

Hampden-Booth Theatre Library, New York, New York

Houghton Library, Harvard University, Cambridge, Massachusetts

Manuscript Division, Library of Congress, Washington, D.C.

Rare Book and Manuscript Library, University Library, University of Illinois at Urbana-Champaign, Urbana, Illinois

Research Center, Chicago History Museum, Chicago, Illinois

Special Collections, Rush Rhees Library, University of Rochester, Rochester, New York

Special Collections Research Center, University of Chicago Library, Chicago, Illinois

Stanley Kimmel Collection, Macdonald-Kelce Library, University of Tampa, Tampa, Florida

Widener Library, Harvard University, Cambridge, Massachusetts

PRINTED SOURCES

PERIODICALS

Albany (N.Y.) *Evening Journal*

American Beacon (Norfolk, Va.)

American Spectator (Boston, Mass.)

The Atlantic Monthly

Baltimore American

Baltimore Patriot and Advertiser

Baltimore Sun

Boston Evening Transcript

Boston Herald

Buffalo (N.Y.) *Times*

California Historical Society Quarterly

The Century Magazine

Chicago Daily Journal

Cleveland Leader

Collier's Weekly

Confederate Veteran

The Cosmopolitan

Daily Inter Ocean (Chicago)

Daily National Republican (Washington, D.C.)

The Figaro

Green Book Album

Harper's New Monthly Magazine

Harper's Weekly

The Illustrated American Magazine

Iowa State Register (Des Moines)

Journal of Southern History

Leisure Hour

BIBLIOGRAPHY

Lincoln Herald

McClure's Magazine

Montgomery (Ala.) Daily Post

New England Magazine

New Orleans Times-Picayune

New York Clipper

New York Daily Tribune

New York Dramatic Mirror

New York Evening Post

New York Herald

New York Press

New York Record

New York Star

New York Sun

New York Theater Magazine

New York Times

North American Review

Philadelphia Inquirer

The Play-Goer and Theatrical Recorder
(New York)

The Programme (New York)

Richmond (Va.) Dispatch

Richmond (Va.) Enquirer

Sacramento Union

San Francisco Examiner

Theater Notebook

Theater Survey

Virginia Magazine of History
and Biography

Washington (D.C.) Evening Star

Wheatley's Gift (Philadelphia)

Wilkes' Spirit of the Times (New York)

BOOKS

Alcott, Louisa May. *Hospital Sketches.* New York: Sagamore, 1957.

Aldrich, Mrs. Thomas Bailey. *Crowding Memories.* Boston: Houghton Mifflin, 1920.

Allen, Gay Wilson. *Melville and His World.* New York: Viking, 1971.

———. *The New Walt Whitman Handbook.* New York: New York University Press, 1975.

———. *The Solitary Singer: A Critical Biography of Walt Whitman.* Chicago: University of Chicago Press, 1985.

Anbinder, Tyler. *Nativism and Slavery: The Northern Know Nothings and the Politics of the 1850s.* New York: Oxford University Press, 1992.

Anonymous, *The Actor, Or, A Peep Behind the Curtain: Being Passages in the Lives of Booth and Some of His Contemporaries.* New York: William H. Graham, 1846.

Archer, Stephen M. *Junius Brutus Booth: Theatrical Prometheus.* Carbondale: Southern Illinois University Press, 1992.

Audubon, John James. *Ornithological Biography: or, An account of the habits of the birds of the United States of America; accompanied by descriptions of the objects represented in the work entitled The birds of America, and interspersed with delineations of American scenery and manners.* Philadelphia: Carey & Hart, 1839.

Badeau, Adam. *Grant in Peace: From Appomattox to Mount McGregor: A Personal Memoir.* Hartford, Conn.: S. S. Scranton, 1887.

———. *Military History of Ulysses S. Grant: From April, 1861, to April, 1865.* New York: D. Appleton, 1868.

———. *The Vagabond.* New York: Rudd & Carleton, 1859.

Baker, Jean H. *Mary Todd Lincoln: A Biography.* New York: Norton, 1987.

Baldwin, Leland. *The Keelboat Age on Western Waters.* Pittsburgh: University of Pittsburgh Press, 1941.

Baltimore Municipal Journal. *Baltimore, 200th Anniversary, 1729–1929.* Baltimore: Fleet-McGinley, c1929.

Bancroft, Hubert Howe. *California Inter Pocula.* San Francisco: History Company, 1888.

Bauer, K. Jack. *The Mexican War: 1846–1848.* New York: Macmillan, 1974.

Baym, Nina, et al., eds. *The Norton Anthology of American Literature.* Vol. 1. New York: Norton, 1989.

Bennett, Betty T., ed. *Lives of the Great Romantics by Their Contemporaries.* Vol. 3, *Godwin, Wollstonecraft & Mary Shelley by Their Contemporaries.* London and Brookfield, Vt.: Pickering & Chatto, 1999.

Bernstein, Iver. *The New York City Draft Riots.* New York: Oxford University Press, 1990.

Black, Brian. *Petrolia.* Baltimore: Johns Hopkins University Press, 2000.

Bloom, Arthur W. *Joseph Jefferson: Dean of the American Theater.* Savannah, Ga.: Frederic C. Beil, 2000.

Booth, John Wilkes. *Right or Wrong, God Judge Me: The Writings of John Wilkes Booth.* Edited by John Rhodehamel and Louise Taper. Urbana: University of Illinois Press, 1997.

Booth, Junius Brutus Sr. *Memoirs of Junius Brutus Booth, from his birth to the present time; with an appendix, containing original letters, from persons of rank and celebrity; and copious extracts from the journal kept by Mr. Booth, during his theatrical tour of the continent.* London: Chapple, Miller, Rowden & E. Wilson, 1817.

Booth, Mary Devlin. *The Letters and Notebooks of Mary Devlin Booth.* Edited by L. Terry Oggel. Contributions in Drama and Theater Studies 23. New York: Greenwood, c1987.

Brandt, Allan M. *No Magic Bullet: A Social History of Venereal Disease in the United States.* New York: Oxford University Press, 1987.

Bristol, Frank Milton. *The Life of Chaplain McCabe.* New York: Fleming H. Revell, 1908.

Brodie, Janet Farrell. *Contraception and Abortion in Nineteenth-Century America.* Ithaca, N.Y.: Cornell University Press, 1994.

Brown, Henry Collins, ed. *Valentine's Manual of Old New York.* New York: Valentine's Manual, 1920.

Browne, D. J. *The Trees of America: Native and foreign, pictorially and botanically delineated, and scientifically and popularly described.* New York: Harper & Brothers, 1846.

Bryan, Vernanne. *Laura Keene: A British Actress on the American Stage.* Jefferson, N.C.: McFarland, 1997.

Bunner, H. C., with E. A. Dithmar, Laurence Hutton, Brander Matthews, and William Winter. *A Portfolio of Players: With a Packet of Notes Thereon.* New York: J. W. Bouton, 1888.

Byron, George Gordon. *Poetical Works of Lord Byron.* Edited by Mathilde Blind. London: Walter Scott, 1886.

Cameron, Kenneth Neill, comp. *Romantic Rebels: Essays on Shelley and His Circle.* Cambridge, Mass.: Harvard University Press, 1973.

Carpenter, Francis B. *Six Months at the White House.* New York: Hurd & Houghton, 1866.

Castellanos, Henry C. *New Orleans As It Was: Episodes of Louisiana Life.* Baton Rouge: Louisiana State University Press, 1978.

Catalog of the Paintings and the Art Treasures of The Players. New York: privately published, 1925.

Christiansen, Richard. *A Theater of Our Own: A History and a Memoir of 1,001 Nights in Chicago.* Evanston, Ill.: Northwestern University Press, 2004.

Clapp, William W. *A Record of the Boston Stage.* Cambridge, Mass.: J. Munroe, 1853.

Clark, Allen C. *Abraham Lincoln in the National Capital.* Washington, D.C.: W. F. Roberts, 1925.

Clarke, Asia Booth. *Booth Memorials: Passages, Incidents and Anecdotes in the Life of Junius Brutus Booth (the elder) by his daughter.* New York: Henry L. Hinton, 1870.

———. *The Elder and the Younger Booth.* Boston: J. R. Osgood, 1882.

————. *John Wilkes Booth: A Sister's Memoir.* Edited by Terry Alford. Jackson: University Press of Mississippi, 1996.

————. *Personal Recollections of the Elder Booth.* London: privately published, 1902.

————. *The Unlocked Book: A Memoir of John Wilkes Booth.* New York: G. P. Putnam's Sons, 1938.

Clarke, James Freeman. *Memorial and Biographical Sketches.* Boston: Houghton, Osgood, 1878.

Cleveland, Grover. *The Letters of Grover Cleveland, 1850–1908.* Edited by Allan Nevins. New York: Houghton Mifflin, 1933.

Clubbe, John. *Byron, Sully and the Power of Portraiture.* Aldershot, Eng.: Ashgate, 2005.

Cohen, Saul B., ed. *The Columbia Gazetteer of the World.* Vol. 1. New York: Columbia University Press, 1998.

Cole, Rodney M., ed. *A Distant War Comes Home: Maine in the Civil War Era.* Camden, Maine: Down East, 1996.

Cone, Andrew, and Walter R. Johns. *Petrolia.* New York: D. Appleton, 1870.

Cook, Adrian. *The Armies of the Streets: The New York City Draft Riots of 1863.* Lexington: University Press of Kentucky, 1974.

Copeland, Charles Townsend. *Edwin Booth.* Boston: Small, Maynard, 1901.

Cowell, Joe. *Thirty Years Passed Among the Players in England and America: Interspersed with Anecdotes and Reminiscences of a Variety of Persons, Directly or Indirectly Connected with the Drama During the Theatrical Life of Joe Cowell, Comedian.* New York: Harper & Brothers, 1844.

Crane, William Carey. *Life and Select Literary Remains of Sam Houston of Texas.* Dallas: William G. Scarff, 1884.

Creahan, John. *The Life of Laura Keene: Actress, Artist, Manager and Scholar.* Philadelphia: Rodgers, 1897.

Dana, Charles A., and J. H. Wilson. *The Life of Ulysses S. Grant: General of the Armies of the United States.* Springfield, Mass.: Gurdon Bill, 1868.

Dawson, Sarah Morgan. *A Confederate Girl's Diary.* Introduction by Warrington Dawson. New York: Houghton Mifflin, 1913.

Day, Roy, ed. *Catalogue of the Paintings and the Art Treasures of The Players.* New York: Players, 1925.

Dempsey, David K. *The Triumphs and Trials of Lotta Crabtree.* New York: William Morrow, 1968.

Derks, Scott. *The Value of a Dollar: Prices and Incomes in the United States, 1860–2004.* Millerton, N.Y.: Grey House, 2004.

Dickens, Charles. *American Notes for General Circulation.* 1842. Reprint, New York: Penguin, 1987.

Donald, David Herbert. *Lincoln.* New York: Simon & Schuster, 1995.

Donohoe, Joseph W., Jr., ed. *The Theatrical Manager in England and America: Players of a Perilous Game.* Princeton, N.J.: Princeton University Press, 1971.

Douglass, Frederick. *Narrative of the Life of Frederick Douglass, An American Slave.* Edited by Houston A. Baker. 1845. Reprint, New York: Penguin, 1986.

Duke, Maurice, and Daniel P. Jordan, eds. *A Richmond Reader: 1733–1983.* Chapel Hill: University of North Carolina Press, 1983.

Dyer, Oliver. *Great Senators of the United States Forty Years Ago.* New York: R. Bonner's Sons, 1889.

Eisler, Benita. *Byron: Child of Passion, Fool of Fortune.* New York: Knopf, 1999.

Ekirch, A. Roger. *At Day's Close: Night in Times Past.* New York: Norton, 2005.

Elliott, Maud Howe. *Lord Byron's Helmet.* Boston: Houghton Mifflin, 1927.

Emmerson, John C. *The steam-boat comes to Norfolk Harbor, and the log of the first ten years, 1815–1825; together with some account of the hotels and taverns that catered to travelers in the steam boats, and of some notable passengers who rode them; as reported by the Norfolk gazette & publick ledger, the American beacon, and the Norfolk & Portsmouth herald.* Portsmouth, Va.: privately published, 1947.

Ernst, Alice Henson. *Trouping in the Oregon Country: A History of Frontier Theater.* Portland: Oregon Historical Society, 1961.

Everett, Barbara. *Young Hamlet: Essays on Shakespeare's Tragedies.* New York: Oxford University Press, 1989.

Fabian, Monroe H. *Mr. Sully, Portrait Painter: The Works of Thomas Sully (1783–1872).* Washington, D.C.: Smithsonian Institution, 1983.

Ferguson, W. J. *I Saw Booth Shoot Lincoln.* Boston: Houghton Mifflin, 1930.

Fields, Barbara Jeanne. *Slavery and Freedom on the Middle Ground: Maryland during the Nineteenth Century.* New Haven, Conn.: Yale University Press, 1985.

Foner, Eric, and John Garraty, eds. *The Reader's Companion to American History.* Boston: Houghton Mifflin, 1991.

Foote, Shelby. *The Civil War, a Narrative.* Vol. 1, *Fort Sumter to Perryville.* New York: Vintage, 1986.

Forbush, Edward H. *A History of the Game Birds, Wild Fowl and Shore Birds of Massachusetts and Adjacent States.* Boston: Wright & Potter, 1912.

Forrest, William S. *Historical and descriptive sketches of Norfolk and vicinity: Including Portsmouth and the adjacent counties, during a period of two hundred years; also sketches of Williamsburg, Hampton, Suffolk, Smithfield, and other places, with descriptions of some of the principal objects of interest in eastern Virginia.* Philadelphia: Lindsay & Blakiston, 1853.

Forrester, Izola L. *This One Mad Act: The Unknown Story of John Wilkes Booth and His Family, by His Granddaughter.* Boston: Hale, Cushman & Flint, 1937.

Francis, John W. *New York During the last Half Century: A Discourse.* New York: John F. Trow, 1857.

Garraty, John, ed. *Encyclopedia of American Biography.* New York: Harper & Row, 1974.

Gilder, Richard Watson. *Grover Cleveland: A Record of Friendship.* New York: Century, 1910.

———. *Letters of Richard Watson Gilder.* Edited by Rosamond Gilder. New York: Houghton Mifflin, 1916.

Godwin, Parke. "Commemorative Address." Program of the Memorial Celebration of the Sixtieth Anniversary of the Birth of Edwin Booth, Madison Square Garden Concert Hall, New York, N.Y., November 13, 1893.

Godwin, William. *Memoirs of Mary Wollstonecraft Godwin.* New York: Gordon, 1972.

Good, Timothy S., ed. *We Saw Lincoln Shot: One Hundred Eyewitness Accounts.* Jackson: University Press of Mississippi, 1995.

Goodale, Katherine Molony. *Behind the Scenes with Edwin Booth.* Boston: Houghton Mifflin, 1931.

Goodwin, Doris Kearns. *Team of Rivals.* New York: Simon & Schuster, 2005.

Gould, Emerson W. *Fifty years on the Mississippi; or, Gould's history of river navigation.* St. Louis: Nixon-Jones, 1889.

Gould, Thomas R. *The Tragedian; An Essay on the Histrionic Genius of Junius Brutus Booth.* New York: Hurd & Houghton, 1868.

Graff, Henry F. *Grover Cleveland.* New York: Times Books, 2002.

Grangé, E., and Xavier de Montépin. *The Corsican Brothers.* New York: Samuel French, 186[?].

Greenslet, Ferris. *The Life of Thomas Bailey Aldrich.* New York: Houghton Mifflin, 1908.

Grossman, Edwina Booth. *Edwin Booth: Recollections by his Daughter and Letters to Her and to his Friends.* New York: Century, 1894.

Grylls, R. Glynn. *Mary Shelley: A Biography.* New York: Oxford University Press, 1938.

Hall, A. O. *The Manhattaner in New Orleans: or, Phases of "Crescent City" Life.* New York: J. S. Redfield, 1851.

Hall, Clayton Coleman, ed. *Baltimore: Its History and Its People.* New York: Lewis Historical, 1912.

Harlow, Alvin F. *Old Bowery Days: The Chronicles of a Famous Street.* New York: D. Appleton, 1931.

Hay, John. *Lincoln and the Civil War in the Diaries and Letters of John Hay.* Edited by Tyler Dennett. New York: Dodd, Mead, 1939.

———. *Lincoln's Journalist: John Hay's Anonymous Writing for the Press, 1860–1864.* Edited by Michael Burlingame. Carbondale: Southern Illinois University Press, 1998.

Henneke, Ben Graf. *Laura Keene: Actress, Innovator and Impresario: A Biography.* Tulsa, Okla.: Council Oak, 1990.

Hepburn, A. Barton. *A History of Currency in the United States.* New York: Augustus M. Kelley, 1967.

Herndon, William H., and Jesse W. Weik. *Herndon's Life of Lincoln: The History and Personal Recollections of Abraham Lincoln.* Edited by Paul M. Angle. Cleveland: World, 1942.

Homberger, Eric. *Mrs. Astor's New York: Money and Social Power in a Gilded Age.* New Haven, Conn.: Yale University Press, 2002.

Honour, Hugh. *Romanticism.* New York: Harper & Row, 1979.

Howard, George W. *The Monumental City: History Resources and Biography, 1628–1880.* Baltimore: J. D. Ehlers, 1873.

Howe, George Frederick. *Chester A. Arthur: A Quarter-Century of Machine Politics.* New York: Dodd, Mead, 1934.

Howe, Julia Ward. *Memoirs of Dr. Samuel Gridley Howe.* Boston: Howe Memorial Committee, 1876.

———. *Reminiscences, 1819–1899.* New York: Negro Universities Press, 1969.

Howe, Samuel Gridley. *Letters and Journals of Samuel Gridley Howe.* Edited by Laura E. Richards. Boston: Dana Estes, 1909.

Hutton, Laurence. *Edwin Booth.* New York: Harper & Brothers, 1893.

Ireland, Joseph Norton. *Records of the New York Stage, from 1750 to 1860.* Vol. 2. New York: T. H. Morrell, 1866.

James, Marquis. *The Raven: A Biography of Sam Houston.* New York: Blue Ribbon, 1929.

Johannsen, Robert W. *Stephen A. Douglas.* New York: Oxford University Press, 1973.

———. *To the Halls of the Montezumas: The Mexican War in the American Imagination.* New York: Oxford University Press, 1985.

Johnson, Allen. *Dictionary of American Biography.* Vol. 1. New York: Charles Scribner's Sons, 1928.

Jordan, Winthrop D. *White Over Black: American Attitudes Toward the Negro, 1550–1812.* New York: Norton, 1977.

Kane, Harnett. *Queen New Orleans, City by the River.* New York: W. Morrow, 1949.

Kendall, John S. *The Golden Age of the New Orleans Theater.* Baton Rouge: Louisiana State University Press, 1952.

Kennedy, William. *O Albany! Improbable City of Political Wizards, Fearless Ethnics, Spectacular Aristocrats, Splendid Nobodies, and Underrated Scoundrels.* New York: Viking, 1983.

Kimmel, Stanley. *The Mad Booths of Maryland.* New York: Bobbs-Merrill, 1940.

Leale, Charles A. *Lincoln's Last Hours: An Address Delivered Before the State of New York Military Order of the Loyal Legion, in the City of New York, February 1909.* New York: privately published, 1909.

Lee, Hermione. *Edith Wharton.* New York: Vintage, 2007.

Leman, Walter. *Memories of an Old Actor.* San Francisco: A. Roman, 1886.

Lester, Charles E. *The Life of Sam Houston.* New York: J. C. Derby, 1855.

Levine, Lawrence. *Highbrow/Lowbrow: The Emergence of Cultural Hierarchy in America.* Cambridge, Mass.: Harvard University Press, 1988.

Lincoln, Abraham. *Abraham Lincoln: His Speeches and Writings.* Edited by Roy Basler. New York: Da Capo, 1990.

Lockridge, Richard. *Darling of Misfortune: Edwin Booth, 1833–1893.* New York: Century, 1932.

Ludlow, Noah. *Dramatic Life As I Found It: A record of personal experience; with an account of the rise and progress of the drama in the West and South.* St. Louis: G. I. Jones, 1880.

Lyon, Isaac S. *Recollections of an Old Cartman, or, Old New York Street Life.* Newark, N.J.: Daily Journal Office, 1872.

MacLiammóir, Micheál. *Put Money in Thy Purse: The Diary of the Film of "Othello."* London: Methuen, 1952.

MacMinn, George. *The Theater of the Golden Era in California.* Caldwell, Idaho: Caxton, 1941.

Mahoney, Ella V. *Sketches of Tudor Hall and the Booth Family.* Belair, Md.: privately published, 1925.

Marchand, Leslie A. *Byron: A Biography.* New York: Knopf, 1957.

Matthews, Brander, and Laurence Hutton, eds. *Actors and Actresses of Great Britain and the United States: From the Days of David Garrick to the Present Time.* Vol. 3, *Kean and Booth; and Their Contemporaries.* New York: Cassell, 1886.

———, eds. *Actors and Actresses of Great Britain and the United States: From the Days of David Garrick to the Present Time.* Vol. 4, *Macready and Forrest; and Their Contemporaries.* New York: Cassell, 1886.

———, eds. *Actors and Actresses of Great Britain and the United States: From the Days of David Garrick to the Present Time.* Vol. 5, *The Present Time.* New York: Cassell, 1886.

———, eds. *Life and Art of Edwin Booth and His Contemporaries.* Boston: L. C. Page, 1886.

Maurice, Arthur Butler. *Fifth Avenue.* New York: Dodd, Mead and Company, 1918.

McCullough, Jack. *Living Pictures on the New York Stage.* Ann Arbor, Mich.: UMI Research Press, 1983.

McKay, Ernest A. *The Civil War and New York City.* Syracuse, N.Y.: Syracuse University Press, 1990.

McLaren, Angus. *A History of Contraception: From Antiquity to the Present Day.* Cambridge, Mass.: B. Blackwell, 1990.

McPherson, James M. *Battle Cry of Freedom: The Civil War Era.* New York: Oxford University Press, 1988.

———, ed. *The Most Fearful Ordeal: Original Coverage of the Civil War by Writers and Reporters of the New York Times.* New York: St. Martin's, 2004.

Miers, Earl Schenck, ed. *Lincoln Day by Day: A Chronology, 1809–1865.* Dayton, Ohio: Morningside, 1991.

Miller, Ernest C. *John Wilkes Booth—Oilman.* New York: Exposition, 1947.

Moore, Edward. *The Foundling: A Comedy; and The Gamester: A Tragedy.* Edited by Anthony Amberg. Newark: University of Delaware Press, 1996.

Mordecai, Samuel. *Virginia, especially Richmond, in by-gone days; with a glance at the present, being reminiscences and last words of an old citizen.* 2nd ed. Richmond, Va.: West & Johnson, 1860.

Morison, Samuel Eliot. *The European Discovery of America: The Northern Voyages A.D. 500–1600.* New York: Oxford University Press, 1971.

Morris, Clara. *Life on the Stage: My Personal Experience and Recollections*. London: Ibister, 1902.

Moses, Montrose, ed. *Representative Plays by American Dramatists from 1765 to the Present Day*. New York: E. P. Dutton, 1925.

Mullan, John, ed. *Lives of the Great Romantics by Their Contemporaries*. Vol. 1, *Shelley*. London: Pickering and Chatto, 1996.

Neeley, Mary Ann. *Old Alabama Town: An Illustrated Guide*. Tuscaloosa: University of Alabama Press, 2002.

Nevins, Allan. *Grover Cleveland: A Study in Courage*. New York: Dodd, Mead, 1933.

Nicolay, John G., and John Hay. *Abraham Lincoln: A History*. 10 vols. New York: Century, 1890.

Nussbaum, Arthur. *A History of the Dollar*. New York: Columbia University Press, 1957.

Oakes, James. *Slavery and Freedom: An Interpretation of the Old South*. New York: Vintage, 1991.

Oettel, Walter. *Walter's Sketch Book of the Players*. New York: Gotham, 1943.

Olson, Sherry. *Baltimore*. Cambridge, Mass.: Ballinger, 1976.

Palmer, Robert. *Deep Blues*. New York: Penguin, 1982.

Parrington, Vernon Louis. *Main Currents in American Thought*. Vol. 3, *The Beginnings of Critical Realism in America 1860–1920*. New York: Harcourt, Brace, 1930.

Phelps, Henry P. *Players of a Century: A Record of the Albany Stage, Including Notices of Prominent Actors Who Have Appeared in America*. Albany, N.Y.: Joseph McDonough, 1880.

Phillips, John S. *The Players: Occasional Pieces*. New York: n.p., 1935.

Pitman, Benn, comp. *The Assassination of President Lincoln and the Trial of the Conspirators: The Courtroom Testimony*. New York: Funk & Wagnalls, 1954.

The Players, Minutes of the First Meeting, December 31, 1888, Together with the Deed of Gift from Edwin Booth. New York: DeVinne, 1908.

Poore, Ben Perley. *Perley's Reminiscences, of Sixty Years in the National Metropolis*. Vol. 1. Philadelphia: Hubbard Brothers, 1886.

Powell, Anthony. *A Dance to the Music of Time: Third Movement*. Chicago: University of Chicago Press, 1995.

Raimond, Jean, and J. R. Watson, eds. *A Handbook to English Romanticism*. New York: St. Martin's, 1992.

Randall, Ruth Painter. *Mary Lincoln: Biography of a Marriage*. Boston: Little, Brown, 1953.

Reignolds-Wilson, Catherine Mary. *Yesterdays with Actors*. Boston: Cupples & Hurd, 1887.

Richards, Laura E. *Samuel Gridley Howe*. New York: Appleton-Century, 1935.

———. *Stepping Westward*. New York: Appleton, 1931.

———, and Maud Howe Elliott. *Julia Ward Howe: 1819–1910*. Vol. 1. Boston: Houghton Mifflin, 1916.

Richardson, Albert D. *A Personal History of Ulysses S. Grant, and a Sketch of Schuyler Colfax*. Hartford, Conn.: American, 1868.

Ripley, Eliza. *Social Life in Old New Orleans*. New York: Appleton, 1912.

Rodriguez, Junius P., ed. *Slavery in the United States: A Social, Political and Historical Encyclopedia, Volume 1*. Santa Barbara, Calif.: ABC-CLIO, 2007.

Rogers, William Warren, Jr. *Confederate Home Front: Montgomery During the Civil War*. Tuscaloosa: University of Alabama Press, 1999.

Rourke, Constance. *Troupers of the Gold Coast: or, the Rise of Lotta Crabtree*. New York: Harcourt, Brace, 1928.

Ruffner, Kevin Conley. *Maryland's Blue and Gray: A Border State's Union and Confederate Junior Officer Corps*. Baton Rouge: Louisiana State University Press, 1997.

Ruggles, Eleanor. *Prince of Players: Edwin Booth.* New York: Norton, 1953.

Ryan, Kate. *Old Boston Museum Days.* Boston: Little, Brown, 1915.

Saint-Gaudens, Augustus. *The Reminiscences of Augustus Saint-Gaudens.* Edited by Homer Saint-Gaudens. New York: Century, 1913.

Samples, Gordon. *Lust for Fame: The Stage Career of John Wilkes Booth.* Jefferson, N.C.: McFarland, 1982.

Scharf, J. Thomas. *The Chronicles of Baltimore: Being a Complete History of "Baltimore Town" and Baltimore City from the Earliest Period to the Present Time.* Baltimore: Turnbull Brothers, 1874.

Shakespeare, William. *The Riverside Shakespeare.* Edited by G. Blakemore Evans. Boston: Houghton Mifflin, 1974.

Shelley, Percy Bysshe. *Complete Poems.* London: Softback Preview, 1993.

Sherman, Robert L. *Chicago Stage: Its Records and Achievements.* Vol. 1, *1834–1871.* Chicago: privately printed, 1947.

Sherman, William Tecumseh. *Memoirs of Gen. W. T. Sherman, Written by Himself.* Vol. 1. New York: Charles L. Webster, 1891.

Sherrard, Owen Aubrey. *A Life of John Wilkes.* London: George Allen & Unwin, 1930.

Siegel, Martin. *New Orleans: A Chronological and Documentary History, 1539–1970.* Dobbs Ferry, N.Y.: Oceana, 1975.

Skinner, Otis. *Footlights and Spotlights: Recollections of My Life on the Stage.* Westport, Conn.: Greenwood, 1924.

———. *The Last Tragedian: Booth Tells His Own Story.* New York: Dodd, Mead, 1939.

———. *Mad Folk of the Theatre: Ten Studies in Temperament.* Indianapolis: Bobbs-Merrill, 1928.

Smiley, Alfred Wilson. *A Few Scraps, Oily and Otherwise.* Oil City, Pa.: Derrick, 1907.

Smith, Solomon. *Theatrical Management in the West and South for Thirty Years.* 1868. Reprint, New York: B. Blom, 1968.

Sollers, John Ford. "The Theatrical Career of John T. Ford." Ph.D. diss., Stanford University, 1962.

Stoddard, W. O. *Inside the White House in War Times.* New York: C. L. Webster, 1890.

Stoddart, J. H. *Recollections of a Player.* New York: Century, 1902.

Stone, William Leete. *History of New York City from the Discovery to the Present Day.* New York: Virtue & Yorston, 1872.

Straus, Ralph. *Carriages and Coaches: Their History and Evolution.* London: Martin Secker, 1912.

Sumner, William G. *A History of American Currency.* New York: Henry Holt, 1874.

Taylor, Tom. *Our American Cousin: A Drama, in Three Acts.* New York: Samuel French, 1869.

Taylor, Tom, and Charles Reade. *Masks and Faces: or, Before and Behind the Curtain: A Comedy in Two Acts.* French's Standard Drama 240. The Acting Edition. New York: S. French, n.d.

Tebbel, John. *A Certain Club: One Hundred Years of The Players.* New York: Wieser & Wieser, 1989.

Tidwell, William A., James O. Hall, and David Winfred Gaddy. *Come Retribution: The Confederate Secret Service and the Assassination of Lincoln.* Jackson: University Press of Mississippi, 1988.

Tocqueville, Alexis de. *Democracy in America.* Edited by J. P. Mayer. Translated by George Lawrence. 1835. Reprint. New York: Harper & Row, 1988.

Townsend, George Allen. *The Life, Crime and Capture of John Wilkes Booth, with a full sketch of the conspiracy of which he was the leader, and the pursuit, trial and execution of his accomplices.* New York: Dick & Fitzgerald, 1865.

Towse, John Ranken. *Sixty Years of the Theater: An Old Critic's Memories.* New York: Funk & Wagnalls, 1916.

Treloar, William Purdie. *Wilkes and the City.* London: John Murray, 1917.

Twain, Mark. *Life on the Mississippi.* New York: Random House, 2007.

United States Bureau of the Census. *Aggregate Amount of Each Description of Persons within the United States of America, and the Territories Thereof, in the Year 1810.* New York: Norman Ross, 1990.

United States Department of Commerce, Bureau of the Census. *Abstract of the Fifth Census of the United States, 1830.* Washington, D.C.: F. P. Blair, 1832.

Vandiver, Frank E. *Mighty Stonewall.* New York: McGraw-Hill, 1957.

Villard, Oswald Garrison. *John Brown: 1800–1859; A Biography Fifty Years After.* Boston: Houghton Mifflin, 1910.

Warren, Marion E., ed. *Baltimore—When She Was What She Used to Be, 1950–1930.* Robert G. Merrick edition. Baltimore: Johns Hopkins University Press, 1983.

Watermeier, Daniel J., ed. *Edwin Booth's Performances: The Mary Isabella Stone Commentaries.* Ann Arbor, Mich.: UMI Research Press, 1990.

Weichmann, Louis J. *A True History of the Assassination of Abraham Lincoln and of the Conspiracy of 1865.* New York: Vintage, 1975.

Wemmlinger, Raymond, et al. *Edwin Booth's Legacy: Treasures from the Hampton-Booth Theatre Collection.* New York: Hampden-Booth Theater Library, 1989.

Wertenbaker, Thomas J. *Norfolk: Historic Southern Port.* Durham, N.C.: Duke University Press, 1931.

Weston, J. M. *Lucretia Borgia. A Drama. In Three Acts.* Adapted from the French of Victor Hugo. *Spencer's Boston Theater,* vol. 5, no. 35. Boston: W. V. Spencer, 1856.

Wharton, Edith. *A Backward Glance.* New York: Simon & Schuster, 1998.

———. *Old New York: Four Novellas.* New York: Scribner, 1995.

Wheeler, George. *Pierpont Morgan and Friends: The Anatomy of a Myth.* Englewood Cliffs, N.J.: Prentice-Hall, 1973.

Whitman, Walt. *Prose Works 1892. Vol. 2, Collect and Other Prose.* Edited by Floyd Stovall. New York: New York University Press, 1964.

Williams, Alfred M. *Sam Houston and the War of Independence in Texas.* Boston: Houghton Mifflin, 1895.

Wilson, Francis. *Francis Wilson's Life of Himself.* New York: Houghton Mifflin, 1924.

———. *John Wilkes Booth: Fact and Fiction of Lincoln's Assassination.* Boston: Houghton Mifflin, 1929.

Wilson, James Grant *The Memorial History of the City of New-York from Its First Settlement to the Year 1892.* Vol. 3. New York: New York History Company, 1893.

Wilson, James Grant, and John Fiske, eds. *Appleton's Cyclopaedia of American Biography.* Vol. 1. New York: D. Appleton, 1888.

Wilson, Philip K., ed. *Midwifery Theory and Practice.* New York: Garland, 1996.

Winter, William. *Between Actor and Critic: Selected Letters of Edwin Booth and William Winter.* Edited by Daniel J. Watermeier. Princeton, N.J.: Princeton University Press, 1971.

———. *Edwin Booth in Twelve Dramatic Characters.* Boston: J. R. Osgood, 1872.

———. *Life and Art of Edwin Booth.* New York: Macmillan, 1893.

———. *Shadows of the Stage.* New York: Macmillan, 1893.

———. *Vagrant Memories: Being Further Recollections of Other Days.* New York: George H. Doran, 1915.

Wood, Virginia S. *Live Oaking: Southern Timber for Tall Ships.* Annapolis, Md.: Naval Institute Press, 1981.

Wooster, Louise C. [anonymous]. *The Autobiography of a Magdalen*. Birmingham, Ala.: Birmingham, 1911.

Wooster, Louise C., and James L. Baggett. *A Woman of the Town: Louise Wooster, Birmingham's Magdalen*. Birmingham, Ala.: Birmingham Public Library Press, 2005.

Wright, William. *The Oil Regions of Pennsylvania*. New York: Harper & Brothers, 1865.

ACKNOWLEDGMENTS

The history I tell is, in large measure, a theatrical history. For three generations, the Booths lived their lives on, and in the shadow of, the stage. To re-create their particular world, it was necessary to gather thousands of pages of primary sources from archives of nineteenth-century American theater history. Reminiscences of the famous clan abound, penned by fellow actors, by legions of journalists, by multitudes of contemporaries and friends. Most important, however, this narrative draws from over one hundred years' worth of private letters, diaries, memoirs, account books, documents, and journals written by the Booths themselves, as well as from the family's huge collection of playbills, paintings, statues, photographs, theatrical costumes, dramatic reviews, and stage props. My first debt is to the librarians, curators, and archivists who guided me on a five-year search through this rich and voluminous record.

In New York, Raymond Wemmlinger, librarian and curator of the Hampden-Booth Theatre Library, gave generous access to the manuscripts, art, and artifacts in his care at 16 Gramercy Park, home of the library and The Players, the club Edwin Booth founded in 1888. Ray was a phenomenal adviser during my visits to the archives and a thoughtful reader of early drafts. (Anyone curious to learn the fate of Edwina Booth would do well to read Ray's haunting novel, *Booth's Daughter*.) I am deeply grateful for his support. At Lincoln Center, the gracious staff at the Billy Rose Theatre Division of the New York Public Library for the Performing Arts, kindly accommodated my digging through boxes of Booth-Grossman family papers. Lisa Bush Hankin, director of Research at Adelson Galleries, was marvelously helpful.

In Cambridge, Massachusetts, I owe a special debt to Susan Halpert, reference librarian at Harvard University's Houghton Library, for lighting my way through the wilderness of Booth and Howe papers there. Others at Houghton were equally generous: to Peter X. Accardo, Denison Beach, James Capobianco, Elizabeth A. Falsey, Mary Haegert, Rachel Howarth, Pamela Madsen, Jennie Rathbun, Emily Walhout, and the late Fredric

Woodbridge Wilson, curator of the Harvard Theatre Collection, I give wholehearted thanks. In Boston, librarians at the Boston Athenaeum, and Anne Trodella of Skinner, Inc., provided much-needed help.

In Washington, D.C., Dr. Georgianna Ziegler, head of Reference at Folger Shakespeare Library, graciously shared her time and insights, steering me toward Booth manuscripts that would prove central to this narrative. Her influence on these pages is substantial. Folger Library's senior photography associate, William Davis, helped me acquire many of the pictures that illustrate this book.

In Florida, Art Bagley, curator of Special Collections at the University of Tampa's MacDonald Kelce Library, kindly allowed me to delve into Stanley Kimmel's vast collection of notes and sources. Mickey Wells, electronic resources librarian, lifted a longlost image from one of Kimmel's negatives: a 1933 photograph of Joseph Edwin Hall, son of the former slaves who lived on the Booth farm, reproduced here.

In Maryland, Laurie Verge, director, Surratt House Museum, M-NCPPC, and Michael W. Kauffman, historian and author of *American Brutus: John Wilkes Booth and the Lincoln Conspiracies,* generously provided copies of Asia Booth Clarke's correspondence. David Angerhofer and Elizabeth A. Proffen of the Maryland Historical Society sent much-needed microfilm. Dan Monahan, superintendent of Green Mount Cemetery, shared photographs of the Booth family plot and verified lot card information, as did Tim Burke of Baltimore Cemetery.

Anna Lee Pauls of Princeton University's Firestone Library provided Adam Badeau's wartime correspondence. Mary M. Huth, head of Special Collections at the University of Rochester Library, gave me access to Edwin Booth's correspondence with John E. Russell. In Pennsylvania, Joseph Shemtov of the Free Library of Philadelphia and Judith Callard of the Germantown Historical Society traced Booth connections to local theaters. Bill Johnson of the Iowa State Historical Museum explained what happened to the guns John Brown and Samuel Gridley Howe ran through Iowa. Lyn Kelsey of the Beth Ahabah Museum and Archives in Richmond, Virginia, sent the writings of a militiaman who stood with John Wilkes Booth at Brown's hanging.

In Illinois, Dr. Alvan Bregman at the Rare Books and Manuscripts Library of the University of Illinois at Urbana-Champaign, pointed me to an extra-illustrated edition of *The Elder and the Younger Booth* bursting with family secrets; his colleague Dennis Sears found key material hidden in the back pages.

The vast resources of the University of Chicago Library enabled me to unravel the Booths' tangled social relationships and to re-create the scenes and settings of their century-long family drama. Since 2006, I have been almost a daily visitor to the library's departments: at Harper, I am grateful to Asahi Hayden; at Regenstein, I owe thanks to Sherry Byrne and Kathleen Arthur, to Microforms expert Ray Gadke, to Map Collection guide Christopher Winters, and to the reference librarians Jeffry Archer, Paul Belloni, Ellen Bryan, Greg Fleming, Sandra Levy, Colleen Mullarkey, Sandy Roscoe, Beverly Sperring, Nancy Spiegel, Rebecca Starkey, and Agnes Tatarka; at the Special Collections Research Center, Christine Colburn, Julia Gardner, Barbara Gilbert, David Pavelitch, and Reina Williams were amazingly kind, as were Alice Schreyer and Judith Dartt.

The historians at the Abraham Lincoln Presidential Library and Museum in Springfield have been great friends to this book. Dr. Thomas F. Schwartz is the Illinois State Historian, the creative mind behind exhibits at the museum, and director of Research at the library. I am indebted to him for his wise counsel, his generosity, his insightful readings of successive drafts, and for cheering this project ever onward. Dr. James M. Cornelius, curator of the Lincoln Collection at the ALPLM, led me on an unforgettable tour of the library's storehouses in search of Booth treasures. His excellent advice and close reading of chapters improved the pages of this book immeasurably. I am very thankful for his help. Thanks also to Jennifer Ericson, Roberta Fairburn, Mary Michals, and Mary Ann Pohl. I owe an extraordinary thanks to the scholar and collector Louise Taper. Through years of indefatigable research, she built the magnificent Taper Collection now housed at the ALPLM. Her work is an inspiration, and her generosity to this project is deeply appreciated.

Beyond library walls, many people were instrumental in bringing the Booths' story to the printed page. The hospitality of the wonderful Maria Capello made research trips to Houghton Library possible; her timely introduction to a literary agent made this project a reality. My teacher Elyce Melmon handed me a pen and turned my thoughts to Shakespeare and Edith Wharton. Castille Hobbs, now a graduate student in library science, volunteered as a research assistant—her creativity and brilliance were a gift. Jessica Kaplan, Clemence Vidal de la Blache, and Caroline Eaton (whose book project, "Becoming Jackie: Jacqueline Bouvier's Life in France," promises to be terrific) gave indispensable help. Herbert Adams, a Maine historian and member of the state legislature, sent Booth material from Portland. Two environmental historians influenced this project: Megan Kate Nelson taught me the significance of swamps and shared sources she discovered while researching her latest book, *Ruin Nation: Destruction and the Civil War;* the late Angela Gugliotta, an expert on the coal and oil regions of western

Pennsylvania, was a valiant guide to Petrolia, elucidating even from her hospital bed the history of the landscape she loved.

Sara Austin, Rachel Barney, Elyce Melmon, Jennie Myers, Lucy Pick, Sandeep Parsad, Meridyth Senes, and John Titone read and commented on an early version of this manuscript. Kathleen D. Morrison and Dean P. Wright scrutinized multiple drafts. For their kindness and support during the writing process, I also wish to thank Chloe Ahmann, Eileen Berger, Andrea Braver, Hilde and Karen Bridges, Mary Bolton, Joanna Busza, Christopher Capozzola, Constance Casey, Albert Colman, Tricia Connell, David Dieguez, Kathryn and Mary Gen Doi, Margaret Farris, Maggie Fezekas, David Finkelstein, Matthew Francis, Julia Goalby, Petra M. Goedegebuerre, Deana Heath, Gwennan Ickes, Vanya Ivanova, Pam Kaye, Julie Kostina, Heather Welch La Rivière, Amy Landry and her family, Gordan Lesic, Allan Lindh, Briana Lindh, Mark Lycett, Martha Nussbaum, Eliza Parker, Nigel Parsad, Javier Ramirez, Larissa Silva, Emily Tancer, Alfred Titone, Jr., Helen Titone, Toby Titone, Stacy Tolbert, Judith Vandegrift, the Whaley family, Vanessa Willetts, David Williamson, Christopher Woods, Bill and Cora Wright, and Ottilie Young. Judith and Barry Bridges have been tireless in their support and encouragement. My father, Joseph R. Titone enthusiastically backed this idea from the get-go: I thank him so much for the inspiration, for helping me hunt sources in the Kimmel Collection, and for buying, as Christmas presents, those crucial reels of microfilm from Harvard Library. Joan Connell and Dean P. Wright, my mother and stepfather, long ago edited my high school history papers. This time around, I owe them an inestimable debt for the Herculean labors they have performed to make this book possible. They found no challenge too great in the pursuit of this goal: their generosity and devotion have been inexhaustible.

I am profoundly grateful to Dominick Anfuso, editor in chief of Free Press, for being the champion of this book. He took a chance on a first-time writer in 2007 when he gave this tale of two brothers the green light. Since then, he has generously provided all the resources necessary to complete the Booths' story—including the most valuable one of all, time. I thank him for his great support and understanding, and for bringing this book to life. To Martha Levin, publisher of Free Press, I also give my gratitude for her tremendous encouragement.

Free Press is a wonderful place to work on a book. For their energies, talents and generosity, I am in awe of Leah Miller, Suzanne Donohue, Charlotte Gill, Carisa Brunetto Hayes, and Nicole Kalian, as well as of Laura Cooke, Maura O'Brien, Alexandra Pisano, Kirsa Rein and Giselle-

Marie Roig. Thanks to Mara Lurie and Tom Pitoniak for taking excellent care of the words, and to Akasha Archer, Charles Corts, Eric Fuentecilla, and John Mercun for doing the same with the pictures.

Martin Beiser, my revered editor, ran every step of the writer's marathon with me. His faith in this story, his embrace of its steadily growing cast of characters, his humor and patience, sustained me through the hardest stretches. "Just write down everything you feel like telling." When cuts were needed, his infallible pen was ready. In our search for a title, he plucked Hamlet's phrase from the heap. I thank him for wanting this book, and for carrying it to the finish line.

To the incomparable Katharine Cluverius, literary agent, I give thanks for seeing the potential of this story when it was still germinating and for sticking with it through thick and thin. With the strategy of a chess master and the courage of cavalry officer, Katharine launched this project. In the years since, she has played many parts in its completion, all of them beautifully— she is adviser, reader, counselor, and deeply valued friend.

Doris Kearns Goodwin has done more for the Booths than I could begin to explain. She has been both teacher and mentor, giving me an education in American history—and in writing biography—obtainable nowhere else. Her friendship and support led directly to this moment, when I am able to thank her for contributing the Foreword to the book that she also taught me how to write. To her kindness, and to that of Richard N. Goodwin, I owe so much.

This book is dedicated to my husband. When the chance to write it came, Jason put his life on hold, shouldering the burden of the "second shift" so I could meet the deadline. He also read and improved every page. Before this time, I considered Jason the love of my life; now, words fall short of expressing what he is to me. Special thanks are due to our son, Nick, who, from the age of two, was my companion on trips to archives across the map. He traveled by jet, Amtrak, subway, even monorail, in search of Booth stuff, and was rolled by stroller through library book stacks across the threshold of The Players. He is now seven, and in my opinion, the greatest boy alive.

INDEX

ABOUT THE AUTHOR

Nora Titone studied history at Harvard University and the University of California, Berkeley. For the past decade, she has worked as a historical researcher specializing in nineteenth-century America. She lives in Chicago. This is her first book.